# INVESTING WITH THE TREND

Since 1996, Bloomberg Press has published books for financial professionals on investing, economics, and policy affecting investors. Titles are written by leading practitioners and authorities, and have been translated into more than 20 languages.

The Bloomberg Financial Series provides both core reference knowledge and actionable information for financial professionals. The books are written by experts familiar with the work flows, challenges, and demands of investment professionals who trade the markets, manage money, and analyze investments in their capacity of growing and protecting wealth, hedging risk, and generating revenue.

For a list of available titles, please visit our Web site at www.wiley.com/go/bloombergpress.

# INVESTING WITH THE TREND

A Rules-Based Approach to
Money Management

**Gregory L. Morris**

**BLOOMBERG PRESS**
An Imprint of
**WILEY**

*To Laura, and our children, Dusti, Grant, Derek, and Kane.*
*And our grandchildren: Katy, Kinsey, Grayson, Connor, and Elaine.*

# Contents

# Foreword

The Greek philosopher Aristotle wrote, "We are what we repeatedly do. Excellence, then, is not an act but a habit."

The same is true of investment. Good investing is not an "event" like finding the next growth company or catching the next market turn. Rather, good investing is a disciplined process that converts research and training into a well-tested methodology, and then makes a habit of following that approach day after day.

Because profits are enjoyable, investors often believe that they are "paid" when their good ideas are comfortably working out, but that is an illusion. If you carefully study the returns of successful investors, you'll find that their profits are more often a sort of delayed payment for actions they took much earlier: maintaining their investment discipline even when it wasn't working in the short run; cutting losses when the evidence changed; and establishing investment positions when it was often uncomfortable to do so.

The financial markets may be efficient, but they are efficient in an interesting way. If all investors were identical and shared the same information, objectives, and temperaments, the markets might be efficient in the "academic" sense, and it would be impossible to outperform a buy-and-hold approach. But in reality, markets are full of greed, fear, uncertainty, and constant second-guessing. In that world, investors are scarcely willing to follow a well-grounded, thoroughly tested discipline once it has become uncomfortable. For those who do, their later success doesn't emerge as "free money." It emerges as delayed payment for the discipline to take scarce, useful actions when other investors were seeking comfort.

For example, it is difficult—particularly after a long market advance—to part with a richly priced investment position as market action begins to deteriorate. When a market advance has been rewarding, the natural inclination is to become attached to those rewards, to fall in love with the bullish "story," and to ignore negative evidence.

It is equally difficult—particularly after a long market decline—to establish an investment position at depressed prices as market action begins to firm. When risk taking has been relentlessly punished, the natural inclination is to avoid risk. That is particularly true if investors have endured a series of whipsaws, where early purchases are followed by immediate price declines and trend-following signals to cut losses.

Discipline requires confidence, and confidence requires evidence. In any investment approach, it is critical to test that discipline against the longest history of data that you can obtain. As an investor, my greatest successes have resulted from the confidence to respond in uncertain environments, based on evidence that had proved to be effective in market cycles again and again throughout history. My single greatest disappointment was the result of a much earlier decision to ignore Depression-era data as outmoded, and then missing a large market rebound while I stress-tested my approach against that data. Test your investment approach in the most challenging conditions you can identify, because someday you will face those conditions.

Greg Morris is among the rare breed of investors who take systematic research, testing, and discipline seriously. Greg is a technical analyst. The book you are reading offers insights that he has gained from his own career as an investment manager. Greg's investment approach is based on indicators that measure price trends, trading volume, the balance of advancing stocks versus declining stocks, and similar considerations. Aside from keeping investors generally aligned with prevailing trends, investment methods like this can be of enormous help in limiting significant market losses.

While my own investment discipline draws from some elements of technical analysis, it is also heavily weighted toward fundamental valuation, stock selection, economic measures, and other factors. Each approach has its benefits and challenges, depending on the market environment. Yet more important than these differences is what both of our approaches share in common, which is the insistence on a systematic investment process.

In addition to sharing the tools and insights of a skilled market technician, Greg shares the three key elements that distinguish an investment discipline from constant guessing:

1. Measuring the weight of the evidence.
2. Rules and guidelines to trade the weight of the evidence.
3. Strict discipline to follow the process.

The importance of each of those words—*evidence*, *rules*, *guidelines*, *discipline*, and, possibly most important, *strict*—can't be understated.

Reliable market indicators are important, but they are not nearly enough. The essential feature of a successful investment discipline is to convert those indicators into objective guidance about when to take action, whether that action is to buy or to sell. Greg Morris brings decades of data and research together into a technically driven, rules-based approach that offers both investors and traders a solid footing to "dance with the trend."

In nearly every long-term pursuit, the secret to success is the same. Find a set of daily actions that you expect to produce good results if you follow them consistently.

Then follow them consistently.

JOHN P. HUSSMAN, PhD
PRESIDENT, HUSSMAN STRATEGIC ADVISORS

# Preface

During tough times in the market, the individual investor is not well served by following the buy-and-hold mentality promulgated by the financial institutions, most mutual funds, and brokerage houses since the early 1950s. The "world of finance" and "Wall Street" have set the stage for investing for the long term in their effort to market themselves and sell investing ideas to an unsuspecting and financially uneducated public. With their big emphasis on diversification and its long-term protection, their confusion between buy and hold and buy and hope, the misinformation continues to pour out of the financial institutions.

Corporate pension plans are being dumped, social security is in the tank, and our financial system is in the midst of a giant restructuring because the stability of the past two decades in the last century has caused prudence, and what used to be called *common sense*, to be set aside for greater leverage and higher risk. Retirees as well as younger investors are learning the hard way that "investing for the long term" has periods where the performance is poor and that those periods can last a decade or much longer.

My decades of experience have taught me that there are times when one should not participate in the markets and are much better off preserving capital because bear markets can set you back for a long time, and they are especially bad when they happen in your later years. Keep in mind that the closer you get to actually needing your serious money for retirement, the worse the effect of a severe bear market can have on your assets. It is critical to understand the concept of avoiding the bad markets and participating in the good ones. It is never too late to invest intelligently for your future.

This is not a storybook. This book is a collection of almost 40 years of being involved in the markets, sharing some things I have learned and truly believe. You will soon find out that there are sections in the book that contain short concepts on various subjects, even one-liners. You will discover early that sometimes I might seem overly passionate about what I'm saying, but hopefully you will realize that is because I have well-formed opinions and just want to ensure that the message is straightforward and easily understood. It is not only a book on trend following but a source of technical analysis information learned over the past 40 years, with quotes, lists, and a host of tidbits that often seem trite, but are usually true.

Some may notice that I repeat myself in a number of places and think that I am old and slipping. While you may be correct, I often did that because it was too important at that point to provide a reference to where it was first said. I believe it is so much easier to make the point again within the context of the current discussion.

Although the book is ultimately about using trend following in a disciplined model for long-term successful investing, it will take a while to get there. I have spent a lot of time on the preparation for understanding the markets, understanding yourself, and understanding things that just don't work, before I get into the subject of the book. You can certainly read the book from front to back, but it would be best to review the table of contents and read first the areas that catch your interest. There are two large research projects inside this book. I had originally thought about writing an academic white paper, but the formality of that exercise was unappealing, so this book is where they ended up. An effort to have all charts and data with an ending date of December 31, 2012, was purposely done, even though I have to be totally honest, I don't know why. People who know me will understand. I also ensure that with each concept I try to show the 20-year results as I think that is a reasonable assumption as to the realistic investment horizon for most people. I have created my own footnote technique because as one gets older the superscript micro type generally used in books just doesn't cut it, plus I prefer all the footnotes to be in a single location in the appendix instead of at the end of each chapter. Furthermore, I have divided the footnotes among academia (A) (articles, white papers, research, etc.), books (B), and websites (W). And finally, in regard to the layout of the book, I have tried to keep comments about charts and graphics such that they are on the same page or at least on opposing pages. There is nothing more frustrating for me than to read about a chart and not be able to see it.

I apologize for the occasional use of mathematics, in particular, equations. I read once that the inclusion of an equation in a book can greatly reduce its sales. That is a sad commentary, so I have tried to keep them only when I believed they were absolutely necessary. Equations are austere, appearing formal and complicated; however, most of the mathematics herein can be classified as arithmetic. If you find that annoying, again, I apologize.

On occasion I am critical of some things, and downright disdainful of others. There is much in modern finance that so blatantly is mere marketing and virtually void of investment substance that it could actually be considered a hoax. I try to be careful with criticism when the results are robust even though I do not believe in the process. When the results of some type of analysis are flawed in ways such that the rules are so complex, have an inordinate number of equations, or entirely too subjective that one could not possibly prove it wrong, I try to state as much. While I write with some certitude, I am fully aware that if I believe I am correct, it does not mean that others are not correct; it just means that I strongly believe what I'm saying. Please do not be offended from my opinions.

The goals for this book are numerous, but if I had to itemize them they would be: Understand . . .

- How markets work and how they have worked in the past.
- The host of misinformation that exists in finance and investments.

- The tools of modern finance and their shortcomings.
- That as a human being, you have horrible natural investment tendencies.
- What risk really is.
- That markets trend and why.
- That there are techniques to managing money that reduce risk consistently and offer hope for long-term success.

If I had to nail down a single goal for the book, it would be to provide substantial evidence that there are ways to be successful at investing that are outside the mainstream of Wall Street. Although it will appear my concern is about modern finance, it is actually directed toward the investment management world and its misuse of the tools of modern finance.

GREGORY L. MORRIS
HORSESHOE BAY, TX

# Acknowledgments

There are people without whom this book could not have been possible. Where do I start? Who do I mention first? This, quite possibly, is more difficult than the book itself.

One must never forget one's roots. There is no doubt in my mind that my parents, Dwight and Mary Morris, are mostly responsible for all the good that I have ever accomplished. Any of the bad surely had to come from being a jet fighter pilot in the U.S. Navy for six years.

I am blessed with a truly wonderful wife, Laura. Her support during this effort was unwavering and fully appreciated. If she would just let me win at golf occasionally. . . .

It is interesting that I am working with Kevin Commins of John Wiley & Sons again. Kevin was the first editor I had when I wrote my "candlestick" book more than 21 years ago. My association with Stephen Isaacs at McGraw-Hill, and now Bloomberg Press, has been long lasting and most enjoyable.

The team at Stadion's portfolio management department was absolutely necessary for the completion of this work (Brad Thompson, Will McGough, Rob Dailey, Clayton Fresk, Clayton Shiver, Clayton Wilkin, John Wiens, Paul Frank, Jonathan Weaver, Danny Mack, and David Pursell). They tirelessly assisted in data acquisition and analysis. Without them the research in Part II would have never been accomplished, certainly not in my lifetime. I truly hate to break out someone in that group as they all made exceptional contributions, but a special thanks to Clayton Fresk who is extremely talented with Microsoft Excel. Clayton produced most of the spreadsheets used in the research and analysis for this book and provided some unique insight into interpreting the data.

I must acknowledge and thank good friend Ted Wong for his Trend Gauge measure and volunteering (I begged) to proof the technical sections of the book. Thanks to George Schade who used his jurist mind to help me provide criticism as long as it is respectful. Doug Short (dshort.com) graciously reproduced a number of his nice graphics into grayscale. Many—in fact, most—of the charts in this book were created with Thomson Reuter's MetaStock software, a product I have used since version one back in 1985.

What an absolute delight to wrap up a long career with my past 14 years at Stadion Money Management, LLC. Tim Chapman and Jud Doherty have been partners, leaders, and friends for all this time. Truly great people! In fact, every employee at Stadion seems to fit the same mold: sharp, hard-working, and loaded with talent. Thanks, Stadion.

As is the accepted standard, and certainly in this case the fact, whatever factual errors and omissions are sadly, but most certainly, my own.

# CHAPTER 1

# Introduction

I have learned a few things over the years and probably retained even fewer. For example, I know that when dealing with the unknown such as the analysis of the stock market, you absolutely cannot speak in absolutes. I also know that random guessing about what to do in the market is a quick path to failure. One needs a process for investing. Any process is better than no process or even worse, a random or constantly changing process. Hopefully, you will find the path to a successful process with this book.

---

The noblest pleasure is the joy of understanding.

*Leonardo da Vinci*

---

How can you even begin to analyze the market if you are not using the correct tools to determine its present state? If you do not fully grasp the present state of the market, your analysis, whether real or anticipated, will be off by an amount equivalent to at least the error of your current analysis. And your error will be compounded based upon the timeframe of your analysis. This highlights why most forecasts are a waste of time.

## Believable Misinformation

One should remember things are quite often not what they seem. It is absolutely amazing to me how much people believe that is not true (the voice of experience speaking). Below are some things that many of us learned in our formative years from our teachers and parents. Most we just accepted as fact because we heard it from people we believed.

Myth: Some believe water runs out of a bathtub faster as it gets toward the end.
Fact: Assuming the tub's sides are cylindrical, the pressure is constant, it only appears to drain faster because you observe it starting to swirl toward the end, something you could not observe when the tub was full. The swirling action deceives one into thinking it is draining faster.

Myth: How many think that George Washington cut down a cherry tree?
Fact: George Washington did not cut down a cherry tree. That was a story told so that adults could teach their children that it was bad to tell lies—even our founding father didn't tell lies. Parson Mason Locke Weems, the author who wrote about it shortly after Washington's death, was trying to humanize Washington.
Myth: Did Washington throw a silver dollar across the Potomac River?
Fact: The Potomac River is almost a mile wide at Mount Vernon and silver dollars did not exist at that time.
Myth: Where was the Battle of Bunker Hill fought?
Fact: It was fought at Breed's Hill in Charleston, Massachusetts.
Myth: Dogs sweat through their tongues.
Fact: Guess what? Dogs don't sweat. Their tongues have large salivary glands that keep them wet.

Okay, the following two examples of believable misinformation are only for the hardy who have found this section interesting. The rest should skip them. They are only for nerds like me.

Myth: How many think that December 21 in the northern hemisphere is the shortest day of the year?
Fact: Most do. However, it is actually the longest astronomical day based on Kepler's Second Law of Planetary Motion (planets, in their elliptical orbits, sweep out equal areas in equal time). When the Earth is closest to the sun, the northern hemisphere is tilted away and a much greater arc is swept in a day's travel than when the Earth is the furthest distance from the sun. If the question were posed as to what is the day with the shortest period of daylight, then it would be correct.

See Figure 1.1 for an illustration of Kepler's Second Law of Planetary Motion.
An additional observation on the tilt of the Earth is that summers in the southern hemisphere are generally warmer than the summers in the northern hemisphere. This can be caused by significantly more ocean in the southern hemisphere but also because the southern hemisphere is tilted toward the sun when the sun is closest to the Earth.

**FIGURE 1.1**  Kepler's Second Law of Planetary Motion

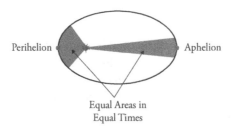

Myth: Bath water drains counterclockwise in the northern hemisphere.

Fact: Another example of how people have believed things that are simply not true is that in the northern hemisphere many will say that water, when draining from a tub, will swirl counterclockwise. Although it very well may do so, it is not for the reason they think it will. This is an example of a little bit of scientific knowledge totally misapplied. The Coriolis Effect (see Figure 1.2) is caused by the earth's rotation and generally applies to large almost frictionless bodies, such as weather systems. This is why in the northern hemisphere, hurricanes rotate counterclockwise, and in the southern hemisphere, they rotate clockwise. The rotational effect is measured in arc seconds (a unit of angular measure equal to 1/60 of an arc minute, or 1/3600 of a degree), which is an extremely small measurement of angular rotation. To apply this principle to the rotation of water draining from a tub is totally incorrect. High pressure and low pressure weather patterns are also reversed—I would love to see a weather reporter from Dallas move to Santiago and adapt to that.

Hopefully, you are getting my point. In the past few years the Internet has been the source and exploitation of much hype and false information. How many times have you received an e-mail from a friend (who probably did not originate it), and believed it to be true but did not bother to check it out, but forwarded it anyhow? You should start verifying them because many of them are a hoax. Believable misinformation flourishes.

**FIGURE 1.2**  Coriolis Effect

If you enjoy this type of information, I would recommend a new book by Samuel Arbesman, *The Half-Life of Facts: Why Everything We Know Has an Expiration Date*. Arbesman is an expert in scientometrics, which looks at how facts are made and remade in the modern world. People often cling to selected "facts" as a way to justify their beliefs about how things work. Arbesman notes, "We persist in only adding facts to our personal store of knowledge that jibe with what we already know, rather than assimilate new facts irrespective of how they fit into our views." (B4) This is known as confirmation bias, which is dealt with in Chapter 6.

A general theme throughout this book is one of separating fact from fiction. Fiction in this case is often a well-accepted theory on finance, economics, or the market in general. If you were caught believing some of the things mentioned in the previous paragraphs, then how much from the world of investing do you believe? Just maybe you have accepted as fact some things that simply are not true. I certainly know that I did.

In this chapter a lot of basic information is provided to assist you in understanding the remainder of this book. There are definitions, mathematical formulae, explanations of anomalies, historical events that affect the data, differing methods of calculation, and a host of other important information normally found in an appendix. It is of such importance to understand this material that it belongs prior to the discussion and not in the appendix, as is usually the custom.

## Indicators and Terminology You Should Be Familiar with

There are basically four different indicator types: differences, ratios, percentage, and cumulative. Differences are most common and should be adjusted for time independent scaling. As the number of issues increase over time, the scaling will get expanded and thresholds that worked in the past will need to be adjusted. One way to do this is to normalize the indicator so the scaling is always between zero and 100. The following section covers many popular indicators and concepts that will help you understand them better when discussed later in the book.

> *Absolute value.* In mathematical script this is denoted with | | around the value in which you want to have its absolute value. Absolute value calculations ignore the sign (positive or negative) of the number. In regard to breadth data, absolute value ignores market direction and only deals with market activity. The absolute value of +3 is 3, and the absolute value of −3 is also 3.
>
> *Accumulated/summed* $\left(\sum\right)$ (also see cumulative below). This is the term used to add up a series of numbers. For example, the advance decline line is an accumulation of the difference between the advances and the declines. That difference is summed with each new day's difference added to the previous value. Also used with the term cumulate. In many formulae in this book it is shown either as Previous Value + Today's Value or $\sum$.

*Alpha.* Alpha is a benchmark relative risk adjusted measure. It is not simply excess return. If markets were truly efficient then there would be no alpha.

*Arithmetic/simple moving averages.* To take an average of just about anything numerical, you add up the numbers and divide by the number of items. For example, if you have $4 + 6 + 2$, the sum is 12, and the average is $12/3 = 4$. A moving average does exactly this but as a new number is added, the oldest number is removed. In the example above, let's say that 8 was the new number, so the sequence would be $6 + 2 + 8$. The first 4 was removed because we are averaging only 3 numbers (3 period moving average). In this case the new average would be $16/3 = 5.33$. So by adding an 8 and removing a 4, we increased the average by 1.33 in this example. For those so inclined: $8 - 4 = 4$, and $4/3 = 1.33$.

In technical analysis the simple or arithmetic average is used extensively. One thing that you should keep in mind is that with the simple average each component is weighted exactly the same. This tends to make the simple average stale if using it for large amounts of data. For example, the popular 200-day average means that the price 200 days ago is carrying the same weight, or having the same effect on the average as the most recent price. It, therefore, is also much slower to change direction. *See exponential average.*

*Average true range* (ATR). Average true range is the process of measuring the price action over a particular period, usually one day. Normally this is done by just looking at the difference between the high and low price of the day. However, ATR also includes the previous days close so that if there is a gap the price action also has that movement included.

*Behavioral finance.* A relative newcomer to the analysis of markets, this is the study of why investors do what they do. "Behavioral finance is the study of the influence of psychology on the behavior of financial practitioners and the subsequent effect on markets" Martin Sewell (W6). "I think of behavioral finance as simply 'open-minded finance'" Thaler (A109).

*Buy and hold.* Buy and hold is the terminology used when discussing the act of making an investment and then just holding it for a very long time. This is more common than most would believe and can be a very bad decision during secular bear periods, which can last on average 17 years.

*Capitalization.* Capitalization refers to the number of shares a company has outstanding multiplied by the price of the stock. Most market indices, such as the S&P 500, NYSE Composite, and the Nasdaq Composite are capitalization weighted, which means the big companies dominate the movement of the index.

*Coefficient of determination.* This measures the proportion of variability in a data set that is explained by another variable. Values can range from 0, indicating that zero percent of the variability of the data set is explained by the other variable, to 1, indicating that all of the variability in a data set is explained by the other variable. It is statistically shown as $R^2$, which is nothing more than the square of correlation.

*Correlation.* A statistical measurement showing dependence between two data sets. Known in statistics and finance as R, it is used to determine the degree of correlation, noncorrelation, or inverse correlation between the two data sets (often an issue such as a mutual fund and its benchmark).

*Cumulative.* Cumulative indicators can be differences, ratios, or percentage. You are adding the daily results to the previous total. The advance decline line is a good example of a cumulative indicator. It is sometimes referred to as accumulate or summed.

*Detrend.* A term to denote when you subtract the price from a moving average of the price. This will amplify the price relative to its smoothed value (moving average). To visualize this, pretend you had the ability to take both ends of the moving average line and pull it taut so that the price line falls into its same relative position to the now straight moving average line. Doing this allows you to see cycles of a length greater than that of the number of periods used in the moving average.

*Divergence.* This is when an indicator and price do not confirm each other. At market tops, many times the price will continue to make new highs, while an indicator will reverse and not make a new high. This is a negative divergence. A positive divergence is at market bottoms when the prices continue to make new lows while the indicator does not and makes higher lows.

*Drawdown.* Drawdown is the percentage that price moves down after making a new all-time high price. Drawdowns of greater than $-20$ percent are known as bear markets. This book tries to convince you that real risk is drawdown and not volatility as modern finance wants you to believe.

*Exponential moving averages.* This method of averaging was developed by scientists, such as Pete Haurlan, in an attempt to assist and improve the tracking of missile guidance systems. More weight is given to the most recent data and it is therefore much faster to change direction. It is sometimes represented as a percentage (trend percent) instead of by the more familiar periods. Here is a formula that will help you convert between the two:

$$K = 2/(N + 1) \text{ where } K = \text{the smoothing constant (trend percent)}$$
$$\text{and } N = \text{periods}$$
$$\text{Algebraically solving for } N: N = (2/K) - 1$$

For example, if you wanted to know the smoothing constant of a 19-period exponential average, you could do the math, $K = 2/(19 + 1) = 2/20 = 0.10$ (smoothing constant) or 10 percent (trend) as it is many times expressed.

Here is something important in regard to exponential moving averages; by the nature of their formula they will always change direction when they move through the price that is used to calculate them. This means that during an uptrend in prices and their exponential average, when the prices drop below the average, the average will immediately begin to decline. A simple or arithmetic average will not do this.

*Filtered wave.* Art Merrill says that it is an amplitude filter to remove the noise by filtering the data. He further states that the important swings in price action are clearly evident. Simply, a filtered wave is a process of removing a predetermined percentage of noise.

*Momentum. See* Rate of Change.

*Normalize.* This is a mathematical procedure to reduce the scaling of unlike data so it can be more easily compared. To normalize a series of data one usually wants the resultant data to fall in a range from zero to 100. The easiest way to do this is by the following formula:

$$\frac{\text{Current Value} - \text{Lowest Value in the Series}}{\text{Highest Value in the Series} - \text{Lowest Value in the Series}} \times 100$$

Some of you might notice that this is similar to the formula for the %K Stochastic indicator, with the exception that for stochastics, the highest and lowest values are set by the number of periods you want to use. Many indicators are served well by looking at their normalized values for a predetermined number of periods. For example, if there was a good identifiable cycle in the market being analyzed, the number of periods of that cycle length might be a good number to use for normalization. A number of the indicators in this book are normalized in that manner.

*Oscillator.* A term used to explain a number of technical indicators such as rate of change, momentum, stochastics, RSI, and so on. These are all indicators that oscillate above and below a common value, many times which is zero. Other times they oscillate between zero and 100.

*Overbought/oversold.* These terms have got to be the most overused and misunderstood terms when talking about the markets. Overbought refers to the time in which the prices have risen to a level that seems as if they cannot go any higher. Oversold is the opposite—prices have dropped to a point it seems as they cannot go any lower. Although this sounds simple enough, the term is usually based on someone's personal observation of price levels and not on sound analysis.

*Overlay.* This refers to the act of putting an indicator on top of another one. A simple example would be displaying a moving average of an indicator on the same plot. In this case the indicator and its moving average would utilize the same scaling. Many times an unrelated indicator can be overlaid on another using totally independent price scaling.

*Peak.* Peak is terminology referring to a peak in prices, usually easy to identify if looking at a price chart, but does depend upon the time frame you are working with. *See* Trough.

*Percentage.* Percentage is generally better than a ratio because you are making the item relative to its related base. For example, the number of new highs by itself can be meaningful in the short term, but over long periods of time and with more and more issues traded, the relationship cannot remain consistent. If you took the number of new highs as a percentage of the total issues traded, then the scaling will always be from zero to 100 and large amounts of data can be viewed with some consistency.

*Rate of change.* Used interchangeably with momentum, rate of change is looking at a piece of data relative to a like piece of data at an earlier time. For example, with stock data, a 10-day rate of change would take today's price and subtract or divide by the stock's price 10 days ago. If one takes the difference in price and then divides by the older price you will see percentage changes. Generally, it is not the value of the rate of change that is important, but the direction and pattern associated with it. However, some oscillators have consistent levels that can be used as overbought and oversold. Rate of change seems to more often than not be in reference to the difference in values, whereas momentum is more often the ratio of values. The line shape will be the same, only the numbers that make up the line will be different.

*Ratio.* A ratio is when you divide one data component by another. This keeps them in perspective and will alleviate many of the problems associated with using just the difference. Sometimes the numerator and denominator are not balanced and you get a nonsymmetrical problem similar to what you get with the Arms Index. This is really not a problem as long as you are aware that it exists. Finally, a ratio of positive numbers (or similar signs) is always going to be greater than zero.

*Real.* Commonly used when referring to data that has been adjusted for the effects of inflation. Most raw data contains the effects of inflation, so by removing inflation from the data, it is called real, such as the real S&P 500. Real = Nominal − Inflation.

*Regression.* This provides us with an equation describing the nature of the relationship between two variables, plus supplies variance measures that allow us to access the accuracy with which the regression equation can predict values on the criterion variable, making it more than just curve-fitting. In modern finance it is used extensively to generate alpha and beta when comparing two issues.

*Semi-log.* Semi-log refers to the price scaling on charts. The abscissa axis is normally the date axis so it cannot be displayed logarithmically. Logarithmic scaling shows percentage moves in price and is much better for viewing long-term data. Note: You cannot use semi-log scaling with any values of zero or negative numbers.

*Smoothing.* This is in reference to averaging data either by a simple or exponential moving average. It is a better adverb to use than always trying to explain that you take the moving average of it or take the exponential moving average of it; just say you are "smoothing" it. It is also used as a verb as in you can "smooth" it.

*Stop loss.* Also known as a protective stop. This is a process in which an investor protects herself against losses larger than desired. There are many types of stop losses, such as a percentage drop from the buying price or a percentage drop from the current or highest price reached.

*Support and resistance.* First the definitions of support and resistance, then an explanation as to what they are. More elaborate definitions are available in almost any text on technical analysis. In fact, one of the best discussions of it is in Steven Achelis' book, *Technical Analysis from A to Z*, where he ties it to supply and demand. Support is the price at which an issue has trouble dropping below. Resistance is the price level that it has trouble rising above.

*Trendiness.* This is my term for a market or any price series to maintain a trend. Of course, the trend must be defined by not only its magnitude but also its duration. Chapter deals with trending markets and this term is used considerably in that chapter.

*Trough.* Trough is terminology referring to a low point in prices, usually easy to identify if looking at a price chart, but does depend upon the time frame you are working with. *See* Peak.

*Volatility.* Volatility is a measure of the movement of a time series, usually of price data, however, not restricted to that. There are many forms of volatility and there is an entire section in this book that discusses it.

*World of finance.* This is a term I use to include financial academia and retail (sell side) Wall Street. There is much in this book that is critical of the world of finance.

There are other terms throughout the book and when I think they need to be defined, the definition is presented on the first appearance of the term.

## Living in the Noise

I'm constantly amazed at the media's attempt to justify every move in the market with something in the news, whether it be economical, political, monetary, or whatever. If the market is up over the past hour, they find a positive news item to justify it. If the market is down, then a negative news item is used. There are other ongoing and constant drumbeats of useless information droning throughout the day while the market is open. Some are just plain wrong, such as "the market is down today because there are more sellers than buyers." It is a free trading market; so for that to work; there has to be the same number of buyers and sellers, no matter what the market is doing. They would be correct if they said that the market sold off today because there was more selling enthusiasm. And finally there is the endless supply of questions for the experts.

Here are some other examples of noise:

"Stocks are under pressure"—Why?
"More sellers than buyers"—Impossible on a share basis.
"What is causing this decline today?"—Always seeking a reason—rarely correct.
"How do you think the market will end this year?"—Forecasting is a fool's game.

"The earnings beat expectations and the stock is down two points"—Sad.

"Cash on the sidelines"—How can that be, when you sell a stock someone has to buy it.

"The latest survey says . . ."—Who cares?

"Breaking news"—It wouldn't be news if it wasn't breaking.

"Countdown clocks"—Media fascination with investors' fear.

"Fair value on morning futures"—Waste of time.

"Sorry Pope Benedict, we have to cut you off because earnings reports are coming out"—Pathetic.

"Asking a long time buy and hold manager what he thinks of the market"—Hmmm, let me guess.

"Brokerage firms offering magical technical analysis software to open an account"—It's the farmer, not the plow.


## Data

I used a great deal of stock market data in this book, primarily the daily series for the Dow Jones Industrial Average and the S&P 500. Reliable data is very important for proper analysis. I have seen references to stock market data back to the early 1800s, but it was spliced together from numerous sources, usually by academics who I think just don't have the same appreciation for accuracy as I do. The two series I used most often have been in existence with original source since the start date of the data I used. Below is some information about that data used in this book.

> *S&P 500.* My series began December 30, 1927. From the beginning until March 3, 1957, it was the S&P 90. There is, however, older data produced by the Cowles Commission back to 1871.
>
> *Dow Industrials.* My series began February 17, 1885, but records show that Charles Henry Dow began the series on July 3, 1884. While Charles Dow began publishing his series in 1897, he maintained the data from 1885. Following the introduction of the 12-stock industrial average in the spring of 1896, Dow, in the autumn of that year, dropped the last nonrailroad stocks in his original index, making it the 20-stock railroad average. Initially the data was known only as the Dow Jones Average. In 1916, the industrial average expanded to 20 stocks; the number was raised again, in 1928, to 30, where it remains today.

Shiller PE and CPI data were obtained from Robert Shiller's website at: www.econ.yale.edu/~shiller/data.htm.

This is monthly data back to 1871 and is updated periodically.

Keeping the data updated is also an important part of analysis; the data sources must be reputable. I use Bloomberg, Thomson Reuters, and Pinnacle Data, and would comfortably recommend them to anyone.

This book is not and never was designed to be a storybook to be read from beginning to end, but is a compilation of information about the markets, the flaws of modern finance, uncovering market history, misconceptions used to promote or market a flawed strategy, and a host of other tidbits. It takes almost two-thirds of the book to get to the "meat" of the book: rules-based trend following models.

Furthermore, I think a money manager, whether managing funds or separate accounts who follows a benchmark or particular style is never asked "why" they manage money that way. Simply, if you are trying to at least track or outperform a benchmark, no one will ask why you try it that way. This is where a rules-based trend following model, which it almost totally unconstrained in what to invest in and especially treats cash as an asset class is completely different. Much of this book is about why I use a rules-based trend following process.

Modern financial theory wants you to believe that the markets do not trend, are efficient, and therefore cannot be exploited for profit. They state that it is random and is normally distributed except for some very long-term periods that last many decades. What they ignore is that the market is made up of people, frail humans who act and invest like humans. Humans can be rational and they can be irrational, rarely knowing which is present and when. Being rational at times and being irrational at times is normal. This is not random behavior and is quite predictable. Hopefully this book demonstrates those failings and offers a solution.

Another focus in this book is the subject of risk. There is a great story about the simplicity of risk analysis told by the late great Peter Bernstein in his book, *Against the Gods*. Blaise Pascal, in scribblings in the margin of his *Pensees* publication, puts for what is now known as *Pascal's Wager*. He asks, "God is, or he is not. Which way should we incline? Reason cannot answer." He explained that belief in God is not a decision. You cannot awake one morning and declare, "Today I think I will decide to believe in God." You believe or you do not believe. Pascal leads us through a decision path that ultimately says that if there is not a God, then it doesn't matter. However, if there is a God, then the decision on how to live your life is important. Salvation is clearly preferable to eternal damnation, the correct decision is to act on the basis that God is. (B7)

I have sprinkled many quotes throughout this book. I like quotes because if something someone has said lasts over the years or is repeated often, it is probably profound. This is not unlike trite expressions, which I believe exist because they are generally true whether you want to believe them or not.

I give a lot of presentations/speeches and each time I learn something. One thing I learned a few years ago is that if you want to present some serious information to an audience that might just not understand your concepts or that resists anything that is new, use humor sparingly. The humor needs to be simple and essentially just witty, but not overly so. You must get them to uncross their arms and smile; this seems to improve their hearing. I have buried a little of that in this book—I think.

Throughout this book, in fact throughout most of my life, I have had a tendency to explain things using multiple approaches in the hope to cover a broader audience.

In fact, you soon learn that I can beat a horse to death at times. If you grasp a concept I am explaining early, please accept my apologies for the remaining explanations.

Finally, here is a short comment about observable information versus actionable information. Often the world of finance will produce very convincing data or charts that show historical information about the markets. The problem is that they are trying to convince you that you should invest a certain way based on that data they have shown. Usually, and more often than not, the data is just showing you about past market history and is really only observable information because you cannot turn that knowledge into an investment strategy or idea. Actionable information, on the other hand, is data or charts that show realistic information that is convertible into a valid investment strategy. Do not misunderstand this, observable information is about studying the past and learning about the markets, which is invaluable, however it takes actionable information to make investment decisions.

---

**NOTE**

Select tables and figures in this book are available online at www.wiley.com/go/morrisinvesting. While they are the same data, the formatting makes them much easier to view and use. Plus they will be updated periodically with more current data. See "About the Online Resources" at the back of the book for more information.

# Market Fiction, Flaws, and Facts

Part I can best be described as the location for things I have learned over the past 40 years about the markets, about investors, and about investment philosophies. These involve many concepts and measurements of the markets that include fiction, flaws, and facts about the markets.

Part I is all about understanding the past and hopefully learning from it. As the old saying goes, "The present is never exactly like the past, but it certainly rhymes," which is helpful to apply when studying the markets. In Part I my opinions are often included, sometimes they are adamant, other times they are merely subjective. I have come to believe strongly in what I say in this book, but also know that just because I believe it, does not always mean it is absolutely fact. I try to say that often so that I don't offend everyone.

There is an old aviation saying, *It is better to be on the ground wishing you were in the air, than in the air, wishing you were on the ground.*

Mark Twain is credited with saying, *It is not what you don't know that will get you into trouble; it is what you know for sure that just ain't so.*

There are things in modern finance that are just plain wrong, more marketing than substance, and I try to dispel much of it in this section. There are many things in modern finance that just don't measure up to their overhyped abilities. I try to point out many of them and offer examples where they are flawed.

Bull markets—Generally defined as moves upward of 20 percent or greater. This is actually a take-off from the more popular definition of a bear market.

Bear markets—Universally defined as declines in the market of 20 percent or more. Drawdowns are moves downward, measured in percentages, with the term *bear market* attached to drawdowns of 20 percent or greater.

Secular markets—Long-term moves in the market, which are defined by long-term swings in valuations, which are caused by changes in inflation.

Market valuations—Generally refers to price earnings ratio, but can involve other fundamental data.

Volatility—The world of finance defines volatility as standard deviation; this book will refute that concept.

Sector analysis—Both Standard & Poor's and Dow Jones have predefined equity market sectors. These are classifications for stocks across broad categories and often used in strategies.

Asset class analysis—These are generally broader than sectors in that they are not tied to equities. Equities could be considered an asset class, along with fixed income, gold, and so on.

Return analysis—Charts of annualized returns over various periods is presented along with various looks at the distribution of returns.

Return distributions—Various charts showing return distributions based on percentages, variability, and segments of the return data.

# CHAPTER 2

# Fictions Told to Investors

Market myths are generally perpetuated by repetition, misleading symbolic connections, and the complete ignoring of facts. The world of finance is full of such tendencies and this section of the book attempts to show you some examples. Please keep in mind that not all of these examples are totally misleading, they are sometimes valid, but have too many holes in them to be worthwhile as investment concepts. And not all are directly related to investing and finance. Enjoy!

## Believable Misinformation in Investing

Remember from Chapter 1 that many of the things we learned when we were young simply are not true? How many things have you learned in regard to investing that also just might not be true?

> Buy and hold is the only way to be successful in the stock market.
> Dollar cost averaging is a good technique.
> Diversification will protect you from bear markets.
> Compounding is the eighth wonder of the world.
> You must remain invested at all times or you will miss the 10 best days each year.
> Average returns are never better than compounded returns.
> Probability and risk are the same thing.
> Equity asset allocation will protect you from bear markets.
> Economists are good at predicting the market.
> Chasing performance is a common technique.

## The Void of Accountability

How often do you watch economists and market experts in the financial media (television, print, etc.) offer strong opinions on the future direction of the economy and the stock market? Do they ever present their track record? Never! In fact, if you pay close attention you will see that most of the "experts" are gaining something from their

15

appearance. I'm shocked and disappointed at the absolute certainty in which they deliver their prognostications.

## Hiding behind Statistics

Have you placed a bet on the market using the Super Bowl indicator? The Super Bowl indicator is based on the premise that if the Super Bowl champion came from the old AFL, now known as the AFC, that the year will bring a down trend in the stock market while a winner from the old NFL, now the NFC, will lead to a bull market. Hopefully you have not made any market decision on this, as that is a classic example of data mining and even then with an inadequate amount of data. This is not, however, uncommon as analysts, the financial media, newsletter writers, bloggers, and so on are constantly using data-mined statistics to make or support their hypothesis.

Figure 2.1 is a histogram of the annual returns on the Dow Industrial Average since 1897. The returns on the left are the down years and the ones on the right are the up years. The up years account for 66 percent of all the years, so if I were selling you a buy-and-hold strategy or an index fund, I could point to this chart and say, "Look the market is up 66 percent of the time," and I would be correct. Is this actionable information? Of course not, it is only observable information and is good because it helps one understand market history and statistics. You just can't make an investment decision based on this information.

Let's play a game. First of all, I promise you that it is a fair game; here are the rules:

It will cost you $10 to play the game.
You can play as many times as you desire.
If you win, you will receive $1 million.
There are no tricks.
The honest mathematical probability of winning is 1 out of 6. Honest! No tricks!

**FIGURE 2.1**   Dow Industrial Annual Return Histogram

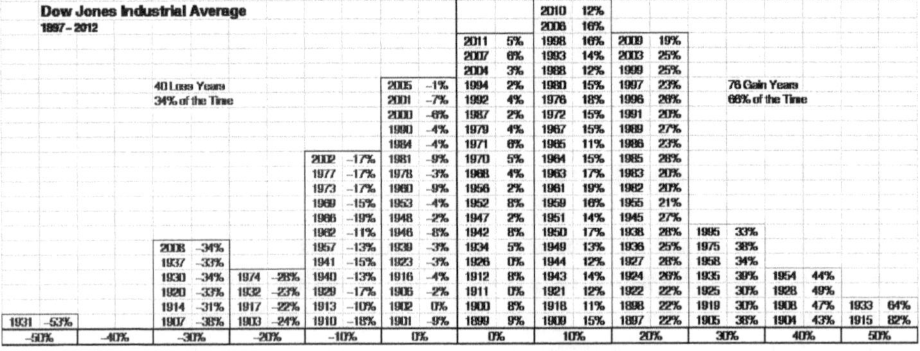

Dow Jones Industrial Average
1897–2012

40 Loss Years — 34% of the Time
76 Gain Years — 66% of the Time

| -50% | -40% | -30% | -20% | -10% | 0% | 0% | 10% | 20% | 30% | 40% | 50% |
|---|---|---|---|---|---|---|---|---|---|---|---|
| | | | | | | | 2012 10% | | | | |
| | | | | | | | 2010 12% | | | | |
| | | | | | | | 2006 16% | | | | |
| | | | | | | 2011 5% | 1998 16% | 2009 19% | | | |
| | | | | | | 2007 6% | 1993 14% | 2003 25% | | | |
| | | | | | 2004 3% | | 1988 12% | 1999 25% | | | |
| | 2008 -34% | | | 2005 -1% | 1994 2% | | 1980 15% | 1997 23% | | | |
| | 1937 -33% | | | 2001 -7% | 1992 4% | | 1976 18% | 1996 26% | | | |
| | | | | 2000 -6% | 1987 2% | | 1972 15% | 1991 20% | | | |
| | | | | 1990 -4% | 1979 4% | | 1967 15% | 1989 27% | | | |
| | | | | 1984 -4% | | 1971 6% | 1965 11% | 1986 23% | | | |
| | | | 2002 -17% | 1981 -9% | | 1970 5% | 1964 15% | 1985 28% | | | |
| | | | 1977 -17% | 1978 -3% | 1968 4% | | 1963 17% | 1983 20% | | | |
| | | | 1973 -17% | 1960 -9% | 1956 2% | | 1961 19% | 1982 20% | | | |
| | | | 1969 -15% | 1953 -4% | | 1952 8% | 1959 16% | 1955 21% | | | |
| | | | 1966 -19% | 1948 -2% | 1947 2% | | 1951 14% | 1945 27% | | | |
| | | | 1962 -11% | 1946 -8% | | 1942 8% | 1950 17% | 1938 28% | 1995 33% | | |
| | | | 1957 -13% | 1939 -3% | | 1934 5% | 1949 13% | 1936 25% | 1975 38% | | |
| | | | 1941 -15% | 1923 -3% | 1926 0% | | 1944 12% | 1927 28% | 1958 34% | | |
| | 1930 -34% | 1974 -28% | 1940 -13% | 1916 -4% | | 1912 8% | 1943 14% | 1924 26% | 1935 39% | 1954 44% | |
| | 1920 -33% | 1932 -23% | 1929 -17% | 1906 -2% | 1911 0% | | 1921 12% | 1922 22% | 1925 30% | 1928 49% | |
| | 1914 -31% | 1917 -22% | 1913 -10% | 1902 0% | | 1900 8% | 1918 11% | 1919 30% | | 1908 47% | 1933 64% |
| 1931 -53% | 1907 -38% | 1903 -24% | 1910 -18% | 1901 -9% | | 1899 9% | 1909 15% | 1897 22% | 1905 38% | 1904 43% | 1915 82% |
| -50% | -40% | -30% | -20% | -10% | 0% | 0% | 10% | 20% | 30% | 40% | 50% |

How many want to play?

When I do this during a presentation most folks raise their hands, a few don't but they are the ones that never raise their hand. I then announce that the game is Russian roulette, and ask, "How many want to play the game now?" No one raises their hands. I then ask, "What happened?" I changed your focus from these goofy statistics to the risk of playing the game and when you found out the risk of playing you were no longer interested. Most do not realize the difference between probability and risk. This is what you need to do with the market, analyze and assess the risk; stop paying attention to the daily noise, and know the difference between actionable information and observable information.

## You Must Remain Invested or You Will Miss the 10 Best Days of the Year

You must remain invested or you will miss the 10 best days each year. How many times have you heard that? While the fact of this matter is true, it is an impossible task to determine the best days beforehand. Let's turn it around and ask what happens if you miss the 10 worst days each year. Figure 2.2 shows the S&P 500 since 1979. The line that moves *down* and to the right is the line representing "missing the 10 best days" argument. Note, in this analysis it was about missing the 10 best (worst) days per year. Again, the argument is factual, it just isn't realistic. The line that moves *up*

**FIGURE 2.2** Missing the Best and the Worst 10 Days Each Year

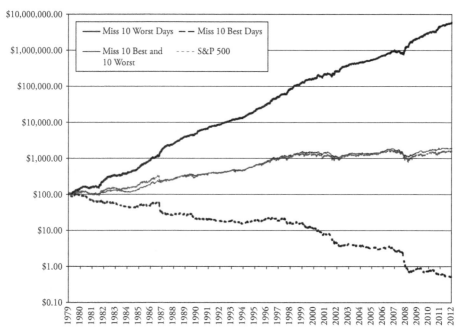

and to the right is the one that "misses the 10 *worst* days." Clearly missing the 10 worst days gives a drastically better performance than missing the 10 best days. The two lines in the middle are the S&P 500 and the line representing "missing both the 10 best and 10 worst days," which you can see are quite close.

I have done this analysis also using the Dow Industrial Average back to 1885 and the results are always the same. I have done this over many varying time periods and again, the results are the same. So, the buy-and-hold pundits and the index investing pundits want to scare you into believing their methods are better. In Chapter 4, the section "The Deception of Average" should be enough to convince you that there is something wrong with that type of thinking. The best days (worst days) in the market are nothing more than interesting statistical anomalies. The argument that missing the best days would reduce the final return of a buy-and-hold strategy is true, but it also provides no information regarding the question of whether one can time the market in that regard. Somewhat like a straw man argument.

Table 2.1 is the data on the "missing days" conundrum. All data is updated through December 31, 2012. All calculations are based solely on price performance with no adjustment for dividends or inflation. It should be clear that if it were possible, missing the worst days each year would be the better strategy. This might be a stretch, but because the missing both best and worst outperforms buy and hold, I think it shows that missing bad market days is more important. It also shows that missing days of high volatility are good. However, the purpose here is to challenge the marketing of buy and hold, which uses the "missing the best days" argument.

Remember, the message is clear and simple: The name of the game is to miss the bad days a lot more than missing the good days. This will play out as this book moves along. Note that most of the best days happen during bad or bear markets, usually tied to an overreaction to a short-term panic decline (you will see this in Table 3.1).

## Diversification Will Protect You?

The world of finance is locked into the risk category of nonsystematic or diversifiable risk, and they do a really good job of it. However, diversifiable risk is a small piece of the big risk pie. There are many trite sayings about diversification, one being: The only thing going up in a bear market is correlation. During big bear markets, correlations move rapidly toward one. This also means that most asset classes fail significantly during severe bear markets. The correlations among them move toward one, which means they become more and more correlated. Correlation is one of the primary components of modern portfolio theory. Diversification is a helpful tool, but it should only be employed to the point where its costs equal its benefits.

You can see in the two charts Figures 2.3 and 2.4 that during up markets, most asset classes are uncorrelated and exhibit significantly different returns. However in the second chart (Figure 2.4), during big bear markets, those same asset classes performed almost identical to each other, which challenges the need for diversification.

**TABLE 2.1**  Best and Worst Days

| Start Year | S&P 500 | | | Dow Industrial Average | | | |
|---|---|---|---|---|---|---|---|
| | 1927 | 1950 | 1980 | 1885 | 1900 | 1950 | 1980 |
| Number of Best Days | 850 | 630 | 330 | 1280 | 1130 | 630 | 330 |
| Number of Worst Days | 850 | 630 | 330 | 1280 | 1130 | 630 | 330 |
| Miss 10 Best of the Year | −17.25% | −12.73% | −15.49% | −16.61 | −16.51 | −13.01% | −14.79 |
| Miss 10 Worst of the Year | 35.70% | 32.44% | 39.26% | 33.68% | 34.25% | 31.66% | 39.47% |
| Miss 10 Best and 10 Worst of the Year | 6.64% | 7.71% | 8.83% | 6.34% | 6.66% | 7.18% | 9.35% |
| Buy and Hold | 5.30% | 7.31% | 8.14% | 4.83% | 5.08% | 6.86% | 8.69% |

**FIGURE 2.3**   Diversification Works

*Source:* Chart courtesy of Stockcharts.com.

**FIGURE 2.4**   Diversification Does Not Work

*Source:* Chart courtesy of Stockcharts.com.

**TABLE 2.2**  Components of the Diversification
Charts (Figures 2.3 and 2.4)

| Asset Class | Vanguard Mutual Fund |
| --- | --- |
| Large Cap | VFINX |
| Small Cap | NAESX |
| Large Cap Value | VIVAX |
| Small Cap Value | VISVX |
| Emerging Markets | VEIEX |
| European | VEURX |
| Pacific | VPACX |
| International Value | VTRIX |
| REIT | VGSIX |
| Total Bond | VBMFX |

The old saying goes, "Diversification works until it doesn't." The asset classes used in these two charts are shown in Table 2.2.

Diversification Works, as you can see in Figure 2.3 over the period from 2000 to October, 2007. . . .

. . . Until it doesn't as you can see in Figure 2.4 over the period from October 2007 to August 2009.

## Dollar Cost Averaging

Dollar cost averaging is simply the act of making like dollar investments on a periodic basis, say every month or every quarter. It is sold as a technique because they want you to believe that no one can outperform the market. There are many papers written on this subject and I don't want to dwell on it. Dollar cost averaging is very dependent on when you start the process. If you start the process at the top of the market, just prior to a large bear market, you will be buying all the way down and this process could last a couple of years. Your average purchase price would probably be somewhere in the middle of the decline. A quick study of equivalent returns would tell you that the following bull move would need to go considerably higher than just half way back up for you to just break even. In addition, it is also critical as to what periodic day or week you choose to make the investment. Should you do it quarterly and invest on the first day of the first week of the quarter, or something else?

The bottom line is that this process is subjected to unknown market risk, which can work for you, but can also work against you. However, I think dollar cost averaging is probably better than buy and hold and it is certainly better than doing nothing, which might also be the same as buy and hold. When I hear someone talk about dollar cost averaging I usually assume it is because they don't know what else to do. Anytime you can get someone to periodically contribute to an investment, you have accomplished something of value.

Table 2.3 is a really simple example of how it works using Apple stock from the year 2011, buying $500 of the stock on the first trading day of each month and determining

**TABLE 2.3**   Dollar Cost Averaging

| Date | Invested | Price per Share | Number of Shares |
|------|----------|-----------------|------------------|
| January | $   500.00 | $329.57 | 1.52 |
| February | $   500.00 | $345.03 | 1.45 |
| March | $   500.00 | $349.31 | 1.43 |
| April | $   500.00 | $344.56 | 1.45 |
| May | $   500.00 | $346.28 | 1.44 |
| June | $   500.00 | $345.51 | 1.45 |
| July | $   500.00 | $343.26 | 1.46 |
| August | $   500.00 | $396.75 | 1.26 |
| September | $   500.00 | $381.03 | 1.31 |
| October | $   500.00 | $374.60 | 1.33 |
| November | $   500.00 | $396.51 | 1.26 |
| December | $   500.00 | $387.93 | 1.29 |
| **Total** | $6,000.00 | $361.70 **Avg.** | 16.65 |
| **Lump** | $6,000.00 | $329.57 | 18.21 |

the results on the day of the last purchase in December. You can see that on the first trading day of December you had accumulated 16.65 shares of Apple stock at an average price of $361.70 per share. The lump sum example assumes you bought all $6,000.00 on the first trading day at $329.57 per share, which gave you 18.21 shares.

From this example, the lump sum investment came out ahead but I think you can see it has a lot to do with the time period for the investment, the volatility of the share prices, and actually, the day of the month that you make the purchase. Some of the advantages of DCA are the affordability factor and the convenience; it can be set up just like any monthly household budget item or expense and also something many people need to keep the process alive. The disadvantages are that lump sum investing can give better returns, but also worse returns, and the disadvantage is you won't know ahead of time. Also, when making numerous DCA investments the fees are generally higher than lump sum. The bottom line is that it helps people make investments on a periodic basis, which is always going to be better than sitting on the sidelines because you don't know what to do. Furthermore, dollar cost averaging becomes less effective as an investor ages because of less time for compounding and free cash is usually a lower percentage of total investment goals.

Jason Zweig, in a *Wall Street Journal* article on May 26, 2009, spoke of Benjamin Graham's comments on dollar cost averaging. Asked if dollar cost averaging could ensure long-term success, Mr. Graham wrote in 1962: "Such a policy will pay off ultimately, regardless of when it is begun, provided that it is adhered to conscientiously and courageously under all intervening conditions." For that to be true, however, the dollar cost averaging investor must "be a different sort of person from the rest of us . . . not subject to the alternations of exhilaration and deep gloom that have accompanied the gyrations of the stock market for generations past." "This," Mr. Graham concluded, "I greatly doubt." He didn't mean that no one can resist being swept up in the gyrating emotions of the crowd. He meant that few people can. To be an intelligent investor, you must cultivate what Mr. Graham called "firmness of character"—the ability to keep your own emotional counsel. (A102)

## Compounding Is the Eighth Wonder of the World

I think it was Albert Einstein who made that comment even though I found no proof that he did. The rest of the quote is: *He who understands it, earns it and he who doesn't, pays it.* I always remind folks that he forgot to include an adjective. *Positive* compounding is the eighth wonder of the world, which is usually associated with saving accounts, and so on. Table 2.4 is a simple example of how one negative year can ruin your retirement plans. Notice that Investment Option B also started out with a phenomenal first year return of +36 percent compared to Option A's return of only +10 percent. Another example of why chasing performance can be very harmful to your wealth.

The investment option B in Table 2.4 would require a return of 16 percent the following year to get back to the 8 percent per year average. Beware of negative returns; they can destroy your financial plans, especially as you lose time to recover the losses.

It is critical for long-term investment success to not track the short-term market movements. Instead one should only try to outperform the markets over the long term. Let's assume that your investment goal is to maintain an annualized return of 10 percent over the next five years as shown in Table 2.5. Here are the hypothetical market returns: +10 percent, +10 percent, +10 percent −10 percent, +10 percent. Those returns look pretty good at first glance even though one of them is negative. However, the impact on the actual investment return is quite different.

**TABLE 2.4** Compounding Example 1

|  | Investment Option A | Investment Option B |
|---|---|---|
| Year 1 | +10% | +36% |
| Year 2 | +6% | +8% |
| Year 3 | +8% | −20% |
| Average | +8% | +8% |
| Growth of $100 | $126 | $117 |
| Compounded Return | +8% | +5.4% |

**TABLE 2.5** Compounding Example 2

| Initial Invested Amount | Return | Balance | Average Compound Return |
|---|---|---|---|
| $100,000 | 10% | $110,000 | 10% |
| Year 2 | 10% | $121,000 | 11% |
| Year 3 | 10% | $133,100 | 11% |
| Year 4 | −10% | $119,790 | 5% |
| Year 5 | 10% | $131,769 | 6% |

The important point is that it only takes one drawdown over any one-year period to destroy compounded returns. In the above example it would take a 33 percent return in year five to return the portfolio to an annualized 10 percent return. This is why most investors' performance is far less than that of the actual market. Compounding is indeed the eighth wonder of the world, but it is only when the returns are positive.

## Relative Performance

First of all, you cannot retire on relative performance. Relative performance is a marketing concept dreamed up by financial pundits who rarely outperformed the market. Figure 2.5 is a table of various asset classes and their relative performance. Keep in mind that each column (year) is totally independent of the other columns, and the assets classes at the top performed better than those at the bottom of each column. You do not know if they both lost money, both made money, one did, or not. It is just simple relative performance. And guess what? You cannot retire on relative returns. Normally this table is displayed in color so the delineation between the squares is more apparent, but showing the actual data was not the purpose of introducing it at this point. You can view the latest version at www.callan.com/research/download/?file=periodic%2ffree%2f655.pdf/.

Often the Callan Periodic Table of Returns is shown to convince investors that chasing performance is a bad idea, as last year's top performer probably won't be the current year's top performer. You can see that sometimes there is a string of consistent top performance, in fact in Figure 2.5 Emerging Markets was the top performer from 2003 to 2007. If an investor caught onto that trend after a few years, it wasn't long before it failed miserably. Sadly, the investor, who probably thought they were genius added money each year and had no money management concepts or loss protection (stop loss) in place. Emerging markets fell to the worst performer in 2008 and showed exceptional relative volatility since. If there was any real value with this it is to learn and understand market history.

This is probably one of the most difficult obstacles to successful investing to overcome. It is human nature to want to be invested in the top-performing stocks, funds, or strategies. Yet, you rarely know they are top performing until after they have had a few good years of top performance. In the old days many picked up the late January issue of Barron's magazine when they showed the performance for all mutual funds for the previous year. Just like the Callan Periodic Table in Figure 2.5, when something is a top performer for a while, it more often than not, does not remain so. Style boxes are another dreadful source of performance chasing. A typical style box created by Morningstar in 1992 is shown in Figure 2.6. This gives investors an orderly classification system for mutual funds, which is unbelievably popular and used extensively to sell mutual funds. Morningstar ranks mutual funds into a five-star scale which forces a normal distribution because the top 10 percent get five stars, the bottom 10 percent get one star, middle 35 percent get three stars, and the other two 22.5 percent groups get four and two stars. Research has shown that investors tend to put money into those with high ratings and withdraw money from those with low ratings, usually when they should be doing the

**FIGURE 2.5** Callan Periodic Table of Relative Returns

Annual Returns for Key Indices (1993–2012) Ranked in Order of Performance

| Rank | 1993 | 1994 | 1995 | 1996 | 1997 | 1998 | 1999 | 2000 | 2001 | 2002 |
|---|---|---|---|---|---|---|---|---|---|---|
| 1 | MSCI Emerging Markets 74.84% | MSCI EAFE 7.78% | S&P 500 Growth 38.13% | S&P 500 Growth 23.97% | S&P 500 Growth 36.52% | S&P 500 Growth 42.16% | MSCI Emerging Markets 66.42% | Russell 2000 Value 22.83% | Russell 2000 Value 14.02% | Barclays Agg 10.26% |
| 2 | MSCI EAFE 32.57% | S&P 500 Growth 3.13% | S&P 500 37.58% | S&P 500 22.96% | S&P 500 33.36% | S&P 500 28.58% | Russell 2000 Growth 43.09% | Barclays Agg 11.63% | Barclays Agg 8.44% | MSCI Emerging Markets -6.00% |
| 3 | Russell 2000 Value 23.77% | S&P 500 1.32% | S&P 500 Value 36.99% | S&P 500 Value 22.00% | Russell 2000 Value 31.78% | MSCI EAFE 20.00% | S&P 500 Growth 28.24% | S&P 500 Value 6.08% | Russell 2000 2.49% | Russell 2000 Value -11.43% |
| 4 | Russell 2000 18.88% | S&P 500 Value -0.64% | Russell 2000 Growth 31.04% | Russell 2000 Value 21.37% | S&P 500 Value 29.98% | S&P 500 Value 14.68% | MSCI EAFE 26.96% | Russell 2000 -3.02% | MSCI Emerging Markets -2.37% | MSCI EAFE -15.94% |
| 5 | S&P 500 Value 18.61% | Russell 2000 Value -1.55% | Russell 2000 28.45% | Russell 2000 16.49% | Russell 2000 22.36% | Barclays Agg 8.70% | Russell 2000 21.26% | S&P 500 -9.11% | Russell 2000 Growth -9.23% | Russell 2000 -20.48% |
| 6 | Russell 2000 Growth 13.36% | Russell 2000 -1.82% | Russell 2000 Value 25.75% | Russell 2000 Growth 11.26% | Russell 2000 Growth 12.95% | Russell 2000 Growth 1.23% | S&P 500 21.04% | MSCI EAFE -14.17% | S&P 500 Value -11.71% | S&P 500 Value -20.85% |
| 7 | S&P 500 10.08% | Russell 2000 Growth -2.43% | Barclays Agg 18.47% | MSCI EAFE 6.05% | Barclays Agg 9.65% | Russell 2000 -2.55% | S&P 500 Value 12.73% | S&P 500 Growth -22.08% | S&P 500 -11.89% | S&P 500 -22.10% |
| 8 | Barclays Agg 9.75% | Barclays Agg -2.92% | MSCI EAFE 11.21% | MSCI Emerging Markets 6.03% | MSCI EAFE 1.78% | Russell 2000 Value -6.45% | Barclays Agg -0.82% | Russell 2000 Growth -22.43% | S&P 500 Growth -12.73% | S&P 500 Growth -23.59% |
| 9 | S&P 500 Growth 1.68% | MSCI Emerging Markets -7.32% | MSCI Emerging Markets -5.21% | Barclays Agg 3.63% | MSCI Emerging Markets -11.59% | MSCI Emerging Markets -25.34% | Russell 2000 Value -1.49% | MSCI Emerging Markets -30.61% | MSCI EAFE -21.44% | Russell 2000 Growth -30.26% |

| Rank | 2003 | 2004 | 2005 | 2006 | 2007 | 2008 | 2009 | 2010 | 2011 | 2012 |
|---|---|---|---|---|---|---|---|---|---|---|
| 1 | MSCI Emerging Markets 56.28% | MSCI Emerging Markets 25.95% | MSCI Emerging Markets 34.54% | MSCI Emerging Markets 32.59% | MSCI Emerging Markets 39.78% | Barclays Agg 5.24% | MSCI Emerging Markets 78.51% | Russell 2000 Growth 29.09% | Barclays Agg 7.84% | MSCI Emerging Markets 18.22% |
| 2 | Russell 2000 Growth 48.54% | Russell 2000 Value 22.25% | MSCI EAFE 13.54% | MSCI EAFE 26.34% | MSCI EAFE 11.17% | Russell 2000 Value -28.92% | Russell 2000 Growth 34.47% | Russell 2000 26.85% | S&P 500 Growth 4.65% | Russell 2000 Value 18.05% |
| 3 | Russell 2000 47.25% | MSCI EAFE 20.25% | S&P 500 Value 6.82% | Russell 2000 Value 23.48% | S&P 500 Growth 9.13% | Russell 2000 -33.79% | MSCI EAFE 31.78% | Russell 2000 Value 24.50% | S&P 500 2.11% | S&P 500 Value 17.68% |
| 4 | Russell 2000 Value 46.03% | Russell 2000 18.33% | S&P 500 4.91% | S&P 500 Value 20.81% | Russell 2000 Growth 7.05% | S&P 500 Growth -34.92% | S&P 500 Growth 31.57% | MSCI Emerging Markets 18.88% | S&P 500 Value -0.48% | MSCI EAFE 17.32% |
| 5 | MSCI EAFE 38.59% | S&P 500 Value 15.71% | Russell 2000 Value 4.71% | Russell 2000 18.37% | Barclays Agg 6.97% | S&P 500 -37.00% | Russell 2000 27.17% | S&P 500 Growth 15.05% | Russell 2000 Growth -2.91% | Russell 2000 16.35% |
| 6 | S&P 500 Value 31.79% | Russell 2000 Growth 14.31% | Russell 2000 4.55% | S&P 500 15.79% | S&P 500 5.49% | Russell 2000 Growth -38.54% | S&P 500 26.47% | S&P 500 15.06% | Russell 2000 -4.18% | S&P 500 16.00% |
| 7 | S&P 500 28.68% | S&P 500 10.88% | Russell 2000 Growth 4.15% | Russell 2000 Growth 13.35% | S&P 500 Value 1.99% | S&P 500 Value -39.22% | S&P 500 Value 21.17% | S&P 500 Value 15.10% | Russell 2000 Value -5.50% | S&P 500 Growth 14.61% |
| 8 | S&P 500 Growth 25.66% | S&P 500 Growth 6.13% | S&P 500 Growth 4.00% | S&P 500 Growth 11.01% | Russell 2000 -1.57% | MSCI EAFE -43.38% | Russell 2000 Value 20.58% | MSCI EAFE 7.75% | MSCI EAFE -12.14% | Russell 2000 Growth 14.59% |
| 9 | Barclays Agg 4.10% | Barclays Agg 4.34% | Barclays Agg 2.43% | Barclays Agg 4.33% | Russell 2000 Value -9.78% | MSCI Emerging Markets -53.18% | Barclays Agg 5.93% | Barclays Agg 6.54% | MSCI Emerging Markets -18.42% | Barclays Agg 4.21% |

*Source:* Courtesy of Callan Associates.

**FIGURE 2.6**   Morningstar Style Box

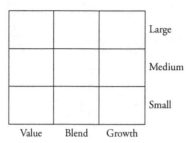

**FIGURE 2.7**   Trend Followers Style Box

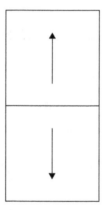

opposite. (A55) In fact, many fund managers are tied to a particular style and measured by how they performed relative to that style. Their benchmark is the style box they have been classified into. If the fund drifts from its designated style, the marketing pressure ensures adherence to the style box. I like to remind investors that when a manager who is tied to a benchmark (style) outperforms it, they call it alpha, however, when the manager under performs the benchmark they like to say it is tracking error.

Later in this book you will see an investment strategy that does not pay any attention to styles or style boxes; however, I can show you a modified style box for a trend following strategy in Figure 2.7. A trend follower is only concerned about uptrends and downtrends. If you feel that you must involve a style box approach, I recommend the one in Figure 2.7.

With all that is arguably wrong with financial theory the next chapter delves into some mathematical anomalies with using simple "bell curve" statistics, which are based on assumptions about the market that just do not play well and in fact are simply erroneous.

# CHAPTER 3

# Flaws in Modern Financial Theory

As an aerospace engineer, my education kept me far removed from the world of finance. Over the past couple of decades my career dropped me solidly into the "world of finance." The *world of finance* is my baked-up term that includes financial academia and, in general, retail (sell side) Wall Street. I honestly believe that the former is the marketing department of the latter.

In engineering we knew that to begin an analysis or delve into a research project, we had to begin with some basic assumptions about things. These assumptions were the starting blocks for the project; they launch the process. Many times, well into the project, it would be obvious that some of the assumptions were just wrong and had to be corrected or removed. The World of Finance over the past 60 years has produced a large number of white papers on financial theories, many of which begin with some basic assumptions. So far, so good!

The markets are efficient.
Investors are rational.
Returns are random.
Returns are normally distributed.
Gaussian (bell-curve) statistics is appropriate for use in finance/investing.
Alpha and beta are independent of correlation.
Volatility is risk.
Is a 60 percent equity/40 percent fixed income appropriate?
Compare forward (guesses) Price Earnings (PE) with long-term trailing (reported) PE.

The remainder of this section covers the challenges I have to the above list. Personally, I think modern finance is almost a hoax, an area of investments that has proliferated into a gigantic sales pitch. Few challenge it, and even fewer fully understand it. I think I could write an entire book about the flaws of modern finance but will try to offer a number of examples of how shallow and truly ineffective some of the concepts are along with examples. Hopefully, I will be successful with some examples that it will at least bring concern on your part and further study into the subject.

I should state that it isn't the problems of modern finance as much as how investment management cherry picks and misuses parts of it for marketing purposes.

## What Modern Portfolio Theory Forgot or Ignored

Recall that the theory assumes that all investors obtain the same information at the same time. Also, that they react similarly and share the same investment goals. Here are some rhetorical questions to challenge those assumptions:

Do people trade/invest using different time horizons? There are now investors/traders who trade in extremely short intervals during the day. There are those who will never hold a position overnight. There are those who let the market determine their holding period. And there are those who buy and hold for very long periods of time.

Are there different views of risk among investors? The really sad part of this questions is that most investors do not fully understand risk and certainly do not know what their risk tolerance is, let alone how to apply it to an investment strategy.

Are there different views of where the same stock's price will be one week, one month, or one year from now? This doesn't need any explanation because if you read financial media or watch television you know there is an unlimited supply of opinions on this.

The Capital Asset Pricing Model (CAPM) assumes that investors agree on return, risk, and correlation characteristics of all assets and invest accordingly. They rarely do. Some of the problems with return, risk, and correlations are dealt with elsewhere in this book. The biggest is that most use very long-term averages of these to assess future valuations. They should use an average that adapts to an investor's investing time horizon.

## Modern Portfolio Theory and the Bell Curve

I'll let Benoit Mandelbrot explain it from his book, *The (Mis)Behavior of Markets* (p. 13). The bell curve fits reality quite poorly. From 1916 to 2003, the daily movements of the Dow Industrials do not spread out on graph paper like a simple bell curve. The far edges flare too high. Theory suggests that over that time, there should be 58 days when the Industrials moved more than 3.4 percent; in fact, there are 1,001 such days. Theory predicts six days of swings beyond 4.5 percent; in fact, there were 366. And swings of more than 7 percent should come once every 300,000 years; in fact, there were 48 such days. Perhaps the assumptions were wrong. (B32)

### Black Monday, October 19, 1987

"The Dow Jones Industrials fell 29.2 percent. The probability of that happening, based on the standard reckoning of financial theorists, was one in 10 to the 50th power;

**FIGURE 3.1**   Normal Distribution Versus Actual Distribution from 2/17/1885 to 12/31/2012

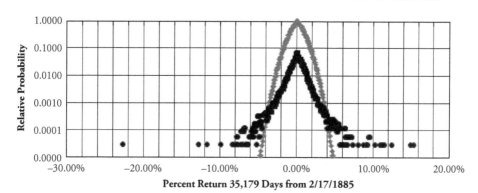

odds so small that they have no meaning. It is a number outside the scale of nature. You could span the powers of ten from the smallest subatomic particle to the breadth of the measurable universe—and still never meet such a number," *The (Mis)Behavior of Markets*, Benoit Mandelbrot (B32). Without knowing how he calculated the returns (daily, weekly, etc.) and the amount of data used in the calculation, it is impossible to re-create his numbers. He stated that on Black Monday the Dow Industrials fell 29.2 percent. Here are the numbers: October 16, 1987, close price was 2,246.74, October 19, 1987, close price was 1,738.74, which is a decline of 22.61 percent. If one used the low of October 19, 1987 (1,677.55), the decline would be −25.33 percent. The message is, however, the same; it was a huge decline and one that statistically should never happen. (B32)

Figure 3.1 shows the huge difference between the distribution of returns from the Gaussian "normal distribution" and the actual distribution of empirical data. This is the daily return of the Dow Industrials from 1885 with the vertical axis being relative probability and the horizontal axis being percent return. The taller peak is the Gaussian normal distribution and the other is the actual returns. You can see the small dot at the far left representing the −22.61 percent day known as Black Monday, October 19, 1987.

## Tails Wagging the Dog

If an asset bubble is defined as 2 standard deviations ($\sigma$, sigma) about its mean, then . . . statistically it won't happen but once every 43 years (four sigma total). Statistics dictate that only once every 1,600 years should such events be followed by a reverse move downward of 2 standard deviations. Sadly, these events happen often. Hence, once again, Gaussian statistics are not appropriate for market data. (B32)

October 2008 had some rare events. Table 3.1 shows 11 days during October 2008 ordered by absolute daily return.

The top three days based upon absolute daily returns are 11.1 percent, 10.9 percent, and −7.9 percent. The mathematical odds of three days with greater than

**TABLE 3.1**   October 2008

| 2008 | Return |
|------|-------:|
| October 13 | **11.1%** |
| October 28 | **10.9%** |
| October 15 | **−7.9%** |
| October 9 | −7.3% |
| October 22 | −5.7% |
| October 7 | −5.1% |
| October 16 | 4.7% |
| October 20 | 4.7% |
| October 24 | −3.6% |
| October 6 | −3.6% |
| October 2 | −3.2% |

7.9 percent moves is: 1 in 10,000,000,000,000,000,000,000 (that's 10 plus 21 zeros). The rise of the term *fat tails* recently is because the world of finance uses the wrong statistical analysis for the market. If the correct analysis were used, the term *fat tails* would not be used, it would have been addressed. This example reminds me of the e-Trade baby exclaiming that the odds are the same as if being eaten by a polar bear and a regular bear in the same day. While I'm critical of the statistics used in modern finance, I think I'm more concerned about their widely held belief as being valid. If you know something has problems, you can adjust accordingly. If you do not realize there are problems, you are in trouble.

My friend Ted Wong (TTSWong Advisory) has this to say about modern finance: "After Markowitz introduced Modern Portfolio Theory (MPT) in the 1950s, which was based on the Gaussian hypothesis, most theoreticians had since moved away from Gaussian statistics. Only the naive research analysts in the financial wire-houses and mutual fund institutions still use normal distributions in their papers. In fact, Benoit Mandelbrot cited in your book was the first to point out in the mid-1960s that the bell curve could not explain many fat tails observed in nature and in the financial markets. Fama and French pointed out that Gaussian statistics was only a special case in the family of Paretian distributions. The latter could account for all forms of fat tails by adjusting the leptokurtosis coefficient." [*Author's note*: Paretian refers to stable distributions, which should be used in modern finance but are rarely used because the mathematics is more complex, anyway that is my opinion. James Weatherall, in *The Physics of Wall Street*, provides a unique history of how Mandelbrot challenged modern finance and made headway, but ultimately did not change anything. (B59)]

"To me, the underlying problem with modern finance is not that Gaussian distributions don't fit the fat tails well. By adjusting the leptokurtosis coefficient, the quasi bell curve can now be bent by the theoreticians to whatever shapes and forms to fit the empirical data. The real issue in modern finance is the "blind" faith in the random walk hypothesis. Both the MPT and the Paretian practitioners assume that market prices behave in a random fashion. The random walk doctrine assumes that price changes are independent variables; that is, today's price change has no relationship with yesterday's or tomorrow's price change. They have hundreds of "proofs" to back up that claim and as a result, financial academia laughs at technical and even fundamental analysts in their efforts to predict future market prices.

"What the random walkers miss is the fact that most technical and quantitative analyses are not intended for predicting daily price changes, which I agree are more or less random. We believe that market prices are not random over a longer period of time. The distributions of totally random price events should have the mean near 0 percent and surrounded by a symmetrical distribution on either side just like the bell curve or the Paretian curve (with fat tails on both sides). If the mean return is located off center and the distributions are asymmetrical around the mean, then one can surely challenge the notion of randomness. Well, look at your Figure 2.1, it's a clear demonstration that over a one-year period, the mean percent return is off center to the right, and the distributions are asymmetrical around the mean. Hence the historical annual return histogram proves that the market is not random. The longer the holding period, the less random (thus more predictable) the market is! Random walks are only random when one walks a short time distance. One can rightfully say that day traders are true random walkers and that technical analysis may not be as useful to them."

## Standard Deviation (Sigma) and Its Shortcomings

*Warning:* This section is for nerds only!

*Definition:* A light year is a distance not a time. It is the distance that light will travel in one year.

Table 3.2 has some numbers that are beyond human capacity to imagine. They are beyond our ability to comprehend. In my normal overkill fashion my goal here is to put these giant numbers into a believable perspective so you will believe that something is wrong with the statistics of modern finance. Black Monday, October 19, 1987, was a decline of 22.61 percent, which was approximately 22 sigma. Twenty-two sigma as shown in Table 3.2, based on Gaussian statistics, should only occur once in every $9.5 \times 10^{103}$ years. That needs to be put into perspective. The speed of light is approximately 186,282 miles per second, so the speed of light in miles per hours is $186,282 \times 60 \times 60 = 670,615,200$ miles per hour. Further expansion shows that the speed of light per day is $670,615,200 \times 24 = 16,094,764,800$ miles per day and so the speed of light per year is $16,094,764,800 \times 365.25 = 5,878,612,843,200$ miles per year. In scientific notation this is expressed as $5.878 \times 10^{12}$. Note that this number is similar to the value for eight sigma (see Table 3.2). To create an impression of sigma that is greater than eight would require the use of terms that deal with the universe, yet I'm going to give it a shot.

Here is a list of galactic-like measurements to help put large sigma events into perspective. There are many wonderful websites on astronomy and such. I checked a number of them and found a general agreement with the numbers used in these examples. Keep in mind that the numbers were generated with a scientific approach,

**TABLE 3.2**  Probability of Events Occurring

| Sigma | Population in Range | Expected Frequency Outside Range (1 in X) | Interpretation |
|---|---|---|---|
| 0.5 | 0.383 | 1.621 | Three times a week |
| 1 | 0.683 | 3.151 | Twice a week |
| 1.5 | 0.866 | 7.484 | Weekly |
| 2 | 0.954 | 21.978 | Every three weeks |
| 2.5 | 0.988 | 80.520 | Quarterly |
| 3 | 0.997 | 370.398 | Yearly |
| 4 | 0.999 (plus one 9) | 15787.193 | Every 43 years |
| 5 | 0.999 (plus three 9s) | $1.744 \times 10^6$ | Every 4,776 years |
| 6 | 0.999 (plus five 9s) | $5.068 \times 10^8$ | Every 1.39 million years |
| 7 | 0.999 (plus eight 9s) | $3.907 \times 10^{11}$ | Every $1.07 \times 10^9$ years |
| 8 | 0.999 (plus fourteen 9s) | $8.037 \times 10^{14}$ | Every $2.20 \times 10^{12}$ years |
| 9 | 0.999 (plus eighteen 9s) | $4.430 \times 10^{18}$ | Every $1.21 \times 10^{16}$ years |
| 10 | 0.999 (plus twenty-eight 9s) | $6.562 \times 10^{22}$ | Every $1.82 \times 10^{20}$ years |
| 12 | 0.999 (plus thirty-two 9s) | $2.815 \times 10^{32}$ | Every $7.71 \times 10^{29}$ years |
| 15 | 0.999 (plus fifty 9s) | $1.362 \times 10^{50}$ | Every $3.73 \times 10^{47}$ years |
| 20 | 0.999 (plus eighty-eight 9s) | $1.816 \times 10^{88}$ | Every $4.97 \times 10^{85}$ years |
| 22 | 0.999 (plus one hundred six 9s) | $3.472 \times 10^{106}$ | Every $9.51 \times 10^{103}$ years |
| 25 | 0.999 (plus one hundred thirty-seven 9s) | $1.636 \times 10^{137}$ | Every $4.48 \times 10^{134}$ years |
| $x$ | Erf($x$/(sqrt(2))) | $1/(1 - \text{Erf}(x/(\text{sqrt}(2))))$ | |

*Note:* Erf (see formula in last row) denotes the error function in statistics and actually has nothing to do with errors. It is related to Gaussian distributions, but is well beyond the purpose of this book. You can find multiple definitions and examples on the Internet. Wolfram Alpha (W11) provides the ability to calculate both of the functions on the bottom row.

not just a guess, but still could be in considerable error. Most of the information can be found on www.universetoday.com.

How many stars are there in the Milky Way galaxy? I found that from a number of different sources this number was fairly consistent and is about 2,500 that are visible to the naked eye on Earth at any one time and 5,800 to 8,000 total visible stars. Now here is the guess of astronomers for the total number of stars in the Milky Way: 200 billion to 400 billion ($4 \times 10^{12}$). Now the Milky Way galaxy is a spiral galaxy that is approximately 100,000 light years across, so you can see that we truly do not know a precise answer other than there are billions of stars in the Milky Way galaxy.

How many galaxies are in the universe? Because we can only see a fraction of the universe, this is impossible to know, but most astronomers have said that there are 100 billion to 200 billion galaxies in the universe. Their recent supercomputer put the number at more than 500 billion, in other words there is an entire galaxy for every star in the Milky Way.

The obvious next question then is how many stars in the universe? Since the determination for the number of galaxies in the universe and the number of stars in each galaxy is clearly a wide-ranging estimate, I'll just use something near the middle of the estimates (aren't you glad I did not use average?). Then, 400 billion galaxies and

400 billion stars in each galaxy equate to 160 trillion stars in the universe. In scientific notation that is $(4 \times 10^{12}) \times (4 \times 10^{12}) = 1.6 \times 10^{25}$. That's a lot of stars, but keep in mind the purpose of this cosmic exercise is to get a perspective on high sigma events. Looking at Table 3.2 you can see that this is close to about an 11 sigma event.

How many atoms in the universe? Let's use the conservative of the estimates just to keep it exciting. If there are 300 billion galaxies in the universe and the number of stars in a galaxy can be 400 billion, then the total number of stars in the universe would be about $1.2 \times 10^{23}$. Always refer to the sigma table to see where these numbers stand relative to large sigma events to keep them in perspective. UniverseToday estimates that on average (there's that concept again) each star can weigh $10^{35}$ grams. Therefore, the total mass of the universe would be about $10^{58}$ grams (Note: Multiplication of exponents is easy, just add them: $23 + 35 = 58$). Because a gram of matter is known to have about $10^{24}$ protons (same as the number of hydrogen atoms), then the total number of atoms in the universe is about $10^{82}$. From Table 3.2 you can extrapolate and see that it is about the same as a 19 sigma event occurring—and Black Monday, October 19, 1987, was a 22 sigma event.

What is the age of the universe? NASA's Wilkinson Microwave Anisotropy Probe has pegged the answer to 13.73 billion years, with a margin of error down to only 120 million years ($1.2 \times 10^8$).

What is the age of the Earth? Plate tectonics has caused rocks to be recycled so it makes it difficult to actually determine the Earth's age. They have found rocks in Michigan and Minnesota that are about 3.6 billion years old ($3.6 \times 10^9$). Western Australia has yielded the oldest rocks thus far at 4.3 billion years. Moon rocks and meteorites have yielded about 4.54 billion years on average, which is also science's determination for the age of the solar system.

What about humans? Currently (seems they are always finding something older) the first homo habilis evolved about 2.3 million years ago—these were the folks that used stone tools and probably not too different than a chimp. According to Recent African Ancestry theory, modern humans evolved in Africa and migrated out of the continent about 50,000 to 100,000 years ago. The forerunner for anatomically modern humans evolved between 400,000 and 250,000 years ago. Finally, many anthropologists agree that the transition to behavioral modernity (culture, language, etc.) happened about 50,000 years ago. We humans are certainly a tiny fraction compared to the universe, and in particular, large sigma events.

Okay, I have thoroughly beat this "perspective" idea to death but hope you found the galactic information entertaining. Basically, and practically, any sigma greater than 4 is usually addressed as infinity. Moreover, in the case of the stock market, that means these events should never happen, yet they do. And way too often! Table 3.2 shows various sigma, the percent of population, the probability of exceeding that sigma, and a calendar based interpretation. I have noticed that Microsoft Excel and Wolfram Alpha produce slightly different values. I think even with the best of intentions when dealing with extremely large or small numbers, one simple rounding error or inappropriate rounding can lead to differences, however, it did not affect the message here.

## Improper Process

When diving into this project on standard deviation and large market moves, I realized that all too often, analysts who are showing similar information are making an egregious error in the calculation. If you wanted to know the standard deviation (sigma) for October 19, 1987 (Black Monday), then you cannot use any data later than or including that day to determine it. I see many times that one will use the calculation of standard deviation on a daily basis up to the day of the analysis, which often includes many years of data that did not exist at the time of the event being analyzed. Table 3.3 shows the 10 largest percentage days in the Dow Industrials since 1885. The Correct Sigma column shows the calculation for past data up to the day before the event, while the Spot Sigma column shows the calculation for the day in question using all the data available up to 12/31/2012, which I don't believe is valid. However, you will notice that there is not a huge difference in the two columns. That is, until you look at the difference and put it into a perspective that the human brain can deal with.

## High Sigma Days We All Remember

In an attempt to portray certain days in the past that we have heard much about, the calculation of sigma expected and observed prior to those days is presented here for events from one sigma up to and including eight sigma. You will notice that at the high sigma data in the tables some of the data was entirely too large or too small to include. Also, the days we are discussing in the section were all much greater than eight sigma days. This analysis is to once again show how often we experience moves in the market that our completely beyond the boundaries of modern finance. Here are the explanations of the headers in the following three tables, October 28 to 29, 1929, October 19, 1987, and all the data up to 12/31/2012.

**TABLE 3.3**  Different Results for Sigma If Not Using Correct Data Periods

| Date | Percent Change | Correct Sigma | Spot Sigma up to 12/31/2012 | Sigma Difference |
|------|----------------|---------------|------------------------------|------------------|
| 10/19/1987 | −22.61% | 21.39 | 21.10 | 0.29 |
| 3/15/1933 | 15.34% | 13.03 | 14.32 | −1.29 |
| 10/6/1931 | 14.87% | 13.90 | 13.88 | 0.02 |
| 10/28/1929 | −12.82% | 13.01 | 11.97 | 1.04 |
| 10/30/1929 | 12.34% | 12.38 | 11.52 | 0.86 |
| 10/29/1929 | −11.73% | 11.84 | 10.95 | 0.89 |
| 9/21/1932 | 11.36% | 9.88 | 10.61 | −0.73 |
| 10/13/2008 | 11.08% | 10.47 | 10.34 | 0.13 |
| 10/28/2008 | 10.88% | 10.25 | 10.15 | 0.10 |
| 10/21/1987 | 10.15% | 9.58 | 9.48 | 0.10 |

Sigma—Standard deviation
    AM – xSD—Percent move representing the average mean (AM) less an "x" sigma move.
        Expected—The number of events expected using statistics.
        Observed—The actual number of events.
        Ratio—The ratio of expected to observed events.
    AM + xSD—Percent move representing the average mean (AM) plus an "x" sigma move.
        Expected—The number of events expected using statistics.
        Observed—The actual number of events.
        Ratio—The ratio of expected to observed events.
    Total Expected—The total of events expected above and below the mean.
    Total Observed—The total of actual events above and below the mean.
    Ratio—The ratio of the Total Expected and Total Observed events.

## Black Monday, October 28 and Black Tuesday, October 29, 1929

Table 3.4 shows the limits for one to eight standard deviations around the arithmetic mean (AM) return for the period from 2/17/1985 until the day before Black Monday, October 28, 1929. There were actually two significant declines during this period. On Monday, October 28, 1929, the Dow Industrials declined 12.82 percent, followed by Tuesday, October 29, 1929, with a decline of 11.73 percent. The total decline from the high price on Monday to the low price on Tuesday was more than 28 percent.

## Black Monday, October 19, 1987

Table 3.5 shows the limits for one to eight sigma around the arithmetic mean (AM) return for the period from 2/17/1985 until the day before Black Monday, October 19, 1987. Black Monday's decline was 22.61 percent, which is less than the two-day decline in October 1929. However, it was twice as large as Black Tuesday, October 29, 1929, which is the day recognized by most historians as the day of the crash.

## 1885–2012

Table 3.6 shows the limits for one to eight sigma around the arithmetic mean (AM) return for the period from 2/17/1885 until 12/31/2012.

## Rolling Returns and Gaussian Statistics

This section attempts to show that high sigma is a much more frequent event than modern finance thinks it is. A number of examples using the Dow Industrials back to 1885 on a daily basis are shown. Each begins with determining a look-back period to determine the average daily return and the standard deviation, and then

**TABLE 3.4**  Black Monday–Tuesday, October 28–29, 1929

2/17/1885–10/26/1929

| Years | Days | Min | Max | Average | Median | Std-Dev |
|---|---|---|---|---|---|---|
| 52.8 | 13,295 | -8.72% | 6.69% | 0.02% | 0.00% | 0.98% |

| Sigma | AM – xSD | Expected | Observed | Ratio | AM + xSD | Expected | Observed | Ratio | Total Expected | Total Observed | Ratio |
|---|---|---|---|---|---|---|---|---|---|---|---|
| 1 | -0.96% | 2,109.32160102 | 1554 | 0.74 | 1.00% | 2,109.32160102 | 1559 | 0.74 | 4,218.64 | 3,113.00 | 0.74 |
| 2 | -1.94% | 302.46300425 | 381 | 1.26 | 1.98% | 302.46300425 | 291 | 0.96 | 604.93 | 672.00 | 1.11 |
| 3 | -2.92% | 17.94689433 | 118 | 6.57 | 2.96% | 17.94689433 | 84 | 4.68 | 35.89 | 202.00 | 5.63 |
| 4 | -3.90% | 0.42106916 | 46 | 109.25 | 3.94% | 0.42106916 | 22 | 52.25 | 0.84 | 68.00 | 80.75 |
| 5 | -4.88% | 0.00381103 | 16 | 4,198.34 | 4.92% | 0.00381103 | 16 | 4,198.34 | 0.01 | 32.00 | 4,198.34 |
| 6 | -5.86% | 0.00001312 | 9 | 686,149.06 | 5.90% | 0.00001312 | 4 | 304,955.14 | 0.00 | 13.00 | 495,552.10 |
| 7 | -6.83% | 0.00000002 | 6 | 352,613,317.82 | 6.88% | 0.00000002 | 0 | — | 0.00 | 6.00 | 176,306,658.91 |
| 8 | -7.81% | — | 3 | — | 7.86% | — | 0 | — | — | 3.00 | — |

36

**TABLE 3.5**  Black Monday, October 19, 1987

### 2/17/1885–10/16/1987

| Years | Days | Min | Max | Average | Median | Std-Dev |
|---|---|---|---|---|---|---|
| 114.4 | 28,831 | −12.82% | 15.34% | 0.02% | 0.02% | 1.05% |

| Sigma | AM−xSD | Expected | Observed | Ratio | AM+xSD | Expected | Observed | Ratio | Total Expected | Total Observed | Ratio |
|---|---|---|---|---|---|---|---|---|---|---|---|
| 1 | −1.03% | 4,574.18962610 | 2940 | 0.64 | 1.07% | 4,574.18962610 | 2872 | 0.63 | 9,148.38 | 5,812.00 | 0.64 |
| 2 | −2.08% | 655.90905420 | 749 | 1.14 | 2.12% | 655.90905420 | 610 | 0.93 | 1,311.82 | 1,359.00 | 1.04 |
| 3 | −3.13% | 38.91891015 | 260 | 6.68 | 3.17% | 38.91891015 | 215 | 5.52 | 77.84 | 475.00 | 6.10 |
| 4 | −4.17% | 0.91311357 | 115 | 125.94 | 4.21% | 0.91311357 | 96 | 105.13 | 1.83 | 211.00 | 115.54 |
| 5 | −5.22% | 0.00826445 | 48 | 5,808.01 | 5.26% | 0.00826445 | 49 | 5,929.01 | 0.02 | 97.00 | 5,868.51 |
| 6 | −6.27% | 0.00002844 | 22 | 773,441.16 | 6.31% | 0.00002844 | 25 | 878,910.40 | 0.00 | 47.00 | 826,175.78 |
| 7 | −7.32% | 0.00000004 | 10 | 271,004,246.61 | 7.36% | 0.00000004 | 13 | 352,305,520.59 | 0.00 | 23.00 | 311,654,883.60 |
| 8 | −8.37% | — | 6 | — | 8.41% | — | 12 | — | — | 18.00 | — |

37

**TABLE 3.6** Full History (1885–2012) of Daily Dow Industrials

2/17/1885–12/31/2012

| Years | Days | Min | Max | Average | Median | Std-Dev |
|---|---|---|---|---|---|---|
| 139.6 | 35,178 | −22.61% | 15.34% | 0.02% | 0.02% | 1.07% |

| Sigma | AM − xSD | Expected | Observed | Ratio | AM + xSD | Expected | Observed | Ratio | Total Expected | Total Observed | Ratio |
|---|---|---|---|---|---|---|---|---|---|---|---|
| 1 | −1.05% | 5,581.17452280 | 3596 | 0.64 | 1.09% | 5,581.17452280 | 3510 | 0.63 | 11,162.34904560 | 7,106.00 | 0.64 |
| 2 | −2.12% | 800.30414167 | 906 | 1.13 | 2.17% | 800.30414167 | 757 | 0.95 | 1,600.60828335 | 1,663.00 | 1.04 |
| 3 | −3.19% | 47.48671296 | 309 | 6.51 | 3.24% | 47.48671296 | 257 | 5.41 | 94.97342591 | 566.00 | 5.96 |
| 4 | −4.26% | 1.11413095 | 131 | 117.58 | 4.31% | 1.11413095 | 115 | 103.22 | 2.22826189 | 246.00 | 110.40 |
| 5 | −5.33% | 0.01008383 | 58 | 5,751.78 | 5.38% | 0.01008383 | 55 | 5,454.28 | 0.02016766 | 113.00 | 5,603.03 |
| 6 | −6.40% | 0.00003471 | 31 | 893,212.62 | 6.45% | 0.00003471 | 28 | 806,772.69 | 0.00006941 | 59.00 | 849,992.66 |
| 7 | −7.47% | 0.00000005 | 13 | 288,740,703.40 | 7.52% | 0.00000005 | 16 | 355,373,173.42 | 0.00000009 | 29.00 | 322,056,938.41 |
| 8 | −8.55% | — | 5 | — | 8.59% | — | 15 | — | — | 20.00 | — |

**FIGURE 3.2** Visual for Look-Back, Look-Forward, and Data Point

**FIGURE 3.3** Five-Year Look-Back and Five-Year Look-Forward Days Outside +/− 3 Sigma

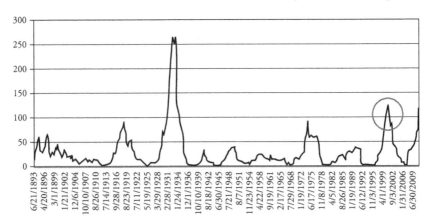

a look-forward period is determined to see if the look-back data continues into the look-forward data. Figure 3.2 is an attempt to help visualize this process. A look-back period is determined (in-sample data) and a look-forward period is also determined (out-of-sample data). The look-back period is used to determine the average daily return and the standard deviation of returns. From that data a range of three sigma about the mean is determined. Then in the look-forward data, the number of daily returns outside the +/− three sigma band are tallied with the total being displaying as a plot; any point on the plot represents the data used in the look-back and the look-forward periods.

In Figure 3.3 a look-back period of 1,260 days (five years) is used to calculate an average daily return and the standard deviation of returns. On 10/24/2002 (circle on Figure 3.3) the average return over the past 1,260 days was 0.07 percent, and the standard deviation over the same period was 0.71 percent. Therefore a three sigma move up was up to 2.21 percent, and a three sigma move down was −2.06 percent. The look-forward period, also 1,260 days, is counting the number of days in which the returns were outside of the look-back range. There were 49 days with returns greater than 2.21 percent and 69 days with returns less than −2.06 percent, for a total number of days with returns outside the +/− 3 sigma range (based on the previous five years) equal to 118. Table 3.7 puts this into another format.

For a +/− 3 sigma event the expected number of observations should be 1.7, whereas there were 118, which is 59 times more than expected (events must be in whole numbers so used 2 for the expected number). Figure 3.3 shows the 1,260-day

**TABLE 3.7**   Table Showing Data in Figure 3.3

| Period | Start Date | End Date | Number of Days/Years | Average Return | Sigma Range | # Days + Sigma | # Days − Sigma |
|--------|-----------|----------|---------------------|----------------|-------------|----------------|----------------|
| Look-back | 10/27/1992 | 10/20/1997 | 1260/5 | 0.07% | −2.06% to 2.21% | | |
| Look-forward | 10/20/1997 | 10/24/2002 | 1260/5 | | | 49 | 69 |

rolling total number of days outside the +/− 3 sigma range. As of 12/31/2007 (five years ago) the total is 116, with an expectation of only 1.7. This is more than 58 times more returns outside the +/− 3 sigma band than expected. Of those 116 days outside the three sigma band, 54 were above 2.45 percent and 62 were below −2.37 percent.

Reducing the look-forward period to one year (252) days while maintaining the five year look-back period yields the chart in Figure 3.4 of rolling number of days outside a +/− 3 sigma (standard deviation) event. Remember that the determination of +/− 3 sigma is determined by the previous five years of data at any point on the chart. For a one-year look-forward there is only an expectation of 0.34 events (days) outside the sigma band.

Taking this concept to another view, Figure 3.5 shows the rolling number of days outside the +/− 3 sigma band for a look-forward of one year and a look-back of 10 years (2,520 days).

Keeping the look-forward period to one year and expanding the look-back period to 20 years (5,020 days) is shown in Figure 3.6. This chart is quite similar to the previous one with only a 10-year look-back. Extrapolating the past into the future always has its surprises. Keeping the look-forward period the same (one year) and increasing the look-back period does not significantly affect the rolling returns outside the sigma range.

**FIGURE 3.4**   Five-Year Look-Back and One-Year Look-Forward Days Outside +/− 3 Sigma

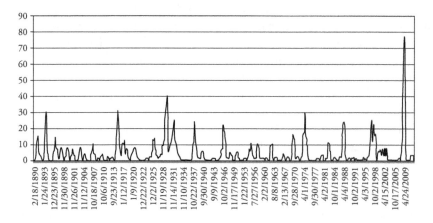

**FIGURE 3.5** Ten-Year Look-Back and One-Year Look-Forward Days Outside +/− 3 Sigma

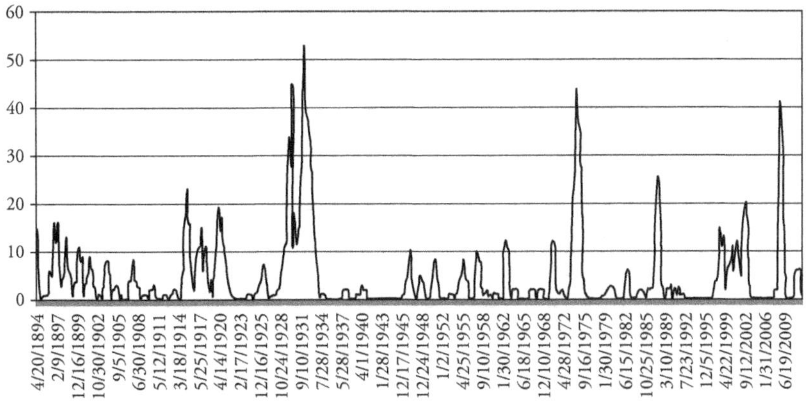

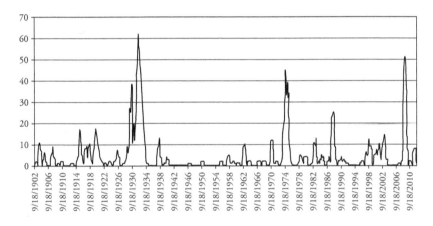

**FIGURE 3.6** Twenty-Year Look-Back and One-Year Look-Forward Days Outside +/− 3 Sigma

Finally, in Figure 3.7, taking a 50-year look-back period (12,600 days), as expected the number of times the following year had exceeded the +/− 3 sigma envelope was similar.

Bottom line: Gaussian (bell-curve) statistics are not appropriate for market analysis, yet modern finance is totally wrapped up in using standard deviation as volatility and then saying that is risk. There are actually two big problems: one is the use of standard deviation to represent risk, and two is that past standard deviation has very little to do with future standard deviation. The first problem does not account for the fact that standard deviation (sigma) is also measuring both upside moves and downside moves with no attempt to separate the two. Clearly, upside volatility is good for long-only strategies. The second problem was adequately covered in this section showing how inadequate standard deviation is from the past in predicting how it would be in the future.

**FIGURE 3.7**  Fifty-Year Look-Back and One-Year Look-Forward Days Outside +/− 3 Sigma

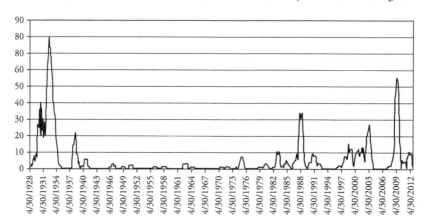

## Risk and Uncertainty

Is volatility risk? (Here we go again.)

In the sterile laboratory of modern finance, risk is defined by volatility as measured by standard deviation; however . . .

It assumes the range of outcomes is a normal distribution (bell curve).
Rarely do the markets yield to normal.

When an investor opens his or her brokerage statement. . . .
It shows the following portfolio data for the last year:

Standard Deviation = .65
Loss for the Year = −35 percent

Which one do you think will catch their attention? I seriously doubt any investor is going to call his or her advisor and complain about a standard deviation of .65. However, the −35 percent loss will get their attention. Even investors who have no knowledge of finance or investments know what risk is—it is the loss of capital.

Risk is not volatility; it is drawdown (loss of capital). However, in the short term, volatility is a good proxy for risk, but over the longer term, drawdown is a much better measure of risk. *Volatility does contribute to risk but it also contributes to market gains.*

Risk and uncertainty are *not* the same thing.

Risk can be measured.

Uncertainty cannot be measured.

A jar contains five red balls and five blue balls. In the old days we called it an urn instead of a jar.

Blindly pick out a ball.

What are the odds of picking a red ball? There are five red balls and the total number of balls is 10. Therefore the odds of picking a red ball are 5/10 = .5 or 50 percent.

**FIGURE 3.8** Nonsystematic and Systematic Risk

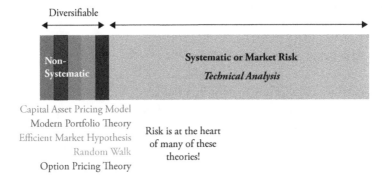

That is Risk! It can be calculated.

Suppose you were not told the number of red or blue balls in the jar.

What are the odds of picking a red ball?

That is Uncertainty!

Figure 3.8 is an attempt to visualize how modern finance is focused on risk, but have you ever wondered or thought about which element of risk they deal with? Actually they do a great job of analyzing risk; risk is at the heart of all the theories of Modern Portfolio Theory (Capital Asset Pricing Model, Efficient Market Hypothesis, Random Walk, Option Pricing Theory, etc.). The risk that they attempt to determine is known as *nonsystematic risk*, or you may have heard it as diversifiable risk. Diversification is a free lunch and should never be ignored. The world of finance is focused on diversifiable or nonsystematic risk. However, there is a much larger piece of the risk pie, and that is called *systematic risk*. Once you have adequately diversified, then it seems that you are only dealing with systematic risk. Systematic risk is what technical analysis attempts to deal with. It is also known as *drawdown, loss of capital*, and in certain situations as a *bear market*.

## Back to the Original Question: Is Volatility Risk?

Two simple price movements are shown in Figure 3.9; which represents more risk, example A or example B?

Modern finance would have you believe that A is riskier because of its volatility. However, you can notice from this overly simple example that the price ended up exactly where it began, therefore you did not make money or lose money. B, based

**FIGURE 3.9** Volatility versus Risk

on the concept of volatility as risk, has no risk according to theory, however, you lost money in the process. I think it is obvious which is risk and which is only theory.

## Is Linear Analysis Good Enough?

Figure 3.10 is known as a Cartesian coordinate system, sometimes referred to as a *scatter diagram*, used often to compare two issues and derive relationships between them. The returns of one are plotted on the $X$ axis (abscissa/horizontal) and the returns of the other are plotted using the $Y$ axis (ordinate/vertical). Those small diamonds are the data points. A concept known as *regression* is then applied by calculating a least squares fit of the data points. This is the straight line that you see below. Then a little high school geometry is used on the equation for a straight line, which is $y = mx + b$, where $m$ is the slope of the line, and $b$ is the where the line crosses the $Y$ axis or $y$–intercept. So once you have the linearly fitted line, you can measure the slope and $y$–intercept and this will give you the beta (slope) and alpha ($y$-intercept).

The following statistical elements can all be derived from simple linear analysis.

Raw Beta
Alpha
$R^2$ (Coefficient of Determination)
$R$ (Correlation)
Standard Deviation of Error
Standard Error of Alpha
Standard Error of Beta

**FIGURE 3.10**   Source of Alpha and Beta from Linear Analysis

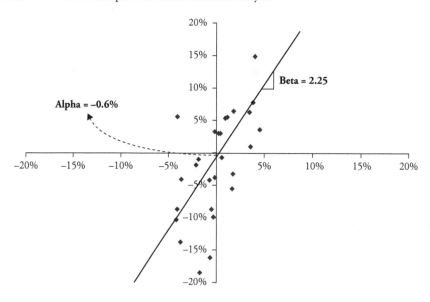

*t*-Test
Significance
Last *T*-Value
Last *P*-Value

## Linear Regression Must Have Correlation

Figure 3.11 is a scatter plot of a fictional fund ABC (*Y* axis) plotted against the S&P 500 (*X* axis). The least squared regression line is plotted and the equation is shown as:

$$Y = 0.5997x + 0.0005, \text{ which means the slope is } .5997$$
$$\text{and the } y\text{-intercept is } 0.0005.$$

A slope of 1.0 would mean that the Beta of the fund compared to the index was the same and the line on the plot would be a quadrant bisector (if the plot were a square, the line would be moving up and to the right at 45 degrees). So, a slope of 0.5997 means the fund has a lower beta than the index. The *y*-intercept is a positive number, although barely, but that means the fund outperformed the index.

$R^2$ is the Coefficient of Determination, also known as the *goodness of fit*. Now I understand that dealing with positive numbers has some advantages, but in most cases $R^2$ is

**FIGURE 3.11** ABC U.S. Equity

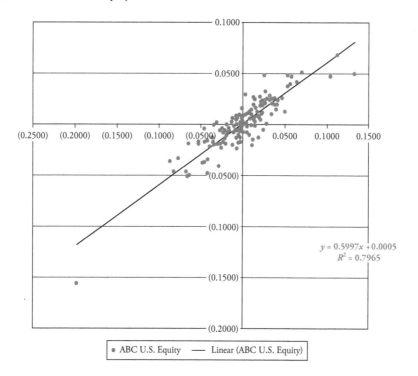

$$y = 0.5997x + 0.0005$$
$$R^2 = 0.7965$$

• ABC U.S. Equity ⸺ Linear (ABC U.S. Equity)

also reducing the amount of information. Let me explain. We know that $R$ is correlation, the statistical measure that shows the relationship between two datasets and how closely they are aligned. That is not the textbook answer for correlation, but will suffice for now. Correlation ranges from $+1$ (totally correlated) to $-1$ (inversely correlated), with 0 being noncorrelated. Nice information to know; is the fund correlated to the market, inversely correlated to the market, or not correlated at all. Squaring correlation will give you an always positive number (remember least squares?) but why remove the information about the level of correlation? $R^2$ will not tell you if it is correlated or inversely correlated. Actually, I think it is the social science's fear of negative numbers. However, in fairness, $R^2$ will show the percent dependency of one variable over the other—in theory.

The $R^2$ in Figure 3.11 is 0.7965, which means there is a fair degree of correlation, we just don't know if it is positive correlation or inverse correlation. To get correlation, merely take the square root of 0.7965 to get $R = 0.8924684$ (yes, an attempt at humor), which means $R$ could also be $-0.8924684$. Anyway, hopefully you get my point.

Finally, notice how the data points are all clustered fairly closely to the least squares line, which visually shows you that this fund is fairly well correlated to the index.

Figure 3.12 shows fund XYZ plotted against an index. Notice that the linear least squared fit equation ($y = 0.5997x + 0.0005$ is exactly the same as the previous example. However the value of $R^2$ is 0.2051, which is considerably different than the previous example. Visually, you can see that the data points are more scattered than in the previous example so just based on the visual observation you know this fund is not nearly as correlated as the previous fund ABC. Yet, we find that the least squares

**FIGURE 3.12**   XYZ U.S. Equity

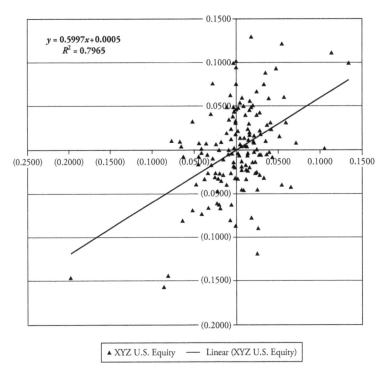

**FIGURE 3.13** ABC and XYZ U.S. Equity

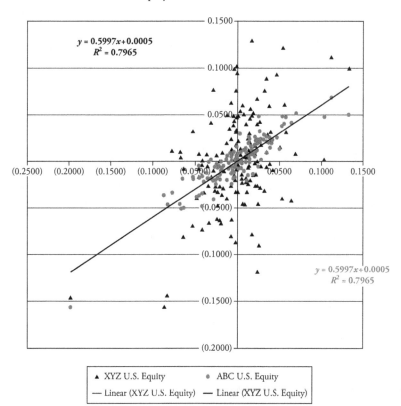

regression line is oriented exactly the same so the values of alpha and beta are the same for this fund (XYZ) as they were for fund (ABC) above.

So what's the difference, you are hopefully asking? The difference is that one fund is not nearly as correlated as the other. We know that they are both positively correlated from visual examination, but unless the value of $R$ (correlation) is shown, we don't know any more about the correlation. This is one of the horrible shortcomings of this type of analysis. Here is the message: If it isn't correlated, then the values derived for alpha and beta are absolutely meaningless. Yet I see publications ranking funds and showing $R^2$, alpha, and beta but never a mention of $R$. Shame on them!

The scatter plot in Figure 3.13 shows both funds plotted with the index. You can clearly see that fund XYZ (triangles) is not nearly as correlated as fund ABC (circles). Yet, the linear statistics of modern finance does not delineate a difference between the two. My only comment to them is: Stay out of aviation.

## The 60/40 Myth Exposed

It is almost impossible to see any performance comparisons that not only show a benchmark, but also show a mix of 60 percent equity and 40 percent fixed income, known as 60/40 in the fund industry. The *efficient frontier* is one of those terms that came from a theory developed decades ago on risk management. Modern finance looks at a plot of returns versus risk, and, of course, by risk, it means standard deviation. This is the first mistake made with this concept. Then it plots a variety of different asset classes on the same plot and derive the efficient frontier, which shows you the level of risk you take for the asset classes you want to invest in. Figure 3.14 shows that efficient frontier curve from 1960 to 2010 (an intermediate bond component was used). Next, if you draw a line that is tangent with the curve and have it cross the vertical return axis at the level for assumed risk free, then the point of tangential is the proper mix of equity and bonds. I did not attempt to do this here as the determination of the risk free rate to use over a 50-year period presents too much subjectivity. From 1960 to present, that mix of stocks and bonds is about 60/40.

The ubiquitous 60/40 ratio of stocks to bonds, which shows up in most performance comparisons, gleans the message that for over 50 years of data nothing has changed? Does anyone actually believe that? Figure 3.15 is a chart showing the efficient frontier for each individual decade in the 1960 to 2010 period. Clearly each decade has its own efficient frontier and its proper mix of equity and bonds. Yet, the world of finance still sticks to the often wrong mix of 60/40. It may very well be a good mix of assets, but the data says it is dynamic and should be reviewed on a periodic basis. Notice that the decades of 1970 and 2000 showed similar downward curves meaning that stocks were not nearly as good as bonds. Conversely the decades of 1980 and 1990 were the opposite.

**FIGURE 3.14**  Efficient Frontier (1960–2010)

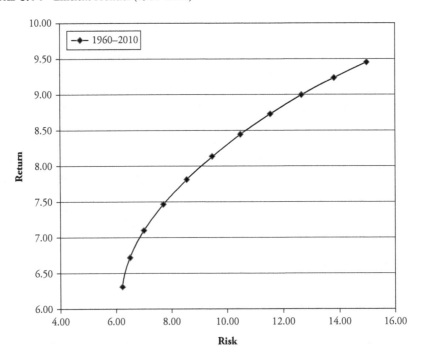

**FIGURE 3.15** Efficient Frontier—Each Decade from 1960 to 2010

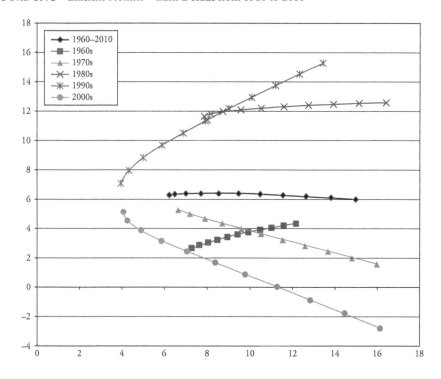

In an interview with Jason Zweig on October 15, 2004, Peter Bernstein said that a rigid allocation policy like 60/40 is another way of passing the buck and avoiding decisions. Did you want to be 40 percent invested in bonds during the 1970s when interest rates soared? Did you want to only be invested 60 percent in equities in the period from 1982 to 2000, which was the greatest bull market in history? Of course not! Markets are dynamic and so should investment strategies. Finally, some analysis will show that a 60/40 portfolio is highly correlated to an all equity portfolio.

## Discounted Cash Flow Model

When studying modern finance, and after years of hearing about the discounted cash flow (DCF) model, I have this to say about the discounted cash flow model. First of all, you must decide on six values about the future. They are shown below. If you have read this book this far, you probably know what is coming next.

Discount Rate
    Cost of Equity, in valuing equity
    Cost of Capital, in valuing the firm
Cash Flows
    Cash Flows to Equity
    Cash Flows to Firm

Growth (to get future cash flows)
    Growth in Equity Earnings
    Growth in Firm Earnings (Operating Income)

The inputs (above) to the DCF process must all be correct or the model fails completely. The odds of successfully coming up with correct (guesses) inputs are extremely low, yet this is used in modern finance routinely. This reminds me of the Kenneth Arrow story on forecasting in Chapter 5. When asked about the discounted cash flow model, I liken it to the Hubble Telescope; move it an inch and all of a sudden you are looking at a different galaxy.

The goal of this chapter at the very minimum is to cause you to challenge what modern finance has provided. I apologize for beating some concepts with a stick but sometimes multiple approaches to show something are better in the hope that one will remain with the reader. There was enough math to scare the average person, the next chapter focuses on the wide use of the term *average*. The goal is to show that using long-term averages can be totally inappropriate for most investors.

# CHAPTER 4

# Misuse of Statistics and Other Controversial Practices

## The Deception of Average

The "World of Finance" is fraught with misleading information. The use of average is one that needs a discussion. Figure 4.1 shows the compounded rates of return for a variety of asset classes. If I were selling you a buy-and-hold strategy, or an index fund, I would love this chart. From this chart showing 85 years of data, I could say that if you had invested in small cap stocks you would have averaged 11.95 percent a year, and if you had invested in large cap stocks you would have averaged 9.85 percent a year. And I would be correct.

I think that most investors have about 20 years, maybe 25 years, in which to accumulate their retirement wealth. In their 20s and 30s, it is difficult to put much money away for many reasons such as: low incomes, children, materialism, college, and so on. Therefore, with that information, what is wrong with this chart? It is for an 85-year investment and people do not have 85 years to invest. As said earlier, most have about 20 years to acquire their retirement wealth and there are many 20-year periods in this chart where the returns were horrible. The bear market that began in 1929 did not fully recover until 1954, a full 25 years later; 1966 took 16 years to recover, 1973 took 10 years, and today's 2000 bear still has not recovered (as of 12/31/2012).

Table 4.1 shows the performance numbers for the asset classes shown in Figure 4.1 (LT—Long Term, IT—Intermediate Term). The cumulative numbers in Table 4.1 begin at 1 on December 31, 1925.

Hint: Be careful when someone uses inappropriate averages; or more accurately, uses averages inappropriately.

Recall in Table 4.1 that the small cap and large cap compounded returns were about 12 percent and 10 percent respectively? Figure 4.2 shows rolling 10-year returns by range since 1900. A rolling return means it shows the periods 1900–1909,

**FIGURE 4.1**   Eighty-Five-Year Returns of Various Assets

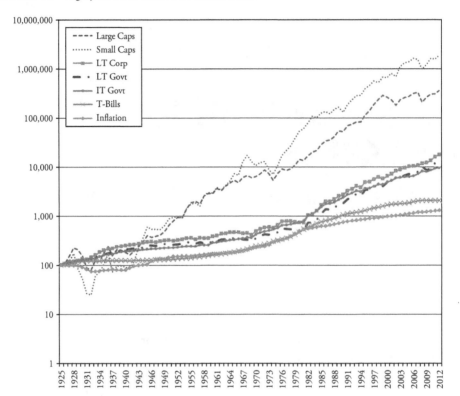

**TABLE 4.1**   Long-Term Performance of Asset Classes

|  | Small Caps | Large Caps | LT Corp. Bonds | LT Govt. Bonds | IT Govt. Bonds | T-Bills | Inflation |
|---|---|---|---|---|---|---|---|
| Cumulative | 18,366.93 | 3,531.23 | 173.08 | 122.13 | 93.00 | 19.58 | 11.81 |
| Annualized | 11.95% | 9.85% | 6.11% | 5.69% | 5.36 | 3.54% | 2.97% |
| Mean | 16.5 | 11.8 | 6.4 | 6.1 | 5.5 | 3.6 | 3.1 |
| Sigma | 32.2 | 20.2 | 8.3 | 9.7 | 5.6 | 3.1 | 4.1 |

*Source:* Morningstar Ibbotson SBBI Yearbook.

1901–1910, 1902–1911, and so on. You can clearly see that the small stock and large stock returns depicted in Table 4.1 fall within the middle range (8 percent–12 percent) in Figure 4.2, yet of all the 10-year rolling periods, only 22 percent of them were in that range. Often average is not very average. It reminds me of the story of the six-foot-tall Texan that drowned while wading across a stream that averaged only three-feet deep.

Another example (and final) shows how easily it is to be confused over what is average. And, of course, this time it is intentional. This example should put it in

**FIGURE 4.2** Distribution of Returns Based on Percentage

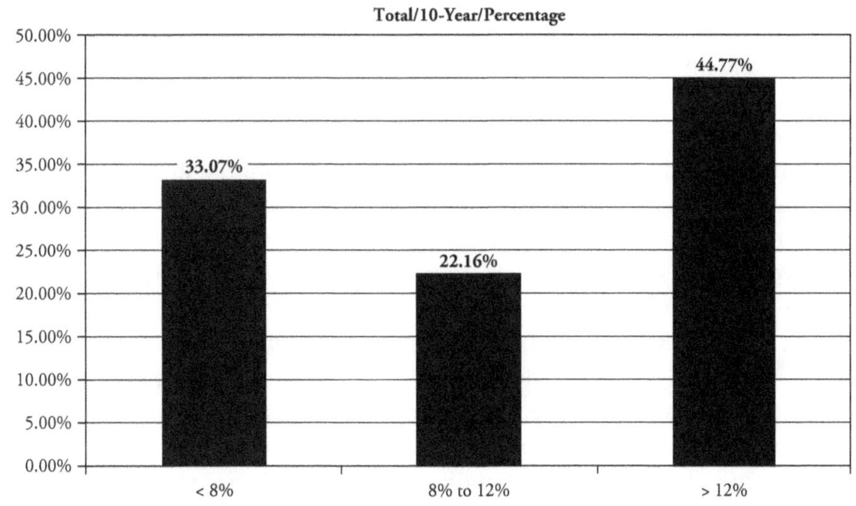

**Total/10-Year/Percentage**

[Bar chart: < 8% = 33.07%, 8% to 12% = 22.16%, > 12% = 44.77%]

perspective. You cannot relate rates of change linearly. In Figure 4.3, point A is 20 miles from point B. If you drive 60 mph going from point A to point B, but returning from point B to point A, you drive 30 mph. What is his average speed for the time you were on the road?

A. 55 mph
B. 50 mph
C. 45 mph
D. 40 mph

Many will answer that it is 45 mph ((60mph + 30mph)/2). However, you cannot average rates of change like you can constants and linear relationships. Distance is rate multiplied by time ($d = rt$). So time ($t$) is distance ($d$)/rate ($r$). The first leg from A to B was 20 miles divided by 60 mph or one-third of an hour. The second leg from B

**FIGURE 4.3** Average of Rates of Change Example

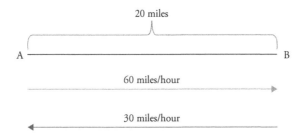

to A was 20 miles divided by 30 mph or two-thirds of an hour. Adding the two times ($\frac{1}{3}$ + $\frac{2}{3}$ = 1 hour) will mean you traveled for one hour and covered a total distance of 40 miles, which has to mean the average speed was 40 mph. Look up harmonic mean if you want more information on this, as it is the correct method to determine central tendency of data when it is in the form of a ratio or rate.

Figure 4.4 shows the 20-year rolling price returns for the Dow Industrials. The range of returns in this 127-year sample (1885–2012) is from a low on 08/31/1949 of −3.71 percent to a high on 3/31/2000 of 14.06 percent which is a 17.77 percent range. To help clarify rolling returns, on 8/31/1949 (low mentioned previously), if investors were in the Dow Industrials from 9/30/1929 until 8/31/1949, they had a return of −3.71 percent. Complementary, if they invested on 4/30/1980, then on 3/31/2000, they had a return of 14.06 percent. The mean return is 5.2 percent and the median return 4.8 percent. When median is less than mean, it simply means more returns were less average. If you recall the long-term assumptions that are often used in the first part of this chapter (Figure 4.1), you can see there is a problem. The magnitude of errors in assumptions of long-term returns cannot be overstated and certainly cannot be ignored. This variability of returns can mean totally different retirement environments for investors who use these long-term assumptions for future returns. It can be the difference between living like a king, or living on government assistance. Institutional investors have the same problems if using these long-term averages.

One of the primary beliefs developed by Markowitz in the 1950s as the architect of Modern Portfolio Theory was the details on the inputs for the efficient investment portfolio. In fact, his focus was hardly on the inputs at all. The inputs that are needed are expected future returns, volatility, and correlations. The industry as a

**FIGURE 4.4** Dow Industrials 20-Year Rolling Returns (1885–2012)

whole took the easy approach to solving this by utilizing long-term averages for the inputs. In other words, one full swing through all the data that was available; and the average is the one used for the inputs into an otherwise fairly good theory. Those long-term inputs are totally inappropriate for the investing horizon of most investors; in fact, I think they are inappropriate for all human beings. While delving into this deeper is not the subject of this book, it once again brings to light the horrible misuse of average. These inputs should use averages appropriate for the investor's accumulation time frame.

## One If by Land, Two If by Sea

Sam Savage is a consulting professor of management science and engineering at Stanford University, and a fellow of the Judge Business School at the University of Cambridge. He wrote an insightful book, *The Flaw of Averages*, in 2009 and included a short piece called "The Red Coats" that fits right into this chapter. Spring 1775: The colonists are concerned about British plans to raid Lexington and Concord, Massachusetts. Patriots in Boston develop a plan that explicitly takes a range of uncertainties into account: The British will come either by land or by sea. These unsung pioneers of modern decision analysis did it just right by explicitly planning for both contingencies. Had Paul Revere and the Minutemen planned for the single average scenario of the British walking up the beach with one foot on the land and one in the sea, the citizens of North America might speak with different accents today. (B50) Incidentally, Dr. Savage's father, Leonard J. Savage, wrote the seminal *The Foundation of Statistics* in 1972 and was a prominent mathematical statistician who collaborated closely with Milton Friedman.

## Everything on Four Legs Is a Pig

Although this is unrelated to investments and finance, it is a story about averages that offers additional support to this topic. Doctors use growth charts (height and weight tables) for a guide on the growth of a child. What folks do not realize is that they were created by actuaries for insurance companies and not doctors. As doctors began to use them the terms *overweight, underweight, obese,* and so on were created based on average. So if your doctor says you are overweight and you need to lose weight, he is also saying you need to lose weight to be average. And from a *Wall Street Journal* article by Melinda Beck on July 24, 2012, "The wide variations are due in part to rising obesity rates, an increase in premature infants who survive, and a population that is growing more diverse. Yet the official growth charts from the Centers for Disease Control (CDC) and Prevention still reflect the size distribution of U.S. children in the 1960s, 1970s, and 1980s. The CDC says it doesn't plan to adjust its charts because it doesn't want the ever-more-obese population to become the new norm." And now you know. (B20)

During my last physical examination, I told my doctor about how these charts on height and weight were just large averages created by actuaries for insurance companies and that I did not mind being above average. The chapter that follows focuses on the multibillion-dollar industry of prediction. I rarely am invited to be on the financial media anymore because I refuse to make a prediction; it is a fool's game.

# CHAPTER 5

# The Illusion of Forecasting

Those who have knowledge don't predict. Those who predict don't have knowledge
*Lao Tzu*

So that there can be no confusion, I want to state my honest heartfelt opinion on forecasting: I adamantly believe there is no one who knows what the market will do tomorrow, next week, next month, next year, or at any time in the future—period.

Hindsight is a wonderful tool to use in order to know why something might have occurred in the past, but rarely is the cause known during the event itself. The prediction business is gigantic. William Sherden, in *The Fortune Sellers*, claimed that in 1998 the prediction business accounted for $200 billion worth of mostly erroneous predictions. (B52) Can you imagine with the growth of the Internet and globalization, what that industry is today? Frightening! As Oaktree Capital Management's Howard Marks says, "You cannot predict, but you can prepare."

Dean Williams, then senior vice president of Batterymarch Financial Management, gave a keynote speech at the Financial Analysts Federation Seminar in August 1981, and made some almost prophetic comments about investing that are as true today as they were then. He spoke about the relationship between physics and investing, but I have previously discussed that subject. Another comment was, "One of the most consuming uses of our time, in fact, has been accumulating information to help us make forecasts of all those things we think we have to predict. Where's the evidence that it works? I've been looking for it. Really! Here are my conclusions: Confidence in a forecast rises with the amount of information that goes into it. But the accuracy of the forecast stays the same." And later, "It's that you can be a successful investor without being a perpetual forecaster. Not only that, I can tell you from personal experience that one of the most liberating experiences you can have is to be asked to go over your firm's economic outlook and say, 'We don't have one.'" He goes on to talk about using simple approaches versus complex ones and delves into the fact that they also must be consistent approaches. This is a must-read; you can find it from an Internet search on Dean Williams Batterymarch. (A107)

Sherden states that the title "second oldest profession" usually goes to lawyers and consultants, but prognosticators are the rightful owners. Early records from 5,000 years ago show that forecasting was practiced in the ancient world in the form of divination, the art of telling the future by seeing patterns and clues in everything from animal entrails to celestial patterns. Isaac Asimov wrote in *Future Days*, such was the eagerness of people to believe these augers that they had great power and could usually count on being well supported by a grateful, or fearful, public. I'm not so sure most of this isn't applicable to today. Sherden did much research into the numbers of people directly involved in forecasting—and this data was from 1998. They are staggering and growing. And let's not forget that one of the largest selling newspapers in the country is the *National Enquirer*. Below are some of the findings on forecasting from Sherden's book. (B52)

> No better than guessing.
> No long-term accuracy.
> Cannot predict turning points.
> No leading forecasters.
> No forecaster was better with specific statistics.
> No one ideology was better.
> Consensus forecasts do not improve accuracy.
> Psychological bias distorts forecasters.
> Increased sophistication does not improve accuracy.
> No improvement over the years.

A weather forecaster will have an exceptional record if he says simply that tomorrow will be just like today. If I were a weather forecaster, I would tend to error on the side of bad weather instead of good weather. Then if you are wrong, most will not notice. It is when you forecast good weather and it is not, then they will notice. Most market prognosticators tend to have a bullish or a bearish bias in their forecasts. Bullish forecasts are generally well accepted especially by the Wall Street community, and bearish forecasting is a giant business because it infringes on investors' fears.

---

Given the difficulties forecasting the future, it is very useful to simply know the present.

*Unknown*

---

Barry Ritholtz (The Big Picture blog) recently pointed out how ridiculous the forecasting business has become. In particular, the end-of-the-year forecasts for the next year or the best stocks to own. Here is an example from the August 14, 2000, issue of *Fortune* magazine by David Rynecki on "10 Stocks to Last the Decade."

**August 14, 2000**

> Nokia (NOK: $54)
> Nortel Networks (NT: $77)
> Enron (ENE: $73)
> Oracle (ORCL: $74)
> Broadcom (BRCM: $237)
> Viacom (VIA: $69)
> Univision (UVN: $113)
> Charles Schwab (SCH: $36)
> Morgan Stanley Dean Witter (MWD: $89)
> Genentech (DNA: $150)

**Closing Prices December 19, 2012**

> Nokia (NOK: $4.22)
> Nortel Networks ($0)
> Enron ($0)
> Oracle (ORCL: $34.22)
> Broadcom (BRCM: $33.28)
> Viacom (VIA: $54.17)
> Univision ($?)
> Charles Schwab (SCH: $14.61)
> Morgan Stanley Dean Witter (MWD: $14.20)
> Genentech (Takeover at $95 share)

Ritholtz goes on to say, "The portfolio managed to lose 74.31 percent, with three bank-ruptcies, one bailout, and not a single winner in the bunch. Even the Roche Holdings take-over of Genentech was for 37 percent below the suggested purchase price. Had you merely bought the S&P 500 Index ETF (SPY), you would have seen a gain of over 23 percent."

On March 11, 2008, CNBC's *Mad Money* host, Jim Cramer emphatically said it was foolish to move money out of Bear Stearns. He claimed that Bear Stearns was just fine. He was totally wrong. A week later JPMorgan agrees on March 16 to buy Bear for $236 million, or $2 a share, representing just over 1 percent of the firm's value at its record high close just 14 months earlier. The deal essentially marked the end of Bear's 85-year run as an independent securities firm. On Monday, March 17, Bear shares closed at $4.81 on opti-mism another buyer may emerge. The average target price: $2. Don't confuse advice from someone in the entertainment business with advice from someone who manages money. In fact, don't pay attention to anyone's predictions. No one knows the future!

## The Reign of Error

In 1987 a book was written entitled *The Great Depression of 1990*, by Dr. Ravi Batra, an SMU professor of economics. Sadly, I bought and read that book. Batra was claimed as one of the great theorist in the world and ranked third in a group of

46 superstars selected from all economists in American and Canadian universities by the learned journal *Economic Inquiry* (October 1978). The foreword was written by world-renowned economist Lester Thurow, who said *The Great Depression of 1990* is crucial reading for everyone who hopes to survive and prosper in the coming economic upheaval. The title for one chapter was "The Great Depression of 1990–96." Not only did he pronounce the beginning of it, he also proclaimed to know the end. The 1990s saw the largest bull market in history, with the Dow Industrials rising from 2,700 to over 11,000 during the decade of the 1990s. By the end of the decade we were flooded with books about the never-ending bull market such as: *Dow 40,000* by Elias, *Dow 36,000* by Glassman and Hassett, and *Dow 100,000* by Kadlec. From 2000 until early 2003, we witnessed a bear market that removed most of the gains of the previous 10 years with the Dow Industrials back down to about 7,350. (B31)

---

We are making forecasts with bad numbers, but bad numbers are all we have.

*Michael Penjer*

---

These forecasts were dead wrong; however, I'm sure the authors sold a lot of books. The bad news in the stock market did not end after the bear market from 2000 to 2003, by March 2009 the Dow Industrials was below the level of the previous bear by another 8 percent. Agencies whose duty is to make forecasts were almost universally wrong during the 2006 to 2007 period with forecasts of the economy, the markets, the world outlook, all positive; even the ones that weren't quite as rosy, were only modestly so. The business magazines were the same. How many forecasts do you find yourself reading and listening to? Did you ever research to see if any of them ever turned out to be correct? Or even close?

Finance is not the same as physics in that no mathematical model can fully capture the large number of always changing economic factors that cause big market moves—the financial meltdown of 2008 is an example. Emanuel Derman says, "In physics, you're playing against God; in finance, you're playing against people." The parallelism between physics and finance has gained support from author Nassim Taleb, who says, "It doesn't meet the very simple rule of demarcation between science and hogwash." Whether invoking the physicist Richard Feyman or the late Fischer Black, the use of mathematical models to value securities is an exercise in estimation. Derman further states, "You need to think about how to account for the mismatch between models and the real world." (A94), (B65)

---

Science is a great many things, but in the end they all return to this: Science is the acceptance of what works and the rejection of what doesn't. That needs more courage that we might think.

*Jacob Bronoski*

---

Long Term Capital Management (LTCM) was started by John Meriwether, who had a great following along with Myron Scholes and Robert Merton, two famous economists. Together they grew LTCM into assets of more than $130 billion, using a model they claimed would achieve exceptional returns without the usual risk. That alone should have been all the warning anyone needed. In 1997, their model did not do well, and by mid-1998 they had lost all of it; they had borrowed more than a trillion dollars to make investments. The story ended in September 1998, when the New York Federal Reserve Bank led a group of organizations to step in and bail them out; shortly thereafter there was no more LTCM. Academics with sophisticated models are a dangerous lot. And here's the best part, just before the demise, Myron Scholes and Robert Merton won the Nobel Prize for economics for their efforts in financial risk control. (B59) (B50)

LTCM was not alone; stories of hundreds of funds have gone out of business after short periods of exceptional success. Rogue trades were rampant. Remember Nick Lesson of Barings Bank? How about Jerome Kerviel of Societe Generale or a host of large banks during the period? The list is long and growing. Enron, WorldCom, Global Crossing were just a few large companies that went bankrupt taking their employees pensions and investments with them. I don't recall anyone ever anticipating any of these failures; forecasters never do.

After the inflationary decade of the 1970s, the price of gold was soaring. In the early 1980s, forecasts of gold reaching unbelievable heights were everywhere. They were supported with the facts that gold's fixed value was released in 1971 and it was free to trade, and trade it did. The Hunt Brothers had bought a large portion of the silver market. No forecaster saw anything but higher prices. I recall buying three 100-ounce bars and wishing I had more money to buy more. You will see in Chapter 11 on drawdowns that gold plummeted in 1981 and it took more than 25 years to get back to its peak. And now the forecasts of gold going to the moon are everywhere. At what point will we start to believe that forecasting is a hoax? This book is about the stock market, where the forecasting business is huge. I can tell you this: stock market forecasters are no different than economic forecasters. The ones who get lucky with a forecast are the ones who have yet to be wrong. I think the worst of them are the ones I call outliers (not to be confused with outlaws); these are the ones who through some stroke of luck make a forecast about something big and it turns out to actually happen. However, rarely in the exact manner of the forecast, but that is soon forgotten as he or she is paraded through the financial media as the guru of the year. They start newsletters, hold conferences, and embark on periods of more and more forecasts because they are now experts. Yet, most rarely make another correct forecast. John Kenneth Galbraith said: "When it comes to the stock market, there are two kinds of investors: those who do not know where it is going and those who do not know that they do not know where it is going." (B31)

## An Investment Professional's Dilemma

When speaking to investment advisors, I often remind them that they must deal with two realities:

1. Your clients expect you to have answers.
2. The market is unpredictable.

Once you have your clients believing #2, then the questions for #1 will be easier to answer. Most advisors and especially their clients get caught up in the moment and are easily swayed into believing that some expert actually knows the future. Or that they focus on the recent past and extrapolate that *ad infinitum.*

"Mind you, you should take economic forecasts—even my own—with a big grain of salt." John Kenneth Galbraith may have been more right than econometricians like to think when he said that "The only function of economic forecasting is to make astrology look respectable."

Nobel Prize–winning economist Kenneth Arrow has his own perspective on forecasting. During World War II, he served as a weather officer in the U.S. Army Air Corps and worked with individuals who were charged with the particularly difficult task of producing month-ahead weather forecasts. As Arrow and his team reviewed these predictions, they confirmed statistically what you and I might just as easily have guessed: The Corps' weather forecasts were no more accurate than random rolls of a die. Understandably, the forecasters asked to be relieved of this seemingly futile duty. Arrow's recollection of his superiors' response was priceless: "The commanding general is well aware that the forecasts are no good. However, he needs them for planning purposes." Peter Bernstein, *Against the Gods.* (B7)

---

You don't need a weatherman to know which way the wind blows.

*Bob Dylan*

---

The book *Dance with Chance* by Spyros Makridakis (an author who wrote a wonderful business forecasting book a couple of decades ago) gives a short story about Karl Popper. Popper was a philosopher of science born in Austria. In the 1930s he leveled a charge against Sigmund Freud, whose psychoanalytical theories had gained widespread acceptance. Popper pointed out that real scientists start with conjectures, which they then try to refute—as well as seeking evidence to support them. Only by failing to disprove their hypotheses, can they prove they were correct. Meanwhile *pseudoscientists*, as Popper called them, only look for events that prove their theories correct. Theories like this are little more than untested assertions. That's not to say the assertions won't eventually turn out to be right, but we can only reach this conclusion once someone has tested them. (B31)

---

Forecasting the future is much more difficult than forecasting the past.

*Unknown*

---

Forecasting the future of monetary, economic, financial, or political possibilities has a serious flaw in that even if your forecast is close to being correct, or even if it is spot on, the assumption about how the market will react is where the big problem lies. There is a flawed belief that positive events from political, economic, and monetary news will reflect positively on the markets. Conversely, negative news events will reflect negatively on the markets. This simply is not true. You can see that there is hardly any useable correlation to these events and the markets; earnings announcements are a perfect example. How many times have they been positive and the stock market did not react accordingly? The gap between a good economic or monetary forecast and the reality of what the market does is huge.

---

There is always a reason for a stock acting the way it does. But also remember that chances are you will not become acquainted with that reason until sometime in the future, when it is too late to act on it profitably.

*Jesse Livermore*

---

The following (slightly modified) comes from Gary Anderson, who wrote the must-read book entitled *The Janus Factor*. The link between fundamentals and price is elastic and rarely still. At times good earnings reports cause the price of a stock to rise, while at other times traders use positive earnings news to sell the same stock. Will a global crisis increase the value of the dollar or send it lower? The linkage between change in the world and change in the market is often ambiguous and sometimes just plain mysterious. In most cases, human beings are clever enough to create plausible stories to account for the market's response to events, but too often only with the aid of hindsight. There is a constant shift in the fundamental reasoning used to support decisions to buy and sell. The financial media is constantly justifying each move in the market with whatever recent event they can find that supports that move. Fundamental conventions supporting buy/sell decisions can vary from period to period and have no place in rational investing. We can draw a useful distinction between reasons and causes. Earnings do not cause prices to move, neither do research reports, news bulletins, talking heads, dividends, stock splits, the economy, peace, or war. These factors may be reasons motivating traders to buy and sell, but the direct cause of a stock's price movement is the buying and selling activity of traders and investors. We focus on causes, not reasons—on what traders do, not why. This is accomplished by measuring price and price derivatives (breadth, relative strength) of price movement. (B64)

## Gurus/Experts

What would we do without all the experts, gurus, pontificators, purveyors of gloom and doom, and, of course, the perma-bulls and perma-bears? First of all a giant industry would be gone, an industry that generates billions of dollars in the USA alone. I'm not going to spend a great deal of time on this, because the website of CXO Advisory Group LLC, CXOadvisory.com, does all the heavy lifting. (W7) They have an entire section devoted to GURUS. Here are the two questions they ask at the beginning of that section: "Can experts, whether self-proclaimed or endorsed by others (publications), provide reliable stock market timing guidance? Do some experts clearly show better intuition about overall market direction than others?" They address these questions with a logical and transparent process. After following more than 60 experts and thousands of observations, near the end of the Guru section, they conclude: "The overall accuracy of the group based on both raw forecast count and on the average of forecaster accuracies (weighting each individual equally) is 47 percent. In summary, stock market experts as a group do not reliably outguess the market. Some experts, though, may be better than others." Hmmm! It seems like a coin toss, on average, would do better.

Additionally, CXOadvisory.com reviews numerous academic papers, and then does its own backup analysis to determine if the paper's author and they agree. An excellent piece when reviewing Charles Manski's July 2010 paper entitled "Policy Analysis with Incredible Certitude," categorizes incredible analytical practices and underlying certitude. These four are:

1. Conventional certitudes (conventional wisdom)—Predictions (indicators) that experts generally accept as accurate, but are not necessarily accurate.
2. Dueling certitudes—Two contradictory predictions that competing experts present as exact, with no expression of uncertainty (leading to conflicting strong investment strategy recommendations).
3. Conflating science and advocacy—Developing arguments (assumptions) that support an investment strategy rather than an investment strategy that supports evidence-based arguments, while portraying the deliberative process as scientific.
4. Wishful extrapolation—Drawing a conclusion about some future situation based on historical tendencies and untenable assumptions (ignoring differences between the historical and future situations, and emphasizing in-sample over out-of-sample testing).

If you have ever watched television, read a newsletter, or attended a seminar, I'm sure the above sounds familiar. People who appear as experts generally aren't any better than the masses, however, when they are wrong, they are rarely held accountable, and never admit it (generally). They will respond that their timing was just off or some catastrophic event caught them off guard, or the worse—wrong for the right reasons. There is a book by Philip Tetlock, *Expert Political Judgement: How Good Is It? How Can We Know?* that deals with the business of prediction. Tetlock claims that the better known and more frequently quoted they are, the less reliable their guesses about the future are likely to be. The accuracy of their predictions actually has an inverse relationship to his or her self-confidence, renown, and depth of knowledge. Listen to experts at your own risk. (B57)

Larry Williams was an active and renowned trader before I even began to show interest in the markets. There is one significant point that Larry has made consistently that needs to be repeated here. If you are going to be mentored by someone, if you are going to read someone's book on trading/investing, if you are going to sign up for a course of instruction from someone, please make sure they are qualified to teach the subject. This does not always translate into how they trade or invest. Like Larry says in his *Trading Lesson 16*, Kareem Abdul Jabar tried coaching and was a disaster at it; Mark Spitz's swimming coach could not swim. However, the bottom line is that the best teachers are probably the ones who actually trade and invest as they have first-hand experience to the nuances of the skill. (A106) This argument is not unlike the one between the ivory tower academics and those involved in the real world applying their craft every day. While they may have considerable talent to offer, your chances are probably better with a real practitioner.

## Masking an Intellectual Void

My formal education was in aerospace engineering. My education in "The World of Finance" came and continues to come from people in the investment industry I have grown to respect. I hate to list some as fear of leaving someone out, but Ed Easterling, John Hussman, and James Montier are certainly at the top of the list. Are these professionals always correct? Of course not, but they usually admit it and they write in such a manner that they know the uncertainty is always there and yet present valid arguments on a wide range of topics and concepts. The rest of the learning comes for reading literally hundreds and hundreds of white papers in finance and economics. This process caused my concern at the insane use of advanced mathematics, usually in the form of partial differential equations, to supposedly assist in making the point that the paper was addressing. I cannot tell you how many times I thought that most of the math was unnecessary and more often than not the paper would have stood alone without the math. In many instances I think there is an attempt by most to overly complicate their work with mathematics with the belief that it brings credibility to their work. Another reason, and one I certainly cannot prove, is that they also know that most people who read their paper, other than their peers, will not grasp the math and just assume it is valid and necessary.

The senior special writer, Carl Bialik, of the *Wall Street Journal*, who writes a section called, "The Numbers Guy" is one of my favorite reads. As I was wrapping up research for this book and thinking that I had included enough opinions about things without substantial evidence, I was delighted to find support from Carl for this section on "Masking an Intellectual Void." On January 4, 2013, he wrote two articles entitled, "Don't Let Math Pull the Wool Over Your Eyes," and "Awed by Equations." Those articles referenced two papers that gave support to my belief in the overuse of mathematics and how readers of white papers generally were impressed with what they actually did not understand. Research was conducted using only the abstracts of two papers, one without math, and one with math; the catch being that the one with math was bogus, totally unrelated to the paper. Yet, the highest percentage of participants who gave the highest rating to the abstract with added math, based on the participants educational degree, was as follows:

> Math, Science, Technology     46 percent
>
> Humanities, Social Science     62 percent
>
> Medicine     64 percent
>
> Other     73 percent

I think this shows that those who had a high probability of not understanding the math gave the paper with the bogus math a higher rating, while those who possibly did understand the math did not. (A31)

$$-e^{\Pi} + (\sin^2 x + \cos^2 x) = 1/\cos 60°$$

This is just my lame attempt at humor. The financial academics have almost universally used partial differential equations in their white papers; I think, more often than not just to hide an intellectual void. Many times, the difficult math is not necessary, but by including it, they know most will never be able to question their work. Sad, indeed! Incidentally, the equation can be simplified to $1 + 1 = 2$.

## Earnings Season

For decades I have watched the parade of earnings announcements and how the media hangs on each one as if it actually had some value other than filling dead air. Figure 5.1 shows the stock price of Amazon back in the 2000 to 2001 bear market. The annotations are from actual earnings forecasts from analysts. If you yell "buy" all the way down, the odds are good that you will eventually be correct. Hopefully, you will still have some money.

---

In our view security analysts as a whole cannot estimate the future earnings pattern of one or more growth stocks with sufficient accuracy to provide a firm basis for valuation in the majority of cases.

*Benjamin Graham*

---

It seems that the media is so focused on earnings reports that they forget to report the actual earnings. Instead their focus is on where the earnings came in relative to the analysts' estimate. After beating up on experts, it is hard to imagine that someone would actually make an investment decision based on an analyst's (expert) guess as to what earnings should be. These analysts are constantly wined and dined by the companies they analyze so, in general, I think they are biased, and almost always to

**FIGURE 5.1**  Buy-and-Sell Recommendations from Earnings Predictions

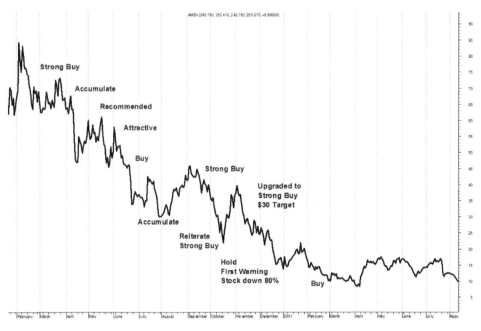

*Source:* Chart courtesy of MetaStock.

the upside. In fact, I think most are really just trend followers, in that they are always forecasting better earnings as markets rise and once a market rolls over and begins to decline they eventually begin to forecast lower earnings.

When asked what investors' greatest problems are, the late Peter Bernstein said, "Extrapolation! They believe the recent past is how the future will be."

## Are Financial Advisors Worth 1 Percent of AUM (Assets under Management)?

People who need advice are least likely to take it.

*Unknown*

Many asset managers hold entirely too many stocks and have become closet benchmark trackers. If they beat their benchmark they call it alpha and when they do not beat their benchmark they call it tracking error. If your investment manager rebalances your portfolio periodically based on a few questions that he required you to answer when setting up the account, here are some things to think about. Usually the risk tolerance and objective questionnaire is much more involved, but here are two questions usually asked:

1. What percentage of current income will you need when you retire?
2. On a scale from 1 to 7 what is your risk tolerance?

Do you honestly believe a person knows the answers to those questions? No way! They will try to answer based on what the advisor has told or suggested to them. The law requires this type of action for advisors, so pick an advisor you think will actually meet your needs and if you are unsure, can point you in the right direction.

## Economists Are Good at Predicting the Market

The economy depends about as much on economists as the weather does on weather forecasters.

*Jean Paul Kauffman*

Just to put this into perspective, the stock market is a component of the index of leading indicators. If the stock market is a good leading indicator of the economy, why ask an economist what the market is going to do? Yet, they are paraded daily across the financial media making forecasts about the markets, political policy, fiscal policy, monetary events, and, yes, occasionally about the economy. When they are correct, they won't let you forget it; when they are wrong no one remembers. Many economists are good when dealing with the economy, but rarely are they good when they stray into other areas.

## News Is Noise

Here is a humorous attempt to portray some of the daily noise often referred to as news. On Wall Street today, news of lower interest rates sent the stock market up, but then the expectation that these rates would be inflationary sent the market down, until the realization that lower rates might stimulate the sluggish economy pushed the market up, before it ultimately went down on fears that an overheated economy would lead to once again an imposition of higher interest rates.

Rolf Dobelli, writing for *The Guardian*, on April 12, 2013, in an article (A105) entitled "News is bad for you—and giving up reading it will make you happier," listed these problems with news:

News misleads.
News is irrelevant.
News has no explanatory power.

News is toxic to your body.
News increases cognitive errors.
News inhibits thinking.
News works like a drug.
News wastes time.
News makes us passive.
News kills creativity.

He claims he has gone without news for four years and says it isn't easy, but it's worth it. (A105) Since he wrote for a news organization I would imagine he is also looking for work.

---

If you can distinguish between good advice and bad advice, then you don't need advice.

*VanRoy's Second Law*

---

When asked at seminars what is the single most important concept to understand when investing, I respond simply that it is to know thyself. The human mind is a horrible investor and the use of heuristics does not help. The next chapter deals with human behavior as it relates to the market.

# CHAPTER 6

# The Enemy in the Mirror

## Real Time versus History

In regard to financial crises, market meltdowns, and so on, when you actually live through it, it is always amplified to the point you think it is the absolute worst ever. After things have faded into history, it never seems as bad. I've been through a bunch of goofy markets, but 2008 seems close to the worst, even though I'm sure it isn't. Being human has some real issues when it comes to the markets. There is an old aviation saying, "It is better to be on the ground wishing you were in the air than being in the air wishing you were on the ground." Another crazy human trait is to wish the markets to be fair, but then search at often great expense for a way to get an edge and win. Opposing that is when you believe the market is unfair, yet you check your portfolio three times a day (see the section "Cognitive Dissonance" in this chapter).

## Behavioral Investing

Heuristic refers to experience-based techniques for problem solving, learning, and discovery. Where an exhaustive search is impractical, heuristic methods are used to speed up the process of finding a satisfactory solution. Examples of this method include using a rule of thumb, an educated guess, an intuitive judgment, or common sense. Heuristics are strategies using readily accessible, though loosely applicable, information to control problem solving in human beings and machines. Heuristics is derived from the same Greek root word from which we derive eureka.

Incidentally, the phrase "rule of thumb" has many origins; I'll pick the one where a man would use his thumb to make various measurements. If you check the Internet you can find many other comments about the origin of "rule of thumb."

There are some great authors that I particularly like when it comes to reading and understanding behavior finance and investing. Here is my short list of favorites:

James Montier (A67) (A68) (A69) (B42) (B43)
Tim Richards (W5)
Hersh Shefrin (A86) (B51)
Thomas Gilovich (B22)
Martin Sewell (W6) (A84)

Most of the following material came from their books (bibliography) or websites. If you haven't read Montier's *Little Book of Behavioral Investing*, you need to, and then read it once a year. I am often asked for advice from young traders and investors. The consistent and most stressed thing I tell them is to learn about yourself. Understanding behavioral biases will help accomplish that.

Because the efficient market hypothesis is widely criticized, the field of behavior finance/investing has surfaced in the past couple of decades as an alternative. The real advantage of understanding these heuristics is that one can learn about one's self and hopefully adjust his or her decision making when it comes to investing.

## Behavioral Biases

Here are the biases that I think are important for investors to consider (alphabetically listed):

### Ambiguity Aversion

- "We don't mind risk but we hate uncertainty," Tim Richards. (W5)
- "People prefer the familiar to the unfamiliar," Hersh Shefrin. (B51)

### Anchoring

- Anchoring is a cognitive heuristic in which decisions are made based on an initial "anchor."
- Reflects the degree to which the initial judgment about an event or situation prohibits one from deviating from that position regardless of new information to the contrary.
- Psychologists have documented that when people make quantitative estimates, their estimates may be heavily influenced by previous values of the item. For example, it is not an accident that used car salespeople always start negotiating with a high price and then work down. The salespeople are trying to get the consumer anchored on the high price so that when they offer a lower price, the consumer will estimate that the lower price represents a good value.
- Anchoring can cause investors to underreact to new information.

- "Our habit of focusing on one salient point and ignoring all others, such as the price at which we buy a stock," Tim Richards. (W5)
- "In the absence of any solid information, past prices are likely to act as anchors for today's prices." "The stock market has a tendency to underreact to fundamental information—be it dividend omission, initiation or an earnings report," James Montier. (B42)

## Availability

- It's different this time!
- Availability is a cognitive heuristic in which a decision maker relies on knowledge that is readily available rather than examining other alternatives or procedures. This leads to arguments like, "smoking is not dangerous since my mother smoked two packs a day and lived to 90."
- "There are situations in which people assess the frequency of a class or the probability of an event by the ease with which instances or occurrences can be brought to mind. For example, one may assess the risk of heart attack among middle-aged people by recalling such occurrences among one's acquaintances. Similarly, one may evaluate the probability that a given business venture will fail by imagining various difficulties it could encounter. This judgmental heuristic is called availability. Availability is a useful clue for assessing frequency or probability, because instances of large classes are usually reached better and faster than instances of less frequent classes. However, availability is affected by factors other than frequency and probability. Consequently, the reliance on availability leads predictable biases," Amos Tversky and Daniel Kahneman. (A95–A97)

## Calendar Effects

- Calendar effects (sometimes less accurately described as *seasonal effects*) are cyclical anomalies in returns, where the cycle is based on the calendar. The most common calendar anomalies are the January effect and the weekend effect.

## Cognitive Dissonance

- "Cognitive dissonance is the mental conflict that people experience when they are presented with evidence that their beliefs or assumptions are wrong," James Montier. (B42)
- "The effect of simultaneously trying to believe two incompatible things at the same time," Tim Richards. (W5)

## Communal Reinforcement

- Communal reinforcement is a social construction in which a strong belief is formed when a claim is repeatedly asserted by members of a community, rather than due to the existence of empirical evidence for the validity of the claim.

## Confirmation Bias

- Confirmation bias is a cognitive bias whereby one tends to notice and look for information that confirms one's existing beliefs, while ignoring anything that contradicts those beliefs. It is a type of selective thinking. This is a heuristic common with newsletter writers. Something has caused them to believe the market will do such and such, and then they search for situations and data that support that belief.
- "Confirmation bias is the technical name for people's desire to find information that agrees with their existing view," James Montier. (B42)

## Disposition Effect

- "The disposition effect can be explained by arguing that investors are predisposed to holding losers too long and selling winners too early," Hersh Shefrin. (B51)
- "Shefrin and Statman predicted that because people dislike incurring losses much more than they enjoy making gains, and people are willing to gamble in the domain of losses, investors will hold onto stocks that have lost value (relative to the reference point of their purchase) and will be eager to sell stocks that have risen in value. They called this the 'disposition effect,'" James Montier. (B42)

## Endowment Effect

- ["This pattern—the fact that people often demand much more to give up an object than they would be willing to pay to acquire it—is called the endowment effect," Richard Thaler.] (W5)
- "The endowment effect is a hypothesis that people value a good more once their property right to it has been established. In other words, people place a higher value on objects they own relative to objects they do not. In one experiment, people demanded a higher price for a coffee mug that had been given to them but put a lower price on one they did not yet own," Martin Sewell. (W6)
- "Both the status quo bias and the endowment effect are part of a more general issue known as loss aversion," James Montier. (B42)
- "Simply put, the endowment effect says that once you own something you start to place a higher value on it than others would," James Montier. (B42)

## Halo Effect

- Experts add little value. Pedigree trumps evidence.
- "The halo effect is a simple, pervasive and powerful psychological bias which sees us anchor onto a single positive feature of a person and then indiscriminately apply it to all of their other traits. So if we perceive someone as physically desirable we're likely to assume that they're attractive in all other ways as well. This is highly fortunate for those beautiful but bad tempered, foul mouthed and cerebrally challenged personalities who commonly grace our multi-media world," Tim Richards. (W5)

- Companies will often attempt to use the halo effect by getting celebrity endorsements from completely unrelated but popular celebrities. Still, trading on such a simple psychological trait would be unlikely to fool savvy investors, you'd think.

## Herding

- ["Herding behavior or 'following the trend' has frequently been observed in the housing market, in the stock market crash of 1987 (see Shiller) and in the foreign exchange market," Frankel and Froot, Allen and Taylor.] (W5)
- ["The behavior, although individually rational, produces group behavior that is, in a well-defined sense, irrational. This herd-like behavior is said to arise from an information cascade," Robert Shiller.] (W5)
- ["We review theory and evidence relating to herd behavior, payoff and reputational interactions, social learning, and informational cascades in capital markets. We offer a simple taxonomy of effects, and evaluate how alternative theories may help explain evidence on the behavior of investors, firms, and analysts. We consider both incentives for parties to engage in herding or cascading, and the incentives for parties to protect against or take advantage of herding or cascading by others," Hirshleifer and Teoh.] (W5)

## Hindsight Bias

- ["The reason for overconfidence may also have to do with hindsight bias, a tendency to think that one would have known actual events were coming before they happened, had one been present then or had reason to pay attention. Hindsight bias encourages a view of the world as more predictable than it really is," Robert Shiller.] (W5)
- "Hindsight bias: a.k.a Monday morning quarterback," Nassim Taleb.
- This is a common heuristic among investors, especially technical analysts, who see situations in the past and actually think they are making a determination that will affect the future—they quite honestly don't realize they are doing it.

## Loss Aversion/Risk Aversion

- Lose sight of the big picture. Focus on short-term losses. Anchor against most recent values. Underweight more aggressive investments.
- ["In prospect theory, loss aversion refers to the tendency for people to strongly prefer avoiding losses than acquiring gains. Some studies suggest that losses are as much as twice as psychologically powerful as gains. Loss aversion was first convincingly demonstrated by Amos Tversky and Daniel Kahneman."] (W5)
- ["The central assumption of the theory is that losses and disadvantages have greater impact on preferences than gains and advantages," Amos Tversky and Daniel Kahneman] (W5)
- ["Numerous studies have shown that people feel losses more deeply than gains of the same value," Amos Tversky and Daniel Kahneman.] (W5)

## Overconfidence

- Everyone believes they are above average. An often quoted test is to ask a group of 50 people to raise their hands if they think they are above average drivers. Most times, considerably more than half of them will raise their hands. People also have a tendency to cling to their assertions about things. With investing, overconfidence can lead to underdiversification. James Montier says this is one of the most common biases.

## Overreaction

- "[I]nvestors overreact to negative news," Hersh Shefrin. (A86)
- "De Bondt and Thaler argued that investors overreact to both bad news and good news. Therefore, overreaction leads past losers to become underpriced and past winners to become overpriced," Hersh Shefrin. (A86)
- "Rather, what we find is apparent Under-reaction at short horizons and apparent overreaction at long horizons," Hersh Shefrin. (A86)
- "What we seem to have is overreaction at very short horizons, say less than one month momentum possibly due to Under-reaction for horizons between three and twelve months (Jegadeesh and Titman) and overreaction for periods longer than one year (De Bondt and Thaler)," Hersh Shefrin.
- "The overreaction evidence shows that over longer horizons of perhaps three to five years, security prices overreact to consistent patterns of news pointing in the same direction," Shleifer.

## Prospect Theory

- Gains are less intense than losses. People hold onto losses too long. People sell winners too soon.
- "Prospect theory was developed by Kahneman and Tversky. In its original form, it is concerned with behavior of decision makers who face a choice between two alternatives. The definition in the original text is: 'Decision making under risk can be viewed as a choice between prospects or gambles.' Decisions subject to risk are deemed to signify a choice between alternative actions, which are associated with particular probabilities (prospects) or gambles. The model was later elaborated and modified," Goldberg and von Nitzsch.
- "Prospect theory has probably done more to bring psychology into the heart of economic analysis than any other approach. Many economists still reach for the expected utility theory paradigm when dealing with problems, however, prospect theory has gained much ground in recent years, and now certainly occupies second place on the research agenda for even some mainstream economists. Unlike much psychology, prospect theory has a solid mathematical basis—making it comfortable for economists to play with. However, unlike expected utility theory which concerns itself with how decisions under uncertainty should be made (a prescriptive approach), prospect theory concerns itself with how decisions are actually made (a descriptive approach)," James Montier. (B42)
- "[G]et-evenitis is central to prospect theory," Hersh Shefrin.

- "[P]rospect theory deals with the way we frame decisions, the different ways we label—or code—outcomes; and how they affect our attitude toward risk," Belsky and Thomas Gilovich. (B22)

## Recency

- "You over focus on the most recent events you've experienced and neglect to worry about older information. We don't so much integrate new information with the old as use it to overwrite our memories," Tim Richards. (W5)

## Representativeness

- Great companies are great investments. People rely on rules of thumb. People see things the way they ought to be.
- ["Many of the probabilistic questions with which people are concerned belong to one of the following types: What is the probability that object A belongs to class B? What is the probability that event A originate from process B? What is the probability that process B will generate event A? In answering such questions, people typically rely on the representativeness heuristic, in which probabilities are evaluated by the degree to which A is representative of B, that is, by the degree to which A resembles B. For example, when A is highly representative of B, the probability that A originates from B is judged to be high. On the other hand, if A is not similar to B, the probability that A originates from B is judged to be low," Amos Tversky and Daniel Kahneman.] (W5)
- "The best explanation to date of the misperception of random sequences is offered by psychologists Daniel Kahneman and Amos Tversky, who attribute it to people's tendency to be overly influenced by judgments of 'representativeness.' Representativeness can be thought of as the reflexive tendency to assess the similarity of outcomes, instances, and categories on relatively salient and even superficial features, and then to use these assessments of similarity as a basis of judgment. People assume that 'like goes with like': Things that go together should look as though they go together. We expect instances to look like the categories of which they are members; thus, we expect someone who is a librarian to resemble the prototypical librarian. We expect effects to look like their causes; thus we are more likely to attribute a case of heartburn to spicy rather than bland food, and we are more inclined to see jagged handwriting as a sign of a tense rather than a relaxed personality," Thomas Gilovich. (B22)

## Selective Thinking

- Selective thinking is the process by which one focuses on favorable evidence in order to justify a belief, ignoring unfavorable evidence.

## Self-Attribution

- "Self-attribution bias occurs when people attribute successful outcomes to their own skill but blame unsuccessful outcomes on bad luck," Hersh Shefrin. (A86)

## Self-Deception

- Self-deception is the process of misleading ourselves to accept as true or valid that which is false or invalid.

## Status Quo Bias

- The status quo bias is a cognitive bias for the status quo; in other words, people tend to be biased toward doing nothing or maintaining their current or previous decision.
- ["The example also illustrates what Samuelson and Zeckhauser (1988) call a status quo bias, a preference for the current state that biases the economist against both buying and selling his wine," Richard Thaler.] (W5)
- ["One implication of loss aversion is that individuals have a strong tendency to remain at the status quo, because the disadvantages of leaving it loom larger than the advantages. Samuelson and Zeckhauser have demonstrated this effect, which they term the status quo bias," Richard Thaler.] (W5)
- "Both the status quo bias and the endowment effect are part of a more general issue known as loss aversion," James Montier. (B42)

## Underreaction

- "In predicting the future, people tend to get anchored by salient past events. Consequently, they underreact," Hersh Shefrin. (A86)
- The underreaction evidence shows that security prices underreact to news such as earnings announcements. If the news is good, prices keep trending up after the initial positive reaction; if the news is bad, prices keep trending down after the initial negative reaction.

## Bias Tracks for Investors

The following is my attempt to tie some of these behavioral biases together and see how they flow from one to another and eventually into technical analysis techniques (italicized).

1. Communal Reinforcement causes Selective Thinking, which causes Confirmation Bias, which can cause Self-Deception, which leads to either Self-Fulfilling or Self-Destructive. If Self-fulfilling, it can lead to using *Price*, which can lead to using *Support and Resistance*. If Self-Destructive it can lead to using *Time*, which can lead to using *Calendar Effects* such as *Weekend Effect, January Barometer, January Effect*, and so on.
2. Status Quo Bias can lead to Anchoring, which can lead to *Support and Resistance*. It can also lead to Loss/Risk Aversion, which can lead to Underreaction, which is typically associated with the *short term*.

3. Self-Deception can lead to Self-Attribution and Overconfidence. Overconfidence can lead to Hindsight Bias and Representativeness. Representativeness can lead to Overreaction, which is typically associated with the *long term*.
4. Since anchoring is often associated with framing, here is a simple example of how framing can work. I ask people how to pronounce the capitol of Kentucky, is it Lewisville, or Loueyville? I just framed the question. I hear an even amount of both from the audience. The correct answer is Frankfurt. This is particularly interesting when I'm doing this while in Kentucky.
5. Herding, disposition, confirmation bias, and representativeness can provide justification for *Trend following*. Information is not dispersed evenly across the investor universe, especially for illiquid assets or if the information has much uncertainty, which leads to underreaction. If investors are reluctant to take small losses then *momentum* is improved by the disposition effect.
6. Herding leads to *Trend analysis*. And finally, Overconfidence can lead to ruin.

Bottom line: You can enter any of these tracks at just about any point and the results will be similar.

## Investor Emotions

I would imagine that everyone has experienced the emotional cycle of investing without a plan. We buy a stock for whatever reason, primarily because we are optimistic about its future. When it does rise in price it creates excitement and as it keeps rising, a state of euphoria is dominating the investor's mind. I can remember 30-plus years ago thinking about quitting my day job during such a period. If the price then drops a bit, it immediately causes anxiety, drops even more and downright fear sets in. Even further price erosion and panic is driving the investor with the absolute depression being the last phase of investor disappointment, usually coinciding with finally selling the stock. However, if still frozen with depression and panic and the price then rises, hope is instilled. Rising prices slowly bring on optimism and the emotional cycle of unplanned, random, guesswork like investor begins again. Figure 6.1 shows this emotional cycle.

## Investors as a Whole Do Poorly

Data has shown that investors as a whole continue to buy and sell at exactly the wrong time. Although we cannot possibly know the specific reasons, a shallow understanding of the human psyche will offer some answers. They react to news without doing any analysis, and it doesn't matter if it is considered good news or bad. Investors become mesmerized by long-running bull markets and absolutely unnerved by bear markets. They, as a whole, try to match the investment acumen of their relatives, neighbors, friends, business associated, and even complete strangers, if they have claimed, even casually, that they have done well in the market.

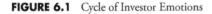

**FIGURE 6.1** Cycle of Investor Emotions

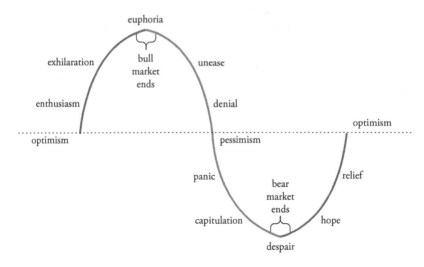

**TABLE 6.1** Twenty-Year Returns of Various Classes and Average Investor

| REITs | Oil | S&P 500 | Gold | Bonds | International | Inflation | Average Investor |
|-------|-----|---------|------|-------|--------------|-----------|------------------|
| 10.9% | 8.6% | 7.8% | 7.6% | 6.5% | 4.0% | 2.5% | 2.1% |

There is a study put out annually by Dalbar, which shows that investors as a whole underperform the markets in a number of different ways. In fact they have consistently underperformed the S&P 500 anywhere from 4 percent to 10 percent per year for the past 27 years (Dalbar began their service in 1984). The percentage might seem small at first glance, but over time it becomes significant. Significant in this example can mean that one may not recover from it. Table 6.1, using data from JP Morgan, shows the 20-year annualized returns for various asset classes and the average investor based on the Dalbar data.

Another study put out by Morningstar's Russell Kinnel on 2/4/2013, shows the same problem; investors as a whole do quite poorly compared to indices. (See Table 6.2.) Basedon all funds, the average investor lagged the average fund by 0.95 percent annualized over the past 10 years.

Buying and selling at the wrong time can be explained by the fact that most investors react to news, whether it is positive or negative, without any detailed analysis. They are mesmerized by seemingly unending uptrends in the market and demoralized by continuing new lows. The bottom line is that they fail to have the discipline to follow a systematic approach that will assist them on detaching their emotions from their decisions. Here is a list of investor faults when it comes to investing. Books are filled with much more and with much more detail, I just wanted to include the ones that I have experienced, with the Lack of Discipline being the one that can cause the most pain.

Lack of discipline
Impatience
Greed
Refusal to accept the truth
No objectivity
Impulse behavior
Avoid false parallels

Your human brain will play tricks on you. If you take an escalator or moving sidewalk when going to work and do so frequently, you will understand. Your brain will cause an automatic (involuntary) action to assist you as you step onto the escalator or moving sidewalk. You might not even realize it. However, if one day the escalator is stopped, and you notice that it is stopped, you will almost stumble as you step onto it because your brain is programmed to assist, and this time that assistance is not helpful, even though you knew it was not moving prior to stepping on it.

Many who are not good at math use heuristics or worse yet, guessing to solve problems. I'll just use a few of the math issues that James Montier has used over the years as examples. (A67) (B43)

*Example A:* You are told that a baseball and bat cost a total of $1.10, and that the bat cost $1 more than the ball. What is the cost of each? The solution involves a really simple eighth grade algebra problem, but most will just guess and their initial guess will probably be that the bat costs a $1 and the ball costs $0.10. Because those numbers just almost pop out at you from the information given. Unfortunately, they forgot the part of the problem that said the bat costs $1 more than the ball. Their usual answer has the difference being $0.90.

**TABLE 6.2**  Investor Performance Compared to Funds

| Category | 10 Years—through December 31, 2012 | | |
| --- | --- | --- | --- |
| | Average Total Return | Asset-Weight Investor Return | Average Fund versus Average Investor |
| U.S. Stock | 7.89 | 6.88 | 1.01 |
| Sector Stock | 9.44 | 9.07 | 0.37 |
| International Equity | 9.95 | 6.84 | 3.11 |
| Balanced | 6.37 | 5.53 | 0.84 |
| Taxable Bond | 5.63 | 4.76 | 0.87 |
| Municipal Bond | 4.06 | 2.71 | 1.35 |
| All Funds | 7.05 | 6.10 | 0.95 |

Let the ball = $X$, then we know that the bat is $X + 100$ (using cents here), so the equation is:

$$X \text{ (ball) } + (X + 100) \text{ (bat)} = 110.$$
Simplifying, it becomes $2X + 100 = 110$,
again, $2X = 110 - 100$,
again, $2X = 10$, or $X = 5 = \$0.05$. Therefore the bat costs $1.05.

*Example B:* You are told that a swimming pool that measures 100 feet by 100 feet has a Lilly pad plant put into it. The plant doubles in size every day. It completely covers the pool in 24 days, how long did it take to cover half of the pool? Most will quickly say 12 days as the word double and 24 just seem to yearn for that. Of course, some will be really hesitant trying to invoke the size of the pool since that was given—it has absolutely nothing to do with the problem. The correct answer is 23 days. Think about it.

*Example C:* Your coffee shop is offering two deals on coffee, the first is 33 percent more coffee, and the second takes 33 percent off the price. Which would you choose? Most would claim they are essentially equal. A discount of 33 percent is the same as getting a 50 percent increase in the amount of coffee. Bottom line: Getting something extra for free feels better than getting the same for less. But, is it?

Most view these options as essentially the same proposition, but they're not. The discount is by far the better deal because most don't realize that, a "50 percent increase in quantity is the same as a 33 percent discount in price." But let's do the math. The initial price is $10 for 10 ounces of coffee. Hopefully, it's obvious that the unit price is therefore $1 per ounce. An extra 33 percent more "free" coffee would bring the total up to 13.3 ounces for $10. That $10 divided by 13.3 ounce gives us a unit price of $0.75 per ounce. With a 33 percent discount off the initial offer, though, the proposition becomes $6.67 for 10 ounces, for a unit price of $0.67 per ounce. After reading this, you will probably pay anything for a cup of coffee.

Now that I hopefully have captured your attention in the first six chapters, let's focus on some facts about the market. The next chapter focuses on bull and bear markets, both cyclical and secular, along with many convincing statistics about them.

# CHAPTER 7

# Market Facts: Bull and Bear Markets

The farther backward you can look, the farther forward you are likely to see.

*Winston Churchill*

## Calendar versus Market Math

There are 365 calendar days per year (365.25 for leap year consideration). There are five market days per week, so five-sevenths of 365 = 260.7 market days per year. Of course, to include leap year using the same methodology, five-sevenths of 365.25 = 260.9 market days per year. Hence, either 260.7 or 260.9 will round to 261 days per year. Next we need to adjust for market holidays, 261 days − 9 holidays = 252 market days per year. Market holidays (Table 7.1) were obtained from the New York Stock Exchange website.

## Stock Exchange Holidays

So now we know that there are 252 market days per year. If we divide that by the number of months per year (12), 252/12 = 21 market days per month. Hence, dividing market days by 12 will yield calendar months.

With this knowledge, we can then determine moving average, ratio, or rates of change values such as:

1 month = 21 market days (for a month you would use 21, not the normal 30/31 days in a month).
3 months = 63 days.
9 months = 189 days (close to the ubiquitous 200 days).

**TABLE 7.1**   Market Holidays (2012)

| | |
|---|---|
| New Year's Day | January 2 |
| Martin Luther King Jr. Day | January 16 |
| Washington's Birthday | February 20 |
| Good Friday | April 6 |
| Memorial Day | May 28 |
| Independence Day | July 4 |
| Labor Day | September 3 |
| Thanksgiving Day | November 22 |
| Christmas Day | December 25 |

## Understanding the Past

Although the old saying goes, the present [market] rarely is the same as the past, but it often rhymes. This is why we study the past so that when similar events unfold in the market, we just might be able to recognize them and know what can possibly happen. Remember, markets constantly change, but people rarely do.

---

All bull markets die, only the cause of death changes.

*James Montier*

---

## Bull Markets

A bull market has many definitions. Usually the one that makes the most sense (cents) is the one that mirrors the definition of a bear market—a move of 20 percent or greater without an opposite move of −20 percent. Table 7.2 shows all bull markets in the S&P 500 Index of greater than 20 percent since 1931 ranked by duration in days. It should be clear that bull markets come in all sizes and durations. The current bull market (as of 12/31/2012) is number 8 in duration.

Figure 7.1 shows the data in Table 7.2 with Percent Gain versus Months duration. The 2009 to 2012 bull market is identified by the square and the average of all bull markets is denoted by the dot. The 2009 to 2012 bull is below the least squares line, which means that for its duration it has not performed as well as the average. However, the 1987 to 2000 bull market could be considered an outlier and if removed (see Figure 7.2), then the 2009 to 2012 bull is closer to average. Although this is foolish, it does show how data can be manipulated, or as Charles Barkley says, "If my aunt were a man, she'd be my uncle."

Bull markets are when investors become genius and overconfidence flourishes. They are the times when capital grows and times are good. Often bull markets are mixed with what appears to be really bad news, whether it is economic, political, or other. An old saying is that bull markets climb a wall of worry. A bull market can cause exceptional complacency and when they begin to roll over into a bear market, most will be in denial and ride much of the bear market down. We won't spend much time

**TABLE 7.2** S&P 500 Bull Markets

| Start | End | Period | % Gain | Calendar Days | Calendar Months | Calendar Years |
|---|---|---|---|---|---|---|
| 12/4/1987 | 3/24/2000 | 87–00 | 582.10% | 4494 | 147.65 | 12.30 |
| 6/13/1949 | 8/2/1956 | 49–56 | 267.10% | 2607 | 85.65 | 7.14 |
| 10/3/1974 | 11/28/1980 | 74–80 | 125.60% | 2248 | 73.86 | 6.15 |
| 7/23/2002 | 10/9/2007 | 02–07 | 96.20% | 1904 | 62.55 | 5.21 |
| 8/12/1982 | 8/25/1987 | 82–87 | 228.80% | 1839 | 60.42 | 5.03 |
| 10/22/1957 | 12/12/1961 | 57–61 | 86.40% | 1512 | 49.68 | 4.14 |
| 4/28/1942 | 5/29/1946 | 42–46 | 157.70% | 1492 | 49.02 | 4.08 |
| 3/9/2009 | 12/31/2012 | **09–12** | 110.81% | 1393 | 45.77 | 3.81 |
| | | | | | | |
| 6/26/1962 | 2/9/1966 | | 79.80% | 1324 | 43.50 | 3.62 |
| 5/26/1970 | 1/11/1973 | 70–73 | 73.50% | 961 | 31.57 | 2.63 |
| 10/7/1966 | 11/29/1968 | 66–68 | 48.00% | 784 | 25.76 | 2.15 |
| 3/14/1935 | 3/10/1937 | 35–37 | 131.60% | 727 | 23.89 | 1.99 |
| 12/30/2027 | 9/16/2029 | | 80.40% | 626 | 20.57 | 1.71 |
| 5/19/1947 | 6/15/1948 | 47–48 | 23.90% | 393 | 12.91 | 1.08 |
| 3/31/1938 | 11/9/1938 | | 62.20% | 223 | 7.33 | 0.61 |
| 4/11/1939 | 10/25/1939 | | 26.80% | 197 | 6.47 | 0.54 |
| 6/10/1940 | 11/7/1940 | | 26.70% | 150 | 4.93 | 0.41 |
| 11/13/2029 | 4/10/1930 | 29–30 | 46.80% | 148 | 4.86 | 0.41 |
| 2/27/1933 | 7/18/1933 | | 120.60% | 141 | 4.63 | 0.39 |
| 10/19/1933 | 2/6/1934 | | 37.30% | 110 | 3.61 | 0.30 |
| 9/21/2001 | 1/4/2002 | | 21.40% | 105 | 3.45 | 0.29 |
| 6/1/1932 | 9/7/1932 | | 111.60% | 98 | 3.22 | 0.27 |
| 12/16/1930 | 2/24/1931 | | 25.80% | 70 | 2.30 | 0.19 |
| 11/20/2008 | 1/6/2009 | | 24.20% | 47 | 1.54 | 0.13 |
| 10/5/1931 | 11/9/1931 | | 30.60% | 35 | 1.15 | 0.10 |
| 6/2/1931 | 6/26/1931 | | 25.80% | 24 | 0.79 | 0.07 |
| | | AVG | 101.99% | 909.69 | 29.89 | 2.49 |

85

**FIGURE 7.1** Bull Markets Gain versus Duration

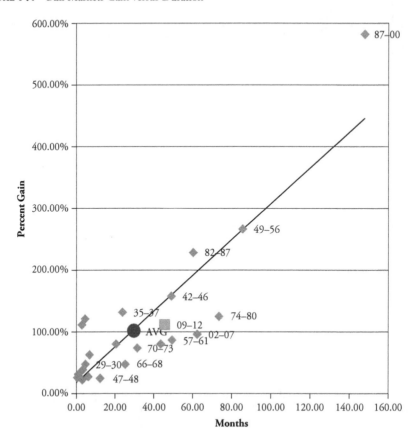

on bull markets because the underlying theme of this book is risk avoidance so the focus is on bear markets and all things associated with them.

## Bear Markets

Figure 7.3 shows the Dow Industrial Average back to 1885 using a semi-log scale in the top plot. The lower plot is a line that zigzags back and forth, known as a filtered wave. That lower line only changes direction *after* a move of at least 20 percent has occurred in the opposite direction. It shows only moves of 20 percent or more. The last move is not valid as it only shows where the last price was from the last move of 20 percent or greater. Most are surprised at the frequency of up and down moves of that magnitude that have occurred in the past 127 years. Notice the three highlighted periods where there were very few up and down moves of greater than 20 percent.

Figure 7.4 is the same as the one above except that it only shows data since 1969 so that you can better see the moves of greater than 20 percent. Notice that there are

**FIGURE 7.2** Bull Markets Gain versus Duration without 1987–2000

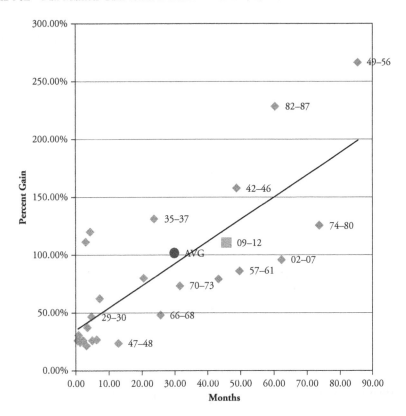

**FIGURE 7.3** Twenty Percent Moves in Dow Industrial Average—Long Term

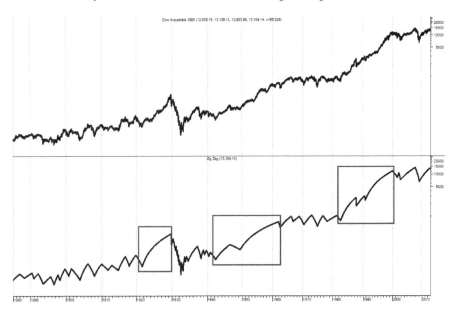

*Source:* Chart from MetaStock.

**FIGURE 7.4**   Twenty Percent Moves in Dow Industrial Average—Medium Term

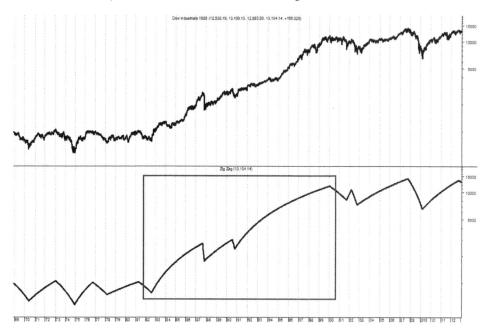

*Source:* Chart from MetaStock.

periods (first half of chart) where there were many up and down moves of greater than 20 percent. These types of moves have also happened on the right edge of the chart since 2000. The period of time between 1982 and 2000 saw relatively few moves in comparison. As will be thoroughly reviewed later, these periods are driven by long-term swings in valuations.

It has long been assumed that moves downward of 20 percent or greater are called *bear markets*. Although this is a subjective call, it is widely accepted and won't be challenged here. Any move downward from a market high is called a *drawdown* and is measured in percentages. Therefore a drawdown of 20 percent or more is also a bear market. Drawdowns are discussed in more detail in Chapter 11. Table 7.3 shows the bear markets in the Dow Industrials since 1885. At the bottom of the table are some statistics to assist you in getting a feel for the averages, and so on.

> *Average.* The same as the mean in statistics, add all values and then divide by the number of items.
>
> *Avg Ex 29.* This is the Average with the 1929 bear removed as it skews the data somewhat.
>
> *Minimum.* The minimum value in that column.
>
> *Maximum.* The maximum value in that column.
>
> *Std. Dev.* This is standard deviation or sigma, which is a measure of the dispersion of the values in the column. About 65 percent of the values will fall within

**TABLE 7.3** Bear Markets in Dow Jones Industrials from 2/17/1885 to 12/31/2012

| Largest to Smallest | Decline from Peak | Return Required for Recovery | Peak Date | Trough Date | Recovery Date | Decline in Days | Decline in Months | Recovery in Days | Recovery in Months | Bear Duration in Days | Bear Duration in Months | Average Drawdown |
|---|---|---|---|---|---|---|---|---|---|---|---|---|
| 1 | −89.19% | 824.72% | 9/3/1929 | 7/8/1932 | 11/23/1954 | 845 | 40.24 | 6464 | 307.81 | 7309 | 348.05 | −55.98% |
| 2 | −53.78% | 116.35% | 10/9/2007 | 3/9/2009 | 12/31/2012 | 355 | 16.90 | 954 | 45.43 | 1309 | 62.33 | −20.67% |
| 3 | −48.54% | 94.34% | 1/19/1906 | 11/15/1907 | 7/28/1915 | 552 | 26.29 | 2192 | 104.38 | 2744 | 130.67 | −18.48% |
| 4 | −46.64% | 87.42% | 6/4/1890 | 8/8/1896 | 1/20/1899 | 1872 | 89.14 | 735 | 35.00 | 2607 | 124.14 | −22.33% |
| 5 | −46.58% | 87.20% | 11/3/1919 | 8/24/1921 | 12/31/1924 | 540 | 25.71 | 1006 | 47.90 | 1546 | 73.62 | −24.10% |
| 6 | −46.14% | 85.67% | 6/17/1901 | 11/9/1903 | 3/24/1905 | 713 | 33.95 | 410 | 19.52 | 1123 | 53.48 | −22.45% |
| 7 | −45.08% | 82.08% | 1/11/1973 | 12/6/1974 | 11/3/1982 | 481 | 22.90 | 1998 | 95.14 | 2479 | 118.05 | −17.30% |
| 8 | −40.13% | 67.02% | 11/21/1916 | 12/19/1917 | 7/9/1919 | 320 | 15.24 | 459 | 21.86 | 779 | 37.10 | −21.39% |
| 9 | −37.85% | 60.89% | 1/14/2000 | 10/9/2002 | 10/3/2006 | 685 | 32.62 | 1003 | 47.76 | 1688 | 80.38 | −13.64% |
| 10 | −36.58% | 57.67% | 2/9/1966 | 5/26/1970 | 11/10/1972 | 1052 | 50.10 | 625 | 29.76 | 1677 | 79.86 | −12.68% |
| 11 | −36.13% | 56.57% | 8/25/1987 | 10/19/1987 | 8/24/1989 | 38 | 1.81 | 468 | 22.29 | 506 | 24.10 | −19.34% |
| 12 | −31.76% | 46.54% | 9/5/1899 | 9/24/1900 | 6/3/1901 | 314 | 14.95 | 202 | 9.62 | 516 | 24.57 | −15.97% |
| 13 | −27.10% | 37.17% | 12/13/1961 | 6/26/1962 | 9/5/1963 | 134 | 6.38 | 301 | 14.33 | 435 | 20.71 | −9.51% |
| 14 | −21.16% | 26.83% | 7/17/1990 | 10/11/1990 | 4/17/1991 | 61 | 2.90 | 129 | 6.14 | 190 | 9.05 | −10.77% |
| 15 | −20.13% | 25.20% | 12/3/1886 | 4/2/1888 | 4/25/1890 | 398 | 18.95 | 623 | 29.67 | 1021 | 48.62 | −8.08% |
| **Average** | **−41.79%** | **71.78%** | | | | **557.33** | **32.26** | **1171.27** | **70.62** | **1728.60** | **102.89** | **−22.58%** |
| **Avg Ex 29** | **−38.40%** | **62.34%** | | | | **536.79** | **25.56** | **793.21** | **37.77** | **1330.00** | **63.33** | **−16.91%** |
| **Minimum** | **−20.13%** | **25.20%** | | | | **38.00** | **1.81** | **129.00** | **6.14** | **190.00** | **9.05** | **−55.98%** |
| **Maximum** | **−89.19%** | **824.72%** | | | | **1872.00** | **89.14** | **6464.00** | **307.81** | **7309.00** | **348.05** | **−8.08%** |
| **Std. Dev.** | **16.48%** | **−14.15%** | | | | **461.33** | **21.97** | **1581.03** | **75.29** | **1742.23** | **82.96** | **11.27%** |
| **Median** | **−40.13%** | **67.02%** | | | | **481.00** | **22.90** | **625.00** | **29.76** | **1309.00** | **62.33** | **−18.48%** |

one standard deviation of the mean, and 95 percent will fall within two standard deviations of the mean.

*Median.* If the data is widely dispersed or has asymptotic outlier data, this is usually a better measure for central tendency than Average.

From Table 7.3 you can see that there were 15 declines of greater than 20 percent in the past 127 years in the Dow Jones Industrial Average. Here are some statistics from the table:

The average decline percentage was −41.79 percent.

The average duration of the decline was 32.26 months.

The average duration of the recovery was 70.62 months.

Therefore, the average bear market from its beginning peak until it had fully returned to that peak lasted 102.89 months or over 8.5 years.

The average percentage gain for the recovery to get back to even was 71.78 percent.

Table 7.4 shows the Bear Markets in the S&P 500 Index since 1927.

From Table 7.4 you can see that there were 10 declines greater than 20 percent in the past 85 years in the S&P 500 Index. Here are some statistics from the table:

The average decline percentage was −40.88%.

The average duration of the decline was 17.07 months.

The average duration of the recovery was 51.23 months.

Therefore, the average bear market from its beginning peak until it had fully returned to that peak lasted 68.3 months or over 5.5 years.

The average percentage gain for the recovery to get back to even was 69.14 percent.

Although the numbers are a little different between the two tables, the Dow Industrials also had 42 more years of data. The message is the same, however, drawdowns of greater than 20 percent (bear markets) can be painful and it takes a long time to recover from them. There will be more detailed coverage of these tables in Chapter 11, Drawdown Analysis.

## Just How Bad Can a Bear Market Be?

In an attempt to show how bad some bear markets can be in not only magnitude but duration, Figure 7.5 shows the S&P 500 beginning in 2000, the Dow Industrials overlaid from 1929, and the Japanese Nikkei 225 overlaid from 1989. All three begin at 0 percent on the left scale. These are inflation adjusted so that you can see the full effect of holding over time. Although we do not know the future, studying the past clearly shows that really bad bear markets can last a very long time.

**TABLE 7.4** Bear Markets in the S&P 500 from 12/30/1927 to 12/31/2012

| Largest to Smallest | Decline from Peak | Return Required for Recovery | Peak Date | Trough Date | Recovery Date | Decline in Days | Decline in Months | Recovery in Days | Recovery in Months | Bear Duration in Days | Bear Duration in Months | Average Drawdown |
|---|---|---|---|---|---|---|---|---|---|---|---|---|
| 1 | -86.19% | 624.09% | 9/16/1929 | 6/1/1932 | 9/22/1954 | 678 | 32.29 | 5571 | 265.29 | 6249 | 297.57 | -52.97% |
| 2 | -56.78% | 131.35% | 10/10/2007 | 3/10/2009 | 12/31/2012 | 355 | 16.90 | 962 | 45.81 | 1317 | 62.71 | -23.11% |
| 3 | -49.15% | 96.65% | 3/27/2000 | 10/10/2002 | 5/31/2007 | 637 | 30.33 | 1166 | 55.52 | 1803 | 85.86 | -22.54% |
| 4 | -48.20% | 93.06% | 1/11/1973 | 10/3/1974 | 7/17/1980 | 436 | 20.76 | 1461 | 69.57 | 1897 | 90.33 | -18.98% |
| 5 | -36.06% | 56.40% | 11/29/1968 | 5/26/1970 | 3/6/1972 | 369 | 17.57 | 451 | 21.48 | 820 | 39.05 | -13.29% |
| 6 | -33.51% | 50.40% | 8/26/1987 | 12/7/1987 | 7/27/1989 | 71 | 3.38 | 414 | 19.71 | 485 | 23.10 | -17.17% |
| 7 | -27.97% | 38.84% | 12/12/1961 | 6/26/1962 | 9/3/1963 | 135 | 6.43 | 299 | 14.24 | 434 | 20.67 | -10.67% |
| 8 | -27.11% | 37.20% | 11/28/1980 | 8/12/1982 | 11/3/1982 | 430 | 20.48 | 58 | 2.76 | 488 | 23.24 | -12.44% |
| 9 | -22.18% | 28.50% | 2/9/1966 | 10/7/1966 | 5/4/1967 | 167 | 7.95 | 143 | 6.81 | 310 | 14.76 | -9.32% |
| 10 | -21.63% | 27.60% | 8/2/1956 | 10/22/1957 | 9/24/1958 | 307 | 14.62 | 233 | 11.10 | 540 | 25.71 | -10.06% |
| **Average** | **-40.88%** | **69.14%** | | | | **358.50** | **17.07** | **1075.80** | **51.23** | **1434.30** | **68.30** | **-19.06%** |
| **Avg Ex 29** | **-35.84%** | **55.87%** | | | | **323.00** | **15.38** | **576.33** | **27.44** | **899.33** | **42.83** | **-15.29%** |
| **Minimum** | **-21.63%** | **27.60%** | | | | **71.00** | **3.38** | **58.00** | **2.76** | **310.00** | **14.76** | **-52.97%** |
| **Maximum** | **-86.19%** | **624.09%** | | | | **678.00** | **32.29** | **5571.00** | **265.29** | **6249.00** | **297.57** | **-9.32%** |
| **Std. Dev.** | **19.95%** | **-16.63%** | | | | **200.78** | **9.56** | **1647.37** | **78.45** | **1788.34** | **85.16** | **12.93%** |
| **Median** | **-34.79%** | **53.34%** | | | | **362.00** | **17.24** | **432.50** | **20.60** | **680.00** | **32.38** | **-15.23%** |

**FIGURE 7.5**   Comparison of Mega-Bear Markets

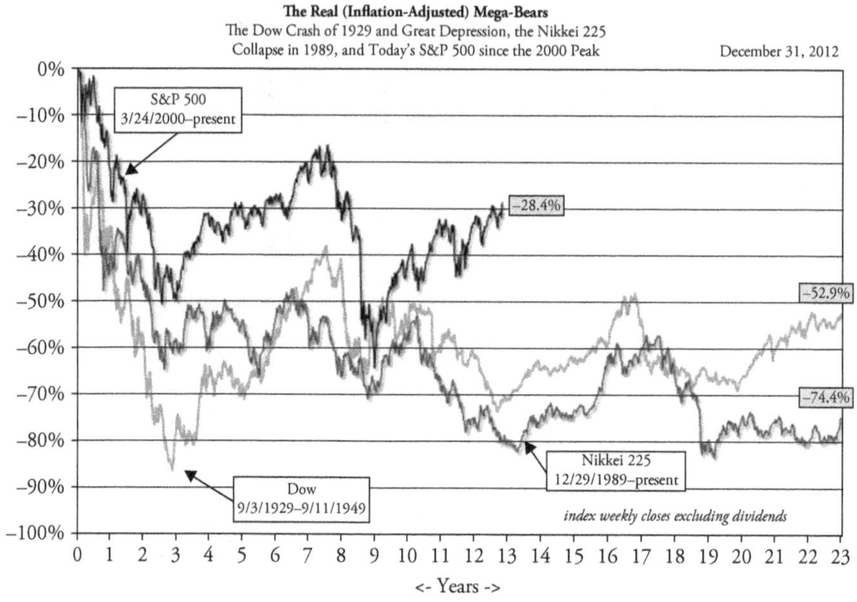

The Real (Inflation-Adjusted) Mega-Bears
The Dow Crash of 1929 and Great Depression, the Nikkei 225
Collapse in 1989, and Today's S&P 500 since the 2000 Peak                 December 31, 2012

*Source:* Chart courtesy of dshort.com.

## Bear Markets and Withdrawals

Table 7.5 shows the last bear market, which began on October 9, 2007, using the
S&P 500 Index price and a typical buy and hold retirement account making periodic
withdrawals. As of 12/31/2012 the bear market had recovered almost all of its losses
but not quite; therefore, a buy-and-hold investor is almost back to breakeven after
5.5 years. However, if one is retired, it generally means one has set up a withdrawal
schedule for income during retirement. In Table 7.5 it is assumed that the retirement
account is withdrawing 6 percent per year adjusted quarterly for 3 percent annualized inflation. The column labeled *Retirement Account* shows the account without
any withdrawals. The column labeled *Account w/Distributions* shows the value of the
account with the withdrawals. The last column shows the percent return to get back
to the initial $100,000 that was in the account when the bear market began. You can
see that in order to return the account to its original $100,000 it would take a return
of more than 99 percent, in other words, one must double his or her money. So when
you are confronted with advice to buy and hold because all bear markets eventually
recover, consider this example.

Figure 7.6 shows the devastating results of being retired during a bear market
while withdrawing money for current income. While the buy and hold strategy eventually begins to recover, the periodic withdrawals from an ever smaller account reach a
state of deteriorating equilibrium. Even buy and hope fails miserably in this environment and when coupled with periodic withdrawals it can be a life changing event.

**TABLE 7.5** Monthly Returns During a Bear Market While Withdrawing from Account

| | | Price Data (6% Withdrawal and 3% Inflation) | | | Retirement Data (6% Withdrawal and 3% Inflation) | | | | |
|---|---|---|---|---|---|---|---|---|---|
| | | S&P 500 | % from Peak | Equivalent Return | Retirement Account | Account w/ Distributions | Monthly Withdrawal | Cummulative Withdrawal | Equivalent Return |
| Previous Peak | 10/9/2007 | 1565.26 | 0.00% | 0.00% | $100,000.00 | $100,000.00 | | | |
| | 10/31/2007 | 1549.38 | −1.01% | 1.02% | $98,985.47 | $98,490.54 | $494.93 | $494.93 | 1.53% |
| | 11/30/2007 | 1481.14 | −5.37% | 5.58% | $94,625.81 | $93,656.52 | $496.16 | $991.09 | 6.77% |
| | 12/31/2007 | 1468.36 | −6.19% | 6.60% | $93,809.34 | $92,351.00 | $497.41 | $1,488.50 | 8.28% |
| | 1/31/2008 | 1378.55 | −11.93% | 13.54% | $88,071.63 | $86,203.84 | $498.65 | $1,987.15 | 16.00% |
| | 2/29/2008 | 1330.63 | −14.99% | 17.63% | $85,010.16 | $82,707.40 | $499.90 | $2,487.04 | 20.91% |
| | 3/31/2008 | 1322.7 | −15.50% | 18.34% | $84,503.53 | $81,713.36 | $501.14 | $2,988.19 | 22.38% |
| | 4/30/2008 | 1385.59 | −11.48% | 12.97% | $88,521.40 | $85,096.16 | $502.40 | $3,490.58 | 17.51% |
| | 5/30/2008 | 1400.38 | −10.53% | 11.77% | $89,466.29 | $85,500.83 | $503.65 | $3,994.24 | 16.96% |
| | 6/30/2008 | 1280 | −18.22% | 22.29% | $81,775.55 | $77,646.06 | $504.91 | $4,499.15 | 28.79% |
| | 7/31/2008 | 1267.38 | −19.03% | 23.50% | $80,969.30 | $76,374.35 | $506.18 | $5,005.33 | 30.93% |
| | 8/29/2008 | 1282.83 | −18.04% | 22.02% | $81,956.35 | $76,797.95 | $507.44 | $5,512.77 | 30.21% |
| | 9/30/2008 | 1166.36 | −25.48% | 34.20% | $74,515.42 | $69,316.64 | $508.71 | $6,021.48 | 44.27% |
| | 10/31/2008 | 968.75 | −38.11% | 61.58% | $61,890.68 | $57,062.72 | $509.98 | $6,531.46 | 75.25% |
| | 11/28/2008 | 896.24 | −42.74% | 74.65% | $57,258.22 | $52,280.38 | $511.26 | $7,042.71 | 91.28% |
| | 12/31/2008 | 903.25 | −42.29% | 73.29% | $57,706.07 | $52,176.76 | $512.53 | $7,555.25 | 91.66% |
| | 1/30/2009 | 825.88 | −47.24% | 89.53% | $52,763.12 | $47,193.62 | $513.82 | $8,069.06 | 111.89% |
| Bottom | 2/27/2009 | 735.09 | −53.04% | 112.93% | $46,962.80 | $41,490.47 | $515.10 | $8,584.16 | 141.02% |
| | 3/31/2009 | 797.87 | −49.03% | 96.18% | $50,973.64 | $44,517.55 | $516.39 | $9,100.55 | 124.63% |
| | 4/30/2009 | 872.81 | −44.24% | 79.34% | $55,761.34 | $48,181.19 | $517.68 | $9,618.23 | 107.55% |
| | 5/29/2009 | 919.14 | −41.28% | 70.30% | $58,721.23 | $50,219.74 | $518.97 | $10,137.20 | 99.12% |
| | 6/30/2009 | 919.32 | −41.27% | 70.26% | $58,732.73 | $49,709.30 | $520.27 | $10,657.47 | 101.17% |
| | 7/31/2009 | 987.48 | −36.91% | 58.51% | $63,087.28 | $52,873.27 | $521.57 | $11,179.04 | 89.13% |
| | 8/31/2009 | 1020.62 | −34.80% | 53.36% | $65,204.50 | $54,124.83 | $522.87 | $11,701.92 | 84.76% |
| | 9/30/2009 | 1057.08 | −32.47% | 48.07% | $67,533.83 | $55,534.17 | $524.18 | $12,226.10 | 80.07% |

(*Continued*)

**TABLE 7.5** Continued

| | Price Data (6% Withdrawal and 3% Inflation) | | | Retirement Data (6% Withdrawal and 3% Inflation) | | | | |
|---|---|---|---|---|---|---|---|---|
| | S&P 500 | % from Peak | Equivalent Return | Retirement Account | Account w/ Distributions | Monthly Withdrawal | Cummulative Withdrawal | Equivalent Return |
| 10/30/2009 | 1036.19 | −33.80% | 51.06% | $66,199.23 | $53,911.21 | $525.49 | $12,751.59 | 85.49% |
| 11/30/2009 | 1095.63 | −30.00% | 42.86% | $69,996.68 | $56,476.97 | $526.81 | $13,278.40 | 77.06% |
| 12/31/2009 | 1115.1 | −28.76% | 40.37% | $71,240.56 | $56,952.47 | $528.12 | $13,806.52 | 75.59% |
| 1/29/2010 | 1073.87 | −31.39% | 45.76% | $68,606.49 | $54,317.25 | $529.44 | $14,335.97 | 84.10% |
| 2/26/2010 | 1104.49 | −29.44% | 41.72% | $70,562.72 | $55,335.27 | $530.77 | $14,866.73 | 80.72% |
| 3/31/2010 | 1169.43 | −25.29% | 33.85% | $74,711.55 | $58,056.69 | $532.09 | $15,398.83 | 72.25% |
| 4/30/2010 | 1186.69 | −24.19% | 31.90% | $75,814.24 | $58,380.14 | $533.42 | $15,932.25 | 71.29% |
| 5/31/2010 | 1089.41 | −30.40% | 43.68% | $69,599.30 | $53,059.62 | $534.76 | $16,467.01 | 88.47% |
| 6/30/2010 | 1030.71 | −34.15% | 51.86% | $65,849.12 | $49,664.55 | $536.09 | $17,003.11 | 101.35% |
| 7/30/2010 | 1101.6 | −29.62% | 42.09% | $70,378.08 | $52,542.93 | $537.44 | $17,540.54 | 90.32% |
| 8/31/2010 | 1049.33 | −32.96% | 49.17% | $67,038.70 | $49,511.03 | $538.78 | $18,079.32 | 101.98% |
| 9/30/2010 | 1141.2 | −27.09% | 37.16% | $72,908.02 | $53,305.65 | $540.13 | $18,619.44 | 87.60% |
| 10/29/2010 | 1183.26 | −24.40% | 32.28% | $75,595.11 | $54,728.81 | $541.48 | $19,160.92 | 82.72% |
| 11/30/2010 | 1180.55 | −24.58% | 32.59% | $75,421.97 | $54,060.63 | $542.83 | $19,703.75 | 84.98% |
| 12/31/2010 | 1257.64 | −19.65% | 24.46% | $80,347.03 | $57,046.61 | $544.19 | $20,247.94 | 75.30% |
| 1/31/2011 | 1286.12 | −17.83% | 21.70% | $82,166.54 | $57,792.92 | $545.55 | $20,793.48 | 73.03% |
| 2/28/2011 | 1327.22 | −15.21% | 17.94% | $84,792.30 | $59,092.87 | $546.91 | $21,340.40 | 69.23% |
| 3/31/2011 | 1325.83 | −15.30% | 18.06% | $84,703.50 | $58,482.71 | $548.28 | $21,888.67 | 70.99% |
| 4/29/2011 | 1363.61 | −12.88% | 14.79% | $87,117.16 | $59,599.54 | $549.65 | $22,438.32 | 67.79% |
| 5/31/2011 | 1345.2 | −14.06% | 16.36% | $85,940.99 | $58,243.87 | $551.02 | $22,989.35 | 71.69% |
| 6/30/2011 | 1320.64 | −15.63% | 18.52% | $84,371.93 | $56,628.08 | $552.40 | $23,541.75 | 76.59% |
| 7/29/2011 | 1292.28 | −17.44% | 21.12% | $82,560.09 | $54,858.24 | $553.78 | $24,095.53 | 82.29% |
| 8/31/2011 | 1218.89 | −22.13% | 28.42% | $77,871.41 | $51,187.62 | $555.17 | $24,650.69 | 95.36% |
| 9/30/2011 | 1131.42 | −27.72% | 38.34% | $72,283.20 | $46,957.74 | $556.55 | $25,207.25 | 112.96% |
| 10/31/2011 | 1253.3 | −19.93% | 24.89% | $80,069.76 | $51,458.22 | $557.95 | $25,765.19 | 94.33% |

| Date | | | | | | | |
|---|---|---|---|---|---|---|---|
| 11/30/2011 | 1246.96 | −20.34% | 25.53% | $79,664.72 | $50,638.57 | $559.34 | $26,324.53 | 97.48% |
| 12/30/2011 | 1257.6 | −19.66% | 24.46% | $80,344.48 | $50,509.92 | $560.74 | $26,885.27 | 97.98% |
| 1/31/2012 | 1312.41 | −16.15% | 19.27% | $83,846.13 | $52,149.15 | $562.14 | $27,447.41 | 91.76% |
| 2/29/2012 | 1365.68 | −12.75% | 14.61% | $87,249.40 | $53,702.31 | $563.55 | $28,010.96 | 86.21% |
| 3/30/2012 | 1408.47 | −10.02% | 11.13% | $89,983.13 | $54,819.98 | $564.95 | $28,575.91 | 82.42% |
| 4/30/2012 | 1397.91 | −10.69% | 11.97% | $89,308.49 | $53,842.60 | $566.37 | $29,142.28 | 85.73% |
| 5/31/2012 | 1310.33 | −16.29% | 19.46% | $83,713.25 | $49,901.54 | $567.78 | $29,710.06 | 100.39% |
| 6/29/2012 | 1362.16 | −12.98% | 14.91% | $87,024.52 | $51,306.19 | $569.20 | $30,279.27 | 94.91% |
| 7/31/2012 | 1379.32 | −11.88% | 13.48% | $88,120.82 | $51,381.90 | $570.63 | $30,849.89 | 94.62% |
| 8/31/2012 | 1406.58 | −10.14% | 11.28% | $89,862.39 | $51,825.33 | $572.05 | $31,421.94 | 92.96% |
| 9/28/2012 | 1440.67 | −7.96% | 8.65% | $92,040.30 | $52,507.89 | $573.48 | $31,995.43 | 90.45% |
| 10/31/2012 | 1412.16 | −9.78% | 10.84% | $90,218.88 | $50,893.87 | $574.92 | $32,570.34 | 96.49% |
| 11/30/2012 | 1416.18 | −9.52% | 10.53% | $90,475.70 | $50,462.40 | $576.35 | $33,146.70 | 98.17% |
| 12/31/2012 | 1426.19 | −8.88% | 9.75% | $91,115.21 | $50,241.29 | $577.79 | $33,724.49 | **99.04%** |

**FIGURE 7.6**  Withdrawals during a Bear Market Can Be Devastating

## Market Volatility

Another shock to people who have not studied market history is the volatility that exists at times. Figure 7.7 shows the S&P 500 real price (real means it does not reflect inflation's affect) and adjusted for dividends. The plot at the bottom shows the 20-year annualized real rate of return. I think it is fairly obvious that returns are not guaranteed over any time period. With the assumption that most investors have about 20 years to really put money away for retirement, a lot has to do with things totally out of your control—like when you were born. Clearly, there are better times to invest than others, usually only known in hindsight.

There are many ways to measure volatility in the market. The world of finance wants you to believe that volatility is risk, and that risk is measured by standard deviation. This would be fine if investors were rational, the markets were efficient, prices were random, and normally distributed. But they aren't.

Figure 7.8 shows price volatility using some of my favorite indicators of volatility. The top plot is the S&P 500 Index from 2008 to December 31, 2012. There are three plots below that show three variations of price volatility.

The second plot from the top shows the volatility of price changes using a technique called *average true range*. This is a preferable method as it takes into account any gaps in price from one day to the next that occur in price histories. The next plot is

**FIGURE 7.7** S&P 500 Real Price and 20-Year Rolling Total Returns

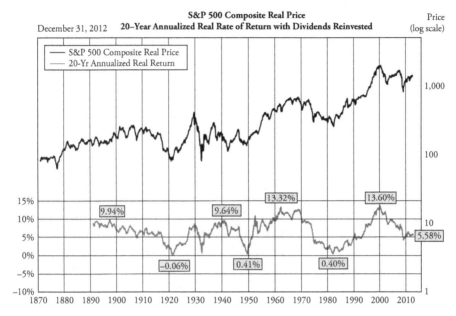

*Source:* Chart courtesy of dshort.com.

**FIGURE 7.8** Volatility Measured Three Ways

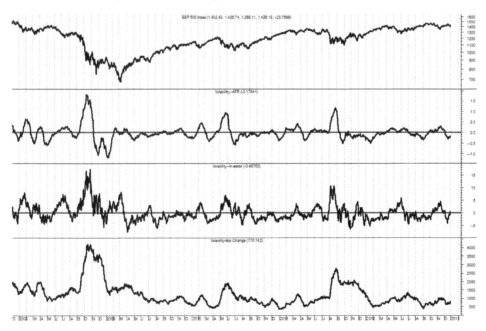

*Source:* Chart courtesy of MetaStock.

simply looking at the percentage price changes each day. The bottom plot shows the volatility of price similar to the one above, only it converts the data to absolute values. All three volatility plots have been smoothed over a 21-day period. I like to use 21 days because that represents the number of market days per month (see beginning of this chapter on Calendar Math).

You can see that during market downturns (see top plot) there is a tendency for volatility to increase. The more extended the down move, the greater the volatility. Volatility is a great measure of investor fear, probably better than most other sentiment indicators, because it is a direct measurement of indecision.

For a long-term perspective, Figure 7.9 shows the 63 day (3 months) absolute percentage change each day for the Dow Industrials back to 1885. The volatility is in the lower plot with a horizontal line at 1.5 percent for reference.

Another way to view volatility is to compare the monthly volatility relative to the yearly volatility. This is shown in Figure 7.10 with the S&P 500 Index in the upper plot, the monthly volatility in the lower plot with the smoother annual volatility overlaid. This method removes the absolute measurement and shows when the shorter-term volatility is greater than its longer term value. For most who want to use a volatility measure on a single issue, this is my preferable method.

Figure 7.11 shows the S&P 500 with the Volatility Index (VIX). VIX is a Chicago Board Options Exchange (CBOE) tradable instrument designed to represent the sentiment of option traders and shows their expectation of 30-day volatility.

**FIGURE 7.9**  Dow Industrial Average Absolute Three-Month Percent Change

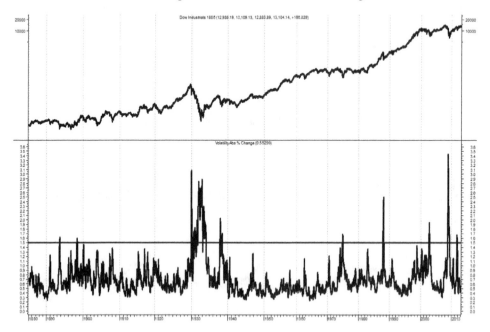

*Source:* Chart courtesy of MetaStock.

**FIGURE 7.10**  Monthly Volatility and Yearly Volatility

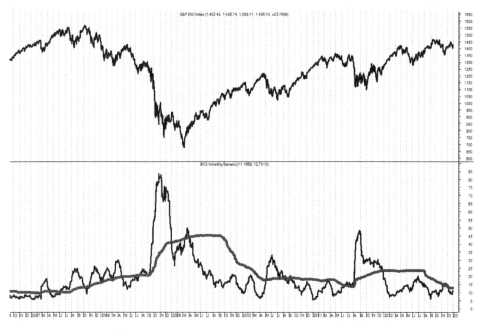

*Source:* Chart courtesy of MetaStock.

**FIGURE 7.11**  S&P 500 and VIX

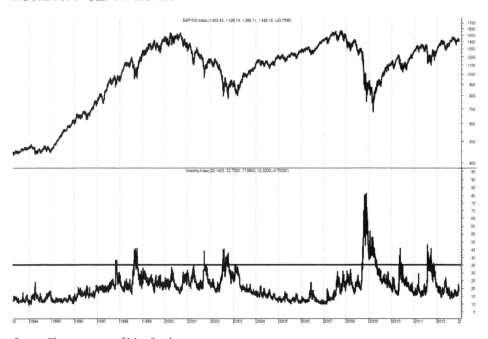

*Source:* Chart courtesy of MetaStock.

It is constructed using the implied volatilities of a wide range of S&P 500 Index options. This volatility is meant to be forward looking and is calculated from both calls and puts.

You can see from Figure 7.11 (S&P 500 on top and VIX on bottom) that whenever the VIX gets above 35 (horizontal line) the market is experiencing large volatility. Notice that there are significant periods without much volatility.

A concept that has surfaced in the past few years is measuring the volatility of volatility. I think this is a valid concept if one measures the volatility of something that is tradable like the VIX shown in Figure 7.11. Figure 7.12 shows the S&P 500 Index in the top plot, the VIX in the middle plot (exactly the same as in Figure 7.11) with the Average True Range version of volatility over 21 days shown in the bottom plot.

The VIX was originally launched in 1993, with a slightly different calculation than the one that is currently employed. The original VIX (which is now VXO) differs from the current VIX in two main respects: It is based on the S&P 100 (OEX) instead of the S&P 500, and it targets at the money options instead of the broad range of strikes utilized by the VIX. The current VIX was reformulated on September 22, 2003, at which time the original VIX was assigned the VXO ticker. VIX futures began trading on March 26, 2004; VIX options followed on February 24, 2006; and two VIX exchange traded notes (VXX and VXZ) were added to the mix on January 30, 2009.

**FIGURE 7.12**   S&P 500, VIX, and VIX Volatility

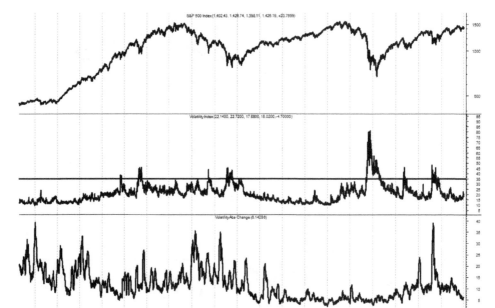

*Source:* Chart Courtesy of MetaStock.

## Highly Volatile Periods

Figure 7.13 shows 18 periods since 1900 in the Dow Industrial Average that were similar in their measure of volatility. I created this because when we get into a volatile period, the usual question asked by many is whether this will be how the markets will be forever. Once again I am reminded of the late Peter Bernstein who said that an investor's biggest mistake is extrapolation—assuming the recent past will also be how the future will be. In Figure 7.13 I used a 5 percent filtered wave, then measured the frequency of the waves within a confined period. The concept of filtered waves is defined in Chapter 1, and again in more detail in Chapter 10.

## Dispersion of Prices

The following concept is from Ed Easterling of Crestmont Research. Although the compounded average annual change in the stock market is about 5 percent over the past 112 years, the range of dispersion in annual returns is dramatic. Table 7.6 presents the distribution of yearly index changes within the range of −5 percent to +5 percent increments during the past century overall (112 years) and during the secular bull (54 years) and bear (58 years) cycles. It becomes clear that moves of +/− 5 percent and to some extent moves of +/− 10 percent on an annual basis are similar across both bull and bear markets, with the bulk (67 percent) of the +10 percent years in secular bull while the secular bears are fairly

**FIGURE 7.13** Dow Industrials Highly Volatile Periods since 1900

*Source:* Chart courtesy of MetaStock.

**TABLE 7.6**  Dispersion of Annual Dow Jones Industrial Prices

| | Percentage of Years During Secular Markets (1901–2012) | | |
|---|---|---|---|
| | 112 Years | 54 Years | 58 Years |
| Range | ALL | BULL (48.2%) | BEAR (51.8%) |
| < −5% | 26% | 7% | 43% |
| −5% to 5% | 21% | 22% | 19% |
| > 5% | 54% | 70% | 38% |
| < −10% | 20% | 4% | 34% |
| −10% to 10% | 33% | 30% | 36% |
| > 10% | 47% | 67% | 29% |
| < −15% | 16% | 0% | 31% |
| −15% to 15% | 49% | 50% | 48% |
| > 15% | 35% | 50% | 21% |
| < −20% | 9% | 0% | 17% |
| −20% to 20% | 65% | 61% | 69% |
| > 20% | 26% | 39% | 14% |
| < −25% | 6% | 0% | 12% |
| −25% to 25% | 74% | 74% | 74% |
| > 25% | 20% | 26% | 14% |
| < −30% | 5% | 0% | 10% |
| −30% to 30% | 84% | 89% | 79% |
| > 30% | 11% | 11% | 10% |
| < −35% | 2% | 0% | 3% |
| −35% to 35% | 90% | 93% | 88% |
| > 35% | 8% | 7% | 9% |
| < −40% | 1% | 0% | 2% |
| −40% to 40% | 94% | 94% | 93% |
| > 40% | 5% | 6% | 5% |
| < −45% | 1% | 0% | 2% |
| −45% to 45% | 96% | 96% | 95% |
| > 45% | 4% | 4% | 3% |
| < −50% | 1% | 0% | 2% |
| −50% to 50% | 97% | 98% | 97% |
| > 50% | 2% | 2% | 2% |

evenly distributed across the range. When the analysis of dispersion expands to annual moves of +/− 15 percent a year, the message is even more pronounced. The secular bulls show no occurrences of −15 percent, with the remaining segments evenly distributed. The secular bears have the largest percentage (48 percent) of their annual returns contained within the +/− 15 percent range. Once you get to the +/− 20 percent dispersions, which are tied to the moves associated with bull-and-bear cyclical markets, the dispersion is fairly consistent for the remaining data. It should be interesting to also note that there were more years deemed as within secular bear markets than in secular bull markets. (B16) (B17)

## Secular Markets

For years (decades) analysts referred to long-term market cycles as *generational markets*. Ed Easterling from Crestmont Research has now defined them for us using a derivative methodology. Previously, most just looked at the price action and when it rose, called it a *bull market*, and when it declined or was flat, called it a *bear market*. I'm going to stick with Easterling's process as it comes with a lot of sound analysis and that removes the subjectivity.

Secular market cycles are long term and have averaged about 25 years over the past 112 years. Secular bear markets average about 11.25 years in length over this period. Keep in mind, however, there are many cyclical bull and bear markets within the longer-term secular bear markets. Because I follow the analysis of Ed Easterling of Crestmont Research, here is my review of his latest book, *Probable Outcomes*, published in 2011. This book, and his previous book, *Unexpected Returns*, are a must-read to understand how long-term markets work.

*Ed Easterling has done it again; provided a big picture approach to the market using time-tested historical data and sound principles. Ed's first book,* Unexpected Returns, *was the first time I had heard of the way secular markets were defined—by valuations.* Probable Outcomes *expands and updates the first book. Easterling builds a methodology that is robust and clearly void of preconceived notions about the future; a refreshing approach rarely seen in books about the stock market.*

*The first part of the book is a lesson in market finance and economics from a practitioner view and not the usual financial academic approach—again quite informative and refreshing. Every concept is supported by data and colorful charts, which make learning and understanding the process enjoyable. He spends a great deal of time and effort to ensure that his explanations are easily understood and succinct. Secular markets are driven by long-term trends in Price Earnings ratios (PE), which, in turn, are driven by inflation/deflation. This removes the scale of time from the secular cycle definition and only uses the trends and cycles of PE and inflation as the identification of secular bear, and bear market cycle beginnings and endings. Simply, a secular bear begins when valuations peak and reverse because of a trend back toward low inflation, then continue to decline throughout the secular period. Once sufficiently low, usually single digit PE, a new secular bull period can begin.*

*The book wraps up with a thorough evaluation of how the current decade (2010–2019) could possibly play out (currently in a secular bear), using a large number of different EPS, PE, and Inflation combination scenarios. The message is clear, there are times (secular bears) that one needs to change their perspective on investing and seek an approach that at a minimum preserves capital so that when the next secular bull market begins, time is not spent trying to recover from the past secular bear. It is sad that most people spend a large part of their investing time trying to recover from previous losses. Understanding the secular approach and making the switch in your investing style (rowing vs. sailing) can lead to a long retirement accompanied by dignity and comfort.*

I did have one question for Ed that somewhat bothered me. He was gracious enough to provide an excellent response.

**My Question**: With the average secular cycle being about 25 years and the total database being 112 years, do you feel there is enough data to be totally confident with your secular market analysis?

**Ed's Answer**: Absolutely. But let's step back for a moment to consider the two types of cycles. You have asked a great question because its answer reveals a lot about secular stock market cycles.

There are two types of cycles: technical cycles and fundamental cycles. Technical cycles generally reflect patterns or levels that have a high propensity to repeat. Technical cycles gain their credibility and validity from a high degree of repeating incidences. The four full secular stock market cycles would hardly be considered high repetition. But secular stock market cycles are not technical cycles.

Secular stock market cycles are fundamentally driven cycles. By fundamentally driven, I mean that economic and inflation factors cause the cycles to occur. Secular stock market cycles are more than patterns, they are reactions to hard drivers. Secular bulls and secular bears are driven by the trend and level of the inflation rate. Secular cycles are the adjustments to financial value that are caused by changes in the inflation rate. Since increases and decreases in the inflation rate change the expected rate of return, stocks and bonds increase or decrease in overall value and thereby add or detract from total return.

Look at the secular bear market of the 1960s and 1970s. Rising inflation caused the valuation of stocks to decline. The market's price/earnings ratio declined from more than 20 to less than 10 over 16 years. Earnings grew and investors received dividends, but the decline in valuation caused returns to be well-below average. Then as the inflation rate turned and declined, the 1980s and 1990s secular bull experienced the benefit of rising valuations as well as earnings growth and dividends.

Okay, one last comment about secular cycles. There is another factor other than inflation that impacts them. The second factor is cash flow. The secular bear of 1929 was caused by deflation. Deflation causes the nominal cash flows from earnings and dividends to decline in amount. So even though the discount rate remains low as inflation neared zero and fell into deflation, the expected future decline in reported cash flows due to deflation caused the present value of the market to decline. P/E fell from more than 20 to less than 10. This is potentially instructive about the future because recent trends in economic growth suggest that it may be slowing from the historical rate averaging 3 percent annual real growth. If economic growth slows, then future earnings growth will slow, too. As a result, the slower growth of cash flows will drive a lower valuation for the market. Growth rate affects the level of P/E.

So we have fundamental principles related to the concepts of cash flow and present value. Then we have four full-cycle examples that are consistent with the well-accepted academic and industry principles. Is four full cycles enough to be confident about the concept of secular stock market cycles? Absolutely!

Thanks Ed.

Easterling points out that these secular periods are not random as they follow each other; he actually calls them cycles. The driver of these cycles is the inflation rate as it moves toward and away from price stability. Trends of rising inflation and deflation drive the market valuation lower and result in low returns. As prices stabilize from either deflation or high inflation, valuations are driven upward and the result is high returns. Keep in mind that this is a process whereby moves away from price stability simultaneously cause PE to decline and low or no returns result. Moves toward price stability simultaneously cause PE to rise and result in high returns.

Furthermore, the relationship among inflation, earnings, and prices is neatly tied together. The S&P 500 is an index of capitalization weighted prices of 500 large cap, blue chip stocks. Inflation is the annual rate of change of the consumer price index, which is a measure of various prices for goods and services. Valuations (earnings) are measured relative to price with the price to earnings ratio (PE). Once again, technical analysis arises because all three measures used to define secular markets are ultimately based on price.

Figure 7.14 shows the monthly S&P 500 back to 1900 along with the 12-month rate of change of the Consumer Price Index (Inflation) and the S&P 500 PE Ratio at the bottom; both the prices and the PE ratio are adjusted for inflation (known as *real*). This makes the PE swings more readily identifiable. You can clearly see from this chart the significant moves in PE (bottom plot) and compare to the moves in the S&P 500 (top plot). The upward moves in the PE Ratio are the secular bulls and the downward moves are the secular bears. The middle plot of inflation shows how it affects valuations over time. Although the specific changes in inflation are not aligned with the peaks and troughs of price or valuation, it is reasonable to assume it leads

**FIGURE 7.14** S&P 500, Inflation (CPI), and Price Earnings Ratio (PE)

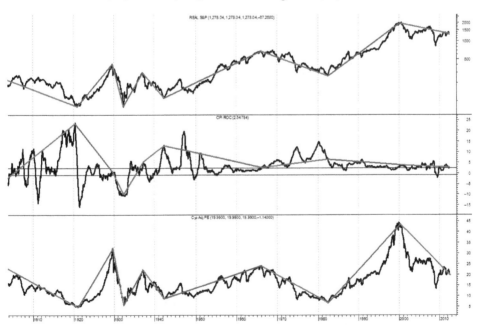

*Source:* Chart courtesy of MetaStock.

**FIGURE 7.15**   Recent S&P 500, Inflation, and PE

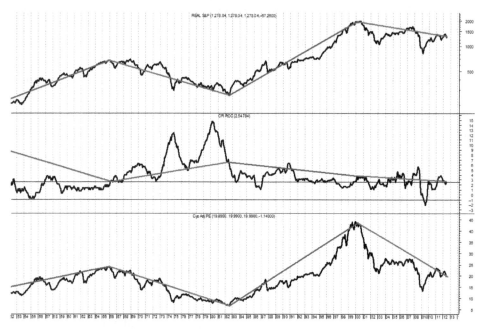

*Source:* Chart courtesy of MetaStock.

them. It does appear that when inflation is within the +2.5% and −1% range (small horizontal lines) its affect is not as great or as timely, and is usually during the Secular Bull markets. I think from this chart, the fact that secular markets are defined by long-term swings in valuations, which are ultimately affected by inflation, bears (sic) out.

Figure 7.15 shows the exact same data as the previous but over a shorter time period so you can see the changes better. This chart shows the data since World War II. The clarity of the secular bull markets and bear markets in the top plot is obvious. The changes in overall inflation in the middle plot, while not as well defined, still exist, and the bottom plot shows the rise and fall of the price earnings ratio in conjunction with the other two.

## Secular Bull Markets

Do not confuse brains with a bull market.

   Don't mistake a bull market for investment skill.

   Martin Pring (strategist for Pring Turner Business Cycle ETF [DBIZ]) describes them as:

> Primary trend changes in secular (and cyclical) bull markets are usually short and shallow and each peak is higher than its predecessor. Investors are routinely assisted from their bad investment decisions by the bull market. Investors' confidence grows

significantly during these times and eventually becomes excessive with the period from 1998 to 1999, known as the dot.com bubble, a classic example. There are geniuses everywhere, and they are paraded hourly on financial television. Investment decisions that are considered irresponsible and careless at the beginning of secular bulls are hailed as perfectly routine as the secular bull matures. The lessons learned in the previous bear market are long forgotten and often you hear "this time is different." When the majority of the above become common, the end of the secular bull is probably near, despite prognostications that it will go much, much higher.

These prognostications are given with extreme determination and confidence. In a secular bull, one can buy and hold, invest in index funds, dollar cost average, just about anything. Here is the problem: most will not realize they are in a secular bull market until it is almost over.

## Secular Bull Markets since 1900

Figure 7.16 shows the four secular bull markets since 1900. It should be clear that a secular bull is a time when caution goes out the window. Unfortunately, most will not realize it until toward the end.

**FIGURE 7.16** Secular Bull Markets since 1900

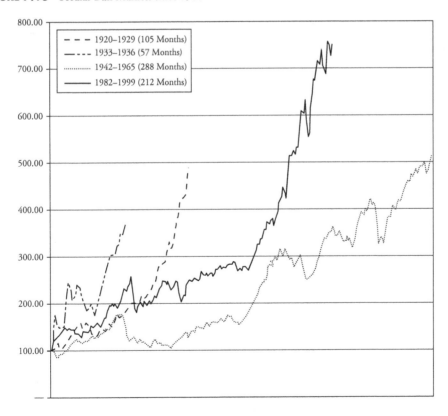

## Secular Bull Data

In Table 7.7 notice that all of the Secular Bull markets started when PE was between 5 and 11, and ended when PE was between 19 and 42. There are charts in Chapter 8 that show the secular changes in valuation.

## Secular Bull Market Composite

The secular bull composite is shown in Figure 7.17. Secular bull markets, if and when you know you are in one, can easily justify some of the investment strategies that this

**TABLE 7.7**  Secular Bull Data

| Start | End | Years | PE Start | PE End | Inflation Start | Inflation End |
|-------|-----|-------|----------|--------|-----------------|---------------|
| 1921 | 1928 | 8 | 5 | 22 | −11% | −2% |
| 1933 | 1936 | 4 | 11 | 19 | −5% | 1% |
| 1942 | 1965 | 24 | 9 | 23 | 11% | 2% |
| 1982 | 1999 | 18 | 7 | 42 | 6% | 2% |

*Source:* CrestmontResearch.com.

**FIGURE 7.17**  Secular Bull Market Composite

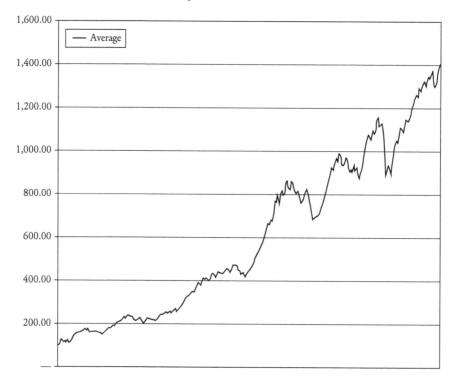

book considers as bad strategies for most investors. Of course, most will not realize they are in a secular bull until it is well developed.

## Secular Bear Markets

Martin Pring says,

> The secular bears are essentially the opposite of the bulls as in general the peaks are lower and the troughs are lower, exhibiting a downward trend. However, keep in mind that they are not always down-trending, and there is sometimes a new high in the middle. The key characteristics are declining price earnings ratio (PE) and low or no returns. Just like the secular bull, every lesson learned is quickly forgotten. Just like a recession cleanses the economy, the secular bear resets everything and removes all the excesses. Most secular bulls end and secular bears begin without there being a condition of excess. The high valuation of the market is the rational result of low inflation. Certainly there are moments of excess, just as normal market volatility creates short periods of excess and the opposite of excess. My key point is that secular tops and bottoms are the result of fundamental conditions rather than irrational emotions. The bearish prognosticators are once again the daily media darlings. And once again, just like in the secular bull, the forecasts are for total gloom and doom. The determination and confidence of these forecasters is convincing, yet eventually wrong. Here is something that is important to remember: Secular bear markets account for over 50% of the total time. In fact, as of 2012, there were actually more years in secular bears than in secular bulls since 1900. The previous two points are true but keep in mind that the period being observed has a secular bear at both ends. Since bears are not necessarily longer than bulls, and vice versa, it's reasonable to say that they are about the same in length on average, but the range of terms varies significantly. Secular bear markets cause investors to seek alternative investments or unconstrained investments that protect them from downside losses. However, just like the secular bull, most will be in denial and not participate in the secular bear properly until sustained losses, and then it will probably be about over.

The next section shows graphics of the various secular bear markets. They were created with monthly data for the S&P 500 from Robert Shiller's database. If yearly data had been used the message would be essentially the same.

## Secular Bear Markets since 1900

Figure 7.18 shows all four of the previous inflation adjusted secular bear markets along with the current one from their starting point on the left side of the graph. Two of the secular bears were shorter and two were longer than the one that began in 2000. One cannot make an investment decision with this information, only an awareness that we are currently in a secular bear market (as of 12/31/2012) and it could last much longer.

**FIGURE 7.18**   Secular Bear Markets since 1900

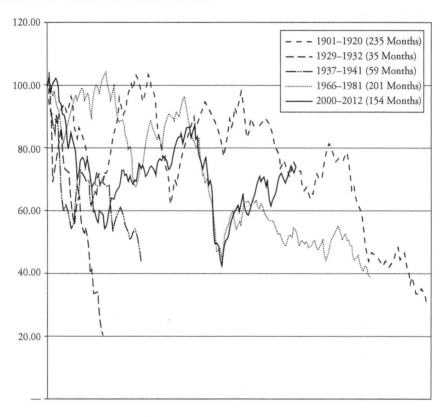

## Secular Bear Data

Ed Easterling says that secular markets are determined by long-term swings in valuations that are driven by inflation. From Table 7.8 you can see that the great depression secular bear did not involve a rise in inflation, but it also only lasted three years. As of this writing, the secular bear that began in 2000 is still in progress.

Notice that the Secular Bear markets started when their PE was between 18 and 42, and ended when their PE was between 5 and 12. The starting PE for the first four Secular Bears was between 18 and 28. The Secular Bear that began in 2000 started at 42, which is an outlier for a starting PE. Chapter 8 shows charts similar to the secular charts displaying the changes in valuations over the various secular cycles.

## Secular Bear Market Composite

Figure 7.19 shows the current secular bear (bold) with the average of the previous secular bears. Again, this information is just for awareness and understanding, you cannot make investment decisions with this type of observation.

**TABLE 7.8**   Secular Bear Data

| Start | End  | Years | PE Start | PE End | Inflation Start | Inflation End |
|-------|------|-------|----------|--------|-----------------|---------------|
| 1901  | 1920 | 20    | 23       | 5      | −2%             | 16%           |
| 1929  | 1932 | 4     | 28       | 8      | 0%              | −10%          |
| 1937  | 1941 | 5     | 18       | 12     | 4%              | 5%            |
| 1966  | 1981 | 16    | 21       | 8      | 3%              | 10%           |
| 2000  | ?    | ?     | 42       | ?      | 3%              | ?             |

*Source:* CrestmontResearch.com.

**FIGURE 7.19**   Secular Bear Market Composite

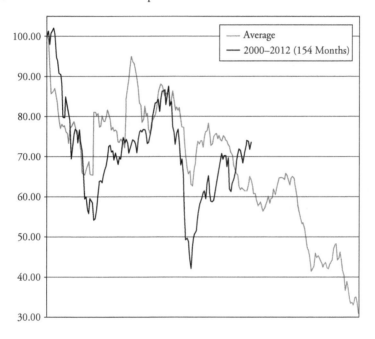

## The Last Secular Bear Market (1966–1982)

Figure 7.20 shows that the last secular bear from 1966 to 1982 went sideways with a number of large cyclical bull markets and bear markets. The message is simple, buy and hold or index investing did not go anywhere for 16 years. That's a long time to not make any money in the market especially when you are in your "retirement wealth accumulation" years. However, if you had a simple trend-following process where you could capture some of the good up moves and avoid most of the big down moves, you would have come out in 1982 significantly better off than buy and hold or index investing.

Notice the percentage moves and the amount of time that each took. When one shows 16 years of data sometimes the compressed data can make it look like the

**FIGURE 7.20**   Secular Bear Market (1966–1982)

frequency of up and down moves is much higher than it actually is. The up moves (cyclical bulls) averaged 23 months in length with an average gain of over 52 percent. The down moves (cyclical bears) averaged almost 19 months with an average decline of −33 percent. Clearly, this falls in line with common knowledge that bull markets last longer than bear markets, even if they are contained in an overall secular bear market.

The next chapter is essentially a continuation of this chapter, delving into market valuations, market sectors, asset classes, various methods to observe returns, and the distribution of those returns.

# CHAPTER 8

# Market Facts: Valuations, Returns, and Distributions

## Market Valuations

Because secular markets are defined by long-term swings in valuations, let's look at the Price Earnings (PE) ratio and study its history. Robert Shiller created a valuable measure of PE valuation that uses trailing (actual) earnings, averaged over a 10-year period. (A87) (A89) Here is how it is calculated:

Use the yearly earning of the S&P 500 for each of the past 10 years.
Adjust these earnings for inflation, using the CPI (i.e., quote each earnings figure in current dollars).
Average these values (i.e., add them up and divide by 10), giving us e10.
Then take the current Price of the S&P 500 and divide by e10.

Figure 8.1 shows the S&P Composite on a monthly basis adjusted for inflation, back to 1871, with a regression line so you can get a feel (visually) of where the current price is relative to the long-term trend of prices. The lower plot is the Shiller PE10 plot with peaks and troughs identified with their values. You can see that all prior secular bears ended with PE10 as a single digit (4.8, 5.6, 9.1, and 6.6). The PE10 on March 9, 2009, only got down to 13.3, which is considerably higher than the level reached by all prior secular bear lows. Based on this simple analogy, I think we have yet to see the secular bear low for this cycle. Remember, it does not mean that the prices have to go lower than they did in 2009; it just means the PE10 should drop to single digits. Remember, PE is a ratio of Price over Earnings. To make the ratio smaller, either the price can decline, the earnings can increase, or a combination of both.

As of December 31, 2012, the PE10 is at 21.3. Referencing the small box in the lower left corner shows that this value is in the fifth quintile of all the PE data. Based on this analysis the market is overvalued.

So when the financial news noise is constantly parading analysts by touting the PE as overvalued or undervalued, you can count on the fact that they are using the forward

**FIGURE 8.1**   S&P Composite and Real Shiller PE10

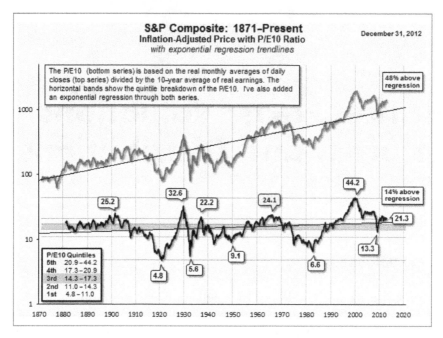

*Source*: Chart courtesy of dshort.com.

PE ratio. The forward ratio is the guess of all the earnings analysts. They are rarely correct. Ignore them.

Finally, Figure 8.2 shows the PE10 in 10 percent increments or deciles. It shows the extreme level reached in the late 1990s from the tech bubble, it shows the 1929 peak, and shows that as of December 31, 2012, we are at the 82 percentile of PE10. This puts the PE10 overvalued on a relative basis, and also on an absolute basis as shown in Figure 8.1. Remember PE10 used real reported (trailing) earnings, not forward (guesses) earnings. As Doug Short says on his website at dshort.com: A more cautionary observation is that when the PE10 has fallen from the top to the second quintile, it has eventually declined to the first quintile and bottomed in single digits. Based on the latest 10-year earnings average, to reach a PE10 in the high single digits would require an S&P 500 price decline below 540. Of course, a happier alternative would be for corporate earnings to continue their strong and prolonged surge. If the 2009 trough was not a PE10 bottom, when might we see it occur? These secular declines have ranged in length from more than 19 years to as few as three. As of December 31, 2012, the current decline in valuations is approaching its 13th year.

## Secular Bear Valuation

Figure 8.3 shows the Shiller PE10 monthly for all the past secular bear markets since 1900, with the current secular bear in bold. What is really interesting about this chart is that most of the secular bears began with PE Ratios in the 20 to 30 range and ended with

**FIGURE 8.2** Shiller PE10 in Deciles

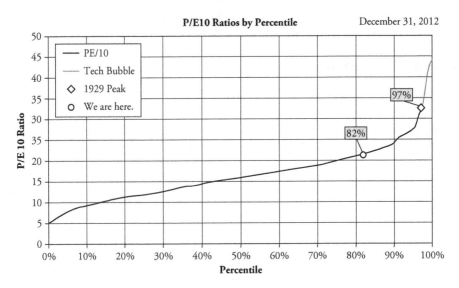

*Source:* Chart courtesy of dshort.com.

**FIGURE 8.3** Secular Bear Market PE since 1900

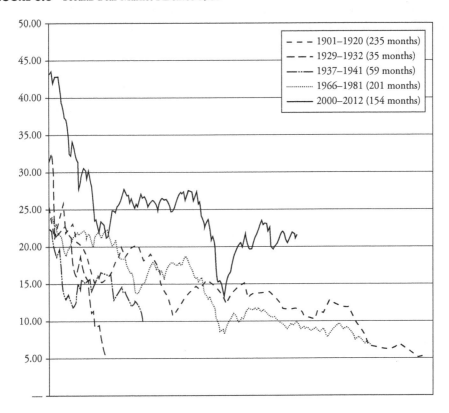

them in the 5 to 10 range. The current secular bear began with a PE in the mid-40s and is now only back down to the level that the previous secular bears began. That could imply that the secular bear that began in 2000 could be a long one. These charts were created using monthly data, if yearly data were used the concept would be even more pronounced.

### Secular Bear Valuation Composite

In Figure 8.4 the current secular bear market valuation is shown in bold, with the other line representing the average of the previous four secular bears. Again, this type of analysis is just an observation and for educational purposes; you cannot make investment decisions from this. Investment decisions come from actionable information and analysis.

### Secular Bull Valuation

Figure 8.5 of secular bull market valuations shows that most of them begin with PE ratios in the 5 to 10 (same as where secular bears end) and they end with PE ratios in the 20 to 30 range. The excessive secular bull of 1982 to 2000 reached unbelievable high valuations. I remember everyone saying that this time was different. Wrong!

### Secular Bull Valuation Composite

The secular bull market valuation composite is shown in Figure 8.6. It is the average of all the secular bull markets since 1900. Since we are currently in a secular bear market, the average of the secular bull markets is shown by itself.

**FIGURE 8.4**   Secular Bear Market PE Composite

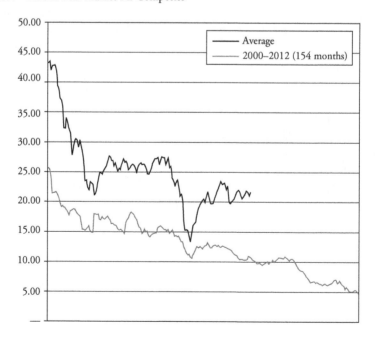

**FIGURE 8.5** Secular Bull Market PE since 1900

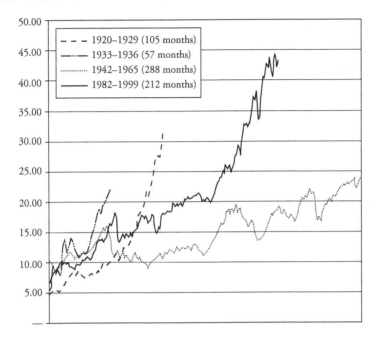

**FIGURE 8.6** Secular Bull Market Composite PE

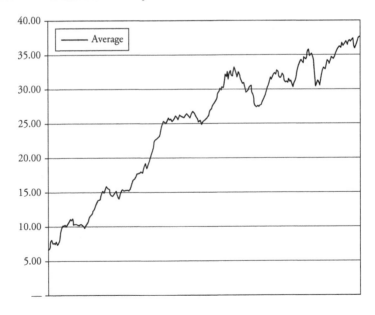

## Market Sectors

I use the sector definitions provided by Standard & Poor's, of which there are 10. The other primary source for sector analysis is Dow Jones. Either is fine, I just prefer the S&P structure because I have been using it for so long. Table 8.1 shows the 10 sectors annual price performance since 1990 and Table 8.2 shows the relative performance of the total returns. When viewing a table of relative returns as in Table 8.2, keep in mind that each column (year) is completely independent of the preceding year or following year. Also the relative ranking shows that those in the top part of the column outperformed those in the lower part of the column, independent of whether the returns were positive, negative, or a combination. Another value of this type of table is to show that picking last year's top performer is not a good strategy. Remember, you cannot retire on relative returns.

This book does not get into the various uses of sectors as investments, but the book would not be complete without the mention of sector rotation and in particular how various sectors rotate in and out of favor based on the phase of the business cycle and the economy. A further delineation of sectors is their propensity to fall within the broad categories of offensive and defensive. This means that when the market is performing poorly, the defensive sectors will generally outperform and when the market is performing well, it is the offensive sectors that are the top performers.

The phases of the economy known as economic expansion and contractions are affected by many events but generally boil down to recessions and periods of expansion. It should be noted, however, that not all contractions end up being recessions. The phases can then be broken down into early cycle, mid-cycle, and late cycle segments of the full cycle. There is a lot of literature available to cover all these details but the point of this discussion is to show the rotational movement of the various sectors through the economic cycle. Figure 8.7 is a graphic showing the sectors and where they fall in the cycle. Figure 8.7 shows the rotation of sectors during an average economic cycle for the past 67 years is courtesy of Sam Stovall, chief equity strategist, S&P Capital IQ. Sam wrote one of the best books on sector rotation years ago, *Standard & Poor's Sector Investing: How to Buy the Right Stock in the Right Industry at The Right Time*, but is currently out of print.

Another excellent study I have seen on the cycles within the phases and what sectors are affected was put out by Fidelity and dated August 23, 2010 (see Table 8.3). It clearly showed that from 1963 through 2010, the following sectors were strongest during the various phases. In each cycle, the top performing sectors are shown with the first being the best of the four and the last being the worst of the top four, which is still the fourth best out of the 10 sectors. (A37)

It was interesting to note in this study that during all of the three cycles, Utilities and Healthcare were the two worst performing of all 10 of the sectors (not shown). They only ranked in the top four during actual recessions. Since recessions are usually identified by the NBER about a year after they begin and sometime not until they have ended, this is not knowledge that you can make investment decisions with.

**TABLE 8.1** Sectors Performance (1990–2012)

| Price Performance | 1990 | 1991 | 1992 | 1993 | 1994 | 1995 | 1996 | 1997 | 1998 | 1999 | 2000 | 2001 | 2002 | 2003 | 2004 | 2005 | 2006 | 2007 | 2008 | 2009 | 2010 | 2011 | 2012 |
|---|---|---|---|---|---|---|---|---|---|---|---|---|---|---|---|---|---|---|---|---|---|---|---|
| Energy | (1.4) | 2.4 | (2.3) | 11.2 | (0.4) | 26.0 | 21.7 | 22.0 | (2.0) | 16.0 | 13.2 | (12.3) | (13.3) | 22.4 | 28.8 | 29.1 | 22.2 | 32.4 | (35.9) | 11.3 | 17.9 | 2.8 | 3.3 |
| Materials | (13.9) | 21.5 | 7.2 | 10.5 | 3.3 | 17.3 | 13.4 | 6.3 | (8.0) | 23.0 | (17.7) | 1.0 | (7.7) | 34.8 | 10.8 | 2.2 | 15.7 | 20.0 | (47.0) | 45.2 | 19.9 | (11.6) | 12.3 |
| Industrials | (10.3) | 26.0 | 6.8 | 15.8 | (4.8) | 35.9 | 22.7 | 25.0 | 9.3 | 19.9 | 4.5 | (7.0) | (27.6) | 29.7 | 16.0 | 0.4 | 11.0 | 9.8 | (41.5) | 17.3 | 23.9 | (2.9) | 12.2 |
| Consumer Discretionary | (14.9) | 38.3 | 17.5 | 12.8 | (9.9) | 18.2 | 10.5 | 32.3 | 39.6 | 24.1 | (20.7) | 1.9 | (24.4) | 36.1 | 12.1 | (7.4) | 17.2 | (14.3) | (34.7) | 38.8 | 25.7 | 4.4 | 21.9 |
| Consumer Staples | 12.4 | 38.4 | 3.0 | (6.3) | 6.8 | 36.2 | 23.2 | 30.5 | 13.9 | (16.6) | 14.5 | (8.3) | (6.3) | 9.2 | 6.0 | 1.3 | 11.8 | 11.6 | (17.7) | 11.2 | 10.7 | 10.5 | 7.8 |
| Health Care | 14.1 | 50.2 | (18.1) | (11.0) | 10.2 | 54.5 | 18.8 | 41.7 | 42.3 | (11.6) | 35.5 | (12.9) | (20.0) | 13.3 | 0.2 | 4.9 | 5.8 | 5.4 | (24.5) | 17.1 | 0.7 | 10.2 | 15.2 |
| Financials | (24.4) | 43.8 | 19.8 | 7.8 | (6.4) | 49.6 | 31.9 | 45.4 | 9.6 | 2.3 | 23.4 | (10.5) | (16.4) | 27.9 | 8.2 | 3.7 | 16.2 | (20.8) | (56.9) | 14.8 | 10.8 | (18.4) | 26.3 |
| Information Technology | 0.5 | 6.6 | 0.6 | 20.5 | 19.1 | 38.8 | 43.3 | 28.1 | 77.6 | 78.4 | (41.0) | (26.0) | (37.6) | 46.5 | 2.1 | 0.4 | 7.7 | 15.5 | (43.7) | 59.9 | 9.1 | 1.3 | 13.5 |
| Telecommunication Services | (17.7) | 7.9 | 11.0 | 10.8 | (8.4) | 37.3 | (2.2) | 37.1 | 49.3 | 17.4 | (39.7) | (13.7) | (35.9) | 3.3 | 16.0 | (9.0) | 32.1 | 8.5 | (33.6) | 2.6 | 12.3 | 0.8 | 7.4 |
| Utilities | (7.3) | 16.0 | 0.3 | 7.8 | (17.2) | 25.2 | 0.2 | 18.4 | 10.0 | (12.8) | 51.7 | (32.5) | (33.0) | 21.1 | 19.6 | 12.8 | 16.9 | 15.8 | (31.5) | 6.8 | 0.9 | 14.8 | (2.9) |
| **S&P 500** | **(6.6)** | **26.3** | **4.5** | **7.1** | **(1.5)** | **34.1** | **20.3** | **31.0** | **26.7** | **19.5** | **(10.1)** | **(13.0)** | **(23.4)** | **26.4** | **9.0** | **3.0** | **13.6** | **3.5** | **(38.5)** | **23.5** | **12.8** | **(0.0)** | **13.4** |

119

**TABLE 8.2**  Sectors Relative Performance (1990–2012)

| Rank | 1990 | 1991 | 1992 | 1993 | 1994 | 1995 | 1996 | 1997 | 1998 | 1999 | 2000 | 2001 | 2002 | 2003 | 2004 | 2005 | 2006 | 2007 | 2008 | 2009 | 2010 | 2011 | 2012 |
|---|---|---|---|---|---|---|---|---|---|---|---|---|---|---|---|---|---|---|---|---|---|---|---|
| Energy | 4 | 11 | 10 | 4 | 5 | 8 | 5 | 9 | 10 | 7 | 5 | 6 | 3 | 7 | 1 | 1 | 2 | 1 | 6 | 8 | 4 | 5 | 10 |
| Materials | 8 | 7 | 4 | 6 | 4 | 11 | 8 | 11 | 11 | 3 | 8 | 2 | 2 | 3 | 6 | 6 | 6 | 2 | 10 | 2 | 3 | 10 | 6 |
| Industrials | 7 | 6 | 5 | 2 | 7 | 6 | 4 | 8 | 9 | 4 | 6 | 3 | 8 | 4 | 4 | 9 | 9 | 6 | 8 | 5 | 2 | 9 | 7 |
| Consumer Discretionary | 9 | 4 | 2 | 3 | 10 | 10 | 9 | 4 | 4 | 2 | 1 | 1 | 7 | 2 | 5 | 10 | 3 | 10 | 5 | 3 | 1 | 4 | 2 |
| Consumer Staples | 2 | 3 | 7 | 10 | 3 | 5 | 3 | 6 | 6 | 11 | 4 | 4 | 1 | 10 | 9 | 7 | 8 | 5 | 1 | 9 | 8 | 2 | 8 |
| Health Care | 1 | 1 | 11 | 11 | 2 | 1 | 7 | 2 | 3 | 9 | 2 | 7 | 5 | 9 | 11 | 3 | 11 | 8 | 2 | 6 | 11 | 3 | 3 |
| Financials | 11 | 2 | 1 | 8 | 8 | 2 | 2 | 1 | 8 | 8 | 3 | 5 | 4 | 5 | 8 | 4 | 5 | 11 | 11 | 7 | 7 | 11 | 1 |
| Information Technology | 3 | 10 | 8 | 1 | 1 | 3 | 1 | 7 | 1 | 1 | 11 | 10 | 11 | 1 | 10 | 8 | 10 | 4 | 9 | 1 | 9 | 6 | 4 |
| Telecommunication Services | 10 | 9 | 3 | 5 | 9 | 4 | 11 | 3 | 2 | 6 | 10 | 9 | 10 | 11 | 3 | 11 | 1 | 7 | 4 | 11 | 6 | 7 | 9 |
| Utilities | 6 | 8 | 9 | 7 | 11 | 9 | 10 | 10 | 7 | 10 | 1 | 11 | 9 | 8 | 2 | 2 | 4 | 3 | 3 | 10 | 10 | 1 | 11 |
| **S&P 500** | 5 | 5 | 6 | 9 | 6 | 7 | 6 | 5 | 5 | 5 | 7 | 8 | 6 | 6 | 7 | 5 | 7 | 9 | 7 | 4 | 5 | 8 | 5 |

**FIGURE 8.7** Sector Rotation Graphic from Sam Stovall

**TABLE 8.3** Sector Performance in Economic Cycle

| Phase | Best | Second Best | Third Best | Fourth Best |
|---|---|---|---|---|
| Early Cycle | Financials | Consumer Discretionary | Information Technology | Industrials |
| Mid Cycle | Information Technology | Industrials | Energy | Materials |
| Late Cycle | Energy | Materials | Consumer Staples | Healthcare |
| During Recession | Consumer Staples | Healthcare | Utilities | Telecom |

However, you can use a momentum analysis and always be in the top four sectors and probably do well. Clearly, this is certainly better than buy and hold or index investing.

Figure 8.8 shows the S&P 500 in the top plot and my Offensive-Defensive Measure in the lower plot. The concept of the Offensive-Defensive Measure is simple.

### The Offensive Components

Consumer Discretionary
Financials
Industrials
Information Technology

### The Defensive Components

Consumer Staples
Utilities
Healthcare
Telecom

**FIGURE 8.8**  Offensive–Defensive Measure

*Source:* Chart courtesy of MetaStock.

You can see that the rally from the left side of the chart to point A (February, 2011) was strong, however, based on the switch from offensive to defensive sectors that occurred at point A the investors were clearly concerned about the market. While the market traded sideways for months (see top plot), the defensive sectors were clearly in the lead causing the offense defense measure to decline. The offense defense measure declined significantly and it wasn't until point B (July 2011) that the market finally gave up and headed south. See the discussion on breadth in the appendix of this book for details as to why this happens this way.

## Sector Rotation in 3-D

Julius de Kempenaer has created a novel way of visualizing sector-rotation or more generally "market-rotation" in such a way that the relative position of all elements in a universe (sectors, asset classes, individual equities, etc.) can be analyzed in one single graph instead of having to browse through all possible combinations. This graphical representation is called a Relative Rotation Graph™ or RRG™. Julius is now working together with Trevor Neil to further research and implement the use of RRGs in the investment process of investment companies, funds, and individual investors. More information can be found on their website www.relativerotationgraphs.com.

A Relative Rotation Graph™ takes two inputs that together combine into an RRG™. I'll use the S&P Sectors for this discussion. The first step is to come up with a measure of relative strength of a sector versus the S&P 500; this is done by taking a ratio between each sector and the S&P 500. Analyzing the slope and pace of these individual RS lines gives a pretty good clue about individual comparisons versus their benchmark. These raw RS lines answer "good" or "bad." However, they do not answer "how good" or "how bad" or "best" and "worst." The reason for this is that Raw RS values (sector/benchmark) for the various elements in the universe are like apples and oranges as they cannot be compared based on their numerical value.

Taking the relative positions of all elements in a universe into account in a uniform way enables "ranking." This process normalizes the various ratios in such a way that their values can be compared as apples to apples, not only against the benchmark but also against each other. The resulting numerical value is known as the JdK RS-Ratio™, the higher the value, the better the relative strength. Additionally, not only the level of the ratio, but also the direction and the pace at which it is moving affects the outcome. A concept similar to the well-known MACD indicator is used to measure the Rate of Change or Momentum of the JdK RS-Ratio™ line. Here also it is important to maintain comparable values so another normalization algorithm is applied to the ROC, this line is known as the JdK RS-Momentum™. The RRG now has JdK RS-Ratio™ for the abscissa (*X* axis) and the JdK RS-Momentum™ for the ordinate (*Y* axis). Graphically, the rotation looks like Figure 8.9.

In Figure 8.10 the sectors that are showing strong relative strength, which is still being pushed higher by strong momentum will show up in the top-right quadrant. By default the Rate of Change will start to flatten first and start to move down. When that happens the sector moves into the bottom-right quadrant. Here we find the sectors that are still showing positive relative strength but with declining momentum. If this deterioration continues the sector will move into the bottom-left quadrant. These are the sectors with negative relative strength, which is being pushed farther down by negative momentum. Once again, by default, the JdK RS-Momentum™ value will start to move up first, which will push the sector into the top-left quadrant. This is where relative strength is still weak (i.e., < 100 on the JdK RS-Ratio™ axis) but its momentum is moving up. Finally, if the strength persists, the sector will be pushed into the top-right quadrant again completing a full rotation.

The next step is to add the third dimension, time, to the plot to visualize the data on a periodic basis and in fact, somewhat like watching a flip chart or animation in

**FIGURE 8.9** Sector Rotation in 3-D

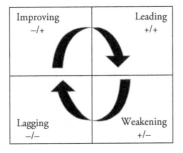

**FIGURE 8.10**   Sector Rotation Graphic

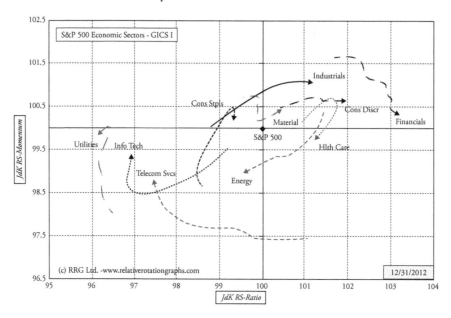

which you can see the movement of each of the sectors around the chart as shown in Figure 8.10.

This technology, in static form, is available on the Bloomberg professional service since January 2011 as a native function (RRG<GO>) where users can set their desired universes, benchmarks, look back periods, and so on. On their aforementioned website Julius and Trevor maintain a number of RRG™s, static and dynamic (animated rotation) on popular universes like the S&P 500 sectors (GICS I & II). Several professional as well as retail software vendors and websites are working to embed the RRG™ technology in their products, which should make this unique visualization tool available to a wider audience.

## Asset Classes

Asset classes can be analyzed exactly the same as market sectors. The only limitation is that they are not tied as closely to economic cycles as sectors so it is more difficult to identify those that are offensive or defensive. Table 8.4 shows the price performance of a multitude of asset classes. Remember, this table is only showing the annual performance of each asset for each year since 1990. Table 8.5 has the asset classes ranked each year numerically. Normally, this type of table is shown with multiple colors, but somewhat difficult in a black-and-white book, so rankings are shown. Again, remember that the rankings only show the relative performance and each year is totally independent of the preceding or following year.

## The Lost Decade

Figure 8.11 shows the S&P 500 Total Return from December 31, 1998, to December 31, 2008. Two huge bear markets and two good bull markets. If you have a strategy that could capture a good portion of those bull markets and avoid a good portion of those bear markets you would do really well. Buy and hold has lost money over this period.

I get asked all the time, "Are we going to have another bear market?" I answer that I can guarantee you that we will; I just have no idea when it will be. However, we can turn to another group of very bright people from the third largest economy in the world and look at their market. Figure 8.12 is the Japanese Nikkei from December 31, 1985, to December 31, 2011, a period of time of 26 years, over a quarter of a century.

Clearly, buy and hold was a devastating investment strategy, and the really bad news is that it still is. Figure 8.13 shows the up and down moves during this period in which a good trend following strategy could have protected you from horrible devastation.

The percentage moves up are shown above the plot and the percentage moves down are below the plot. These are the percentage moves for each of the up and downs you see on the chart. There were five cyclical bull moves of greater than 60 percent during this period. There were also five cyclical bear moves of greater than −40 percent. Remember, a 40 percent loss, requires a gain of 66 percent just to get back to even. The small box in the lower right edge shows the decline from the market top in late December 1989 (−73.3 percent). A 73 percent decline requires a gain of 285 percent to get back even. Most people won't live long enough for that to happen.

**FIGURE 8.11**   Lost Decade

*Source:* Chart courtesy of MetaStock.

**TABLE 8.4**  Asset Class Performance (1990–2012)

| Price Performance | 1990 | 1991 | 1992 | 1993 | 1994 | 1995 | 1996 | 1997 | 1998 | 1999 | 2000 |
|---|---|---|---|---|---|---|---|---|---|---|---|
| S&P 500 | -3.11% | 30.47% | 7.62% | 10.08% | 1.32% | 37.58% | 22.96% | 33.36% | 28.58% | 21.04% | -9.11% |
| S&P 500 Growth | 0.20% | 38.37% | 5.06% | 1.68% | 3.13% | 38.13% | 23.97% | 36.52% | 42.16% | 28.24% | -22.08% |
| S&P 500 Value | -6.85% | 22.56% | 10.52% | 18.61% | -0.64% | 36.99% | 22.00% | 29.98% | 14.69% | 12.73% | 6.08% |
| Russell 2000 | -19.48% | 46.04% | 18.41% | 18.88% | -1.82% | 28.45% | 16.49% | 22.36% | -2.55% | 21.26% | -3.02% |
| Russell 2000 Growth | -17.42% | 51.19% | 7.77% | 13.37% | -2.43% | 31.04% | 11.26% | 12.95% | 1.23% | 43.09% | -22.43% |
| Russell 2000 Value | -21.77% | 41.70% | 29.14% | 23.77% | -1.54% | 25.75% | 21.37% | 31.78% | -6.45% | -1.49% | 22.83% |
| EAFE | -23.45% | 12.14% | -12.18% | 32.57% | 7.78% | 11.21% | 6.05% | 1.78% | 20.00% | 26.96% | -14.17% |
| BarCap Agg Bond | 8.96% | 16.00% | 7.40% | 9.75% | -2.92% | 18.46% | 3.64% | 9.64% | 8.70% | -0.82% | 11.63% |
| 2 Year Treasury | 9.20% | 11.73% | 6.31% | 5.46% | 0.26% | 11.13% | 4.71% | 6.45% | 6.57% | 1.90% | 7.57% |
| 3 Year Treasury | 9.58% | 13.53% | 6.62% | 6.83% | -1.52% | 13.83% | 3.89% | 7.11% | 8.28% | 1.43% | 9.71% |
| 5 Year Treasury | 8.69% | 14.64% | 5.77% | 9.42% | -4.26% | 16.93% | 2.32% | 8.03% | 9.81% | -2.54% | 11.88% |
| 10 Year Treasury | 6.88% | 17.18% | 6.50% | 12.08% | -8.29% | 23.58% | 0.04% | 11.16% | 12.77% | -8.25% | 14.86% |
| 30 Year Treasury | 4.77% | 17.54% | 6.79% | 19.16% | -11.99% | 34.08% | -4.54% | 15.21% | 17.57% | -15.13% | 20.05% |
| MBS | 10.72% | 15.72% | 6.96% | 6.84% | -1.61% | 16.80% | 5.35% | 9.49% | 6.96% | 1.86% | 11.16% |
| Investment Grade Corporate Bonds | 7.05% | 18.51% | 8.69% | 12.16% | -3.93% | 22.25% | 3.28% | 10.23% | 8.57% | -1.96% | 9.08% |
| High Yield Bonds | -4.36% | 39.17% | 17.44% | 16.69% | -1.06% | 20.44% | 11.32% | 13.27% | 2.95% | 2.51% | -5.17% |
| Gold | -3.11% | -8.56% | -5.73% | 17.68% | -2.17% | 0.98% | -4.59% | -21.41% | -0.83% | 0.85% | -5.44% |
| Silver | -19.63% | -7.93% | -4.94% | 39.39% | -5.18% | 6.02% | -6.70% | 24.96% | -16.51% | 6.49% | -14.17% |
| Oil | 30.61% | -32.91% | 1.99% | -27.33% | 25.34% | 10.08% | 32.58% | -31.94% | -31.46% | 111.75% | 4.69% |
| Commodities | 29.08% | -6.13% | 4.42% | -12.33% | 5.29% | 20.33% | 33.92% | -14.07% | -35.75% | 40.92% | 49.74% |

| Price Performance | 2001 | 2002 | 2003 | 2004 | 2005 | 2006 | 2007 | 2008 | 2009 | 2010 | 2011 | 2012 |
|---|---|---|---|---|---|---|---|---|---|---|---|---|
| S&P 500 | −11.89% | −22.10% | 28.68% | 10.86% | 4.91% | 15.79% | 5.59% | −37.00% | 26.47% | 15.06% | 2.11% | 15.65% |
| S&P 500 Growth | −12.73% | −23.59% | 25.66% | 6.13% | 4.00% | 11.01% | 9.13% | −34.92% | 31.57% | 15.05% | 4.65% | 15.17% |
| S&P 500 Value | −11.71% | −20.85% | 31.79% | 15.71% | 5.82% | 20.81% | 1.99% | −39.22% | 21.17% | 15.10% | −0.48% | 16.41% |
| Russell 2000 | 2.49% | −20.48% | 47.25% | 18.33% | 4.55% | 18.37% | −1.57% | −33.79% | 27.17% | 26.85% | −4.18% | 16.35% |
| Russell 2000 Growth | −9.23% | −30.26% | 48.54% | 14.31% | 4.15% | 13.35% | 7.05% | −38.54% | 34.47% | 29.09% | −2.91% | 14.59% |
| Russell 2000 Value | 14.02% | −11.43% | 46.03% | 22.25% | 4.71% | 23.48% | −9.78% | −28.92% | 20.58% | 24.50% | −5.50% | 18.05% |
| EAFE | −21.44% | −15.94% | 38.59% | 20.25% | 13.54% | 26.34% | 11.17% | −43.38% | 31.78% | 7.75% | −12.14% | 17.32% |
| BarCap Agg Bond | 8.43% | 10.26% | 4.10% | 4.34% | 2.43% | 4.33% | 6.97% | 5.24% | 5.93% | 6.54% | 7.84% | 4.22% |
| 2 Year Treasury | 7.91% | 6.87% | 2.23% | 0.75% | 1.45% | 3.81% | 7.50% | 7.43% | 1.05% | 2.28% | 1.46% | 0.28% |
| 3 Year Treasury | 9.21% | 9.60% | 2.71% | 1.27% | 0.94% | 3.58% | 8.66% | 9.32% | 0.96% | 4.14% | 3.39% | 0.57% |
| 5 Year Treasury | 7.51% | 12.35% | 2.51% | 2.40% | 0.02% | 2.81% | 10.42% | 13.28% | −1.47% | 6.76% | 9.21% | 2.27% |
| 10 Year Treasury | 4.26% | 14.62% | 1.32% | 4.83% | 1.99% | 1.36% | 9.76% | 20.06% | −9.71% | 7.90% | 17.15% | 4.18% |
| 30 Year Treasury | 3.55% | 16.25% | 0.78% | 8.88% | 8.78% | −1.13% | 10.37% | 41.20% | −25.98% | 8.65% | 35.50% | 2.48% |
| MBS | 8.22% | 8.75% | 3.07% | 4.70% | 2.61% | 5.22% | 6.90% | 8.34% | 5.89% | 5.37% | 6.23% | 2.59% |
| Investment Grade | | | | | | | | | | | | |
| Corporate Bonds | 10.31% | 10.12% | 8.24% | 5.39% | 1.68% | 4.30% | 4.56% | −4.94% | 18.68% | 9.00% | 8.15% | 9.82% |
| High Yield Bonds | 4.54% | −1.89% | 28.15% | 10.87% | 2.72% | 11.74% | 2.24% | −26.39% | 57.51% | 15.19% | 4.38% | 15.58% |
| Gold | 0.75% | 25.57% | 19.89% | 4.65% | 17.77% | 23.20% | 31.92% | 4.32% | 25.04% | 29.24% | 8.93% | 8.26% |
| Silver | −1.20% | 3.21% | 27.87% | 14.25% | 29.57% | 46.09% | 14.42% | −26.90% | 57.46% | 80.28% | −8.00% | 6.28% |
| Oil | −25.97% | 57.26% | 4.23% | 33.61% | 40.48% | 0.02% | 57.25% | −53.54% | 77.94% | 15.15% | 8.15% | −7.09% |
| Commodities | −31.93% | 32.07% | 20.72% | 17.28% | 25.55% | −15.09% | 32.67% | −46.49% | 13.49% | 9.02% | −1.18% | 0.08% |

**TABLE 8.5** Asset Class Relative Performance (1990–2012)

| Relative Performance | 1990 | 1991 | 1992 | 1993 | 1994 | 1995 | 1996 | 1997 | 1998 | 1999 | 2000 | 2001 | 2002 | 2003 | 2004 | 2005 | 2006 | 2007 | 2008 | 2009 | 2010 | 2011 | 2012 |
|---|---|---|---|---|---|---|---|---|---|---|---|---|---|---|---|---|---|---|---|---|---|---|---|
| S&P 500 | 12 | 6 | 7 | 12 | 5 | 2 | 4 | 2 | 2 | 7 | 16 | 16 | 18 | 6 | 10 | 8 | 7 | 15 | 15 | 8 | 9 | 12 | 5 |
| S&P 500 Growth | 11 | 5 | 15 | 18 | 4 | 1 | 3 | 1 | 1 | 4 | 19 | 17 | 19 | 9 | 12 | 12 | 10 | 9 | 14 | 6 | 10 | 9 | 7 |
| S&P 500 Value | 15 | 7 | 4 | 6 | 7 | 3 | 5 | 4 | 5 | 8 | 11 | 15 | 17 | 5 | 6 | 7 | 5 | 18 | 17 | 10 | 8 | 14 | 3 |
| Russell 2000 | 17 | 2 | 2 | 5 | 12 | 6 | 7 | 6 | 16 | 6 | 13 | 11 | 16 | 2 | 4 | 10 | 6 | 19 | 13 | 7 | 4 | 17 | 4 |
| Russell 2000 Growth | 16 | 1 | 6 | 9 | 14 | 5 | 9 | 9 | 14 | 2 | 20 | 14 | 20 | 1 | 7 | 11 | 8 | 12 | 16 | 4 | 3 | 16 | 8 |
| Russell 2000 Value | 19 | 3 | 1 | 3 | 10 | 7 | 6 | 3 | 17 | 16 | 2 | 1 | 14 | 3 | 2 | 9 | 3 | 20 | 12 | 11 | 5 | 18 | 1 |
| EAFE | 20 | 15 | 20 | 2 | 2 | 16 | 10 | 17 | 3 | 5 | 18 | 18 | 15 | 4 | 3 | 5 | 2 | 5 | 18 | 5 | 15 | 20 | 2 |
| BarCap Agg Bond | 6 | 11 | 8 | 13 | 15 | 12 | 14 | 12 | 8 | 15 | 6 | 4 | 7 | 14 | 17 | 15 | 12 | 13 | 7 | 14 | 17 | 7 | 12 |
| 2 Year Treasury | 5 | 16 | 13 | 17 | 6 | 17 | 12 | 16 | 12 | 11 | 10 | 6 | 11 | 18 | 20 | 18 | 14 | 11 | 6 | 16 | 20 | 13 | 18 |
| 3 Year Treasury | 4 | 14 | 11 | 16 | 9 | 15 | 13 | 15 | 10 | 13 | 8 | 3 | 9 | 16 | 19 | 19 | 15 | 10 | 4 | 17 | 19 | 11 | 17 |
| 5 Year Treasury | 7 | 13 | 14 | 14 | 17 | 13 | 16 | 14 | 7 | 18 | 5 | 7 | 6 | 17 | 18 | 20 | 16 | 6 | 3 | 18 | 16 | 3 | 16 |
| 10 Year Treasury | 9 | 10 | 12 | 11 | 19 | 8 | 17 | 10 | 6 | 19 | 4 | 9 | 5 | 19 | 14 | 16 | 17 | 8 | 2 | 19 | 14 | 2 | 13 |
| 30 Year Treasury | 10 | 9 | 10 | 4 | 20 | 4 | 18 | 7 | 4 | 20 | 3 | 10 | 4 | 20 | 11 | 6 | 19 | 7 | 1 | 20 | 13 | 1 | 15 |
| MBS | 3 | 12 | 9 | 15 | 11 | 14 | 11 | 13 | 11 | 12 | 7 | 5 | 10 | 15 | 15 | 14 | 11 | 14 | 5 | 15 | 18 | 8 | 14 |
| Investment Grade Corporate Bonds | 8 | 8 | 5 | 10 | 16 | 9 | 15 | 11 | 9 | 17 | 9 | 2 | 8 | 12 | 13 | 17 | 13 | 16 | 9 | 12 | 12 | 6 | 9 |
| High Yield Bonds | 14 | 4 | 3 | 8 | 8 | 10 | 8 | 8 | 13 | 10 | 14 | 8 | 13 | 7 | 9 | 13 | 9 | 17 | 10 | 2 | 6 | 10 | 6 |
| Gold | 13 | 19 | 19 | 7 | 13 | 20 | 19 | 19 | 15 | 14 | 15 | 12 | 3 | 11 | 16 | 4 | 4 | 3 | 8 | 9 | 2 | 4 | 10 |
| Silver | 18 | 18 | 18 | 1 | 18 | 19 | 20 | 5 | 18 | 9 | 17 | 13 | 12 | 8 | 8 | 2 | 1 | 4 | 11 | 3 | 1 | 19 | 11 |
| Oil | 1 | 20 | 17 | 20 | 1 | 18 | 2 | 20 | 19 | 1 | 12 | 19 | 1 | 13 | 1 | 1 | 18 | 1 | 20 | 1 | 7 | 5 | 20 |
| Commodities | 2 | 17 | 16 | 19 | 3 | 11 | 1 | 18 | 20 | 3 | 1 | 2 | 2 | 10 | 5 | 3 | 20 | 2 | 19 | 13 | 11 | 15 | 19 |

**FIGURE 8.12**  Lost Quarter of a Century

*Source:* Chart courtesy of MetaStock.

**FIGURE 8.13**  Nikkei 225 (1984–2012)

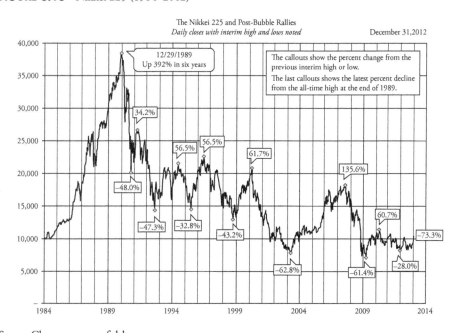

*Source:* Chart courtesy of dshort.com.

Finally, please notice that Figure 8.13 covers approximately 30 years of data and that the point on the right end (most recent value) is approximately equal to the starting point back in the mid-1980s; certainly the lost three decades. Buy and Hold is Buy and Hope.

## Market Returns

It is always good to see how the markets have performed in the past. With the advent of the internet, globalization, minute-by-minute news, investors have a natural tendency to focus on the short term. Without a knowledge of the long-term performance of the markets, that short-term orientation can cause one to be totally out of touch with the reality that the market does not always go up. The following charts will show annualized returns for the S&P 500 price, total return, and inflation adjusted total return over various periods. These types of charts are also known as rolling return charts. As an example using the 10-year annualized rolling return, the data begins in 1928, so the first data point would not be until 1938 and be the 10-year annualized return from 1928 to 1938, the next data point would be for the 10-year period from 1929 to 1939, the third from 1930 to 1940, and so on.

Figure 8.14 shows the 1-year annualized return for the S&P price. It should be obvious that one-year returns are all over the place, oscillating between highs in the 40 percent to 50 percent range, and lows in the −15 percent to −25 percent range. Following Figure 8.14 are the 3-year (Figure 8.15), 5-year (Figure 8.16), 10-year (Figure 8.17), and 20-year (Figure 8.18) charts of annualized returns with the average for all the data shown in the chart caption. Following the 20-year chart is a further analysis for the 20-year period.

**FIGURE 8.14**  One-Year Annualized Return of S&P 500 Price

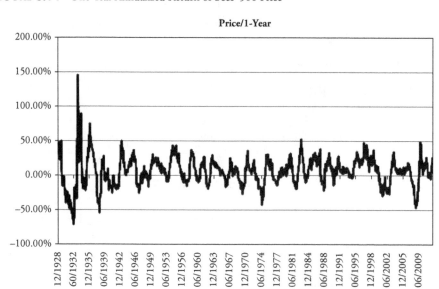

When you look at the rolling returns for three years (Figure 8.15), it dampens out the oscillations somewhat but there are still many periods of exceptional movement both up and down.

Once you get to the five-year rolling returns (Figure 8.16), the range has been reduced from the shorter periods and you can begin to see up-and-down trends in the rolling return data.

**FIGURE 8.15**  Three-Year Annualized Return of S&P 500 Price

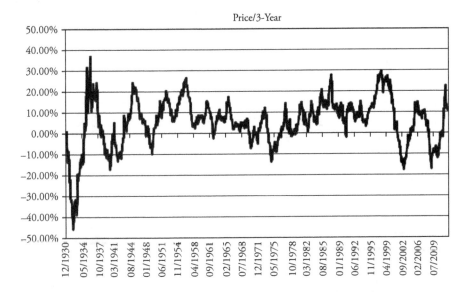

**FIGURE 8.16**  Five-Year Annualized Return of S&P 500 Price

**FIGURE 8.17**  Ten-Year Annualized Return of S&P 500 Price

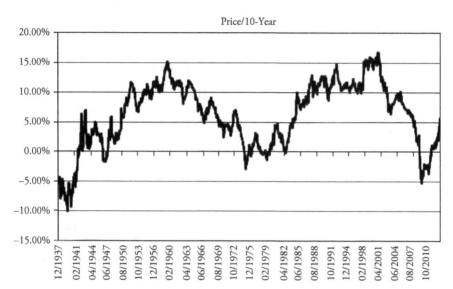

**FIGURE 8.18**  Twenty-Year Annualized Return of S&P 500 Price

The 10-year return chart now clearly shows up-and-down trends in the data (see Figure 8.17).

The 20-year rolling return chart (Figure 8.18) continues to reduce the short-term volatility in the chart and the up-and-down trends become clear.

Since I adamantly believe that most investors have about 20 years to really put money away in a serious manner for retirement, the following two charts show returns over 20 years for total return (Figure 8.19) and inflation-adjusted total return (Figure 8.20).

**FIGURE 8.19** Twenty-Year Annualized Total Return for S&P 500

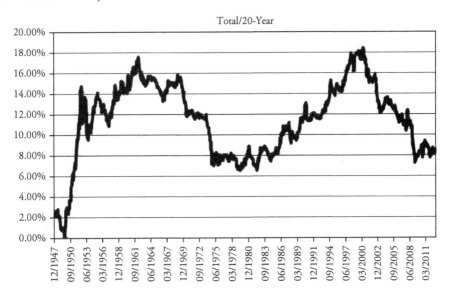

**FIGURE 8.20** Twenty-Year Annualized Total Return for S&P 500 Inflation Adjusted

For most analysis the Price chart is more than adequate. In the world of finance there is an almost universal demand for the Total Return chart; however, I think that if you are going to insist on Total Return, you should then also insist on Inflation Adjusted Total Return. Using the three preceding 20-year charts and the averages shown, you can see that the average for Price is 6.97 percent, Total Return is 11.32 percent, and Inflation Adjusted Total Return is 7.19 percent. What this says is that the effect of including dividends (Total Return) and the effect of Inflation often neutralize each other.

Table 8.6 shows the annualized returns for the S&P 500 for price, total return, and inflation-adjusted total return for the following periods: 1-year, 2-year, 3-year, 5-year, 10-year, and 20-year periods.

Table 8.7 shows the minimum and maximum returns, along with the range of returns, their mean, median, and variability about their mean (Standard Deviation).

## Distribution of Returns

The range of return data is very easy to calculate because it is simply the difference between the largest and the smallest values in a data set. Thus, range, including any outliers, is the actual spread of data. Range equals the difference between highest and lowest observed values. However, a great deal of information is ignored when computing the range, because only the largest and smallest data values are considered. The range value of a data set is greatly influenced by the presence of just one unusually large or small value (outlier). The disadvantage of using range is that it does not measure the spread of most of the values—it only measures the spread between highest and lowest values. As a result, other measures are required in order to give a better picture of the data spread. The monthly returns for the S&P 500 begin with December 1927, so as of December 2012, there are 1,020 months (85 years) of data.

Additional charts show the distribution of data in various ways using the 20-year annualized returns of the S&P 500 inflation-adjusted total return data for rolling 20-year

**TABLE 8.6**  Average and Median Returns for 1, 2, 3, 5, 10, and 20 Years

| Data | Statistic | 1 Year | 2 Year | 3 Year | 5 Year | 10 Year | 20 Year |
|------|-----------|--------|--------|--------|--------|---------|---------|
| Price | Average | 7.35% | 6.09% | 5.72% | 5.86% | 6.29% | 6.97% |
|  | Median | 8.10% | 7.28% | 6.75% | 6.73% | 7.24% | 7.17% |
| Total | Average | 11.21% | 9.97% | 9.62% | 9.86% | 10.46% | 11.32% |
|  | Median | 11.94% | 11.45% | 11.02% | 10.75% | 10.69% | 11.68% |
| Inf Adj TR | Average | 7.82% | 6.53% | 6.16% | 6.28% | 6.63% | 7.19% |
|  | Median | 8.07% | 7.21% | 6.64% | 6.76% | 7.15% | 7.86% |

**TABLE 8.7**  Range of Returns for 1, 2, 3, 5, 10, and 20 Years

| Parameter | Monthly | 1 Year | 2 Year | 3 Year | 5 Year | 10 Year | 20 Year |
|-----------|---------|--------|--------|--------|--------|---------|---------|
| Minimum | −29.94% | −70.13% | −57.28% | −45.53% | −22.01% | −9.90% | −3.60% |
| Maximum | 39.14% | 146.28% | 48.81% | 37.14% | 29.47% | 16.75% | 14.38% |
| Range | 69.08% | 216.40% | 106.09% | 82.67% | 51.48% | 26.65% | 17.98% |
| Mean | 0.58% | 7.35% | 6.09% | 5.72% | 5.86% | 6.29% | 6.97% |
| Median | 0.87% | 8.10% | 7.28% | 6.75% | 6.73% | 7.24% | 7.17% |
| Std. Dev. | 5.51% | 20.83% | 14.24% | 11.45% | 8.24% | 5.44% | 3.29% |

periods. Twenty-year returns from the S&P 500 with 1,020 months of data would yield 778 data points. Return distributions can be thought of like this: Each bar represents the proportion of the returns that meet a percentage division of the data, mathematical division of the data, or statistical division of the data. The following are definitions of the various distribution methods as shown in the title of the following figures.

> *Decile.* One of 10 groups containing an equal number of the items that make up a frequency distribution. The range of returns is determined by the difference between the minimum and maximum returns in the series, then divided by 10 to create 10 equal groups.
>
> *Quartile.* The calculation is similar to decile (above) but with only four groupings.

Note: This use of decile and quartile does not follow the standard definition or calculation method often used in statistics.

> *Standard deviation.* A statistical measure of the amount by which a set of values differs from the arithmetical mean, equal to the square root of the mean of the differences' squares. Figure 8.21 shows the percentage of the data that is included in a standard deviation. You can see that the mean is the peak and that 68.2 percent of the data is within one standard deviation from the mean, and 95.4 percent of the data is within two standard deviations of the mean.
>
> *Percentage.* A proportion stated in terms of one-hundredths that is calculated by multiplying a fraction by 100.

Figure 8.22 shows the 20-year rolling returns using inflation adjusted total return data distributed by quartiles. From the chart you can see that 13.24 percent of the returns fall into the first quartile or lowest 25 percent of the data, 28.15 percent in the second, 32.90 percent in the third, and 25.71 percent in the fourth quartile or highest 25 percent of the data.

**FIGURE 8.21**  Normal Distribution

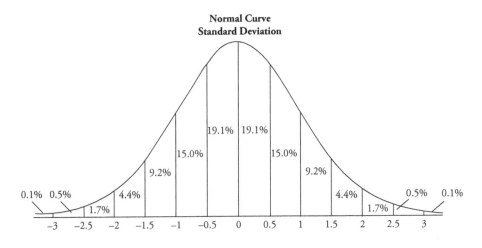

**FIGURE 8.22**  Distribution of Inflation-Adjusted 20-Year Returns by Quartile

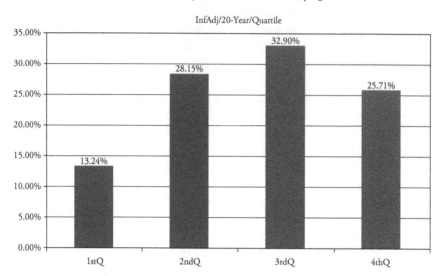

Figure 8.23 shows the same data but in a decile distribution where each bar represents 10 percent of the number of data items. For example 8.23 percent of the data fell in the highest 10 percent of the data.

Figure 8.24 shows the distribution of the data based on variance from the mean or standard deviation. You can see that the two middle bars, each represents 34.1 percent of the data (68.2 percent total) that is one standard deviation from the mean. As an example 33.68 percent of the 20-year rolling returns data was within one standard deviation above the mean of all the data. You can also surmise that the two bars on the

**FIGURE 8.23**  Distribution of Inflation-Adjusted 20-Year Returns by Decile

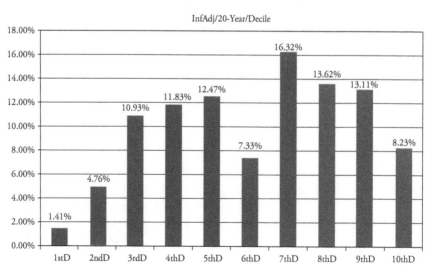

right represent 50 percent of all the data and 53.86 percent (33.68 + 20.18) of the returns. Overly simplifying this one then knows that there were more returns greater than the mean. However, there is an asymmetrical distribution between the returns that are outside of one standard deviation from the mean, with the larger percentage to the downside.

Figure 8.25 shows the 20-year rolling returns of the S&P 500 inflation adjusted total return within percentage ranges. The bar on the left shows all the returns of less than 8 percent, which accounted for more than 50 percent of all returns (51.41 percent), while the bar on the right shows returns of greater than 12 percent accounted

**FIGURE 8.24** Distribution of Inflation-Adjusted 20-Year Returns by Standard Deviation

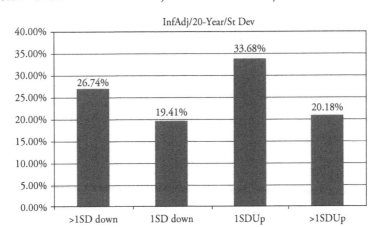

**FIGURE 8.25** Distribution of Inflation-Adjusted 20-Year Returns by Percentage Ranges

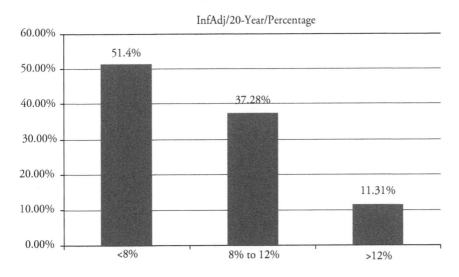

for only 11.31 percent of all returns. The bar in the middle is the range of returns between 8 percent and 12 percent, which accounted for 37.28 percent of all returns. Recall the discussion in Chapter 4 on the deception of average, and once again the average 8 percent to 12 percent return is not average.

When the market starts to decline significantly it is not the same as when someone yells "fire" in a theater. In a theater everyone is running for the exits. In a big decline in the market, you can run for the exits, but first you have to find someone to replace you—you must find a buyer. Big difference! This chapter has attempted to stick to what I believe are market facts and essential information you should understand in regard to how markets work and have worked in the past. If one does not know market history, it would be very difficult to keep a focus on what the possibilities are in the future.

This concludes Part I where I have attempted to show you the many popular beliefs about the market that are used by academia and Wall Street to help sell their products. Part I also wraps up with what I believe to be truisms about the market. Part II has an introductory chapter on technical analysis and is followed by two chapters on extensive research into trend determination and risk/drawdowns.

# PART II

# Market Research

Part II is devoted to technical market research, after an introduction to technical analysis.

Trend analysis, which is essentially what this book is all about, is dealt with in Chapter 10. Thorough research is included in an attempt to quantify the fact that markets, in general, trend much more than not. This is presented with tables containing a wide array of market indices both domestic and international. The trend analysis is then presented on all of the Standard & Poor's GICS sectors, industry groups, and industries. Additional tables of trend analysis are also included in Appendix B.

The concept that risk is drawdown is presented in Chapter 11, with a thorough analysis of past drawdowns from the Dow Jones Industrial Average beginning in 1885 and the S&P 500 Index since 1927, both in price and total return. Drawdowns of other asset classes are also presented.

Remember: All of the financial theories and all of the fundamentals will never be any better than what the trend of the market will allow.

# CHAPTER 9

# Why Technical Analysis?

Technical analysis offers an unbiased truth about the markets.

If one is going to follow and utilize a particular discipline, hopefully they have done a thorough investigation as to the benefits and pitfalls of that discipline. I share a short story from the mid-1970s, a period of my life when I was a Navy fighter pilot, and, of course, knew everything. I had a few thousand dollars that I wanted to invest. I honestly can't recall my source for research, but I'm almost positive I didn't pay for any of it; probably a trip to the Public Library and probably the Value Line Investment Survey. This is a giant black ring binder with a single page dedicated to a single stock in the Value Line universe of about 1,700 issues. I know the research was quite thorough and it probably took me a few months to even work up the nerve to actually speculate (I called it *invest* back then) in the market. I don't even recall the small brokerage firm I used, but I do remember that discount firms were being talked about but none were in existence then (I think). There was no FNN (Financial News Network), CNBC, Fox Business, or Bloomberg television in those days.

My research efforts involved the typical fundamental review looking for stocks that met a host of different criteria using ratios such as price to earnings, price to dividend, price to book, and so on. I do know that the price to sales ratio had not been created yet. I think it was developed by Ken Fisher in the 1970s and became widely used in the 1980s. So I buy two stocks in late 1972; I remember that one of them was UAL (United Airlines). Clearly my bias for aviation was part of the decision—a bias that this book is trying to teach is totally wrong. For two months they went straight up. I have to be honest, I thought I was truly brilliant. I was euphoric. Then in early 1973, my brilliance turned to anxiety when the prices of both stocks started to decline. Fear of losing money was now dominating my thought process. Strangely, nothing entered my mind in regard to selling those stocks, or putting a stop loss order in (doubt I even knew what that was then), I just knew I was right and was going to prove it. Well, as I recall I held those two stocks until sometime in 1975. They had declined with the market and by the end of 1974 were down 75 percent from where I bought them. I had no stops, I had no plan, I had no money management, I had nothing but an ego that kept me totally wrong for two years. The market started up in early 1975 and I was so happy to unload them for a few percentage points above their bottom, I swore

I'd never gamble in the market again. However, I remember that it sure made me feel good to buy a stock because the financial ratios were good. Fortunately, I quickly learned that feeling good has very little to do with making money in the markets.

It was then that I read a book, suggested by a good friend, called *The Art of Low Risk Investing*, by Michael Zahorchak. I had previously read a few other books on technical analysis but none of them involved a process; they usually dealt with chart patterns, and so on. Zahorchak offered a complete and rational technical process to investing. The book has long been out of print, but I'm sure you can find it on eBay or somewhere. If you are having doubts about technical analysis, this book will correct that. I have never deviated from technical analysis since that experience in the mid-1970s; I believe it is the best way to help investors control their emotions during the investment process.

Figure 9.1 shows the NYSE Composite Index with my interpretation of the Zahorchak method overlaid. Whenever the Zahorchak method line is above zero (horizontal line), one should be invested in equities and when below zero, one should be invested in cash or cash equivalents. One could further fine-tune it by using various levels for different asset commitments to enhance the process. The Zahorchak method uses only weekly data, uses moving averages of 5, 15, and 40 on the NYSE Composite Index and the NYSE Advance Decline Line for its signals. The same process is then applied to stocks for selection. A complete set of rules is given on how to make trades from that data. (B61)

Now, within technical analysis there are many varied approaches. Many of which I have tried, but was not successful. I like to say that I have a master's degree in what not to do as those lessons came at a significant cost. As I have aged, I have slowly

**FIGURE 9.1**   Zahorchak Method

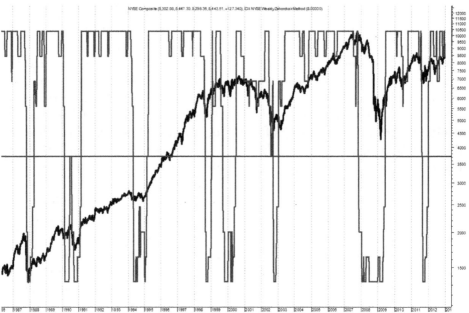

*Source:* Chart courtesy of MetaStock.

learned not to speak in absolutes about the market, as any approach that one can use to be successful is the right approach for that person. Just because I don't care for some approach does not mean that someone else cannot use it successfully.

There are different types of market analysis. The most widely used is fundamental analysis, which focuses is on multiples or fundamental ratios. Almost 90 percent of these ratios use price, usually in the numerator or sometimes in the denominator. Price earnings ratio, price to sales, price to dividends, price to book ratio, and so on, are just a few of them.

Technical analysis, however, is the analysis of price. Price is what we buy. When you buy a stock, you are not buying the earnings, the products, the management, dividends; you are buying the stock at a market generated price. Those other things might be why you buy it, but they are not what you are buying, you are buying the stock, not the company.

Trend determination is the trend of the price that we are analyzing. Trend analysis is a significant part of what this book is all about. Breadth analysis is a derivative of price movement. Breadth analysis is dealt with extensively in the appendix. It is a critical contribution to technical analysis. Relative strength analysis is the analysis of one group relative to another. An example of relative strength is the relationship between small capitalization stocks and large capitalization stocks. However, most importantly, technical analysis bridges the gap between doing the analysis and taking action—it is just the next step.

## What Is Technical Analysis?

Martin Pring says the art of technical analysis is to identify trend changes at an early stage and to maintain an investment position until the weight of the evidence indicates that the trend has reversed. Although there are other definitions, Pring's definition is the one I agree with. It is primarily used two ways: predictive and reactive. Most newsletter writers, television experts, brokerage firm analysts use it to predict the market. The reactive mode means that it is used to measure what the market is doing, then just react to that information. The subject of this book is all about the latter. React, don't predict. For additional reading on technical analysis, I strongly recommend *Technical Analysis*, by Charlie Kirkpatrick and Julie Dahlquist. It is the best single volume on technical analysis there is. (B27)

## I Use Technical Analysis Because . . .

It is something we can believe in and rely on. It removes the destructive emotions of fear, hope, and greed.

---

Individuals who cannot master their emotions are ill-suited to profit from the investment process.

*Benjamin Graham (the great value investor)*

---

It keeps our perceptions clear.

---

It ain't what you know that gets you into trouble, it's what you know for sure that just ain't so.

*Mark Twain*

---

*And the absolute most important thing technical analysis does is it gives us discipline.*

I want to share a story with you. I have been on a diet my entire adult life. Seriously! Last spring my wife and I were driving in the north Georgia mountains one Sunday afternoon. I stopped at an old filling station for gas. It had the old style pumps so I had to go inside to pay for the gas. I see a candy bar near the register and buy it. As I'm walking back to the car, I can see my wife giving me "that look." You know that look, don't you? I get in the car and she says, "You just don't have any discipline." I said, "That's not true, because you don't know how many of these I wanted."

I tell that story because discipline is not a knob or a lever that you can subjectively set each day. Discipline is something that must be instilled into your life and your work. I think everyone will agree that when it comes to investing, a disciplined approach is probably going to be a better approach. I'll take that one step further and say that a disciplined life is probably going to be a good life. Discipline is a critical element for success in the stock market and in life.

## The Challenge of Technical Analysis

---

I know of no way of judging the future but by the past.

*Patrick Henry*

---

Warning: I share passionate opinions in this section. I am approaching 40 years as being actively involved in technical analysis; you can assume correctly that I have some strong opinions on things. To be perfectly honest, those opinions have changed from time to time, but I do want to share them here. Does this mean that I think I am correct and anything I question is wrong? Not at all, most of technical and, in particular, market analysis is arguable and controversial. I just focus on what works for me.

What is technical analysis? Books are filled with definitions and interpretations on technical analysis. A significant part of technical analysis is the art of studying the past, attempting to identify a pattern or event that seems to represent or reflect the market being studied, and then believing that it will work with some certainty in the foreseeable future.

My definition for technical analysis and my adherence to using it comes from a belief that everyone needs something to believe in or rely on. I believe in technical analysis because of its close relationship to the supply and demand of the market. Fundamental analysis, which is by far a more popular method of analysis, is generally flawed in that it does not address the issue of "when." When should I buy or when should I sell? Researching the hundreds of different fundamental ratios is the full-time job of thousands of securities analysts. However, think about this simple fact. Almost all fundamental ratios involve price. So why not analyze price? Most forms of technical analysis do just that.

Is technical analysis the same as market timing? Sometimes it is, sometimes it isn't. Market timing has received a bad rap, especially by those who believe it is a process by some who blindly follow some overoptimized mechanical system without utilizing money management or an asset commitment plan. In that regard, its bad rap is appropriate. The analysis of risk and reward is not market timing in the sense that many think of when using that often misused term. Determining when the market has too much risk is not market timing, but prudent and discretionary investment decision making. Next time you hear a brokerage firm analyst mention that no one can time the market, or that technical analysis does not work, ask to see his record during the bear markets of 2000 to 2002 or 2007 to 2009. Heck, he probably wasn't a stockbroker then anyway. I hate it when I call salespeople stockbrokers. They are not stockbrokers, as that is what the company they work for is called; they are salespeople for a stockbroker. I feel better now.

I have a cassette tape that I received from Sedge Coppock, the founder of the San Antonio firm, Trendex. This was in 1983 when I was heading a group of technical analysts in Dallas and wanted him to come up and speak to us. He declined but sent a tape, which was about 30 minutes in length in which he said how inept most investors were at controlling their emotions and that even worse than that was when they sought advice from a stockbroker. Sedge did not hold stockbrokers in high regard. I was fortunate to attend the Market Technician's Association annual seminar in Naples, Florida in 1989 when Edwin Sedgwick Chittenden Coppock received their highest award, the MTA Annual Award. He passed away the next year.

Another challenge to technical analysis is that of whether it is an art or a science. I cannot believe anyone would seriously ask this, and suspect the question comes almost totally from the nonscientific or the innumerate among us. I do believe that scientists, engineers, and mathematically inclined investors migrate toward technical analysis over time because of its ability to look back in history and see how supply and demand played out. It is certainly a more analytical approach to market analysis.

Many claim that technical analysis is science. My response is that the person making the claim is neither a scientist nor an engineer, and clearly doesn't know the difference between art and science. Finance and economics are considered social sciences, which is a wide swath into the wrong direction. Neither are science, they are arts. You don't get a bachelor of science degree in them; you get a bachelor of arts degree. Here's the difference between art and science. Science is when you can reliably repeat something within predefined parameters. For example, I know that at sea level, with the ambient temperature at 59 degrees Fahrenheit or 15 degrees Centigrade ($59 - 32 = 27$. $27 / 9 = 3$. $3 \times 5 = 15$), and the atmospheric pressure is 29.92 inches or 1,013 millibars that pure water $H_2O$, in laboratory conditions will boil at 212 degrees Fahrenheit or 100 degrees Centigrade. I'll bet a large sum of money on it. I can't think of anything in finance, economics, or technical analysis in which I would do that.

Those who get excited and experience a warm feeling about the overused adjectives of quality, strong, healthy, and so on, when Wall Street talks about investing in specific companies are surely the ones who think technical analysis is witchcraft. Years ago I used to be entertained by watching *Wall Street Week*, and was humored by the fundamental analysts who would talk endlessly about how they liked to pick good quality companies and hold onto them. They then quickly point out the Ibbotson study that shows that equities have performed at about a 9-plus percent annual rate for the past 100 years. Hogwash! While the study is true, it is totally irrelevant as one does not have a 100-year investment horizon, and is therefore not applicable to humans. Most investors have a good 20-year period in which to make their serious investments. There were many 20-year periods in the past 100 years that resulted in negative or inadequate returns. The most egregious example is if you had bought in 1929, you did not break even until 1954; 25 years later. And guess what, getting even is not what investing is all about.

A good detective will tell you that some of the least reliable information comes from eye witnesses. When people observe an event, it seems their background, education, and other influences unrelated to the observed event, color their perception of what occurred. Most will also be influenced by what they hear from others. This is also amplified by a number of individual studies done by behavior psychologists. In a nutshell, they all agree that groups of people will tend to amplify the consensus view rather than challenge it. A group's ability to focus on common knowledge and uncover anything new is commonplace. Plus the fact that if someone in the group is acknowledged as an expert, their opinion can totally dominate the thinking for the group and can lead to what is known as the *herd* mentality. Talk radio is a perfect example of this.

---

The riskiest moment is when you are right. That's when you're in the most trouble, because you tend to overstay the good decisions.

*Peter Bernstein*

---

I don't want to turn this into a science book, but I am adamant about correcting the proliferation of bad or incorrect information that exists in the financial markets and by showing you similar misconceptions that you may have believed before is the best way to get your attention. In a previous chapter there was a discussion about believable misinformation; if you found that you believed one or more of those misconceptions, then how many market-related ones do you also believe?

Technical analysis will let you deal with reality and keep you from falling victim every time the financial news offers their expert opinion on why the markets did today what they did. I remember when the Indonesian earthquake tidal waves killed thousands of people, but you could not begin to know how many during the initial broadcasts. Most news sources were stating guesses anywhere from 15,000 to well over 150,000. Many news sources cannot even keep the number consistent within their own articles. Do you think they can also tell you why the markets did what they did on a daily basis? Stick to technical analysis, it will increase your understanding of the markets, if only by the fact that you are uncovering information about market behavior.

Here are some comments on technical analysis that I read more than 35 years ago in *The Commodities Futures Game* by Richard Teweles, and believe to be just as valid today. Almost all methods of technical analysis generate useful information, which if used for nothing more than uncovering and organizing facts about market behavior will increase the investor's understanding of the markets. The investor is made painfully aware that technical competence does not ensure competent investing. Speculators who lose money do so not always because of bad analysis, but because of the inability to transform their analysis into sound practice. Bridging the gap between analysis and action requires overcoming the threat of greed, hope, and fear.

Technical analysis is the art of analysis that will keep your emotions from being a part of your investment decision making. While not infallible, it certainly gives you the tools to do so. It will also assist you in overcoming the human traits of ignorance and bliss. Ignorance is an intellectual state and appears to be chronic in many people as regards to the stock market. Bliss is an emotional state and it characterizes many investors as long as the market is going up. Deluded by emotions, one cannot begin to be successful in the investing arena without some means of controlling greed, fear, and hope. This is what I think technical analysis does best.

## Technical Indicators

Those who cannot remember the past are condemned to repeat it.

*George Santayanna*

An indicator is defined by Webster as a pointer or directing device, an instrument for measuring or recording. What then is a technical indicator? Technical indicators are mathematical manipulations of data so that specific values or levels can reflect the market or security being indicated upon (analyzed). There are other types of market indicators that are commonly used, such as: economic time series, interest rates, and so on. Stock market indicators utilize open, high, low, close, volume, and open interest, which are the basic components of stock and futures data.

He who does not know the supreme certainty of mathematics is wallowing in confusion.

*Leonardo da Vinci*

I hope that the mention of mathematics doesn't scare anyone. You don't always have to understand mathematics to know that it will work. Most people believe that Leonardo da Vinci was a mathematician, when he was actually far from it. He had a close friendship with Luca Pacioli, who inspired Leonardo. Leonardo did, however, create a number of mathematical instruments and measuring devices, but his knowledge of mathematics was not exceptional; his friendship with one, whose mathematical knowledge was exceptional, was where the confusion may lie. One word of caution here, do not confuse mathematics with numerology.

One of the first, and possibly still best, indicators is the moving average. In the early days of technical analysis there was only a moving average. It wasn't as specifically defined as it is today by adjectives such as: simple, exponential, weighted, triangular, variable, and so on. Using a columnar pad and a pencil, one could easily calculate a simple (arithmetic) moving average, especially a 10-period simple average. This average smoothed price movements and reduced or eliminated any cyclic action whose period was less than that of the average. In other words, it helped eliminate noise and made the prices easier to follow.

The ability to visually display an indicator made computers the ideal mechanism for significant advances in technical analysis. Today, with most technical analysis software packages, you can manipulate data in their formulary and immediately see the results visually. Incidentally, formulary is a word coined by John Sweeney (Technical Editor, *Stocks & Commodities*), which refers to the system or technique of building or constructing indicators by using predefined mathematical operations and functions.

Remember: Learn not only the capabilities of your technical tools, but more importantly, learn their limitations.

Indicators come in all types: those that indicate overbought and oversold, those that try to follow a trend, those that indicate reversals of trends, those that indicate excess, and a host of others. You can use an indicator without actually knowing the exact mathematical calculations—honest. Display the indicator with the security you want to analyze, using as much data as you can (the more, the better). Attempt to identify times when the indicator reaches a certain threshold or value and the security responds in the same manner. It will be rare to find an indicator that perfectly correlates with the security, so learn to accept something less than 100 percent. Experiment with small changes in the parameters that make up the indicator to see if the results improve. Once you have it where you like it, try it on another security. Yes, you have just discovered one of the difficulties of over fitting an indicator to specific data.

This is commonly referred to as *curve fitting*, which works well in the past and rarely so in the future. That is a statistical reference used when performing regression analysis. It works great on the data being used, but is basically worthless with anything else. That is why so many indicators seem to work on some things and fail miserably on others. This is also quite common among those selling systems and "get rich quick" products.

## Some Things That Bother Me

*Warning!* This section is loaded with my personal opinions.

As I have stated earlier I believe technical analysis is much more art than science; the science part is more related to the process of research than the actual analysis. A lot of esoteric analysis has attached itself to technical analysis, probably because they involve numbers or charts. Before moving forward with this section, I adamantly want to state that with technical analysis being essentially an art; then almost anything goes as long as the user is comfortable with it. Bottom line is that if it works for you, go for it. I guess the engineer in me wants to ensure the methods I use are based on sound and reasonable principles and at most, don't violate any principles of analysis that I believe in. If I hit on something you disagree with, please understand I'm just expressing my personal opinion, which, of course, could be totally wrong. Isaac Asimov was one of my favorite authors, scientists, and researchers. In an article entitled, "The Relativity of Wrong," he used the curvature of the Earth to help explain how differences in perceived facts should be held.

---

When people thought the Earth was flat, they were wrong. When people thought the Earth was spherical, they were wrong. But if you think that thinking the Earth is spherical is just as wrong as thinking the Earth is flat, then your view is wronger than both of them put together. The basic trouble, you see, is that people think that "right" and "wrong" are absolute; that everything that isn't perfectly and completely right is totally and equally wrong.

*Isaac Asimov*

---

In Nate Silver's book, *The Signal and the Noise,* he shows concern about the honest evaluation of the performance of predictive models. We keep being bombarded by stories of data mining, when the facts show that most statistical models have high rates of error, especially true in modern finance. This does not mean they are not useful, but they have a quantifiable chance to fail. (B54) This all goes back to the difference between an art and a science. Technical analysis is an art that can use some scientific processes in its practice. If someone is mathematically inclined such as an engineer or a scientist, then I think the probability of them using technical analysis in its purest form (first order) is more likely than when someone from the arts uses it. While the following comments on various elements of technical analysis (second order) cause me concern, it shouldn't bother you if you disagree on my interpretation of their merits, only the realization that you and I disagree.

---

Criticism is always a kind of compliment.

*John Maddox*

---

## Bold Statements about an Indicator's Value/Worth

An issue that is of concern is when someone makes the statement that an indicator is not good because they have back-tested it. Well, therein is a big problem because not everyone uses an indicator the same way. You cannot judge an indicator's usefulness for someone else, only yourself. As an example, I use stochastics more as a trend measure and normalization measure whereas I think the majority uses it as an over-bought oversold indicator. I also always use stops instead of a reversal signal of the indicator that gave the buy signal, many do not. Therefore, when you hear someone make a bold statement about an indicator's worth, ask them for very specific details on how they tested it.

## Fibonacci Numbers

Often a simple mathematical series of numbers can sometimes get misinterpreted (promoted) to be something magical. My personal favorite sequence is 6, 28, 496, 2,520, 8,128, and 24,601. I'll explain them at the end of this section. Personally, I see no value in the actual numbers that make up the Fibonacci series, a series developed by an Italian mathematician (Fibonacci) in the thirteenth century to help understand the propagation of rabbits. First I must say that I do value the ratio of the numbers that are expanded in a Fibonacci-like series (0, 1, 1, 2, 3, 5, 8, 13, 21, 34, 55, 89, . . .). That ratio is 0.618 (and its reciprocal is 1.618), often called the *golden ratio* because of its wide occurrence in nature, usually with a jaundiced eye. Here is a fact: the actual numbers in the Fibonacci series have little to do with the ratio. Any two numbers expanded in the same manner will produce the same golden ratio. Here is a test: Try it with 2 and 19. Add them together, and then add the total to the previous number just like in the Fibonacci series (2 + 19 = 21, 19 + 21 = 40, 21 + 40 = 61, etc.). Expand this until you get to four digit numbers so that the accuracy will be acceptable (2, 19, 21, 40, 61, 101, 162, 263, 425, 688, 1,113, 1,801, 2,914, 4,716, . . .). The last two numbers in this sequence are the two numbers that I will use for this example: 2,914 and 4,716. Now divide the first number by the second number and you will get 0.618. This is exactly the same as with the value obtained using the Fibonacci series of numbers. So why did I pick 2 and 19 for this example? Hint: The second letter in the alphabet is B. What is the 19th letter? S. BS! And that is what numerology is all about.

I can find no source that explains why the series of Fibonacci numbers begins at zero. If I were tasked with mathematically identifying the propagation of rabbits, I think I would at least have to begin the series at 2. The fact of the matter is that the series can begin anywhere, even negative numbers as long as the expansion follows the correct formula. It is the ratio that is important, not the actual numbers in the series. So, when you hear someone say they are going to use a 34-day moving average because 34 is a Fibonacci number, you can immediately begin to doubt the rest of their analysis. Just so you know: the Fibonacci expansion of 1 plus the square root of 5 divided by 2 will work with any two numbers, even negative numbers. Sorry, no magic here, just numerology. As far as Elliott Wave theory goes, there are often so many complications and conditions introduced into using this type of analysis, that it is incapable of being proved wrong. Sometimes I think it gets adjusted more often than earnings estimates. However, it is always convincing to align the workings of the market with what appears to be pure mathematics. In the series of numbers introduced at the beginning of this section, 6, 28, 496, and 8,128, are known as perfect numbers; this means the sum of their divisors (other than the number itself) is also equal to the number. For example: $6 = 1 + 2 + 3$, and $28 = 1 + 2 + 4 + 7 + 14$. I like 2,520 because it is the smallest integer than is divisible by all integers from 1 to 10 inclusive. Finally, I like 24,601 as it is the prisoner number of Jean Valjean from Victor Hugo's *Les Misérables*. Incidentally, 24,601 has prime factors of 73 and 337. I like these numbers solely for their mathematical uniqueness; and like many number sequences, they have no use in technical market analysis. Possibly Keno!

## Retracements

Many use the Fibonacci ratio for percentage retracements. These retracements are generally derivations and powers of the expansion formula 1 plus the square root of 5 divided by 2. They are generated by looking at ratios of the supposed Fibonacci numbers themselves, such as dividing any number by the one that immediately follows it, which yields the popular 0.618. The complement of that is 0.382, which can also be found by dividing any number in the series by the number two places later in the sequence. 0.236 is often used as it is created by dividing any number by the number that is three places later in the series. I have often wondered where the 0.50 ratio came from; it is just the ratio of the second (1) and third (2) number in the series. I'm not sure that this process could ever end. Add to the Fibonacci retracements, those of Edson Gould, which were 33 percent and 67 percent, and all of a sudden, with some percentage of error involved, you have covered over 50 percent of the entire data being analyzed—a coin toss would be better. I could carry this further by adding the retracement values of others; Gann comes to mind. The bottom line is simply that with enough percentage retracements provided, one of them is bound to be close to a reversal point, however, you won't know which one it is until you invoke hindsight.

## Reversal and Continuation Patterns

If I drew a pattern that looked like a head and shoulders pattern on a white board, most would be able to identify it. However, if it is a reversal pattern (which the head and shoulders pattern is), then shouldn't it be reversing something? It should appear in an uptrend. If not, one is working in isolation and will be often wrong.

Figure 9.2 is a picture of a classic pattern known as a *head and shoulders top* pattern. However, I challenge this type of labeling because we don't know if it is in an uptrend or not. If the graphic showed an uptrend in prices preceding the pattern with at least as much price movement as the neckline to the head, then I would agree that this is a head and shoulders top. There is no difference with Japanese candle patterns, a subject I have written endlessly about in the third edition of my *Candlestick Charting Explained*, in which I took an engineering approach to validate the patterns and wrote honestly about them. Classic chart patterns or candlestick patterns used in isolation are dangerous. If they are reversal patterns, then they must reverse something, and that is the preceding trend.

Figure 9.3 is a Japanese candle pattern known as the *evening star*. It is a bearish reversal pattern because it reverses an uptrend—as shown by the three vertical lines

**FIGURE 9.2**  Head and Shoulders Top?

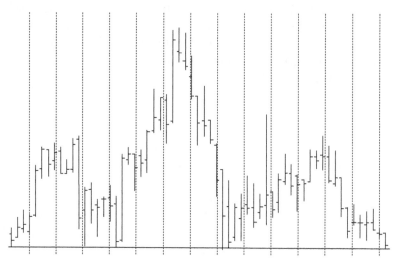

*Source:* Chart courtesy of MetaStock.

**FIGURE 9.3**  Japanese Evening Star Pattern?

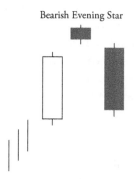

Bearish Evening Star

preceding it. If those uptrend lines were not there, I would say that this pattern looks like an evening star, but until we know what trend it is in, cannot say for sure.

The same exact analysis can be attributed to continuation patterns, both classical and candlestick. If a bullish continuation pattern is identified, please ensure that it is in an uptrend, otherwise it is not a bullish continuation pattern.

## Japanese Candle Patterns

I spent a considerable amount of time in Japan with my friend Takehiro Hikita in the early 1990s. He translated most of the Japanese books on candle patterns and was insistent on me learning exactly how they should be interpreted and used. I cannot tell you how often I see candle patterns being misused, including the previous topic on not identifying a trend first. Why are single-day candle patterns not recommended for trading? Every day the market sends a message. Here is what I say about single day candlesticks: They are not candle patterns in that they allow you to see the evolution of trader psychology through multiple days like you can with more complex candle patterns. I also say single candlesticks still send a message that should neither be traded nor ignored. Can you use candle patterns on intraday or weekly data? Of course you can; however, I don't recommend it. The Japanese were adamant about the period of time between the close of one day and the open of the next day as being critically important to the psychological evolution of traders in developing the pattern. With intraday charts, that time period is just the next data tick, not a lot of time to develop a thought. Weekly candlesticks truly voids the concept as the open is Monday's open, the close is Friday's close, the high is the high for the week (could occur on any day), and the low is the low for the week (again, it could occur on any day of the week). In fact, the open, high, and low could all occur on Monday, with the close on Friday. The trading activity for the last four days of the week would not be seen in a weekly candlestick. However, as with any art form, if it works for you, use it.

## Analyzing Time Series That Does Not Trade

Can you do technical analysis on a time series that doesn't trade? For example, I see a lot of moving averages, trendlines, and support and resistance lines on charts of economic data like the Baltic Dry Index, the advance decline line, or the Index of Leading Indicators. Does the Baltic Dry Index trade? How about the Index of Leading Indicators? Are investors/traders making investment/trading decisions on the data that makes up that index? How can something that is not traded have support and resistance? It can't, it is just analysis by those who truly don't understand what they are doing. Computer software has caused a lot of this and new (sometimes older) analysts are analyzing every chart they see—most in futility. I think much of it is because they are just playing with their software.

Almost all references on supply and demand are directly tied to price. This involves the pricing of goods and services, as well as securities. It seems that some analysts have not understood this concept and draw trendlines all over a chart without any real understanding as to what it is they are trying to accomplish, unless, of course, it is to support (sic) their hypotheses.

## Support and Resistance

Can you use support and resistance for oscillators, ratios, and accumulated or summed values like you do with price-based issues? I believe this is carrying the supply and demand analysis a little too far, yet many analysts are doing it. Can an oscillator made up of internal breadth components have a support line or a resistance line? No, but it can reach certain levels on a consistent basis and if that is what is being represented, then so be it, but it is not support or resistance. Similarly, I see some who will draw trendlines across moving average peaks or troughs. This is irrelevant analysis and does not represent any type of support or resistance. Like most things, there are exceptions to all this. An analyst may point out that the 200-day moving average offers support for the issue being analyzed. This may well hold out to be true, only because of that particular moving average's popularity. It probably would not hold true if an average that is less familiar or a totally random average were picked, say 163 periods.

Also, and in fairness to these analysts, drawing trendlines on some indicators such as the advance decline line is not done to identify support and resistance, but to assist the analyst in identifying divergence with price. This is one reason drawing trendlines on rates of change oscillators is not support and resistance identification.

The message is simple: If it does not trade, don't do technical analysis on it.

## Multicollinearity

If you find a group of indicators that are essentially telling you the same thing and with consistency, you need to pick one of them to use and then drop the others. If they are all saying the same thing they are not assisting you in your analysis. This is known as *multicollinearity* and is a trap you need to avoid. Ensure that you are using indicators that measure the markets differently, and are diversified. While breadth indicators are different than most price-based indicators, there are many price and breadth indicators that are essentially revealing the same thing.

Table 9.1 is from Stockcharts.com's Chart School showing the various categories with a few samples of the indicators contained in each category.

**TABLE 9.1**  Multicollinearity Example

| Category | Indicators |
| --- | --- |
| Momentum | Rate of Change |
| | Stochastics |
| | Relative Strength Index |
| | Commodity Channel Index |
| | Williams %R |
| | Chande StochRSI |
| | Hutson TRIX |
| | Ultimate Oscillator |
| | Aroon |
| Trend | Moving Averages |
| | Moving Average Convergence Divergence |
| | Average True Range |
| | Wilder's DMI and ADX |
| | Price Oscillator |
| Volume | Accumulation Distribution |
| | Chaikin Money Flow |
| | Volume Rate of Change |
| | Volume Oscillator |
| | Demand Index |
| | On Balance Volume |
| | Money Flow Index |

Many times, investors think that they are more correct in their analysis if many indicators are telling them the same thing (see section on behavioral biases and in particular confirmation bias). They are supportive of your analysis only if the indicators are not collinear. If they are collinear, then the support the investor feels from having a lot of indications agree is misleading and dangerous. The support for their analysis gives them a false confidence. This occurs in many things, more information is not always better information.

## Analysis versus Reporting

Are you an investor or a story teller?

*Barry Ritholtz*

I see hundreds of charts with analysis on the Internet, newsletters, and many are sent to me for feedback. More often than not, I see a beautiful example of the analyst unknowingly utilizing the remarkable and always correct technique of hindsight. A beautiful chart with some indicators is presented and the analysis discusses the signals from the indicator or an obvious divergence between the prices and the indicator, but sadly all that took place a few weeks ago or more. Identification of chart patterns, whether classical or candlestick, usually only occur sometime after they have matured and often too late to act on. Analysis is accomplished at the cold hard right-hand edge of the chart. Reporting is the analysis that is accomplished elsewhere on the chart. Hindsight is great for observable information about how markets and techniques reacted in the past, but it never works for tomorrow. Learn from the past, just don't trade from it.

## Analog Charts

My main problem is that they are an example of recency bias. Recency bias was defined in Chapter 6, but is related to thinking one can determine the next color on a roulette wheel from observation. The market is impacted by events each year that affect the decision making of investors and rarely, if ever, do these types of events reoccur. Often I have observed analog charts with huge amounts of data where the small arrows used to point out the correlation can be many months in width. Remember, it might rhyme, but it doesn't repeat. In support of analog charts, the fact of which I agree is that investor behavior does repeat and repeat often and this alone may be the true benefit of analog charts.

## Polls and Surveys

With the Internet and 24/7 media, there are polls and surveys for everything imaginable. Rarely are the actual questions presented to the viewer, only the results with an error probability, which I think they just make up to add to the credibility of the poll. If you have ever tracked the polls over time, you know that rarely is there any timely information, and more than likely there is never any actionable information. If you see the results that you do not like, change the channel or go to another website. Poll and survey questions can be constructed in a way to generate the answers that the pollster desires. This is called *framing* and is mentioned elsewhere in this book.

## Miscellaneous

There are a number of analysis techniques that have attached themselves to technical analysis that I do not use. I have spent a lot of time in the early days studying them, and decided they were not for me as they involve entirely too much subjectivity in their process. Although I think some analysts use them beneficially, I think most will never be able to do so. Some have to be restated more often than earnings reports. Here are some questions for those who believe full moons affect investors: When is the moon not full? If the sky is overcast, is it still a full moon? If it is a full moon in Texas, is it a full moon in India? A full moon is solely based on the relationship of the observer and the light of the sun shining on it. In other words, you must know where you are on Earth in order to know when there will be a full moon. Ironically, the most perfect full moon is when it is in a lunar eclipse, an event in which the Earth blocks the sun from illuminating the moon. Just something to think about! And to correlate market events to full moons is downright scary—a classic case of mistaking correlation with causation.

Cyclical events, those with consistent periodicity such as planets and other orbiting bodies, especially those with human identified frequency, say the Moon, which orbits Earth every 28 days (27.322 to be exact) can cause many examples of apparent correlation, but woefully short on causation. Just think of all the human-like events that occur once per month! And I'm not even going to address the issue of whether viewing the orbit from Earth or elsewhere.

Seasonality is popular among some, but I always want to ask them just one simple question: Would you actually make a trading decision based solely upon seasonality? Most will say they use it to help confirm, and that has merit. Just because February 25 has historically been a good day for the stock market, does not mean it will be a good one this year. An often touted example is the "sell in May and go away," where there is significant statistical proof that the period from May through October performs worse than the November through April period. I have dealt with using statistics in earlier chapters so you know my opinion on this; seasonality is just statistics. In my opinion, seasonality is a perfect example of observable information; you just can't make a trading decision based on it.

Let's say you tested the "Sell in May" concept by first choosing exactly when to sell and exactly when to buy again in November and the results over the past 60 years shows it worked 75 percent of the time. I'm not even going to address the issue of how to determine "it worked" but only that it was profitable on an absolute basis. Now, armed with that statistic, would you actually sell in May and buy again next November? I seriously doubt it. It just might be the beginning of a period of time that contributes to the 25 percent of the time it doesn't work—maybe for the next four to five years. Would you stick with it? Of course not, investing decisions based solely on statistical evidence are unsound.

A mechanically inclined person can make a reasonable assumption about how a clock works even though having never seen the inside of one. Even with the addition of drawings and descriptions about how it works, one can probably get it very close to being correct. However, until one sees the actual workings, one is never really quite certain.

My opinions on these esoteric analysis techniques are directly tied to my use of technical analysis to actually manage money. I do, however, believe those who use technical analysis to make forecasts, find these techniques easy to use and justify.

And finally, no indicator is right all of the time; fortunately you don't have to be right all of the time. You just need to ensure that you do not hold onto losers and keep your emotions out of the game. Choose some good reliable indicators and stick with them. Learn how they respond during different market environments and master the interpretation of them. And remember, when your favorite indicator fails you, avoid thinking that this time is different, it probably is not.

It is time to move from some of my strong opinions about the market to research into how to determine if a market trends whether it be up, down, or both and then a convincing section on what truly is risk. I strongly believe risk is the loss of capital and not volatility as the "world of finance" would have you believe.

# CHAPTER 10

# Market Trend Analysis

This chapter focuses on trends in the market—an explanation as to why markets trend, reasons why it is good to know that markets trend, then finally, a large research section into how much markets trend. This analysis will initially be shown on 109 market indices that involve domestic, international, and commodity sectors. Following that the full list of all S&P GICS sectors, industry groups, and industries are shown following the same format. There is a great amount of data in this chapter. I try to slice through it with simple analysis, keeping in mind that lots of data does not equate to information.

## Why Markets Trend

Trends in markets are generally caused by short-term supply and demand imbalances with a heavy overdose of human emotion. When you buy a stock, you know that someone had to sell it to you. If the market has been rising recently, then you know you will probably pay a higher price for it and the seller also knows he can get a higher price for it. The buying enthusiasm is much greater than the selling enthusiasm. I hate it when the financial media makes a comment when the market is down by saying that there are more sellers than buyers. They clearly do not understand how these markets work. Based on shares there are always the same number of buyers and sellers; it is the buying and selling enthusiasm that changes. Finally, trending is a positive feedback process. Even Isaac Newton believed in trends with his first law of motion, which stated an object at rest stays at rest and an object in motion stays in motion with the same speed and in the same direction unless acted on by an unbalanced force. Hey, an apple will continue to fall until it hits the ground. Positive feedback is the direct result of an investor's confidence in the price trend. When prices rise, investors confidently buy into higher and higher prices.

## Supply and Demand

A buyer of a stock, which is the *demand*, bids for a certain amount of stock at a certain price. A seller, which is the *supply*, offers a certain amount at a certain price. I think it is fair to say that one buys a stock with the anticipation that they can sell it later to someone at a higher price. Not an unreasonable desire, and probably what drives most investors. The buyer has no idea who will sell it to him, or why they would sell it to him. He may assume that he and the seller have a complete disagreement on the future value of that stock. And that might be correct, however, the buyer will never know. In fact, the buyer just might be the seller's person who buys it from him at a higher price.

The reasons for buying and selling stock are complex and impossible to quantify. However when they eventually agree, what is it that they agreed on? Was it the earnings of the company? Was it the products the company produces? Was it the management team? Was it the amount of the stock's dividend? Was it the sales revenues? It was none of those things, the transaction was settled because they agreed on the price of the stock, and that alone determines profit or loss. Changes in supply and demand are reflected immediately in price, which is an instantaneous assessment of supply and demand.

## What Do You Know about This Chart?

In Figure 10.1 I have removed the price scale, the dates, and the name of this issue; now let me ask you some questions about this issue.

1. Is this a chart of daily prices, weekly prices, or 30-minute prices?
2. Is this a chart of a stock, a commodity, or a market index?

Okay, I'll give you this much, it is a daily price chart of a stock over a period of about six years. Now, some more questions:

**FIGURE 10.1**  Chart without Price, Name, or Dates

*Source:* Chart courtesy of MetaStock.

3. During this period of time, there were 11 earnings announcements. Can you show me where one of those announcements occurred and if you could, were the earnings report considered good or bad?
4. Also during the period of time for this chart, there were seven Federal Open Market Committee (FOMC) announcements. Can you tell me where one of them occurred and was the announcement considered good or bad?
5. Does this stock pay a dividend?
6. Hurricane Katrina occurred during this period displayed on this chart, can you tell me where it is?
7. Finally, would you want to buy this stock at the beginning of the period displayed and then sell it at the end of the period (right side of chart)?

I doubt, in fact, I *know* you cannot answer most of the above questions with any tool other than guessing. The point of this exercise is to point out that there is always and ever noise in stock prices. This noise comes in hundreds of different colors, sizes, shapes, and media formats. The bottom line is that it is just noise. The financial media bombards us all day long with noise. I do not think they do it maliciously; they do it because they believe they are giving you valuable information to help you make investment decisions. Nothing could be further from the truth. Of course, question number 7 is the one question that most can answer because from the chart a buy-and-hold investment during the data displayed clearly resulted in no investment growth.

However, let me tell you what I see as shown in Figure 10.2. I see two really good uptrends and if I had a trend-following methodology that could capture 65 percent

**FIGURE 10.2** Chart with Only Trends

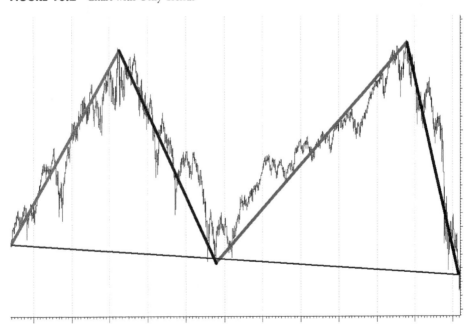

*Source:* Chart courtesy of MetaStock.

to 75 percent of those uptrends I would be happy. I also see two good downtrends, and if I had a methodology that could avoid about 75 percent of them, I would also be happy. If you could do that for the amount of time shown on the chart below, then you would come out considerably better off than the buy and hold investor. I generally only participate in the long side of the market and move to cash or cash equivalents when defensive. However, a long–short strategy could possibly derive even greater profit.

## Trend versus Mean Reversion

I prefer to use a market analysis methodology called *trend following*. Sometimes it should be called *trend continuation*. Why? Trend analysis works on the thoroughly researched concept that once a trend is identified, it has a reasonable probability to continue. I know that is the case because most of the time markets are trending markets and I see no reason to adopt a different strategy during a period of mean reverting, such as is experienced in the market from time to time. You can think of trend following as a positive feedback mechanism. Mean reverting measures are those that oscillate between predetermined parameters; oftentimes the selection of those parameters is the problem. Mean reversion strategies are clearly superior during those volatile sideways times but the implementation of a mean reverting process requires a level of guessing that I refuse to be a part of. You can think of mean reversion as a negative feedback mechanism.

In technical analysis there are many mean reverting measures that could be used. They are the ones where you frequently hear the terms overbought and oversold. Overbought means the measurement shows that prices have moved upward to a limit that is predefined. Oversold means the opposite: prices have moved down to a predetermined level. The problem with that type of indicator or measurement is that a parameter needs to be set beforehand to know what the overbought and oversold levels are. Also, if you believe something mean reverts, you will probably have difficulty in determining the rate of reversion. For mean reversion to be relevant, there must be a meaning tied to average (mean) and since most market data does not adhere to normal distributions, the mean isn't as meaningful (sic). Kind of like charting net worth and removing billionaires to make the data less skewed and therefore a more meaningful average.

Clearly, mean reverting measurements would work better in highly volatile markets, such as we witness from time to time. One might ask the question: Why don't you incorporate both into your model? A fair question, but one that shows the inquiry is forgetting that hindsight is not an analysis tool that will serve you well. When do you switch from one strategy (trend following) to the other (mean reversion)? Therein lays the problem.

Another question that might be asked is why not use adaptive measures to help identify the two types of markets. Again, another fair question! I think the lag between the two types of markets and the fact that often there is no clear period of delineation is the issue. It is a natural instinct to want to change the strategy in order to respond more quickly from one to the other. Natural instincts are what we are trying to avoid, simply because they are generally wrong, and painfully wrong at the worst times.

The transition from trend following to mean reversion can be difficult to see except with 20/20 hindsight. For example, when you view a chart, which clearly has gone from trending to reversion, from that point if we had used a simple mean reverting measurement, we would have looked like geniuses. However, in reality, periods like that have existed many times in the past in overall trending markets. Then the next problem becomes when to move away from a mean reverting strategy back to a trend following one. Again, hindsight always gives the precise answer, but in reality it is extremely difficult to implement in real time.

The bottom line is that with markets that generally trend most of the time, keeping a set of rules and stop loss levels in place, will probably always win over the long term. Sharpshooting the process is the beginning of the end. Trend following is somewhat similar to a momentum strategy except for two significant differences. One, momentum strategies generally rank past performance for selection, and two, often they do not utilize stop-loss methods, instead move in and out of top performers. They both rely on the persistence of price behavior.

## Trend Analysis

If one is going to be a trend follower, what is the first thing that must be done (rhetorical)? In order to be a trend follower you must first determine the minimum length trend you want to identify. You cannot follow every little up and down move in the market; you must decide what the minimum trend length is that you want to follow. Once this is done, you can then develop trend-following indicators using parameters that will help identify trends in the market based on the minimum length you have decided on.

Figure 10.3 is an example of various trend-following periods. The top plot is the Nasdaq Composite index. The second plot is a filtered wave showing the trend analysis for a fairly short-term–oriented trend system. This is for traders and those who want to try to capture every small up and down in the market; a process that is not adopted by this author. The third plot is the ideal trend system, where it is obvious that you buy at the long-term bottom and sell at the long-term top. You must realize that this trend analysis can *only* be done with perfect 20/20 hindsight, and is probably even more difficult than the short-term process shown in the second plot. The bottom plot is a trend analysis process that is at the heart of the concepts discussed in this book. It is a trend-following process that realizes you cannot participate in every small up and down move, but try to capture most of the up moves and avoid most of the down moves.

There is a concept developed by the late Arthur Merrill called Filtered Waves. (B40) A filtered wave is the measurement of price movements in which only the movement that exceeds a predetermined percentage is counted. The price component used in this concept needs to be decided on as to whether to use just the closing prices

**FIGURE 10.3**   Trend Length and Frequency

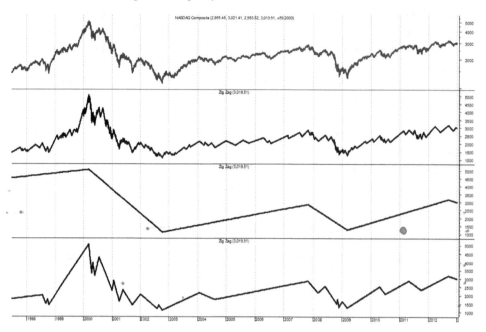

*Source:* Chart courtesy of MetaStock.

for the filtered wave or use a combination of high and low prices. This would mean that while prices are rising the high would be used and while prices are falling the low price would be used. I personally prefer the high and low prices as they truly reflect the price movements, whereas the closing prices only would eliminate some of the data. For example, in Figure 10.4, the background plot is the S&P 500 Index with both the close C and the high low H-L filtered waves overlaid on the prices. You can see that the H-L filtered wave techniques picks up more of the data; in fact, it shows a move of 5 percent in the middle of the plot that the Close only version did not show. In this particular example the zigzag line uses a filter of 5 percent, which means that each time it changes direction, it had previously moved at least 5 percent in the opposite direction. There is one exception to this and that is the last move of the zigzag line (there is a similar discussion in an earlier chapter). It merely moves to the most recent close regardless of the percentage moved so it must be ignored.

The bottom plot in Figure 10.5 shows the filtered wave by breaking down the up moves and down moves and then counting the number of periods that were in each move. There are three horizontal lines on that plot, the middle one is at zero, which is where the filtered wave changes direction. In this example the top and bottom lines are at +21 and −21 periods, which mean that anytime the filtered wave exceeds those lines above or below, the trend has lasted at least 21 periods. Notice that in this example there was a period at the beginning (highlighted) where the market moved up and down in 5 percent or greater moves with high frequency but never lasted long enough to exceed the 21 boundaries. Then in the second half of the chart, there were

**FIGURE 10.4** Difference between Filtered Wave Using Close and High–Low

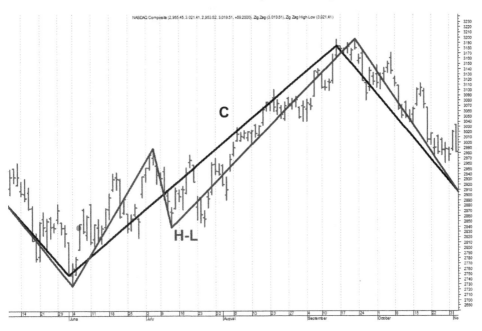

*Source:* Chart courtesy of MetaStock.

**FIGURE 10.5** Trend Analysis Example

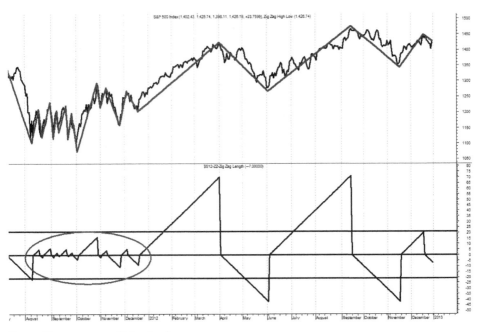

*Source:* Chart courtesy of MetaStock.

two good moves that did exceed the 21 boundaries. This is a good example of a chart where there was a trendless market (first half) and a trending market (second half). I used the high–low filtered wave of 5 percent and 21 days for the minimum length because that is what I prefer to use for most trend analysis.

The following research was conducted using the high–low filtered wave using various percentages and various trend length measures. The research was conducted on a wide variety of market prices, such as most domestic indices, most foreign indices, all of the S&P sectors and industry groups; 109 issues in all. I offer commentary throughout so you can see that this was a robust process. Any indices or price series that is missing was probably because of an inadequate amount of data, as you need a few years of data to determine a series' trendiness. The goal of this research was to determine that markets generally trend and if there are some markets that trend better than others. Following this large section, the trend analysis will be shown using the S&P GICS data on sectors, industry groups, and industries.

Table 10.1 is the complete list of indices used in this study along with the beginning date of the data.

**TABLE 10.1**   Indices Used in Trend Analysis

| Index Name | Start Date |
| --- | --- |
| AMEX Composite | 12/27/1995 |
| AMEX Oil Index | 10/25/1984 |
| AMEX Pharmaceutical Index | 4/21/1992 |
| Argentina MerVal | 6/3/1991 |
| Australia All Ordinaries | 1/4/1982 |
| Austria ATX | 10/28/1991 |
| Belgium BEL-20 | 1/2/1992 |
| Brazil Bovespa | 11/22/1996 |
| Chile IGPA General Index | 12/4/1996 |
| Chile IPSA | 12/4/1996 |
| China Shanghai Composite | 12/19/1990 |
| CRB Index | 1/2/1980 |
| Czech Republic PX | 7/16/2004 |
| Denmark Copenhagen 20 | 2/2/2001 |
| DJ Wilshire US Small Cap | 3/14/2005 |
| Dow Industrials 1885 | 02/17/1885 |
| Dow Jones Composite | 1/3/1995 |
| Dow Jones Euro Stoxx | 2/17/1998 |
| Dow Jones Euro Stoxx 50 | 3/2/1998 |
| Dow Jones Stoxx | 2/17/1998 |
| Dow Jones Transport | 1/2/1990 |
| Dow Jones Utilities | 1/2/1990 |
| Dow Jones Wilshire 5000 Composite Index | 11/10/1980 |
| Dow Jones Wilshire REIT Index | 5/3/2004 |
| Dow Jones Wilshire REIT Total Return Index | 5/3/2004 |
| Egypt CMA | 1/27/1999 |
| EURONEXT 100 | 3/15/2002 |
| Finland HSE General Index | 3/1/1991 |

**TABLE 10.1**  Continued

| Index Name | Start Date |
| --- | --- |
| France CAC 40 | 8/19/1988 |
| Germany DAX | 12/14/1993 |
| Global Dow | 9/12/2008 |
| Gold and Silver Mining | 12/20/1983 |
| Gold Base Price Handy & Harman | 1/30/1920 |
| Gold Bugs (AMEX) | 5/6/1996 |
| Gold Mining Stocks | 9/17/1993 |
| Greece General Share | 1/2/1991 |
| Hanoi SE Index | 4/21/2009 |
| Healthcare Index (S&P) | 4/29/2002 |
| Hong Kong Hang Seng | 1/4/1982 |
| Ibex 35 | 9/6/1991 |
| India BSE 30 | 1/1/1990 |
| Indonesia Jakarta Composite | 4/6/1990 |
| Israel TA-100 | 6/17/1996 |
| Italy FTSE MIB Index | 4/3/2003 |
| Japan Nikkei 225 | 1/4/1982 |
| Johannesburg All Shares | 4/22/2002 |
| Major Market Index | 4/15/1983 |
| Malaysia KLSE Composite | 1/4/1982 |
| Mexico IPC | 1/2/1987 |
| Morgan Stanley Consumer Index | 10/23/1992 |
| Morgan Stanley Cyclical Index | 10/23/1992 |
| MSCI EAFE | 12/31/1969 |
| MSCI EM | 12/31/1987 |
| NASDAQ 100 | 2/4/1985 |
| NASDAQ Composite | 2/5/1971 |
| Netherlands AEX General | 1/3/1983 |
| Norway Oslo All Share Composite | 2/5/2001 |
| Norway Oslo OBX Top 25 | 9/21/2004 |
| NYSE Composite | 12/31/1965 |
| Pakistan Karachi 100 | 5/25/1994 |
| Peru Lima General | 1/27/1999 |
| Philippines PSE Composite | 1/2/1987 |
| Russell 1000 | 6/29/1987 |
| Russell 1000 Growth | 8/31/1992 |
| Russell 1000 Value | 8/31/1992 |
| Russell 2000 | 12/29/1978 |
| Russell 2000 Growth | 12/29/1978 |
| Russell 2000 Value | 12/29/1978 |
| Russell 3000 | 6/29/1987 |
| S&P 100 Index | 1/2/1976 |
| S&P 1500 INDEX | 8/30/2001 |
| S&P 400 Index | 3/11/1992 |
| S&P 500 Index | 12/30/1927 |
| S&P 500 Total Return | 1/4/1988 |
| S&P 600 Index | 11/21/1994 |
| S&P CNX NIFTY (India) | 2/8/2000 |
| S&P Cons Discretionary Sector | 9/11/1989 |
| S&P Cons Staples Sector | 9/11/1989 |

*(Continued)*

**TABLE 10.1**  Continued

| Index Name | Start Date |
|---|---|
| S&P Energy Sector | 9/11/1989 |
| S&P Equal Weight | 11/7/2000 |
| S&P Financials Sector | 9/11/1989 |
| S&P Healthcare Sector | 9/11/1989 |
| S&P Industrials Sector | 9/11/1989 |
| S&P Materials Sector | 9/11/1989 |
| S&P MIDCAP INDEX | 1/2/1981 |
| S&P Technology Sector | 9/11/1989 |
| S&P Telecomm Sector | 9/11/1989 |
| S&P Utilities Sector | 9/11/1989 |
| S&P/TSX 60 CAPPED (Canada) | 11/20/2000 |
| S&P/TSX 60 INDEX (Canada) | 12/31/1998 |
| S&P/TSX Composite (Canada) | 1/2/1980 |
| Silver Base Price Handy & Harman | 2/15/1996 |
| Singapore Straits Times | 8/31/1999 |
| Slovakia SAX | 1/27/1999 |
| South Korea Seoul Composite | 5/3/1983 |
| S&P 500 Tot Ret Inflation Adj | 1/4/1988 |
| Spain Madrid General | 8/1/1984 |
| Sri Lanka All Share | 6/14/1993 |
| Swedish OMX 30 | 9/30/1986 |
| Switzerland Swiss Market | 1/4/1988 |
| Taiwan Weighted | 1/5/1981 |
| Thailand SET | 1/4/1982 |
| Turkey ISE National-100 | 1/4/1988 |
| United Kingdom FTSE 100 | 1/3/1984 |
| US Dollar Index | 11/8/1985 |
| Value Line Index (Arithmetic) | 1/2/1980 |
| Value Line Index (Geometric) | 12/15/1983 |
| Venezuela IBC | 12/31/1993 |
| Viet Nam Index | 5/13/2002 |

Because of space limitations in a book, I had to break up the giant spreadsheets that were used for this trend analysis. Hopefully, it will be clear with the commentary associated with each table.

I did multiple sets of data runs, but will explain the process by showing just one of them. Table 10.2 is the data run through all 109 indices for the 5 percent filtered wave and 21 days for the trend to be identified. The first column is the name of the index (they are in alphabetical order), the next four columns are the results of the data runs for the total trend percentage, the uptrend percentage, the downtrend percentage, and the ratio of uptrends to downtrends.

Total reflects the amount of time relative to the amount of all data available that the index was in a trend mode defined by the filtered wave and trend time; in the case below a trend had to last at least 21 days and a move of 5 percent or greater. The up

**TABLE 10.2** Trends of 21 Days with 5 Percent Filter

| All | 21 Day/5% | | | |
|---|---|---|---|---|
| Index Name | Total | Up | Down | U/D Ratio |
| AMEX Composite | 71.18 | 56.16 | 15.03 | 3.74 |
| AMEX Oil Index | 62.97 | 41.86 | 21.11 | 1.98 |
| AMEX Pharmaceutical Index | 70.91 | 44.5 | 26.41 | 1.69 |
| Argentina MerVal | 33.23 | 24.22 | 9.012 | 2.69 |
| Australia All Ordinaries | 84.78 | 59.6 | 25.18 | 2.37 |
| Austria ATX | 64.6 | 47.03 | 17.57 | 2.68 |
| Belgium BEL-20 | 67.4 | 46.36 | 21.04 | 2.20 |
| Brazil Bovespa | 33.67 | 28.01 | 5.658 | 4.95 |
| Chile IGPA General Index | 87.35 | 54.51 | 32.83 | 1.66 |
| Chile IPSA | 70.06 | 44.17 | 25.89 | 1.71 |
| China Shanghai Composite | 48.85 | 25.72 | 23.13 | 1.11 |
| CRB Index | 87.57 | 53.45 | 34.12 | 1.57 |
| Czech Republic PX | 58.61 | 36.88 | 21.73 | 1.70 |
| Denmark Copenhagen 20 | 57.15 | 44.97 | 12.18 | 3.69 |
| DJ Wilshire US Small Cap | 55.88 | 45.85 | 10.03 | 4.57 |
| Dow Industrials 1885 | 76.98 | 55.06 | 21.93 | 2.51 |
| Dow Jones Composite | 71.66 | 50.2 | 21.46 | 2.34 |
| Dow Jones Euro Stoxx | 57.03 | 42.47 | 14.56 | 2.92 |
| Dow Jones Euro Stoxx 50 | 50.21 | 38.39 | 11.82 | 3.25 |
| Dow Jones Stoxx | 64.87 | 48.45 | 16.42 | 2.95 |
| Dow Jones Transport | 53.42 | 39.15 | 14.26 | 2.74 |
| Dow Jones Utilities | 75.64 | 54.77 | 20.87 | 2.62 |
| DJ Wilshire 5000 Composite | 81.47 | 59.02 | 22.45 | 2.63 |
| Dow Jones Wilshire REIT | 50.94 | 42.01 | 8.925 | 4.71 |
| DJ Wilshire REIT Total Return | 52.2 | 44.28 | 7.921 | 5.59 |
| Egypt CMA | 67.41 | 50.87 | 16.53 | 3.08 |
| EURONEXT 100 | 58.62 | 47.67 | 10.95 | 4.35 |
| Finland HSE General Index | 52.78 | 36.63 | 16.15 | 2.27 |
| France CAC 40 | 56.3 | 41.43 | 14.88 | 2.78 |
| Germany DAX | 53.21 | 43.04 | 10.17 | 4.23 |
| Global Dow | 64.43 | 45.04 | 19.39 | 2.32 |
| Gold and Silver Mining | 18.27 | 8.126 | 10.15 | 0.80 |
| Gold Base Price Handy & Harman | 46.38 | 25.17 | 21.21 | 1.19 |
| Gold Bugs (AMEX) | 13.85 | 6.805 | 7.044 | 0.97 |
| Gold Mining Stocks | 30.22 | 14.97 | 15.26 | 0.98 |
| Greece General Share | 48.61 | 29.53 | 19.08 | 1.55 |
| Hanoi SE Index | 34.7 | 8.944 | 25.75 | 0.35 |
| Healthcare Index (S&P) | 74.1 | 48.34 | 25.75 | 1.88 |
| Hong Kong Hang Seng | 56.3 | 40.35 | 15.95 | 2.53 |
| Ibex 35 | 50.86 | 38.04 | 12.82 | 2.97 |
| India BSE 30 | 42.16 | 30.12 | 12.04 | 2.50 |
| Indonesia Jakarta Composite | 64.65 | 44.16 | 20.49 | 2.16 |
| Israel TA-100 | 63.88 | 46.81 | 17.07 | 2.74 |
| Italy FTSE MIB Index | 54.22 | 41.87 | 12.35 | 3.39 |
| Japan Nikkei 225 | 62.79 | 43.93 | 18.86 | 2.33 |
| Johannesburg All Shares | 61.24 | 51.91 | 9.333 | 5.56 |

*(Continued)*

**TABLE 10.2** Continued

| All | 21 Day/5% | | | |
|---|---|---|---|---|
| Index Name | Total | Up | Down | U/D Ratio |
| Major Market Index | 74.82 | 55.55 | 19.28 | 2.88 |
| Malaysia KLSE Composite | 73.46 | 50.2 | 23.26 | 2.16 |
| Mexico IPC | 53.87 | 43.18 | 10.68 | 4.04 |
| Morgan Stanley Consumer Index | 80.56 | 60.7 | 19.86 | 3.06 |
| Morgan Stanley Cyclical Index | 58.98 | 44.76 | 14.23 | 3.15 |
| MSCI EAFE | 84.76 | 56.48 | 28.28 | 2.00 |
| MSCI EM | 76.57 | 54.06 | 22.51 | 2.40 |
| NASDAQ 100 | 54.28 | 40.96 | 13.33 | 3.07 |
| NASDAQ Composite | 73.67 | 50.23 | 23.44 | 2.14 |
| Netherlands AEX General | 67.81 | 50.14 | 17.67 | 2.84 |
| Norway Oslo All Share Composite | 64.01 | 51.16 | 12.86 | 3.98 |
| Norway Oslo OBX Top 25 | 48.37 | 40.84 | 7.526 | 5.43 |
| NYSE Composite | 84.77 | 59.02 | 25.74 | 2.29 |
| Pakistan Karachi 100 | 53.13 | 37.87 | 15.26 | 2.48 |
| Peru Lima General | 71.67 | 43.77 | 27.9 | 1.57 |
| Philippines PSE Composite | 62.2 | 39.98 | 22.23 | 1.80 |
| Russell 1000 | 75.67 | 57.62 | 18.05 | 3.19 |
| Russell 1000 Growth | 72.59 | 53.38 | 19.2 | 2.78 |
| Russell 1000 Value | 70.47 | 50.82 | 19.65 | 2.59 |
| Russell 2000 | 74.81 | 51.3 | 23.51 | 2.18 |
| Russell 2000 Growth | 73.98 | 53.45 | 20.53 | 2.60 |
| Russell 2000 Value | 82.58 | 66.17 | 16.41 | 4.03 |
| Russell 3000 | 76.28 | 58.12 | 18.16 | 3.20 |
| S&P 100 Index | 74.79 | 53 | 21.79 | 2.43 |
| S&P 1500 INDEX | 68 | 50.35 | 17.65 | 2.85 |
| S&P 400 Index | 68.89 | 54.12 | 14.77 | 3.67 |
| S&P 500 Index | 81.6 | 57.21 | 24.39 | 2.35 |
| S&P 500 Total Return | 83.39 | 64.18 | 19.21 | 3.34 |
| S&P 600 Index | 60.88 | 46.02 | 14.85 | 3.10 |
| S&P CNX NIFTY (India) | 49.11 | 37.29 | 11.81 | 3.16 |
| S&P Cons Discretionary Sector | 69.9 | 50.52 | 19.38 | 2.61 |
| S&P Cons Staples Sector | 71.14 | 52.35 | 18.79 | 2.79 |
| S&P Energy Sector | 87.3 | 62.67 | 24.63 | 2.54 |
| S&P 500 Equal Weight | 61.35 | 41.5 | 19.84 | 2.09 |
| S&P Financials Sector | 62.86 | 40.67 | 22.19 | 1.83 |
| S&P Healthcare Sector | 77.15 | 54.03 | 23.12 | 2.34 |
| S&P Industrials Sector | 74.24 | 51.94 | 22.31 | 2.33 |
| S&P Materials Sector | 66.41 | 45.32 | 21.09 | 2.15 |
| S&P MIDCAP INDEX | 76.28 | 57.58 | 18.69 | 3.08 |
| S&P Technology Sector | 59.58 | 41.61 | 17.96 | 2.32 |
| S&P Telecomm Sector | 72.02 | 46.11 | 25.91 | 1.78 |
| S&P Utilities Sector | 81.02 | 55.71 | 25.3 | 2.20 |
| S&P/TSX 60 CAPPED (Canada) | 74.31 | 52.23 | 22.08 | 2.37 |
| S&P/TSX 60 (Canada) | 68.3 | 49.23 | 19.07 | 2.58 |
| S&P/TSX Composite (Canada) | 79 | 56.15 | 22.85 | 2.46 |
| Silver Base Price Handy & Harman | 62.35 | 38.04 | 24.31 | 1.57 |
| Singapore Straits Times | 49 | 31.33 | 17.67 | 1.77 |

**TABLE 10.2**  Continued

| All | 21 Day/5% | | | |
|---|---|---|---|---|
| Index Name | Total | Up | Down | U/D Ratio |
| Slovakia SAX | 84.97 | 48.66 | 36.31 | 1.34 |
| South Korea Seoul Composite | 54.09 | 34.39 | 19.7 | 1.75 |
| S&P 500 Tot Ret Inflation Adj | 82.57 | 62.2 | 20.36 | 3.05 |
| Spain Madrid General | 64.68 | 42.89 | 21.79 | 1.97 |
| Sri Lanka All Share | 76.99 | 44.69 | 32.3 | 1.38 |
| Swedish OMX 30 | 56.65 | 42.08 | 14.57 | 2.89 |
| Switzerland Swiss Market | 72.39 | 55.74 | 16.65 | 3.35 |
| Taiwan Weighted | 56.23 | 37.97 | 18.26 | 2.08 |
| Thailand SET | 62.21 | 42.41 | 19.81 | 2.14 |
| Turkey ISE National-100 | 18.51 | 16.05 | 2.46 | 6.52 |
| United Kingdom FTSE 100 | 72.85 | 52.11 | 20.74 | 2.51 |
| US Dollar Index | 96.17 | 48.83 | 47.33 | 1.03 |
| Value Line Index (Arithmetic) | 79.98 | 57.05 | 22.93 | 2.49 |
| Value Line Index (Geometric) | 77.38 | 53.43 | 23.95 | 2.23 |
| Venezuela IBC | 67.02 | 42.41 | 24.61 | 1.72 |
| Viet Nam Index | 59.18 | 25.95 | 33.23 | 0.78 |
| **Statistics** | | | | |
| Mean | 64.53 | 45.29 | 19.24 | 2.61 |
| Average Deviation | 11.68 | 8.52 | 4.99 | 0.75 |
| Median | 66.41 | 46.11 | 19.38 | 2.49 |
| Minimum | 13.85 | 6.81 | 2.46 | 0.35 |
| Maximum | 96.17 | 66.17 | 47.33 | 6.52 |
| Sigma | 15.16 | 11.57 | 6.76 | 1.05 |
| Geometric Mean | 62.11 | 42.96 | 17.92 | 2.40 |
| Harmonic Mean | 58.35 | 38.59 | 16.12 | 2.14 |
| Kurtosis | 1.40 | 1.99 | 2.30 | 2.11 |
| Skewness | −0.93 | −1.21 | 0.63 | 1.05 |
| Trimmed Mean—20% | 65.74 | 46.55 | 19.04 | 2.52 |

measure is just the percentage of the uptrend relative to the amount of data. Similarly, the downtrend is the percentage of the downtrend to the amount of data. If you add the uptrend and downtrend you will get the total trend. The last column is the U/D Ratio, which is merely the uptrend percentage divided by the downtrend percentage. If you look at the first entry in Table 10.2, the AMEX Composite trends 71.18 percent of the time, with 56.16 percent of the time in an uptrend and 15.03 percent of the time in a downtrend. The U/D Ratio is 3.74, which means the AMEX Composite trends up almost 4 (3.74) times more than it trends down. You can verify the amount of data in the Indices Date table shown early to see if it was adequate enough for trend analysis. It is not shown, but the complement of the total would give you the amount of time the index was trendless.

At the bottom of each table is a grouping of statistical measures for the various columns. Here are the definitions of those statistics:

*Mean.* In statistics this is the arithmetic average of the selected cells. In Excel, this is the Average function (go figure). It is a good measure as long as there are no large outliers in the data being analyzed.

*Average deviation.* This is a function that returns the average of the absolute deviations of data points from their mean. It can be thought of as a measure of the variability of the data.

*Median.* This function measures central tendency, which is the location of the center of a group of numbers in a statistical distribution. It is the middle number of a group of numbers; that is, half the numbers have values that are greater than the median, and half the numbers have values that are less than the median. For example, the median of 2, 3, 3, 5, 7, and 10 is 4. If there are a wide range of values that are outliers, then median is a better measure than mean or average.

*Minimum.* Shows the value of the minimum value of the cells that are selected.

*Maximum.* Shows the value of the maximum value of the cells that are selected.

*Sigma.* Also known as standard deviation. It is a measure of how widely values are dispersed from their mean (average).

*Geometric mean.* First of all, it is only good for positive numbers and can be used to measure growth rates, etc. It will always be a smaller number than the mean.

*Harmonic mean.* Simply the reciprocal of the arithmetic mean, or could be stated as the arithmetic mean of the reciprocals. It is a value that is always less than the geometric mean, and like the geometric mean, can only be calculated on positive numbers and generally used for rates and ratios.

*Kurtosis.* This function characterizes the relative peakedness or flatness of a distribution compared with the normal distribution (bell curve). If the distribution is "tall" then it reflects positive kurtosis, while a relatively flat or short distribution (relative to normal) reflects a negative kurtosis.

*Skewness.* This characterizes the degree of symmetry of a distribution about its mean. Positive skewness reflects a distribution that has long tails of positive values, while negative skewness reflects a distribution with an asymmetric tail extending toward more negative values.

*Trimmed mean (20 percent).* This is a great function. It is the same as the Mean, but you can select any number or percentage of numbers (sample size) to be eliminated at the extremes. A great way to eliminate the outliers in a data set.

## Trendiness Determination Method One

This methodology for trend determination looks at the average of multiple sets of raw data. An example of just one set of the data was shown previously in Table 10.2, which looks at a filtered wave of 5 percent and a minimum trend length of 21 days. Following Table 10.3 is an explanation of the column headers for Trendiness One in the analysis tables that follow.

*Trendiness average.* This is the simple average of all the total trending expressed as a percentage. The components that make up this average are the total

**TABLE 10.3** Trendiness One Explanation

| Trendiness | | Avg. | Up Trendiness | |
|---|---|---|---|---|
| Average | Rank | U/D | WtdAvg | Rank |

trendiness of all the raw data tables in which the total average is the average of the uptrends and downtrends as a percentage of the total data in the series.

*Rank.* This is just a numerical ranking of the trendiness average with the largest total average equal to a rank of 1.

*Avg. U/D.* This is the average of all the raw data tables' ratio of uptrends to downtrends. Note: If the value of the Avg. U/D is equal to 1, it means that the uptrends and downtrends were equal. If it is less than 1, then there were more downtrends.

*Uptrendiness WtdAvg.* This is the product of column Trendiness Average and column Avg. U/D. Here the Total Trendiness (sum of up and down) is multiplied by their ratio, which gives a weighted portion to the upside when the ratio is high. If the average of the total trendiness is high and the uptrendiness is considerably larger than the downtrendiness, then this value (WtdAvg) will be high.

*Rank.* This is a numerical ranking of the Up Trendiness WtdAvg with the largest value equal to a rank of 1.

Table 10.4 shows the complete results using Trendiness One methodology.

## Trendiness Determination Method Two

The second method of trend determination uses the raw data averages. For example, the up value is calculated by using the raw data up average compared to the raw data total average, which therefore means it only is using the amount of data that is trending and not the full data set of the series. This way the results are dealing only with the trending portion of the index, and if you think about it, when the minimum trend length is high and the filtered wave is low, there might not be that much trending. Table 10.5 shows the column headers followed by their definitions.

*Up.* This is the average of the raw data Up Trends as a percentage of the Total Trends.

*Down.* This is the average of the raw data Down Trends as a percentage of the Total Trends.

*Up rank.* This is the numerical ranking of the Up column, with the largest value equal to a rank of 1.

Table 10.6 shows the results using Trendiness Two methodology.

**TABLE 10.4** Trendiness One Table

| Index Name | Trendiness | | Avg. | Up Trendiness | |
|---|---|---|---|---|---|
| | Average | Rank | U/D | WtdAvg | Rank |
| AMEX Composite | 80.49 | 41 | 3.38 | 271.90 | 6 |
| AMEX Oil Index | 74.51 | 61 | 1.96 | 146.23 | 76 |
| AMEX Pharmaceutical Index | 81.68 | 37 | 1.74 | 142.38 | 80 |
| Argentina MerVal | 50.48 | 102 | 2.41 | 121.53 | 94 |
| Australia All Ordinaries | 90.94 | 4 | 2.28 | 207.75 | 28 |
| Austria ATX | 76.85 | 57 | 2.24 | 172.31 | 55 |
| Belgium BEL-20 | 78.16 | 50 | 2.15 | 168.18 | 59 |
| Brazil Bovespa | 48.29 | 105 | 3.44 | 165.90 | 61 |
| Chile IGPA General Index | 90.17 | 6 | 1.66 | 149.32 | 74 |
| Chile IPSA | 80.43 | 42 | 1.63 | 131.41 | 88 |
| China Shanghai Composite | 62.87 | 97 | 1.17 | 73.82 | 104 |
| CRB Index | 92.69 | 2 | 1.42 | 131.59 | 87 |
| Czech Republic PX | 69.81 | 79 | 1.65 | 115.13 | 96 |
| Denmark Copenhagen 20 | 72.47 | 71 | 2.76 | 200.23 | 32 |
| DJ Wilshire US Small Cap | 66.74 | 89 | 3.12 | 208.53 | 26 |
| Dow Industrials 1885 | 86.07 | 19 | 2.27 | 195.02 | 38 |
| Dow Jones Composite | 78.81 | 45 | 2.49 | 196.51 | 37 |
| Dow Jones Euro Stoxx | 70.26 | 76 | 2.37 | 166.81 | 60 |
| Dow Jones Euro Stoxx 50 | 64.79 | 92 | 2.51 | 162.47 | 65 |
| Dow Jones Stoxx | 76.85 | 56 | 2.53 | 194.67 | 39 |
| Dow Jones Transport | 69.39 | 81 | 2.24 | 155.18 | 71 |
| Dow Jones Utilities | 83.77 | 28 | 2.43 | 203.64 | 30 |
| DJ Wilshire 5000 Composite | 88.07 | 10 | 2.62 | 230.54 | 16 |
| Dow Jones Wilshire REIT | 64.13 | 95 | 3.46 | 221.59 | 21 |
| DJ Wilshire REIT Total Return | 64.34 | 93 | 4.14 | 266.38 | 7 |
| Egypt CMA | 73.73 | 65 | 2.82 | 207.83 | 27 |
| EURONEXT 100 | 70.41 | 73 | 3.67 | 258.45 | 10 |
| Finland HSE General Index | 63.57 | 96 | 2.09 | 133.08 | 86 |
| France CAC 40 | 69.78 | 80 | 2.45 | 171.01 | 57 |
| Germany DAX | 67.81 | 85 | 3.44 | 233.49 | 14 |
| Global Dow | 74.55 | 60 | 1.95 | 145.64 | 77 |
| Gold and Silver Mining | 38.35 | 107 | 0.90 | 34.66 | 107 |
| Gold Base Price Handy & Harman | 49.21 | 103 | 1.20 | 59.26 | 105 |
| Gold Bugs (AMEX) | 32.56 | 108 | 1.04 | 33.76 | 108 |
| Gold Mining Stocks | 48.18 | 106 | 1.07 | 51.61 | 106 |
| Greece General Share | 62.60 | 98 | 1.27 | 79.60 | 102 |
| Hanoi SE Index | 49.16 | 104 | 0.44 | 21.73 | 109 |
| Healthcare Index (S&P) | 84.22 | 24 | 1.94 | 163.54 | 62 |
| Hong Kong Hang Seng | 69.98 | 78 | 2.22 | 155.21 | 70 |
| Ibex 35 | 67.58 | 86 | 2.42 | 163.36 | 63 |
| India BSE 30 | 57.04 | 101 | 2.29 | 130.77 | 90 |
| Indonesia Jakarta Composite | 73.88 | 64 | 2.04 | 150.64 | 73 |
| Israel TA-100 | 77.53 | 52 | 2.57 | 199.63 | 35 |
| Italy FTSE MIB Index | 64.28 | 94 | 2.48 | 159.60 | 68 |
| Japan Nikkei 225 | 75.65 | 59 | 1.95 | 147.74 | 75 |
| Johannesburg All Shares | 72.84 | 68 | 4.53 | 330.27 | 1 |

**TABLE 10.4** Continued

| Index Name | Trendiness | | Avg. | Up Trendiness | |
|---|---|---|---|---|---|
| | Average | Rank | U/D | WtdAvg | Rank |
| Major Market Index | 84.49 | 20 | 2.68 | 226.54 | 20 |
| Malaysia KLSE Composite | 82.64 | 32 | 1.96 | 162.02 | 66 |
| Mexico IPC | 68.41 | 84 | 3.35 | 229.30 | 17 |
| Morgan Stanley Consumer Index | 87.52 | 12 | 2.96 | 259.01 | 9 |
| Morgan Stanley Cyclical Index | 69.12 | 83 | 2.32 | 160.59 | 67 |
| MSCI EAFE | 89.91 | 7 | 1.99 | 178.96 | 52 |
| MSCI EM | 84.27 | 23 | 2.21 | 186.22 | 49 |
| NASDAQ 100 | 65.28 | 91 | 2.86 | 186.56 | 48 |
| NASDAQ Composite | 81.32 | 38 | 2.19 | 177.69 | 53 |
| Netherlands AEX General | 78.28 | 49 | 2.45 | 191.77 | 43 |
| Norway Oslo All Share Composite | 73.70 | 66 | 3.74 | 275.40 | 5 |
| Norway Oslo OBX Top 25 | 60.77 | 100 | 4.88 | 296.50 | 3 |
| NYSE Composite | 89.89 | 8 | 2.41 | 217.05 | 22 |
| Pakistan Karachi 100 | 67.51 | 87 | 2.06 | 139.15 | 83 |
| Peru Lima General | 80.33 | 43 | 1.78 | 142.75 | 79 |
| Philippines PSE Composite | 74.47 | 62 | 1.66 | 123.72 | 93 |
| Russell 1000 | 83.72 | 29 | 3.02 | 252.92 | 11 |
| Russell 1000 Growth | 80.55 | 40 | 2.61 | 209.84 | 23 |
| Russell 1000 Value | 78.58 | 47 | 2.26 | 177.52 | 54 |
| Russell 2000 | 83.02 | 30 | 2.07 | 171.63 | 56 |
| Russell 2000 Growth | 82.05 | 35 | 2.31 | 189.76 | 47 |
| Russell 2000 Value | 87.53 | 11 | 3.69 | 322.90 | 2 |
| Russell 3000 | 84.38 | 22 | 2.95 | 248.63 | 12 |
| S&P 100 Index | 83.97 | 27 | 2.27 | 190.61 | 46 |
| S&P 1500 INDEX | 78.57 | 48 | 2.58 | 202.70 | 31 |
| S&P 400 Index | 78.80 | 46 | 3.01 | 237.45 | 13 |
| S&P 500 Index | 88.78 | 9 | 2.25 | 199.91 | 33 |
| S&P 500 Total Return | 86.90 | 16 | 3.21 | 278.62 | 4 |
| S&P 600 Index | 71.77 | 72 | 2.55 | 183.16 | 50 |
| S&P CNX NIFTY (India) | 62.26 | 99 | 2.88 | 179.06 | 51 |
| S&P Cons Discretionary Sector | 76.96 | 55 | 2.71 | 208.53 | 25 |
| S&P Cons Staples Sector | 80.19 | 44 | 2.49 | 199.75 | 34 |
| S&P Energy Sector | 92.31 | 3 | 2.52 | 232.75 | 15 |
| S&P 500 Equal Weight | 72.75 | 69 | 2.19 | 158.98 | 69 |
| S&P Financials Sector | 74.40 | 63 | 1.73 | 128.41 | 91 |
| S&P Healthcare Sector | 86.97 | 15 | 2.21 | 192.24 | 41 |
| S&P Industrials Sector | 82.49 | 33 | 2.05 | 169.05 | 58 |
| S&P Materials Sector | 77.15 | 54 | 2.01 | 154.98 | 72 |
| S&P MIDCAP INDEX | 84.10 | 25 | 2.71 | 228.13 | 19 |
| S&P Technology Sector | 70.34 | 74 | 2.05 | 144.50 | 78 |
| S&P Telecomm Sector | 80.79 | 39 | 1.71 | 138.25 | 84 |
| S&P Utilities Sector | 87.37 | 13 | 2.19 | 191.14 | 44 |
| S&P/TSX 60 CAPPED (Canada) | 81.78 | 36 | 2.43 | 198.35 | 36 |
| S&P/TSX 60 (Canada) | 77.47 | 53 | 2.50 | 193.45 | 40 |
| S&P/TSX Composite (Canada) | 87.29 | 14 | 2.20 | 191.92 | 42 |
| Silver Base Price Handy & Harman | 72.55 | 70 | 1.44 | 104.30 | 100 |
| Singapore Straits Times | 65.83 | 90 | 1.67 | 109.63 | 97 |
| Slovakia SAX | 90.31 | 5 | 1.28 | 115.54 | 95 |
| South Korea Seoul Composite | 67.39 | 88 | 1.59 | 107.17 | 99 |

*(Continued)*

**TABLE 10.4**   Continued

| Index Name | Trendiness | | Avg. | Up Trendiness | |
|---|---|---|---|---|---|
| | Average | Rank | U/D | WtdAvg | Rank |
| S&P 500 Tot Ret Inflation Adj | 86.25 | 18 | 3.05 | 262.89 | 8 |
| Spain Madrid General | 78.14 | 51 | 1.79 | 140.12 | 82 |
| Sri Lanka All Share | 83.98 | 26 | 1.29 | 108.17 | 98 |
| Swedish OMX 30 | 70.18 | 77 | 2.72 | 190.76 | 45 |
| Switzerland Swiss Market | 82.10 | 34 | 2.79 | 229.22 | 18 |
| Taiwan Weighted | 69.20 | 82 | 1.82 | 125.61 | 92 |
| Thailand SET | 73.51 | 67 | 1.88 | 138.19 | 85 |
| Turkey ISE National-100 | 32.02 | 109 | 4.43 | 141.83 | 81 |
| United Kingdom FTSE 100 | 82.77 | 31 | 2.53 | 209.34 | 24 |
| US Dollar Index | 95.16 | 1 | 1.08 | 102.65 | 101 |
| Value Line Index (Arithmetic) | 86.60 | 17 | 2.36 | 204.40 | 29 |
| Value Line Index (Geometric) | 84.44 | 21 | 1.93 | 162.59 | 64 |
| Venezuela IBC | 76.70 | 58 | 1.70 | 130.78 | 89 |
| Viet Nam Index | 70.31 | 75 | 1.08 | 75.84 | 103 |
| **Statistics** | | | | | |
| Mean | 74.81 | | 2.33 | 174.47 | |
| Average Deviation | 9.27 | | 0.56 | 44.70 | |
| Median | 76.96 | | 2.27 | 172.31 | |
| Minimum | 32.02 | | 0.44 | 21.73 | |
| Maximum | 95.16 | | 4.88 | 330.27 | |
| Sigma | 12.25 | | 0.77 | 58.11 | |
| Geometric Mean | 73.59 | | 2.20 | 161.93 | |
| Harmonic Mean | 72.03 | | 2.04 | 142.11 | |
| Kurtosis | 2.08 | | 1.30 | 0.52 | |
| Skewness | −1.24 | | 0.64 | −0.05 | |
| Trimmed Mean—20% | 76.18 | | 2.29 | 174.81 | |

**TABLE 10.5**   Trendiness Two Explanation

| While in Trend | | |
|---|---|---|
| Up | Down | Up Rank |

## Comparison of the Two Trendiness Methods

Figure 10.6 compares the rankings using both "Trendiness" methods. Keep in mind we are only using uptrends, downtrends, and a derivative of them, which is up over down ratio. The plot below is informally called a *scatter plot* and deals with the relationships between two sets of paired data. The equation of the regression line is from high school geometry and follows the expression: $y = mx + b$, where $m$ is the slope and $b$ is the $y$-intercept (where it crosses the $y$ axis); $x$ is known as the independent

**TABLE 10.6** Trendiness Two Table

| Index Name | While in Trend | | |
| | Up/Tot | Dn/Tot | Up Rank |
|---|---|---|---|
| AMEX Composite | 76.98% | 23.02% | 8 |
| AMEX Oil Index | 66.24% | 33.76% | 77 |
| AMEX Pharmaceutical Index | 63.58% | 36.42% | 87 |
| Argentina MerVal | 70.23% | 29.77% | 46 |
| Australia All Ordinaries | 69.52% | 30.48% | 52 |
| Austria ATX | 68.65% | 31.35% | 61 |
| Belgium BEL-20 | 68.21% | 31.79% | 68 |
| Brazil Bovespa | 74.77% | 25.23% | 15 |
| Chile IGPA General Index | 62.34% | 37.66% | 91 |
| Chile IPSA | 61.97% | 38.03% | 95 |
| China Shanghai Composite | 54.10% | 45.90% | 103 |
| CRB Index | 58.45% | 41.55% | 98 |
| Czech Republic PX | 62.22% | 37.78% | 94 |
| Denmark Copenhagen 20 | 72.37% | 27.63% | 28 |
| DJ Wilshire US Small Cap | 74.27% | 25.73% | 19 |
| Dow Industrials 1885 | 69.23% | 30.77% | 54 |
| Dow Jones Composite | 71.23% | 28.77% | 38 |
| Dow Jones Euro Stoxx | 69.78% | 30.22% | 50 |
| Dow Jones Euro Stoxx 50 | 70.54% | 29.46% | 45 |
| Dow Jones Stoxx | 71.39% | 28.61% | 35 |
| Dow Jones Transport | 68.29% | 31.71% | 67 |
| Dow Jones Utilities | 70.76% | 29.24% | 41 |
| DJ Wilshire 5000 Composite | 72.34% | 27.66% | 29 |
| Dow Jones Wilshire REIT | 76.41% | 23.59% | 10 |
| DJ Wilshire REIT Total Return | 79.56% | 20.44% | 3 |
| Egypt CMA | 73.69% | 26.31% | 22 |
| EURONEXT 100 | 77.86% | 22.14% | 7 |
| Finland HSE General Index | 67.49% | 32.51% | 69 |
| France CAC 40 | 70.69% | 29.31% | 43 |
| Germany DAX | 76.73% | 23.27% | 9 |
| Global Dow | 65.57% | 34.43% | 81 |
| Gold and Silver Mining | 48.11% | 51.89% | 108 |
| Gold Base Price Handy & Harman | 54.64% | 45.36% | 102 |
| Gold Bugs (AMEX) | 51.30% | 48.70% | 107 |
| Gold Mining Stocks | 52.05% | 47.95% | 104 |
| Greece General Share | 55.26% | 44.74% | 101 |
| Hanoi SE Index | 31.12% | 68.88% | 109 |
| Healthcare Index (S&P) | 66.04% | 33.96% | 79 |
| Hong Kong Hang Seng | 68.60% | 31.40% | 63 |
| Ibex 35 | 69.99% | 30.01% | 49 |
| India BSE 30 | 68.93% | 31.07% | 57 |
| Indonesia Jakarta Composite | 66.95% | 33.05% | 72 |
| Israel TA-100 | 71.90% | 28.10% | 31 |
| Italy FTSE MIB Index | 70.12% | 29.88% | 48 |
| Japan Nikkei 225 | 65.66% | 34.34% | 80 |

*(Continued)*

**TABLE 10.6**  Continued

| Index Name | While in Trend | | |
| --- | --- | --- | --- |
| | Up/Tot | Dn/Tot | Up Rank |
| Johannesburg All Shares | 81.41% | 18.59% | 2 |
| Major Market Index | 72.75% | 27.25% | 27 |
| Malaysia KLSE Composite | 66.08% | 33.92% | 78 |
| Mexico IPC | 76.30% | 23.70% | 11 |
| Morgan Stanley Consumer Index | 74.68% | 25.32% | 16 |
| Morgan Stanley Cyclical Index | 68.48% | 31.52% | 66 |
| MSCI EAFE | 66.56% | 33.44% | 75 |
| MSCI EM | 68.72% | 31.28% | 59 |
| NASDAQ 100 | 73.88% | 26.12% | 20 |
| NASDAQ Composite | 68.54% | 31.46% | 65 |
| Netherlands AEX General | 70.74% | 29.26% | 42 |
| Norway Oslo All Share Composite | 78.82% | 21.18% | 5 |
| Norway Oslo OBX Top 25 | 82.86% | 17.14% | 1 |
| NYSE Composite | 70.61% | 29.39% | 44 |
| Pakistan Karachi 100 | 66.54% | 33.46% | 76 |
| Peru Lima General | 63.81% | 36.19% | 86 |
| Philippines PSE Composite | 62.28% | 37.72% | 93 |
| Russell 1000 | 75.06% | 24.94% | 14 |
| Russell 1000 Growth | 72.16% | 27.84% | 30 |
| Russell 1000 Value | 69.06% | 30.94% | 56 |
| Russell 2000 | 67.34% | 32.66% | 70 |
| Russell 2000 Growth | 69.62% | 30.38% | 51 |
| Russell 2000 Value | 78.59% | 21.41% | 6 |
| Russell 3000 | 74.56% | 25.44% | 18 |
| S&P 100 Index | 69.33% | 30.67% | 53 |
| S&P 1500 INDEX | 71.79% | 28.21% | 32 |
| S&P 400 Index | 74.59% | 25.41% | 17 |
| S&P 500 Index | 69.21% | 30.79% | 55 |
| S&P 500 Total Return | 76.12% | 23.88% | 12 |
| S&P 600 Index | 71.37% | 28.63% | 36 |
| S&P CNX NIFTY (India) | 73.86% | 26.14% | 21 |
| S&P Cons Discretionary Sector | 73.02% | 26.98% | 24 |
| S&P Cons Staples Sector | 71.17% | 28.83% | 39 |
| S&P Energy Sector | 71.59% | 28.41% | 33 |
| S&P 500 Equal Weight | 68.66% | 31.34% | 60 |
| S&P Financials Sector | 63.20% | 36.80% | 88 |
| S&P Healthcare Sector | 68.78% | 31.22% | 58 |
| S&P Industrials Sector | 66.98% | 33.02% | 71 |
| S&P Materials Sector | 66.66% | 33.34% | 74 |
| S&P MIDCAP INDEX | 72.86% | 27.14% | 26 |
| S&P Technology Sector | 66.92% | 33.08% | 73 |
| S&P Telecomm Sector | 63.06% | 36.94% | 89 |
| S&P Utilities Sector | 68.61% | 31.39% | 62 |
| S&P/TSX 60 CAPPED (Canada) | 70.79% | 29.21% | 40 |
| S&P/TSX 60 (Canada) | 71.32% | 28.68% | 37 |
| S&P/TSX Composite (Canada) | 68.58% | 31.42% | 64 |

**TABLE 10.6** Continued

| Index Name | While in Trend | | |
| --- | --- | --- | --- |
| | Up/Tot | Dn/Tot | Up Rank |
| Silver Base Price Handy & Harman | 58.78% | 41.22% | 97 |
| Singapore Straits Times | 62.30% | 37.70% | 92 |
| Slovakia SAX | 56.08% | 43.92% | 100 |
| South Korea Seoul Composite | 61.19% | 38.81% | 96 |
| S&P 500 Tot Ret Inflation Adj | 75.15% | 24.85% | 13 |
| Spain Madrid General | 64.01% | 35.99% | 85 |
| Sri Lanka All Share | 56.21% | 43.79% | 99 |
| Swedish OMX 30 | 72.97% | 27.03% | 25 |
| Switzerland Swiss Market | 73.27% | 26.73% | 23 |
| Taiwan Weighted | 64.06% | 35.94% | 84 |
| Thailand SET | 64.99% | 35.01% | 83 |
| Turkey ISE National-100 | 79.17% | 20.83% | 4 |
| United Kingdom FTSE 100 | 71.56% | 28.44% | 34 |
| US Dollar Index | 51.85% | 48.15% | 105 |
| Value Line Index (Arithmetic) | 70.19% | 29.81% | 47 |
| Value Line Index (Geometric) | 65.56% | 34.44% | 82 |
| Venezuela IBC | 63.02% | 36.98% | 90 |
| Viet Nam Index | 51.69% | 48.31% | 106 |
| **Statistics** | | | |
| Mean | 68.04% | 31.96% | |
| Average Deviation | 5.46% | 5.46% | |
| Median | 69.21% | 30.79% | |
| Minimum | 31.12% | 17.14% | |
| Maximum | 82.86% | 68.88% | |
| Sigma | 7.66% | 7.66% | |
| Geometric Mean | 67.53% | 31.15% | |
| Harmonic Mean | 66.92% | 30.41% | |
| Kurtosis | 446.17% | 446.17% | |
| Skewness | −148.50% | 148.50% | |
| Trimmed Mean—20% | 68.78% | 31.22% | |

**FIGURE 10.6** Scatter Plot of Trendiness One versus Trendiness Two

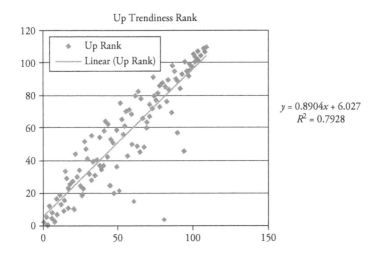

$y = 0.8904x + 6.027$
$R^2 = 0.7928$

variable or the predictor variable and $y$ is the dependent variable or response variable. The expression that defines the regression (linear least squares) shows that the slope of the line ($m$) is 0.8904. The line crosses the $y$ (vertical) axis at 6.027, which is $b$. $R^2$, which is also known as the *coefficient of determination*, is 0.7928. From $R^2$, we can easily see that the correlation $R$ is 0.8904 (square root of $R^2$). We know this is a highly positive correlation because we can visually verify it simply from the orientation of the slope. We can interpret $m$ as the value of $y$ when $x$ is zero and we can interpret $b$ as the amount that $y$ increases when $x$ increases by one. From all of this one can determine the amount that one variable influences the other. Sorry, I beat this to death; you can probably find simpler explanations in a high school statistics textbook.

## Trendless Analysis

This is a rather simple but complementary (intentional spelling) method that helps to validate the other two processes. This method focuses on the lack of a trend, or the amount of trendless time is in the data. The first two methods focused on trending and this one is focused on nontrending, all using the same raw data. Determining markets that do not trend will serve two purposes. One is to not use conventional trend-following techniques on them, and two, it can be good for mean reversion analysis. Table 10.7 shows the column headers; the definitions follow.

**TABLE 10.7**  Trendless Analysis Explanation

| Up | Down | Trendless | Rank |
| --- | --- | --- | --- |

*Up.* This is the Total Trend average from Trendiness One multiplied by the Up Total from Trendiness Two.

*Down.* This is the Total Trend average from Trendiness One multiplied by the Down Total from Trendiness Two.

*Trendless.* This is the complement of the sum of the Up and Down values (1 − (Up + Down)).

*Rank.* This is the numerical rank of the Trendless column with the largest value equal to a rank of 1.

Table 10.8 shows the results using the Trendless methodology.

## Comparison of Trendiness One Rank and Trendless Rank

Although I think this was quite obvious, Figure 10.7 shows the analysis math is consistent and acceptable. These two series should essentially be inversely correlated, and they are with coefficient of determination equal to one.

**TABLE 10.8** Trendless Analysis Table

| Index Name | Up | Down | Trendless | Rank |
|---|---|---|---|---|
| AMEX Composite | 61.97% | 18.53% | 19.51% | 69 |
| AMEX Oil Index | 49.36% | 25.15% | 25.49% | 49 |
| AMEX Pharmaceutical Index | 51.93% | 29.74% | 18.32% | 73 |
| Argentina MerVal | 35.45% | 15.03% | 49.52% | 8 |
| Australia All Ordinaries | 63.22% | 27.71% | 9.06% | 106 |
| Austria ATX | 52.76% | 24.09% | 23.15% | 53 |
| Belgium BEL-20 | 53.32% | 24.84% | 21.84% | 60 |
| Brazil Bovespa | 36.11% | 12.18% | 51.71% | 5 |
| Chile IGPA General Index | 56.21% | 33.95% | 9.83% | 104 |
| Chile IPSA | 49.84% | 30.58% | 19.57% | 68 |
| China Shanghai Composite | 34.01% | 28.86% | 37.13% | 13 |
| CRB Index | 54.17% | 38.51% | 7.31% | 108 |
| Czech Republic PX | 43.44% | 26.38% | 30.19% | 31 |
| Denmark Copenhagen 20 | 52.45% | 20.03% | 27.53% | 39 |
| DJ Wilshire US Small Cap | 49.57% | 17.18% | 33.26% | 21 |
| Dow Industrials 1885 | 59.59% | 26.49% | 13.93% | 91 |
| Dow Jones Composite | 56.13% | 22.68% | 21.19% | 65 |
| Dow Jones Euro Stoxx | 49.03% | 21.23% | 29.74% | 34 |
| Dow Jones Euro Stoxx 50 | 45.71% | 19.09% | 35.21% | 18 |
| Dow Jones Stoxx | 54.86% | 21.99% | 23.15% | 54 |
| Dow Jones Transport | 47.39% | 22.00% | 30.61% | 29 |
| Dow Jones Utilities | 59.28% | 24.49% | 16.23% | 82 |
| DJ Wilshire 5000 Composite | 63.70% | 24.36% | 11.93% | 100 |
| Dow Jones Wilshire REIT | 49.00% | 15.13% | 35.87% | 15 |
| DJ Wilshire REIT Total Return | 51.19% | 13.15% | 35.66% | 17 |
| Egypt CMA | 54.33% | 19.40% | 26.27% | 45 |
| EURONEXT 100 | 54.82% | 15.59% | 29.59% | 37 |
| Finland HSE General Index | 42.90% | 20.67% | 36.43% | 14 |
| France CAC 40 | 49.32% | 20.45% | 30.22% | 30 |
| Germany DAX | 52.03% | 15.78% | 32.19% | 25 |
| Global Dow | 48.88% | 25.67% | 25.45% | 50 |
| Gold and Silver Mining | 18.45% | 19.90% | 61.65% | 3 |
| Gold Base Price Handy & Harman | 26.89% | 22.32% | 50.79% | 7 |
| Gold Bugs (AMEX) | 16.70% | 15.85% | 67.44% | 2 |
| Gold Mining Stocks | 25.08% | 23.10% | 51.82% | 4 |
| Greece General Share | 34.59% | 28.01% | 37.40% | 12 |
| Hanoi SE Index | 15.30% | 33.86% | 50.84% | 6 |
| Healthcare Index (S&P) | 55.62% | 28.60% | 15.78% | 86 |
| Hong Kong Hang Seng | 48.01% | 21.97% | 30.02% | 32 |
| Ibex 35 | 47.30% | 20.28% | 32.42% | 24 |
| India BSE 30 | 39.32% | 17.72% | 42.96% | 9 |
| Indonesia Jakarta Composite | 49.46% | 24.42% | 26.12% | 46 |
| Israel TA-100 | 55.75% | 21.78% | 22.47% | 58 |
| Italy FTSE MIB Index | 45.07% | 19.21% | 35.72% | 16 |
| Japan Nikkei 225 | 49.67% | 25.98% | 24.35% | 51 |

*(Continued)*

**TABLE 10.8**  Continued

| Index Name | Up | Down | Trendless | Rank |
|---|---|---|---|---|
| Johannesburg All Shares | 59.30% | 13.54% | 27.16% | 42 |
| Major Market Index | 61.47% | 23.02% | 15.51% | 90 |
| Malaysia KLSE Composite | 54.61% | 28.04% | 17.36% | 78 |
| Mexico IPC | 52.19% | 16.21% | 31.59% | 26 |
| Morgan Stanley Consumer Index | 65.36% | 22.16% | 12.48% | 98 |
| Morgan Stanley Cyclical Index | 47.33% | 21.78% | 30.88% | 27 |
| MSCI EAFE | 59.85% | 30.06% | 10.09% | 103 |
| MSCI EM | 57.92% | 26.36% | 15.73% | 87 |
| NASDAQ 100 | 48.23% | 17.05% | 34.72% | 19 |
| NASDAQ Composite | 55.74% | 25.58% | 18.68% | 72 |
| Netherlands AEX General | 55.37% | 22.90% | 21.72% | 61 |
| Norway Oslo All Share Composite | 58.09% | 15.61% | 26.30% | 44 |
| Norway Oslo OBX Top 25 | 50.36% | 10.41% | 39.23% | 10 |
| NYSE Composite | 63.47% | 26.42% | 10.11% | 102 |
| Pakistan Karachi 100 | 44.92% | 22.59% | 32.49% | 23 |
| Peru Lima General | 51.26% | 29.07% | 19.67% | 67 |
| Philippines PSE Composite | 46.38% | 28.09% | 25.53% | 48 |
| Russell 1000 | 62.84% | 20.88% | 16.28% | 81 |
| Russell 1000 Growth | 58.13% | 22.43% | 19.45% | 70 |
| Russell 1000 Value | 54.27% | 24.31% | 21.42% | 63 |
| Russell 2000 | 55.91% | 27.11% | 16.98% | 80 |
| Russell 2000 Growth | 57.13% | 24.92% | 17.95% | 75 |
| Russell 2000 Value | 68.80% | 18.74% | 12.47% | 99 |
| Russell 3000 | 62.91% | 21.47% | 15.62% | 88 |
| S&P 100 Index | 58.22% | 25.76% | 16.03% | 83 |
| S&P 1500 INDEX | 56.41% | 22.16% | 21.43% | 62 |
| S&P 400 Index | 58.78% | 20.02% | 21.20% | 64 |
| S&P 500 Index | 61.45% | 27.33% | 11.22% | 101 |
| S&P 500 Total Return | 66.15% | 20.75% | 13.10% | 94 |
| S&P 600 Index | 51.23% | 20.55% | 28.23% | 38 |
| S&P CNX NIFTY (India) | 45.99% | 16.27% | 37.74% | 11 |
| S&P Cons Discretionary Sector | 56.20% | 20.76% | 23.04% | 55 |
| S&P Cons Staples Sector | 57.07% | 23.12% | 19.81% | 66 |
| S&P Energy Sector | 66.08% | 26.23% | 7.69% | 107 |
| S&P 500 Equal Weight | 49.95% | 22.80% | 27.25% | 41 |
| S&P Financials Sector | 47.03% | 27.38% | 25.60% | 47 |
| S&P Healthcare Sector | 59.82% | 27.16% | 13.03% | 95 |
| S&P Industrials Sector | 55.25% | 27.24% | 17.51% | 77 |
| S&P Materials Sector | 51.43% | 25.72% | 22.85% | 56 |
| S&P MIDCAP INDEX | 61.28% | 22.82% | 15.90% | 85 |
| S&P Technology Sector | 47.07% | 23.27% | 29.66% | 36 |
| S&P Telecomm Sector | 50.95% | 29.84% | 19.21% | 71 |
| S&P Utilities Sector | 59.95% | 27.42% | 12.63% | 97 |
| S&P/TSX 60 CAPPED (Canada) | 57.89% | 23.89% | 18.22% | 74 |
| S&P/TSX 60 (Canada) | 55.25% | 22.21% | 22.53% | 57 |

**TABLE 10.8** Continued

| Index Name | Up | Down | Trendless | Rank |
|---|---|---|---|---|
| S&P/TSX Composite (Canada) | 59.86% | 27.43% | 12.71% | 96 |
| Silver Base Price Handy & Harman | 42.65% | 29.91% | 27.45% | 40 |
| Singapore Straits Times | 41.01% | 24.82% | 34.17% | 20 |
| Slovakia SAX | 50.65% | 39.67% | 9.69% | 105 |
| South Korea Seoul Composite | 41.24% | 26.15% | 32.61% | 22 |
| S&P 500 Tot Ret Inflation Adj | 64.82% | 21.43% | 13.75% | 92 |
| Spain Madrid General | 50.02% | 28.12% | 21.86% | 59 |
| Sri Lanka All Share | 47.21% | 36.77% | 16.02% | 84 |
| Swedish OMX 30 | 51.21% | 18.97% | 29.82% | 33 |
| Switzerland Swiss Market | 60.16% | 21.94% | 17.90% | 76 |
| Taiwan Weighted | 44.33% | 24.87% | 30.80% | 28 |
| Thailand SET | 47.77% | 25.73% | 26.49% | 43 |
| Turkey ISE National-100 | 25.35% | 6.67% | 67.98% | 1 |
| United Kingdom FTSE 100 | 59.23% | 23.54% | 17.23% | 79 |
| US Dollar Index | 49.34% | 45.82% | 4.84% | 109 |
| Value Line Index (Arithmetic) | 60.79% | 25.81% | 13.40% | 93 |
| Value Line Index (Geometric) | 55.36% | 29.09% | 15.56% | 89 |
| Venezuela IBC | 48.34% | 28.37% | 23.30% | 52 |
| Viet Nam Index | 36.34% | 33.97% | 29.69% | 35 |
| **Statistics** | | | | |
| Mean | 51.10% | 23.71% | 25.19% | |
| Average Deviation | 7.42% | 4.39% | 9.27% | |
| Median | 52.03% | 23.27% | 23.04% | |
| Minimum | 15.30% | 6.67% | 4.84% | |
| Maximum | 68.80% | 45.82% | 67.98% | |
| Sigma | 10.28% | 5.92% | 12.25% | |
| Geometric Mean | 49.70% | 22.93% | 22.50% | |
| Harmonic Mean | 47.64% | 22.01% | 19.90% | |
| Kurtosis | 245.72% | 191.06% | 207.66% | |
| Skewness | −134.87% | 42.01% | 123.61% | |
| Trimmed Mean—20% | 52.30% | 23.58% | 23.82% | |

**FIGURE 10.7** Trendiness One versus Trendless Scatter Plot

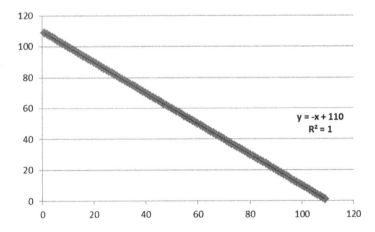

The following tables take the data from the full 109 indices and subdivide it into sectors, international, domestic, and time frames to ensure there is robustness across a variety of data. There are many indices that appear in many if not most of these tables, but keeping data of that sort for comparison with others that are not so widely diversified will enhance the research. These tables show all three trend method results. This first table consists of all the index data. The remaining ones contain subsets of the All table, such as Domestic, International, Commodities, Sectors, Data > 2000, Data > 1990, and Data > 1980. The reason for the data subsets is to ensure there is a robust analysis in place across various lengths of data, which means multiple bull-and-bear cyclical markets are considered, in addition to secular markets. The Data > 2000 means that the data starts sometime prior to 2000 and therefore totally contains the secular bear market that began in 2000.

## All Trendiness Analysis

Table 10.9 contains data from all of the 109 indices in the analysis. The first column contains letters identifying the subcategory for each issue as follows:

I – International
S – Sector
C – Commodity
Blank – Domestic

## Trend Table Selective Analysis

In this section, I will demonstrate more details on selected issues from Table 10.9 to show how the data can be utilized.

Using the Trendiness One Rank, you can see that the U.S. Dollar Index is number one. You can also see it is the worst for being Trendless (last column), which one would expect. However, if you look at the Trendiness One and Trendiness Two Up Ranks, you see that it did not rank well. This can only be interpreted that the U.S. Dollar Index is a good downtrending issue, but not a good uptrending one based on this relative analysis with 109 various indices. This is made clear from the long trendline drawn from the first data point to the last data point and is clearly in a downtrend. Figure 10.8 shows the U.S. Dollar Index with a 5 percent filtered wave overlaid on it. The lower plot shows the filtered wave of 5 percent measuring the number of days during each up and down move. The two horizontal lines are at +21 and −21, which means that movements inside that band are not counted in the trendiness or trendless calculations. The only difference between what this chart shows and what the table data measures is the fact that the table is averaging a number of different filtered waves and trend lengths.

Let's now look at the worst trendiness index and see what we can find out about it (Table 10.9). The Trendiness One rank and the Trendless Rank confirm that this is not a good trending index. Furthermore, the Up Trendiness in both One and Two

**TABLE 10.9** All Three Trend Analyses on All Indices

| | | Trendiness One | | | | | Trendiness Two | | | Trendless Analysis | | | |
| | | Trendiness | | Avg. | Up Trendiness | | While in Trend | | | | | | |
| | Index Name | Average | Rank | /D | WtdAvg | Rank | Up/Tot | Dn/Tot | Up Rank | Up | Down | Trendless | Rank |
|---|---|---|---|---|---|---|---|---|---|---|---|---|---|
| | AMEX Composite | 80.49 | 41 | 3.38 | 271.90 | 6 | 76.98% | 23.02% | 8 | 61.97% | 18.53% | 19.51% | 69 |
| C | AMEX Oil Index | 74.51 | 61 | 1.96 | 146.23 | 76 | 66.24% | 33.76% | 77 | 49.36% | 25.15% | 25.49% | 49 |
| S | AMEX Pharmaceutical Index | 81.68 | 37 | 1.74 | 142.38 | 80 | 63.58% | 36.42% | 87 | 51.93% | 29.74% | 18.32% | 73 |
| I | Argentina MerVal | 50.48 | 102 | 2.41 | 121.53 | 94 | 70.23% | 29.77% | 46 | 35.45% | 15.03% | 49.52% | 8 |
| I | Australia All Ordinaries | 90.94 | 4 | 2.28 | 207.75 | 28 | 69.52% | 30.48% | 52 | 63.22% | 27.71% | 9.06% | 106 |
| I | Austria ATX | 76.85 | 57 | 2.24 | 172.31 | 55 | 68.65% | 31.35% | 61 | 52.76% | 24.09% | 23.15% | 53 |
| I | Belgium BEL-20 | 78.16 | 50 | 2.15 | 168.18 | 59 | 68.21% | 31.79% | 68 | 53.32% | 24.84% | 21.84% | 60 |
| I | Brazil Bovespa | 48.29 | 105 | 3.44 | 165.90 | 61 | 74.77% | 25.23% | 15 | 36.11% | 12.18% | 51.71% | 5 |
| I | Chile IGPA General Index | 90.17 | 6 | 1.66 | 149.32 | 74 | 62.34% | 37.66% | 91 | 56.21% | 33.95% | 9.83% | 104 |
| I | Chile IPSA | 80.43 | 42 | 1.63 | 131.41 | 88 | 61.97% | 38.03% | 95 | 49.84% | 30.58% | 19.57% | 68 |
| I | China Shanghai Composite | 62.87 | 97 | 1.17 | 73.82 | 104 | 54.10% | 45.90% | 103 | 34.01% | 28.86% | 37.13% | 13 |
| C | CRB Index | 92.69 | 2 | 1.42 | 131.59 | 87 | 58.45% | 41.55% | 98 | 54.17% | 38.51% | 7.31% | 108 |
| I | Czech Republic PX | 69.81 | 79 | 1.65 | 115.13 | 96 | 62.22% | 37.78% | 94 | 43.44% | 26.38% | 30.19% | 31 |
| I | Denmark Copenhagen 20 | 72.47 | 71 | 2.76 | 200.23 | 32 | 72.37% | 27.63% | 28 | 52.45% | 20.03% | 27.53% | 39 |
| I | DJ Wilshire US Small Cap | 66.74 | 89 | 3.12 | 208.53 | 26 | 74.27% | 25.73% | 19 | 49.57% | 17.18% | 33.26% | 21 |
| I | Dow Industrials 1885 | 86.07 | 19 | 2.27 | 195.02 | 38 | 69.23% | 30.77% | 54 | 59.59% | 26.49% | 13.93% | 91 |
| I | Dow Jones Composite | 78.81 | 45 | 2.49 | 196.51 | 37 | 71.23% | 28.77% | 38 | 56.13% | 22.68% | 21.19% | 65 |
| I | Dow Jones Euro Stoxx | 70.26 | 76 | 2.37 | 166.81 | 60 | 69.78% | 30.22% | 50 | 49.03% | 21.23% | 29.74% | 34 |
| I | Dow Jones Euro Stoxx 50 | 64.79 | 92 | 2.51 | 162.47 | 65 | 70.54% | 29.46% | 45 | 45.71% | 19.09% | 35.21% | 18 |
| I | Dow Jones Stoxx | 76.85 | 56 | 2.53 | 194.67 | 39 | 71.39% | 28.61% | 35 | 54.86% | 21.99% | 23.15% | 54 |
| I | Dow Jones Transport | 69.39 | 81 | 2.24 | 155.18 | 71 | 68.29% | 31.71% | 67 | 47.39% | 22.00% | 30.61% | 29 |
| I | Dow Jones Utilities | 83.77 | 28 | 2.43 | 203.64 | 30 | 70.76% | 29.24% | 41 | 59.28% | 24.49% | 16.23% | 82 |
| I | DJ Wilshire 5000 Composite | 88.07 | 10 | 2.62 | 230.54 | 16 | 72.34% | 27.66% | 29 | 63.70% | 24.36% | 11.93% | 100 |
| S | DJ Wilshire REIT | 64.13 | 95 | 3.46 | 221.59 | 21 | 76.41% | 23.59% | 10 | 49.00% | 15.13% | 35.87% | 15 |
| S | DJ Wilshire REIT Total Return | 64.34 | 93 | 4.14 | 266.38 | 7 | 79.56% | 20.44% | 3 | 51.19% | 13.15% | 35.66% | 17 |
| I | Egypt CMA | 73.73 | 65 | 2.82 | 207.83 | 27 | 73.69% | 26.31% | 22 | 54.33% | 19.40% | 26.27% | 45 |
| I | EURONEXT 100 | 70.41 | 73 | 3.67 | 258.45 | 10 | 77.86% | 22.14% | 7 | 54.82% | 15.59% | 29.59% | 37 |
| I | Finland HSE General Index | 63.57 | 96 | 2.09 | 133.08 | 86 | 67.49% | 32.51% | 69 | 42.90% | 20.67% | 36.43% | 14 |

(*Continued*)

185

**TABLE 10.9** Continued

| Index Name | | Trendiness One | | | | | Trendiness Two | | | | | | |
|---|---|---|---|---|---|---|---|---|---|---|---|---|---|
| | | Trendiness | | Avg. | Up Trendiness | | While in Trend | | | Trendless Analysis | | | |
| | | Average | Rank | /D | WtdAvg | Rank | Up/Tot | Dn/Tot | Up Rank | Up | Down | Trendless | Rank |
| France CAC 40 | I | 69.78 | 80 | 2.45 | 171.01 | 57 | 70.69% | 29.31% | 43 | 49.32% | 20.45% | 30.22% | 30 |
| Germany DAX | I | 67.81 | 85 | 3.44 | 233.49 | 14 | 76.73% | 23.27% | 9 | 52.03% | 15.78% | 32.19% | 25 |
| Global Dow | I | 74.55 | 60 | 1.95 | 145.64 | 77 | 65.57% | 34.43% | 81 | 48.88% | 25.67% | 25.45% | 50 |
| Gold and Silver Mining | C | 38.35 | 107 | 0.90 | 34.66 | 107 | 48.11% | 51.89% | 108 | 18.45% | 19.90% | 61.65% | 3 |
| Gold Base Price Handy & Harman | C | 49.21 | 103 | 1.20 | 59.26 | 105 | 54.64% | 45.36% | 102 | 26.89% | 22.32% | 50.79% | 7 |
| Gold Bugs (AMEX) | C | 32.56 | 108 | 1.04 | 33.76 | 108 | 51.30% | 48.70% | 107 | 16.70% | 15.85% | 67.44% | 2 |
| Gold Mining Stocks | C | 48.18 | 106 | 1.07 | 51.61 | 106 | 52.05% | 47.95% | 104 | 25.08% | 23.10% | 51.82% | 4 |
| Greece General Share | I | 62.60 | 98 | 1.27 | 79.60 | 102 | 55.26% | 44.74% | 101 | 34.59% | 28.01% | 37.40% | 12 |
| Hanoi SE Index | I | 49.16 | 104 | 0.44 | 21.73 | 109 | 31.12% | 68.88% | 109 | 15.30% | 33.86% | 50.84% | 6 |
| Healthcare Index (S&P) | S | 84.22 | 24 | 1.94 | 163.54 | 62 | 66.04% | 33.96% | 79 | 55.62% | 28.60% | 15.78% | 86 |
| Hong Kong Hang Seng | I | 69.98 | 78 | 2.22 | 155.21 | 70 | 68.60% | 31.40% | 63 | 48.01% | 21.97% | 30.02% | 32 |
| Ibex 35 | I | 67.58 | 86 | 2.42 | 163.36 | 63 | 69.99% | 30.01% | 49 | 47.30% | 20.28% | 32.42% | 24 |
| India BSE 30 | I | 57.04 | 101 | 2.29 | 130.77 | 90 | 68.93% | 31.07% | 57 | 39.32% | 17.72% | 42.96% | 9 |
| Indonesia Jakarta Composite | I | 73.88 | 64 | 2.04 | 150.64 | 73 | 66.95% | 33.05% | 72 | 49.46% | 24.42% | 26.12% | 46 |
| Israel TA-100 | I | 77.53 | 52 | 2.57 | 199.63 | 35 | 71.90% | 28.10% | 31 | 55.75% | 21.78% | 22.47% | 58 |
| Italy FTSE MIB Index | I | 64.28 | 94 | 2.48 | 159.60 | 68 | 70.12% | 29.88% | 48 | 45.07% | 19.21% | 35.72% | 16 |
| Japan Nikkei 225 | I | 75.65 | 59 | 1.95 | 147.74 | 75 | 65.66% | 34.34% | 80 | 49.67% | 25.98% | 24.35% | 51 |
| Johannesburg All Shares | I | 72.84 | 68 | 4.53 | 330.27 | 1 | 81.41% | 18.59% | 2 | 59.30% | 13.54% | 27.16% | 42 |
| Major Market Index | I | 84.49 | 20 | 2.68 | 226.54 | 20 | 72.75% | 27.25% | 27 | 61.47% | 23.02% | 15.51% | 90 |
| Malaysia KLSE Composite | I | 82.64 | 32 | 1.96 | 162.02 | 66 | 66.08% | 33.92% | 78 | 54.61% | 28.04% | 17.36% | 78 |
| Mexico IPC | I | 68.41 | 84 | 3.35 | 229.30 | 17 | 76.30% | 23.70% | 11 | 52.19% | 16.21% | 31.59% | 26 |
| Morgan Stanley Consumer Index | S | 87.52 | 12 | 2.96 | 259.01 | 9 | 74.68% | 25.32% | 16 | 65.36% | 22.16% | 12.48% | 98 |
| Morgan Stanley Cyclical Index | S | 69.12 | 83 | 2.32 | 160.59 | 67 | 68.48% | 31.52% | 66 | 47.33% | 21.78% | 30.88% | 27 |
| MSCI EAFE | I | 89.91 | 7 | 1.99 | 178.96 | 52 | 66.56% | 33.44% | 75 | 59.85% | 30.06% | 10.09% | 103 |
| MSCI EM | I | 84.27 | 23 | 2.21 | 186.22 | 49 | 68.72% | 31.28% | 59 | 57.92% | 26.36% | 15.73% | 87 |
| NASDAQ 100 | I | 65.28 | 91 | 2.86 | 186.56 | 48 | 73.88% | 26.12% | 20 | 48.23% | 17.05% | 34.72% | 19 |
| NASDAQ Composite | I | 81.32 | 38 | 2.19 | 177.69 | 53 | 68.54% | 31.46% | 65 | 55.74% | 25.58% | 18.68% | 72 |
| Netherlands AEX General | I | 78.28 | 49 | 2.45 | 191.77 | 43 | 70.74% | 29.26% | 42 | 55.37% | 22.90% | 21.72% | 61 |
| Norway Oslo All Share Composite | I | 73.70 | 66 | 3.74 | 275.40 | 5 | 78.82% | 21.18% | 5 | 58.09% | 15.61% | 26.30% | 44 |
| Norway Oslo OBX Top 25 | I | 60.77 | 100 | 4.88 | 296.50 | 3 | 82.86% | 17.14% | 1 | 50.36% | 10.41% | 39.23% | 10 |

| | Index | | | | | | | | | | | | |
|---|---|---|---|---|---|---|---|---|---|---|---|---|---|
| | NYSE Composite | 89.89 | 8 | 2.41 | 217.05 | 22 | 70.61% | 29.39% | 44 | 63.47% | 26.42% | 10.11% | 102 |
| I | Pakistan Karachi 100 | 67.51 | 87 | 2.06 | 139.15 | 83 | 66.54% | 33.46% | 76 | 44.92% | 22.59% | 32.49% | 23 |
| I | Peru Lima General | 80.33 | 43 | 1.78 | 142.75 | 79 | 63.81% | 36.19% | 86 | 51.26% | 29.07% | 19.67% | 67 |
| I | Philippines PSE Composite | 74.47 | 62 | 1.66 | 123.72 | 93 | 62.28% | 37.72% | 93 | 46.38% | 28.09% | 25.53% | 48 |
| | Russell 1000 | 83.72 | 29 | 3.02 | 252.92 | 11 | 75.06% | 24.94% | 14 | 62.84% | 20.88% | 16.28% | 81 |
| | Russell 1000 Growth | 80.55 | 40 | 2.61 | 209.84 | 23 | 72.16% | 27.84% | 30 | 58.13% | 22.43% | 19.45% | 70 |
| | Russell 1000 Value | 78.58 | 47 | 2.26 | 177.52 | 54 | 69.06% | 30.94% | 56 | 54.27% | 24.31% | 21.42% | 63 |
| | Russell 2000 | 83.02 | 30 | 2.07 | 171.63 | 56 | 67.34% | 32.66% | 70 | 55.91% | 27.11% | 16.98% | 80 |
| | Russell 2000 Growth | 82.05 | 35 | 2.31 | 189.76 | 47 | 69.62% | 30.38% | 51 | 57.13% | 24.92% | 17.95% | 75 |
| | Russell 2000 Value | 87.53 | 11 | 3.69 | 322.90 | 2 | 78.59% | 21.41% | 6 | 68.80% | 18.74% | 12.47% | 99 |
| | Russell 3000 | 84.38 | 22 | 2.95 | 248.63 | 12 | 74.56% | 25.44% | 18 | 62.91% | 21.47% | 15.62% | 88 |
| | S&P 100 Index | 83.97 | 27 | 2.27 | 190.61 | 46 | 69.33% | 30.67% | 53 | 58.22% | 25.76% | 16.03% | 83 |
| | S&P 1500 INDEX | 78.57 | 48 | 2.58 | 202.70 | 31 | 71.79% | 28.21% | 32 | 56.41% | 22.16% | 21.43% | 62 |
| | S&P 400 Index | 78.80 | 46 | 3.01 | 237.45 | 13 | 74.59% | 25.41% | 17 | 58.78% | 20.02% | 21.20% | 64 |
| | S&P 500 Index | 88.78 | 9 | 2.25 | 199.91 | 33 | 69.21% | 30.79% | 55 | 61.45% | 27.33% | 11.22% | 101 |
| | S&P 500 Total Return | 86.90 | 16 | 3.21 | 278.62 | 4 | 76.12% | 23.88% | 12 | 66.15% | 20.75% | 13.10% | 94 |
| | S&P 600 Index | 71.77 | 72 | 2.55 | 183.16 | 50 | 71.37% | 28.63% | 36 | 51.23% | 20.55% | 28.23% | 38 |
| I | S&P CNX NIFTY (India) | 62.26 | 99 | 2.88 | 179.06 | 51 | 73.86% | 26.14% | 21 | 45.99% | 16.27% | 37.74% | 11 |
| S | S&P Cons Discretionary Sector | 76.96 | 55 | 2.71 | 208.53 | 25 | 73.02% | 26.98% | 24 | 56.20% | 20.76% | 23.04% | 55 |
| S | S&P Cons Staples Sector | 80.19 | 44 | 2.49 | 199.75 | 34 | 71.17% | 28.83% | 39 | 57.07% | 23.12% | 19.81% | 66 |
| S | S&P Energy Sector | 92.31 | 3 | 2.52 | 232.75 | 15 | 71.59% | 28.41% | 33 | 66.08% | 26.23% | 7.69% | 107 |
| S | S&P 500 Equal Weight | 72.75 | 69 | 2.19 | 158.98 | 69 | 68.66% | 31.34% | 60 | 49.95% | 22.80% | 27.25% | 41 |
| S | S&P Financials Sector | 74.40 | 63 | 1.73 | 128.41 | 91 | 63.20% | 36.80% | 88 | 47.03% | 27.38% | 25.60% | 47 |
| S | S&P Healthcare Sector | 86.97 | 15 | 2.21 | 192.24 | 41 | 68.78% | 31.22% | 58 | 59.82% | 27.16% | 13.03% | 95 |
| S | S&P Industrials Sector | 82.49 | 33 | 2.05 | 169.05 | 58 | 66.98% | 33.02% | 71 | 55.25% | 27.24% | 17.51% | 77 |
| S | S&P Materials Sector | 77.15 | 54 | 2.01 | 154.98 | 72 | 66.66% | 33.34% | 74 | 51.43% | 25.72% | 22.85% | 56 |
| S | S&P MIDCAP INDEX | 84.10 | 25 | 2.71 | 228.13 | 19 | 72.86% | 27.14% | 26 | 61.28% | 22.82% | 15.90% | 85 |
| S | S&P Technology Sector | 70.34 | 74 | 2.05 | 144.50 | 78 | 66.92% | 33.08% | 73 | 47.07% | 23.27% | 29.66% | 36 |
| S | S&P Telecomm Sector | 80.79 | 39 | 1.71 | 138.25 | 84 | 63.06% | 36.94% | 89 | 50.95% | 29.84% | 19.21% | 71 |
| S | S&P Utilities Sector | 87.37 | 13 | 2.19 | 191.14 | 44 | 68.61% | 31.39% | 62 | 59.95% | 27.42% | 12.63% | 97 |
| I | S&P/TSX 60 CAPPED (Canada) | 81.78 | 36 | 2.43 | 198.35 | 36 | 70.79% | 29.21% | 40 | 57.89% | 23.89% | 18.22% | 74 |
| I | S&P/TSX 60 (Canada) | 77.47 | 53 | 2.50 | 193.45 | 40 | 71.32% | 28.68% | 37 | 55.25% | 22.21% | 22.53% | 57 |
| I | S&P/TSX Composite (Canada) | 87.29 | 14 | 2.20 | 191.92 | 42 | 68.58% | 31.42% | 64 | 59.86% | 27.43% | 12.71% | 96 |

(Continued)

TABLE 10.9 Continued

| | Index Name | Trendiness One | | | | | Trendiness Two | | | Trendless Analysis | | | |
|---|---|---|---|---|---|---|---|---|---|---|---|---|---|
| | | Trendiness | | Avg. | Up Trendiness | | | While in Trend | | | | | |
| | | Average | Rank | /D | WtdAvg | Rank | Up/Tot | Dn/Tot | Up Rank | Up | Down | Trendless | Rank |
| C | Silver Base Price Handy & Harman | 72.55 | 70 | 1.44 | 104.30 | 100 | 58.78% | 41.22% | 97 | 42.65% | 29.91% | 27.45% | 40 |
| I | Singapore Straits Times | 65.83 | 90 | 1.67 | 109.63 | 97 | 62.30% | 37.70% | 92 | 41.01% | 24.82% | 34.17% | 20 |
| I | Slovakia SAX | 90.31 | 5 | 1.28 | 115.54 | 95 | 56.08% | 43.92% | 100 | 50.65% | 39.67% | 9.69% | 105 |
| I | South Korea Seoul Composite | 67.39 | 88 | 1.59 | 107.17 | 99 | 61.19% | 38.81% | 96 | 41.24% | 26.15% | 32.61% | 22 |
| I | S&P 500 Tot Ret Inflation Adj | 86.25 | 18 | 3.05 | 262.89 | 8 | 75.15% | 24.85% | 13 | 64.82% | 21.43% | 13.75% | 92 |
| I | Spain Madrid General | 78.14 | 51 | 1.79 | 140.12 | 82 | 64.01% | 35.99% | 85 | 50.02% | 28.12% | 21.86% | 59 |
| I | Sri Lanka All Share | 83.98 | 26 | 1.29 | 108.17 | 98 | 56.21% | 43.79% | 99 | 47.21% | 36.77% | 16.02% | 84 |
| I | Swedish OMX 30 | 70.18 | 77 | 2.72 | 190.76 | 45 | 72.97% | 27.03% | 25 | 51.21% | 18.97% | 29.82% | 33 |
| I | Switzerland Swiss Market | 82.10 | 34 | 2.79 | 229.22 | 18 | 73.27% | 26.73% | 23 | 60.16% | 21.94% | 17.90% | 76 |
| I | Taiwan Weighted | 69.20 | 82 | 1.82 | 125.61 | 92 | 64.06% | 35.94% | 84 | 44.33% | 24.87% | 30.80% | 28 |
| I | Thailand SET | 73.51 | 67 | 1.88 | 138.19 | 85 | 64.99% | 35.01% | 83 | 47.77% | 25.73% | 26.49% | 43 |
| I | Turkey ISE National-100 | 32.02 | 109 | 4.43 | 141.83 | 81 | 79.17% | 20.83% | 4 | 25.35% | 6.67% | 67.98% | 1 |
| I | United Kingdom FTSE 100 | 82.77 | 31 | 2.53 | 209.34 | 24 | 71.56% | 28.44% | 34 | 59.23% | 23.54% | 17.23% | 79 |
| C | US Dollar Index | 95.16 | 1 | 1.08 | 102.65 | 101 | 51.85% | 48.15% | 105 | 49.34% | 45.82% | 4.84% | 109 |
| C | Value Line Index (Arithmetic) | 86.60 | 17 | 2.36 | 204.40 | 29 | 70.19% | 29.81% | 47 | 60.79% | 25.81% | 13.40% | 93 |
| | Value Line Index (Geometric) | 84.44 | 21 | 1.93 | 162.59 | 64 | 65.56% | 34.44% | 82 | 55.36% | 29.09% | 15.56% | 89 |
| I | Venezuela IBC | 76.70 | 58 | 1.70 | 130.78 | 89 | 63.02% | 36.98% | 90 | 48.34% | 28.37% | 23.30% | 52 |
| I | Viet Nam Index | 70.31 | 75 | 1.08 | 75.84 | 103 | 51.69% | 48.31% | 106 | 36.34% | 33.97% | 29.69% | 35 |
| | **Statistics** | | | | | | | | | | | | |
| | Mean | 74.81 | | 2.33 | 174.47 | | 68.04% | 31.96% | | 51.10% | 23.71% | 25.19% | |
| | Average Deviation | 9.27 | | 0.56 | 44.70 | | 5.46% | 5.46% | | 7.42% | 4.39% | 9.27% | |
| | Median | 76.96 | | 2.27 | 172.31 | | 69.21% | 30.79% | | 52.03% | 23.27% | 23.04% | |
| | Minimum | 32.02 | | 0.44 | 21.73 | | 31.12% | 17.14% | | 15.30% | 6.67% | 4.84% | |
| | Maximum | 95.16 | | 4.88 | 330.27 | | 82.86% | 68.88% | | 68.80% | 45.82% | 67.98% | |
| | Sigma | 12.25 | | 0.77 | 58.11 | | 7.66% | 7.66% | | 10.28% | 5.92% | 12.25% | |
| | Geometric Mean | 73.59 | | 2.20 | 161.93 | | 67.53% | 31.15% | | 49.70% | 22.93% | 22.50% | |
| | Harmonic Mean | 72.03 | | 2.04 | 142.11 | | 66.92% | 30.41% | | 47.64% | 22.01% | 19.90% | |
| | Kurtosis | 2.08 | | 1.30 | 0.52 | | 446.17% | 446.17% | | 245.72% | 191.06% | 207.66% | |
| | Skewness | -1.24 | | 0.64 | -0.05 | | -148.50% | 148.50% | | -134.87% | 42.01% | 123.61% | |
| | Trimmed Mean – 20% | 76.18 | | 2.29 | 174.81 | | 68.78% | 31.22% | | 52.30% | 23.58% | 23.82% | |

**FIGURE 10.8** Trend Analysis of U.S. Dollar Index Chart

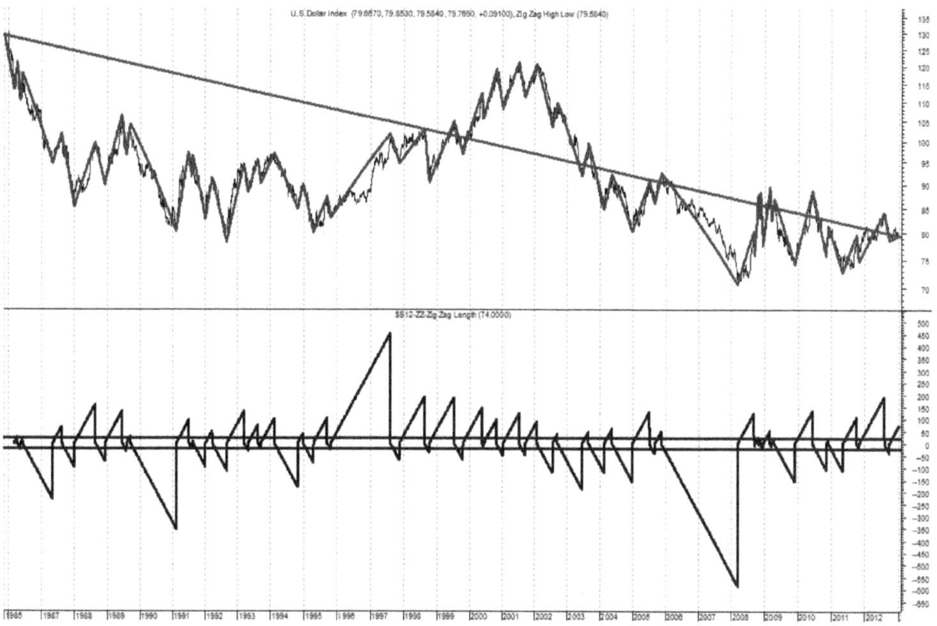

*Source:* Chart courtesy of MetaStock.

also shows that it ranks low (109 and 81) in the Trendiness One, which is measuring the trendiness based on all the data, and that the rank in Trendiness Two is high (4). Remember that Trendiness Two only looks at the trending data, not all of the data. Therefore, you can say that this index when in a trending mode, tends to trend up well, but the problem is that it isn't in a trending mode often (see Table 10.11).

Figure 10.9 shows the Turkey ISE National-100 index with the same format as the earlier analysis. Notice that it is generally in an uptrend based on the long-term trend line. From the bottom plot you can see that there is very little movement of trends outside of the +21 and −21 day bands. Bottom line is that this index doesn't trend well, and is quite volatile in its price movements; if you are trend follower; don't waste your time with this one. A question that might arise is that it is also clear from the top plot that it is in an uptrend, so if you used a larger filtered wave and/or different trend length, it might yield different results. My response to that is simply: of course it will, you can fit the analysis to get any results you want, especially with all this wonderful hindsight. Bad approach to successful trend following.

Using the same data table, let's look at an index that ranks high in the uptrend rankings (Table 10.9). From the table it ranks as middle of the road relatively based on Trendiness One and Trendless rank. However, the rank for Up Trendiness One and Trendiness Two Up rank is high (both are 5). This means that most of the trendiness is to the upside with only moderate downtrends (see Table 10.12).

**TABLE 10.10** Trend Analysis of U.S. Dollar Index

| | Trendiness One | | | | | | Trendiness Two | | | | Trendless Analysis | | | |
| | Trendiness | | Avg. | Up Trendiness | | | While in Trend | | | | | | | |
| Index Name | Average | Rank | U/D | WrdAvg | Rank | | Up/Tot | Dn/Tot | Up Rank | | Up | Down | Trendless | Rank |
|---|---|---|---|---|---|---|---|---|---|---|---|---|---|---|
| C U.S. Dollar Index | 95.16 | 1 | 1.08 | 102.65 | 101 | | 51.85% | 48.15% | 105 | | 49.34% | 45.82% | 4.84% | 109 |

190

**TABLE 10.11**  Trend Analysis of Turkey ISE National-100

| | Trendiness One | | | | | | Trendiness Two | | | | Trendless Analysis | | |
| | Trendiness | | Avg. | Up Trendiness | | | While in Trend | | | | | | |
| Index Name | Average | Rank | U/D | WtdAvg | Rank | | Up/Tot | Dn/Tot | Up Rank | | Up | Down | Trendless | Rank |
|---|---|---|---|---|---|---|---|---|---|---|---|---|---|---|
| 1  Turkey ISE National-100 | 32.02 | 109 | 4.43 | 141.83 | 81 | | 79.16% | 20.83% | 4 | | 25.35% | 6.67% | 67.98% | 1 |

191

**FIGURE 10.9**   Trend Analysis of Turkey ISE National-100 Chart

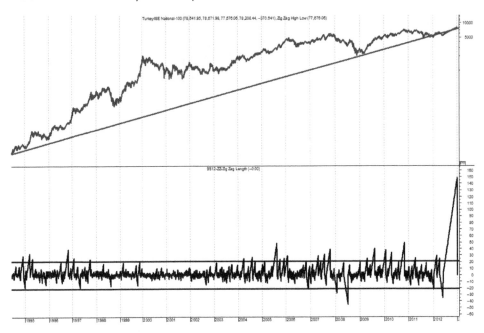

*Source:* Chart courtesy of MetaStock.

Figure 10.10 shows the Norway Oslo Index clearly in an uptrend. The bottom plot shows that most of the spikes of trend length are above the +21 band level and very few are below the −21 band level. This confirms the data in the table.

In order to carry this analysis to fruition, let's look at the index with the worst uptrend rank (Table 10.9). From the table the Trendiness One and Two Up ranks are dead last (109). The Trendiness One overall rank is 104, which is almost last, and the trendless rank is 6, which confirms that data (see Table 10.13).

Figure 10.11 shows that the Hanoi SE Index is clearly in a downtrend; however, the bottom plot shows that very few trends are outside the bands. And the ones that move well outside the bands are the downtrends. As before, one can change the analysis and get desired results, but that is not how it should be done. One note, however, is that this index does not have a great deal of data compared to most of the others and this should be a consideration in the overall analysis.

## Indices Analysis Summary

The analysis of the various rankings for the indices shows that the data in the table is robust and accurate. In summary, there are two types of overall trendiness measures; Trendiness One uses all of the data to determine trendiness, and Trendless uses only the trending data determined by the filtered wave value and the trend length. Of

**TABLE 10.12** Trend Analysis of Norway Oslo All Share Composite

| Index Name | Trendiness One | | | | | | Trendiness Two | | | | | Trendless Analysis | | | |
| | Trendiness | | Avg. | Up Trendiness | | | While in Trend | | | | | | | | |
| | Average | Rank | U/D | WtdAvg | Rank | | Up/Tot | Dn/Tot | Up Rank | | | Up | Down | Trendless | Rank |
|---|---|---|---|---|---|---|---|---|---|---|---|---|---|---|---|
| I Norway Oslo All Share Composite | 73.70 | 66 | 3.74 | 275.40 | 5 | | 78.82% | 21.18% | 5 | | | 58.09% | 15.61% | 26.30% | 44 |

**FIGURE 10.10**  Trend Analysis of Norway Oslo All Share Composite Chart

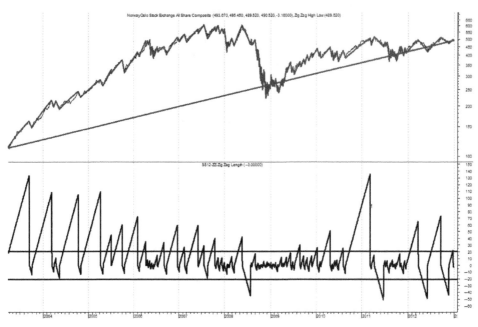

*Source:* Chart courtesy of MetaStock.

**FIGURE 10.11**  Trend Analysis of Hanoi SE Index Chart

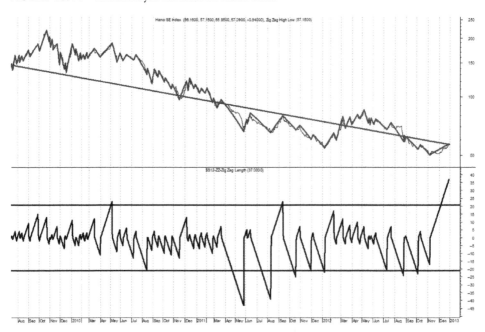

*Source:* Chart courtesy of MetaStock.

**TABLE 10.13** Trend Analysis of Hanoi SE Index

| Index Name | Trendiness One | | | | | | Trendiness Two | | | | Trendless Analysis | | |
| | Trendiness | | Avg. | Up Trendiness | | | While in Trend | | | | | | |
| | Average | Rank | U/D | WtdAvg | Rank | Up/Tot | Dn/Tot | Up Rank | Up | Down | Trendless | Rank |
|---|---|---|---|---|---|---|---|---|---|---|---|---|
| 1  Hanoi SE Index | 49.16 | 104 | 0.44 | 21.73 | 109 | 31.12% | 68.88% | 109 | 15.30% | 33.86% | 50.84% | 6 |

course, Trendiness One is the complement of Trendless analysis. They are still measuring trendiness, just in two different arenas. There are also two measures of Up Trendiness using the same concept. This could have just as easily been a ranking of down trendiness, but I think up trendiness is more prevalent in most markets.

Appendix B contains a number of tables that show the tables ordered by their ranks, which makes it easier to find the ranking you are looking for.

The following tables show various subsets of the All table just analyzed.

## Domestic Trendiness

Table 10.14 contains only the domestic issues.

## International Trendiness

Table 10.15 contains only the international issues.

## Commodity Trendiness

Table 10.16 contains only the commodity-based issues.

## Sector Trendiness

Table 10.17 contains only the sector-related issues.

**TABLE 10.14** Domestic Trendiness

| Index Name | Trendiness One | | | | | Trendiness Two | | | | | | |
| | Trendiness | | Avg. | Up Trendiness | | While in Trend | | | Trendless Analysis | | | |
| | Average | Rank | U/D | WtdAvg | Rank | Up | Down | Up Rank | Up | Down | Trendless | Rank |
|---|---|---|---|---|---|---|---|---|---|---|---|---|
| AMEX Compsite | 80.49 | 20 | 3.38 | 271.90 | 3 | 76.98% | 23.02% | 2 | 61.97% | 18.53% | 19.51% | 11 |
| DJ Wilshire US Small Cap | 66.74 | 29 | 3.12 | 208.53 | 13 | 74.27% | 25.73% | 8 | 49.57% | 17.18% | 33.26% | 2 |
| Dow Industrials 1885 | 86.07 | 8 | 2.27 | 195.02 | 19 | 69.23% | 30.77% | 23 | 59.59% | 26.49% | 13.93% | 23 |
| Dow Jones Composite | 78.81 | 21 | 2.49 | 196.51 | 18 | 71.23% | 28.77% | 17 | 56.13% | 22.68% | 21.19% | 10 |
| Dow Jones Stoxx | 76.85 | 25 | 2.53 | 194.67 | 20 | 71.39% | 28.61% | 15 | 54.86% | 21.99% | 23.15% | 6 |
| Dow Jones Transport | 69.39 | 28 | 2.24 | 155.18 | 30 | 68.29% | 31.71% | 28 | 47.39% | 22.00% | 30.61% | 3 |
| Dow Jones Utilities | 83.77 | 14 | 2.43 | 203.64 | 15 | 70.76% | 29.24% | 18 | 59.28% | 24.49% | 16.23% | 17 |
| DJ Wilshire 5000 Composite | 88.07 | 3 | 2.62 | 230.54 | 8 | 72.34% | 27.66% | 12 | 63.70% | 24.36% | 11.93% | 28 |
| Major Market Index | 84.49 | 9 | 2.68 | 226.54 | 10 | 72.75% | 27.25% | 11 | 61.47% | 23.02% | 15.51% | 22 |
| NASDAQ 100 | 65.28 | 30 | 2.86 | 186.56 | 23 | 73.88% | 26.12% | 9 | 48.23% | 17.05% | 34.72% | 1 |
| NASDAQ Composite | 81.32 | 18 | 2.19 | 177.69 | 25 | 68.54% | 31.46% | 27 | 55.74% | 25.58% | 18.68% | 13 |
| NYSE Composite | 89.89 | 1 | 2.41 | 217.05 | 11 | 70.61% | 29.39% | 19 | 63.47% | 26.42% | 10.11% | 30 |
| Russell 1000 | 83.72 | 15 | 3.02 | 252.92 | 5 | 75.06% | 24.94% | 5 | 62.84% | 20.88% | 16.28% | 16 |
| Russell 1000 Growth | 80.55 | 19 | 2.61 | 209.84 | 12 | 72.16% | 27.84% | 13 | 58.13% | 22.43% | 19.45% | 12 |
| Russell 1000 Value | 78.58 | 23 | 2.26 | 177.52 | 26 | 69.06% | 30.94% | 25 | 54.27% | 24.31% | 21.42% | 8 |
| Russell 2000 | 83.02 | 16 | 2.07 | 171.63 | 27 | 67.34% | 32.66% | 29 | 55.91% | 27.11% | 16.98% | 15 |
| Russell 2000 Growth | 82.05 | 17 | 2.31 | 189.76 | 22 | 69.62% | 30.38% | 21 | 57.13% | 24.92% | 17.95% | 14 |
| Russell 2000 Value | 87.53 | 4 | 3.69 | 322.90 | 1 | 78.59% | 21.41% | 1 | 68.80% | 18.74% | 12.47% | 27 |
| Russell 3000 | 84.38 | 11 | 2.95 | 248.63 | 6 | 74.56% | 25.44% | 7 | 62.91% | 21.47% | 15.62% | 20 |
| S&P 100 Index | 83.97 | 13 | 2.27 | 190.61 | 21 | 69.33% | 30.67% | 22 | 58.22% | 25.76% | 16.03% | 18 |
| S&P 1500 INDEX | 78.57 | 24 | 2.58 | 202.70 | 16 | 71.79% | 28.21% | 14 | 56.41% | 22.16% | 21.43% | 7 |
| S&P 400 Index | 78.80 | 22 | 3.01 | 237.45 | 7 | 74.59% | 25.41% | 6 | 58.78% | 20.02% | 21.20% | 9 |
| S&P 500 Index | 88.78 | 2 | 2.25 | 199.91 | 17 | 69.21% | 30.79% | 24 | 61.45% | 27.33% | 11.22% | 29 |

*(Continued)*

197

**TABLE 10.14** Continued

| Index Name | Trendiness One | | | | | | Trendiness Two | | | Trendless Analysis | | | |
|---|---|---|---|---|---|---|---|---|---|---|---|---|---|
| | Trendiness | | Avg. | Up Trendiness | | | While in Trend | | | | | | |
| | Average | Rank | U/D | WtdAvg | Rank | | Up | Down | Up Rank | Up | Down | Trendless | Rank |
| S&P 500 Total Return | 86.90 | 5 | 3.21 | 278.62 | 2 | 76.12% | 23.88% | 3 | 66.15% | 20.75% | 13.10% | 26 |
| S&P 600 Index | 71.77 | 27 | 2.55 | 183.16 | 24 | 71.37% | 28.63% | 16 | 51.23% | 20.55% | 28.23% | 4 |
| S&P Equal Weight | 72.75 | 26 | 2.19 | 158.98 | 29 | 68.66% | 31.34% | 26 | 49.95% | 22.80% | 27.25% | 5 |
| S&P MIDCAP INDEX | 84.10 | 12 | 2.71 | 228.13 | 9 | 72.86% | 27.14% | 10 | 61.28% | 22.82% | 15.90% | 19 |
| S&P 500 Tot Ret Inflation Adj | 86.25 | 7 | 3.05 | 262.89 | 4 | 75.15% | 24.85% | 4 | 64.82% | 21.43% | 13.75% | 24 |
| Value Line Index (Arithmetic) | 86.60 | 6 | 2.36 | 204.40 | 14 | 70.19% | 29.81% | 20 | 60.79% | 25.81% | 13.40% | 25 |
| Value Line Index (Geometric) | 84.44 | 10 | 1.93 | 162.59 | 28 | 65.56% | 34.44% | 30 | 55.36% | 29.09% | 15.56% | 21 |
| **Statistics** | | | | | | | | | | | | |
| Mean | 81.13 | | 2.61 | 211.55 | 15.50 | 71.72% | 28.28% | 15.50 | 58.19% | 22.94% | 18.87% | |
| Average Deviation | 5.00 | | 0.33 | 30.04 | 7.50 | 2.47% | 2.47% | 7.50 | 4.29% | 2.43% | 5.00% | |
| Median | 83.37 | | 2.54 | 203.17 | 15.50 | 71.38% | 28.62% | 15.50 | 58.50% | 22.74% | 16.63% | |
| Minimum | 65.28 | | 1.93 | 155.18 | 1.00 | 65.56% | 21.41% | 1.00 | 47.39% | 17.05% | 10.11% | |
| Maximum | 89.89 | | 3.69 | 322.90 | 30.00 | 78.59% | 34.44% | 30.00 | 68.80% | 29.09% | 34.72% | |
| Sigma | 6.44 | | 0.42 | 38.74 | 8.80 | 3.05% | 3.05% | 8.80 | 5.38% | 3.04% | 6.44% | |
| Geometric Mean | 80.87 | | 2.58 | 208.36 | 12.04 | 71.66% | 28.12% | 12.04 | 57.95% | 22.74% | 17.93% | |
| Harmonic Mean | 80.59 | | 2.55 | 205.40 | 7.51 | 71.59% | 27.95% | 7.51 | 57.69% | 22.53% | 17.10% | |
| Kurtosis | 0.49 | | 0.10 | 1.00 | -1.20 | -33.35% | -33.34% | -1.20 | -37.63% | -47.28% | 49.10% | |
| Skewness | -1.05 | | 0.73 | 0.97 | 0.00 | 27.76% | -27.76% | 0.00 | -30.23% | -8.41% | 105.13% | |
| Trimmed Mean – 20% | 81.91 | | 2.57 | 208.18 | 15.50 | 71.61% | 28.39% | 15.50 | 58.37% | 22.99% | 18.09% | |

**TABLE 10.15** International Trendiness

| | Trendiness One | | | | | Trendiness Two | | | Trendless Analysis | | | |
| | Trendiness | | Avg. | Up Trendiness | | While in Trend | | | | | | |
| Index Name | Average | Rank | U/D | WtdAvg | Rank | Up | Down | Up Rank | Up | Down | Trendless | Rank |
|---|---|---|---|---|---|---|---|---|---|---|---|---|
| Argentina MerVal | 50.48 | 52 | 2.41 | 121.53 | 46 | 70.23% | 29.77% | 21 | 35.45% | 15.03% | 49.52% | 4 |
| Australia All Ordinaries | 90.94 | 1 | 2.28 | 207.75 | 10 | 69.52% | 30.48% | 25 | 63.22% | 27.71% | 9.06% | 55 |
| Austria ATX | 76.85 | 19 | 2.24 | 172.31 | 21 | 68.65% | 31.35% | 28 | 52.76% | 24.09% | 23.15% | 37 |
| Belgium BEL-20 | 78.16 | 15 | 2.15 | 168.18 | 23 | 68.21% | 31.79% | 31 | 53.32% | 24.84% | 21.84% | 41 |
| Brazil Bovespa | 48.29 | 54 | 3.44 | 165.90 | 25 | 74.77% | 25.23% | 8 | 36.11% | 12.18% | 51.71% | 2 |
| Chile IGPA General Index | 90.17 | 3 | 1.66 | 149.32 | 32 | 62.34% | 37.66% | 44 | 56.21% | 33.95% | 9.83% | 53 |
| Chile IPSA | 80.43 | 12 | 1.63 | 131.41 | 41 | 61.97% | 38.03% | 48 | 49.84% | 30.58% | 19.57% | 44 |
| China Shanghai Composite | 62.87 | 47 | 1.17 | 73.82 | 54 | 54.10% | 45.90% | 53 | 34.01% | 28.86% | 37.13% | 9 |
| Czech Republic PX | 69.81 | 35 | 1.65 | 115.13 | 48 | 62.22% | 37.78% | 47 | 43.44% | 26.38% | 30.19% | 21 |
| Denmark Copenhagen 20 | 72.47 | 29 | 2.76 | 200.23 | 11 | 72.37% | 27.63% | 13 | 52.45% | 20.03% | 27.53% | 27 |
| Dow Jones Euro Stoxx | 70.26 | 32 | 2.37 | 166.81 | 24 | 69.78% | 30.22% | 24 | 49.03% | 21.23% | 29.74% | 24 |
| Dow Jones Euro Stoxx 50 | 64.79 | 44 | 2.51 | 162.47 | 27 | 70.54% | 29.46% | 20 | 45.71% | 19.09% | 35.21% | 12 |
| Egypt CMA | 73.73 | 25 | 2.82 | 207.83 | 9 | 73.69% | 26.31% | 10 | 54.33% | 19.40% | 26.27% | 31 |
| EURONEXT 100 | 70.41 | 30 | 3.67 | 258.45 | 4 | 77.86% | 22.14% | 5 | 54.82% | 15.59% | 29.59% | 26 |
| Finland HSE General Index | 63.57 | 46 | 2.09 | 133.08 | 40 | 67.49% | 32.51% | 32 | 42.90% | 20.67% | 36.43% | 10 |
| France CAC 40 | 69.78 | 36 | 2.45 | 171.01 | 22 | 70.69% | 29.31% | 19 | 49.32% | 20.45% | 30.22% | 20 |
| Germany DAX | 67.81 | 39 | 3.44 | 233.49 | 5 | 76.73% | 23.27% | 6 | 52.03% | 15.78% | 32.19% | 17 |
| Global Dow | 74.55 | 22 | 1.95 | 145.64 | 34 | 65.57% | 34.43% | 38 | 48.88% | 25.67% | 25.45% | 34 |
| Greece General Share | 62.60 | 48 | 1.27 | 79.60 | 52 | 55.26% | 44.74% | 52 | 34.59% | 28.01% | 37.40% | 8 |
| Hanoi SE Index | 49.16 | 53 | 0.44 | 21.73 | 55 | 31.12% | 68.88% | 55 | 15.30% | 33.86% | 50.84% | 3 |
| Hong Kong Hang Seng | 69.98 | 34 | 2.22 | 155.21 | 30 | 68.60% | 31.40% | 29 | 48.01% | 21.97% | 30.02% | 22 |
| Ibex 35 | 67.58 | 40 | 2.42 | 163.36 | 26 | 69.99% | 30.01% | 23 | 47.30% | 20.28% | 32.42% | 16 |
| India BSE 30 | 57.04 | 51 | 2.29 | 130.77 | 43 | 68.93% | 31.07% | 26 | 39.32% | 17.72% | 42.96% | 5 |
| Indonesia Jakarta Composite | 73.88 | 24 | 2.04 | 150.64 | 31 | 66.95% | 33.05% | 33 | 49.46% | 24.42% | 26.12% | 32 |

(*Continued*)

**TABLE 10.15** Continued

| Index Name | Trendiness One | | | | | Trendiness Two | | | Trendless Analysis | | | |
|---|---|---|---|---|---|---|---|---|---|---|---|---|
| | Trendiness | | Avg. | Up Trendiness | | | While in Trend | | | | | |
| | Average | Rank | U/D | WtdAvg | Rank | Up | Down | Up Rank | Up | Down | Trendless | Rank |
| Israel TA-100 | 77.53 | 17 | 2.57 | 199.63 | 12 | 71.90% | 28.10% | 14 | 55.75% | 21.78% | 22.47% | 39 |
| Italy FTSE MIB Index | 64.28 | 45 | 2.48 | 159.60 | 29 | 70.12% | 29.88% | 22 | 45.07% | 19.21% | 35.72% | 11 |
| Japan Nikkei 225 | 75.65 | 21 | 1.95 | 147.74 | 33 | 65.66% | 34.34% | 37 | 49.67% | 25.98% | 24.35% | 35 |
| Johannesburg All Shares | 72.84 | 28 | 4.53 | 330.27 | 1 | 81.41% | 18.59% | 2 | 59.30% | 13.54% | 27.16% | 28 |
| Malaysia KLSE Composite | 82.64 | 9 | 1.96 | 162.02 | 28 | 66.08% | 33.92% | 36 | 54.61% | 28.04% | 17.36% | 47 |
| Mexico IPC | 68.41 | 38 | 3.35 | 229.30 | 6 | 76.30% | 23.70% | 7 | 52.19% | 16.21% | 31.59% | 18 |
| MSCI EAFE | 89.91 | 4 | 1.99 | 178.96 | 20 | 66.56% | 33.44% | 34 | 59.85% | 30.06% | 10.09% | 52 |
| MSCI EM | 84.27 | 6 | 2.21 | 186.22 | 18 | 68.72% | 31.28% | 27 | 57.92% | 26.36% | 15.73% | 50 |
| Netherlands AEX General | 78.28 | 14 | 2.45 | 191.77 | 16 | 70.74% | 29.26% | 18 | 55.37% | 22.90% | 21.72% | 42 |
| Norway Oslo All Share Composite | 73.70 | 26 | 3.74 | 275.40 | 3 | 78.82% | 21.18% | 4 | 58.09% | 15.61% | 26.30% | 30 |
| Norway Oslo OBX Top 25 | 60.77 | 50 | 4.88 | 296.50 | 2 | 82.86% | 17.14% | 1 | 50.36% | 10.41% | 39.23% | 6 |
| Pakistan Karachi 100 | 67.51 | 41 | 2.06 | 139.15 | 38 | 66.54% | 33.46% | 35 | 44.92% | 22.59% | 32.49% | 15 |
| Peru Lima General | 80.33 | 13 | 1.78 | 142.75 | 35 | 63.81% | 36.19% | 42 | 51.26% | 29.07% | 19.67% | 43 |
| Philippines PSE Composite | 74.47 | 23 | 1.66 | 123.72 | 45 | 62.28% | 37.72% | 46 | 46.38% | 28.09% | 25.53% | 33 |
| S&P CNX NIFTY (India) | 62.26 | 49 | 2.88 | 179.06 | 19 | 73.86% | 26.14% | 9 | 45.99% | 16.27% | 37.74% | 7 |
| S&P/TSX 60 CAPPED(Canada) | 81.78 | 11 | 2.43 | 198.35 | 13 | 70.79% | 29.21% | 17 | 57.89% | 23.89% | 18.22% | 45 |
| S&P/TSX 60 (Canada) | 77.47 | 18 | 2.50 | 193.45 | 14 | 71.32% | 28.68% | 16 | 55.25% | 22.21% | 22.53% | 38 |
| S&P/TSX Composite (Canada) | 87.29 | 5 | 2.20 | 191.92 | 15 | 68.58% | 31.42% | 30 | 59.86% | 27.43% | 12.71% | 51 |
| Singapore Straits Times | 65.83 | 43 | 1.67 | 109.63 | 49 | 62.30% | 37.70% | 45 | 41.01% | 24.82% | 34.17% | 13 |
| Slovakia SAX | 90.31 | 2 | 1.28 | 115.54 | 47 | 56.08% | 43.92% | 51 | 50.65% | 39.67% | 9.69% | 54 |
| South Korea Seoul Composite | 67.39 | 42 | 1.59 | 107.17 | 51 | 61.19% | 38.81% | 49 | 41.24% | 26.15% | 32.61% | 14 |

| | | | | | | | | | | | |
|---|---|---|---|---|---|---|---|---|---|---|---|
| Spain Madrid General | 40 | 21.86% | 28.12% | 50.02% | 41 | 64.01% | 35.99% | 37 | 140.12 | 1.79 | 16 | 78.14 |
| Sri Lanka All Share | 49 | 16.02% | 36.77% | 47.21% | 50 | 56.21% | 43.79% | 50 | 108.17 | 1.29 | 7 | 83.98 |
| Swedish OMX 30 | 23 | 29.82% | 18.97% | 51.21% | 12 | 72.97% | 27.03% | 17 | 190.76 | 2.72 | 33 | 70.18 |
| Switzerland Swiss Market | 46 | 17.90% | 21.94% | 60.16% | 11 | 73.27% | 26.73% | 7 | 229.22 | 2.79 | 10 | 82.10 |
| Taiwan Weighted | 19 | 30.80% | 24.87% | 44.33% | 40 | 64.06% | 35.94% | 44 | 125.61 | 1.82 | 37 | 69.20 |
| Thailand SET | 29 | 26.49% | 25.73% | 47.77% | 39 | 64.99% | 35.01% | 39 | 138.19 | 1.88 | 27 | 73.51 |
| Turkey ISE National-100 | 1 | 67.98% | 6.67% | 25.35% | 3 | 79.17% | 20.83% | 36 | 141.83 | 4.43 | 55 | 32.02 |
| United Kingdom FTSE 100 | 48 | 17.23% | 23.54% | 59.23% | 15 | 71.56% | 28.44% | 8 | 209.34 | 2.53 | 8 | 82.77 |
| Venezuela IBC | 36 | 23.30% | 28.37% | 48.34% | 43 | 63.02% | 36.98% | 42 | 130.78 | 1.70 | 20 | 76.70 |
| Viet Nam Index | 25 | 29.69% | 33.97% | 36.34% | 54 | 51.69% | 48.31% | 53 | 75.84 | 1.08 | 31 | 70.31 |
| **Statistics** | | | | | | | | | | | | |
| Mean | | 28.05% | 23.40% | 48.55% | | 67.54% | 32.46% | | 164.25 | 2.32 | | 71.95 |
| Average Deviation | | 8.30% | 5.12% | 6.57% | | 5.80% | 5.80% | | 40.94 | 0.61 | | 8.30 |
| Median | | 27.16% | 23.89% | 49.67% | | 68.65% | 31.35% | | 162.02 | 2.22 | | 72.84 |
| Minimum | | 9.06% | 6.67% | 15.30% | | 31.12% | 17.14% | | 21.73 | 0.44 | | 32.02 |
| Maximum | | 67.98% | 39.67% | 63.22% | | 82.86% | 68.88% | | 330.27 | 4.88 | | 90.94 |
| Sigma | | 11.23% | 6.54% | 8.99% | | 8.31% | 8.31% | | 55.12 | 0.85 | | 11.23 |
| Geometric Mean | | 25.84% | 22.37% | 47.48% | | 66.92% | 31.53% | | 153.58 | 2.16 | | 70.94 |
| Harmonic Mean | | 23.48% | 21.11% | 45.93% | | 66.13% | 30.65% | | 136.77 | 1.98 | | 69.70 |
| Kurtosis | | 211.76% | 27.07% | 267.46% | | 585.62% | 585.62% | | 1.36 | 1.54 | | 2.12 |
| Skewness | | 93.41% | -3.96% | -127.13% | | -158.25% | 158.25% | | 0.50 | 0.95 | | -0.93 |
| Trimmed Mean – 20% | | 27.29% | 23.36% | 49.41% | | 68.14% | 31.86% | | 161.81 | 2.25 | | 72.71 |

**TABLE 10.16** Commodity Trendiness

| | Trendiness One | | | | | Trendiness Two | | | Trendless Analysis | | | |
| | Trendiness | | Avg. | Up Trendiness | | While in Trend | | | | | | |
| Index Name | Average | Rank | U/D | WtdAvg | Rank | Up | Down | Up Rank | Up | Down | Trendless | Rank |
|---|---|---|---|---|---|---|---|---|---|---|---|---|
| AMEX Oil Index | 74.51 | 3 | 1.96 | 146.23 | 1 | 66.24% | 33.76% | 1 | 49.36% | 25.15% | 25.49% | 6 |
| CRB Index | 92.69 | 2 | 1.42 | 131.59 | 2 | 58.45% | 41.55% | 3 | 54.17% | 38.51% | 7.31% | 7 |
| Gold and Silver Mining | 38.35 | 7 | 0.90 | 34.66 | 7 | 48.11% | 51.89% | 8 | 18.45% | 19.90% | 61.65% | 2 |
| Gold Base Price Handy & Harman | 49.21 | 5 | 1.20 | 59.26 | 5 | 54.64% | 45.36% | 4 | 26.89% | 22.32% | 50.79% | 4 |
| Gold Bugs (AMEX) | 32.56 | 8 | 1.04 | 33.76 | 8 | 51.30% | 48.70% | 7 | 16.70% | 15.85% | 67.44% | 1 |
| Gold Mining Stocks | 48.18 | 6 | 1.07 | 51.61 | 6 | 52.05% | 47.95% | 5 | 25.08% | 23.10% | 51.82% | 3 |
| Silver Base Price Handy & Harman | 72.55 | 4 | 1.44 | 104.30 | 3 | 58.78% | 41.22% | 2 | 42.65% | 29.91% | 27.45% | 5 |
| US Dollar Index | 95.16 | 1 | 1.08 | 102.65 | 4 | 51.85% | 48.15% | 6 | 49.34% | 45.82% | 4.84% | 8 |
| **Statistics** | | | | | | | | | | | | |
| Mean | 62.90 | | 1.26 | 83.01 | | 55.18% | 44.82% | | 35.33% | 27.57% | 37.10% | |
| Average Deviation | 20.83 | | 0.26 | 38.18 | | 4.48% | 4.48% | | 13.55% | 7.88% | 20.83% | |
| Median | 60.88 | | 1.14 | 80.96 | | 53.35% | 46.65% | | 34.77% | 24.13% | 39.12% | |
| Minimum | 32.56 | | 0.90 | 33.76 | | 48.11% | 33.76% | | 16.70% | 15.85% | 4.84% | |
| Maximum | 95.16 | | 1.96 | 146.23 | | 66.24% | 51.89% | | 54.17% | 45.82% | 67.44% | |
| Sigma | 24.15 | | 0.34 | 43.93 | | 5.76% | 5.76% | | 15.16% | 10.06% | 24.15% | |
| Geometric Mean | 58.71 | | 1.23 | 72.19 | | 54.93% | 44.47% | | 32.25% | 26.11% | 26.86% | |
| Harmonic Mean | 54.66 | | 1.20 | 62.26 | | 54.68% | 44.10% | | 29.24% | 24.81% | 16.36% | |
| Kurtosis | -1.69 | | 1.98 | -1.72 | | 77.34% | 77.34% | | -215.25% | 8.99% | -168.59% | |
| Skewness | 0.19 | | 1.37 | 0.24 | | 95.42% | -95.42% | | -1.96% | 95.42% | -18.89% | |
| Trimmed Mean – 20% | 62.90 | | 1.26 | 83.01 | | 55.18% | 44.82% | | 35.33% | 27.57% | 37.10% | |

**TABLE 10.17** Sector Trendiness

| | Trendiness One | | | | | Trendiness Two | | | Trendless Analysis | | | |
| | Trendiness | | Avg. | Up Trendiness | | While in Trend | | | | | | |
| Index Name | Average | Rank | U/D | WtdAvg | Rank | Up | Down | Up Rank | Up | Down | Trendless | Rank |
|---|---|---|---|---|---|---|---|---|---|---|---|---|
| AMEX Pharmaceutical Index | 81.68 | 7 | 1.74 | 142.38 | 14 | 63.58% | 36.42% | 14 | 51.93% | 29.74% | 18.32% | 10 |
| Dow Jones Wilshire REIT | 64.13 | 16 | 3.46 | 221.59 | 4 | 76.41% | 23.59% | 2 | 49.00% | 15.13% | 35.87% | 1 |
| DJ Wilshire REIT Total Return | 64.34 | 15 | 4.14 | 266.38 | 1 | 79.56% | 20.44% | 1 | 51.19% | 13.15% | 35.66% | 2 |
| Healthcare Index (S&P) | 84.22 | 5 | 1.94 | 163.54 | 10 | 66.04% | 33.96% | 13 | 55.62% | 28.60% | 15.78% | 12 |
| Morgan Stanley Consumer | 87.52 | 2 | 2.96 | 259.01 | 2 | 74.68% | 25.32% | 3 | 65.36% | 22.16% | 12.48% | 15 |
| Morgan Stanley Cyclical | 69.12 | 14 | 2.32 | 160.59 | 11 | 68.48% | 31.52% | 9 | 47.33% | 21.78% | 30.88% | 3 |
| S&P Cons Discretionary Sector | 76.96 | 11 | 2.71 | 208.53 | 5 | 73.02% | 26.98% | 4 | 56.20% | 20.76% | 23.04% | 6 |
| S&P Cons Staples Sector | 80.19 | 9 | 2.49 | 199.75 | 6 | 71.17% | 28.83% | 6 | 57.07% | 23.12% | 19.81% | 8 |
| S&P Energy Sector | 92.31 | 1 | 2.52 | 232.75 | 3 | 71.59% | 28.41% | 5 | 66.08% | 26.23% | 7.69% | 16 |
| S&P Financials Sector | 74.40 | 12 | 1.73 | 128.41 | 16 | 63.20% | 36.80% | 15 | 47.03% | 27.38% | 25.60% | 5 |
| S&P Healthcare Sector | 86.97 | 4 | 2.21 | 192.24 | 7 | 68.78% | 31.22% | 7 | 59.82% | 27.16% | 13.03% | 13 |
| S&P Industrials Sector | 82.49 | 6 | 2.05 | 169.05 | 9 | 66.98% | 33.02% | 10 | 55.25% | 27.24% | 17.51% | 11 |
| S&P Materials Sector | 77.15 | 10 | 2.01 | 154.98 | 12 | 66.66% | 33.34% | 12 | 51.43% | 25.72% | 22.85% | 7 |

*(Continued)*

**TABLE 10.17** Continued

| Index Name | Trendiness One | | | | | Trendiness Two | | | | | | |
| | Trendiness | | Avg. | Up Trendiness | | While in Trend | | | Trendless Analysis | | | |
| | Average | Rank | U/D | WrdAvg | Rank | Up | Down | Up Rank | Up | Down | Trendless | Rank |
|---|---|---|---|---|---|---|---|---|---|---|---|---|
| S&P Technology Sector | 70.34 | 13 | 2.05 | 144.50 | 13 | 66.92% | 33.08% | 11 | 47.07% | 23.27% | 29.66% | 4 |
| S&P Telecomm Sector | 80.79 | 8 | 1.71 | 138.25 | 15 | 63.06% | 36.94% | 16 | 50.95% | 29.84% | 19.21% | 9 |
| S&P Utilities Sector | 87.37 | 3 | 2.19 | 191.14 | 8 | 68.61% | 31.39% | 8 | 59.95% | 27.42% | 12.63% | 14 |
| **Statistics** | | | | | | | | | | | | |
| Mean | 78.75 | | 2.39 | 185.82 | | 69.30% | 30.70% | | 54.45% | 24.29% | 21.25% | |
| Average Deviation | 6.85 | | 0.49 | 35.61 | | 3.83% | 3.83% | | 4.96% | 3.84% | 6.85% | |
| Median | 80.49 | | 2.20 | 180.09 | | 68.55% | 31.45% | | 53.59% | 25.97% | 19.51% | |
| Minimum | 64.13 | | 1.71 | 128.41 | | 63.06% | 20.44% | | 47.03% | 13.15% | 7.69% | |
| Maximum | 92.31 | | 4.14 | 266.38 | | 79.56% | 36.94% | | 66.08% | 29.84% | 35.87% | |
| Sigma | 8.45 | | 0.66 | 42.92 | | 4.80% | 4.80% | | 6.07% | 4.86% | 8.45% | |
| Geometric Mean | 78.31 | | 2.32 | 181.35 | | 69.14% | 30.32% | | 54.15% | 23.74% | 19.62% | |
| Harmonic Mean | 77.86 | | 2.25 | 177.12 | | 68.99% | 29.90% | | 53.85% | 23.08% | 17.94% | |
| Kurtosis | -0.70 | | 2.15 | -0.72 | | -17.23% | -17.23% | | -48.32% | 77.90% | -70.37% | |
| Skewness | -0.39 | | 1.48 | 0.55 | | 64.11% | -64.11% | | 59.72% | -112.18% | 38.86% | |
| Trimmed Mean – 20% | 78.82 | | 2.31 | 184.16 | | 69.01% | 30.99% | | 54.15% | 24.69% | 21.18% | |

## Data with History Prior to 2000

Table 10.18 contains all the issues that have data that began prior to 2000. This table contains more issues than the following two tables as each of them reduces the number of issues by increasing the amount of data by using an earlier starting date.

## Data with History Prior to 1990

Table 10.19 contains all the issues that have data that began prior to 1990.

## Data with History Prior to 1980

Table 10.20 contains all the issues that have data that began prior to 1980. This is the table with the longest set of data and hence, the fewest number of issues.

**TABLE 10.18**  Trend Analysis on Indices with Data History Prior to 2000

| Secular Bear Market | Index Name | Trendiness One | | | | | Trendiness Two | | | Trendless Analysis | | | |
|---|---|---|---|---|---|---|---|---|---|---|---|---|---|
| | | Trendiness | | Avg. | Up Trendiness | | While in Trend | | | | | | |
| | | Average | Rank | U/D | WtdAvg | Rank | Up | Down | Up Rank | Up | Down | Trendless | Rank |
| | AMEX Compsite | 80.49 | 39 | 3.38 | 271.90 | 3 | 76.98% | 23.02% | 3 | 61.97% | 18.53% | 19.51% | 53 |
| C | AMEX Oil Index | 74.51 | 57 | 1.96 | 146.23 | 62 | 66.24% | 33.76% | 64 | 49.36% | 25.15% | 25.49% | 35 |
| S | AMEX Pharmaceutical Index | 81.68 | 35 | 1.74 | 142.38 | 65 | 63.58% | 36.42% | 72 | 51.93% | 29.74% | 18.32% | 57 |
| I | Argentina MerVal | 50.48 | 85 | 2.41 | 121.53 | 79 | 70.23% | 29.77% | 35 | 35.45% | 15.03% | 49.52% | 7 |
| I | Australia All Ordinaries | 90.94 | 4 | 2.28 | 207.75 | 21 | 69.52% | 30.48% | 40 | 63.22% | 27.71% | 9.06% | 88 |
| I | Austria ATX | 76.85 | 54 | 2.24 | 172.31 | 44 | 68.65% | 31.35% | 48 | 52.76% | 24.09% | 23.15% | 38 |
| I | Belgium BEL-20 | 78.16 | 47 | 2.15 | 168.18 | 48 | 68.21% | 31.79% | 55 | 53.32% | 24.84% | 21.84% | 45 |
| I | Brazil Bovespa | 48.29 | 87 | 3.44 | 165.90 | 50 | 74.77% | 25.23% | 9 | 36.11% | 12.18% | 51.71% | 5 |
| I | Chile IGPA General Index | 90.17 | 6 | 1.66 | 149.32 | 60 | 62.34% | 37.66% | 76 | 56.21% | 33.95% | 9.83% | 86 |
| I | Chile IPSA | 80.43 | 40 | 1.63 | 131.41 | 73 | 61.97% | 38.03% | 79 | 49.84% | 30.58% | 19.57% | 52 |
| I | China Shanghai Composite | 62.87 | 82 | 1.17 | 73.82 | 87 | 54.10% | 45.90% | 87 | 34.01% | 28.86% | 37.13% | 10 |
| C | CRB Index | 92.69 | 2 | 1.42 | 131.59 | 72 | 58.45% | 41.55% | 82 | 54.17% | 38.51% | 7.31% | 90 |
| | Dow Industrials 1885 | 86.07 | 19 | 2.27 | 195.02 | 28 | 69.23% | 30.77% | 42 | 59.59% | 26.49% | 13.93% | 73 |
| | Dow Jones Composite | 78.81 | 43 | 2.49 | 196.51 | 27 | 71.23% | 28.77% | 28 | 56.13% | 22.68% | 21.19% | 49 |
| I | Dow Jones Euro Stoxx | 70.26 | 66 | 2.37 | 166.81 | 49 | 69.78% | 30.22% | 38 | 49.03% | 21.23% | 29.74% | 26 |
| I | Dow Jones Euro Stoxx 50 | 64.79 | 80 | 2.51 | 162.47 | 53 | 70.54% | 29.46% | 34 | 45.71% | 19.09% | 35.21% | 12 |
| | Dow Jones Stoxx | 76.85 | 53 | 2.53 | 194.67 | 29 | 71.39% | 28.61% | 25 | 54.86% | 21.99% | 23.15% | 39 |
| | Dow Jones Transport | 69.39 | 70 | 2.24 | 155.18 | 57 | 68.29% | 31.71% | 54 | 47.39% | 22.00% | 30.61% | 22 |
| | Dow Jones Utilities | 83.77 | 27 | 2.43 | 203.64 | 23 | 70.76% | 29.24% | 30 | 59.28% | 24.49% | 16.23% | 65 |
| | DJ Wilshire 5000 Composite | 88.07 | 10 | 2.62 | 230.54 | 11 | 72.34% | 27.66% | 20 | 63.70% | 24.36% | 11.93% | 82 |
| I | Egypt CMA | 73.73 | 61 | 2.82 | 207.83 | 20 | 73.69% | 26.31% | 14 | 54.33% | 19.40% | 26.27% | 31 |
| I | Finland HSE General Index | 63.57 | 81 | 2.09 | 133.08 | 71 | 67.49% | 32.51% | 56 | 42.90% | 20.67% | 36.43% | 11 |
| I | France CAC 40 | 69.78 | 69 | 2.45 | 171.01 | 46 | 70.69% | 29.31% | 32 | 49.32% | 20.45% | 30.22% | 23 |
| I | Germany DAX | 67.81 | 74 | 3.44 | 233.49 | 9 | 76.73% | 23.27% | 4 | 52.03% | 15.78% | 32.19% | 18 |
| C | Gold and Silver Mining | 38.35 | 89 | 0.90 | 34.66 | 90 | 48.11% | 51.89% | 91 | 18.45% | 19.90% | 61.65% | 3 |

| | | | | | | | | | | | | | |
|---|---|---|---|---|---|---|---|---|---|---|---|---|---|
| C | Gold Base Price Handy & Harman | 49.21 | 86 | 1.20 | 59.26 | 88 | 54.64% | 45.36% | 86 | 26.89% | 22.32% | 50.79% | 6 |
| C | Gold Bugs (AMEX) | 32.56 | 90 | 1.04 | 33.76 | 91 | 51.30% | 48.70% | 90 | 16.70% | 15.85% | 67.44% | 2 |
| C | Gold Mining Stocks | 48.18 | 88 | 1.07 | 51.61 | 89 | 52.05% | 47.95% | 88 | 25.08% | 23.10% | 51.82% | 4 |
| I | Greece General Share | 62.60 | 83 | 1.27 | 79.60 | 86 | 55.26% | 44.74% | 85 | 34.59% | 28.01% | 37.40% | 9 |
| I | Hong Kong Hang Seng | 69.98 | 68 | 2.22 | 155.21 | 56 | 68.60% | 31.40% | 50 | 48.01% | 21.97% | 30.02% | 24 |
| I | Ibex 35 | 67.58 | 75 | 2.42 | 163.36 | 51 | 69.99% | 30.01% | 37 | 47.30% | 20.28% | 32.42% | 17 |
| I | India BSE 30 | 57.04 | 84 | 2.29 | 130.77 | 75 | 68.93% | 31.07% | 45 | 39.32% | 17.72% | 42.96% | 8 |
| I | Indonesia Jakarta Composite | 73.88 | 60 | 2.04 | 150.64 | 59 | 66.95% | 33.05% | 59 | 49.46% | 24.42% | 26.12% | 32 |
| I | Israel TA-100 | 77.53 | 49 | 2.57 | 199.63 | 26 | 71.90% | 28.10% | 22 | 55.75% | 21.78% | 22.47% | 43 |
| I | Japan Nikkei 225 | 75.65 | 56 | 1.95 | 147.74 | 61 | 65.66% | 34.34% | 66 | 49.67% | 25.98% | 24.35% | 36 |
| | Major Market Index | 84.49 | 20 | 2.68 | 226.54 | 15 | 72.75% | 27.25% | 19 | 61.47% | 23.02% | 15.51% | 72 |
| I | Malaysia KLSE Composite | 82.64 | 31 | 1.96 | 162.02 | 54 | 66.08% | 33.92% | 65 | 54.61% | 28.04% | 17.36% | 61 |
| I | Mexico IPC | 68.41 | 73 | 3.35 | 229.30 | 12 | 76.30% | 23.70% | 5 | 52.19% | 16.21% | 31.59% | 19 |
| S | Morgan Stanley Consumer | 87.52 | 12 | 2.96 | 259.01 | 5 | 74.68% | 25.32% | 10 | 65.36% | 22.16% | 12.48% | 80 |
| S | Morgan Stanley Cyclical | 69.12 | 72 | 2.32 | 160.59 | 55 | 68.48% | 31.52% | 53 | 47.33% | 21.78% | 30.88% | 20 |
| I | MSCI EAFE | 89.91 | 7 | 1.99 | 178.96 | 41 | 66.56% | 33.44% | 62 | 59.85% | 30.06% | 10.09% | 85 |
| I | MSCI EM | 84.27 | 23 | 2.21 | 186.22 | 39 | 68.72% | 31.28% | 47 | 57.92% | 26.36% | 15.73% | 69 |
| | NASDAQ 100 | 65.28 | 79 | 2.86 | 186.56 | 38 | 73.88% | 26.12% | 13 | 48.23% | 17.05% | 34.72% | 13 |
| | NASDAQ Composite | 81.32 | 36 | 2.19 | 177.69 | 42 | 68.54% | 31.46% | 52 | 55.74% | 25.58% | 18.68% | 56 |
| I | Netherlands AEX General | 78.28 | 46 | 2.45 | 191.77 | 33 | 70.74% | 29.26% | 31 | 55.37% | 22.90% | 21.72% | 46 |
| | NYSE Composite | 89.89 | 8 | 2.41 | 217.05 | 16 | 70.61% | 29.39% | 33 | 63.47% | 26.42% | 10.11% | 84 |
| I | Pakistan Karachi 100 | 67.51 | 76 | 2.06 | 139.15 | 68 | 66.54% | 33.46% | 63 | 44.92% | 22.59% | 32.49% | 16 |
| I | Peru Lima General | 80.33 | 41 | 1.78 | 142.75 | 64 | 63.81% | 36.19% | 71 | 51.26% | 29.07% | 19.67% | 51 |
| I | Philippines PSE Composite | 74.47 | 58 | 1.66 | 123.72 | 78 | 62.28% | 37.72% | 78 | 46.38% | 28.09% | 25.53% | 34 |
| I | Russell 1000 | 83.72 | 28 | 3.02 | 252.92 | 6 | 75.06% | 24.94% | 8 | 62.84% | 20.88% | 16.28% | 64 |

*(Continued)*

**TABLE 10.18** Continued

| Secular Bear Market | | Trendiness One | | | | | Trendiness Two | | | | Trendless Analysis | | | |
|---|---|---|---|---|---|---|---|---|---|---|---|---|---|---|---|
| | | Trendiness | | Avg. | Up Trendiness | | While in Trend | | | | | | | | |
| Index Name | | Average | Rank | U/D | WtdAvg | Rank | Up | Down | Up Rank | Up | Up | Down | Trendless | Rank |
| Russell 1000 Growth | | 80.55 | 38 | 2.61 | 209.84 | 17 | 72.16% | 27.84% | 21 | 58.13% | 22.43% | 19.45% | 54 |
| Russell 1000 Value | | 78.58 | 45 | 2.26 | 177.52 | 43 | 69.06% | 30.94% | 44 | 54.27% | 24.31% | 21.42% | 47 |
| Russell 2000 | | 83.02 | 29 | 2.07 | 171.63 | 45 | 67.34% | 32.66% | 57 | 55.91% | 27.11% | 16.98% | 63 |
| Russell 2000 Growth | | 82.05 | 34 | 2.31 | 189.76 | 37 | 69.62% | 30.38% | 39 | 57.13% | 24.92% | 17.95% | 58 |
| Russell 2000 Value | | 87.53 | 11 | 3.69 | 322.90 | 1 | 78.59% | 21.41% | 2 | 68.80% | 18.74% | 12.47% | 81 |
| Russell 3000 | | 84.38 | 22 | 2.95 | 248.63 | 7 | 74.56% | 25.44% | 12 | 62.91% | 21.47% | 15.62% | 70 |
| S&P 100 Index | | 83.97 | 26 | 2.27 | 190.61 | 36 | 69.33% | 30.67% | 41 | 58.22% | 25.76% | 16.03% | 66 |
| S&P 400 Index | | 78.80 | 44 | 3.01 | 237.45 | 8 | 74.59% | 25.41% | 11 | 58.78% | 20.02% | 21.20% | 48 |
| S&P 500 Index | | 88.78 | 9 | 2.25 | 199.91 | 24 | 69.21% | 30.79% | 43 | 61.45% | 27.33% | 11.22% | 83 |
| S&P 500 Total Return | | 86.90 | 16 | 3.21 | 278.62 | 2 | 76.12% | 23.88% | 6 | 66.15% | 20.75% | 13.10% | 76 |
| S&P 600 Index | | 71.77 | 64 | 2.55 | 183.16 | 40 | 71.37% | 28.63% | 26 | 51.23% | 20.55% | 28.23% | 28 |
| S | S&P Cons Discretionary Sector | 76.96 | 52 | 2.71 | 208.53 | 19 | 73.02% | 26.98% | 16 | 56.20% | 20.76% | 23.04% | 40 |
| S | S&P Cons Staples Sector | 80.19 | 42 | 2.49 | 199.75 | 25 | 71.17% | 28.83% | 29 | 57.07% | 23.12% | 19.81% | 50 |
| S | S&P Energy Sector | 92.31 | 3 | 2.52 | 232.75 | 10 | 71.59% | 28.41% | 23 | 66.08% | 26.23% | 7.69% | 89 |
| S | S&P Financials Sector | 74.40 | 59 | 1.73 | 128.41 | 76 | 63.20% | 36.80% | 73 | 47.03% | 27.38% | 25.60% | 33 |
| S | S&P Healthcare Sector | 86.97 | 15 | 2.21 | 192.24 | 31 | 68.78% | 31.22% | 46 | 59.82% | 27.16% | 13.03% | 77 |
| S | S&P Industrials Sector | 82.49 | 32 | 2.05 | 169.05 | 47 | 66.98% | 33.02% | 58 | 55.25% | 27.24% | 17.51% | 60 |
| S | S&P Materials Sector | 77.15 | 51 | 2.01 | 154.98 | 58 | 66.66% | 33.34% | 61 | 51.43% | 25.72% | 22.85% | 41 |
| S | S&P MIDCAP INDEX | 84.10 | 24 | 2.71 | 228.13 | 14 | 72.86% | 27.14% | 18 | 61.28% | 22.82% | 15.90% | 68 |
| S | S&P Technology Sector | 70.34 | 65 | 2.05 | 144.50 | 63 | 66.92% | 33.08% | 60 | 47.07% | 23.27% | 29.66% | 27 |
| S | S&P Telecomm Sector | 80.79 | 37 | 1.71 | 138.25 | 69 | 63.06% | 36.94% | 74 | 50.95% | 29.84% | 19.21% | 55 |
| S | S&P Utilities Sector | 87.37 | 13 | 2.19 | 191.14 | 34 | 68.61% | 31.39% | 49 | 59.95% | 27.42% | 12.63% | 79 |
| I | S&P/TSX 60 (Canada) | 77.47 | 50 | 2.50 | 193.45 | 30 | 71.32% | 28.68% | 27 | 55.25% | 22.21% | 22.53% | 42 |
| I | S&P/TSX Composite (Canada) | 87.29 | 14 | 2.20 | 191.92 | 32 | 68.58% | 31.42% | 51 | 59.86% | 27.43% | 12.71% | 78 |

| | | | | | | | | | | | | |
|---|---|---|---|---|---|---|---|---|---|---|---|---|
| C | Silver Base Price Handy & Harman | 72.55 | 63 | 1.44 | 104.30 | 84 | 58.78% | 41.22% | 81 | 42.65% | 29.91% | 27.45% | 29 |
| I | Singapore Straits Times | 65.83 | 78 | 1.67 | 109.63 | 81 | 62.30% | 37.70% | 77 | 41.01% | 24.82% | 34.17% | 14 |
| I | Slovakia SAX | 90.31 | 5 | 1.28 | 115.54 | 80 | 56.08% | 43.92% | 84 | 50.65% | 39.67% | 9.69% | 87 |
| I | South Korea Seoul Composite | 67.39 | 77 | 1.59 | 107.17 | 83 | 61.19% | 38.81% | 80 | 41.24% | 26.15% | 32.61% | 15 |
| I | S&P 500 Tot Ret Inflation Adj | 86.25 | 18 | 3.05 | 262.89 | 4 | 75.15% | 24.85% | 7 | 64.82% | 21.43% | 13.75% | 74 |
| I | Spain Madrid General | 78.14 | 48 | 1.79 | 140.12 | 67 | 64.01% | 35.99% | 70 | 50.02% | 28.12% | 21.86% | 44 |
| I | Sri Lanka All Share | 83.98 | 25 | 1.29 | 108.17 | 82 | 56.21% | 43.79% | 83 | 47.21% | 36.77% | 16.02% | 67 |
| I | Swedish OMX 30 | 70.18 | 67 | 2.72 | 190.76 | 35 | 72.97% | 27.03% | 17 | 51.21% | 18.97% | 29.82% | 25 |
| I | Switzerland Swiss Market | 82.10 | 33 | 2.79 | 229.22 | 13 | 73.27% | 26.73% | 15 | 60.16% | 21.94% | 17.90% | 59 |
| I | Taiwan Weighted | 69.20 | 71 | 1.82 | 125.61 | 77 | 64.06% | 35.94% | 69 | 44.33% | 24.87% | 30.80% | 21 |
| I | Thailand SET | 73.51 | 62 | 1.88 | 138.19 | 70 | 64.99% | 35.01% | 68 | 47.77% | 25.73% | 26.49% | 30 |
| I | Turkey ISE National-100 | 32.02 | 91 | 4.43 | 141.83 | 66 | 79.17% | 20.83% | 1 | 25.35% | 6.67% | 67.98% | 1 |
| I | United Kingdom FTSE 100 | 82.77 | 30 | 2.53 | 209.34 | 18 | 71.56% | 28.44% | 24 | 59.23% | 23.54% | 17.23% | 62 |
| C | US Dollar Index | 95.16 | 1 | 1.08 | 102.65 | 85 | 51.85% | 48.15% | 89 | 49.34% | 45.82% | 4.84% | 91 |
| | Value Line Index (Arithmetic) | 86.60 | 17 | 2.36 | 204.40 | 22 | 70.19% | 29.81% | 36 | 60.79% | 25.81% | 13.40% | 75 |
| | Value Line Index (Geometric) | 84.44 | 21 | 1.93 | 162.59 | 52 | 65.56% | 34.44% | 67 | 55.36% | 29.09% | 15.56% | 71 |
| I | Venezuela IBC | 76.70 | 55 | 1.70 | 130.78 | 74 | 63.02% | 36.98% | 75 | 48.34% | 28.37% | 23.30% | 37 |
| | **Statistics** | | | | | | | | | | | | |
| | Mean | 75.84 | | 2.24 | 170.76 | | 67.70% | 32.30% | | 51.54% | 24.30% | 24.16% | |
| | Average Deviation | 9.40 | | 0.47 | 41.31 | | 4.87% | 4.87% | | 7.59% | 4.00% | 9.40% | |
| | Median | 78.28 | | 2.25 | 171.01 | | 68.78% | 31.22% | | 52.76% | 24.31% | 21.72% | |
| | Minimum | 32.02 | | 0.90 | 33.76 | | 48.11% | 20.83% | | 16.70% | 6.67% | 4.84% | |
| | Maximum | 95.16 | | 4.43 | 322.90 | | 79.17% | 51.89% | | 68.80% | 45.82% | 67.98% | |
| | Sigma | 12.67 | | 0.63 | 53.25 | | 6.44% | 6.44% | | 10.29% | 5.56% | 12.67% | |
| | Geometric Mean | 74.51 | | 2.15 | 160.37 | | 67.37% | 31.71% | | 50.20% | 23.63% | 21.36% | |
| | Harmonic Mean | 72.75 | | 2.05 | 145.35 | | 67.02% | 31.17% | | 48.32% | 22.81% | 18.81% | |
| | Kurtosis | 2.55 | | 0.94 | 0.53 | | 83.18% | 83.19% | | 199.39% | 316.83% | 255.41% | |
| | Skewness | -1.45 | | 0.38 | -0.12 | | -97.06% | 97.06% | | -124.52% | 60.76% | 145.40% | |
| | Trimmed Mean – 20% | 77.57 | | 2.23 | 171.57 | | 68.39% | 31.61% | | 52.78% | 24.12% | 22.43% | |

**TABLE 10.19**  Trend Analysis on Indices with Data History Prior to 1990

| | | Trendiness One | | | | | Trendiness Two | | | | | | |
| | | Trendiness | | Avg. | Up Trendiness | | While in Trend | | | Trendless Analysis | | | |
| | Index Name | Average | Rank | U/D | WtdAvg | Rank | Up | Down | Up Rank | Up | Down | Trendless | Rank |
|---|---|---|---|---|---|---|---|---|---|---|---|---|---|
| C | AMEX Oil Index | 74.51 | 40 | 1.96 | 146.23 | 42 | 66.24% | 33.76% | 42 | 49.36% | 25.15% | 25.49% | 17 |
| I | Australia All Ordinaries | 90.94 | 4 | 2.28 | 207.75 | 15 | 69.52% | 30.48% | 25 | 63.22% | 27.71% | 9.06% | 53 |
| C | CRB Index | 92.69 | 2 | 1.42 | 131.59 | 48 | 58.45% | 41.55% | 53 | 54.17% | 38.51% | 7.31% | 55 |
| | Dow Industrials 1885 | 86.07 | 16 | 2.27 | 195.02 | 20 | 69.23% | 30.77% | 27 | 59.59% | 26.49% | 13.93% | 41 |
| | Dow Jones Transport | 69.39 | 48 | 2.24 | 155.18 | 39 | 68.29% | 31.71% | 36 | 47.39% | 22.00% | 30.61% | 9 |
| | Dow Jones Utilities | 83.77 | 23 | 2.43 | 203.64 | 17 | 70.76% | 29.24% | 19 | 59.28% | 24.49% | 16.23% | 34 |
| | DJ Wilshire 5000 Composite | 88.07 | 8 | 2.62 | 230.54 | 7 | 72.34% | 27.66% | 14 | 63.70% | 24.36% | 11.93% | 49 |
| I | France CAC 40 | 69.78 | 47 | 2.45 | 171.01 | 34 | 70.69% | 29.31% | 21 | 49.32% | 20.45% | 30.22% | 10 |
| C | Gold and Silver Mining | 38.35 | 55 | 0.90 | 34.66 | 56 | 48.11% | 51.89% | 56 | 18.45% | 19.90% | 61.65% | 2 |
| C | Gold Base Price Handy & Harman | 49.21 | 54 | 1.20 | 59.26 | 55 | 54.64% | 45.36% | 54 | 26.89% | 22.32% | 50.79% | 3 |
| I | Hong Kong Hang Seng | 69.98 | 46 | 2.22 | 155.21 | 38 | 68.60% | 31.40% | 33 | 48.01% | 21.97% | 30.02% | 11 |
| I | India BSE 30 | 57.04 | 53 | 2.29 | 130.77 | 49 | 68.93% | 31.07% | 29 | 39.32% | 17.72% | 42.96% | 4 |
| I | Japan Nikkei 225 | 75.65 | 39 | 1.95 | 147.74 | 41 | 65.66% | 34.34% | 44 | 49.67% | 25.98% | 24.35% | 18 |
| I | Major Market Index | 84.49 | 17 | 2.68 | 226.54 | 11 | 72.75% | 27.25% | 13 | 61.47% | 23.02% | 15.51% | 40 |
| I | Malaysia KLSE Composite | 82.64 | 27 | 1.96 | 162.02 | 37 | 66.08% | 33.92% | 43 | 54.61% | 28.04% | 17.36% | 30 |
| I | Mexico IPC | 68.41 | 50 | 3.35 | 229.30 | 8 | 76.30% | 23.70% | 3 | 52.19% | 16.21% | 31.59% | 7 |
| I | MSCI EAFE | 89.91 | 5 | 1.99 | 178.96 | 31 | 66.56% | 33.44% | 41 | 59.85% | 30.06% | 10.09% | 52 |
| I | MSCI EM | 84.27 | 20 | 2.21 | 186.22 | 30 | 68.72% | 31.28% | 31 | 57.92% | 26.36% | 15.73% | 37 |
| | NASDAQ 100 | 65.28 | 52 | 2.86 | 186.56 | 29 | 73.88% | 26.12% | 8 | 48.23% | 17.05% | 34.72% | 5 |
| | NASDAQ Composite | 81.32 | 31 | 2.19 | 177.69 | 32 | 68.54% | 31.46% | 35 | 55.74% | 25.58% | 18.68% | 26 |
| I | Netherlands AEX General | 78.28 | 34 | 2.45 | 191.77 | 24 | 70.74% | 29.26% | 20 | 55.37% | 22.90% | 21.72% | 23 |
| I | NYSE Composite | 89.89 | 6 | 2.41 | 217.05 | 12 | 70.61% | 29.39% | 22 | 63.47% | 26.42% | 10.11% | 51 |
| I | Philippines PSE Composite | 74.47 | 41 | 1.66 | 123.72 | 52 | 62.28% | 37.72% | 51 | 46.38% | 28.09% | 25.53% | 16 |
| I | Russell 1000 | 83.72 | 24 | 3.02 | 252.92 | 4 | 75.06% | 24.94% | 6 | 62.84% | 20.88% | 16.28% | 33 |
| | Russell 2000 | 83.02 | 25 | 2.07 | 171.63 | 33 | 67.34% | 32.66% | 37 | 55.91% | 27.11% | 16.98% | 32 |
| | Russell 2000 Growth | 82.05 | 30 | 2.31 | 189.76 | 28 | 69.62% | 30.38% | 24 | 57.13% | 24.92% | 17.95% | 27 |
| | Russell 2000 Value | 87.53 | 9 | 3.69 | 322.90 | 1 | 78.59% | 21.41% | 2 | 68.80% | 18.74% | 12.47% | 48 |

| | Index | | | | | | | | | | | |
|---|---|---|---|---|---|---|---|---|---|---|---|---|
| | Russell 3000 | 84.38 | 19 | 2.95 | 248.63 | 5 | 74.56% | 25.44% | 7 | 62.91% | 21.47% | 15.62% | 38 |
| | S&P 100 Index | 83.97 | 22 | 2.27 | 190.61 | 27 | 69.33% | 30.67% | 26 | 58.22% | 25.76% | 16.03% | 35 |
| | S&P 500 Index | 88.78 | 7 | 2.25 | 199.91 | 18 | 69.21% | 30.79% | 28 | 61.45% | 27.33% | 11.22% | 50 |
| | S&P 500 Total Return | 86.90 | 13 | 3.21 | 278.62 | 2 | 76.12% | 23.88% | 4 | 66.15% | 20.75% | 13.10% | 44 |
| S | S&P Cons Discretionary Sector | 76.96 | 38 | 2.71 | 208.53 | 14 | 73.02% | 26.98% | 10 | 56.20% | 20.76% | 23.04% | 19 |
| S | S&P Cons Staples Sector | 80.19 | 33 | 2.49 | 199.75 | 19 | 71.17% | 28.83% | 18 | 57.07% | 23.12% | 19.81% | 24 |
| S | S&P Energy Sector | 92.31 | 3 | 2.52 | 232.75 | 6 | 71.59% | 28.41% | 15 | 66.08% | 26.23% | 7.69% | 54 |
| S | S&P Financials Sector | 74.40 | 42 | 1.73 | 128.41 | 50 | 63.20% | 36.80% | 49 | 47.03% | 27.38% | 25.60% | 15 |
| S | S&P Healthcare Sector | 86.97 | 12 | 2.21 | 192.24 | 22 | 68.78% | 31.22% | 30 | 59.82% | 27.16% | 13.03% | 45 |
| S | S&P Industrials Sector | 82.49 | 28 | 2.05 | 169.05 | 35 | 66.98% | 33.02% | 38 | 55.25% | 27.24% | 17.51% | 29 |
| S | S&P Materials Sector | 77.15 | 37 | 2.01 | 154.98 | 40 | 66.66% | 33.34% | 40 | 51.43% | 25.72% | 22.85% | 20 |
| S | S&P MIDCAP INDEX | 84.10 | 21 | 2.71 | 228.13 | 10 | 72.86% | 27.14% | 12 | 61.28% | 22.82% | 15.90% | 36 |
| S | S&P Technology Sector | 70.34 | 44 | 2.05 | 144.50 | 43 | 66.92% | 33.08% | 39 | 47.07% | 23.27% | 29.66% | 13 |
| S | S&P Telecomm Sector | 80.79 | 32 | 1.71 | 138.25 | 46 | 63.06% | 36.94% | 50 | 50.95% | 29.84% | 19.21% | 25 |
| S | S&P Utilities Sector | 87.37 | 10 | 2.19 | 191.14 | 25 | 68.61% | 31.39% | 32 | 59.95% | 27.42% | 12.63% | 47 |
| I | S&P/TSX 60 (Canada) | 77.47 | 36 | 2.50 | 193.45 | 21 | 71.32% | 28.68% | 17 | 55.25% | 22.21% | 22.53% | 21 |
| I | S&P/TSX Composite (Canada) | 87.29 | 11 | 2.20 | 191.92 | 23 | 68.58% | 31.42% | 34 | 59.86% | 27.43% | 12.71% | 46 |
| I | South Korea Seoul Composite | 67.39 | 51 | 1.59 | 107.17 | 53 | 61.19% | 38.81% | 52 | 41.24% | 26.15% | 32.61% | 6 |
| I | S&P 500 Tot Ret Inflation Adj | 86.25 | 15 | 3.05 | 262.89 | 3 | 75.15% | 24.85% | 5 | 64.82% | 21.43% | 13.75% | 42 |
| I | Spain Madrid General | 78.14 | 35 | 1.79 | 140.12 | 45 | 64.01% | 35.99% | 48 | 50.02% | 28.12% | 21.86% | 22 |
| I | Swedish OMX 30 | 70.18 | 45 | 2.72 | 190.76 | 26 | 72.97% | 27.03% | 11 | 51.21% | 18.97% | 29.82% | 12 |
| I | Switzerland Swiss Market | 82.10 | 29 | 2.79 | 229.22 | 9 | 73.27% | 26.73% | 9 | 60.16% | 21.94% | 17.90% | 28 |
| I | Taiwan Weighted | 69.20 | 49 | 1.82 | 125.61 | 51 | 64.06% | 35.94% | 47 | 44.33% | 24.87% | 30.80% | 8 |
| I | Thailand SET | 73.51 | 43 | 1.88 | 138.19 | 47 | 64.99% | 35.01% | 46 | 47.77% | 25.73% | 26.49% | 14 |
| I | Turkey ISE National-100 | 32.02 | 56 | 4.43 | 141.83 | 44 | 79.17% | 20.83% | 1 | 25.35% | 6.67% | 67.98% | 1 |
| I | United Kingdom FTSE 100 | 82.77 | 26 | 2.53 | 209.34 | 13 | 71.56% | 28.44% | 16 | 59.23% | 23.54% | 17.23% | 31 |
| C | U.S. Dollar Index | 95.16 | 1 | 1.08 | 102.65 | 54 | 51.85% | 48.15% | 55 | 49.34% | 45.82% | 4.84% | 56 |
| C | Value Line Index (Arithmetic) | 86.60 | 14 | 2.36 | 204.40 | 16 | 70.19% | 29.81% | 23 | 60.79% | 25.81% | 13.40% | 43 |

(Continued)

**TABLE 10.19** Continued

| Index Name | Trendiness One | | | | | Trendiness Two | | | Trendless Analysis | | | |
| | Trendiness | | Avg. | Up Trendiness | | While in Trend | | | | | | |
| | Average | Rank | U/D | WtdAvg | Rank | Up | Down | Up Rank | Up | Down | Trendless | Rank |
|---|---|---|---|---|---|---|---|---|---|---|---|---|
| Value Line Index (Geometric) | 84.44 | 18 | 1.93 | 162.59 | 36 | 65.56% | 34.44% | 45 | 55.36% | 29.09% | 15.56% | 39 |
| **Statistics** | | | | | | | | | | | | |
| Mean | 78.40 | | 2.30 | 180.20 | | 68.47% | 31.53% | | 53.82% | 24.58% | 21.60% | |
| Average Deviation | 8.79 | | 0.43 | 38.79 | | 4.14% | 4.14% | | 7.25% | 3.58% | 8.79% | |
| Median | 82.30 | | 2.26 | 188.16 | | 69.07% | 30.93% | | 55.56% | 25.04% | 17.70% | |
| Minimum | 32.02 | | 0.90 | 34.66 | | 48.11% | 20.83% | | 18.45% | 6.67% | 4.84% | |
| Maximum | 95.16 | | 4.43 | 322.90 | | 79.17% | 51.89% | | 68.80% | 45.82% | 67.98% | |
| Sigma | 12.24 | | 0.60 | 50.83 | | 5.87% | 5.87% | | 9.84% | 5.31% | 12.24% | |
| Geometric Mean | 77.15 | | 2.22 | 171.32 | | 68.20% | 31.04% | | 52.62% | 23.95% | 18.96% | |
| Harmonic Mean | 75.43 | | 2.13 | 157.93 | | 67.91% | 30.58% | | 50.90% | 23.06% | 16.71% | |
| Kurtosis | 4.51 | | 2.35 | 1.16 | | 268.34% | 268.34% | | 335.26% | 603.36% | 451.11% | |
| Skewness | -1.88 | | 0.67 | -0.12 | | -122.48% | 122.48% | | -156.32% | 63.85% | 188.09% | |
| Trimmed Mean – 20% | 80.16 | | 2.28 | 180.39 | | 69.02% | 30.98% | | 55.07% | 24.50% | 19.84% | |

**TABLE 10.20** Trend Analysis on Indices with Data History Prior to 1980

| | | Trendiness One | | | | | Trendiness Two | | | | Trendless Analysis | | |
|---|---|---|---|---|---|---|---|---|---|---|---|---|---|
| | | Trendiness | | Avg. | Up Trendiness | | While in Trend | | | | | | |
| | Index Name | Average | Rank | U/D | WtdAvg | Rank | Up | Down | Up Rank | Up | Down | Trendless | Rank |
| C | CRB Index | 92.69 | 1 | 1.42 | 131.59 | 13 | 58.45% | 41.55% | 13 | 54.17% | 38.51% | 7.31% | 14 |
| | Dow Industrials 1885 | 86.07 | 9 | 2.27 | 195.02 | 6 | 69.23% | 30.77% | 7 | 59.59% | 26.49% | 13.93% | 6 |
| | DJ Wilshire 5000 Composite | 88.07 | 5 | 2.62 | 230.54 | 2 | 72.34% | 27.66% | 2 | 63.70% | 24.36% | 11.93% | 10 |
| C | Gold Base Price Handy & Harman | 49.21 | 14 | 1.20 | 59.26 | 14 | 54.64% | 45.36% | 14 | 26.89% | 22.32% | 50.79% | 1 |
| I | MSCI EAFE | 89.91 | 2 | 1.99 | 178.96 | 10 | 66.56% | 33.44% | 12 | 59.85% | 30.06% | 10.09% | 13 |
| | NASDAQ Composite | 81.32 | 13 | 2.19 | 177.69 | 11 | 68.54% | 31.46% | 10 | 55.74% | 25.58% | 18.68% | 2 |
| | NYSE Composite | 89.89 | 3 | 2.41 | 217.05 | 3 | 70.61% | 29.39% | 3 | 63.47% | 26.42% | 10.11% | 12 |
| | Russell 2000 | 83.02 | 11 | 2.07 | 171.63 | 12 | 67.34% | 32.66% | 11 | 55.91% | 27.11% | 16.98% | 4 |
| | Russell 2000 Growth | 82.05 | 12 | 2.31 | 189.76 | 9 | 69.62% | 30.38% | 5 | 57.13% | 24.92% | 17.95% | 3 |
| | Russell 2000 Value | 87.53 | 6 | 3.69 | 322.90 | 1 | 78.59% | 21.41% | 1 | 68.80% | 18.74% | 12.47% | 9 |
| | S&P 100 Index | 83.97 | 10 | 2.27 | 190.61 | 8 | 69.33% | 30.67% | 6 | 58.22% | 25.76% | 16.03% | 5 |
| | S&P 500 Index | 88.78 | 4 | 2.25 | 199.91 | 5 | 69.21% | 30.79% | 8 | 61.45% | 27.33% | 11.22% | 11 |
| I | S&P/TSX Composite (Canada) | 87.29 | 7 | 2.20 | 191.92 | 7 | 68.58% | 31.42% | 9 | 59.86% | 27.43% | 12.71% | 8 |
| | Value Line Index (Arithmetic) | 86.60 | 8 | 2.36 | 204.40 | 4 | 70.19% | 29.81% | 4 | 60.79% | 25.81% | 13.40% | 7 |
| | **Statistics** | | | | | | | | | | | | |
| | Mean | 84.03 | | 2.23 | 190.09 | | 68.09% | 31.91% | | 57.54% | 26.49% | 15.97% | |
| | Average Deviation | 5.80 | | 0.33 | 33.09 | | 3.62% | 3.62% | | 5.41% | 2.57% | 5.80% | |
| | Median | 86.95 | | 2.26 | 191.26 | | 69.22% | 30.78% | | 59.72% | 26.12% | 13.05% | |
| | Minimum | 49.21 | | 1.20 | 59.26 | | 54.64% | 21.41% | | 26.89% | 18.74% | 7.31% | |
| | Maximum | 92.69 | | 3.69 | 322.90 | | 78.59% | 45.36% | | 68.80% | 38.51% | 50.79% | |
| | Sigma | 10.53 | | 0.56 | 56.49 | | 5.70% | 5.70% | | 9.60% | 4.35% | 10.53% | |
| | Geometric Mean | 83.21 | | 2.17 | 180.19 | | 67.85% | 31.46% | | 56.46% | 26.18% | 14.21% | |
| | Harmonic Mean | 82.13 | | 2.10 | 166.06 | | 67.60% | 31.03% | | 54.89% | 25.89% | 13.17% | |
| | Kurtosis | 10.89 | | 3.52 | 3.60 | | 239.84% | 239.84% | | 915.76% | 473.44% | 1088.87% | |
| | Skewness | -3.15 | | 0.76 | -0.01 | | -99.77% | 99.78% | | -272.38% | 134.75% | 314.59% | |
| | Trimmed Mean – 20% | 86.21 | | 2.20 | 189.92 | | 68.33% | 31.67% | | 59.16% | 26.13% | 13.79% | |

## Trend Analysis on the S&P GICS Data

Next I conduct a similar study on the 95 S&P GICS Sectors, Industry Groups, and Industries. This is a different study in that the parameters for determination of trending markets were greatly expanded. The number of days for trend determination was tabulated for days from 15 to 65. The filtered wave percentage was also expanded from 5 percent to 11 percent. All of the analysis that was included in the previous section was done on these 95 sectors and industry groups.

The Global Industry Classification Standard (GICS) is an industry taxonomy developed by MSCI and Standard & Poor's (S&P) for use by the global financial community. The GICS structure consists of 10 sectors, 24 industry groups, 68 industries and 154 subindustries into which S&P has categorized all major public companies. The system is similar to ICB (Industry Classification Benchmark), a classification structure maintained by Dow Jones Indexes and FTSE Group.

### S&P Sectors, Industry Groups, and Industries

The numerical identification is exactly the same used by Standard & Poor's in their GICS classification methodology. Most, but not all, of the GICS database began in 1989, in fact there were only 21 series that did not begin in 1989. When viewing the analysis that follows, you can cross-reference this table if one particular sector or industry seems to trend outside the average, then check the start date as it might not have enough data for good analysis. Table 10.21 shows all the GICS data and each starting date.

### GICS Total Summary

Table 10.22 shows the robustness of the analysis. It is entirely too much data to put into a table in a book, but is displayed here merely as proof (only partial data is shown). The raw data will be removed for the remainder of this analysis, only showing the average rankings and relative rankings. This is a table that shows the total trend (up and down) for all the raw data used in the analysis, with filtered waves from 5 percent to 11 percent and trend lengths from 15 to 65 days. The table is presented here just to give you an idea as to how much analysis went into this. A summary table follows that is much easier to view.

The GICS Summary tables are shown below but without the vast amount of raw data, only the name of the classification, the average of all the raw calculations, and the relative rank of each. Following these tables are tables using the same analysis that was conducted previously on the 109 indices.

**TABLE 10.21**  GICS Sectors, Industry Groups, and Industries

| Start Date | GICS TOTAL Summary |
|---|---|
| 9/11/1989 | 10 Energy |
| 9/11/1989 | 101010 Energy Equipment & Services |
| 9/11/1989 | 101020 Oil Gas & Consumable Fuels |
| 9/11/1989 | 15 Materials |
| 9/11/1989 | 151010 Chemicals |
| 9/11/1989 | 151020 Construction Materials |
| 9/11/1989 | 151030 Containers & Packaging |
| 9/11/1989 | 151040 Metals & Mining |
| 9/11/1989 | 151050 Paper & Forest Products |
| 9/11/1989 | 20 Industrials |
| 9/11/1989 | 2010 Capital Goods |
| 9/11/1989 | 201010 Aerospace & Defense |
| 9/11/1989 | 201020 Building Products |
| 9/11/1989 | 201030 Construction & Engineering |
| 9/11/1989 | 201040 Electrical Equipment |
| 9/11/1989 | 201040 Electronic Equipment Instruments & Components |
| 9/11/1989 | 201050 Industrial Conglomerates |
| 9/11/1989 | 201060 Machinery |
| 6/30/1996 | 201070 Trading Companies & Distributors |
| 9/11/1989 | 2020 Commercial & Professional Services |
| 9/11/1989 | 202010 Commercial Services & Supplies |
| 8/29/2008 | 202020 Professional Services |
| 9/11/1989 | 2030 Transportation |
| 9/11/1989 | 203010 Air Freight & Logistics |
| 9/11/1989 | 203020 Airlines |
| 9/11/1989 | 203040 Road & Rail |
| 9/11/1989 | 25 Consumer Discretionary |
| 9/11/1989 | 2510 Automobiles & Components |
| 9/11/1989 | 251010 Auto Components |
| 9/11/1989 | 251020 Automobiles |
| 9/11/1989 | 2520 Consumer Durables & Apparel |
| 9/11/1989 | 252010 Household Durables |
| 9/11/1989 | 252020 Leisure Equipment & Products |
| 9/11/1989 | 252030 Textiles Apparel & Luxury Goods |
| 9/11/1989 | 2530 Consumer Services |
| 9/11/1989 | 253010 Hotels Restaurants & Leisure |
| 4/28/2005 | 253020 Diversified Consumer Services |
| 9/11/1989 | 2540 Media |
| 9/11/1989 | 254010 Media |
| 9/11/1989 | 2550 Retailing |
| 11/4/2002 | 255010 Distributors |
| 10/29/2002 | 255020 Internet & Catalog Retail |
| 9/11/1989 | 255030 Multiline Retail |
| 9/11/1989 | 255040 Specialty Retail |
| 9/11/1989 | 30 Consumer Staples |
| 9/11/1989 | 3010 Food & Staples Retailing |
| 9/11/1989 | 301010 Food & Staples Retailing |

*(Continued)*

**TABLE 10.21**  Continued

| Start Date | GICS TOTAL Summary |
| --- | --- |
| 9/11/1989 | 3020 Food Beverage & Tobacco |
| 9/11/1989 | 302010 Beverages |
| 9/11/1989 | 302020 Food Products |
| 9/11/1989 | 302030 Tobacco |
| 9/11/1989 | 3030 Household & Personal Products |
| 9/11/1989 | 303010 Household Products |
| 9/11/1989 | 303020 Personal Products |
| 9/11/1989 | 35 Health Care |
| 9/11/1989 | 3510 Health Care Equipment & Services |
| 9/11/1989 | 351010 Health Care Equipment & Supplies |
| 9/11/1989 | 351020 Health Care Providers & Services |
| 4/27/2006 | 351030 Health Care Technology |
| 1/7/2000 | 3520 Pharmaceuticals Biotechnology & Life Sciences |
| 9/11/1989 | 352010 Biotechnology |
| 9/11/1989 | 352020 Pharmaceuticals |
| 4/27/2006 | 352030 Life Sciences Tools & Services |
| 9/11/1989 | 40 Financials |
| 9/11/1989 | 4010 Banks |
| 9/11/1989 | 401010 Commercial Banks |
| 5/2/2003 | 401020 Thrifts & Mortgage Finance |
| 9/11/1989 | 4020 Diversified Financials |
| 5/1/2003 | 402010 Diversified Financial Services |
| 5/6/2003 | 402020 Consumer Finance |
| 5/2/2003 | 402030 Capital Markets |
| 9/11/1989 | 4030 Insurance |
| 9/11/1989 | 403010 Insurance |
| 10/9/2001 | 4040 Real Estate |
| 10/9/2001 | 404020 Real Estate Investment Trusts (REITs) |
| 8/2/2006 | 404030 Real Estate Management & Development |
| 9/11/1989 | 45 Information Technology |
| 9/11/1989 | 4510 Software & Services |
| 1/4/1999 | 451010 Internet Software & Services |
| 9/11/1989 | 451020 IT Services |
| 9/11/1989 | 451030 Software |
| 9/11/1989 | 4520 Technology Hardware & Equipment |
| 9/11/1989 | 452010 Communications Equipment |
| 9/11/1989 | 452020 Computers & Peripherals |
| 6/28/1996 | 452040 Office Electronics |
| 5/2/2003 | 4530 Semiconductors & Semiconductor Equipment |
| 9/11/1989 | 453010 Semiconductors & Semiconductor Equipment |
| 9/11/1989 | 50 Telecommunication Services |
| 9/11/1989 | 501010 Diversified Telecommunication Services |
| 7/1/1993 | 501020 Wireless Telecommunication Services |
| 9/11/1989 | 55 Utilities |
| 9/11/1989 | 551010 Electric Utilities |
| 9/11/1989 | 551020 Gas Utilities |
| 8/31/1999 | 551030 Multi-Utilities |
| 4/28/2005 | 551050 Independent Power Producers & Energy Traders |

**TABLE 10.22** GICS Trend Analysis of Wide Variety of Trends (Partial Data)

| | 15d5%T | 15d7%T | 15d9%T | 15d11%T | 21d5%T | 21d7%T | 21d9%T | 21d11%T | 30d5%T | 30d7%T |
|---|---|---|---|---|---|---|---|---|---|---|
| 10 Energy | 68.63 | 82.67 | 89.78 | 91.72 | 61.35 | 78.36 | 84.82 | 88.17 | 51.89 | 73.25 |
| 101010 Energy Equipment & Services | 47.31 | 64.80 | 79.70 | 83.47 | 35.84 | 53.83 | 69.05 | 75.44 | 24.46 | 43.32 |
| 101020 Oil Gas & Consumable Fuels | 70.59 | 85.32 | 90.20 | 92.22 | 63.13 | 80.60 | 85.24 | 88.67 | 53.91 | 75.38 |
| 15 Materials | 74.58 | 86.74 | 91.58 | 91.39 | 66.41 | 80.88 | 87.28 | 88.27 | 59.16 | 73.78 |
| 151010 Chemicals | 71.42 | 84.85 | 93.65 | 92.27 | 65.12 | 80.28 | 90.79 | 89.47 | 54.87 | 70.04 |
| 151020 Construction Materials | 43.06 | 59.99 | 74.54 | 82.35 | 29.89 | 49.21 | 64.23 | 75.72 | 15.80 | 37.40 |
| 151030 Containers & Packaging | 72.79 | 87.38 | 93.05 | 96.26 | 63.73 | 80.72 | 90.01 | 95.04 | 51.49 | 70.48 |
| 151040 Metals & Mining | 59.11 | 75.73 | 86.36 | 90.54 | 50.37 | 69.08 | 81.14 | 85.97 | 36.39 | 59.76 |
| 151050 Paper & Forest Products | 60.11 | 79.26 | 86.88 | 88.50 | 50.58 | 73.79 | 84.45 | 85.83 | 37.43 | 63.93 |

*(Continued)*

**TABLE 10.22** Continued

| | 30d9%T | 30d11%T | 40d5%T | 40d7%T | 40d9%T | 40d11%T | 65d5%T | 65d7%T | 65d9%T | 65d11%T | Average | Rank |
|---|---|---|---|---|---|---|---|---|---|---|---|---|
| 10 Energy | 80.63 | 85.15 | 41.16 | 63.50 | 73.69 | 81.68 | 22.51 | 44.58 | 60.07 | 70.65 | 69.71 | 41 |
| 101010 Energy Equipment & Services | 60.56 | 67.91 | 14.05 | 33.57 | 48.62 | 60.52 | 7.03 | 19.28 | 27.06 | 41.33 | 47.86 | 89 |
| 101020 Oil Gas & Consumable Fuels | 80.99 | 86.27 | 42.71 | 64.34 | 74.74 | 83.33 | 21.85 | 50.44 | 65.43 | 75.25 | 71.53 | 38 |
| 15 Materials | 82.65 | 84.39 | 50.38 | 69.03 | 79.10 | 81.98 | 28.80 | 53.40 | 60.77 | 72.32 | 73.14 | 31 |
| 151010 Chemicals | 82.64 | 85.63 | 44.48 | 64.81 | 77.85 | 82.63 | 25.37 | 49.52 | 68.53 | 74.56 | 72.44 | 33 |
| 151020 Construction Materials | 55.22 | 69.31 | 8.32 | 28.39 | 44.11 | 57.18 | 1.80 | 15.08 | 26.97 | 37.48 | 43.80 | 90 |
| 151030 Containers & Packaging | 84.76 | 90.27 | 40.07 | 61.90 | 77.80 | 86.05 | 22.00 | 37.63 | 57.86 | 69.98 | 71.46 | 39 |
| 151040 Metals & Mining | 74.45 | 80.74 | 28.10 | 50.37 | 67.45 | 76.69 | 9.82 | 26.28 | 43.01 | 57.07 | 60.42 | 71 |
| 151050 Paper & Forest Products | 76.30 | 80.65 | 25.84 | 52.92 | 69.81 | 76.44 | 6.08 | 31.01 | 45.53 | 56.07 | 61.57 | 67 |

**TABLE 10.23** Summary of GICS Trend Analysis

| | Total | | Up | | Down | | U/D Ratio |
|---|---|---|---|---|---|---|---|
| | Average | Rank | Average | Rank | Average | Rank | Average |
| 10 Energy | 69.71 | 41 | 47.99 | 42 | 20.80 | 42 | 3.06 |
| 101010 Energy Equipment & Services | 47.86 | 89 | 30.70 | 83 | 15.53 | 81 | |
| 101020 Oil Gas & Consumable Fuels | 71.53 | 38 | 47.87 | 43 | 22.74 | 23 | 2.83 |
| 15 Materials | 73.14 | 31 | 50.27 | 31 | 22.09 | 30 | 2.54 |
| 151010 Chemicals | 72.44 | 33 | 52.22 | 23 | 19.56 | 56 | 3.08 |
| 151020 Construction Materials | 43.80 | 90 | 25.29 | 92 | 17.47 | 73 | |
| 151030 Containers & Packaging | 71.46 | 39 | 44.40 | 58 | 26.19 | 7 | 1.79 |
| 151040 Metals & Mining | 60.42 | 71 | 36.68 | 74 | 22.40 | 27 | 1.68 |
| 151050 Paper & Forest Products | 61.57 | 67 | 38.46 | 72 | 21.99 | 32 | |
| 20 Industrials | 77.55 | 18 | 56.54 | 9 | 20.75 | 43 | 3.03 |
| 2010 Capital Goods | 77.07 | 20 | 55.40 | 13 | 21.24 | 39 | 2.83 |
| 201010 Aerospace & Defense | 77.98 | 16 | 61.30 | 5 | 16.12 | 79 | |
| 201020 Building Products | 57.99 | 74 | 36.14 | 76 | 21.04 | 40 | 2.00 |
| 201030 Construction & Engineering | 52.55 | 82 | 29.88 | 86 | 21.27 | 38 | 1.47 |
| 201040 Electrical Equipment | 68.94 | 42 | 49.59 | 34 | 18.54 | 64 | 3.15 |
| 201040 Electronic Equip Instruments & Components | 54.73 | 80 | 34.73 | 80 | 19.02 | 61 | |
| 201050 Industrial Conglomerates | 68.76 | 43 | 48.07 | 41 | 20.07 | 49 | 2.82 |
| 201060 Machinery | 71.64 | 36 | 48.15 | 40 | 22.72 | 24 | 2.43 |
| 201070 Trading Companies & Distributors | 62.80 | 64 | 43.10 | 62 | 18.43 | 67 | 2.63 |
| 2020 Commercial & Professional Services | 77.63 | 17 | 54.05 | 19 | 23.21 | 21 | 2.58 |
| 202010 Commercial Services & Supplies | 77.53 | 19 | 54.19 | 18 | 22.95 | 22 | 2.62 |
| 202020 Professional Services | 60.85 | 70 | 41.44 | 67 | 18.49 | 66 | |
| 2030 Transportation | 73.93 | 27 | 51.21 | 26 | 22.19 | 28 | 3.13 |
| 203010 Air Freight & Logistics | 62.98 | 62 | 37.50 | 73 | 24.46 | 15 | |
| 203020 Airlines | 50.02 | 86 | 27.59 | 90 | 21.51 | 36 | |
| 203040 Road & Rail | 66.22 | 51 | 46.57 | 45 | 18.86 | 63 | 3.04 |
| 25 Consumer Discretionary | 78.40 | 14 | 59.13 | 8 | 18.95 | 62 | 4.39 |
| 2510 Automobiles & Components | 61.53 | 68 | 35.71 | 78 | 24.81 | 12 | 1.72 |

*(Continued)*

**TABLE 10.23** Continued

| | Total | | Up | | Down | | U/D Ratio |
|---|---|---|---|---|---|---|---|
| | Average | Rank | Average | Rank | Average | Rank | Average |
| 251010 Auto Components | 65.58 | 54 | 40.15 | 69 | 24.48 | 14 | 1.73 |
| 251020 Automobiles | 54.60 | 81 | 31.61 | 82 | 21.60 | 35 | 1.84 |
| 2520 Consumer Durables & Apparel | 76.73 | 22 | 54.33 | 16 | 22.03 | 31 | 2.85 |
| 252010 Household Durables | 71.54 | 37 | 48.75 | 37 | 22.11 | 29 | 2.53 |
| 252020 Leisure Equipment & Products | 66.45 | 49 | 42.86 | 64 | 22.41 | 26 | 2.68 |
| 252030 Textiles Apparel & Luxury Goods | 67.17 | 48 | 48.67 | 38 | 17.78 | 70 | 3.42 |
| 2530 Consumer Services | 75.01 | 25 | 53.82 | 22 | 20.57 | 44 | |
| 253010 Hotels Restaurants & Leisure | 74.48 | 26 | 53.91 | 20 | 19.90 | 52 | |
| 253020 Diversified Consumer Services | 50.49 | 85 | 28.90 | 89 | 20.06 | 50 | |
| 2540 Media | 71.66 | 35 | 44.96 | 55 | 25.94 | 9 | 2.69 |
| 254010 Media | 71.70 | 34 | 45.03 | 53 | 25.93 | 10 | 2.74 |
| 2550 Retailing | 67.69 | 46 | 47.34 | 44 | 19.54 | 57 | 3.23 |
| 255010 Distributors | 65.57 | 55 | 45.03 | 54 | 19.67 | 54 | |
| 255020 Internet & Catalog Retail | 37.09 | 93 | 27.16 | 91 | 8.73 | 94 | |
| 255030 Multiline Retail | 64.19 | 57 | 43.95 | 60 | 19.35 | 59 | |
| 255040 Specialty Retail | 65.90 | 52 | 44.42 | 57 | 20.56 | 45 | 2.85 |
| 30 Consumer Staples | 87.73 | 1 | 67.22 | 1 | 20.32 | 46 | 3.53 |
| 3010 Food & Staples Retailing | 80.15 | 9 | 55.70 | 12 | 23.55 | 18 | 2.67 |
| 301010 Food & Staples Retailing | 80.15 | 8 | 55.70 | 11 | 23.54 | 19 | 2.67 |
| 3020 Food Beverage & Tobacco | 86.32 | 2 | 61.19 | 7 | 24.80 | 13 | 2.62 |
| 302010 Beverages | 81.70 | 6 | 61.20 | 6 | 19.93 | 51 | 3.30 |
| 302020 Food Products | 86.19 | 3 | 64.07 | 4 | 21.93 | 33 | 3.07 |
| 302030 Tobacco | 69.93 | 40 | 49.20 | 35 | 19.57 | 55 | |
| 3030 Household & Personal Products | 83.01 | 4 | 66.65 | 2 | 16.18 | 78 | |
| 303010 Household Products | 81.77 | 5 | 64.84 | 3 | 16.65 | 76 | |
| 303020 Personal Products | 68.33 | 44 | 50.94 | 28 | 16.39 | 77 | |
| 35 Health Care | 80.41 | 7 | 56.36 | 10 | 23.24 | 20 | 3.61 |
| 3510 Health Care Equipment & Services | 78.78 | 13 | 54.29 | 17 | 23.68 | 17 | 2.57 |
| 351010 Health Care Equipment & Supplies | 76.77 | 21 | 54.62 | 15 | 21.47 | 37 | 2.75 |
| 351020 Health Care Providers & Services | 72.81 | 32 | 49.15 | 36 | 22.53 | 25 | 2.93 |

| | | | | | | | |
|---|---|---|---|---|---|---|---|
| 351030 Health Care Technology | 42.05 | 91 | 30.06 | 85 | 11.17 | 92 | 2.00 |
| 3520 Pharmaceuticals Biotechnology & Life Sciences | 79.13 | 12 | 49.67 | 33 | 28.57 | 2 | 2.05 |
| 352010 Biotechnology | 55.36 | 77 | 35.60 | 79 | 18.30 | 68 | 2.31 |
| 352020 Pharmaceuticals | 78.32 | 15 | 51.34 | 25 | 26.15 | 8 | |
| 352030 Life Sciences Tools & Services | 62.82 | 63 | 50.51 | 30 | 11.56 | 90 | |
| 40 Financials | 68.22 | 45 | 48.44 | 39 | 19.09 | 60 | 3.46 |
| 4010 Banks | 66.26 | 50 | 45.70 | 50 | 19.70 | 53 | 3.36 |
| 401010 Commercial Banks | 65.74 | 53 | 43.01 | 63 | 21.91 | 34 | 2.51 |
| 401020 Thrifts & Mortgage Finance | 59.32 | 72 | 29.38 | 88 | 29.22 | 1 | 0.99 |
| 4020 Diversified Financials | 64.01 | 58 | 45.66 | 51 | 17.70 | 71 | 3.67 |
| 402010 Diversified Financial Services | 54.97 | 79 | 35.95 | 77 | 18.52 | 65 | |
| 402020 Consumer Finance | 55.06 | 78 | 39.39 | 70 | 14.90 | 84 | |
| 402030 Capital Markets | 57.58 | 75 | 41.16 | 68 | 15.48 | 82 | |
| 4030 Insurance | 73.19 | 29 | 45.71 | 47 | 26.73 | 5 | 1.83 |
| 403010 Insurance | 73.19 | 29 | 45.71 | 47 | 26.73 | 5 | 1.83 |
| 4040 Real Estate | 63.29 | 61 | 51.16 | 27 | 11.23 | 91 | |
| 404020 Real Estate Investment Trusts (REITs) | 63.29 | 60 | 50.68 | 29 | 11.72 | 89 | |
| 404030 Real Estate Management & Development | 23.17 | 95 | 17.96 | 95 | 4.54 | 95 | |
| 45 Information Technology | 64.34 | 56 | 43.73 | 61 | 19.41 | 58 | |
| 4510 Software & Services | 62.46 | 66 | 44.08 | 59 | 17.21 | 74 | 3.06 |
| 451010 Internet Software & Services | 37.05 | 94 | 25.23 | 93 | 10.84 | 93 | |
| 451020 IT Services | 61.22 | 69 | 45.08 | 52 | 15.15 | 83 | 4.08 |
| 451030 Software | 58.65 | 73 | 41.75 | 66 | 15.72 | 80 | 3.68 |
| 4520 Technology Hardware & Equipment | 62.56 | 65 | 44.46 | 56 | 16.89 | 75 | 3.12 |
| 452010 Communications Equipment | 55.41 | 76 | 39.23 | 71 | 14.90 | 85 | 3.12 |
| 452020 Computers & Peripherals | 63.83 | 59 | 42.59 | 65 | 20.11 | 48 | 2.88 |
| 452040 Office Electronics | 41.38 | 92 | 25.04 | 94 | 14.80 | 86 | |
| 4530 Semiconductors & Semiconductor Equip | 51.41 | 84 | 30.19 | 84 | 20.13 | 47 | |
| 453010 Semiconductors & Semiconductor Equip | 48.24 | 88 | 32.23 | 81 | 14.76 | 87 | |
| 50 Telecommunication Services | 75.85 | 23 | 49.88 | 32 | 25.23 | 11 | 2.47 |

*(Continued)*

**TABLE 10.23** Continued

| | Total | | Up | | Down | | U/D Ratio |
|---|---|---|---|---|---|---|---|
| | Average | Rank | Average | Rank | Average | Rank | Average |
| 501010 Diversified Telecommunication Services | 75.30 | 24 | 46.45 | 46 | 27.98 | 3 | 1.96 |
| 501020 Wireless Telecommunication Services | 48.26 | 87 | 29.77 | 87 | 17.49 | 72 | 2.33 |
| 55 Utilities | 79.60 | 11 | 53.89 | 21 | 24.44 | 16 | 2.09 |
| 551010 Electric Utilities | 79.64 | 10 | 51.68 | 24 | 26.73 | 4 | 2.09 |
| 551020 Gas Utilities | 73.80 | 28 | 55.17 | 14 | 17.90 | 69 | 3.35 |
| 551030 Multi-Utilities | 67.53 | 47 | 45.71 | 49 | 20.86 | 41 | 2.46 |
| 551050 Ind Power Producers & Energy Traders | 51.70 | 83 | 36.50 | 75 | 13.55 | 88 | 2.46 |
| **Statistics** | | | | | | | |
| Mean | 66.04 | | 45.22 | | 19.95 | | 2.71 |
| Average Deviation | 9.52 | | 8.03 | | 3.38 | | 0.50 |
| Median | 67.17 | | 45.71 | | 20.11 | | 2.71 |
| Minimum | 23.17 | | 17.96 | | 4.54 | | 0.99 |
| Maximum | 87.73 | | 67.22 | | 29.22 | | 4.39 |
| Sigma | 12.18 | | 10.27 | | 4.46 | | 0.65 |
| Geometric Mean | 64.72 | | 43.93 | | 19.33 | | 2.62 |
| Harmonic Mean | 63.07 | | 42.47 | | 18.46 | | 2.52 |
| Kurtosis | 0.83 | | -0.19 | | 0.92 | | 0.22 |
| Skewness | -0.80 | | -0.28 | | -0.60 | | -0.10 |
| Trimmed Mean – 20% | 66.98 | | 45.42 | | 20.17 | | 2.71 |

## GICS Summary

Table 10.23 contains all of the averages of the various filtered wave and trend days analysis categorized into Total Trendiness, Uptrends, Downtrends, and the ratio of up to downtrends. You will notice that there are missing data in the U/D Ratio column. This is because of a couple of different things.

1. There were a few of the series that just did not have a long enough data history.
2. When you mix a small filtered wave with a long trend expectation, you will find that some series just do not have an Uptrend, a Downtrend, or both. Division does not work well with a zero for numerator or denominator.

On first glance at the above table of all GICS issues, it could be noticed that all of the ones that have numerical codes starting with the number 3 are ranked high in the Total Trendiness. While I think this is poor analysis, let's see if there is anything there. Oh my, yes there is, all of them are part of Consumer Staples or Healthcare. Both of these sectors are typically defensive in nature and usually with less volatility. If you refer to the table at the beginning of this section that has 109 market indices, it also contains 16 sectors or industries. Consumer Staples is ranked in that table using Trendiness One as number 3, while the Healthcare sector is ranked number 14. Remember that these are relative ranks, but the results confirm that Staples and Healthcare are good trending issues. Does this hold up for other defensive issues such as Utilities and Telecom? The Utilities sector and the Electric Utilities industry rank 14 and 13 in overall trendiness, however, the other utility industries do not rank high. Telecom sector ranks 23, with diversified telecom industry at 25 and wireless at 89. It should also be noted when doing this type of analysis that the wireless data begins 4 years later than the other, but I don't see that as a hindrance.

Let's now look at which GICS issues are not good at trending (Table 10.24). The top five are Internet Software and Services, Internet and Catalog Retail, Health Care Technology, Office Electronics, and Construction Materials. With this wide dispersion of industries, let's first check the data. First note that of the 95 GICS issues, only 20 (21 percent) have data less than the majority, which all begin in 1989. Four of the poor trending issues are in this category. Only Construction Materials began in 1989. Since this analysis is measuring relative trendiness one would then need to go to each individual issue and chart it as was done in the previous section.

## GICS Summary Table (With Inadequate Periods of Analysis Removed)

## GICS Table for All Trends Up to and Including 30 Days

Table 10.25 shows the analysis on the GICS data in the same manner as the earlier analysis on the 109 market indices. A review of the details in that section might be helpful.

**TABLE 10.24** Summary of GICS Trend Analysis with Short Data History Issues Removed

| All GICS With U/D Full Data History | Total | | Up | | Down | | U/D Ratio |
|---|---|---|---|---|---|---|---|
| | Average | Rank | Average | Rank | Average | Rank | Average |
| 10 Energy | 69.71 | 41 | 47.99 | 42 | 20.80 | 42 | 3.06 |
| 101020 Oil Gas & Consumable Fuels | 71.53 | 38 | 47.87 | 43 | 22.74 | 23 | 2.83 |
| 15 Materials | 73.14 | 31 | 50.27 | 31 | 22.09 | 30 | 2.54 |
| 151010 Chemicals | 72.44 | 33 | 52.22 | 23 | 19.56 | 56 | 3.08 |
| 151030 Containers & Packaging | 71.46 | 39 | 44.40 | 58 | 26.19 | 7 | 1.79 |
| 151040 Metals & Mining | 60.42 | 71 | 36.68 | 74 | 22.40 | 27 | 1.68 |
| 20 Industrials | 77.55 | 18 | 56.54 | 9 | 20.75 | 43 | 3.03 |
| 2010 Capital Goods | 77.07 | 20 | 55.40 | 13 | 21.24 | 39 | 2.83 |
| 201020 Building Products | 57.99 | 74 | 36.14 | 76 | 21.04 | 40 | 2.00 |
| 201030 Construction & Engineering | 52.55 | 82 | 29.88 | 86 | 21.27 | 38 | 1.47 |
| 201040 Electrical Equipment | 68.94 | 42 | 49.59 | 34 | 18.54 | 64 | 3.15 |
| 201050 Industrial Conglomerates | 68.76 | 43 | 48.07 | 41 | 20.07 | 49 | 2.82 |
| 201060 Machinery | 71.64 | 36 | 48.15 | 40 | 22.72 | 24 | 2.43 |
| 201070 Trading Companies & Distributors | 62.80 | 64 | 43.10 | 62 | 18.43 | 67 | 2.63 |
| 2020 Commercial & Professional Services | 77.63 | 17 | 54.05 | 19 | 23.21 | 21 | 2.58 |
| 202010 Commercial Services & Supplies | 77.53 | 19 | 54.19 | 18 | 22.95 | 22 | 2.62 |
| 2030 Transportation | 73.93 | 27 | 51.21 | 26 | 22.19 | 28 | 3.13 |
| 203040 Road & Rail | 66.22 | 51 | 46.57 | 45 | 18.86 | 63 | 3.04 |
| 25 Consumer Discretionary | 78.40 | 14 | 59.13 | 8 | 18.95 | 62 | 4.39 |
| 2510 Automobiles & Components | 61.53 | 68 | 35.71 | 78 | 24.81 | 12 | 1.72 |
| 251010 Auto Components | 65.58 | 54 | 40.15 | 69 | 24.48 | 14 | 1.73 |
| 251020 Automobiles | 54.60 | 81 | 31.61 | 82 | 21.60 | 35 | 1.84 |
| 2520 Consumer Durables & Apparel | 76.73 | 22 | 54.33 | 16 | 22.03 | 31 | 2.85 |
| 252010 Household Durables | 71.54 | 37 | 48.75 | 37 | 22.11 | 29 | 2.53 |
| 252020 Leisure Equipment & Products | 66.45 | 49 | 42.86 | 64 | 22.41 | 26 | 2.68 |
| 252030 Textiles Apparel & Luxury Goods | 67.17 | 48 | 48.67 | 38 | 17.78 | 70 | 3.42 |
| 2540 Media | 71.66 | 35 | 44.96 | 55 | 25.94 | 9 | 2.69 |
| 254010 Media | 71.70 | 34 | 45.03 | 53 | 25.93 | 10 | 2.74 |
| 2550 Retailing | 67.69 | 46 | 47.34 | 44 | 19.54 | 57 | 3.23 |
| 255040 Specialty Retail | 65.90 | 52 | 44.42 | 57 | 20.56 | 45 | 2.85 |
| 30 Consumer Staples | 87.73 | 1 | 67.22 | 1 | 20.32 | 46 | 3.53 |
| 3010 Food & Staples Retailing | 80.15 | 9 | 55.70 | 12 | 23.55 | 18 | 2.67 |
| 301010 Food & Staples Retailing | 80.15 | 8 | 55.70 | 11 | 23.54 | 19 | 2.67 |
| 3020 Food Beverage & Tobacco | 86.32 | 2 | 61.19 | 7 | 24.80 | 13 | 2.62 |
| 302010 Beverages | 81.70 | 6 | 61.20 | 6 | 19.93 | 51 | 3.30 |

| | | | | | | | |
|---|---|---|---|---|---|---|---|
| 302020 Food Products | 86.19 | 3 | 64.07 | 4 | 21.93 | 33 | 3.07 |
| 35 Health Care | 80.41 | 7 | 56.36 | 10 | 23.24 | 20 | 3.61 |
| 3510 Health Care Equipment & Services | 78.78 | 13 | 54.29 | 17 | 23.68 | 17 | 2.57 |
| 351010 Health Care Equipment & Supplies | 76.77 | 21 | 54.62 | 15 | 21.47 | 37 | 2.75 |
| 351020 Health Care Providers & Services | 72.81 | 32 | 49.15 | 36 | 22.53 | 25 | 2.93 |
| 3520 Pharmaceuticals Biotechnology & Life Sciences | 79.13 | 12 | 49.67 | 33 | 28.57 | 2 | 2.00 |
| 352010 Biotechnology | 55.36 | 77 | 35.60 | 79 | 18.30 | 68 | 2.05 |
| 352020 Pharmaceuticals | 78.32 | 15 | 51.34 | 25 | 26.15 | 8 | 2.31 |
| 40 Financials | 68.22 | 45 | 48.44 | 39 | 19.09 | 60 | 3.46 |
| 4010 Banks | 66.26 | 50 | 45.70 | 50 | 19.70 | 53 | 3.36 |
| 401010 Commercial Banks | 65.74 | 53 | 43.01 | 63 | 21.91 | 34 | 2.51 |
| 401020 Thrifts & Mortgage Finance | 59.32 | 72 | 29.38 | 88 | 29.22 | 1 | 0.99 |
| 4020 Diversified Financials | 64.01 | 58 | 45.66 | 51 | 17.70 | 71 | 3.67 |
| 4030 Insurance | 73.19 | 29 | 45.71 | 47 | 26.73 | 5 | 1.83 |
| 403010 Insurance | 73.19 | 29 | 45.71 | 47 | 26.73 | 5 | 1.83 |
| 4510 Software & Services | 62.46 | 66 | 44.08 | 59 | 17.21 | 74 | 3.06 |
| 451020 IT Services | 61.22 | 69 | 45.08 | 52 | 15.15 | 83 | 4.08 |
| 451030 Software | 58.65 | 73 | 41.75 | 66 | 15.72 | 80 | 3.68 |
| 4520 Technology Hardware & Equipment | 62.56 | 65 | 44.46 | 56 | 16.89 | 75 | 3.12 |
| 452010 Communications Equipment | 55.41 | 76 | 39.23 | 71 | 14.90 | 85 | 3.12 |
| 452020 Computers & Peripherals | 63.83 | 59 | 42.59 | 65 | 20.11 | 48 | 2.88 |
| 50 Telecommunication Services | 75.85 | 23 | 49.88 | 32 | 25.23 | 11 | 2.47 |
| 501010 Diversified Telecommunication Services | 75.30 | 24 | 46.45 | 46 | 27.98 | 3 | 1.96 |
| 55 Utilities | 79.60 | 11 | 53.89 | 21 | 24.44 | 16 | 2.33 |
| 551010 Electric Utilities | 79.64 | 10 | 51.68 | 24 | 26.73 | 4 | 2.09 |
| 551020 Gas Utilities | 73.80 | 28 | 55.17 | 14 | 17.90 | 69 | 3.35 |
| 551030 Multi-Utilities | 67.53 | 47 | 45.71 | 49 | 20.86 | 41 | 2.46 |
| **Statistics** | | | | | | | |
| Mean | 70.64 | | 47.98 | | 21.83 | | 2.71 |
| Average Deviation | 6.81 | | 5.89 | | 2.60 | | 0.50 |
| Median | 71.59 | | 48.03 | | 21.92 | | 2.71 |
| Minimum | 52.55 | | 29.38 | | 14.90 | | 0.99 |
| Maximum | 87.73 | | 67.22 | | 29.22 | | 4.39 |
| Sigma | 8.27 | | 7.77 | | 3.29 | | 0.65 |
| Geometric Mean | 70.15 | | 47.33 | | 21.58 | | 2.62 |
| Harmonic Mean | 69.65 | | 46.63 | | 21.33 | | 2.52 |
| Kurtosis | -0.54 | | 0.37 | | -0.34 | | 0.22 |
| Skewness | -0.17 | | -0.14 | | 0.11 | | -0.10 |
| Trimmed Mean – 20% | 70.86 | | 48.15 | | 21.80 | | 2.71 |

**TABLE 10.25** GICS Analysis for All Trends Up to 30-Day Duration

| GICs—Data up to and Including 30 Day Trends | Trendiness One | | | | | Trendiness Two | | | Trendless Analysis | | | |
|---|---|---|---|---|---|---|---|---|---|---|---|---|
| | Trendiness | | Avg. | Up Trendiness | | | While in Trend | | | | | |
| | Average | Rank | U/D | WtdAvg | Rank | Up/Tot | Dn/Tot | Up Rank | Up | Down | Trendless | Rank |
| 10 Energy | 78.03 | 41 | 1.99 | 155.47 | 42 | 68.37% | 31.63% | 30 | 53.36% | 24.68% | 21.97% | 54 |
| 101010 Energy Equipment & Services | 58.81 | 88 | 1.94 | 114.02 | 77 | 68.49% | 31.51% | 28 | 40.28% | 18.53% | 41.19% | 7 |
| 101020 Oil Gas & Consumable Fuels | 79.38 | 39 | 1.84 | 146.14 | 56 | 66.64% | 33.36% | 48 | 52.89% | 26.48% | 20.62% | 56 |
| 15 Materials | 80.59 | 32 | 1.93 | 155.21 | 44 | 66.66% | 33.34% | 47 | 53.72% | 26.87% | 19.41% | 63 |
| 151010 Chemicals | 80.09 | 33 | 2.28 | 182.47 | 17 | 68.73% | 31.27% | 26 | 55.04% | 25.04% | 19.91% | 62 |
| 151020 Construction Materials | 54.73 | 90 | 1.35 | 73.74 | 92 | 56.97% | 43.03% | 89 | 31.18% | 23.55% | 45.27% | 5 |
| 151030 Containers & Packaging | 81.33 | 29 | 1.45 | 117.98 | 74 | 58.80% | 41.20% | 84 | 47.82% | 33.51% | 18.67% | 66 |
| 151040 Metals & Mining | 70.80 | 69 | 1.49 | 105.56 | 80 | 61.06% | 38.94% | 78 | 43.23% | 27.57% | 29.20% | 26 |
| 151050 Paper & Forest Products | 72.31 | 63 | 1.56 | 112.62 | 78 | 62.00% | 38.00% | 73 | 44.83% | 27.48% | 27.69% | 32 |
| 20 Industrials | 84.22 | 21 | 2.33 | 196.04 | 13 | 66.98% | 33.02% | 43 | 56.41% | 27.81% | 15.78% | 74 |
| 2010 Capital Goods | 83.87 | 23 | 2.17 | 181.94 | 18 | 65.99% | 34.01% | 54 | 55.35% | 28.52% | 16.13% | 72 |
| 201010 Aerospace & Defense | 85.36 | 16 | 3.02 | 257.55 | 6 | 74.37% | 25.63% | 4 | 63.48% | 21.88% | 14.64% | 79 |
| 201020 Building Products | 66.98 | 75 | 1.48 | 99.19 | 84 | 59.10% | 40.90% | 83 | 39.59% | 27.39% | 33.02% | 20 |
| 201030 Construction & Engineering | 63.99 | 80 | 1.35 | 86.32 | 88 | 57.81% | 42.19% | 88 | 37.00% | 26.99% | 36.01% | 15 |
| 201040 Electrical Equipment | 77.13 | 46 | 2.21 | 170.37 | 26 | 68.76% | 31.24% | 25 | 53.04% | 24.10% | 22.87% | 49 |
| 201040 Electronic Equipment Instruments & Components | 65.26 | 78 | 1.60 | 104.62 | 81 | 60.02% | 39.98% | 80 | 39.17% | 26.09% | 34.74% | 17 |
| 201050 Industrial Conglomerates | 76.91 | 47 | 2.02 | 155.64 | 40 | 66.19% | 33.81% | 52 | 50.91% | 26.00% | 23.09% | 48 |
| 201060 Machinery | 79.30 | 40 | 1.85 | 146.89 | 54 | 65.79% | 34.21% | 57 | 52.17% | 27.13% | 20.70% | 55 |
| 201070 Trading Companies & Distributors | 72.01 | 66 | 1.99 | 143.65 | 60 | 65.61% | 34.39% | 60 | 47.25% | 24.77% | 27.99% | 29 |
| 2020 Commercial & Professional Services | 85.39 | 15 | 1.90 | 162.61 | 34 | 63.43% | 36.57% | 65 | 54.16% | 31.22% | 14.61% | 80 |
| 202010 Commercial Services & Supplies | 85.15 | 18 | 1.93 | 164.33 | 32 | 63.73% | 36.27% | 63 | 54.26% | 30.88% | 14.85% | 77 |
| 202020 Professional Services | 68.50 | 73 | 2.41 | 164.94 | 31 | 71.58% | 28.42% | 11 | 49.04% | 19.47% | 31.50% | 22 |
| 2030 Transportation | 81.83 | 27 | 1.99 | 163.16 | 33 | 65.96% | 34.04% | 55 | 53.98% | 27.85% | 18.17% | 68 |
| 203010 Air Freight & Logistics | 73.07 | 60 | 1.31 | 95.46 | 85 | 58.16% | 41.84% | 87 | 42.50% | 30.57% | 26.93% | 35 |
| 203020 Airlines | 62.08 | 85 | 1.11 | 68.98 | 93 | 50.58% | 49.42% | 93 | 31.40% | 30.68% | 37.92% | 10 |
| 203040 Road & Rail | 74.63 | 54 | 2.03 | 151.60 | 48 | 64.95% | 35.05% | 62 | 48.48% | 26.16% | 25.37% | 41 |
| 25 Consumer Discretionary | 85.29 | 17 | 2.52 | 215.00 | 10 | 71.17% | 28.83% | 12 | 60.70% | 24.59% | 14.71% | 78 |
| 2510 Automobiles & Components | 72.61 | 61 | 1.25 | 90.89 | 86 | 56.57% | 43.43% | 91 | 41.08% | 31.53% | 27.39% | 34 |

| | | | | | | | | | | | | |
|---|---|---|---|---|---|---|---|---|---|---|---|---|
| 251010 Auto Components | 74.49 | 55 | 1.50 | 111.99 | 79 | 61.75% | 38.25% | 74 | 45.99% | 28.49% | 25.51% | 40 |
| 251020 Automobiles | 66.96 | 76 | 1.31 | 87.93 | 87 | 58.44% | 41.56% | 86 | 39.13% | 27.83% | 33.04% | 19 |
| 2520 Consumer Durables & Apparel | 84.32 | 20 | 2.02 | 170.30 | 27 | 66.22% | 33.78% | 51 | 55.84% | 28.48% | 15.68% | 75 |
| 252010 Household Durables | 79.40 | 38 | 1.87 | 148.85 | 51 | 65.79% | 34.21% | 58 | 52.23% | 27.17% | 20.60% | 57 |
| 252020 Leisure Equipment & Products | 77.14 | 45 | 1.66 | 127.86 | 67 | 62.53% | 37.47% | 72 | 48.23% | 28.91% | 22.86% | 50 |
| 252030 Textiles Apparel & Luxury Goods | 75.88 | 48 | 2.29 | 173.47 | 25 | 67.04% | 32.96% | 42 | 50.87% | 25.01% | 24.12% | 47 |
| 2530 Consumer Services | 83.80 | 24 | 2.16 | 181.15 | 21 | 67.54% | 32.46% | 40 | 56.60% | 27.20% | 16.20% | 71 |
| 253010 Hotels Restaurants & Leisure | 83.23 | 26 | 2.25 | 187.03 | 16 | 68.47% | 31.53% | 29 | 56.99% | 26.24% | 16.77% | 69 |
| 253020 Diversified Consumer Services | 63.50 | 81 | 1.35 | 85.72 | 89 | 56.94% | 43.06% | 90 | 36.16% | 27.34% | 36.50% | 14 |
| 2540 Media | 79.47 | 36 | 1.50 | 119.58 | 72 | 62.53% | 37.47% | 71 | 49.70% | 29.78% | 20.53% | 59 |
| 254010 Media | 79.47 | 37 | 1.51 | 119.60 | 71 | 62.54% | 37.46% | 70 | 49.70% | 29.77% | 20.53% | 58 |
| 2550 Retailing | 77.30 | 43 | 2.06 | 159.09 | 38 | 68.21% | 31.79% | 33 | 52.73% | 24.58% | 22.70% | 52 |
| 255010 Distributors | 75.33 | 49 | 2.00 | 150.35 | 49 | 58.62% | 41.38% | 85 | 44.16% | 31.17% | 24.67% | 46 |
| 255020 Internet & Catalog Retail | 47.42 | 93 | 3.29 | 155.96 | 39 | 72.96% | 27.04% | 6 | 34.59% | 12.82% | 52.58% | 2 |
| 255030 Multiline Retail | 73.98 | 57 | 1.99 | 147.31 | 53 | 66.55% | 33.45% | 49 | 49.24% | 24.75% | 26.02% | 38 |
| 255040 Specialty Retail | 74.35 | 56 | 1.91 | 141.76 | 62 | 67.83% | 32.17% | 37 | 50.43% | 23.92% | 25.65% | 39 |
| 30 Consumer Staples | 92.37 | 1 | 2.75 | 254.00 | 7 | 71.59% | 28.41% | 10 | 66.13% | 26.25% | 7.63% | 94 |
| 3010 Food & Staples Retailing | 87.08 | 11 | 2.07 | 179.86 | 23 | 68.30% | 31.70% | 31 | 59.47% | 27.61% | 12.92% | 84 |
| 301010 Food & Staples Retailing | 87.08 | 10 | 2.07 | 179.85 | 24 | 68.29% | 31.71% | 32 | 59.47% | 27.61% | 12.92% | 85 |
| 3020 Food Beverage & Tobacco | 91.26 | 2 | 2.11 | 192.55 | 14 | 67.74% | 32.26% | 39 | 61.82% | 29.44% | 8.74% | 93 |
| 302010 Beverages | 88.44 | 7 | 2.56 | 226.16 | 8 | 70.75% | 29.25% | 14 | 62.58% | 25.87% | 11.56% | 88 |
| 302020 Food Products | 91.05 | 3 | 2.47 | 225.13 | 9 | 67.82% | 32.18% | 38 | 61.75% | 29.30% | 8.95% | 92 |
| 302030 Tobacco | 79.85 | 35 | 2.26 | 180.11 | 22 | 69.05% | 30.95% | 22 | 55.14% | 24.71% | 20.15% | 60 |
| 3030 Household & Personal Products | 90.08 | 4 | 3.07 | 276.63 | 4 | 72.55% | 27.45% | 7 | 65.35% | 24.73% | 9.92% | 91 |
| 303010 Household Products | 89.36 | 5 | 2.91 | 259.99 | 5 | 70.23% | 29.77% | 17 | 62.76% | 26.60% | 10.64% | 90 |
| 303020 Personal Products | 77.78 | 42 | 2.56 | 199.00 | 12 | 71.63% | 28.37% | 9 | 55.72% | 22.06% | 22.22% | 53 |
| 35 Health Care | 88.65 | 6 | 2.05 | 181.62 | 19 | 68.78% | 31.22% | 24 | 60.97% | 27.68% | 11.35% | 89 |
| 3510 Health Care Equipment & Services | 86.01 | 12 | 1.95 | 167.89 | 29 | 66.79% | 33.21% | 45 | 57.45% | 28.56% | 13.99% | 83 |
| 351010 Health Care Equipment & Supplies | 84.68 | 19 | 2.21 | 187.24 | 15 | 68.91% | 31.09% | 23 | 58.35% | 26.33% | 15.32% | 76 |
| 351020 Health Care Providers & Services | 81.64 | 28 | 1.96 | 160.38 | 35 | 68.12% | 31.88% | 34 | 55.61% | 26.03% | 18.36% | 67 |
| 351030 Health Care Technology | 49.70 | 92 | 2.59 | 128.56 | 66 | 70.26% | 29.74% | 16 | 34.92% | 14.78% | 50.30% | 3 |

(Continued)

227

**TABLE 10.25** Continued

| | Trendiness One | | Avg. | Up Trendiness | | Trendiness Two | | | Trendless Analysis | | | |
| GICs—Data up to and Including 30 Day Trends | Trendiness | | | | | While in Trend | | | | | | |
| | Average | Rank | U/D | WtdAvg | Rank | Up/Tot | Dn/Tot | Up Rank | Up | Down | Trendless | Rank |
|---|---|---|---|---|---|---|---|---|---|---|---|---|
| 3520 Pharmaceuticals Biotechnology & Life Sci | 87.44 | 8 | 1.50 | 131.53 | 65 | 60.29% | 39.71% | 79 | 52.72% | 34.72% | 12.56% | 87 |
| 352010 Biotechnology | 67.26 | 74 | 1.73 | 116.08 | 76 | 63.71% | 36.29% | 64 | 42.85% | 24.41% | 32.74% | 21 |
| 352020 Pharmaceuticals | 87.14 | 9 | 1.65 | 143.93 | 59 | 62.72% | 37.28% | 68 | 54.65% | 32.49% | 12.86% | 86 |
| 352030 Life Sciences Tools & Services | 69.80 | 71 | 4.52 | 315.72 | 1 | 81.86% | 18.14% | 1 | 57.14% | 12.66% | 30.20% | 24 |
| 40 Financials | 77.26 | 44 | 2.00 | 154.38 | 47 | 63.20% | 36.80% | 66 | 48.83% | 28.43% | 22.74% | 51 |
| 4010 Banks | 74.83 | 51 | 1.96 | 146.48 | 55 | 66.15% | 33.85% | 53 | 49.50% | 25.34% | 25.17% | 44 |
| 401010 Commercial Banks | 74.65 | 53 | 1.67 | 124.87 | 68 | 62.60% | 37.40% | 69 | 46.73% | 27.92% | 25.35% | 42 |
| 401020 Thrifts & Mortgage Finance | 69.70 | 72 | 0.94 | 65.37 | 94 | 48.83% | 51.17% | 94 | 34.03% | 35.67% | 30.30% | 23 |
| 4020 Diversified Financials | 72.31 | 62 | 2.20 | 159.21 | 37 | 67.83% | 32.17% | 36 | 49.05% | 23.27% | 27.69% | 33 |
| 402010 Diversified Financial Services | 63.06 | 82 | 1.58 | 99.86 | 83 | 59.82% | 40.18% | 81 | 37.72% | 25.33% | 36.94% | 13 |
| 402020 Consumer Finance | 62.47 | 83 | 2.34 | 145.90 | 57 | 72.17% | 27.83% | 8 | 45.09% | 17.39% | 37.53% | 12 |
| 402030 Capital Markets | 64.42 | 79 | 2.48 | 159.53 | 36 | 73.91% | 26.09% | 5 | 47.62% | 16.81% | 35.58% | 16 |
| 4030 Insurance | 80.90 | 30 | 1.51 | 121.92 | 69 | 61.31% | 38.69% | 76 | 49.60% | 31.30% | 19.10% | 64 |
| 403010 Insurance | 80.90 | 30 | 1.51 | 121.92 | 69 | 61.31% | 38.69% | 76 | 49.60% | 31.30% | 19.10% | 64 |
| 4040 Real Estate | 71.02 | 67 | 4.44 | 315.56 | 2 | 79.66% | 20.34% | 2 | 56.57% | 14.45% | 28.98% | 28 |
| 404020 Real Estate Investment Trusts (REITs) | 70.96 | 68 | 4.11 | 291.71 | 3 | 77.97% | 22.03% | 3 | 55.33% | 15.63% | 29.04% | 27 |
| 45 Information Technology | 74.68 | 52 | 1.95 | 145.32 | 58 | 66.92% | 33.08% | 44 | 49.98% | 24.71% | 25.32% | 43 |
| 4510 Software & Services | 73.65 | 58 | 2.11 | 155.04 | 45 | 66.72% | 33.28% | 46 | 49.14% | 24.51% | 26.35% | 37 |
| 451010 Internet Software & Services | 46.82 | 94 | 3.07 | 143.62 | 61 | 69.81% | 30.19% | 18 | 32.69% | 14.14% | 53.18% | 1 |
| 451020 IT Services | 72.15 | 64 | 2.51 | 181.40 | 20 | 70.36% | 29.64% | 15 | 50.77% | 21.39% | 27.85% | 31 |
| 451030 Software | 70.63 | 70 | 2.19 | 154.76 | 46 | 67.16% | 32.84% | 41 | 47.44% | 23.20% | 29.37% | 25 |
| 4520 Technology Hardware & Equipment | 72.01 | 65 | 2.34 | 168.20 | 28 | 70.79% | 29.21% | 13 | 50.98% | 21.04% | 27.99% | 30 |
| 452010 Communications Equipment | 66.25 | 77 | 2.35 | 155.62 | 41 | 69.29% | 30.71% | 21 | 45.91% | 20.35% | 33.75% | 18 |
| 452020 Computers & Peripherals | 73.42 | 59 | 1.80 | 132.41 | 64 | 65.96% | 34.04% | 56 | 48.43% | 25.00% | 26.58% | 36 |

| | | | | | | | | | | | | |
|---|---|---|---|---|---|---|---|---|---|---|---|---|
| 452040 Office Electronics | 52.62 | 91 | 1.96 | 103.17 | 82 | 66.32% | 33.68% | 50 | 34.90% | 17.72% | 47.38% | 4 |
| 4530 Semiconductors & Semiconductor Equipment | 62.35 | 84 | 1.29 | 80.13 | 91 | 55.88% | 44.12% | 92 | 34.84% | 27.51% | 37.65% | 11 |
| 453010 Semiconductors & Semiconductor Equipment | 58.82 | 87 | 1.99 | 117.13 | 75 | 64.99% | 35.01% | 61 | 38.23% | 20.59% | 41.18% | 8 |
| 50 Telecommunication Services | 83.96 | 22 | 1.61 | 135.19 | 63 | 63.06% | 36.94% | 67 | 52.95% | 31.01% | 16.04% | 73 |
| 501010 Diversified Telecommunication Services | 83.39 | 25 | 1.43 | 119.21 | 73 | 61.54% | 38.46% | 75 | 51.32% | 32.07% | 16.61% | 70 |
| 501020 Wireless Telecommunication Services | 57.95 | 89 | 1.47 | 85.22 | 90 | 59.37% | 40.63% | 82 | 34.40% | 23.54% | 42.05% | 6 |
| 55 Utilities | 85.80 | 14 | 1.93 | 165.27 | 30 | 68.61% | 31.39% | 27 | 58.87% | 26.93% | 14.20% | 81 |
| 551010 Electric Utilities | 85.91 | 13 | 1.72 | 147.86 | 52 | 65.61% | 34.39% | 59 | 56.37% | 29.54% | 14.09% | 82 |
| 551020 Gas Utilities | 80.07 | 34 | 2.63 | 210.49 | 11 | 69.30% | 30.70% | 20 | 55.49% | 24.58% | 19.93% | 61 |
| 551030 Multi-Utilities | 74.90 | 50 | 2.00 | 149.47 | 50 | 67.99% | 32.01% | 35 | 50.93% | 23.97% | 25.10% | 45 |
| 551050 Independent Power Producers & Energy Traders | 61.70 | 86 | 2.52 | 155.44 | 43 | 69.69% | 30.31% | 19 | 43.00% | 18.71% | 38.30% | 9 |
| Average Deviation | 8.12 | | 0.43 | 36.49 | | 0.04 | 0.04 | | 0.07 | 0.04 | 0.08 | |
| Geometric Mean | 74.54 | | 1.98 | 147.43 | | 0.66 | 0.34 | | 0.49 | 0.25 | 0.23 | |
| Harmonic Mean | 73.72 | | 1.90 | 139.97 | | 0.65 | 0.33 | | 0.48 | 0.25 | 0.21 | |
| Kurtosis | 0.36 | | 4.41 | 1.66 | | 1.11 | 1.11 | | -0.39 | 0.70 | 0.36 | |
| Maximum | 92.37 | | 4.52 | 315.72 | | 0.82 | 0.51 | | 0.66 | 0.36 | 0.53 | |
| Mean | 73.74 | | 2.07 | 152.37 | | 0.66 | 0.35 | | 0.48 | 0.26 | 0.25 | |
| Median | 75.11 | | 1.99 | 150.97 | | 0.66 | 0.33 | | 0.50 | 0.26 | 0.23 | |
| Minimum | 8.12 | | 0.43 | 36.49 | | 0.04 | 0.04 | | 0.07 | 0.04 | 0.08 | |
| Sigma | 12.25 | | 0.64 | 51.66 | | 0.08 | 0.06 | | 0.09 | 0.05 | 0.10 | |
| Skewness | -0.74 | | 1.67 | 1.02 | | -0.22 | 0.22 | | -0.43 | -0.82 | 0.74 | |
| Trimmed Mean – 20% | 76.21 | | 1.98 | 150.21 | | 0.66 | 0.34 | | 0.50 | 0.26 | 0.24 | |

**TABLE 10.26**   Trend Analysis in Secular Bear Markets

| Secular Bears | Total Trend | Up Trend | Down Trend | Up/Down Ratio |
|---|---|---|---|---|
| 1901–1920 | 89.07% | 50.81% | 38.26% | 1.33 |
| 1929–1932 | 18.39% | 14.8% | 3.59% | 4.13 |
| 1937–1941 | 63.46% | 39.84% | 23.63% | 1.69 |
| 1966–1981 | 65.59% | 37.22% | 28.36% | 1.31 |
| 2000–20?? | 71.9% | 52.74% | 19.15% | 2.75 |

## Trend Analysis in Secular Bear Markets

Table 10.26 shows the trend analysis for the periods when the Dow Industrials was in a secular bear market. Although these results are not as robust as the research in this chapter, and uses the 21-day trend without a move of more than 5 percent as the measure, it does show by example the message. Without studying the markets, one might assume that secular bear markets are mainly down trending markets. Hopefully this table dispels that notion and shows that during secular bear markets a strong tendency to trend still exists.

If there is a single takeaway from all this analysis on market trends, it is this: markets trend. Herding causes demand, which is the opposite of economic supply and demand (A104). The stock market is a demand event. Some issues trend better when in uptrends than in downtrends, while the reverse holds true for some. From the tables in this chapter and in the appendix, you should be able to discern which indices, sectors, or industries are better for trending.

# CHAPTER 11

# Drawdown Analysis

While the world of finance believes risk is measured by volatility (standard deviation), it is my belief that loss of capital is risk and not volatility. In Figure 11.1, example A ends where it begins with zero gain or loss, yet modern finance says it is risky because it is volatile. Example B shows the end price lower than the beginning price so it shows a loss. Modern finance, in this instance, would say there is no risk because there is no volatility. I think you can draw your own conclusions. Volatility can contribute to risk, but it also can contribute to price gains. Loss of capital is simple and reasonable to use as a risk measure, and in this chapter, risk is defined by drawdown.

## What Is Drawdown?

Drawdown is the percentage that price has moved down from its previous all-time high price.

> Drawdown is risk.
> Drawdown is systematic risk.
> Drawdown is loss of capital.
> Drawdown can last longer than you can.
> Drawdown can ruin your retirement plans.

## Drawdown Terminology

The following describes the nomenclature used in Figure 11.2.

> Magnitude: Drawdown *Magnitude* is the percentage that price has moved down from its previous all-time high.
> Decline: Drawdown *Decline* is the amount of time the market declined from an all-time high to the trough.
> Duration: Drawdown *Duration* is the total amount of time that it took the price to recover to is previous all-time high.
> Recovery: Drawdown *Recovery* is the time it took from the trough to get back to an all-time high.

231

**FIGURE 11.1**   Volatility versus Risk

**FIGURE 11.2**   Drawdown Terminology Chart

*Source:* Chart courtesy of MetaStock.

**TABLE 11.1**   Drawdown Terminology Table

| % Decline | |
|---|---|
| 0–5% | Noise |
| 5–10% | Pull Back |
| 10–20% | Correction |
| > 20% | Bear Market |

Although the terminology for drawdowns is subjective, I'll stick with the ones that Sam Stovall (Standard & Poor's) uses, as they are as good as any. I have often thought one more term for bear markets greater than −40 percent would be good, such as Super Bear, but I have other battles to fight. See Table 11.1.

## The Mathematics of Drawdown and Equivalent Return

Recovering from a severe drawdown takes an extraordinary return just to get back to where you were. This is sometimes referred to as *equivalent return* and is represented by this formula:

$$\text{Percent Drawdown}/(1 - \text{Percent Drawdown}) - 1$$

If you don't have a calculator or table handy, just divide the percent decline by its complement (100 − percent), and then mentally place the decimal in the appropriate place. This is best done in privacy and not on a stage in front of many people.

From Figure 11.3 you can see that if you lose 50 percent, then it takes a 100 percent gain to get back to even. When was the last time you doubled your money? A 100 percent gain is the same as doubling your money. The recent bear market that began on October 9, 2007, dropped more than 55 percent, you can see that to recover it takes a gain of more than 122 percent to get back to even. One thing the graphic clearly shows is that the larger the loss, the gain required to recover becomes even greater.

## Cumulative Drawdown

Figure 11.4 is an example of cumulative drawdown. The line that moves across the tops of the price data (top plot) only moves up with the data and sideways when the data does not move up; in other words, it is constantly reflecting the price's all-time high value. The bottom plot is the percentage decline from that all-time high line. Whenever that line is at the top it means that price in the top plot is at its all-time high. As the line in the bottom plot declines it moves in percentages of where it was last at its all-time high price. In the example shown, a new all-time high in price is reached at the vertical line labeled A. The bottom plot shows that as prices move down from that point, the drawdown also moves in conjunction with price. The horizontal line that goes through the lower part of the drawdown plot is at −10 percent. You can't read the dates at the bottom, but it took almost six months before the prices recovered to point B and then moved above the level they had reached at point A. This is an example of drawdown that had a magnitude of −17 percent shown by the lowest point reached on the drawdown line in the bottom plot. The drawdown also lasted (duration) almost six months as shown by the time between line A and line B.

Figure 11.5 shows the percentage of drawdown over the entire history of the Dow Industrials since 1885. The top portion is the Dow Industrials plotted using semi-log scaling and the bottom plot is the drawdown percentage. The darker horizontal line through the bottom plot is the mean or average of the drawdown over the full time period since 1885. Its value is −22.1 percent. The other horizontal lines are shown at zero (top line), −20 percent, −35 percent, −50 percent, and −65 percent, I think the thing that stands out from this chart is that the period from 1929 through 1954 suffered an enormous drawdown not only in magnitude but also in duration. The low was on June 28, 1932 at −88.67 percent. The equivalent return to get back to even from that point was a gain of more than 783 percent. That is why it took almost 25 years to accomplish.

**FIGURE 11.3**  Mathematics of Equivalent Return

**The Break-Even Curve**
What percentage gain is required to recover from a loss?
It grows exponentially as the loss increases.

| Loss | Gain Needeed to Recovery |
|------|--------------------------|
| 0%   | 0.0%                     |
| 10%  | 11.1%                    |
| 15%  | 17.6%                    |
| 20%  | 25.0                     |
| 25%  | 33.3%                    |
| 30%  | 42.9%                    |
| 35%  | 53.8%                    |
| 40%  | 66.7%                    |
| 45%  | 81.8%                    |
| 50%  | 100.0%                   |
| 55%  | 122.2%                   |
| 60%  | 150.0%                   |
| 65%  | 185.7%                   |
| 70%  | 233.3%                   |
| 75%  | 300.0%                   |
| 80%  | 400.0%                   |
| 85%  | 566.7%                   |
| 90%  | 900.0%                   |
| 95%  | 1900.0%                  |

Percent Gain Needed = $1/(1 - $ Percent Loss$) - 1$

*Source:* Chart courtesy of dshort.com.

**FIGURE 11.4**  Cumulative Drawdown Example

*Source:* Chart courtesy of MetaStock.

**FIGURE 11.5** Dow Industrials Cumulative Drawdown (1885–2012)

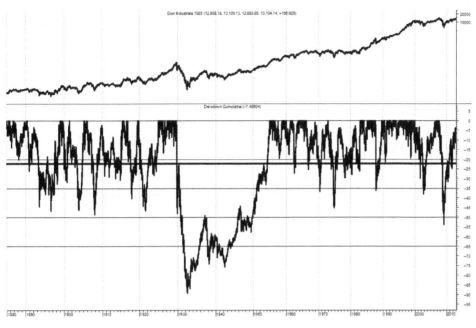

*Source:* Chart courtesy of MetaStock.

Because the depression-era drawdown distorts the other drawdowns, Figure 11.6 shows exactly the same data since about 1954, eliminating the scaling affect from the −88 percent depression era drawdown. The drawdown in 2008 clearly stands out as the biggest in modern times at −53.78 percent on March 9, 2009. As of this writing, that drawdown has yet to recover. It should be noted that all of the time that the drawdown line in the bottom plot is not back up to the top (0 percent), the market is in a "state of drawdown," which is noted by the duration, not just the amount of the decline, which is the magnitude.

Remember: Every bear market ends, but rarely when you are still trying to pick the bottom.

## S&P 500 Drawdown Analysis

The following data is from the S&P 500 Index, not adjusted for dividends or inflation, over the period from December 30, 1927, through December 31, 2012. It was a period that consisted of 21,353 market days and 1,016.81 calendar months. The S&P 500 has been widely regarded as the best single gauge of the large cap U.S. equities market since the index was first published in 1957 and back filled to 1927 with the S&P 90. The index has more than US$5.58 trillion benchmarked, with index assets comprising approximately US$1.31 trillion of this total. The index includes 500 leading companies in leading industries of the U.S. economy, capturing 75 percent coverage of U.S. equities.

**FIGURE 11.6**   Dow Industrials Cumulative Drawdown (1954–2012)

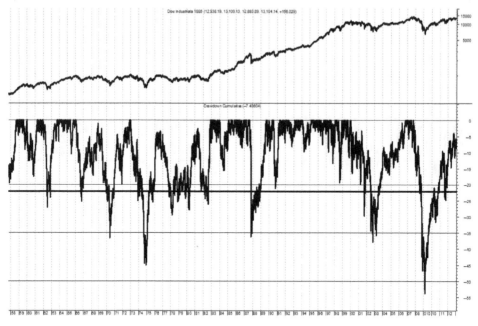

*Source:* Chart courtesy of MetaStock.

## Drawdown Decline — S&P 500

Table 11.2 is focused only on the percentage decline of the various drawdowns. The columns in the table are defined as follows:

> *Drawdown range.* This is the percentage of drawdown decline, it is divided into various ranges which make up the rows in the table. The top row of data is for drawdowns with declines greater than 20 percent and the bottom row is the data for all drawdowns.
>
> *Average max drawdown.* This is the average of all the drawdowns for the percentage decline in the first column.
>
> *Average days in decline.* This is the average number of market days that the drawdowns were in the decline whose percentage decline is defined by the first column.
>
> *Average months in drawdown.* This is simply a calculation of dividing the average market days in decline by 21, which is the average number of market days per month, which yields calendar months.
>
> *Total days in decline.* This is the sum of all the days the particular decline range was in decline.
>
> *Total months in decline.* This is the total market days in decline divided by 21.
>
> *Percentage of time spent in decline.* This is the percentage of time that the declines were in a state of decline based on the total number of market days for the period of analysis.

**TABLE 11.2** S&P 500 Drawdown Decline Data

| Drawdown Range | | Average Max Drawdown | Average Days in Decline | Average Months in Decline | Total Days in Decline | Total Months in Decline | Percentage of Time Spent in Decline |
|---|---|---|---|---|---|---|---|
| −100% | −20% | −40.88% | 359 | 17.07 | 3,585 | 171 | 16.79% |
| −15% | −19.99% | −19.63% | 47 | 2.21 | 93 | 4 | 0.44% |
| −10% | −14.99% | −11.54% | 102 | 4.84 | 813 | 39 | 3.81% |
| −5% | −9.99% | −7.00% | 23 | 1.10 | 806 | 38 | 3.77% |
| −0.01% | −4.99% | −1.19% | 4 | 0.19 | 1,510 | 72 | 7.07% |
| All DDs | | −2.89% | 16 | 0.76 | 6,807 | 324 | 31.88% |

From Table 11.2 you can see that all drawdowns greater than 20 percent, which are also called *bear markets*, were in a state of decline for almost 17 percent of the time, in other words bear market declines accounted for 17 percent of the total time from 1927 to 2012. The bottom row in the table above shows that all drawdowns (DD), no matter what their magnitude spent almost 32 percent of the time declining.

## Drawdown Recovery—S&P 500

*Drawdown recovery* is the term used to define the time spent from when a drawdown bottoms (hits its absolute lowest point and greatest percentage of decline) and completely recovers (gets back up to where the drawdown began). The columns in Table 11.3 are similar to the Drawdown Decline table in Table 11.2; we are just discussing the last portion of the drawdown here instead of the first portion.

Following a similar discussion as was done in the Drawdown Decline analysis, we can see that Drawdown Recoveries where the magnitude of the drawdown was greater than 20 percent took more than 50 percent of the total time to recover. Remember that recoveries from declines always take longer than the declines. This is generally defined by the fact that declines (selling) are more emotionally driven so usually are quicker and more abrupt. There is a new column in the Drawdown Recovery table and it is called *Average Gain to Recovery*. This is the percentage of gain (recovery) needed to get back to where the drawdown began. See the earlier part of this section that talks about equivalent return for more information. From the Table 11.3 you can see that for drawdowns greater than 20 percent, on average it takes a gain of more than 69 percent to get back to even. Remember we are dealing with averages in these tables. Elsewhere in the book are tables showing each of the drawdowns that were greater than 20 percent.

## Drawdown Duration—S&P 500

Drawdown Duration is shown in Table 11.4; this is the total amount of time that a complete drawdown occurred. The previous two tables dealt with the decline and the recovery, this table is the total of those two.

**TABLE 11.3**  S&P 500 Drawdown Recovery Data

| Drawdown Range | | Average Gain to Recovery | Average Days to Recover | Average Months to Recover | Total Days in Recovery | Total Months in Recovery | Percentage of Time Spent in Recovery |
|---|---|---|---|---|---|---|---|
| −100% | −20% | 69.14% | 1,075 | 51.18 | 10,748 | 511.81 | 50.33% |
| −15% | −19.99% | 24.42% | 72 | 3.40 | 143 | 6.81 | 0.67% |
| −10% | −14.99% | 13.04% | 53 | 2.52 | 424 | 20.19 | 1.99% |
| −5% | −9.99% | 7.53% | 31 | 1.50 | 1,100 | 52.38 | 5.15% |
| −0.01% | −4.99% | 1.21% | 3 | 0.14 | 1,114 | 53.05 | 5.22% |
| All DDs | | 2.98% | 32 | 1.52 | 13,529 | 644.24 | 63.36% |

**TABLE 11.4**  S&P 500 Drawdown Duration Data

| Drawdown Range | | Average Duration of Drawdown (Days) | Average Duration of Drawdown (Months) | Total Duration of Drawdown (Days) | Total Duration of Drawdown (Months) | Percentage of Time Spent in Drawdown |
|---|---|---|---|---|---|---|
| −100% | −20% | 1,433 | 68.25 | 14,333 | 682.52 | 67.12% |
| −15% | −19.99% | 118 | 5.62 | 236 | 11.24 | 1.11% |
| −10% | −14.99% | 155 | 7.36 | 1,237 | 58.90 | 5.79% |
| −5% | −9.99% | 54 | 2.59 | 1,906 | 90.76 | 8.93% |
| −0.01% | −4.99% | 7 | 0.34 | 2,624 | 124.95 | 12.29% |
| All DDs | | 48 | 2.28 | 20,336 | 968.38 | 95.24% |

Drawdowns of greater than 20 percent averaged 1,433 days, which is more than 68 months, or about 5.6 years. The total number of days of all drawdowns greater than 20 percent was 14,333 market days or 682 months, which is more than 56 years. Now the real eye-catcher in this table is the last row that shows all drawdowns regardless of the percentage decline. It shows that the market from 1927 to 2012 was in a state of drawdown for more than 95 percent of the time. In other words, the market was making new all-time highs less than 5 percent of the time.

## The Drawdown Message — S&P 500

With all the above tables about the various stages of drawdown, the information taken from the Drawdown Duration table in Table 11.5 is the real message from this Drawdown Analysis; the percentage of time that the market, in this case the S&P 500 Index, has spent in a state of drawdown. In other words, the amount of time that the market has spent just to get back to where it had already been before is what most folks do not realize. *If you even eliminated the noise, which are the drawdowns of less than 5 percent, the market has been in a state of drawdown for 82.95 percent of the time.*

**TABLE 11.5** S&P 500 Time Spent in Drawdown

| Drawdown Range | | Percent of Time Spent in Drawdown |
|---|---|---|
| −100% | −20% | 67.12% |
| −15% | −19.99% | 1.11% |
| −10% | −14.99% | 5.79% |
| −5% | −9.99% | 8.93% |
| −0.01% | −4.99% | 12.29% |
| **All Drawdowns** | | **95.24%** |

## Alternative Method

Figure 11.7 and the analysis below shows an alternative method to validate this drawdown analysis. In this mathematical process, the amount of time spent making new all-time highs was calculated using the same S&P 500 data. The top plot is the S&P 500 price shown plotted using semi-log scaling. The jagged line that moves along the top of the data is a line representing the all-time high price. It only moves up when the S&P is making a new all-time high and moves sideways when the S&P is declining below its previous all-time high. The second plot is a calculation to identify only the days in which the all-time high line in the top plot was moving upward, in other words the days in which the S&P 500 was making a new all-time high. The third plot has two lines; one is a summation of the second plot or the running sum of all the days

**FIGURE 11.7** Alternative Drawdown Method for S&P 500

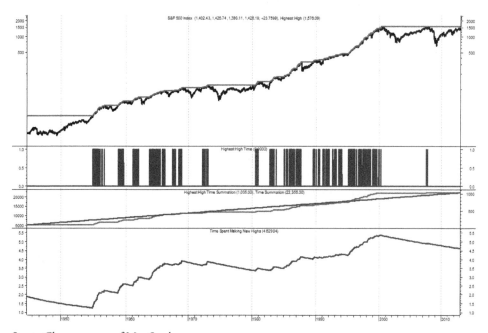

*Source:* Chart courtesy of MetaStock.

making a new all-time high in price. The second line in the third plot is just calculating all the days of data in the S&P 500 by using the simple concept of Close price not equal to zero and then doing the running summation. The bottom plot is the percent of the new all-time highs summation to the total of all days of data. You can see (trust me) that the percentage of time the S&P 500 was making new all-time highs is 4.63 percent. In the previous drawdown analysis it was shown that all drawdowns contained 95.24 percent of the data. 100 percent − 95.24 percent = 4.76 percent, which is only 0.13 percent difference between the two totally independent calculations.

## Average Drawdown — S&P 500

An additional calculation has been added to Table 11.4—S&P 500 Drawdown Duration Data and is shown in Table 11.6 as two new columns; the average of the average drawdown for each percentage category, and the total average of all drawdowns.

While the data in the previous tables breaks down the drawdowns over various ranges of percentage of decline, a common mistake in the world of finance is to focus on a term called *maximum drawdown* when comparing two issues, such as two mutual funds. One must keep in mind that maximum drawdown is a one-time isolated event and could be misleading. Here is an example: Let's assume we are looking at two mutual funds, each with a 20-year history of net asset value (NAV). Fund A has a maximum drawdown of 45 percent and Fund B has a maximum drawdown of 30 percent. Which fund do you prefer? Most will say that Fund B is better because it has a smaller maximum drawdown. And they would be correct, but I think they need to view more information from the 20 years of data. What if Fund B had 12 additional drawdowns of 25 percent each and Fund A had additional drawdowns with the largest being only 12 percent. Now which fund do you like? While the maximum drawdown is greater on Fund A, all of the remaining drawdowns are considerably less than those for Fund B. This is why I prefer to look at Average Drawdown as shown in Table 11.6.

## Distribution of Drawdowns — S&P 500

Figure 11.8 shows all drawdowns that were greater than 15 percent. You can see that for the period from 1927 to 2012, the S&P 500 had 2 drawdowns in the 15–19.99 percent range, 2 in the 20–24.99 percent range, and so on, for a total of 12 drawdowns of magnitude greater than 15 percent. Interestingly, there were no drawdowns in the 40–44.99 percent range. I would guess that once a market has declined over 40 percent that it creates so much fear it cannot stop until it moves further first.

Figure 11.9 shows all drawdowns no matter how small. You can see that there were 424 drawdowns, with 369 of them less than 5 percent. Five percent declines are generally considered just noise and part of the market pricing mechanism. Drawdowns between 5 percent and 10 percent are considered pullbacks; there were 35 pullbacks during this period. Corrections are drawdowns between 10 percent and 20 percent, you can see that there were 10 (total of 10–14.99 percent and 15–19.99 percent). There were 10 drawdowns of 20 percent or greater. Also notice that Figure 11.8 is reflected in Figure 11.9, just that 3 more distribution percentages were added to the left.

**TABLE 11.6** S&P 500 Average Drawdown

| Drawdown Range | | Drawdown Duration | | | | | Average Average Drawdown | Average Drawdown |
|---|---|---|---|---|---|---|---|---|
| | | Average Duration of Drawdown (Days) | Average Duration of Drawdown (Months) | Total Duration of Drawdown (Days) | Total Duration of Drawdown (Months) | Percentage of Time Spent in Drawdown | | |
| −100% | −20% | 1,433 | 68.25 | 14,333 | 682.52 | 67.12% | −19.06% | −23.32% |
| −15% | −19.99% | 118 | 5.62 | 236 | 11.24 | 1.11% | −10.87% | |
| −10% | −14.99% | 155 | 7.36 | 1,237 | 58.90 | 5.79% | −5.55% | |
| −5% | −9.99% | 54 | 2.59 | 1,906 | 90.76 | 8.93% | −3.29% | |
| −0.01% | −4.99% | 7 | 0.34 | 2,624 | 124.95 | 12.29% | −0.66% | |
| All DDs | | 48 | 2.28 | 20,336 | 968.38 | 95.24% | −1.45% | |

**FIGURE 11.8**  S&P 500 Distribution of Drawdowns Greater than 15 Percent

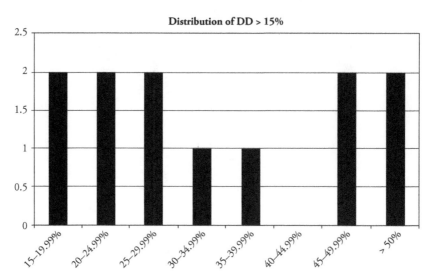

**FIGURE 11.9**  S&P 500 Distribution of All Drawdowns

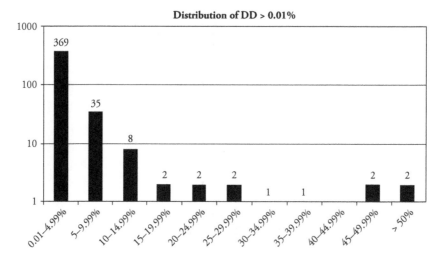

## Cumulative Drawdown for S&P 500

Figure 11.10 shows you a visual of all drawdowns during the analysis period. The 1929 Drawdown is clearly exceptional not only in magnitude of decline but also duration; so much so that it skews the visual affect of the remaining drawdowns.

## S&P 500 Index Excluding the 1929 Bear Market

Often it is good to remove some statistical outliers such as the giant drawdown/bear market that began in 1929 and lasted until 1954, 25 years total duration. The tables that follow (Table 11.7, Table 11.8, and Table 11.9) show the S&P 500 from 1927 to

**FIGURE 11.10**  S&P 500 Cumulative Drawdown Chart

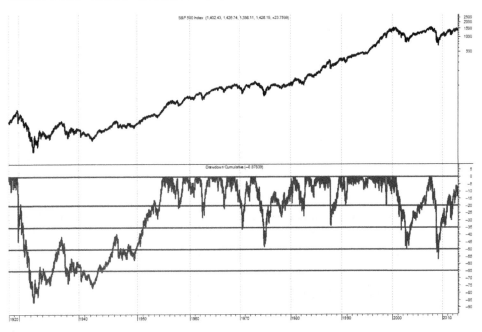

*Source:* Chart courtesy of MetaStock.

**TABLE 11.7**  S&P 500 Drawdown Decline Data Excluding 1929 Bear Market

| Drawdown Range | | Average Max Drawdown | Average Days in Decline | Average Months in Decline | Total Days in Decline | Total Months in Decline | Percentage of Time Spent in Decline |
|---|---|---|---|---|---|---|---|
| −100% | −20% | −35.84% | 323 | 15.38 | 2,907 | 138 | 13.61% |
| −15% | −19.99% | −19.63% | 47 | 2.21 | 93 | 4 | 0.44% |
| −10% | −14.99% | −11.54% | 102 | 4.84 | 813 | 39 | 3.81% |
| −5% | −9.99% | −7.00% | 23 | 1.10 | 806 | 38 | 3.77% |
| −0.01% | −4.99% | −1.19% | 4 | 0.19 | 1,510 | 72 | 7.07% |
| All DDs | | −2.69% | 14 | 0.69 | 6,129 | 292 | 28.70% |

2012 with exactly the same data as the previous respective tables; however, this time the great depression drawdown has been removed from the data.

The Average Max Drawdown has decreased from −40.88 percent to only −35.84 percent for drawdowns more than 20 percent. You can look at the numbers for the remaining columns and see that they are all reduced, however, not by nearly as much as I would have guessed prior to doing the analysis.

Recovery data seems to have been reduced significantly more when removing the 1929 depression drawdown. This is because not only was the magnitude of that bear market over −86 percent, but it also lasted for more than 25 years.

**TABLE 11.8**   S&P 500 Drawdown Recovery Data Excluding 1929 Bear Market

| Drawdown Range | | Average Gain to Recovery | Average Days to Recover | Average Months to Recover | Total Days in Recovery | Total Months in Recovery | Percentage of Time Spent in Recovery |
|---|---|---|---|---|---|---|---|
| −100% | −20% | 55.87% | 575 | 27.40 | 5,178 | 246.57 | 24.25% |
| −15% | −19.99% | 24.42% | 72 | 3.40 | 143 | 6.81 | 0.67% |
| −10% | −14.99% | 13.04% | 53 | 2.52 | 424 | 20.19 | 1.99% |
| −5% | −9.99% | 7.53% | 31 | 1.50 | 1,100 | 52.38 | 5.15% |
| −0.01% | −4.99% | 1.21% | 3 | 0.14 | 1,114 | 53.05 | 5.22% |
| All DDs | | 2.77% | 19 | 0.90 | 7,959 | 379.00 | 37.27% |

Because the Recovery numbers were significantly reduced with the removal of the 1929 bear market, it also stands to reason that the duration numbers would also be significantly reduced. And Table 11.9 confirms that is the case.

### Drawdowns Greater than 20 Percent Are Bear Markets

Although this is also shown in Chapter 7, it is appropriate to include with this section of the book on Drawdown Analysis because bear markets are merely drawdowns of 20 percent or greater. Table 11.10 shows all the drawdowns (bear markets) of 20 percent or greater in the S&P 500 Index since 12/30/1927. Here is a brief description of the statistics that are at the bottom of Table 11.10.

> *Average.* The same as the mean in statistics; add all values and then divide by the number of items.
>
> *Avg Ex 29.* This is the Average with the 1929 bear market removed as it skews the data somewhat.
>
> *Minimum.* The minimum value in that column.
>
> *Maximum.* The maximum value in that column.
>
> *Std. Dev.* This is standard deviation or sigma, which is a measure of the dispersion of the values in the column. About 65 percent of the values will fall within one standard deviation of the mean, and 95 percent will fall within two standard deviations of the mean.
>
> *Median.* If the data is widely dispersed or has asymptotic outlier data, this is usually a better measure for central tendency than Average.

The number two drawdown as of 12/31/2012 is still in progress. While its magnitude of decline was −56.78 percent, the duration is still in progress and only fourth in rank as the current number 3 and 4 drawdowns, while not as steep, lasted longer.

**TABLE 11.9** S&P 500 Drawdown Duration Data Excluding 1929 Bear Market

| Drawdown Range | | Drawdown Duration | | | | | |
|---|---|---|---|---|---|---|---|
| | | Average Duration of Drawdown (Days) | Average Duration of Drawdown (Months) | Total Duration of Drawdown (Days) | Total Duration of Drawdown (Months) | Percentage of Time Spent in Drawdown | Average Average Drawdown | Average Drawdown |
| -100% | -20% | 898 | 42.78 | 8,085 | 385.00 | 37.86% | -15.29% | -10.95% |
| -15% | -19.99% | 118 | 5.62 | 236 | 11.24 | 1.11% | -10.87% | |
| -10% | -14.99% | 155 | 7.36 | 1,237 | 58.90 | 5.79% | -5.55% | |
| -5% | -9.99% | 54 | 2.59 | 1,906 | 90.76 | 8.93% | -3.29% | |
| -0.01% | -4.99% | 7 | 0.34 | 2,624 | 124.95 | 12.29% | -0.66% | |
| All DDs | | 33 | 1.59 | 14,088 | 670.86 | 65.98% | -1.33% | |

245

**TABLE 11.10** Bear Markets in S&P 500 from 12/30/1927 to 12/31/2012

| Largest to Smallest | Decline from Peak | Return Required for Recovery | Peak Date | Trough Date | Recovery Date | Decline in Days | Decline in Months | Recovery in Days | Recovery in Months | Bear Duration in Days | Bear Duration in Months | Average Drawdown |
|---|---|---|---|---|---|---|---|---|---|---|---|---|
| 1 | −86.19% | 624.09% | 9/16/1929 | 6/1/1932 | 9/22/1954 | 678 | 32.29 | 5,571 | 265.29 | 6,249 | 297.57 | −52.97% |
| **2** | −56.78% | 131.35% | 10/10/2007 | 3/10/2009 | **12/31/2012** | 355 | 16.90 | 962 | 45.81 | 1,317 | 62.71 | −23.11% |
| 3 | −49.15% | 96.65% | 3/27/2000 | 10/10/2002 | 5/31/2007 | 637 | 30.33 | 1,166 | 55.52 | 1,803 | 85.86 | −22.54% |
| 4 | −48.20% | 93.06% | 1/11/1973 | 10/3/1974 | 7/17/1980 | 436 | 20.76 | 1,461 | 69.57 | 1,897 | 90.33 | −18.98% |
| 5 | −36.06% | 56.40% | 11/29/1968 | 5/26/1970 | 3/6/1972 | 369 | 17.57 | 451 | 21.48 | 820 | 39.05 | −13.29% |
| 6 | −33.51% | 50.40% | 8/26/1987 | 12/7/1987 | 7/27/1989 | 71 | 3.38 | 414 | 19.71 | 485 | 23.10 | −17.17% |
| 7 | −27.97% | 38.84% | 12/12/1961 | 6/26/1962 | 9/3/1963 | 135 | 6.43 | 299 | 14.24 | 434 | 20.67 | −10.67% |
| 8 | −27.11% | 37.20% | 11/28/1980 | 8/12/1982 | 11/3/1982 | 430 | 20.48 | 58 | 2.76 | 488 | 23.24 | −12.44% |
| 9 | −22.18% | 28.50% | 2/9/1966 | 10/7/1966 | 5/4/1967 | 167 | 7.95 | 143 | 6.81 | 310 | 14.76 | −9.32% |
| 10 | −21.63% | 27.60% | 8/2/1956 | 10/22/1957 | 9/24/1958 | 307 | 14.62 | 233 | 11.10 | 540 | 25.71 | −10.06% |
| **Average** | −40.88% | 69.14% | | | | 358.50 | 17.07 | 1,075.80 | 51.23 | 1,434.30 | 68.30 | −19.06% |
| **Avg Ex 29** | −35.84% | 55.87% | | | | 323.00 | 15.38 | 576.33 | 27.44 | 899.33 | 42.83 | −15.29% |
| **Minimum** | −21.63% | 27.60% | | | | 71.00 | 3.38 | 58.00 | 2.76 | 310.00 | 14.76 | −52.97% |
| **Maximum** | −86.19% | 624.09% | | | | 678.00 | 32.29 | 5,571.00 | 265.29 | 6,249.00 | 297.57 | −9.32% |
| **Std. Dev.** | 19.95% | −16.63% | | | | 200.78 | 9.56 | 1,647.37 | 78.45 | 1,788.34 | 85.16 | 12.93% |
| **Median** | −34.79% | 53.34% | | | | 362.00 | 17.24 | 432.50 | 20.60 | 680.00 | 32.38 | −15.23% |

## S&P Total Return Analysis

This data is not as robust as the price data but does reflect the reality of the markets for buy and hold or index investing in which one received and reinvests the dividends earned by the individual stocks that make up the index. This data begins on March 31, 1936, so therefore will not include the great depression drawdown that began in 1929. Tables 11.11 through 11.13, Figures 11.11 and 11.12, and Table 11.14 follow the format of the preceding sections.

## Drawdown Decline — S&P Total Return

**TABLE 11.11**   S&P 500 Total Return Drawdown Decline Data

| Drawdown Range | | Average Max Drawdown | Average Days in Decline | Average Months in Decline | Total Days in Decline | Total Months in Decline | Percentage of Time Spent in Decline |
|---|---|---|---|---|---|---|---|
| −100% | −20% | −35.68% | 297 | 14.12 | 2,965 | 141 | 15.37% |
| −15% | −19.99% | −18.72% | 48 | 2.30 | 193 | 9 | 1.00% |
| −10% | −14.99% | −11.69% | 88 | 4.17 | 1,402 | 67 | 7.27% |
| −5% | −9.99% | −6.89% | 24 | 1.16 | 1,189 | 57 | 6.16% |
| −0.01% | −4.99% | −1.11% | 4 | 0.18 | 2,293 | 109 | 11.89% |
| All DDs | | −2.37% | 18 | 0.86 | 7,707 | 367 | 39.95% |

## Drawdown Recovery — S&P Total Return

**TABLE 11.12**   S&P 500 Total Return Drawdown Recovery Data

| Drawdown Range | | Average Gain to Recovery | Average Days to Recover | Average Months to Recover | Total Days in Recovery | Total Months in Recovery | Percentage of Time Spent in Recovery |
|---|---|---|---|---|---|---|---|
| −100% | −20% | 55.47% | 532 | 25.32 | 5,318 | 253.24 | 27.57% |
| −15% | −19.99% | 23.04% | 98 | 4.65 | 391 | 18.62 | 2.03% |
| −10% | −14.99% | 13.24% | 58 | 2.78 | 933 | 44.43 | 4.84% |
| −5% | −9.99% | 7.40% | 27 | 1.30 | 1,339 | 63.76 | 6.94% |
| −0.01% | −4.99% | 1.12% | 3 | 0.13 | 1,607 | 76.52 | 8.33% |
| All DDs | | 2.43% | 22 | 1.06 | 9,520 | 453.33 | 49.35% |

# Drawdown Duration—S&P Total Return

**TABLE 11.13** S&P 500 Total Return Drawdown Duration Data

| Drawdown Range | | Average Duration of Drawdown (Days) | Average Duration of Drawdown (Months) | Total Duration of Drawdown (Days) | Total Duration of Drawdown (Months) | Percentage of Time Spent in Drawdown | Average Average Drawdown | Average Drawdown |
|---|---|---|---|---|---|---|---|---|
| -100% | -20% | 828 | 39.44 | 8,283 | 394.43 | 42.94% | -15.40% | -9.68% |
| -15% | -19.99% | 146 | 6.95 | 584 | 27.81 | 3.03% | -9.95% | |
| -10% | -14.99% | 146 | 6.95 | 2,335 | 111.19 | 12.10% | -5.37% | |
| -5% | -9.99% | 52 | 2.46 | 2,528 | 120.38 | 13.10% | -3.28% | |
| -0.01% | -4.99% | 6 | 0.30 | 3,900 | 185.71 | 20.22% | -0.63% | |
| All DDs | | 40 | 1.92 | 17,227 | 820.33 | 89.30% | -1.20% | |

## Distribution of Drawdowns Greater than 15 Percent — S&P Total Return

**FIGURE 11.11** S&P 500 Total Return Distributions Greater than 15 Percent

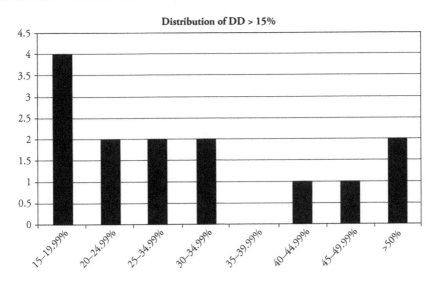

## Distribution of All Drawdowns — S&P Total Return

**FIGURE 11.12** S&P 500 Total Return Distributions

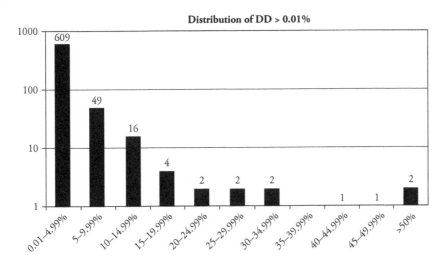

# Bear Markets—S&P Total Return

**TABLE 11.14** S&P 500 Total Return Bear Markets (3/31/1936 to 12/31/2012)

| Largest to Smallest | Decline from Peak | Return Required for Recovery | Peak Date | Trough Date | Recovery Date | Decline in Days | Decline in Months | Recovery in Days | Recovery in Months | Bear Duration in Days | Bear Duration in Months | Average Drawdown |
|---|---|---|---|---|---|---|---|---|---|---|---|---|
| 1 | -55.25% | 123.47% | 10/9/2007 | 3/9/2009 | 4/2/2012 | 355 | 16.90 | 774 | 36.86 | 1,129 | 53.76 | -21.13% |
| 2 | -51.33% | 105.45% | 3/10/1937 | 3/31/1938 | 5/31/1944 | 267 | 12.71 | 1,543 | 73.48 | 1,810 | 86.19 | -25.85% |
| 3 | -47.41% | 90.17% | 9/1/2000 | 10/9/2002 | 10/23/2006 | 525 | 25.00 | 1,017 | 48.43 | 1,542 | 73.43 | -21.38% |
| 4 | -44.80% | 81.17% | 1/11/1973 | 10/3/1974 | 7/9/1976 | 436 | 20.76 | 445 | 21.19 | 881 | 41.95 | -17.36% |
| 5 | -32.93% | 49.10% | 8/25/1987 | 10/19/1987 | 5/15/1989 | 38 | 1.81 | 397 | 18.90 | 435 | 20.71 | -16.04% |
| 6 | -32.59% | 48.34% | 11/29/1968 | 5/26/1970 | 3/15/1971 | 369 | 17.57 | 203 | 9.67 | 572 | 27.24 | -12.19% |
| 7 | -26.88% | 36.76% | 12/12/1961 | 6/26/1962 | 4/15/1963 | 135 | 6.43 | 201 | 9.57 | 336 | 16.00 | -10.57% |
| 8 | -25.22% | 33.72% | 5/29/1946 | 5/19/1947 | 9/30/1949 | 243 | 11.57 | 595 | 28.33 | 838 | 39.90 | -12.35% |
| 9 | -20.21% | 25.34% | 2/9/1966 | 10/7/1966 | 3/23/1967 | 167 | 7.95 | 114 | 5.43 | 281 | 13.38 | -8.36% |
| 10 | -20.16% | 25.25% | 11/28/1980 | 8/12/1982 | 10/7/1982 | 430 | 20.48 | 39 | 1.86 | 469 | 22.33 | -8.78% |
| Average | -35.68% | 55.47% | | | | 296.50 | 14.12 | 532.80 | 25.37 | 829.30 | 39.49 | -15.40% |
| Avg Ex 29 | -33.50% | 50.38% | | | | 290.00 | 13.81 | 506.00 | 24.10 | 796.00 | 37.90 | -14.76% |
| Minimum | -20.16% | 25.25% | | | | 38.00 | 1.81 | 39.00 | 1.86 | 281.00 | 13.38 | -25.85% |
| Maximum | -55.25% | 123.47% | | | | 525.00 | 25.00 | 1,543.00 | 73.48 | 1,810.00 | 86.19 | -8.36% |
| Std. Dev. | 13.05% | -11.54% | | | | 153.33 | 7.30 | 469.19 | 22.34 | 522.57 | 24.88 | 5.95% |
| Median | -32.76% | 48.72% | | | | 311.00 | 14.81 | 421.00 | 20.05 | 705.00 | 33.57 | -14.20% |

## Dow Jones Industrial Average Drawdown Analysis

This section follows the same order and format of the previous section on the S&P 500 Index drawdown, however, the only difference is that the analysis is done on the Dow Jones Industrial Average. (See Tables 11.15 through 11.19, Figures 11.13 through 11.15, and additional Tables 11.20 through 11.23.) The Dow Jones Industrial Average, also referred to as *The Dow*, is a price-weighted measure of 30 U.S. blue-chip companies. The Dow covers all industries with the exception of transportation and utilities, which are covered by the Dow Jones Transportation Average and Dow Jones Utility Average. Although stock selection is not governed by quantitative rules, a stock typically is added to the Dow only if the company has an excellent reputation, demonstrates sustained growth and is of interest to a large number of investors. Maintaining adequate sector representation within the indexes is also a consideration in the selection process.

The following data is from the Dow Jones Industrial Average, not adjusted for dividends or inflation, over the period from February 17, 1885, through December 31, 2012. The drawdown analysis for the Dow Industrials consists of 35,179 market days which translates into 1,675.19 calendar months.

### Drawdown Decline — Dow Jones Industrial Average

**TABLE 11.15**  Dow Industrials Drawdown Decline Data

| Drawdown Range | | Average Max Drawdown | Average Days in Decline | Average Months in Decline | Total Days in Decline | Total Months in Decline | Percentage of Time Spent in Decline |
|---|---|---|---|---|---|---|---|
| −100% | −20% | −41.79% | 557 | 26.54 | 8,360 | 398 | 23.76% |
| −15% | −19.99% | −17.68% | 165 | 7.88 | 827 | 39 | 2.35% |
| −10% | −14.99% | −12.25% | 43 | 2.07 | 564 | 27 | 1.60% |
| −5% | −9.99% | −7.03% | 23 | 1.11 | 866 | 41 | 2.46% |
| −0.01% | −4.99% | −1.15% | 4 | 0.17 | 1,821 | 87 | 5.18% |
| All DDs | | −3.01% | 22 | 1.05 | 12,438 | 592 | 35.36% |

## Drawdown Recovery — Dow Jones Industrial Average

**TABLE 11.16**  Dow Industrials Drawdown Recovery Data

| Drawdown Range | | Average Gain to Recovery | Average Days to Recover | Average Months to Recover | Total Days in Recovery | Total Months in Recovery | Percentage of Time Spent in Recovery |
|---|---|---|---|---|---|---|---|
| −100% | −20% | 71.78% | 1,170 | 55.73 | 17,554 | 835.90 | 49.90% |
| −15% | −19.99% | 21.48% | 125 | 5.97 | 627 | 29.86 | 1.78% |
| −10% | −14.99% | 13.95% | 73 | 3.46 | 944 | 44.95 | 2.68% |
| −5% | −9.99% | 7.56% | 33 | 1.55 | 1,205 | 57.38 | 3.43% |
| −0.01% | −4.99% | 1.17% | 2 | 0.11 | 1,140 | 54.29 | 3.24% |
| All DDs | | 3.11% | 38 | 1.81 | 21,470 | 1,022.38 | 61.03% |

## Drawdown Duration — Dow Jones Industrial Average

**TABLE 11.17**  Dow Industrials Drawdown Duration Data

| Drawdown Range | | Average Duration of Drawdown (Days) | Average Duration of Drawdown (Months) | Total Duration of Drawdown (Days) | Total Duration of Drawdown (Months) | Percentage of Time Spent in Drawdown |
|---|---|---|---|---|---|---|
| −100% | −20% | 1,728 | 82.27 | 25,914 | 1,234.00 | 73.66% |
| −15% | −19.99% | 291 | 13.85 | 1,454 | 69.24 | 4.13% |
| −10% | −14.99% | 116 | 5.52 | 1,508 | 71.81 | 4.29% |
| −5% | −9.99% | 56 | 2.67 | 2,071 | 98.62 | 5.89% |
| −0.01% | −4.99% | 6 | 0.28 | 2,961 | 141.00 | 8.42% |
| All DDs | | 60 | 2.85 | 33,908 | 1,614.67 | 96.39% |

## The Drawdown Message — Dow Jones Industrial Average

**TABLE 11.18**  Dow Industrials Time Spent in Drawdown

| Drawdown Range | | Percent of Time Spent in Drawdown |
|---|---|---|
| −100% | −20% | 73.66% |
| −15% | −19.99% | 4.13% |
| −10% | −14.99% | 4.29% |
| −5% | −9.99% | 5.89% |
| −0.01% | −4.99% | 8.42% |
| All Drawdowns | | 96.39% |

# Average Drawdown—Dow Jones Industrial Average

**TABLE 11.19** Dow Industrials Average Drawdown

| Drawdown Range | | Drawdown Duration | | | | Percentage of Time Spent in Drawdown | Average Average Drawdown | Average Drawdown |
|---|---|---|---|---|---|---|---|---|
| | | Average Duration of Drawdown (Days) | Average Duration of Drawdown (Months) | Total Duration of Drawdown (Days) | Total Duration of Drawdown (Months) | | | |
| −100% | −20% | 1,728 | 82.27 | 25,914 | 1,234.00 | 73.66% | −19.51% | −22.10% |
| −15% | −19.99% | 291 | 13.85 | 1,454 | 69.24 | 4.13% | −8.70% | |
| −10% | −14.99% | 116 | 5.52 | 1,508 | 71.81 | 4.29% | −5.20% | |
| −5% | −9.99% | 56 | 2.67 | 2,071 | 98.62 | 5.89% | −3.42% | |
| −0.01% | −4.99% | 6 | 0.28 | 2,961 | 141.00 | 8.42% | −0.67% | |
| All DDs | | 60 | 2.85 | 33,908 | 1,614.67 | 96.39% | −1.52% | |

253

## Distribution of Drawdowns — Dow Jones Industrial Average

**FIGURE 11.13**  Dow Industrials Distribution of Drawdowns Greater than 15 Percent

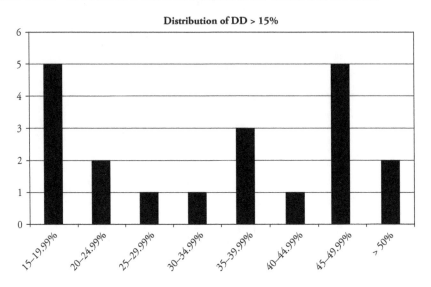

**FIGURE 11.14**  Dow Industrials Distribution of All Drawdowns

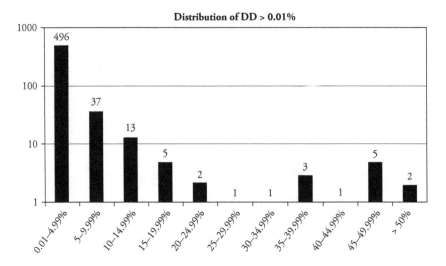

## Cumulative Drawdown for Dow Industrials

**FIGURE 11.15** Dow Industrials Cumulative Drawdown

*Source:* Chart courtesy of MetaStock.

## Dow Industrials Excluding the 1929 Bear Market

**TABLE 11.20** Dow Industrials Drawdown Decline Excluding 1929 Bear Market

| Drawdown Range | | Average Max Drawdown | Average Days in Decline | Average Months in Decline | Total Days in Decline | Total Months in Decline | Percentage of Time Spent in Decline |
|---|---|---|---|---|---|---|---|
| −100% | −20% | −38.40% | 537 | 25.56 | 7,515 | 358 | 21.36% |
| −15% | −19.99% | −17.68% | 165 | 7.88 | 827 | 39 | 2.35% |
| −10% | −14.99% | −12.25% | 43 | 2.07 | 564 | 27 | 1.60% |
| −5% | −9.99% | −7.03% | 23 | 1.11 | 866 | 41 | 2.46% |
| −0.01% | −4.99% | −1.15% | 4 | 0.17 | 1,821 | 87 | 5.18% |
| All DDs | | −2.86% | 21 | 0.98 | 11,593 | 552 | 32.95% |

**TABLE 11.21** Dow Industrials Drawdown Recovery Excluding 1929 Bear Market

| Drawdown Range | | Average Gain to Recovery | Average Days to Recover | Average Months to Recover | Total Days in Recovery | Total Months in Recovery | Percentage of Time Spent in Recovery |
|---|---|---|---|---|---|---|---|
| −100% | −20% | 62.34% | 792 | 37.72 | 11,091 | 528.14 | 31.53% |
| −15% | −19.99% | 21.48% | 125 | 5.97 | 627 | 29.86 | 1.78% |
| −10% | −14.99% | 13.95% | 73 | 3.46 | 944 | 44.95 | 2.68% |
| −5% | −9.99% | 7.56% | 33 | 1.55 | 1,205 | 57.38 | 3.43% |
| −0.01% | −4.99% | 1.17% | 2 | 0.11 | 1,140 | 54.29 | 3.24% |
| All DDs | | 2.95% | 27 | 1.26 | 15,007 | 714.62 | 42.66% |

**TABLE 11.22** Dow Industrials Drawdown Duration Excluding 1929 Bear Market

| Drawdown Range | | Average Duration of Drawdown (Days) | Average Duration of Drawdown (Months) | Total Duration of Drawdown (Days) | Total Duration of Drawdown (Months) | Percentage of Time Spent in Drawdown | Average Average Drawdown | Average Drawdown |
|---|---|---|---|---|---|---|---|---|
| -100% | -20% | 1,329 | 63.29 | 18,606 | 886.00 | 52.89% | -16.91% | -13.17% |
| -15% | -19.99% | 291 | 13.85 | 1,454 | 69.24 | 4.13% | -8.70% | |
| -10% | -14.99% | 116 | 5.52 | 1,508 | 71.81 | 4.29% | -5.20% | |
| -5% | -9.99% | 56 | 2.67 | 2,071 | 98.62 | 5.89% | -3.42% | |
| -0.01% | -4.99% | 6 | 0.28 | 2,961 | 141.00 | 8.42% | -0.67% | |
| All DDs | | 47 | 2.24 | 26,600 | 1,266.67 | 75.61% | -1.42% | |

# Drawdowns Greater than 20 Percent Are Bear Markets

**TABLE 11.23** Dow Industrials Bear Markets (2/17/1885 to 12/31/2012)

| Largest to Smallest | Decline from Peak | Return Required for Recovery | Peak Date | Trough Date | Recovery Date | Decline in Days | Decline in Months | Recovery in Days | Recovery in Months | Bear Duration in Days | Bear Duration in Months | Average Drawdown |
|---|---|---|---|---|---|---|---|---|---|---|---|---|
| 1 | −89.19% | 824.72% | 9/3/1929 | 7/8/1932 | 11/23/1954 | 845 | 40.24 | 6,464 | 307.81 | 7,309 | 348.05 | −55.98% |
| 2 | −53.78% | 116.35% | 10/9/2007 | 3/9/2009 | **12/31/2012** | 355 | 16.90 | 954 | 45.43 | 1,309 | 62.33 | −20.67% |
| 3 | −48.54% | 94.34% | 1/19/1906 | 11/15/1907 | 7/28/1915 | 552 | 26.29 | 2,192 | 104.38 | 2,744 | 130.67 | −18.48% |
| 4 | −46.64% | 87.42% | 6/4/1890 | 8/8/1896 | 1/20/1899 | 1,872 | 89.14 | 735 | 35.00 | 2,607 | 124.14 | −22.33% |
| 5 | −46.58% | 87.20% | 11/3/1919 | 8/24/1921 | 12/31/1924 | 540 | 25.71 | 1,006 | 47.90 | 1,546 | 73.62 | −24.10% |
| 6 | −46.14% | 85.67% | 6/17/1901 | 11/9/1903 | 3/24/1905 | 713 | 33.95 | 410 | 19.52 | 1,123 | 53.48 | −22.45% |
| 7 | −45.08% | 82.08% | 1/11/1973 | 12/6/1974 | 11/3/1982 | 481 | 22.90 | 1,998 | 95.14 | 2,479 | 118.05 | −17.30% |
| 8 | −40.13% | 67.02% | 11/21/1916 | 12/19/1917 | 7/9/1919 | 320 | 15.24 | 459 | 21.86 | 779 | 37.10 | −21.39% |
| 9 | −37.85% | 60.89% | 1/14/2000 | 10/9/2002 | 10/3/2006 | 685 | 32.62 | 1,003 | 47.76 | 1,688 | 80.38 | −13.64% |
| 10 | −36.58% | 57.67% | 2/9/1966 | 5/26/1970 | 11/10/1972 | 1,052 | 50.10 | 625 | 29.76 | 1,677 | 79.86 | −12.68% |
| 11 | −36.13% | 56.57% | 8/25/1987 | 10/19/1987 | 8/24/1989 | 38 | 1.81 | 468 | 22.29 | 506 | 24.10 | −19.34% |
| 12 | −31.76% | 46.54% | 9/5/1899 | 9/24/1900 | 6/3/1901 | 314 | 14.95 | 202 | 9.62 | 516 | 24.57 | −15.97% |
| 13 | −27.10% | 37.17% | 12/13/1961 | 6/26/1962 | 9/5/1963 | 134 | 6.38 | 301 | 14.33 | 435 | 20.71 | −9.51% |
| 14 | −21.16% | 26.83% | 7/17/1990 | 10/11/1990 | 4/17/1991 | 61 | 2.90 | 129 | 6.14 | 190 | 9.05 | −10.77% |
| 15 | −20.13% | 25.20% | 12/3/1886 | 4/2/1888 | 4/25/1890 | 398 | 18.95 | 623 | 29.67 | 1,021 | 48.62 | −8.08% |
| **Average** | −41.79% | 71.78% | | | | 557.33 | 32.26 | 1,171.27 | 70.62 | 1,728.60 | 102.89 | −22.58% |
| **Avg Ex 29** | −38.40% | 62.34% | | | | 536.79 | 25.56 | 793.21 | 37.77 | 1,330.00 | 63.33 | −16.91% |
| **Minimum** | −20.13% | 25.20% | | | | 38.00 | 1.81 | 129.00 | 6.14 | 190.00 | 9.05 | −55.98% |
| **Maximum** | −89.19% | 824.72% | | | | 1,872.00 | 89.14 | 6,464.00 | 307.81 | 7,309.00 | 348.05 | −8.08% |
| **Std. Dev.** | 16.48% | −14.15% | | | | 461.33 | 21.97 | 1,581.03 | 75.29 | 1,742.23 | 82.96 | 11.27% |
| **Median** | −40.13% | 67.02% | | | | 481.00 | 22.90 | 625.00 | 29.76 | 1,309.00 | 62.33 | −18.48% |

## Dow Industrials Total Return Analysis

This data is only available beginning on March 31, 1963. (See Tables 11.24 through 11.26 and Figures 11.16 and 11.17, followed by Table 11.27.)

### Drawdown Decline — Dow Industrials Total Return

**TABLE 11.24**   Dow Industrials Total Return Drawdown Decline Data

| Drawdown Range | | Average Max Drawdown | Average Days in Decline | Average Months in Decline | Total Days in Decline | Total Months in Decline | Percentage of Time Spent in Decline |
|---|---|---|---|---|---|---|---|
| −100% | −20% | −32.63% | 293 | 13.96 | 2,346 | 112 | 18.68% |
| −15% | −19.99% | −17.35% | 97 | 4.61 | 387 | 18 | 3.08% |
| −10% | −14.99% | −12.33% | 75 | 3.59 | 528 | 25 | 4.20% |
| −5% | −9.99% | −6.94% | 24 | 1.13 | 922 | 44 | 7.34% |
| −0.01% | −4.99% | −1.08% | 4 | 0.17 | 1,632 | 78 | 12.99% |
| All DDs | | −2.33% | 12 | 0.55 | 5,815 | 277 | 46.29% |

### Drawdown Recovery — Dow Industrials Total Return

**TABLE 11.25**   Dow Industrials Total Return Drawdown Recovery Data

| Drawdown Range | | Average Gain to Recovery | Average Days to Recover | Average Months to Recover | Total Days in Recovery | Total Months in Recovery | Percentage of Time Spent in Recovery |
|---|---|---|---|---|---|---|---|
| −100% | −20% | 48.44% | 339 | 16.14 | 2,712 | 129.14 | 21.59% |
| −15% | −19.99% | 20.99% | 86 | 4.08 | 343 | 16.33 | 2.73% |
| −10% | −14.99% | 14.06% | 60 | 2.88 | 423 | 20.14 | 3.37% |
| −5% | −9.99% | 7.46% | 31 | 1.48 | 1,215 | 57.86 | 9.67% |
| −0.01% | −4.99% | 1.10% | 2 | 0.11 | 1,042 | 49.62 | 8.30% |
| All DDs | | 2.38% | 11 | 0.54 | 5,735 | 273.10 | 45.66% |

# Drawdown Duration—Dow Industrials Total Return

**TABLE 11.26** Dow Industrials Total Return Drawdown Duration Data

| Drawdown Range | | Average Duration of Drawdown (Days) | Average Duration of Drawdown (Months) | Total Duration of Drawdown (Days) | Total Duration of Drawdown (Months) | Percentage of Time Spent in Drawdown | Average Average Drawdown | Average Drawdown |
|---|---|---|---|---|---|---|---|---|
| −100% | −20% | 632 | 30.11 | 5,058 | 240.86 | 40.27% | −14.12% | −7.73% |
| −15% | −19.99% | 183 | 8.69 | 730 | 34.76 | 5.81% | −8.51% | |
| −10% | −14.99% | 136 | 6.47 | 951 | 45.29 | 7.57% | −5.38% | |
| −5% | −9.99% | 55 | 2.61 | 2,137 | 101.76 | 17.01% | −3.30% | |
| −0.01% | −4.99% | 6 | 0.29 | 2,674 | 127.33 | 21.29% | −0.63% | |
| All DDs | | 23 | 1.09 | 11,550 | 550.00 | 91.95% | −1.20% | |

## Distribution of Drawdowns — Dow Industrials Total Return

**FIGURE 11.16**  Dow Industrials Total Return Distribution of Drawdowns Greater than 15%

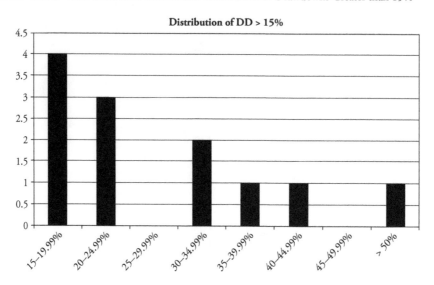

**FIGURE 11.17**  Dow Industrials Total Return Distribution of Drawdowns

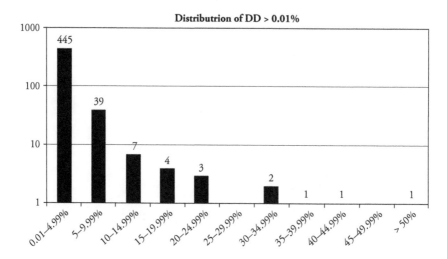

# Bear Markets for Dow Industrials Total Return

**TABLE 11.27**  Dow Industrials Total Return Bear Markets (3/31/1963 to 12/31/2012)

| Largest to Smallest | Decline from Peak | Return Required for Recovery | Peak Date | Trough Date | Recovery Date | Decline in Days | Decline in Months | Recovery in Days | Recovery in Months | Bear Duration in Days | Bear Duration in Months | Average Drawdown |
|---|---|---|---|---|---|---|---|---|---|---|---|---|
| 1 | −51.78% | 107.38% | 10/9/2007 | 3/9/2009 | 4/23/2011 | 355 | 16.90 | 541 | 25.76 | 896 | 42.67 | −20.95% |
| 2 | −40.75% | 68.79% | 1/11/1973 | 12/6/1974 | 1/12/1976 | 483 | 23.00 | 278 | 13.24 | 761 | 36.24 | −16.51% |
| 3 | −35.69% | 55.49% | 8/25/1987 | 10/19/1987 | 7/12/1989 | 38 | 1.81 | 437 | 20.81 | 475 | 22.62 | −17.60% |
| 4 | −34.80% | 53.38% | 1/14/2000 | 10/9/2002 | 12/14/2004 | 685 | 32.62 | 549 | 26.14 | 1,234 | 58.76 | −11.92% |
| 5 | −32.25% | 47.60% | 5/14/1969 | 5/26/1970 | 3/15/1971 | 263 | 12.52 | 204 | 9.71 | 467 | 22.24 | −14.72% |
| 6 | −23.27% | 30.33% | 2/9/1966 | 10/7/1966 | 9/25/1967 | 168 | 8.00 | 243 | 11.57 | 411 | 19.57 | −10.38% |
| 7 | −22.18% | 28.50% | 12/31/1976 | 2/28/1978 | 8/13/1979 | 293 | 13.95 | 369 | 17.57 | 662 | 31.52 | −9.43% |
| 8 | −20.34% | 25.54% | 7/17/1990 | 10/11/1990 | 3/5/1991 | 61 | 2.90 | 99 | 4.71 | 160 | 7.62 | −11.43% |
| Average | −32.63% | 48.44% | | | | 293.25 | 13.96 | 340.00 | 16.19 | 633.25 | 30.15 | −14.12% |
| Avg Ex 29 | −29.90% | 42.65% | | | | 284.43 | 13.54 | 311.29 | 14.82 | 595.71 | 28.37 | −13.14% |
| Minimum | −20.34% | 25.54% | | | | 38.00 | 1.81 | 99.00 | 4.71 | 160.00 | 7.62 | −20.95% |
| Maximum | −51.78% | 107.38% | | | | 685.00 | 32.62 | 549.00 | 26.14 | 1,234.00 | 58.76 | −9.43% |
| Std. Dev. | 10.65% | −9.63% | | | | 216.79 | 10.32 | 162.20 | 7.72 | 332.34 | 15.83 | 4.01% |
| Median | −33.53% | 50.43% | | | | 278.00 | 13.24 | 323.50 | 15.40 | 568.50 | 27.07 | −13.32% |

## Gold Drawdown

Drawdowns are not restricted to the stock market; they can be analyzed on any time series data. Figure 11.18 is a chart of gold. This shows the price of gold in the top plot since 1967 and its cumulative drawdown in the bottom plot. The two horizontal lines in the drawdown plot are at −20 percent and −50 percent. I think it is clear that anyone who bought gold in the Hunt Brothers 1981 silver era and also the ending of the exceptional inflationary period of the 1970s, held an investment from 1980 until 2008 before the price of gold recovered. Twenty-eight years is a really long time to hold a loser. With gold's recent surge to new highs, the time value of money would probably continue to erode this 1980 investment, even though those folks are at least feeling better now.

## Japan's Nikkei 225 Drawdown

Figure 11.19 is of the Japanese stock market and its drawdown. I think at this point no commentary is needed as you can see that the Nikkei started dropping in late 1989 and is down in the −75 percent area since the end of 2008.

## Copper Drawdown

Copper is often referred to as *Doctor Copper* as many think it is a measure of economic activity, especially in the construction industry. Figure 11.20 is a chart of copper since

**FIGURE 11.18**  Gold Cumulative Drawdown

*Source:* Chart courtesy of MetaStock.

**FIGURE 11.19** Nikkei Cumulative Drawdown

*Source:* Chart courtesy of MetaStock.

**FIGURE 11.20** Copper Cumulative Drawdown

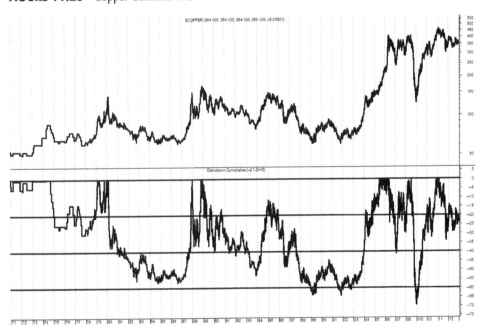

*Source:* Chart courtesy of MetaStock.

1971 with its cumulative drawdown in the bottom plot. Clearly, copper as an investment has spent an enormous amount of time in a state of drawdown.

## Drawdown Intensity Evaluator (DIE)

In an attempt to further evaluate the pain of drawdown, I have created an indicator that measures not only the magnitude of the drawdown, but also the duration.
Remember it is not just how big the drop in price is, but also how long it takes to
recover. Figure 11.21 helps you understand how this concept works. The top plot
is a price series, the middle plot (with the circles) is the cumulative drawdown, and
the bottom plot is the Drawdown Intensity Evaluator (DIE). You can see at point
A on the middle plot that a drawdown began and did not end until point D, in this
example (Consumer Staples) a time period from the end of 1998 until the middle
of 2006. You also see that the DIE was at zero at point A and again at point D
(vertical lines). From the middle plot of cumulative drawdown you can see that the
point of maximum drawdown is at point B (early 2000), which also corresponded
with an initial peak in DIE. The middle plot of drawdown shows point C, which
occurred in early 2003 and is not as low as point B, in fact, in this example point B
is −32.5 percent and point C is −27.4 percent. However, when you look at the bottom plot of DIE the highest point is at point C. This is because even though point

**FIGURE 11.21**    Drawdown Intensity Evaluator (DIE) Explanation

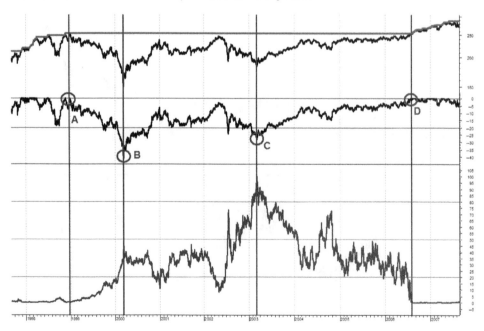

*Source:* Chart courtesy of MetaStock.

**FIGURE 11.22** Drawdown Intensity Evaluator and Normalized Version

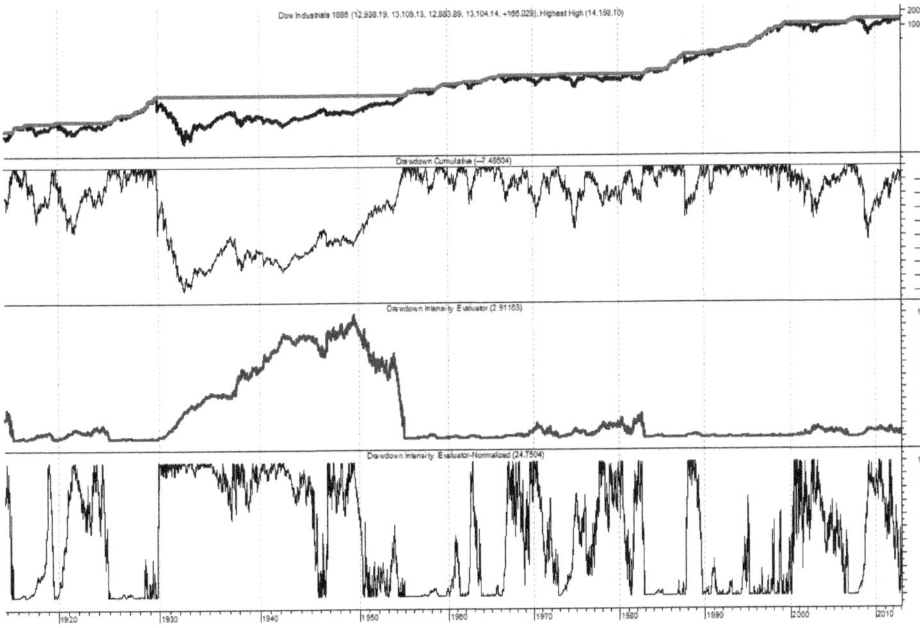

*Source:* Chart courtesy of MetaStock.

C occurred three years after point B, the pain of holding an investment during this time increased because the drawdown was still significant even though it wasn't at its maximum. After point C you can see that the drawdown slowing started to decrease but did not get back to its starting point (A) for more than three years (point D). DIE represents the pain of drawdown using not only magnitude but also, and equally important, the duration.

The DIE in Figure 11.21 uses the data for the entire period, to determine the pain. The next example, Figure 11.22, is an attempt to normalize the information using a four-year look-back. Normalizing data in this case resets the drawdown numbers and gives us a better picture of current conditions relative to a recent period of time and is particularly useful for long duration drawdowns. This means that it is measuring DIE over a moving four-year window. Figure 11.22 is a chart of the Dow Industrial Average in the top plot, with the cumulative drawdown in the second plot. The third plot is the Drawdown Intensity Evaluator, or DIE. The bottom plot is the DIE that has been normalized over a four-year period. The data begins in 1969. The DIE is a relatively simple process as it merely calculates the percentage of drawdown and multiplies it by the number of cumulative days it is in drawdown. An example here is in 1987 when there was a large drawdown but it did not last very long, in fact, the market completely recovered in only two years.

The world of finance, with its inadequate mathematics, inappropriate statistics, and faulty assumptions wants investors to believe that risk is volatility as represented by Standard Deviation (sigma). Although volatility is a contributor to drawdown it is also a contributor to price gains. Risk is loss of capital and that is best measured by drawdown. An investment strategy that attempts to tackle and limit drawdowns will be a more comfortable "Investment Ride" for most investors.

This wraps up Part II, which was heavily focused on research. Let's now move to why we want to understand all this—building a trend-following rules-based model designed to participate as much as possible in the good times, trying to avoid the bad times, and most of all, keep the subjectivity out of the process.

# Rules-Based Money Management

Part III is where it all comes together. All of the knowledge learned about the markets, investor behavior, and technical research on risk and trends is culminated in developing a rules-based trend-following model. It took almost 61.8 percent of the book to get to this point.

---

If you buy the why, the how is infinitely bearable.

*Friedrich Nitsche*

---

Part III begins with a chapter on popular indicators that are used throughout this section or at least derivations of these indicators.

In Part III I walk you through the involved process of creating and maintaining a rules-based trend-following model, affectionately called *Dance with the Trend*. Throughout this part I show many technical indicators that I have developed and used over the years, and give suggestions on how to determine the best parameters to use for each one. Although I do not believe that I have discovered anything special, I do know that what works for one may or may not work for another. I do not dive into specifics for individual indicators but try to give you guidelines on how to determine the parameters that best meet your goals. I hope this section of the book is a convincing testimony as to the need for a good technical model, along with rules and guidelines, for long-term successful investing. And don't forget the discipline, an equal partner in this process.

It doesn't have to be perfect to be good.

And now, let's dance with the trend.

# CHAPTER 12

# Popular Indicators and Their Uses

To begin Part III, we need to review a few basic technical indicators that are referenced frequently. Their concepts are used throughout this part of the book. Remember Part III is the creating of the weight of the evidence to identify trends in the overall market, a ranking and selection process for finding securities to buy based on their individual and relative momentum, a set of rules and guidelines to provide you with a checklist on how to trade the information, and the results of my rules-based trend following strategy called *Dance with the Trend*.

## Moving Averages and Smoothing

Most times daily stock market data is too volatile to analyze properly. There needs to be a way of removing much of this daily volatility. There is a way, and that is the subject of this section on smoothing techniques. Smoothing refers to the act of making the time series data smoother to remove oscillations, but keeping the general trend. It is a better adverb to use than always trying to explain that you take a moving average of it or take the exponential average of it; just say you are smoothing it. Some of the advantages of doing this are:

- Reduces the day-to-day fluctuations.
- Makes it easier to identify trends.
- Makes it easier to see changes in trend.
- Provides initial support and resistance levels.
- Much better for trend following.

One of the simplest market systems created, the moving average, works almost as well as the best of the complicated smoothing techniques. A moving average is exactly the same as a regular average (mean) except that it "moves" because it is continuously updated as new data become available. Each data point in a moving average is given equal weight in the computation; hence the term *arithmetic* or *simple* is sometimes used when referring to a moving average.

A moving average smoothes a sequence of numbers so that the effects of short-term fluctuations are reduced, while those of longer-term fluctuations remain relatively unchanged. Obviously, the time span of the moving average will alter its characteristics.

J. M. Hurst, in *The Profit Magic of Stock Transaction Timing* (1970), explained these alterations with three general rules:

1. A moving average of any given time span exactly reduces the magnitude of the fluctuations of durations equal to that time span to zero.
2. The same moving average also greatly reduces (but does not eliminate) the magnitude of all fluctuations of duration less than the time span of the moving average.
3. All fluctuations that are greater than the time span of the average "come through," or are present in the resulting moving average line. Those with durations just a little greater than the span of the average are greatly reduced in magnitude, but the effect lessens as periodicity duration increases. Very long duration periodicities come through nearly unscathed.

## Simple or Arithmetic Moving Average

To take an average of just about any set of numbers or prices, you add up the numbers then divide by the number of items. For example, if you have $4 + 6 + 2$, the sum is 12, and the average is $12/3 = 4$. A moving average does exactly this, but as a new number is added, the oldest number is removed. In the previous example, let's say that 8 is the new number, so the new sequence would be $6 + 2 + 8$. The original first number (4) was removed because we are only adding the most recent three numbers. In this case the new average would be $16/3 = 5.33$. So by adding an 8 and removing a 4, we increased the average by 1.33 in this example. For those so inclined, here's the math: $8 - 4 = 4$, and $4/3 = 1.33$.

Another feature of the simple moving average is that each component is treated equally, that is, it carries an equal weight in the calculation of the average. This is shown graphically in Figure 12.1. Note that it does not matter how many data points you are averaging, they each carry an equal contribution to the value of the average.

**FIGURE 12.1**   Arithmetic Average Component Weighting

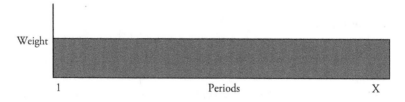

Because of the equal weighting of the data components in a simple moving average, the larger the average, the slower it will react to changes in price. I'll share a little story about price charts and moving averages. Back in the 1980s there was one of the original online services called Prodigy. At one point they started to provide some simple stock charts with a single moving average on them. I kept looking at it and knew something was wrong because I had studied and created these types of charts for years. I finally discovered that they were using separate scales for the price and the price's moving average. Although the values would be correct, the display was not because the average was using its isolated price scale. I wrote (yes, there was no e-mail then) them and explained. The first response was denial that they could be doing it wrong. I mailed them some charts showing their way and the proper way to display moving averages over price by sharing the same vertical scale. It took a long time and many letters before I finally convinced someone that they had it wrong. In appreciation they sent me a small digital clock worth about $1.25 (battery not included).

## Exponential Moving Average

This method of averaging was developed by scientists, such as Pete Haurlan, in an attempt to assist and improve the tracking of missile guidance systems. More weight is given to the most recent data, and it is therefore much faster to change direction and respond to changes in price. It is sometimes represented as a percentage (trend percent) instead of by the more familiar periods. For example, to calculate a 5 percent exponential average, you would take the last closing price and multiply it by 5 percent, then add this result to the value of the previous period's exponential average value multiplied by the complement, which in this case is $1 - .05 = .95$. Here is a formula that will help you convert between the two:

$K = 2/(N + 1)$ where $K$ is the smoothing constant (trend percent) and $N$ is the number of periods.

Algebraically solving for $N$: $N = (2/K) - 1$.

For example, if you wanted to know the smoothing constant of a 19-period exponential average, you could do the math, $K = 2/(19 + 1) = 2/20 = 0.10$ (smoothing constant) or 10 percent trend as it is many times expressed. In the example previously that used a 5 percent exponential average, the math is as follows:

5 percent Exp Avg = (Current price × 0.05) + (Previous Exp Avg × 0.95)

Figure 12.2 shows how the weight of each component affects the average. The most recent data is represented by the far right on the graph.

Now for the really important piece of knowledge about the difference between the simple moving average and the exponential moving average. Notice in Figure 12.3 how long it takes the simple average (dashed) to reverse direction to the upside. From the time the price line climbs through the dashed line, it takes five to six days before the dashed line begins to rise in this example (upward arrow—SMA). In fact,

**FIGURE 12.2**   Exponential Average Component Weighting

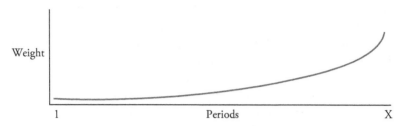

**FIGURE 12.3**   Difference between Simple Average (SMA) and Exponential Average (EMA)

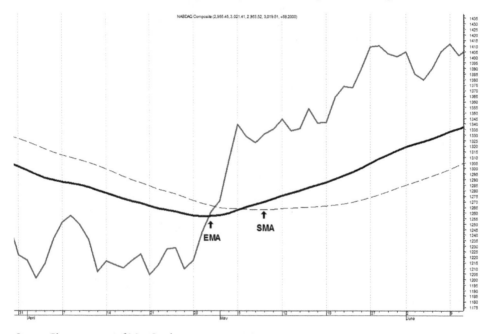

*Source:* Chart courtesy of MetaStock.

immediately after the price goes below the dashed line, the dashed line is still falling. Both averages used the same number of periods.

Now note how quickly the darker exponential average changes direction when the price line moves through it (upward arrow—EMA). Immediately! Yes, because of the *mathematics the exponential average will always change direction as soon as the price line moves through it.* That is why the exponential average is used, because it hugs the data tighter and eliminates much of the lag that is present in the simple average.

Now when it comes to the question as to which is better, the answer is always that it depends on what you are trying to accomplish. Sometimes the simple average is better because of its lag, and sometimes not. The same goes for the exponential average, sometimes it is better, sometimes not. Personally, I have found that the exponential average is better for longer-term analysis, say more than 65 periods (days). However, that becomes a personal preference as you build experience.

## Stochastics

George Lane promoted it and Ralph Dystant probably created it, however I know that Tim Slater, the creator of CompuTrac software in 1978 probably was the one that coined the name *Stochastics*. This is an odd name as stochastic is a mathematical term that refers to the evolution of a random variable over time. Stochastics is a range-based indicator that normalizes price data over a selected period of time, usually 14 periods or days. It basically shows where the most recent price is relative to the full range of prices over the selected number of periods. This display of price location within a range of prices is scaled between 0 and 100. Usually there are two versions, one called %K, which is the raw calculation and %D, which is just a three-period moving average of %K. Don't get me started why there are two names for a calculation and its smoothed value. I met George Lane a number of times and found him to be a delightful gentleman; George passed away in 2008.

Personally, this is about my favorite price-based indicator. It seems that almost everyone uses Stochastics as an overbought/oversold indicator. While it is good in a trading range or sideways market, it does not work well in a trending market when used this way. However, it is also an excellent trend measure. This is good because many stocks and markets trend more than they go sideways. So how does it work as a trend measure? If you think about the formula and realize that as long as prices are rising, then %K is going to remain at or near its highest level, say over 80. Therefore, as long as %K is over 80, you can assume you are in an uptrending market. Likewise, when %K is below 20 for a period of time, you are in a downtrending market. Personally, I like to use %D instead of %K for trend analysis, as it is smoother with less false signals. Figure 12.4 shows a 14-day Stochastic with the S&P 500 Index above. The three horizontal lines on the Stochastic are at 20, 50, and 80.

If you use Stochastics as an overbought/oversold indicator, it will work better if you only take signals that are aligned with a longer-term trend. For example, if the general trend of the market is up, then only adhere to the buy signals from Stochastics. Finally, you are not restricted to the 80 and 20 levels to determine overbought and oversold, you can use any levels you feel comfortable with. In fact, if using %D for trend following, also using 30 and 70 will help eliminate whipsaws.

One of the really unique properties of this indicator is that it can be used to normalize data. Let me explain. If you wanted to see data prices that were contained within a range between 0 and 100, then this formula would do that. For example if you had a year's worth of data, which is about 252 trading days, merely set the number of periods for %K to 252 and you would be able to see where prices moved over the last year. This becomes especially valuable when comparing two different stocks or indices. It should also be noted that Stochastics was designed to be used with data that contains the High, Low, and Close price. It can work with close-only data but the formula must be adjusted accordingly.

**FIGURE 12.4**  Stochastics Example

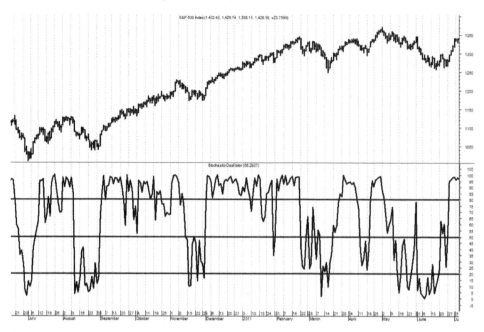

*Source:* Chart courtesy of MetaStock.

## RSI (Relative Strength Index)

RSI was one of the first truly original momentum oscillator indicators that was created prior to desktop or personal computers. Welles Wilder laid out the concept on a columnar pad. Basically, RSI takes a weighted average of the last 14 days' (if using 14 for the number of periods) up closes and divides by the last 14 days' down closes. It is then normalized so that the indicator always reads between 0 and 100. Parameters often associated with RSI for overbought are when RSI is over 70, and oversold when it is below 30.

The Relative Strength Index (RSI) can be used a number of different ways. Probably the most common is to use it the same as Stochastics in an overbought/oversold manner. Whenever RSI rises above 70 and then reverses direction and drops below 70, that is a sign that the down closes have increased relative to the up close and the market is declining. Although this method seems to always be popular, using RSI as a trend measure and one to help spot divergences with price seems like two better uses for RSI. Figure 12.5 shows RSI with the S&P 500 Index above. The horizontal lines on RSI are at 30, 50, and 70.

RSI is probably one of the most popular indicators ever developed. I think that is because most could not generate the formula themselves if it were not a mainstay in almost every technical analysis software package. Wilder developed it using a

**FIGURE 12.5**  RSI Example

*Source:* Chart courtesy of MetaStock.

columnar pad and had to come up with a way to do a weighted average of the up and down closes. It is not a true weighted average but gets the job done. One of the really big problems that I see with RSI is that in long continuous trends, it can be using some relatively old data as part of its calculation. Here's an example, say the stock is in an uptrend and has been for a while. The denominator is the average of the down closes in the last 14 days. If the uptrend is strong, there might not be any down closes for a period of time. If there were not any in the last 14 days, without the Wilder smoothing technique, the denominator would be equal to zero, and that would render the indicator useless. Because of this situation, the calculation for RSI can use relatively old data. That is why RSI seems to work well as a divergence indicator, because of the old data. This is generally caused by the fact that the previous up trend keeps the denominator, which uses down closes fairly inactive, but once the down closes started hitting again, it had a strong effect on RSI.

## Moving Average Convergence Divergence (MACD)

MACD is a concept using two exponential averages developed by Gerald Appel. It was originally developed as the difference between the 12 and 26 day exponential averages; the same as a moving average crossover system with the periods of the two averages being 12 and 26. The resulting difference, called the MACD line, is then smoothed with a nine-day exponential average, which is referred to as the *signal line*. Gerald Appel originally designed this indicator using different parameters for buy and sell signals, but that seems to have faded away and almost everyone now uses the 12–26–9 combination for both buy and sell. The movement of the MACD line is the measurement of the difference between the two moving averages. When MACD is at its highest point, it just means that the two averages are at their greatest distance apart (with short above long). And when the MACD is at its lowest level, it just means the two averages are at their greatest distance apart when the short average is below the long average. It really is a simple concept and is a wonderful example of the benefit of charting, because it is so easy to see. MACD, and in particular, the concept behind it, is an excellent technical indicator for trend determination. Not only that, but it also shows some information that can be used to determine overbought and oversold, as well as divergence. You could say it does almost everything. Figure 12.6 shows the MACD with the S&P 500 Index above. The solid line is the 12–26 MACD line and the dotted line is the nine period average.

Please keep this in mind: Although MACD is a valuable indicator for trend analysis, it is only the difference between two exponential moving averages. In fact, if you used price and one moving average it would be similar in that one of the moving averages was using a period of one. This is not rocket science! Figure 12.6 is an example of MACD with its signal line.

**FIGURE 12.6**   MACD Example

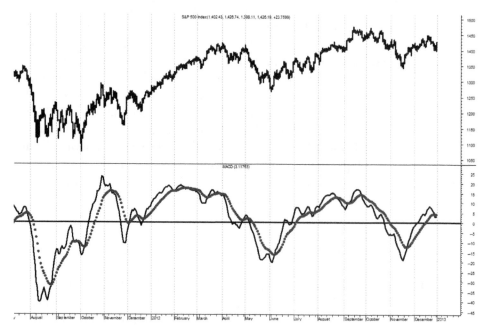

*Source:* Chart courtesy of MetaStock.

## A Word of Caution

Technical indicators generally deal with price and volume. Price involves the open, high, low, and close values. There are literally hundreds, if not thousands, of technical indicators that utilize these price components. These indicators use various parameters to make the indicator useful in analyzing the market. Generally, the Relative Strength Index (RSI) is considered an overbought/oversold indicator, while Moving Average Convergence Divergence (MACD) is considered a trend indicator. With an intentional reworking of the parameters used in each, Figure 12.7 shows both the RSI and MACD of the S&P 500 Index. Notice that they both look almost exactly the same. When you are working with only price or its components you must be careful to not overanalyze or overoptimize the indicator or you will just be looking at the same information. See the section on Multicollinearity in Chapter 9 for more evidence of this potential problem.

There are a host of money management techniques that have surfaced in the investment community. Each has its merits and each has its shortcomings. This section is provided to complement the book's completeness, and does not dwell into the details.

## The Binary Indicator

This part of the book also shows many charts of market data and indicators. Many will include what is called a *binary measure*. Binary means that it only gives two signals; it

**FIGURE 12.7** RSI and MACD Example

*Source:* Chart courtesy of MetaStock.

is either on or off similar to a simple digital signal. Figure 12.8 is a chart of an index in the top plot and an indicator in the bottom plot. The signals generated by the indicator are whenever it crosses the zero line shown on the lower plot. Whenever the indicator is above the line, it means the trend is up and whenever the indicator is below the line it means the trend is down (not up). To further simplify that concept, the tooth-like pattern, called the *binary* and is overlaid on the indicator, which gives the exact same information without all the volatility of the indicator. Notice that when the indicator is above the horizontal signal line that the binary is also above the line, and whenever the indicator is below the horizontal line, so is the binary. With that, we can then plot the binary directly on top of the index in the top plot and see the signals. In fact, now with this knowledge, the entire bottom plot could be removed and no essential information would be lost.

Other conventions adapted to Part III of this book that you need to know are that when discussing indicators or market measures, there are parameters used to give them specific values based on periods. A period can be any measure of time, hourly, daily, weekly, and so on. Here we will always stick to using daily analysis unless addressed locally. The term *issue* or *security* is often used; I will stick to using ETFs as the investment vehicle.

When showing many measures that are in the same category, such as ranking measures, I attempt to show them individually, but over the same period of time using the same ETF, such as the SPY.

**FIGURE 12.8**   Binary Indicator Example

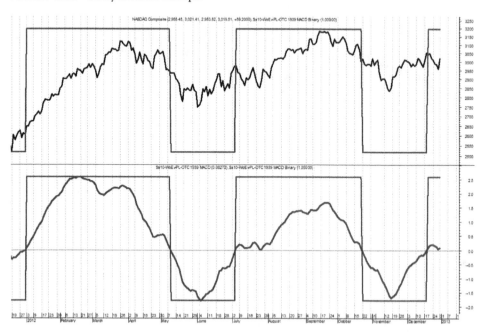

*Source:* Chart courtesy of MetaStock.

## How Compound Measures Work

Before moving on, a concept needs to be understood. Figure 12.9 will help you understand how a compound measure works. First, you need to know that this is not a complex system, as the signals work whenever two of the three indicators are in agreement the compound measure moves in the same direction. This means that all three could be signaling, but it only takes two to accomplish the goal. In Figure 12.9 the top plot is the Nasdaq Composite. The next three plots contain the binary indicators for the three components, in this example they are called 1, 2, and 3. There are four instances of signals from those three components, labeled in the top plot as A, B, C, and D. Let's go through them starting with signal A. Notice that there are two vertical lines, with the first one being created by indicator 3. Notice how indicator 3 dropped from its high position to its low position; that is a binary signal from indicator 3. The next vertical line shows up when indicator 2 drops to its low position. We now have two of the three indicators dropping to their low position, which means the compound binary indicator overlaid on the Nasdaq Composite in the top plot now drops to its low position.

The second signal at B occurs when both indicator 2 and 3 both drop to their low position at the same time, once again this is a signal for the compound binary in the top plot to drop to its low position. Moving over to signal C, you can see that indicator 3 rose to its top position followed a few days later by indicator 2 rising to its

**FIGURE 12.9**   Compound Measures Example 1

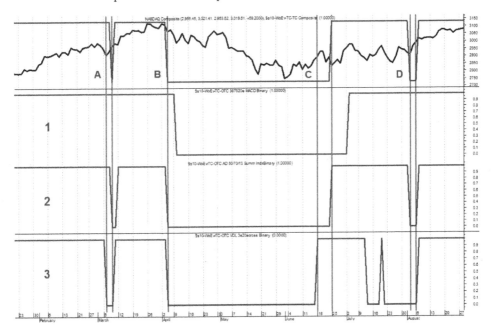

*Source:* Chart courtesy of MetaStock.

top position, which in turn causes the compound binary in the top plot to rise to its top position. Example D below shows indicator 2 dropping to its low position. This has caused the compound binary to drop because if you will notice, indicator 3 had already dropped to its low position many days prior to that of indicator 2. In example D, notice that both indicator 2 and 3 both rose on the same day and indicated by the rightmost vertical line, which of course caused the compound binary to also rise. The concept is simple; it only takes two of the three indicators to control the compound binary in the top plot. It does not matter which two it is or in what combination. As you can hopefully see, the process could be expanded to using five indicators and using the best three of the five.

Now try to figure out the compound measure below without any visual or verbal assistance. In Figure 12.10 the top plot contains the Nasdaq Composite and the compound binary. There are binaries for three indicators below and they work just like the example above, any two that are on is a signal for the compound binary to move in the same direction. Good luck.

**FIGURE 12.10**   Compound Measures Example 2

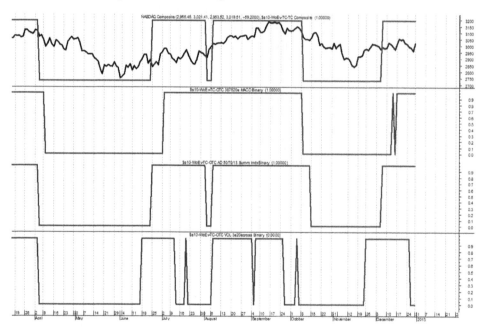

*Source:* Chart courtesy of MetaStock.

# CHAPTER 13

# Measuring the Market

## Weight of the Evidence Measures

I have been fond of a weight of the evidence approach for more than 30 years. The concept of "weight of the evidence" came from Stan Weinstein who published the newsletter, *The Professional Tape Reader*, and author of *Secrets for Profiting in Bull and Bear Markets*. Back in the early 1980s, most analysis was done manually. We did not have computers, Internet, or e-mail. Our data came from subscriptions or newspapers. I was a religious user of the *Barron's* Market Laboratory pages. I was working with Norm North of N-Squared Computing then, designing technical analysis software (yes, it was DOS-based and ran on 5.25" floppies). Norm had started a database of about 130 items from the market lab pages and each Saturday, I would go to the nearby hotel, buy a copy of *Barron's*, update the database then upload it to CompuServe so our clients could download it—all at the lightning fast speed of 300 baud. I'm somewhat of a packrat, and have many ring binders full of charts and notes; Figure 13.1 is the weight of the evidence approach I used back then. Wish I could print like that now.

I have totally stopped using the sentiment measures because I think the data collection process is not reliable. If you have ever taken a survey, especially an unsolicited survey, you can probably guess where I'm coming from. However, that does not mean the data isn't worthwhile, just not for me. There is, however, an excellent service provided by Jason Goepfert called Sentiment Trader at www.sentimentrader.com. Jason provided an example of a sentiment indicator that can be used in trend analysis. Figure 13.2 is the put/call ratio, which tends to trend along with the market. We see a higher average range during bear markets and a lower average range during bull markets. That has changed a little bit over the past decade, as there has been a structural shift to higher put/call ratios—more hedging from nervous investors who have been whacked with two big bear markets. But you can still see the trend in the ratio from a bull market to the next bear market.

I also no longer use any of the NYSE member/specialist data or odd-lot data as most doesn't seem as valid today as then. Now, the technical trend-following measures

**FIGURE 13.1**  Greg Morris' Weight of the Evidence Worksheet from Mid-1980s

| | BULLISH + | NEUTRAL N | BEARISH − | REMARKS |
|---|---|---|---|---|
| MEMBER SHORTS | < 81% | 81%-86% | > 86% | smart money |
| SPC SHORTS | < 45% | 45%-50% | > 50% | smart money, but usually 4-6 mo. early |
| PUB / SPC | > 5.00 | 3-5 | < 3.00 | |
| MBR - SPC SHORTS | > 50% | 35%-50% | < 35% | floor traders, smart on the big moves (short term) |
| MBR PURCH - SALES | < -4.00 | | > -4.00 | |
| ODD SHORTS BULL ONLY | > 6% | | ——— | less informed, especially intermediate term |
| PUB SHORTS | > 18% | 10%-18% | < 10.00 | less informed |
| TOT SHORTS | > 10% | 7%-10% | < 7% | less informed overall opinion |
| AMEX SPEC | < 7% | 7%-15% | > 15% | shows speculative attitude, usually late in a major trend |
| OTC SPEC | < 50% | 50%-80% | > 80% | same as above |
| 15-40 A-D LINE | 15 > 40 | | 15 < 40 | pure Zahorchek |
| SUM (NH - NL) | trending up | # wk change | trending down | good long term trend - takes 2 successive moves to change trend |
| ACT UP - ACT DN | < 0 | 0 - 4.00 | > 4.00 | big money, usually wrong |
| VOL UP - VOL DN | > 10.00 | | < 10.00 | technical |
| NH - NL | > 0 | | < 0 | technical |
| TRIN | > 9.50 | 9.5 - 10.5 | < 10.50 | technical |
| 40 DET NYSI | > 0 | | < 0 | technical |
| PUT % CALL | > 55% | 35%-55% | < 35% | usually wrong, small speculators |
| UNWEIGHT 5-30 | 5 > 30 | | 5 < 30 | |
| FED INDICATOR | > 3.0 | > +.5  < 0 | < -2.5 | |
| DJIA YIELD BEAR ONLY | ——— | | < 4.00% | fundamental |
| FREE RESERVES | > -50 | | < -50 | |
| DISCOUNT vs T-BILL | T.B < DISC | | T.B > DISC | |
| FED FUNDS vs MA | FF < MA b/103 | | FF > MA b/103 | |
| GROUP INTENSITY | > 0 | | < 0 | |
| INSIDERS | < 2.00 | | > 2.00 | smart money ? |
| INVESTORS | < 30% | 30%-70% | > 70% | |
| MUTUAL FUND | > 11% | 7%-8% | < 7% | holding cash at the wrong time -- usually late trend followers |
| MARGIN DEBT | > MA | | < MA | smart money |
| FCB CASH ACCT + MARG | > MA | | < MA | less informed, usually do the wrong thing during initial moves. |
| SHORT INTEREST | > MA | | < MA | potential supply |

**FIGURE 13.2**  Jason Goepfert's Equity Put/Call Ratio Analysis

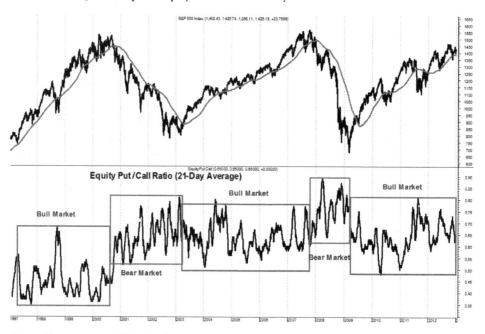

*Source:* Chart courtesy of MetaStock.

that make up the weight of the evidence consist of price, breadth, and relative strength indicators.

## A Note on Optimization

When evaluating indicators to be considered for trend following, you cannot optimize over long-term periods and then just pick the best performing indicator. That is a guarantee of failure and probably quite soon. Optimization is a great process in which to discover areas to avoid, but a poor process to actually determine parameters. If you do try to optimize then please read some good book on the downfalls of doing so. Optimization in the wrong hands is extremely dangerous. One area of value is to plot all of parameter's performance and look for plateaus (box) where the parameter performed steadily over a range of similar values. Picking a spike (circle) is the worst thing you can do as the parameter surrounding the spike are probably closer to where you will see the actual results. See Figure 13.3.

## Indicator Evaluation Periods

Indicators need to be evaluated over cyclical bull and bear markets, secular markets, periods covering calendar-based times, randomly selected periods, and almost any other period selection process you want to try. Remember, the goal is to find

**FIGURE 13.3**   Optimized Results Showing Good and Bad Areas

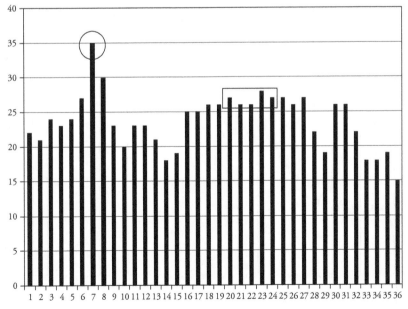

parameters that meet the needs of the model you are trying to create. You want indicators whose statistics over various times provide the safety and return that you expect of them. Ideally, you want to test the indicators with a certain portion of your data, get the parameters that work well, and then check it on the remaining portion of your data. This is known as *in sample* and *out of sample* testing. If the indicator continues to perform on the previously unused data, then you probably have something.

Figure 13.4 shows the Nasdaq Composite Average and the S&P 500 Index. The vertical lines are placed at each low and high that can be used to determine the evaluation periods. You must be careful with this and include the significant peaks and troughs when viewed over the long term. In fact, using a weekly price chart is probably better for this than using a daily price chart.

The remainder of this section covers many of the weight of the evidence indicators (measures) that are good for trend following. These can be separated into three broad categories: price, breadth, and relative strength.

## Price-Based Indicators

Price-based means that the indicator is measuring movement in price instruments; whether it be from an index such as the Nasdaq Composite Average, the S&P 500, or from an individual security, such as an ETF, a stock, a mutual fund, and so on. I use the Nasdaq Composite for my price guide because it is a high beta index that contains

**FIGURE 13.4**   Indicator Evaluation Periods

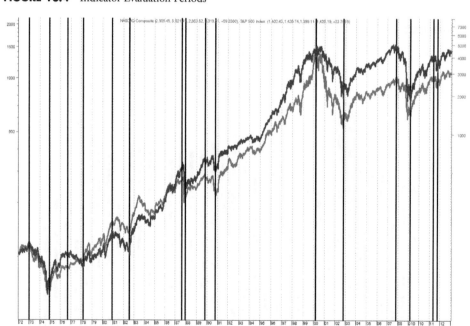

*Source:* Chart courtesy of MetaStock.

small caps, mid-caps, large caps, technology, just about everything except financials, and also has some dogs. If you are going to be a trend follower, then you want to follow a price-based index that moves; it doesn't matter if it is up or down, it just needs to do so in a big way, and the Nasdaq Composite fills the bill.

## Price Short Term

The short version of price is more for shorter-term assessment of trendiness. It is simply looking at the price relationship in the 5 to 21 day range. If you were using multiple price measures on the same index, then this is the one that would turn on first and also turn off first; it is the quickest to respond to changes in price direction. Many times a short-term measure is not actually used in the weight of the evidence calculation, but serves a weight of the evidence model well with an advance warning of things to come.

## Price Medium Term

This is another price trend measure that uses a different analytical technique and different look-back period than the Trend Capturing component. This Price Medium measure is basically looking at the price relationships over a three- to four-week period. If the short-term price measure isn't used, then this is the one that will lead the changed in direction of the index being followed.

## Price Long Term

This price trend measure is similar to Price Medium but looking at the price relationship over a four- to eight-week period. Generally the Price Medium indicator will turn on first and if the trend is sustained the Price Long measure will turn on thus providing confirmation of the trend and further building the point total of the cumulative weight of the evidence.

Figure 13.5 is an example of the Price Long measure. Although this is almost too much data on one chart, you can focus on the binary overlay on the top plot and can see that it does a good job of tagging the uptrends, which is all we want it to do.

Figure 13.6 shows the same price measure as the one above, just a smaller time frame. It becomes much clearer that the binary line overlaid on the top price data moves in conjunction with the indicator in the bottom plot, the price long measure. Whenever the price long indicator moves above the horizontal line, the binary moves to the top, and whenever the price long drops below the horizontal line, the binary drops back to the bottom. You can then see that whenever the binary is at the top, it is signaling an uptrend and whenever it is at the bottom it is signaling no uptrend (down trend or sideways). This concept is quite valuable since it allows you to view only the binary to know what the indicator is doing. So is this indicator perfect? Of course not, you can see there was a whipsaw signal (short and wrong, but also quickly

**FIGURE 13.5**   Price Long Term (1998–2012)

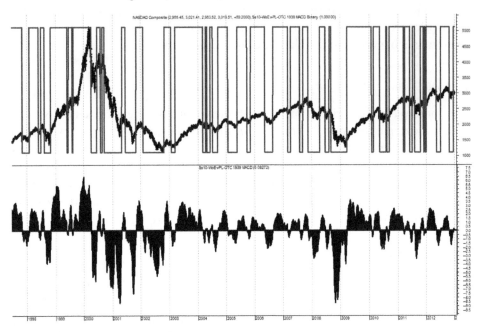

*Source:* Chart courtesy of MetaStock.

**FIGURE 13.6**   Price Long Term (2009–2012)

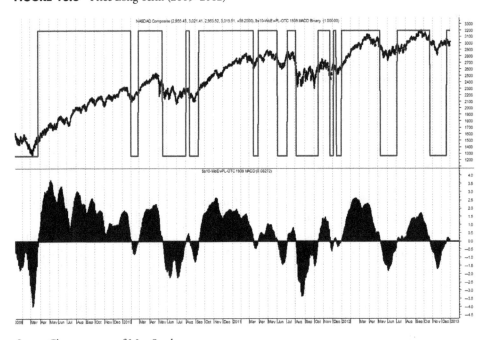

*Source:* Chart courtesy of MetaStock.

reversed) near the right center of the chart where the binary was at the top for only a very short period of time. As I have said before and will no doubt say again, I know these measures will be wrong at times, but they are not going to stay wrong because they react to the market. Because these indicators are all trend following, they will reverse a wrong direction almost as fast as they identify it in the first place. That is exactly what you want them to do and it is also why I use a weight of the evidence approach, which means I rely on a basket of technical measures. Sort of a democratic approach, if you will.

Table 13.1 is an example of the detailed research behind each of the various indicators used in the weight of the evidence. This example is over the period from 1980 to 2012, however, it should be run over many different periods (see Figure 13.4) to find consistency.

Here is an explanation of the various parameters in Table 13.1:

*Parameter.* These are the variable parameters used to test the indicator's usefulness in identifying trends. They can be discovered by optimization, or just a visual analysis of the indicator. They are then spread about to cover a wide range of analysis for the indicator.

*Winning years.* The percentage of years that the trading ended higher than the close from the previous year.

*Trades per year.* This is the number of closed trades per year.

*Average return per year.* Determined by looking at the total return for the entire run, and then dividing it by the number of years.

*Total return.* The total return from the system using the selected parameter.

*Compounded annual return.* The gain each year that would be required in order to achieve the total gain for the analysis period.

*Compounded annual return while invested.* The annual gain that would be required to achieve the total gain, excluding cash positions, over the period being analyzed.

*Percentage of time invested.* The percentage of time that actual trades were placed and not in cash.

*Ulcer index.* A measure of downside volatility also covered in the ranking measure section of this book.

*Largest trade loss.* A single trade that resulted in the largest loss.

*Maximum drawdown.* The maximum decline of the system measured from the highest level that the system had reached. Keep in mind this is a one-time isolated event.

*Ulcer performance index.* The compounded annual return divided by the Ulcer index, this is a performance measure similar to the Sharp ratio, the Sortino ratio, and the Treynor ratio. All are risk-adjusted measures of performance.

Although the calculation of all the various measures of an indicator's ability to work over a vast number of trials and time segments, one still has to determine "Where's the beef?" Of all that data generated, shouldn't you list the categories from

**TABLE 13.1**   Price Long-Term Performance Statistics

WoEv – Price Long Team
12/01/1980–12/31/2012
NASDAQ
Statistics from Ultra Financial Systems

| Parameter | Winning Years | Trades Per Year | Average Return Per Trade | Total Return | Compounded Annual Return | Compounded Annual Return While Invested | Percentage of Time Invested | Ulcer Index | Largest Trade Loss | Maximum Drawdown | Ulcer Performance Index |
|---|---|---|---|---|---|---|---|---|---|---|---|
| 1.00 | 63.64% | 2.68 | 3.12% | 817.41% | 7.15% | 20.12% | 37.66% | 13.95% | −8.48% | −35.48% | 51.25% |
| 0.80 | 72.73% | 2.52 | 4.19% | 1,634.06% | 9.29% | 22.97% | 42.99% | 11.20% | −7.89% | −34.33% | 82.95% |
| 0.60 | 69.70% | 2.43 | 4.95% | 2,488.97% | 10.67% | 23.55% | 47.92% | 10.08% | −7.75% | −32.35% | 105.85% |
| 0.40 | 63.64% | 2.31 | 5.61% | 3,188.24% | 11.49% | 22.77% | 53.03% | 10.74% | −9.31% | −37.17% | 106.98% |
| 0.20 | 78.79% | 2.24 | 6.12% | 3,731.11% | 12.03% | 21.71% | 57.80% | 11.06% | −9.98% | −36.19% | 108.77% |
| 0.00 | 69.70% | 2.15 | 6.34% | 3,654.53% | 11.96% | 19.96% | 62.05% | 12.42% | −11.01% | −36.25% | 96.30% |
| −0.20 | 69.70% | 2.27 | 5.92% | 3,412.49% | 11.72% | 18.32% | 65.91% | 12.06% | −9.80% | −29.84% | 97.18% |
| −0.40 | 66.67% | 2.40 | 5.46% | 3,009.20% | 11.30% | 16.53% | 70.00% | 13.97% | −10.38% | −39.19% | 80.89% |
| −0.60 | 63.64% | 2.15 | 6.36% | 2,603.02% | 10.82% | 14.98% | 73.58% | 14.45% | −10.07% | −39.25% | 74.88% |
| −0.80 | 69.70% | 1.99 | 6.15% | 1,566.61% | 9.16% | 12.04% | 77.07% | 20.25% | −14.99% | −51.22% | 45.23% |
| −1.00 | 66.67% | 1.90 | 6.40% | 1,373.94% | 8.74% | 11.05% | 79.98% | 21.76% | −13.97% | −53.30% | 40.17% |
| **Buy & Hold** | | | | | | | | | | | |
| NASDAQ | 66.67% | | | 1,373.58% | 8.74% | 8.74% | 100.00% | 36.58% | | −77.93% | 23.89% |
| NYSE | 72.73% | | | 888.72% | 7.40% | 7.40% | 100.00% | 14.94% | | −59.01% | 49.53% |
| S&P | 72.73% | | | 939.42% | 7.57% | 7.57% | 100.00% | 17.13% | | −56.78% | 44.19% |

best to worst inasmuch as their contribution to what you looking for? I think so, definitely so. One method and the one I use is to ask some sharp folks who are deeply familiar with the indicator and the output to give me their input as to the order in which the parameter analysis should be viewed. And to keep this as a robust process, it is done each year. Often there isn't much change, but sometimes someone gets a more involved feeling after working with these almost every day as to which is more important than another. Sometimes the overall relative ranking of these gets changed.

Table 13.2 shows that each column of data is ranked based on its relative importance as determined by the individuals involved in the portfolio management process. This relative input is then weighted based on the level it has reached in the vetting process. There is an old forecasting axiom that says the average of all estimates is probably going to work better than trying to select the single best guess.

Note: The columns with Inverted at the top mean that the smaller the value, the better it is performing.

The relative ranking is then placed alongside the parameter output to see where the current parameter being used and followed immediately by the ranking of the output components shown in the first column of Table 13.2. This process allows you to see how the parameters change over time compared to the one currently in use. Note that the parameters in the first column of Table 13.1 are in numerical order, so while this is a change in the relative ranking, if the change in the parameter is small then generally no changes will be made to the parameter in this weight of the evidence indicator. However, it will be watched over time and if there is an obvious drift away from the parameter being used, a change will be considered.

The above performance statistical information provided for the price long weight of the evidence will not be included in all of the indicators that are used as this section would get overly long. However, when something stands out that will provide additional insight into this process; the information will definitely be shown. However, do not fear; a chart or two will be shown for each measure.

## Risk Price Trend

The risk price trend is in the lower plot of Figure 13.7, while the top plot is the Nasdaq Composite and the risk price trend binary. This measure uses the MACD concept with considerably longer parameters for both the short- and long components. You can see from the binary that it does a relatively good job of picking out the trends of the market.

## Adaptive Trend

The adaptive trend measure incorporates the most recent 21 days of market data to compute volatility based on an average true range methodology. This process always considers the previous day's close price in the current day's high low range to ensure we are using days that gap either up or down to their fullest benefit. When the price is trading above the adaptive trend, a positive signal is generated; and when below, a

**TABLE 13.2** Price Long-Term Performance Statistics Ranking

| Weight | 2% | Inverted 4% | 9% | 7% | 2% | 15% | Inverted 5% | Inverted 18% | 15% | 11% | 13% | 100% |
|---|---|---|---|---|---|---|---|---|---|---|---|---|
| Rank | Winning Years | Trades per Year | Avg Return per Trade | Total Return | Annual Return | Annual Invested Return | % Time Invested | Ulcer Index | Largest Trade Loss | Max DD | Ulcer Perf. Index | Total |
| 7 | 9 | 11 | 11 | 11 | 11 | 5 | 1 | 7 | 3 | 4 | 9 | 7 |
| 4 | 2 | 10 | 10 | 8 | 8 | 2 | 2 | 4 | 2 | 3 | 6 | 5 |
| 1 | 3 | 9 | 9 | 7 | 7 | 1 | 3 | 1 | 1 | 2 | 3 | 3 |
| 3 | 9 | 7 | 7 | 4 | 4 | 3 | 4 | 2 | 4 | 7 | 2 | 4 |
| 2 | 1 | 5 | 5 | 1 | 1 | 4 | 5 | 3 | 6 | 5 | 1 | 4 |
| 6 | 3 | 3 | 3 | 2 | 2 | 6 | 6 | 6 | 9 | 6 | 5 | 6 |
| 5 | 3 | 6 | 6 | 3 | 3 | 7 | 7 | 5 | 5 | 1 | 4 | 5 |
| 9 | 7 | 8 | 8 | 5 | 5 | 8 | 8 | 8 | 8 | 8 | 7 | 8 |
| 8 | 9 | 3 | 2 | 6 | 6 | 9 | 9 | 9 | 7 | 9 | 8 | 7 |
| 10 | 3 | 2 | 4 | 9 | 9 | 10 | 10 | 10 | 11 | 10 | 10 | 9 |
| 11 | 7 | 1 | 1 | 10 | 10 | 11 | 11 | 11 | 10 | 11 | 11 | 9 |

290

**FIGURE 13.7** Risk Price Trend

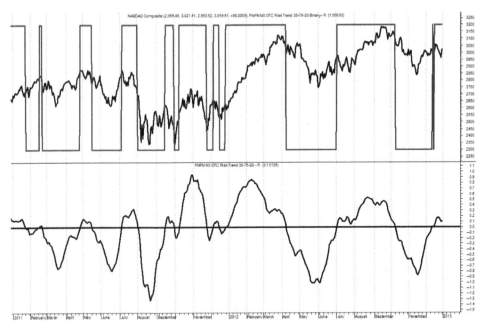

*Source:* Chart courtesy of MetaStock.

negative signal is in place. This is clearly shown in Figure 13.8 with the adaptive trend binary overlaid on the price chart at top. Whenever the binary is at the top, it is showing an uptrend, and when at the bottom, a downtrend.

## Breadth-Based Indicators

Breadth contributes significantly to trend analysis and is thoroughly described in this chapter and the Appendix. Breadth-based indicators offer an unweighted view of market action, a valuable view that is often obscured by price or capitalization weighted indices.

### Advances/Declines

The advance/decline component measures the relationship of advancing issues to declining issues. Advancing issues outnumbering declining issues is a positive event as more participation is taking place in the equity markets. However, an inverse relationship (decliners outnumber advancers) would be a clear sign of weakness to a price movement. There is a recent example of the clear divergence in the price movement and market internal movement during much of 2007 and particularly in the fourth quarter of 2007. From early October 2007 to late October 2007 we saw a distinct positive price trend

**FIGURE 13.8**   Adaptive Trend

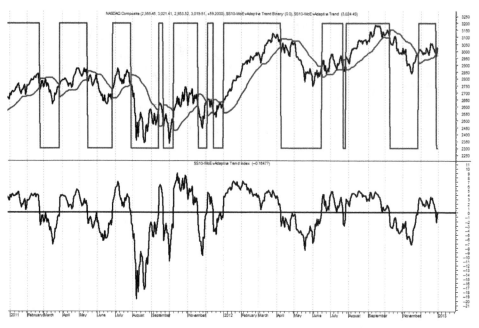

*Source:* Chart courtesy of MetaStock.

while the advance decline measure was rapidly declining. By late October the markets were reaching all time new highs. What you were reading and hearing in the news was all positive, "The market reached an all-time new high." According to the price movement things couldn't have looked better. However, the advance/decline measure was telling us a very different story as declining issues continued to outnumber advancing issues. This forewarning was signaling increased risk as the upward price movement was not being supported by broad participation. At that time, the advance/decline component was negative; hence, it was not contributing to the weight of the evidence total. Divergences can cue us to be prepared in the event the price action reverses rapidly. In fact, that is exactly what happened and it was the beginning of the 2007 to 2009 bear market.

Figure 13.9 shows the deterioration in the advance decline measure in 2007. You can see that while the market was reaching new highs, the advance decline measure never even got back up to its horizontal signal line. Breadth does this time and time again. It almost always leaves the party early and is a great tool to have in your arsenal as a trend follower.

Figure 13.10 is the same indicator but plotted with the same data used throughout this section so cross reference is easier.

## Up Volume/Down Volume

This Breadth measure gives us an internal look at the volume behind the price action by looking at the relationship of the volume in advancing issues versus the volume

**FIGURE 13.9** Advance Decline Measure—2007

*Source:* Chart courtesy of MetaStock.

**FIGURE 13.10** Advance Decline Measure

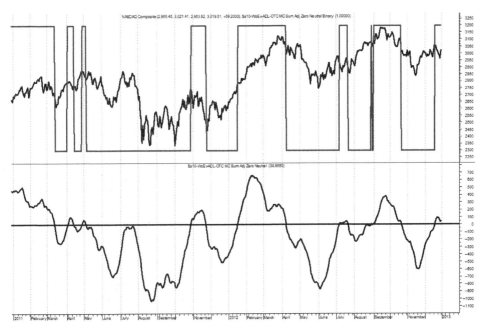

*Source:* Chart courtesy of MetaStock.

in declining issues. Again, by removing the capitalization weighting of the price movement that can drive the index price, this measure gives us an internal view of what is going on behind a price movement. Generally, if there is strong up volume relative to down volume it is a positive sign that the positive price movement is being supported. However, if there is positive price movement, but down volume is greater than up volume it is a sign that the price movement lacks participating volume. In this case the up volume/down volume measure would not contribute to the weight of the evidence leading to a lower total level signaling increased risk. Figure 13.11 is the up volume/down volume weight of the evidence measure. You might notice that the signal line (horizontal line) is not at zero like many use, but in this case it is at +400. The parameter analysis identified that this was a significantly better signal level. You can see that the up and down volume has been quite weak since and before the peak in prices, which occurred in the middle of the time period shown.

## New Highs/New Lows

The High/Low Breadth measure looks at the relationship between issues reaching new 52-week new high values to issues hitting new 52-week new low values. Generally, when the number of issues reaching new 52-week highs are outpacing the number

**FIGURE 13.11**   Up Volume/Down Volume Measure

*Source:* Chart courtesy of MetaStock.

reaching new 52-week lows there is a positive indication in support of positive price action. The flip side of more new lows to new highs is a negative indication, and this lets us know that there is potential risk that the price action and prices could possibly turn quickly in the other direction. When this indicator is on we have internal support for positive price movement and it adds to the point value of the weight of the evidence.

Note: See Appendix C for High Low Validation Measure for expanded information.

This weight of the evidence measure is a little different than the previous ones in that signals are generated by the crossing of the indicator's moving average shown in Figure 13.12 the bottom plot as the dotted line. You can see the binary in the top plot makes seeing these crossings quite easy.

## Breadth Combination Measure

The combination breadth measure (Figure 13.13) uses advancing and declining issues as well as advancing volume and declining volume by weighting the significant volume days inside of the indicator. This component serves to underweight insignificant price movements if the volume is weak while weighting the more significant price movements when volume is significant. This measure was created out of concern for days such as the Friday that follows Thanksgiving, a partial day of trading, and always

**FIGURE 13.12** New Highs/New Lows Measure

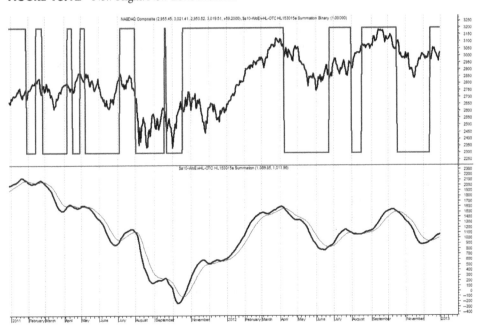

*Source:* Chart courtesy of MetaStock.

**FIGURE 13.13**   Breadth Combination Measure

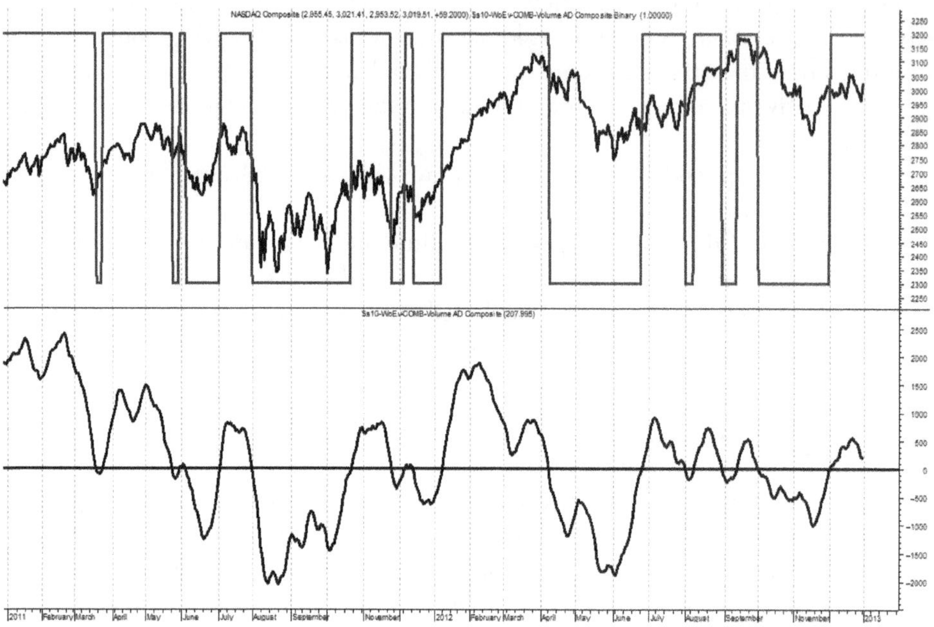

*Source:* Chart courtesy of MetaStock.

with very low volume. The downside of using breadth is that it does not matter if the day is shortened or the trading is light, you will always end up with a full complement of breadth data. Remember, breadth does not measure magnitude directly, only direction. In this measure, when the up volume is below a predetermined moving average, then only the advances are used. If the up volume is above this average, then the product of advances and up volume is used. The same concept is applied to the declines and the down volume.

## Breadth Is Not Always Internal Data

There are a number of breadth-based measures that do not use internal market data such as advances, declines, up volume, down volume, new highs, or new lows. A concept known as the *Percent Participation Index* is used by many analysts. The concept is simple yet revealing, it measures the number of stocks in an index as to where they are relative to their moving average. For example, many use a 200-day Participation Index, which shows the percent of stocks that make up the index that are above their own 200-day moving average. Figure 13.14 shows the Nasdaq Composite in the top plot with its 200-day simple moving average. The bottom plot is the 200-day participation index, which shows the percentage of all Nasdaq Composite stocks that are above their respective 200-day simple moving averages.

**FIGURE 13.14** Nasdaq Percent of Issues Above Their 200-Day Moving Average

*Source:* Chart courtesy of Stockcharts.com.

Figure 13.15 is similar to the previous one except that it shows the 50-day participation index.

## Slope of Moving Average

A longer-term big picture measure of market movements can be accomplished by calculating the slope of a moving average, in this case the 252-day moving average. This is the type of market measure that can be used as a filter for parameter changes. For example, whenever the histogram in the lower plot of Figure 13.16 is above the zero line, the stops can be looser, the buying requirements can be looser, and even other market measure parameters could be lengthened. If it is below the horizontal line, then revert back to the tighter set of parameters.

## World Market Climate

This is a breadth measure that uses a basket of international indices and their respective moving average relationship. For this example, this measure uses a basket of

**FIGURE 13.15**   Nasdaq Percent of Issues above Their 50-Day Moving Average

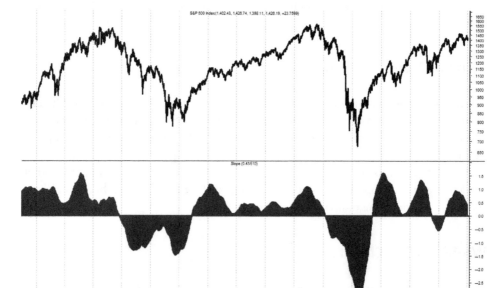

*Source:* Chart courtesy of Stockcharts.com.

**FIGURE 13.16**   Slope of Moving Average

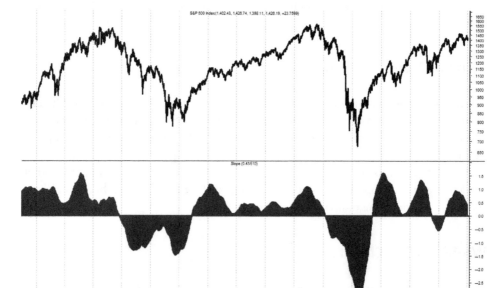

*Source:* Chart courtesy of MetaStock.

international stock market indices and their 50-day exponential average. The measure is bounded between zero and 100 because all that is being done is determining the percentage of the basket of indices that are above their 50-day exponential average. Complementarily, this will also tell you the percent below their 50-day moving average. Figure 13.17 has the World Market Climate shown in the top plot with lines drawn at 80 percent, 50 percent, and 30 percent. The bottom plot is the MSCI EAFE Index, which is a broad-based international index using markets from Europe, Australasia, and the Far East. Australasia is Australia, New Guinea, New Zealand, and their neighboring islands. Clearly the goal of EAFE is to include a broad international exposure outside North America. The EAFE in the bottom plot is shown with a 200-day exponential moving average just for reference.

**FIGURE 13.17** World Market Climate

*Source:* Chart courtesy of MetaStock.

## Cyclical Market Measure

This measure looks for longer-term price trends to identify cyclical bull or bear environments. For this example, I use the basket of international markets discussed in the previous measure. The concept is unique yet simple; it measures the direction of longer term averages and uses a filter of 0.05 percent before a reversal of the average is identified. Figure 13.18 shows the Cyclical Market Measure in the top plot with a horizontal line at 50 percent and the MSCI EAFE Index in the bottom plot with a 126-day simple moving average. One could use any values for the length of the moving average, both for the smoothing of the EAFE in the lower plot to the calculation of trending percentage that makes up the Cyclical Market Measure.

**FIGURE 13.18**   Cyclical Market Measure

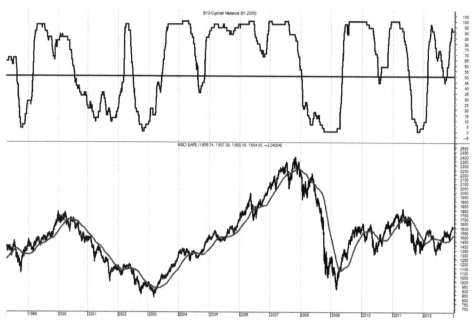

*Source:* Chart courtesy of MetaStock.

## Relative Strength

Back in the 1970s we used to have an indicator that looked at the volume on the American Stock Exchange (AMEX), also known as *the curb*, and the volume on the New York Stock Exchange (NYSE) known as *the big board*. It was called *The Speculation Index*. The AMEX consisted of small, relatively illiquid issues, generally all that could not make the listing requirements of the NYSE. The ratio of AMEX volume to NYSE volume was thought to represent excessive optimism when it reached a certain level. In perfect hindsight I think if we had used it as a trend indicator it would have been more valuable. Identify the rising path of speculation and as the volume of the AMEX increased relative to that of the NYSE, you would be in a good uptrend.

**Note:** In 2008, the AMEX was acquired by the NYSE Euronext, which announced that the exchange would be renamed the NYSE Alternext US. The latter was renamed NYSE Amex Equities in March 2009. These changes have made stand-alone AMEX trading volumes difficult to source and track, as a result of which the speculation index has lost much of its relevance as a measure of speculative activity.

### Small Cap versus Large Cap Component

Small cap participation is critical for sustained uptrends in the market because small caps reflect speculation and speculation is a requirement for uptrends. For small capitalization issues the Russell 2000 Index is used and for large capitalization issues the venerable

**FIGURE 13.19** Small Cap versus Large Cap Measure

*Source:* Chart courtesy of MetaStock.

S&P 500 Index is used. The math is simply to create the ratio of the small to large, then use technical analysis to provide a normalized trend measure. In Figure 13.19 the typical Nasdaq Composite is in the top plot along with the small cap large cap binary. The middle plot is just the ratio of the small to large issues, and the lower plot is the small cap large cap weight of the evidence measure. In this example you can see that small caps dominated the up move near the center of the chart, but have been relatively weak since. If you think about it, small caps also more closely relate to breadth.

### Growth versus Value Component

This component of relative strength measures the difference between growth stocks and value stocks. Now this will shock most folks who have studied the markets, but I use small cap issues for both the growth and value components. I was initially concerned that small cap value was almost an oxymoron, but the data has proved time and time again that it is perfectly valid. Figure 13.20 shows the growth value ratio in the middle with the growth value weight of the evidence measure in the bottom plot and its binary overlaid in the top plot.

### Breadth versus Price Component

There is only one more relative strength measure to view, the relationship between breadth and price. For breadth, a relationship between the advancing issues and the

**FIGURE 13.20**   Growth versus Value Measure

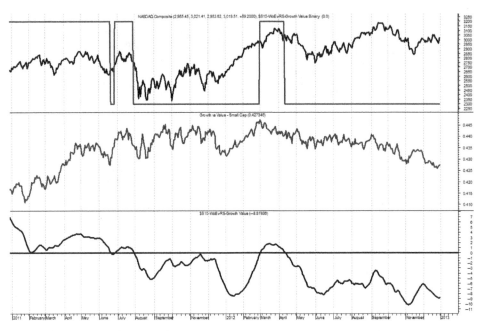

*Source:* Chart courtesy of MetaStock.

declining issues is used, while the Nasdaq Composite is used for price. The middle
plot in Figure 13.21 shows the raw ratio of those two, with the price to breadth
weight of the evidence measure in the lower plot and its binary in the top plot. This
is an excellent example of how technical manipulation of the data can turn that noisy
middle plot into something like the bottom plot, and a good trend measure.

### Relative Strength Compound Measure

This compound measure (see Chapter 12) is designed to measure market sentiment.
Are investors actively taking investment risk? Or are they behaving much more bear-
ishly? Again, there are three indicators that drive this component and are shown
above. These indicators look at the relationship between small cap issues versus large
cap issues, growth-oriented issues versus value issues, and breadth measurements versus price measurements. For example, when small caps are dominant (small caps outperforming large caps) it is generally a sign of more speculation taking place in the
markets as investors are willing to accept more risk. This is generally a good sign and
it is during these environments that the markets generally perform well historically.
When large caps are dominant it is usually the result of a flight to quality as investors
are taking risk off the table. This type of investor sentiment usually results in less favorable market conditions. A similar relationship exists between growth and value. When

**FIGURE 13.21**   Breadth versus Price Measure

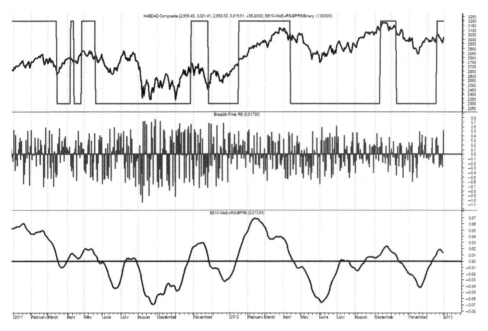

*Source:* Chart courtesy of MetaStock.

growth issues are outperforming it is generally because the market is pricing in favorable growth estimates, and conversely, when value issues are dominating it is because the market is no longer pricing in such optimistic positive growth estimates. The breadth versus price measurement is similar to an equal weighted measurement versus a capitalization weighted measurement. Again, we are using three indicators in this component for confirmation purposes. When this relative strength component is on it is adding value to the weight of the evidence of the model by letting me know that the sentiment in the markets is favorable and is viewed more as a trend confirmation measure versus a trend identification measure. Figure 13.22 is a chart showing lots of data but includes all three components of the relative strength measure. The top plot is the Nasdaq Composite with the compound binary measure overlaid. The binary measure for each of the components is also shows overlaid on their respective plots.

Figure 13.23 is the same as the preceding figure, but with less data displayed.

## Dominant Index

A concept known as the *Dominant Index* measures the relative strength between the Nasdaq Composite and the New York Stock Exchange (NYSE) Composite. The Nasdaq is generally dominated by small capitalization issues and the NYSE is dominated by large capitalization issues. Therefore, a measure that shows which is outperforming is

**FIGURE 13.22**  Relative Strength Compound Measure (1999–2012)

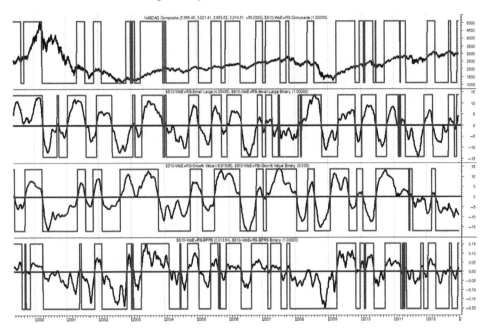

*Source:* Chart courtesy of MetaStock.

**FIGURE 13.23**  Relative Strength Compound Measure (2008–2012)

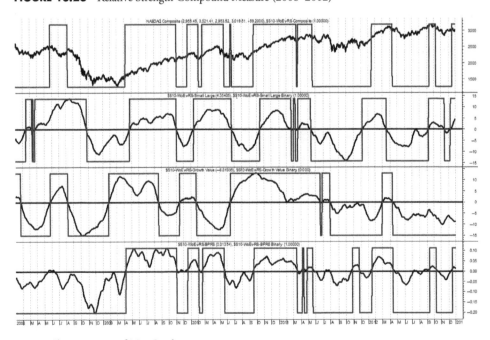

*Source:* Chart courtesy of MetaStock.

**FIGURE 13.24** Dominate Index Concept

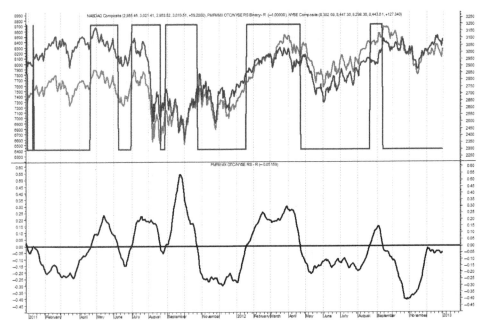

*Source:* Chart courtesy of MetaStock.

also showing whether small cap issues are outperforming large cap issues or vice versa. Figure 13.24 shows the Nasdaq Composite and the NYSE Composite in the top plot with the relationship between the two displayed in the bottom plot. Whenever the line is above the horizontal line, it means the Nasdaq is performing better than the NYSE. In the last decade the Nasdaq has grown considerably with many more large cap issues, which somewhat hampers this measure.

## Trend Capturing Measure

This is a truly important compound measure, which can drive the weight of the evidence or hold it back. The trend capturing measure, like many compound measures consists of three independent indicators of trend, and in this case two are based on breadth and one on price. Any two measures saying there is an uptrend will work.

### Advance Decline Component

The advance decline component of the trend capturing measure uses the advances and declines difference and then mathematically puts that difference into a relationship similar to MACD. (See Figure 13.25.) The signals are given by the crossing of that formula with its shorter term (10–18 periods) exponential moving average.

### Up Volume/Down Volume Component

The up volume/down volume component of the trend capturing measure (see Figure 13.26) uses the up volume and the down volume in a similar manner as the advance and decline measure in Figure 13.25. One could assume that these would be very similar as they are tied to the same price movement, one by daily changes, and one by the amount of volume behind those changes. However, in the up volume/down volume, the parameters used are somewhat longer than in the advance decline component.

### Price Component

The price component of the trend capturing measure (Figure 13.27), like the other two components uses a similar relationship, but this one uses parameters that are longer than the other two.

### Trend Capturing Compound Measure

This is a major component of my model because it ties directly with the investment philosophy of identifying positive market trends that have a high probability of continuing into the future. I never predict; I only have an expectation that the identified trend will continue. This component is a composite of three technical measurements. One is a price measure, and the other two are breadth measures, one of which uses up

**FIGURE 13.25**   Advance Decline Component of Trend Capturing Measure

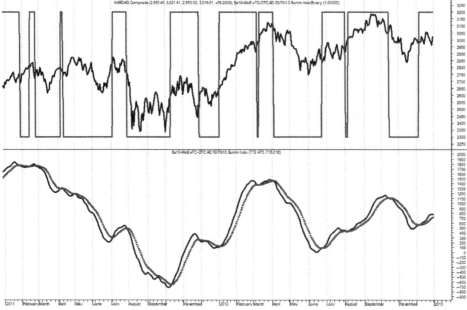

*Source:* Chart courtesy of MetaStock.

**FIGURE 13.26**   Up Volume/Down Volume Component of Trend Capturing Measure

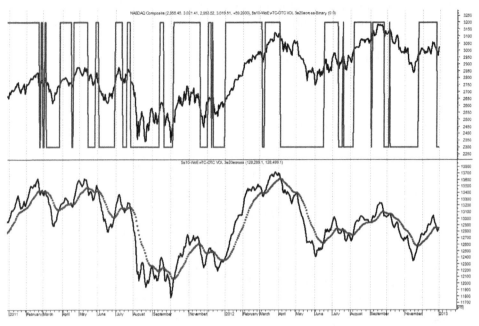

*Source:* Chart courtesy of MetaStock.

**FIGURE 13.27**   Price Component of Trend Capturing Measure

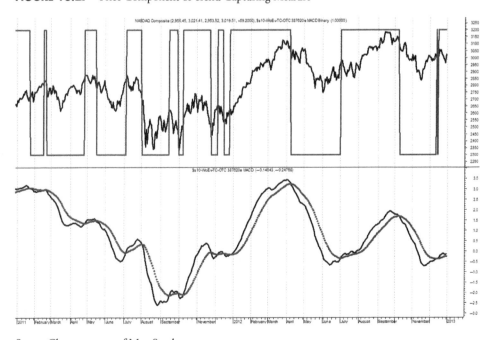

*Source:* Chart courtesy of MetaStock.

and down volume, and the other uses advancing and declining issues (see Figures 13.26 and 13.27). I use multiple indicators for confirmation purposes. For instance, when the first of these three indicators turns positive it is telling us there is a positive price trend developing. When the second of these indicators turns positive it provides confirmation of the trend, and if the third turns positive as well I know I have a very solid trend in place. See Figure 13.28.

## LTM—Long-Term Measure

Sometimes a good way to dampen things is to utilize a longer-term overlay measure such as this Long-Term Measure (LTM). There are multiple ways to smooth out the noise in data, one, the moving average, we have discussed at length. The other, using weekly data often does the same thing, and sometimes even better. The long-term measure uses only weekly data. It has many components such as weekly advances and declines, weekly new high/new low data, weekly up volume and down volume data, plus a price component that measures the relationship among many market indices and tracks their position relative to their long-term moving average. All of that data is calculated and then put together in a fairly complex manner to give the binary indicator shown in the top plot of Figure 13.29. It has an intermediate level, sort of a transition zone so that as the long term components go from being on to off, they pause in the transition zone to ensure there is follow through. This is a fairly slow

**FIGURE 13.28**    Trend Capturing Measure (2012)

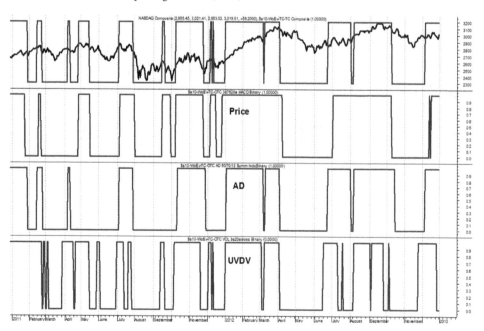

*Source:* Chart courtesy of MetaStock.

**FIGURE 13.29** Long-Term Measure (1994–2012)

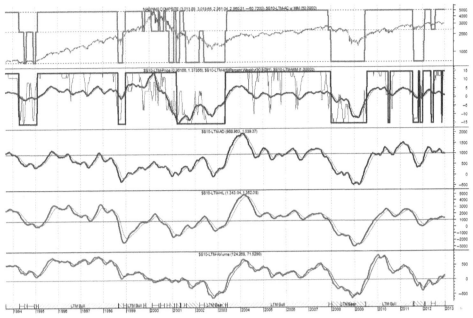

*Source:* Chart courtesy of MetaStock.

moving measure and is best used to identify cyclical moves in the market. The best place to find weekly breadth data is from Dow Jones and Company, in either Barron's or the Wall Street Journal. See the Appendix on breadth to understand why you cannot combine the daily breadth to get the weekly data.

Figure 13.30 shows the long-term measure over a shorter time frame so you can better see the action of each measure.

## Bull Market Confirmation Measure

The Bull Market Confirmation Measure is about as simple as it can get. (See Figure 13.31.) It just uses a 50 moving average and a filter to identify bull moves. It is calculated on the average price of the high, low, and close $((H + L + C) / 3)$. The difference between the average price and its 50 period simple moving average is then adjusted to identifying only times when it is outside of the −5 percent and −10 percent range. As the average price drops below the −5 percent value it is a sell signal and when it rises above the −10 percent it is the buy signal. These crossover percentages are determined based on the price series you are using. They will probably be different for each one.

Figures 13.31 and 13.32 is the Bull Market Confirmation measure with less data so you can see the turning points easier.

**FIGURE 13.30**   Long-Term Measure (2011–2012)

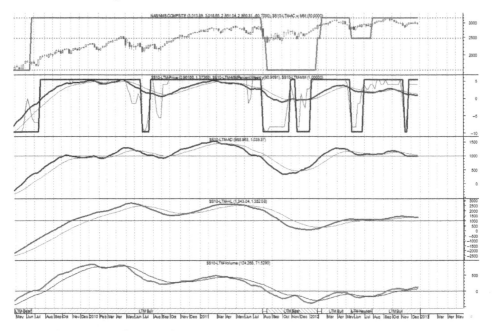

*Source:* Chart courtesy of MetaStock.

**FIGURE 13.31**   Bull Market Confirmation Measure (1964–2012)

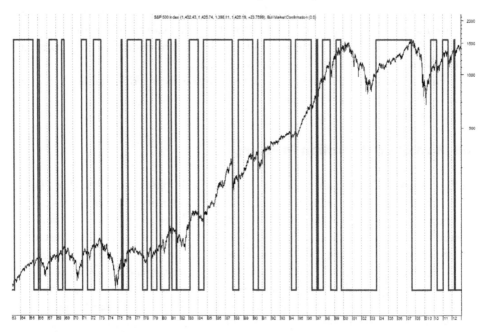

*Source:* Chart courtesy of MetaStock.

**FIGURE 13.32**   Bull Market Confirmation Measure (1999–2012)

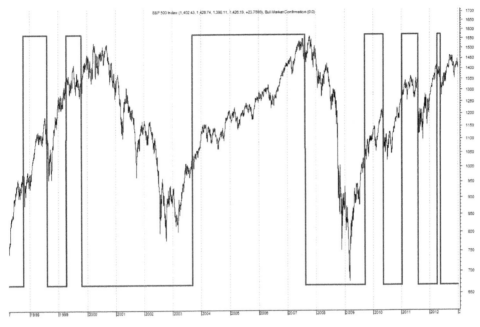

*Source:* Chart courtesy of MetaStock.


## Initial Trend Measures (ITM)

A significant enhancement to a trend following model is an early warning set of indi-cators. I call them *Initial Trend Measures*, or *Early Trend Measures*. They are designed to measure trends just like the weight of the evidence measure does, but use shorter term parameters in an attempt to pick up or identify the trend at an earlier stage in its development. You can use as many short-term trend measures as you need, but usually 3 is more than enough, if you have them in different categories of trend measurement, such as price, breadth, and relative strength.

Figure 13.33 is one of the Initial Trend Measures that utilizes up volume com-pared to down volume. It can be either the Nasdaq data or the NYSE data. The top plot is the Nasdaq bar chart with the indicator's binary wave overlaid on the price bars. Recall that the binary is at the top when the indicator is above its moving average and at the bottom when it is below its moving average.

Figure 13.34 shows the Initial Trend Measure, which uses the advance decline data. Just like the other weight of the evidence measures this uses an MACD approach.

Figure 13.35 is another ITM, this one uses price, and in this case it is the Nasdaq Composite Index that is used. This measure is similar to the trend measure mentioned earlier but uses short-term parameters.

Figure 13.36 is a similar initial trend measure, but this one uses the NYSE Composite Index for price.

**FIGURE 13.33**   Up Volume/Down Volume Initial Trend Measure

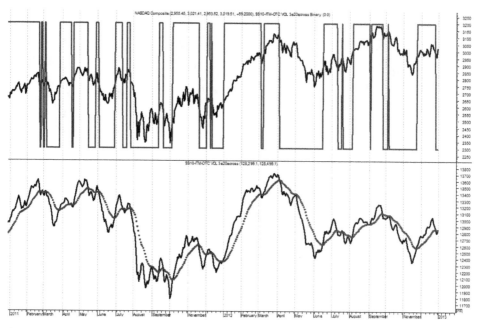

*Source:* Chart courtesy of MetaStock.

**FIGURE 13.34**   Advance Decline Initial Trend Measure

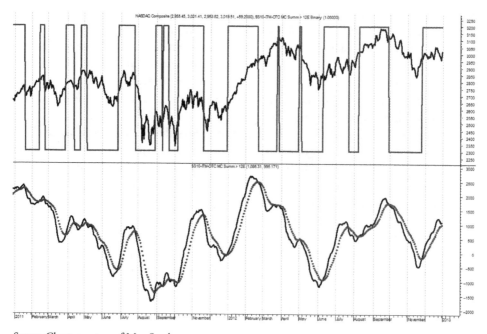

*Source:* Chart courtesy of MetaStock.

**FIGURE 13.35** Price Initial Trend Measure

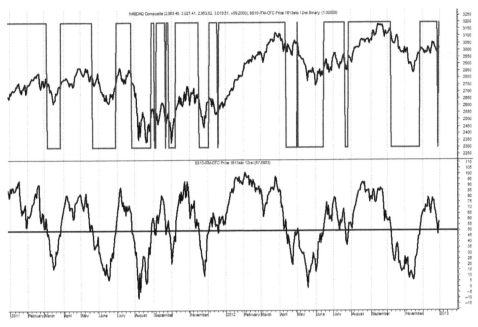

*Source:* Chart courtesy of MetaStock.

**FIGURE 13.36** NYSE Price Initial Trend Measure

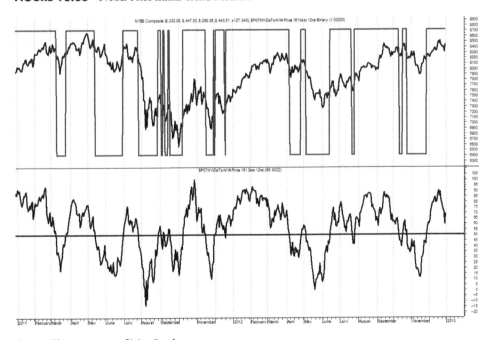

*Source:* Chart courtesy of MetaStock.

The Initial Trend Measures provide an alert mechanism for the weight of the evidence. You will also see their use in Chapter 14 when used along with the trade up rules.

## Trend Gauge

A concept that was introduced to me by my friend Ted Wong (TTSWong Advisory) is the use of multiple market indices and measuring their relationship to their moving average. Trend Gauge is comprised of Mega Trend Plus and Trend Strength. A concept that attempts to identify overall trendiness in the market is always going to be a valuable tool for a trend follower. For purposes of this example I selected the ubiquitous 200-day exponential average and then smoothed the results with a three-day arithmetic average. There are a number of modifications one could do with this concept, including optimizing the moving average lengths for each of the market indices. I say that with this warning, optimization must be done properly to avoid curve fitting and was discussed earlier in this chapter. I would start with moving average lengths that are closely tied to the trend lengths I want to focus on and then use a short-term noise reduction smoothing like I did in this example.

### Mega Trend Plus

Mega Trend Plus is constructed by selecting 11 major indexes with the longest historical database. One could easily make the case for more or less indices and which indices are to be included. I would suggest using enough indices to give you broad coverage over how you plan to make investments. The Mega Trend Plus is also used in the Long-Term Measure (LTM), but in that case it uses weekly data. Clearly if you are going to have a focus on international securities, you would want to include international indices. The list of indices used in this example is:

Nasdaq Composite
S&P 500
S&P 100
Russell 2000
Russell 2000 Growth
Russell 2000 Value
New York Composite
Dow Jones Industrials
Dow Jones Transports
Dow Jones Utilities
Value Line Geometric

When the index is greater than its exponential moving average (EMA), it receives a +1, below its EMA, it receives a −1. Then the scores from all 11 indexes are summed and then normalized so the composite will have a range between 0 percent and 100 percent. An uptrending market is called when the composite is greater than or equal to 85 percent. A downtrending market is when the composite is less than or equal to 15 percent. Once a threshold is crossed, the market stance stays until the opposite threshold is penetrated. Hence Mega Trend Plus is a digital meter: either bull or bear. Figure 13.37 shows the S&P 500 in the top plot, Mega Trend Plus in the lower plot, and the Mega Trend Plus binary overlaid on the S&P 500. The binary is at +1 whenever Mega Trend Plus is greater than or equal to 85, at −1 whenever Mega Trend Plus is less than or equal to 15, and at zero when it is between 15 and 85. You can see that is does a reasonable job of trend identification. This is a weight of the evidence approach that is totally related to the concepts in this book.

## Trend Strength

Trend Strength is a different composite, which is the sum of 11 ratios. For each market index, a ratio is calculated with this formula: (price/EMA−1) × 100 percent. The EMA lengths are identical to those used in Mega Trend Plus. The ratio depicts how far away (up or down) the index is positioned relative to its EMA. Hence Trend Strength is an oscillating analog meter that measures the momentum of each of the 11 market indexes (see Figure 13.38).

Trend Gauge combines the readings from both the digital and analog meters (Mega Trend Plus and Trend Strength). It represents a weight of evidence approach in determining both the direction (digital) and the strength (analog) of the overall market trend. Figure 13.39 shows the S&P 500 in the top plot and Trend Gauge in the

**FIGURE 13.37** Mega Trend Plus

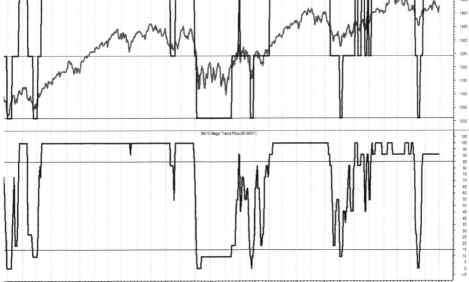

*Source:* Chart courtesy of MetaStock.

**FIGURE 13.38**   Trend Strength

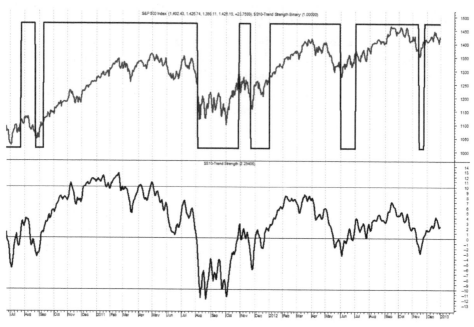

*Source:* Chart courtesy of MetaStock.

**FIGURE 13.39**   Trend Gauge

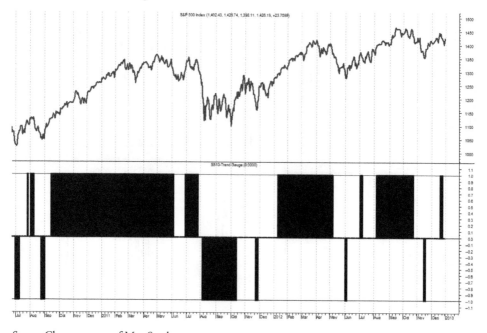

*Source:* Chart courtesy of MetaStock.

**FIGURE 13.40** Trend Gauge Over Longer Time Frame

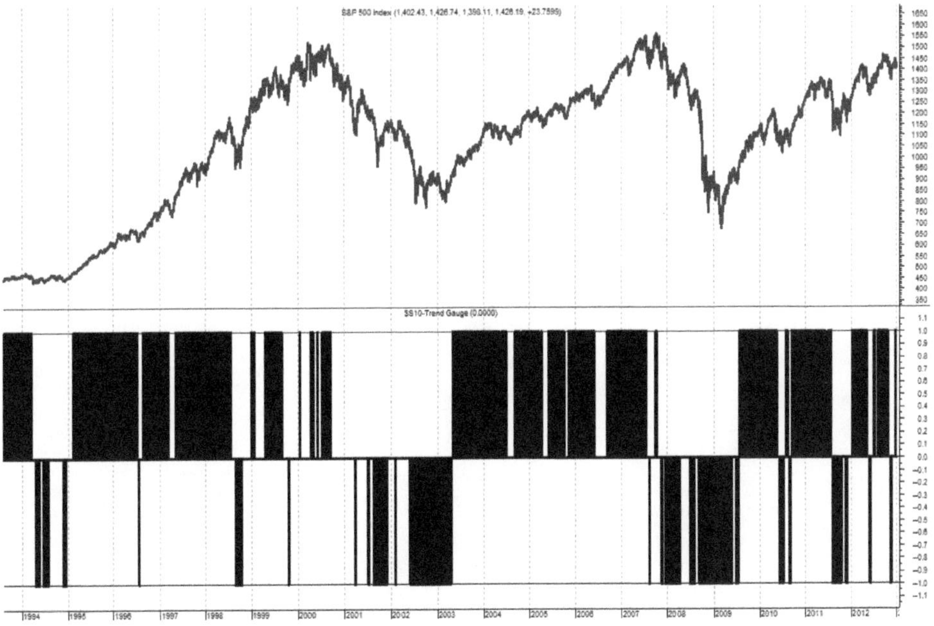

*Source:* Chart courtesy of MetaStock.

lower plot. Whenever the Trend Gauge is at +1 it has identified an uptrend, when at −1 it has identified a downtrend, and when at 0, there is neither an up- or downtrend (neutral).

Figure 13.40 is the same data as in Figure 13.39, just over a much longer time frame. The beginning date in Figure 13.40 is 1992.

Measuring the market is a significant component to a good trend following, rules-based model. This chapter has introduced many measures that can be used individually or in groups to assist in trend identification. Clearly there were many measures introduced and hopefully you can find a few that will fit your needs. Also, hopefully you will not use all of them as many are similar with minor deviations in their concept.

# CHAPTER 14

# Security Ranking, Selection, Rules, and Guidelines

It is not uncommon for investors to believe that the more information they have, the better their chance at choosing good investments. Financial websites offer alerts on stocks, the economy, and just about anything you think you might need. The sad part is that the investor thinks every iota of information is important and tries to draw a conclusion from it. The conclusion may turn out to be correct, but it is usually not. The investor is trying to tie each item of news to the movement of a stock, which generally never seems to work; just a few minutes watching the financial media should tell you that it doesn't work. Human emotions make the investor feel good about having news that supports their beliefs, but rarely do those emotions contribute to investment success. I find it amazing how many times I go into an office and find the financial television playing, sometimes muted, but probably only when they see me coming. Too much information can lead to a total disarray of investment ideas and decisions. Keep it simple, turn off the outside noise, and use a technical approach to determine which issues to buy and sell. You'll be healthier.

## Ranking Measures

Ranking measures are the technical indicators used to determine which issues to buy based on their trendiness. They can be assigned as mandatory or tie-breaker ranking measures. The mandatory ones are the ranking measures that have to meet certain requirements before an issue can be bought. The tie-breaker ranking measures are there to assist in issue selection but are not mandatory.

Ranking measures can be used with individual stocks, Exchange Traded Funds (ETFs), mutual funds, and bonds; however, there must be a process for selecting them if for any other reason than to reduce the number down to a useable amount. For example in an exchange-traded fund (ETF)-only strategy, consider that there are nearly 1,400 ETFs and a fully invested portfolio might only have positions in 20 ETFs. Ranking measures are indicators, mainly of price or price relationships that assist in the determination of whether an issue is in an uptrend.

Throughout this section, the charts show the exchange-traded fund SPY in the top plot whenever possible, the ranking measure in the bottom plot, and the ranking measure's binary overlaid on the SPY in the top plot. Some exceptions to using SPY are when volume is needed for the ranking measure, in which case another broad-based ETF will be used. A discussion of the parameters that can be used for each ranking measure is also included. I do not go into excruciating analysis on each chart as the concept is really simple. The binary is the signal line and it only represents the ranking measure's signals exactly. Not all ranking measures have a binary signal as they are used for confirmation of a trend direction. The discussion for each ranking measure is varied as some are fairly simple to understand and won't involve a detailed discussion. I certainly am not the type that discusses each wiggle and waggle of the indicator.

## Trend

Trend is the name given to a derivative of an indicator originally created by Jim Ritter of Stratagem Software. He wrote about it in the December 1992 (V. 12:12, 534–534) issue of *Stocks & Commodities* magazine, in an article, "Create a Hybrid Indicator." Trend is a simple concept, yet powerful combination of two overbought oversold indicators: Stochastics (%K) and Relative Strength Index (RSI). The indicator uses 50 percent of each one in combination and while both are range-bound between zero and 100, the combination is also range-bound between zero and 100. Stochastics, normally much quicker to react to price changes, is dampened by the usually slower to react RSI. In combination you have an indicator that shows strong trend measurements whenever it is above a predetermined threshold.

### Parameters

The Stochastic needs to be much longer than when used by itself while RSI can be used close to its original value. The Stochastic range of 20 to 30 should work well with the final value determined by the length trend you want to follow. The RSI range can vary but you don't want to make it too long as it is already a slower reacting measure. Finally, the threshold used for Trend should be in the 50 to 60 range, again dependent on how soon you want the signal, remembering that early signals will also give more whipsaws.

The examples of Trend in Figure 14.1 have the threshold drawn at 50, which is a good all-around value. The concept is simply that whenever Trend is above 50, the ETF is in an uptrend, and whenever Trend is below 50, it is not in an uptrend. The binary is overlaid on the price plot (top) so you can see the signals better. Notice that when prices are in an uptrend, the binary is usually at the top, and when prices are not, it is at the bottom. Notice in the middle of the plot there were a number of quick signals in succession; this is why one should not rely on a single indicator for analysis.

**FIGURE 14.1** Trend

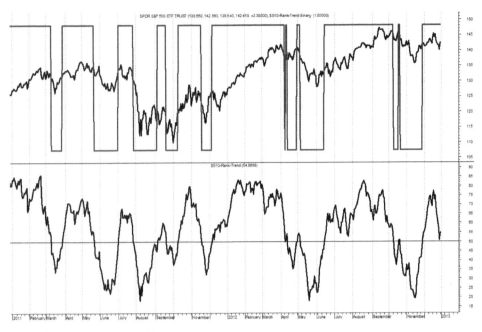

*Source:* Chart courtesy of MetaStock.

## Trend Rate of Change (ROC)

This is merely the five-day rate of change of Trend. Why would you use that? When viewing a lot of data on a spreadsheet that does not contain any charts, and you see the value for Trend is 65, you also need to know if it is rising through 65 or declining through it. A snapshot of the data can be dangerous if you don't also look at the direction the indicator is moving. Figure 14.2 is a chart of the five-day rate of change of Trend. You can see that while Trend is still slightly positive (above the 50 line) it is declining (see Figure 14.1). Then when you compare it with the Trend ROC in Figure 14.2, it is showing significant weakness. Of course, showing the five-day rate of change of an indicator without showing the indicator itself is foolish; it was done here so that you could see the measure being discussed.

### Parameters

This can be almost any value you desire based on what you are using it for. I used it here to see the short-term trend of an indicator so five days is just about right. If you were using rate of change as an indicator for measuring the strength of an ETF or an index, then a longer period would probably be more appropriate. I use 21 days when I use ROC by itself.

**FIGURE 14.2**   Trend Rate of Change

*Source:* Chart courtesy of MetaStock.

Figure 14.3 shows the Trend with the five-day rate of change of Trend overlaid (lighter). This is the way that all the mandatory ranking measures and some of the tie-breakers measures are shown. You can see from this that the Trend is above 50, but the five-day rate of change is deteriorating and is well below zero (negative).

## Trend Diffusion

This is also known as *Detrend*, which is a technique where you subtract the value of an indicator's moving average from the value of the indicator. It is a simple concept, actually, and not unlike the difference between two moving averages with one average being equal to 1, or MACD for that matter. Technical analysis is ripe with simple diversions from concepts and often with someone's name attached to the front if it—don't get me started on that one. Figure 14.4 is the same Trend as previously discussed except that it is the 15-day Detrend of Trend, or Trend Diffusion. The middle plot is the Trend with the lighter line being a 15 day simple moving average of the Trend. The bottom plot is the Trend Diffusion, which is simply the difference between the Trend and its own 15-day moving average. You can see this when the Trend moves above its moving average, the Trend Diffusion moves above the zero line. Similarly, when-ever the Trend moves below its 15-day moving average in the middle plot, the Trend Diffusion moves below the zero line in the bottom plot. The information from the

**FIGURE 14.3**   Trend with Trend Rate of Change

*Source:* Chart courtesy of MetaStock.


**FIGURE 14.4**   Trend and Trend Diffusion

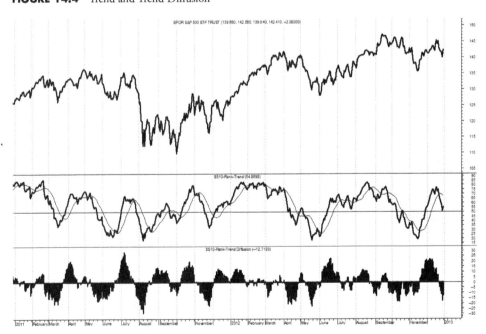

*Source:* Chart courtesy of MetaStock.

15-day Trend Diffusion is absolutely no different that the information in the middle plot showing the Trend and its 15-day moving average, just easier to visualize.

### Parameters

The example in Figure 14.4 uses 15 days, which is three weeks. Parameters need to be chosen based on the time frame for your analysis. A range from 10 to 30 is probably adequate for Trend Diffusion.

## Price Momentum

This indicator looks back at the price today compared to X days ago. It is created by calculating the difference between the sum of all recent gains and the sum of all recent losses and then dividing the results by the sum of all price movement over the period being analyzed. This oscillator is similar to other momentum indicators such as RSI and Stochastics because it is range bound, in this case from $-100$ to $+100$.

### Parameters

Price Momentum is very close to being the same as rate of change; generally the only difference between the two is the scaling of the data. Momentum oscillates above and below zero and yields absolute values, while the Rate of Change moves between zero and 100 and yields relative values. The shape of the line, however, is similar. With momentum, the threshold is shown at 50 but could be higher if requiring more stringent ranking requirements.

Figure 14.5 shows the Price Momentum ranking measure (dark line) and its five-day rate of change (lighter line). You can see that the Price Momentum is weak and the ROC is negative and declining.

## Price Performance

This indicator shows the recent performance based on its actual rate of change for multiple periods, added together, and then divided by the number of rates of change used. In this example I used three rates of change of 5, 10, and 21 days, which equates to 1 week, 2 weeks, and 1 month. Simply calculate each rate of change, add them together, and then divide by three. This gives an equal weighting to rates of change over various days.

### Parameters

Like many indicators the parameters used are totally dependent on what you are trying to accomplish. Here I am trying only to identify ETFs that are in an uptrend.

Figure 14.6 shows the Price Performance measure using the three rates of change mentioned above. There is no need to show the typical five-day rate of change of this indicator since it is in itself a rate of change indicator.

**FIGURE 14.5** Price Momentum and Momentum Rate of Change

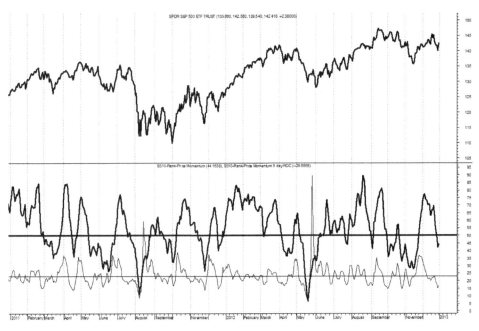

*Source:* Chart courtesy of MetaStock.

**FIGURE 14.6** Price Performance

*Source:* Chart courtesy of MetaStock.

## Relationship to Stop

This is the percentage that price is below its previous 21-day highest close. This is an extremely important ranking measure and here's why. If you are using a system that always uses stop loss placement (hopefully you are), then you certainly would not want to buy an ETF that was already close to its stop. This is the case when using trailing stops, if using portfolio stops, or stops based on the purchase price, this measure does not come into play. I like to use stops during periods of low risk of 5 percent below where the closing price had reached its highest value over the past 21 days. If you think about this, this means that as prices decline from a new high, then the stop baseline is set at that point and the percentage decline is measured from there.

### *Parameters*

In most cases this is a variable parameter determined by the risk that you have assessed in the market or in the holding. I prefer very tight stops in the early stages of an uptrend because I know there are going to be times when it does not work, and when those times happen, I want out. The setting of stop loss levels is entirely too subjective, but I would say that as risk lessens, the stops should become looser allowing for more daily volatility in the price action.

Figure 14.7 shows the 5 percent trailing stop using the highest closing price over the past 21 days. The two lines are drawn at zero and −5 percent. When this measure is at zero, it means that the price is at its highest level in the past 21 days. The line then continuously shows where the price is relative to the moving 21-day highest closing price. When it drops below the −5 percent line, then the stop has been hit and the holding should be sold. Please notice that I did not beat around the bush on that last sentence. When a stop is hit, sell the holding. Like Forrest Gump, that is all I'm going to say about that.

## Relative Performance

This indicator shows the recent performance of an ETF relative to that of the S&P 500. Often there is a tendency to show the performance relative to the total return version of the S&P 500. This is only advisable if you are actually measuring and using the total return version of an ETF. In addition, most measurements are of a time frame where the total return does not come into play. However, purists may want one over the other, and the results will be satisfactory if used consistently. Usually the data analyzed is price-based; therefore, the relative performance should be using the price only S&P 500 Index. Also when comparing an ETF to an index, one must be careful when comparing say the SPY with the S&P 500 Index, two issues that should track relatively close to each other. The mathematics can blow up on you, so just be cognizant of this situation. Hence, the example in the chart below has switched from using SPY to using the EFA exchange-traded fund. Finally, you cannot simply divide the ETF by the index and plot it, or you will have a lot of noise with no clear indication

**FIGURE 14.7** Relation to Stop

*Source:* Chart courtesy of MetaStock.

as to the relative performance. I like to normalize the ratio of the two over a time period that is appropriate for my work, in this case over 65 days. This can further be expanded, similar to the Price Performance measure covered previously, and also use another normalization period, say 21 days, then average them. Additionally, you can then smooth the results to help remove some noise. Remember you are only trying to assess relative performance here.

### Parameters

This, like many ranking measures, is based totally on personal preference and also on the time frame you are using for analysis. In this example, I normalized the ratio with 65 and 21 days, then smoothed the result with the difference between their 15 and 50 day exponential average.

Figure 14.8 shows EFA relative to the S&P 500 Index. Whenever it is above the horizontal zero line, then EFA is outperforming the S&P 500. This would be considered an alpha-generating ranking measure if your benchmark is the S&P 500.

## Power Score

This is a combination indicator that takes four indicators into account to get a composite score. They are Trend, Price Momentum, Price Performance, and Relationship

**FIGURE 14.8**   Relative Performance

*Source:* Chart courtesy of MetaStock.

to Stop. Additionally, the PowerScore also factors in the five-day rates of change of the Price Momentum and Trend measures.

### Parameters

There are not really any parameters to discuss with PowerScore because it is created by using four of the mandatory ranking measures. The concept here can be as broad or as narrow as needed. Using only the mandatory ranking measures seems reasonable; however, the PowerScore is unlimited in what components can be used.

Figure 14.9 shows the PowerScore with a horizontal line at the value of 100. Based on the calculations of the components for this indicator, whenever PowerScore is above 100, then it is saying that the components are collectively saying the ETF is in an uptrend. This could be considered a composite measure, but unlike the ones referred to in the weight of the evidence components, this one uses all components.

### Efficiency Ratio

This ratio shows how much price movement in the past 21 days was essentially noise. It is a measure of the smoothness of the 21-day rate of change. It was created years ago by Perry Kaufman. This is an excellent ranking measure but you need to know that it is an absolute measure of how an ETF gets from point A to point B, in this case from

**FIGURE 14.9** PowerScore

*Source:* Chart courtesy of MetaStock.

21 days ago until today. Figure 14.10 is an example of how to think about this. If you were interested in two funds, fund 1 (solid line) and fund B (thicker dashed line), measuring their price movements of the same period of time, then which of the two would you prefer? The one that smoothly rose from point A to point B, or the one that had erratic movements up and down but ended up at the same place? I think everyone agrees that the smoother ride, or the solid line, is preferable.

## Parameters

I use 15 or 21 days, but as always, this is more dependent on your trading style and time frame of reference. The value should closely mirror what the minimum length trend you are trying to identify, independent of direction.

**FIGURE 14.10** Efficiency Ratio Explanation

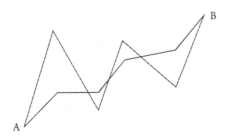

**FIGURE 14.11**   Efficiency Ratio

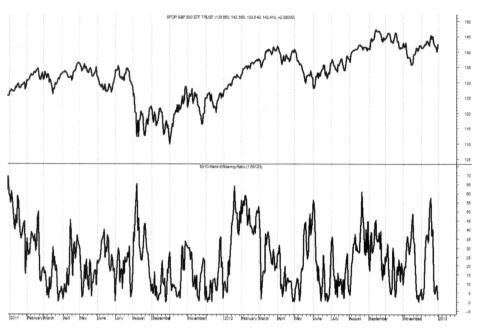

*Source:* Chart courtesy of MetaStock.

Figure 14.11 shows the 21-day efficiency ratio for SPY. You can see that whenever the ETF is trending, the Efficiency Ratio rises, and when the ETF is range-bound and moving sideways, the Efficiency Ratio remains low. In other words, a high efficiency ratio means the ride is more comfortable. It is moving efficiently.

## Average Drawdown

If you read the section in this book on Drawdown Analysis (Chapter 11), then you know exactly what this ranking measure accomplishes. The concept of average Drawdown for analysis and using it for a ranking measure are considerably different. To utilize average drawdown as a ranking measure you need to use a moving average drawdown, such as over the past year. This is because an issue that has been in a state of drawdown for a number of years will not give you the ranking data that is needed for a frame of reference over the past few months. A moving average of drawdown will help reset the drawdown as time moves forward.

### Parameters

I like to see the average drawdown over the past year, which is on average 252 market days. This is enough time for a measurement, but short enough to get a feel for how long it remains in a state of drawdown.

**FIGURE 14.12**   Average Drawdown

*Source:* Chart courtesy of MetaStock.

Figure 14.12 shows the average drawdown over the past 252 days. The horizontal line is drawn at −5 percent as a reference. The lower plot is the cumulative drawdown with the horizontal line being the long-term average.

### Relative Average Drawdown

Figure 14.13 shows the difference between the average drawdown of the issue compared to that of the S&P 500 Index. This is shown here only as an example of another type of ranking measure, and certainly would never qualify as a mandatory ranking measure.

### Price × Volume

Figure 14.14 shows the 21-day simple average of the volume times the close price. The purpose here is to show if the issue has enough liquidity to be traded. The ranking measures should always give a quick view on a variety of indicators and this one might show you immediately if there is enough trading volume to give you the liquidity you would need to trade it. Of course, the ideal solution is to have a good relationship with the trading desk that you will be using as they can give you up-to-date information on what volume you can trade.

**FIGURE 14.13**    Relative Average Drawdown

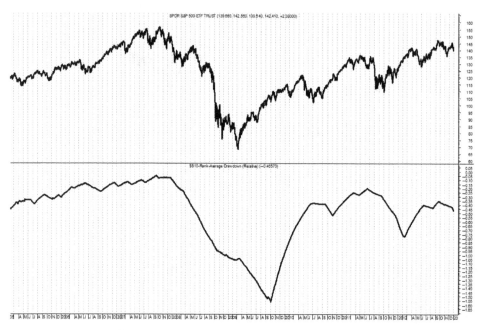

*Source:* Chart courtesy of MetaStock.

**FIGURE 14.14**    Price × Volume

*Source:* Chart courtesy of MetaStock.

## Adaptive Trend

Adaptive Trend is an intermediate trend measure that changes based on the volatility of the price movements. The Adaptive Trend measure incorporates the most recent 21 days of market data to compute volatility based on a true range methodology. This process always considers the previous day's close price in the current day's high–low range to ensure we are using days that gap either up or down to their fullest benefit. When the price is trading above the Adaptive Trend a positive signal is generated and when below a negative signal is in place. The chart in Figure 14.15 shows the Adaptive Trend as an oscillator above and below zero so that when it is above zero it means the price is above the Adaptive Trend and when below zero, price is below the Adaptive Trend. The top plot shows the Adaptive Trend binary. If you prefer, the horizontal line at zero is the adaptive trend, similar to the Trend Diffusion discussed earlier.

**FIGURE 14.15** Adaptive Trend

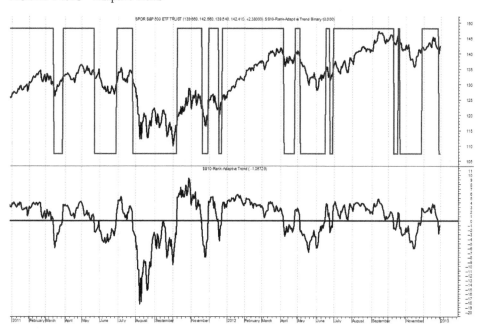

*Source:* Chart courtesy of MetaStock.

## Weighted Performance

Figure 14.16 is a weighted average of the 1-, 3-, 5-, 10-, and 21-day rates of change. One can argue that it is difficult to decide which exact period to measure for performance and I would not disagree. The method takes a number of periods into consideration and averages them for a single result. One could carry this concept further and weight each of the measurements and have a double-weighted performance measure.

**FIGURE 14.16**  Weighted Performance

*Source:* Chart courtesy of MetaStock.

You should, however, try to keep things simple, as complexity has a greater tendency to fail.

## Slow Trend

This measure, shown in Figure 14.17, is similar to Trend, but uses a longer period for its calculation. This concept can be used on many of the ranking measures as a second line of defense or confirmation. The faster version is good for initial selection, and the slower version is good for adding to positions (trading up).

## Ulcer Index

The Ulcer Index (Figure 14.18) takes into account only the downward volatility for an issue plus uses price crossover technique with a 21-period average. This concept was first written about by Peter Martin in *The Investor's Guide to Fidelity Funds*, in 1989. (B37)

## Sortino Ratio

Figure 14.19 shows the downside risk after the return of the issue falls below that of the 13-week T-bill yield. It is a risk-adjusted return like the Sharpe Ratio, but only

**FIGURE 14.17**   Slow Trend

*Source:* Chart courtesy of MetaStock.

**FIGURE 14.18**   Ulcer Index

*Source:* Chart courtesy of MetaStock.

**FIGURE 14.19**   Sortino Ratio

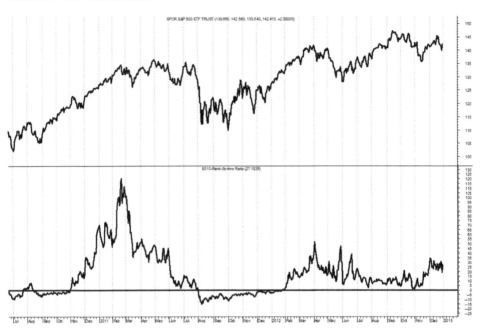

*Source:* Chart courtesy of MetaStock.

penalizes downward volatility whereas the Sharpe Ratio uses sigma (standard deviation). This is also similar to the Treynor ratio, which uses beta as the denominator and
expected return for the numerator.

### Beta

Figure 14.20 is the issue's beta based on the past 126 days (6 months). The same issue
exists here as with the Relative Performance earlier. You cannot measure beta unless it
is measured against something, in this case the S&P 500. Therefore, be careful when
comparing a large cap ETF to a large cap benchmark, small cap ETF to a small cap
benchmark, and so on.

### Relationship to Moving Average

Figure 14.21 shows the percent above or below the simple 65-day exponential moving
average. This is similar to detrend or diffusion. I think here the value is that one should
always pick a moving average period to use and stick with it so that you get a feel for
its action during certain market movements. In other words, you become accustomed
to how this moving average works over time. I equate this to using only one wedge

**FIGURE 14.20**    Beta

*Source:* Chart courtesy of MetaStock.

**FIGURE 14.21**    Relationship to Moving Average

*Source:* Chart courtesy of MetaStock.

in golf instead of multiple ones. Most of us cannot devote the time to practice with multiple wedges, so learn one and stick with it.

## Correlation

Correlation is an attempt to find a close relationship with an index such as the S&P 500. This is another one of those ranking measures you need to be careful not to compare a like ETF to a similar index. For example, the mathematics of correlation would blow up if you tried to compare the ETF SPY with the S&P 500 Index. In Figure 14.22 whenever the line is near the top of the plot, then it is saying the correlation of the top plot is correlated to the benchmark being used. When the market is advancing, you want highly correlated holdings. When the market is declining, or you see it begin to roll over in a topping manner, you want to move into less correlated holdings. You must keep in mind that you are still a momentum player and even though you want less correlation to the market, they still must be advancing on an individual basis.

---

Correlation is not always causation, but don't try explaining that to your dog when he hears the can opener.

*Tom McClellan*

---

**FIGURE 14.22**  Correlation

*Source:* Chart courtesy of MetaStock.

## Pullback Rally Analysis

The Pullback Rally Analysis is not a ranking measure but a technique for determining the relative strength of issues by looking at the most recent rally from a previous pullback. Measure the amount of the pullback in percent, then measure the current rally up to the current date in percent. The concept is fairly simple, those issues that dropped the least in the pullback, will probably outperform in the following rally. This concept measures the percentage move during the pullback, the percentage to date of the current rally, and the percentage to date from the beginning of the pullback. This is a great method to see strength outside of the snapshot of the ranking measures. Figure 14.23 shows an example on how to determine the dates for the beginning and end of the pullback. From the chart you can see a peak at point A with a pullback down to point B. The rally is then measured from point B to the current date.

A ratio of the percentage move of the current rally to the percentage move of the previous pullback is calculated. Another calculation is percentage the current price is from the beginning of the pullback (previous high). This data, when ranked, will help you determine strength in the rally as compared to the previous pullback. Often the stronger issues in a pullback are the leaders during the rally.

Table 14.1 shows the data for the Pullback Rally Analysis. You can see from Table 14.1, even a quick glance shows that the international ETFs are outperforming, not

**FIGURE 14.23**  Pullback Rally Period Example

*Source:* Chart courtesy of MetaStock.

**TABLE 14.1** Pullback Rally Analysis

| ETF Pullback Rally Strength | Last Close | % Pullback 9/21/2012 11/16/2012 | % Rally 11/16/2012 12/31/2012 | Ratio % Pullback % Rally | % Prev. High 9/21/2012 12/31/2012 |
|---|---|---|---|---|---|
| **Broad** | | | | | |
| SPY  SPDR S&P 500 ETF Trust | 142.41 (1.7%) | -6.51% | 4.43% | 0.68 | -2.37% |
| OEF  iShares S&P 100 IDX Fund | 64.69 (1.67%) | -8.03% | 3.97% | 0.49 | -4.38% |
| ONEQ  Fidelity Nasdaq Compsite Index Tracking Stock | 118.41 (1.52%) | -10.02% | 5.29% | 0.53 | -5.26% |
| QQQ  PowerShares QQQ Trust Series 1 | 65.13 (2.12%) | -11.19% | 4.54% | 0.41 | -7.16% |
| DIA  SPDR Dow Jones Industrial Average ETF Trust | 130.58 (1.17%) | -7.29% | 3.96% | 0.54 | -3.61% |
| NYC  iShares NYSE Composite Index Fund | 76.69 (0.85%) | -5.98% | 6.00% | 1.00 | -0.34% |
| MDY  SPDR S&P MidCap 400 ETF Trust | 185.71 (1.63%) | -4.91% | 6.88% | 1.40 | 1.63% |
| IJR  iShares Core S&P Small Cap | 78.1 (1.91%) | -8.60% | 8.29% | 0.96 | -1.03% |
| IWM  iShares Trust Russell 2000 Index Fund | 84.32 (2.17%) | -9.38% | 8.83% | 0.94 | -1.38% |
| VTI  Vanguard Total Stock Market | 73.28 (1.81%) | -7.05% | 5.06% | 0.72 | -2.35% |
| **Style** | | | | | |
| IWO  iShares Trust Russell 2000 Growth | 95.31 (2.09%) | -9.77% | 7.94% | 0.81 | -2.61% |
| IWN  iShares Trust Russell 2000 Value | 75.51 (2.07%) | -9.10% | 9.40% | 1.03 | -0.55% |
| IJT  iShares S&P SmallCap 600 Growth Index Fund | 84.04 (2.05%) | -8.57% | 7.65% | 0.89 | -1.58% |
| IJS  iShares S&P SmallCap 600 Value Index Fund | 80.91 (1.94%) | -8.61% | 9.26% | 1.08 | -0.15% |
| IJK  iShares S&P Midcap 400 Growth Index Fund | 114.41 (1.66%) | -4.66% | 5.57% | 1.20 | 0.65% |
| IJJ  iShares S&P Midcap 400 value Index Fund | 88.14 (1.49%) | -6.25% | 7.78% | 1.24 | 1.04% |
| IVW  iShares S&P 500 Growth Index Fund | 75.74 (1.81%) | -7.69% | 3.50% | 0.45 | -4.47% |
| IVE  iShares S&P 500 Value Index Fund | 66.39 (1.68%) | -6.11% | 5.65% | 0.92 | -0.81% |
| **Sector** | | | | | |
| XLI  Industrial Select Sector SPDR Fund | 37.9 (1.83%) | -3.94% | 6.70% | 1.70 | 2.50% |
| XLP  Consumer Staples Sector SPDR Fund | 34.9 (1.31%) | -4.31% | 1.42% | 0.33 | -2.95% |
| XLY  Consumer Discretionary Sector SPDR Fund | 47.44 (2%) | -4.94% | 5.00% | 1.01 | -0.19% |
| XLV  Health Care Select Sector SPDR Fund | 39.88 (1.07%) | -3.14% | 2.44% | 0.78 | -0.77% |
| XLF  Financial Select Sector SPDR Fund | 16.39 (1.3%) | -3.47% | 7.26% | 2.09 | 3.54% |
| XLU  Utilities Select Sector SPDR Fund | 34.92 (1.37%) | -4.62% | 1.63% | 0.35 | -3.06% |
| XLK  Technology Select Sector SPDR Fund | 28.85 (1.73%) | -12.22% | 4.30% | 0.35 | -8.44% |
| XLE  Energy Select Sector SPDR Fund | 71.42 (2.28%) | -7.71% | 3.63% | 0.47 | -4.36% |

| Ticker | Name | | | | | |
|---|---|---|---|---|---|---|
| XLB | Materials Select Sector SPDR Fund | 37.54 (1.96%) | −6.90% | 7.69% | 1.11 | 0.25% |
| IYR | iShares Trust DJ US Real Estate Index | 64.67 (0.92%) | −5.94% | 4.49% | 0.76 | −1.71% |
| XHB | SPDR S&P Homebuilders | 26.6 (2.7%) | −4.01% | 6.87% | 1.71 | 2.58% |

**Intl**

| Ticker | Name | | | | | |
|---|---|---|---|---|---|---|
| VEU | Vanguard FTSE All World ex US | 45.75 (1.71%) | −5.84% | 8.75% | 1.50 | 2.39% |
| IEV | iShares Trust S&P Europe 350 | 39.3 (1.71%) | −5.84% | 10.30% | 1.76 | 3.86% |
| ILF | iShares S&P Latin America 40 Index Fund | 43.84 (1.25%) | −6.26% | 7.27% | 1.16 | 0.55% |
| EWZ | iShares MSCI Brazil (Free) Index Fund | 55.94 (1.23%) | −8.71% | 9.56% | 1.10 | 0.02% |
| EEM | iShares MSCI Emerging Markets Index Fund | 44.35 (1.49%) | −3.27% | 9.75% | 2.98 | 6.16% |
| EWJ | iShares MSCI Japan Index Fund | 9.75 (0.83%) | −3.15% | 7.62% | 2.42 | 4.22% |
| EFA | iShares MSCI EAFE Index Fund | 56.86 (1.52%) | −4.50% | 9.16% | 2.03 | 4.24% |
| ACWI | iShares MSCI ACWI Indx Fund | 48.08 (1.52%) | −4.98% | 6.42% | 1.29 | 1.11% |
| ACWX | iShares MSCI ACWI ex US Index Fund | 41.88 (1.21%) | −4.50% | 8.53% | 1.89 | 3.64% |
| FXI | iShares FTSE China 25 Index Fund | 40.45 (2.28%) | 2.95% | 13.08% | 4.44 | 16.42% |
| EWC | iShares MSCI Canada Index Fund | 28.4 (1.43%) | −6.16% | 4.80% | 0.78 | −1.66% |
| EWA | iShares MSCI Australia Index Fund | 25.14 (1.82%) | −1.53% | 5.67% | 3.71 | 4.06% |
| EWW | iShares MSCI Mexico Investable Market Co | 70.53 (1.58%) | −0.45% | 9.62% | 21.44 | 9.13% |
| GXG | Global × FTSE Colombia 20 | 22.24 (0.82%) | −2.80% | 6.87% | 2.45 | 3.88% |

**Other/Misc**

| Ticker | Name | | | | | |
|---|---|---|---|---|---|---|
| XLE | Energy Select Sector SPDR Fund | 71.42 (2.28%) | −7.71% | 3.63% | 0.47 | −4.36% |
| KRE | SPDR S&P Regional Banking | 27.97 (0.97%) | −8.88% | 5.52% | 0.62 | −3.85% |
| KBE | SPDR S&P Bank | 23.83 (1.15%) | −5.34% | 5.91% | 1.11 | 0.25% |
| IBB | iShares Nasdaq Biotechnology Index Fund | 137.22 (1.69%) | −9.06% | 4.25% | 0.47 | −5.20% |
| VXX | BARCLAYS BkPLCiPthS&pP500VIXShrtTrmFt ETN | 31.81 (−10.22%) | −0.29% | −8.28% | 28.78 | −8.54% |
| GLD | SPDR Gold Trust | 162.02 (0.92%) | −3.54% | −2.33% | 0.66 | −5.78% |
| SLV | iShares Silver Trust | 29.37 (0.93%) | −6.78% | −5.90% | 0.87 | −12.28% |
| DVY | iShares Trusts DJ Select Dividend Index Fund | 57.24 (1.47%) | −5.38% | 3.23% | 0.60 | −2.32% |
| SDY | SPDR S&P Dividend | 58.16 (1.5%) | −3.77% | 3.43% | 0.91 | −0.46% |
| MOO | Market Vectors Agribusiness | 52.76 (1.55%) | −4.57% | 5.75% | 0.00 | 0.92% |

only in the rally phase (% Rally) but also are now almost all above where the previous high (beginning of pullback) began (% Prev. High). The iShares FTSE China 25 Index Fund also performed well during the pullback phase with the only international ETF with a gain for that period of 2.95 percent, while the others were losses. The Ratio column shows the ratio of the percent of rally compared to the percent of pullback. The pullback is completed so only the extent of the rally is unknown. This ratio will show ETFs that performed in a couple of ways. One is that if the ETF did not decline much during the pullback *and* rises quickly in the rally, it will have a large ratio. For example, in the Broad category, the SPDR S&P MidCap 400 ETF Trust (MDY) has a ratio of 1.40, highest in that category. This is because it was the best performer (least decline) in the pullback phase and ranked third in performance in the rally phase. This would indicate that MDY is a strong performer and a candidate to consider for buying. The last column, % Previous High will also show you which ETFs are making new highs from the beginning of the pullback. This method of selection shows which issues are strong on a relative basis. In fact, it will also tell you which sectors and styles are strongest if you use ETFs that are tied to those strategies.

## Pair Analysis

I remember following Martin Zweig years ago and in fact used one of the techniques he described in his book, *Winning on Wall Street*, in the mid-1980s. In it he described a really simple technique using his unweighted index (ZUPI) and on a weekly basis trading it whenever it moved 4 percent or more. If it moved up 4 percent in a week, he bought, if it moved down 4 percent in one week, he sold. Positions were held until the next opposing signal—just that simple. The problem I had back then was not only not following it but trying to tweak it into something better. Eventually experience told me that he had already been down that road and I was the beneficiary of the results. Anyway, I took this concept and used it on Index/ETF pairs, actually calculating the ratio of Index/ETF pairs and using the weekly movement of 4 percent to swap between the numerator and the denominator. It really works well with asset classes that are not correlated, such as equity versus fixed income or equity versus gold, and so on. Figure 14.24 shows an example of this pair strategy the S&P 600 small cap index (IJR) versus the BarCap 7–10 Year Treasury index (IEF). The ratio line is the typical price line with the binary signal line overlaid while the lower plot is the percent up and down moves for each weekly data point. Remember, this is a weekly chart. Whenever the ratio line moves by 4 percent in a week as shown by the lower plot moving above or below the horizontal lines shown as +4 percent and −4 percent, the binary line overlaid on the price ratio changes direction. Repeated moves in the same direction are ignored.

The ratio significantly outperformed each of the individual components (IJR and IEF) and the S&P 500. Figure 14.25 shows the performance of the ratio with the numerator and denominator swapped whenever there was a move of 4 percent or greater, the performance of the individual components that make up the ratio, and the S&P 500.

**FIGURE 14.24**  IJR/IEF Pair Ratio with 4 Percent Weekly Change

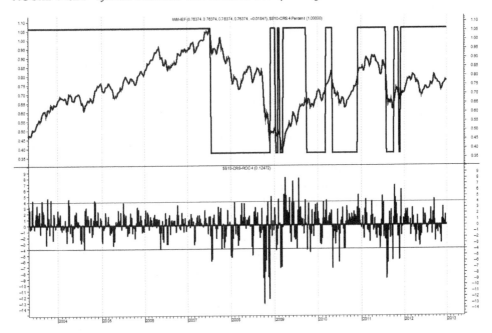

*Source:* Chart courtesy of MetaStock.

**FIGURE 14.25**  Pair and Individual Components

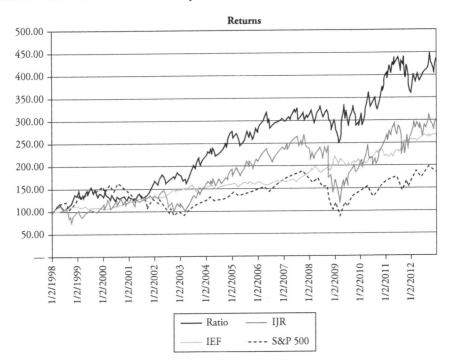

Table 14.2 shows the annualized performance statistics from 01/02/1998 until 12/28/2012 (weekly data). The Sharpe Ratio is slightly modified in that the return is used as the numerator without a reduction for risk-free return. The Ratio rotation strategy outperformed in annualized return, and when compared to the equity component it reduced the Drawdown (DD) considerably, improved the Sharpe Ratio, and lowered the Ulcer Index.

I also found that smoothing the ratio with just a two-period moving average greatly enhanced the performance because it reduced the number of trades. Trying different percentages other than Zweig's 4 percent worked well occasionally, but overall, the 4 percent on weekly data yielded the most robust results time and time again. The real advantage for a pair rotation strategy is when it is used as a core holding situation. In other words, if a strategy required a core holding percentage but that core could be actively managed, this would give an actively managed core holding that would have much lower drawdowns than a buy-and-hold core, and with considerably better returns. Table 14.3 shows the pairs used with an equal allocation of 25 percent each given to the four pairs. This adds up to an allocation of 100 percent, but in this example it means 100 percent of the core and the core percentage of total allocation is determined by the strategy, often 50 percent.

Figure 14.26 shows the results using the four different pairs in a core rotation strategy compared to buy and hold of the S&P 500. The drawdown in 2008 was limited to only 14 percent, and other than that was a nice ride. The average drawdown (see Table 14.4) is only 20 percent of the maximum drawdown. I was curious about the lack of performance in 2012 and found it was the fact that in the Gold/20-Year Treasury pair gold was the holding the entire period.

Table 14.4 shows the performance statistics for the Core Rotation Strategy (CRS) compared to the S&P 500. In this rotation strategy example each of the pairs were smoothed by their two-period average prior to measuring the 4 percent rate of change.

**TABLE 14.2**  IJR/IEF Pair Performance Statistics

| January 2, 1998–December 28, 2012 | Annualized Return | Sigma (Std. Deviation) | Maximum DD | Average DD | Sharpe Ratio | Ulcer Index |
|---|---|---|---|---|---|---|
| IJR | 7.59% | 23.12% | −57.38% | −10.62% | 0.33 | 15.46% |
| IEF | 6.79% | 6.59% | −9.43% | −2.32% | 1.03 | 3.23% |
| **Ratio of IJR/IEF** | 10.24% | 15.25% | −24.85% | −6.40% | 0.67 | 8.38% |
| S&P 500 | 4.32% | 19.21% | −54.71% | −15.88% | 0.23 | 20.45% |

**TABLE 14.3**  Core Rotation Pairs

|  | Index 1 | ETF 1 | Index 2 | ETF 2 | Allocation % |
|---|---|---|---|---|---|
| Pair 1 | S&P 400 Mid Cap | MDY | BarCap 3–7 Year Treasure | IEI | 25.0% |
| Pair 2 | S&P 600 Small Cap | IJR | BarCap 7–10 Year Treasury | IEF | 25.0% |
| Pair 3 | Nasdaq 100 | QQQ | BarCap US MBS | MBB | 25.0% |
| Pair 4 | London Gold (PM) | GLD | BarCap 20+ Year Treasury | TLT | 25.0% |

**FIGURE 14.26** Pair Analysis versus S&P 500

**TABLE 14.4** Performance Comparison between Core
Rotation Strategy and S&P 500

|  | CRS | S&P 500 |
|---|---|---|
| Return | 13.43% | 4.33% |
| Standard Deviation | 11.65% | 19.19% |
| Sharpe Ratio | 1.15 | 0.23 |
| Maximum Drawdown | −14.43% | −54.71% |
| Average Drawdown | −3.39% | −15.88% |

This process removes many of the signals and while not affecting the results that much, reduces the number of trades significantly.

Figure 14.27 is the drawdown of the core rotation strategy compared to the S&P 500. You can see that the cumulative drawdown for the rotation strategy is considerably less than the drawdown of the index. The average drawdown for the rotation strategy was −3.39 percent, while the average drawdown for the S&P 500 was −15.88 percent. This would make for a very comfortable core considering the exceptional returns and reduced risk statistics from just holding the index in a buy-and-hold situation.

**FIGURE 14.27**   Core Rotation Strategy and S&P 500 with Drawdowns

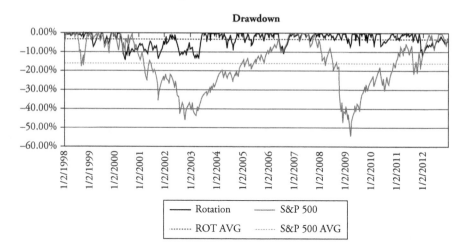

This core rotation strategy still meets the requirement of an always invested core while actively switching between four pairs of equity, gold, and fixed income ratios.

## Ranking and Selection

Ranking and Selection is another critical component to a rules-based model. Once you have measured the market, you need to determine what to buy. This is the technical process of determining securities that meet the rules when the time to buy arrives.

### Mandatory Measures

Once you have your collection of ranking measures, you need to determine which are to be used along with the rules and guidelines as mandatory ranking measures. This means that you predefine the value range that they must be in before you can purchase that ETF. This is necessary to keep the subjectivity out of the process.

### Tie-Breaker Measures

Once you have determined your mandatory ranking measures, the remaining ranking measures are considered tie-breaker ranking measures. These are used to help in the selection process, especially when there are hundreds of issues that qualify based on the mandatory measures. You can further reduce these into categories if desired, such as frontline tie-breakers, those you use more often than the others.

## Ranking Measures Worksheet

Table 14.5 is a partial view of the ranking measures worksheet. It only shows the top 50 to 60 issues as an example since there are more than 1,400 ETFs in the full listing. One really important concept to grasp when looking at technical values in a spreadsheet is that you are only seeing a snapshot in time. Here is an example, let's say that the Trend value is of primary importance and you have two ETFs, one with a Trend of 60 and one with a trend of 70, which would you choose? Well, the quick answer is probably 70 as that is a stronger trend measure than 60. However, don't you also need to know which direction the trend indicator is heading? If the trend that was at 60 was in an uptrend, while the one with the trend measure at 70 was in a downtrend, a completely different picture is presented. This is why all of the mandatory ranking measures also show their individual five-day rate of change, so that you can glean from the spreadsheet not only the absolute value of the ranking measure, but also the direction it is headed. It should be noted that any short-term period for rate of change will work.

## Ranking Measures Are All About Momentum

Throughout this chapter it should be obvious that the ranking and selection process is centered on the concept known as *momentum*. Simply said, I want to buy an ETF that exhibits an upward trend that is determined by a number of different technical measures.

A final thought on momentum is that every day, in almost every newspaper's business section there is an excellent list of stocks to buy. It is called the *52-week new high list*, or often *stocks making new highs*. If you were to only use this readily available tool, along with a simple stop-loss strategy, you would probably do much better at investing in the market. Sadly, many investors think about buying stocks like they think about buying something at Walmart, they look for bargains. Although this is a valid method also known as *value investing*, it is very difficult to put into action and seems better in theory. When you buy a stock, you buy it simply because you think you can sell it later at a higher price, I think momentum will work much better in that regard.

# Rules and Guidelines

Rules and guidelines are a critical element to a good trend-following model. Once you have the weight of the evidence measure telling you what the market is currently doing, the rules and guidelines provide the necessary process on how to invest based on that measure. If there was a simple answer as to why they are necessary, it is to invoke an objective approach, one that does as much as possible to remove the frail human element in the model. Rules are mandatory, while guidelines are not. That being said, if a guideline is to be ignored, one needs to ensure there is ample supporting evidence to allow it. Basically, the strategy I use is one of a conservative buyer and an aggressive seller. After many decades in aviation and the always increasing use of checklists, the rules and guidelines are no different for maintaining a nondiscretionary strategy than

**TABLE 14.5**  Ranking Measures Worksheet

| | | | PwrScore | Trend | Trnd5ROC | PrMo | PMo5ROC | PrPerf | 21dHHV | ER | AvgDD |
|---|---|---|---|---|---|---|---|---|---|---|---|
| Mean | | | 104.12 | 54 | -11.95 | 47.2 | -9.65 | 0.63 | -1.13 | 23.15 | -1.53 |
| Median | | | 92.94 | 55 | -23.18 | 41.3 | -40.37 | -1.19 | -2.18 | 10.75 | -0.43 |
| StdDev | | | 31.62 | 17.62 | 10.61 | 12.5 | 23.7 | 1.81 | 1.11 | 15.83 | 3.87 |
| Style | Ticker | Name | PwrScore | Trend | Trnd5ROC | PrMo | PMo5ROC | PrPerf | 21dHHV | ER | AvgDD |
| IC | DXJ | WISDOMTREE JAPAN HEDGED EQ | 190.25 | 87.96 | 1.85 | 85.9 | -1.55 | 6.36 | 0 | 68.61 | -8.59 |
| EEM | EEM | ISHARES MSCI EMERGING MKT IN | 160.92 | 81.53 | 5.35 | 65.8 | -17.8 | 3.6 | 0 | 49.45 | -7.66 |
| IC | EWY | ISHARES MSCI SOUTH KOREA IND | 159.15 | 80.36 | 3.07 | 65.2 | -22.21 | 3.63 | 0 | 52.09 | -6.09 |
| IC | EWJ | ISHARES MSCI JAPAN INDEX FD | 158.2 | 79.76 | -4.45 | 76.3 | -6.99 | 2.7 | -0.51 | 46.58 | -7.91 |
| IR | EFA | ISHARES MSCI EAFE INDEX FUND | 141.93 | 78.17 | -4.76 | 62 | -24.68 | 1.8 | 0 | 34.17 | -5.6 |
| IC | TUR | ISHARES MSCI TURKEY INVSTBLE | 150.96 | 77.76 | 5.62 | 58.2 | -4.26 | 5.03 | 0 | 28.68 | -6.32 |
| IC | EWG | ISHARES MSCI GERMANY INDEX | 144.21 | 76.66 | -7.69 | 65 | -18.23 | 2.62 | -0.11 | 40.9 | -8.64 |
| IR | IEFA | ISHARES CORE MSCI EAFE ETF | 143.54 | 76.56 | -6.36 | 64.7 | -17.82 | 2.32 | 0 | 38.05 | |
| IG | IPK | SPDR S&P INT'L TECHNOLOGY SECT | 149.47 | 74.59 | 3.83 | 60.5 | -9.2 | 4.37 | 0 | 28.15 | -7.43 |
| IC | AUSE | WISDOMTREE AUSTRALIA DIVIDEN | 124.77 | 69.5 | -5.68 | 53.2 | -23.77 | 2.06 | 0 | 22.47 | -6.44 |
| IG | RXI | ISHARES S&P CONSUMER DISCRET | 126.65 | 68.38 | -9.68 | 56.9 | -19.11 | 1.7 | -0.27 | 22.46 | -1.22 |
| SB | IJR | ISHARES CORE S&P SMALL-CAP E | 123.71 | 67.47 | -9.8 | 55.2 | -18.1 | 1.51 | -0.46 | 21.8 | -2 |
| FIN | XLF | FINANCIAL SELECT SECTOR SPDR | 125.17 | 67.47 | -9.58 | 57.5 | -21.16 | 2.08 | -1.86 | 18.67 | -3.37 |
| IG | ACWI | ISHARES MSCI ACWI INDEX FUND | 116.1 | 67.01 | -9.91 | 48.7 | -30.19 | 0.96 | -0.52 | 14.7 | -2.67 |
| MB | IJH | ISHARES CORE S&P MIDCAP ETF | 113.83 | 64.49 | -13.87 | 49.6 | -27.12 | 0.79 | -1.08 | 12.88 | -1.66 |
| HY | JNK | SPDR BARCLAYS HIGH YIELD BD | 109.85 | 64.33 | -17.82 | 46.1 | -35.97 | 0.04 | -0.63 | 5.73 | 0.74 |
| MB | MDY | SPDR S&P MIDCAP 400 ETF TRST | 114.85 | 64.11 | -15.86 | 51 | -29.51 | 0.96 | -1.24 | 15.78 | -1.59 |
| IND | XLI | INDUSTRIAL SELECT SECT SPDR | 112.62 | 63.99 | -13.03 | 49.3 | -31.17 | 0.84 | -1.46 | 10.99 | -1.89 |
| LB | RSP | GUGGENHEIM S&P 500 EQUAL WEI | 110.11 | 61.76 | -15.64 | 49 | -31.62 | 0.84 | -1.51 | 10.26 | -0.93 |
| LV | IWD | ISHARES RUSSELL 1000 VALUE | 105.08 | 59.36 | -15.63 | 47 | -27.7 | 0.63 | -1.87 | 4.88 | -0.46 |

| | | Mean | 586.32 | 2.86 | 0.54 | 58.18 | 7.5 | 52.02 | 0.52 | 1.75 | −1.99 | |
| | | Median | 1.81 | −1.82 | −1.31 | 58.46 | 9.56 | 27.24 | 1 | 0.18 | −7.4 | |
| | | StdDev | 2904.7 | 13.95 | 1.16 | 18.81 | 5.74 | 73.76 | 0.58 | 3.03 | 9.04 | |
| Style | Ticker | Name | PxV | AT | WgtPerf | OldTrend | UI | Sortino | Beta | +−65 | RelPerf | Price |
|---|---|---|---|---|---|---|---|---|---|---|---|---|
| IC | DXJ | WISDOMTREE JAPAN HEDGED EQ | 40.63 | 7.91 | 3.31 | 88.27 | 7.527 | 37.89 | 0.9 | 10.8 | 15.35 | 36.88 |
| EEM | EEM | ISHARES MSCI EMERGING MKT IN | 2103.8 | 4.55 | 2.56 | 82.88 | 7.894 | 46.71 | 1.18 | 5.43 | 5 | 44.35 |
| IC | EWY | ISHARES MSCI SOUTH KOREA IND | 103.38 | 4.93 | 2.9 | 82.57 | 8.66 | 34.06 | 1.27 | 6.46 | 4 | 63.35 |
| IC | EWJ | ISHARES MSCI JAPAN INDEX FD | 249.23 | 4.25 | 1.22 | 81.67 | 2.877 | 16.14 | 0.84 | 5.31 | 16.44 | 9.75 |
| IR | EFA | ISHARES MSCI EAFE INDEX FUND | 1006.45 | 3.17 | 1.22 | 79.55 | 7.744 | 49.24 | 1.13 | 4.38 | 3.97 | 56.86 |
| IC | TUR | ISHARES MSCI TURKEY INVSTBLE | 18.19 | 5.13 | 2.9 | 79.86 | 28.66 | 62.14 | 0.82 | 8.62 | 7.01 | 66.78 |
| IC | EWG | ISHARES MSCI GERMANY INDEX | 63.54 | 4.09 | 1.43 | 79.78 | 13.82 | 48.92 | 1.48 | 5.91 | 6.3 | 24.7 |
| IR | IEFA | ISHARES CORE MSCI EAFE ETF | 11.15 | 98.03 | 1.47 | 80.18 | | | | | | 50.85 |
| IG | IPK | SPDR S&P INT TECHNOLOGY SECT | 0.28 | 5.3 | 3.29 | 78.37 | 7.949 | 28.55 | 1.06 | 8.01 | 5.37 | 27.11 |
| IC | AUSE | WISDOMTREE AUSTRALIA DIVIDEN | 0.27 | 3.22 | 2.06 | 76.11 | 4.676 | 41.76 | 1.05 | 5.15 | 6.1 | 58.17 |
| IG | RXI | ISHARES S&P CONSUMER DISCRET | 4.34 | 2.69 | 1.43 | 75.37 | 13.39 | 52.67 | 0.98 | 4.21 | 8.01 | 61.71 |
| SB | IJR | ISHARES CORE S&P SMALL-CAP E | 84.99 | 2.71 | 1.34 | 73.87 | 7.982 | 30.07 | 1.01 | 2.72 | 17.94 | 78.1 |
| FIN | XLF | FINANCIAL SELECT SECTOR SPDR | 762.86 | 2.81 | 0.98 | 71.03 | 16.41 | 38.11 | 1.11 | 2.92 | 9.06 | 16.39 |
| IG | ACWI | ISHARES MSCI ACWI INDEX FUND | 61.52 | 2.11 | 0.9 | 73.33 | 8.091 | 51.37 | 1.02 | 2.29 | −2.56 | 48.08 |
| MB | IJH | ISHARES CORE S&P MIDCAP ETF | 115.45 | 1.95 | 0.73 | 71.51 | 9.795 | 36.89 | 1.01 | 2.46 | 9.03 | 101.7 |
| HY | JNK | SPDR BARCLAYS HIGH YIELD BD | 154.71 | 0.52 | −0.09 | 70.93 | 5.826 | 87.64 | 0.28 | 0.88 | 1.06 | 40.71 |
| MB | MDY | SPDR S&P MIDCAP 400 ETF TRST | 451.06 | 2.15 | 0.87 | 71.26 | 9.882 | 37.6 | 1.02 | 2.68 | 7.16 | 185.7 |
| IND | XLI | INDUSTRIAL SELECT SECT SPDR | 325.87 | 1.91 | 0.75 | 69.69 | 6.747 | 28.79 | 1.09 | 2.56 | 12.67 | 37.9 |
| LB | RSP | GUGGENHEIM S&P 500 EQUAL WEI | 38.58 | −0.17 | 0.78 | 68.33 | 9.333 | 39.07 | 1.04 | 1.95 | 1.62 | 53.32 |
| LV | IWD | ISHARES RUSSELL 1000 VALUE | 181.88 | −0.45 | 0.62 | 66.41 | 9.982 | 33.32 | 1.01 | 1.11 | 2 | 72.82 |

a checklist is for a pilot. In aviation, checklists grew in length over time because as accidents or incidents happened a checklist item was created to help prevent it in the future. There is an old axiom about checklists that said behind every item on a checklist, there is a story. Same philosophy goes for rules and guidelines in an investment strategy. A checklist (rules) ensures portfolio managers follow all procedures precisely and unfailingly. This overcomes the problem with experienced managers thinking they can accomplish the task and do not need any assistance. That attitude is costly.

## Buy Rules

B1—If asset commitment calls for an amount greater than 50 percent, then only 50 percent will be committed, with remainder the next day, ensuring objectives remain aligned. Forty percent can be the maximum per day if necessary for Guideline G6. This rule keeps the asset purchases to a maximum for any single day. It would not be prudent to go into the market at 100 percent on one day.

B2—No Buy Days are (1) FOMC announcement day, (2) First/Last day of calendar quarter, (3) days in which the market has reduced hours. FOMC announcement days are typically high-volatility days and the end/beginning of a quarter involves a lot of window dressing. Leave the noise alone.

B3—No buying unless 50 (this can also be a percentage) tradable ETFs (not counting noncorrelated) have:

Weight of the Evidence: Weak: Trend > 60, Intermediate: Trend > 55, Strong: Trend > 50

I call this the "soup on the shelf" rule. If you have been to a large grocery store lately and strolled down the aisle that has soup, you probably noticed there are thousands of cans of soup with hundreds of blends, styles, and so on to choose from. Now imagine your spouse has sent you to the store to buy soup. When you turn down the soup aisle, you notice they are essentially empty except for two cans of rhubarb turnip barley in cream sauce. You probably aren't going to buy any soup that day. The market is similar, especially during the early stages of an uptrend, there just isn't much to choose from. In addition, the early stages have stricter buying requirements so the number of issues to pick from could be very small, if any. Because you *never* violate the rules, a rule to protect you during this period was created, hence rule B3.

B4—No buying on days when stops on current holdings are hit and assets sold. This is usually the first hint that the ensuing uptrend is faltering. It just doesn't make sense as a trend follower to be buying on the same day as you are selling something that has hit its stop. The argument that one holding might not be correlated is weak in this example as with proper trading up, weak holdings should have been previously traded.

B5—No buying on days when the Nasdaq or S&P 500 is down greater than 1.0 percent (the indices used need to be tied you what you are using in the trend measures). Simply, this means that if the market as determined by the S&P 500 and/or Nasdaq Composite is down more than 1 percent during the day, something is wrong with the uptrend and it is better to not buy that day. An argument from bargain hunters or value investors would be that one would get a better price on that day if the uptrend resumed. I can't argue with that but I'm not a value investor or a bargain hunter. It seems many investors want to buy stocks at bargain prices and I can understand that. However, we are not buying soap at a discount store; we are buying a tradable investment vehicle whose price is determined by buyers and sellers. Moreover, you only want to buy what is going up.

## Sell Rules

S1—If stops are hit with End of Day data and still in place at 30 minutes (this time period is based solely on your comfort level) after the open the next day, a sell is initiated; if not in place at the 30-minute point, the issue falls under intraday monitoring (see S2).

S2—Intraday monitoring of Price and Trend between the hours of 30 minutes after the open until 60 minutes before the close, will invoke a Sell order sent to brokers for execution. Once an issue hits its stop, then a 30-minute period is allowed before it is sold. With the constant barrage of Internet and financial media trying to be first with breaking news, often the story is presented incorrectly, and it can have an effect on a large stock, an industry, or even a sector and cause a big sell-off. Usually, if the story was reported in error or incorrectly, and then reported correctly, the issue quickly recovers. Most of this happens in a very short period of time. The 30-minute rule will help avoid most of these short-term sell-off with quick recoveries.

S3—In a broad-based sell-off and stops are hit, holdings hitting stops can begin liquidating before the 30-minute limit.

S4—If a holding has experienced a sharp run-up in price, once it reaches a 20 percent gain, sell 50 percent of the holding and invest in another holding or a new holding. This is just a prudent way of locking in exceptional gains.

S5—Any holding that is still being held after experiencing S4, once a gap open (above previous day's high) occurs, a further reduction in the holding is warranted. Additionally, this can also anticipate a blow-off move or island reversal while protecting most gains but still allowing for more upside, although limited exposure. This is not a good process when trading only one issue, but is prudent when trading many issues with the ability to always find something else to trade.

## Trade Up Rules

T1—With Weight of the Evidence strong: If stops are hit, but limited to single sector/industry/style, replace next day as long as the Initial Trend Measures are all indicating an uptrend.

T2—With Weight of the Evidence strong: If stops are hit on more than one sector/industry/style, reenter when Initial Trend Measures are all indicating an uptrend or Initial Trend Measures are improving, as long as there is no deterioration in the weight of the evidence.

T3—With Weight of the Evidence at an intermediate level: If stops are hit, but limited to single sector/industry group, replace next day as long as Initial Trend Measures are all indicating an uptrend.

T4—With Weight of the Evidence at an intermediate level: If stops are hit on more than a single sector/industry/style, the normal Buy rules apply.

T5—There is no trading up when weight of the evidence or initial trend measures are deteriorating. Clearly in this situation there is something not good about the uptrend and it is not a time to trade up.

## Guidelines

*Note:* Guidelines are used as reminders and offer the opportunity to be ignored but only after considerable deliberation and examining all other possibilities. The absolute most important guideline is the first one, G1.

G1—In the event a situation arises in which there is not a rule or guideline, a conservative solution will be decided on and implemented based on immediate needs. A new guideline or rule will be developed only after the event/conflict has totally passed. This is a critically important guideline to ensure the "heat of the moment" is not used to create or change a rule. The absolute worst time to create or change a rule is when you are emotionally concerned about something that just seems to not be working correctly. In the 1970s, the Navy F-4J Phantom jet had analog instruments and compared to today's electronic technology, was antiquated. We had to memorize what we called *initial action items* for emergency procedures; these were designed to handle the quick and necessary steps to shut down an engine because of fire, no oil pressure, and so on. During simulator (talk about antiquated compared to now) many would pull the wrong lever or shut off the wrong switch during the emotional surge that comes with bright red flashing lights and loud horns. I was not excluded from that group, but found that when something happened that required immediate action, winding the clock (they weren't electric back then) for a few seconds to rid yourself of the adrenalin rush would allow you to perform better during the procedure. Beside the reasons given for S1 previously, this falls in line with that thinking.

G2—Try to adhere to this if possible: Weak Weight of the Evidence: SPY, MDY, DIA (ensure liquidity), Intermediate Weight of the Evidence: Styles and Sectors, Strong Weight of the Evidence: Wide Open (a pilot term meaning full throttle). The mandatory ranking measures will dominate this guideline.

G3—European ETFs need to be monitored closely after 1 pm to ensure adequate execution time. This is because when the Europe markets close, liquidity in those issues becomes a problem.

G4—Every day when invested, trading up needs to be evaluated. Often this involves selling the poor performing holding and buying additional amounts of current holdings.

G5—All buy candidates should be determined by:

–Rising mandatory ranking components using a chart of the Ranking Measures.

–An awareness of the issue's price support and resistance levels.

G6—Always be aware of the Prudent Man concept. This is sort of a catch all to make one think about an action that has not been adequately covered with rules or guidelines. If deciding to do something as far as asset commitment or ETF selection, one needs to be prepared to stand in front of the boss and explain it.

There are a host of additional rules and guidelines that can be created. I would caution you on trying to develop a rule for every inconsistency or disappointment that surfaces while trading with a model. There is probably a good equilibrium about the depth and number of rules is best. I strongly suggest adding rules rationally and unemotionally.

## Asset Commitment Tables

In addition to measuring what the market is doing (weight of the evidence) and a set of rules and guidelines to tell you how to invest based on what the market is doing, you then need a set of tables for each strategy to show you the asset commitment (equity exposure goal) levels to be invested to for each Weight of the Evidence scenario. Table 14.6 is an example table showing the Initial Trend Measure Level (ITM), Weight

**TABLE 14.6** Asset Commitment Table

| ITM | WoEv | Points | Asset Commitment % |
|-----|--------|--------|--------------------|
| 0 | Red | 0 | 0 |
| 1 | Red | 1 | 0 |
| 2 | Red | 2 | 0 |
| 3 | Red | 3 | 20 |
| 0 | Orange | 4 | 0 |
| 1 | Orange | 5 | 0 |
| 2 | Orange | 6 | 20 |
| 3 | Orange | 7 | 70 |
| 0 | Yellow | 8 | 50 |
| 1 | Yellow | 9 | 50 |
| 2 | Yellow | 10 | 100 |
| 3 | Yellow | 11 | 100 |
| 0 | Green | 12 | 100 |
| 1 | Green | 13 | 100 |
| 2 | Green | 14 | 100 |
| 3 | Green | 15 | 100 |

**TABLE 14.7**  Alternative Asset Commitment Table

| ITM | WoEv | Points | Asset Commitment % |
|-----|------|--------|--------------------|
| 0 | Red | 0 | 0 |
| 1 | Red | 1 | 0 |
| 2 | Red | 2 | 0 |
| 3 | Red | 3 | 5 |
| 0 | Yellow | 4 | 15 |
| 1 | Yellow | 5 | 15 |
| 2 | Yellow | 6 | 25 |
| 3 | Yellow | 7 | 50 |
| 0 | Green | 8 | 100 |
| 1 | Green | 9 | 100 |
| 2 | Green | 10 | 100 |
| 3 | Green | 11 | 100 |

of the Evidence (WoEv), the Points assigned to each level, and the Asset Commitment Level Percentage (Asset Commitment percent). This is merely a sample and should be based on your risk preferences and objectives. As you can see even with the Weight of the Evidence at its lowest level as long as the much shorter term trend measures (ITM) are all saying there is an uptrend, one can commit equity to the market.

An alternative and more conservative asset commitment table is shown in Table 14.7. It is easier and a more simple process to divide the Weight of the Evidence into only three levels, with the middle or intermediate level being the transition zone.

The rules and guidelines offer a few exceptions to the above table of asset commitment, but only based on fairly rare events. Following the rules and commitment levels will lead to an objective process, which is the ultimate goal.

This chapter contains many measures one can use to determine which holdings should be bought. Many are only valuable in assisting in the selection process. If you consider the fact that you might only need to purchase a few holdings and there are more than 1,400 available, you need a strong set of technical measures to help you reduce the number of issues into a more manageable number. There are some that were identified as mandatory measures, which means these are the ones that have the best track record at identifying early when a holding is in an uptrend. I am positive there are many momentum indicators that are not in this chapter, but these are the ones that I have used for many years. Just keep in mind what the goal of this is: to remove human input into the selection process.

# CHAPTER 15

# Putting It All Together: The "Dancing with the Trend" Model

One of the basic premises for model development is the concept of Occam's Razor. Occam's (or Ockham's) razor is a principle attributed to the 14th-century logician and Franciscan friar William of Ockham. This is the basic premise of all scientific and theory building. The simpler of two methods is preferable. Simplest may not be best, but is a good start.

---

Everything should be made as simple as possible, but not simpler.

*Albert Einstein*

---

It is the only form that takes its own advice: Keep things simple. A model built on sound principles will probably survive the tumult of the markets much longer and better than an overly complex model. Complexity has a tendency to fail, and unfortunately, usually at the worst time. I always think about the complex algorithms used by Long Term Capital in 1998, when they began to fail miserably. Their complete failure and the foolish effort to tweak them almost took the New York Fed down with them. It seems that too often investors associate complexity with viability. That is just not correct.

---

Simplicity is the ultimate sophistication.

*Leonardo da Vinci*

---

There are three primary components to a sound model, and just like a three-legged stool, a model must be stable in all environments. They are:

1. Weight of the evidence measurement of market movement.
2. Rules and guidelines to show how to trade the weight of the evidence information.
3. Strict discipline to follow the process with confidence.

Remove any one of those components, and like the legs on a three-legged stool, the model will tumble. The following discusses each of these components and how they fit together to produce a comfortable rules-based trend-following model. I mention comfortable because you must be comfortable with your model or you will constantly challenge it and probably abandon it if not. The only thing that really matters when judging a strategy is actual, real-time, verifiable results. Everything else is just window dressing.

## Weight of the Evidence

The "Dancing with the Trend" model described herein uses a basket of technical measures to determine the overall risk levels in the market place. The model has been constructed so that each technical measure (see Chapter 13) carries a specified weight based on extensive research. These weights (percentage points) are cumulated to derive a total model point measure to build the weight of the evidence. This approach gives one the ability to protect assets in difficult market environments (low weight of the evidence totals) while also allowing one to make tactical shifts to better performing assets when the investment environment is more favorable (high weight of the evidence totals).

Each of the weight of the evidence components is assigned a weight based on their percentage contribution to the overall model, with the total of all components equal to 100. The weight of the evidence is further broken into four different levels in this example. For example, if the sum of the weights of the indicators is equal to 65, the model would be deemed to be yellow as the yellow range is from 51 to 80. These ranges and the number of ranges are determined during model development and research. Sometimes only three ranges are necessary, and, in fact, for most it is advisable. In this example, I have four ranges, with the middle two considered as transition ranges. This allows the model to absorb some market volatility without penalizing the process.

    0–30 = Red
    31–50 = Orange
    51–80 = Yellow
    81–100 = Green

An alternative range could also be used. One must decide on how close the stops are in order to determine how many levels, and in particular the middle or transitional levels are used. Like the porridge in the three bears' story, one is going to be just right (for your model).

0–30 = Red
31–70 = Yellow
71–100 = Green

These levels serve the model concept as they determine what set of rules to use to buy, sell, or trade up (trade up is the act of replacing current poor relative performing holdings with better performing holdings). Asset allocation (equity exposure) values are also a function of the weight of the evidence level. There are also three additional Initial Trend Measures (ITM), which provide guidance to the buying and trading up process using the point system. These help refine the various levels using shorter term trend measures.

The weight of the evidence model uses these primary components that, when used together, help determine the most appropriate asset allocation level as measured by the model. The terminology below of "turning on" refers to the fact that the measurement is indicating a positive or upward trend. In this example, the price-based components are:

Trend Capturing (one component)
Price Short
Price Medium
Price Long
Adaptive Trend

The next group of components fall into the category of Market Breadth measures. Market Breadth indicators allow one to look at the market internals that are not always reflected in the price action of the market. This is much like a physical examination performed by your doctor. You might be feeling fine but when the doctor runs his diagnostic tests he is getting an internal look that can potentially find a health risk that you were not aware of. That is the precise reason it is recommended you have routine physical exams. I'll spend some time here to illustrate how such Breadth measures can be used to evaluate potential risk in the markets that is not readily apparent in the price action alone.

To use a very simplistic example, let's focus on the Dow Jones Industrial Average Index (DJIA), which is comprised of 30 large blue-chip issues. If IBM (or another of the high priced stocks in the index) was up 15 percent on the day, but the other 29 DJIA stocks were down slightly, the DJIA could possibly still be up for the day because of the large price contribution from IBM. The price movement of the index would be showing a positive action. However, if you look at the fact that only one of the 30 was up while 29 were down a much different picture of the overall health of the market is yielded. Since DJIA is a price-weighted index, this example demonstrates how a high priced stock can influence the average. Similarly, capitalization weighted indices (S&P 500) can have cases were the top 10 percent of the components will

**FIGURE 15.1**   Why Breadth Is Used

*Source:* Chart courtesy of MetaStock.

influence the daily return of the index. Additionally, the Nasdaq 100 index, which comprises the top capitalization stocks in the Nasdaq Composite shows that the top 10 stocks of the Nasdaq 100 account for about 43 percent of the movement of the entire Nasdaq 100 index. The largest capitalization stock in the index can be up $20 for the day and the smallest capitalization stock can be down one cent for the day, but with breadth, they evenly cancel each other out. Breadth, on the other hand, shows the true internal action of an index from treating all issues equally. Therefore, Breadth measures will generally begin to decline prior to price or cap weighted indexes at market tops. Tom McClellan is fond of saying that breadth arrives at the party on time, but always leaves early.

During periods of market distribution or the long drawn-out topping process, investors will tend to move from their more illiquid higher risk holdings (usually small cap issues) into what they perceive as less risky large capitalization blue chip stocks. This serves to drive price and capitalization indices (which most are) higher, while breadth, being equally weighted, shows that most issues are declining. As the breadth measures turn off it reduces risk by tightening your sell criteria.

Figure 15.1 is an example from 2007 in which the price-based capitalization index moved higher (top plot of S&P 500), the breadth-based advance decline measure (bottom plot) moved lower.

Here are the breadth-based measures used in this example of the weight of the evidence used in the Dance with the Trend model:

Advance/Decline
New Highs/New Lows
Up Volume/Down Volume
Breadth Combination
Trend Capturing (2 components)

The single remaining weight of the evidence component is the relative strength measure. Recall that it is a compound measure using small cap versus large cap, growth versus value, and breadth versus price (see Figure 13.24 and Figure 13.25). Figure 15.2 shows the Nasdaq Composite in the top plot with the total weight of the evidence overlaid on it and below are all nine weight of the evidence binary indicators. You can see from the individual binaries that they turn on and off independently. As one binary comes on the total weight of the evidence in the top plot moves up based upon how many points that binary was worth.

**FIGURE 15.2** Weight of the Evidence Explanation 1

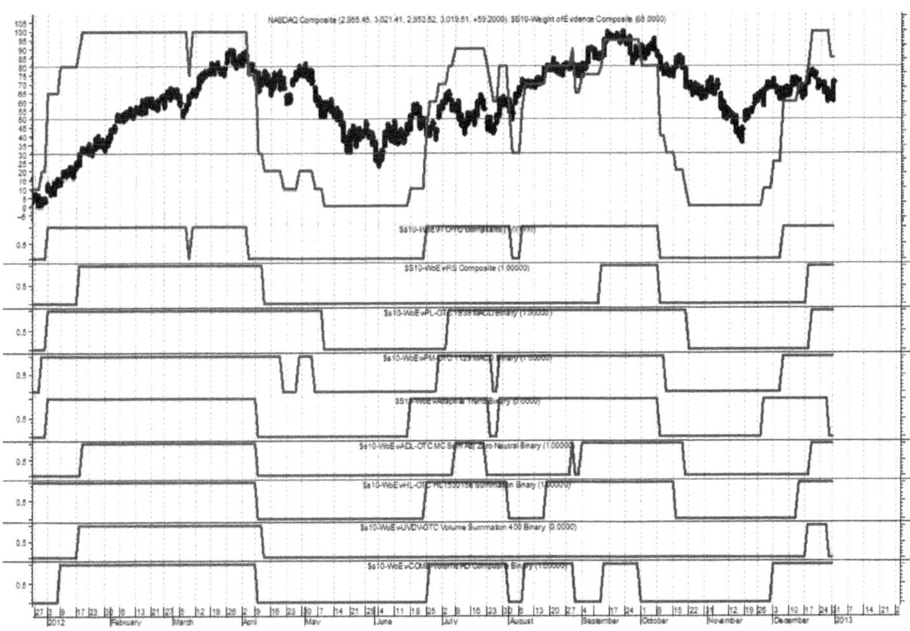

*Source:* Chart courtesy of MetaStock.

Figure 15.3 shows an example of the weight of the evidence in the top plot overlaid on the Nasdaq Composite going from 100 just after the first vertical line down to zero just before the second vertical line. The weight of the evidence component binaries are all shown below. You can see that as they turn off, the total weight of the evidence line in the top plot declines based on the percentage value of the binary that turned off. Below are the dates and names of the weight of the evidence components and when they turned off. You can see that it took from 5/4/2010 until 5/20/2010 for

**FIGURE 15.3**   Weight of the Evidence Explanation 2

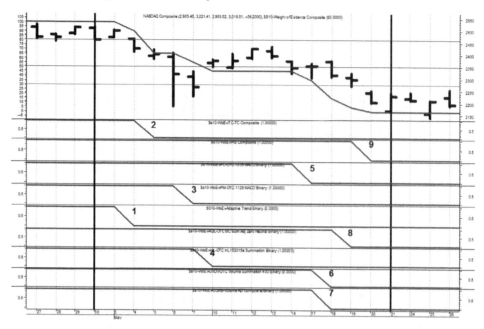

*Source:* Chart courtesy of MetaStock.

all of them to turn off and take the weight of the evidence from 100 to zero. However, don't forget as the weight of the evidence transitions through the four zones the stops on each holding are tighter so a nearly defensive position was reached by 5/7/2010.

1. 5/4/2010 Adaptive Trend
2. 5/5/2010 Trend Capturing
3. 5/7/2010 Price Medium
4. 5/10/2010 High Low
5. 5/17/2010 Price Long
6. 5/18/2010 Up Volume Down Volume
7. 5/18/2010 Breadth Combination
8. 5/19/2010 Advance Decline
9. 5/20/2010 Relative Strength

Figure 15.4 shows the total weight of the evidence with the Nasdaq Composite overlaid. When the weight of the evidence is at the top, which is 100, it means all of the components are saying the trend is up. When it is at the bottom, which is zero, it means all of the components are saying the trend is not up. The three horizontal lines are at 80, 50, and 30, which break the weight of the evidence into four sections, which are described in the next section. I think you can clearly see that when the weight of the evidence is strong (> 50), the market is generally in an uptrend.

**FIGURE 15.4**  Weight of the Evidence Explanation 3

*Source:* Chart courtesy of MetaStock.

## Investing with the Weight of the Evidence

When all of the indicators are "on" you have very strong uptrends occurring, and they have been confirmed by a number of weight of the evidence indicators so there is strong confirmation of the trends in place. There is a strong relative strength relationship in that there is ample speculation taking place in the markets to help drive upward price movement and investor sentiment is good. In addition, the positive price movement is being fully supported by the internal breadth measures. This is a favorable time to be invested, and this is when you want to participate in the equity markets because of the favorable opportunity of market gains.

However, when all of the indicators are off, a negative or insufficient uptrend is in place and there is no confirmation of a solid positive trend. The relative strength relationship is showing unfavorable market sentiment, which leads to less than favorable market conditions. In addition, the breadth measures are telling you that the market internals are weak. This is a time when the risk of negative price movement is at its greatest, and the time to be invested in much safer assets such as cash or cash equivalents until market conditions improve.

Transitional markets occur when the weight of the evidence is either increasing or decreasing. If the weight of the evidence is increasing one will generally begin increasing the equity allocations as evidence builds until you get to a point where most or all of the indicators are on at which time you would have generally moved to a fully invested position. When the weight of the evidence is declining, the stops that are in place on every holding in the portfolio are tightened. These stops, which act as a downside protection mechanism in the event the market price action reverses suddenly, control the sell side discipline, and if these stops are hit the positions are sold. Stopped out positions are not replaced until you once again begin to see an improvement in the market's performance or the weight of the evidence, depending on the rules and guidelines. Therefore, as the weight of the evidence continues to decline (indicators turning off) and holdings continue to hit stop loss levels one is naturally decreasing the equity allocation until such time that you might be fully defensive. Figure 15.5 shows the Nasdaq Composite with the weight of the evidence composite overlaid and the four levels defined previously.

Table 15.1 shows in table form what Figure 11.5 displays visually.

The technical measures are based on sound principles, solid research, and are applied with uncompromised discipline. This approach to trend following for money

**FIGURE 15.5**   Weight of the Evidence Levels

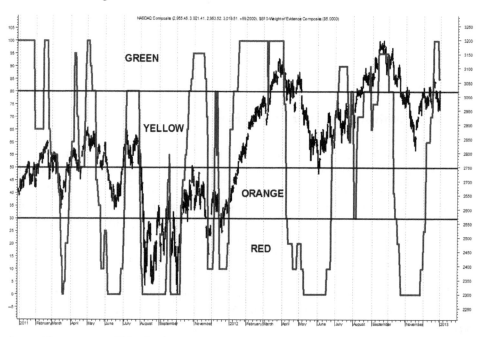

*Source:* Chart courtesy of MetaStock.

**TABLE 15.1**   Weight of the Evidence Levels Table

| WoEv Color | WoEv Level | Posture | Stops | Trade Up? |
|---|---|---|---|---|
| Green | 81–100 | Fully Invested | Loose | Active |
| Yellow | 51–80 | Selectively Invested | Normal | Defensive |
| Orange | 31–50 | Defensive | Tight | No |
| Red | 0–30 | Fully Defensive | Very Tight | No |

management provides a level of comfort to investing in the equities market that few can question.

## Ranking and Selection

Chapter 14 presented all of the ranking measures and details on each one. Here I just bring them into the full picture of how the overall model works. From the ETF universe (currently about 1,400), using the mandatory ranking measures of Trend, Price Performance, Relative Performance, and Risk Adjusted Return Measures, a fully invested portfolio will contain anywhere from 12 to 18 holdings. Clearly this number is decided by the strategy team or the investment committee and is used here merely as an example. The Ranking Measures bring the giant universe of possible ETFs down to only the ones qualified for investment based upon their technical and risk performance. Figure 15.6 helps visualize this ranking and selection process.

Figure 15.7 is a sample of the ranking measures that are mandatory with some of the top-rated ETFs based on the value of Trend. In this particular example you can see that many fixed income issues ranked high, plus the energy ETFs, and a few equity-based ETFs. From this I would guess the market was in a transition area going from up to down or vice versa because not many equity related ETFs are performing well.

Figure 15.8 shows not only the mandatory ranking measures, but also the tie-breakers, all of which were covered in detail in Chapter 14. The conditional formatting allowed in spreadsheet software is invaluable for this process. If the negative numbers are displayed and easily determined it drastically speeds up and simplifies the selection process.

## Discipline

Up to this point in the book, I have given many examples of discipline and its constant need when using an objective model. It is mentioned again here because it is a critically important component. In fact, I think discipline is the sole reason most analysts fail when using a model.

**FIGURE 15.6**  ETF Universe Reduced by Ranking Measures

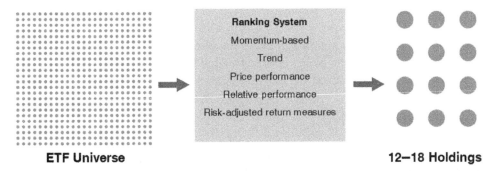

ETF Universe

Ranking System
Momentum-based
Trend
Price performance
Relative performance
Risk-adjusted return measures

12–18 Holdings

**FIGURE 15.7**  Mandatory Ranking Measures

Mandatory Ranking Measures

| Ticker | Name | PwrScore | Trend | Trnd5ROC | PrMo | PMo5ROC | PrPerf | 21dHHV |
|---|---|---|---|---|---|---|---|---|
| EWP | ISHARES MSCI SPAIN CAPPED ET | 194.9 | 87.63 | 8.01 | 79.35 | 12.83 | 7.92 | 0 |
| FAN | FIRST TRUST GLOBAL WIND | 183.88 | 83.04 | 8.26 | 76.17 | 5.12 | 4.68 | 0 |
| TAN | GUGGENHEIM SOLAR ETF | 176.74 | 81.25 | 10.57 | 71.07 | -7.1 | 14.42 | 0 |
| FEZ | SPDR EURO STOXX 50 ETF | 170.05 | 76.7 | 11.33 | 69.42 | 35.94 | 3.92 | 0 |
| EZU | ISHARES MSCI EMU ETF | 167.35 | 76.08 | 11.3 | 67.83 | 44.06 | 3.44 | 0 |
| XOP | SPDR S&P OIL & GAS EXP & PR | 170.84 | 75.32 | 24.32 | 67.92 | 24.1 | 7.6 | 0 |
| VCIT | VANGUARD INT-TERM CORPORATE | 140.09 | 75.07 | 0.28 | 54.09 | -20.03 | 0.93 | 0 |
| DSUM | POWERSHARES CHINESE YUAN DIM | 145.67 | 72.13 | 6.44 | 62.59 | -9.45 | 1.16 | -0.22 |
| VTIP | VANGUARD SHORT-TERM TIPS | 150.24 | 71.43 | 2.42 | 58.56 | 13.39 | 0.25 | 0 |
| BIV | VANGUARD INTERMEDIATE-TERM B | 115.45 | 70.37 | -4.48 | 44.52 | -25.31 | 0.63 | -0.07 |
| CIU | ISHARES INTERMEDIATE CREDIT | 119.44 | 69.34 | -3.89 | 49.61 | -9.17 | 0.49 | 0 |
| AGG | ISHARES CORE TOTAL US BOND M | 113.76 | 68.94 | -3.7 | 44.25 | -22.01 | 0.58 | -0.01 |
| IEI | ISHARES 3-7 YEAR TREASURY BO | 114.58 | 68.83 | -5.7 | 45.4 | -21.8 | 0.42 | -0.07 |
| STPZ | PIMCO 1-5 YEAR US TIPS INDEX | 149.78 | 67.95 | 2.51 | 61.45 | 22.85 | 0.38 | 0 |
| BSV | VANGUARD SHORT-TERM BOND ETF | 112.58 | 67.18 | -6.38 | 45.33 | -13.92 | 0.14 | -0.07 |
| QQQ | POWERSHARES QQQ NASDAQ 100 | 144.29 | 66.47 | 25.49 | 55.19 | 43.71 | 2.63 | 0 |
| IEF | ISHARES 7-10 YEAR TREASURY B | 106.41 | 66.34 | -9.21 | 39.91 | -34.37 | 0.55 | -0.38 |
| IJR | ISHARES CORE S&P SMALL-CAP E | 145.08 | 65.74 | 17.24 | 56.4 | 44.37 | 2.95 | 0 |
| VMBS | VANGUARD MORTGAGE-BACKED SEC | 110.35 | 65.52 | -10.36 | 44.58 | -27.78 | 0.41 | -0.17 |
| LQD | ISHARES IBOXX INVESTMENT GRA | 116.16 | 65.48 | -2.47 | 49.6 | -6.56 | 1.13 | -0.05 |

**FIGURE 15.8**  Mandatory and Tie-Breaker Ranking Measures

| | | Mandatory Ranking Measures | | | | | | | Tie Breaker Ranking Measures | | | | | | | | | | |
|---|---|---|---|---|---|---|---|---|---|---|---|---|---|---|---|---|---|---|---|
| Ticker | Name | Pwr Score | Trend | Trnd5 ROC | PrMo | PMo5 ROC | PrPerf | 21d HHV | ER | AvgDD | PxV | AT | WgtPerf | Old Trend | UI | Sortino | Beta | +-65 | Rel Perf |
| EWP | ISHARES MSCI SPAIN CAPPED ET | 194.9 | 87.63 | 8.01 | 79.35 | 12.83 | 7.92 | 0 | 59.76 | -5.39 | 24.86 | 9.19 | 4.48 | 88.27 | 14.3949 | 41.12 | 1.2 | 12.83 | 14.81 |
| FAN | FIRST TRUST GLOBAL WIND | 183.88 | 83.04 | 8.26 | 76.17 | 5.12 | 4.68 | 0 | 58.29 | -3.82 | 0.92 | 5.97 | 2.39 | 84.44 | 29.6592 | 72.47 | 1.04 | 8.96 | 7.97 |
| TAN | GUGGENHEIM SOLAR ETF | 176.74 | 81.25 | 10.57 | 71.07 | -7.1 | 14.42 | 0 | 53.96 | -13.32 | 17.18 | 17.09 | 7.33 | 82.41 | 50.4799 | 32.98 | 2.15 | 21.25 | 7.4 |
| FEZ | SPDR EURO STOXX 50 ETF | 170.05 | 76.7 | 11.33 | 69.42 | 35.94 | 3.92 | 0 | 36.09 | -1.77 | 46.11 | 5.16 | 2.34 | 81.21 | 12.7303 | 39.15 | 1.18 | 6.99 | 13.29 |
| EZU | ISHARES MSCI EMU ETF | 167.35 | 76.08 | 11.3 | 67.83 | 44.06 | 3.44 | 0 | 32.11 | -1.31 | 133.64 | 4.69 | 2.1 | 81 | 13.4553 | 47.35 | 1.06 | 6.5 | 12.41 |
| XOP | SPDR S&P OIL & GAS EXP & PR | 170.84 | 75.32 | 24.32 | 67.92 | 24.1 | 7.6 | 0 | 40.51 | -2.32 | 285.78 | 8.64 | 5.49 | 78.97 | 10.9938 | 45.25 | 1.32 | 9.66 | 8.71 |
| VCIT | VANGUARD INT-TERM CORPORATE | 140.09 | 75.07 | 0.28 | 54.09 | -20.03 | 0.93 | 0 | 17.95 | -2.49 | 22.43 | 1.31 | 0.56 | 76.93 | -4.6558 | -56.09 | 0.17 | 0.93 | 10.05 |
| DSUM | POWERSHARES CHINESE YUAN DIM | 145.67 | 72.13 | 6.44 | 62.59 | -9.45 | 1.16 | -0.22 | 26.1 | -0.16 | 0.61 | 1.33 | 0.57 | 73.07 | 5.6828 | -1.48 | 0.1 | 1.58 | 10.23 |
| VTIP | VANGUARD SHORT-TERM TIPS | 150.24 | 71.43 | 2.42 | 58.56 | 13.39 | 0.25 | 0 | 16 | | 6.08 | 0.49 | 0.12 | 75.19 | | | 0.05 | 0.31 | 3.38 |
| BIV | VANGUARD INTERMEDIATE-TERM B | 115.45 | 70.37 | -4.48 | 44.52 | -25.31 | 0.63 | -0.07 | 3.37 | -3.93 | 15.7 | 0.97 | 0.35 | 73.96 | -6.4866 | -71.31 | 0.08 | 0.67 | 7.49 |
| CIU | ISHARES INTERMEDIATE CREDIT | 119.44 | 69.34 | -3.89 | 49.61 | -9.17 | 0.49 | 0 | 3.05 | -1.04 | 55.44 | 0.75 | 0.25 | 73.53 | -3.6138 | -85.94 | 0.09 | 0.49 | 5.36 |
| AGG | ISHARES CORE TOTAL US BOND M | 113.76 | 68.94 | -3.7 | 44.25 | -22.01 | 0.58 | -0.01 | 1.69 | -1.93 | 93.52 | 0.8 | 0.36 | 73.64 | -4.6605 | -85.69 | 0.09 | 0.63 | 4.85 |
| IEI | ISHARES 3-7 YEAR TREASURY BO | 114.58 | 68.83 | -5.7 | 45.4 | -21.8 | 0.42 | -0.07 | 2.38 | -0.34 | 204.67 | 0.66 | 0.23 | 73.28 | -1.7227 | -77.52 | 0.02 | 0.58 | 4.68 |
| STPZ | PIMCO 1-5 YEAR US TIPS INDEX | 149.78 | 67.95 | 2.51 | 61.45 | 22.85 | 0.38 | 0 | 23.47 | -0.35 | 6.47 | 0.62 | 0.21 | 73.45 | -1.7435 | -66.66 | 0.08 | 0.43 | 3.9 |
| BSV | VANGUARD SHORT-TERM BOND ETF | 112.58 | 67.18 | -6.38 | 45.33 | -13.92 | 0.14 | -0.07 | 0.78 | 0.28 | 75.53 | 0.26 | 0.07 | 72.56 | -2.4625 | -160.71 | 0.03 | 0.21 | 2.24 |
| QQQ | POWERSHARES QQQ NASDAQ 100 | 144.29 | 66.47 | 25.49 | 55.19 | 43.71 | 2.63 | 0 | 18.61 | -0.49 | 2547.33 | 3.65 | 2.14 | 71.46 | 9.886 | 64.77 | 0.94 | 4.03 | -0.75 |
| IEF | ISHARES 7-10 YEAR TREASURY B | 106.41 | 66.34 | -9.21 | 39.91 | -34.37 | 0.55 | -0.38 | 9.72 | -3.26 | 118.05 | 1 | 0.28 | 70.2 | -6.0226 | -53.09 | 0.02 | 0.62 | 7.63 |
| IJR | ISHARES CORE S&P SMALL-CAP E | 145.08 | 65.74 | 17.24 | 56.4 | 44.37 | 2.95 | 0 | 17.27 | -0.07 | 116.47 | 3.95 | 2.01 | 71.99 | 16.6479 | 54.15 | 1.12 | 4.07 | -0.35 |
| VMBS | VANGUARD MORTGAGE-BACKED SEC | 110.35 | 65.52 | -10.36 | 44.58 | -27.78 | 0.41 | -0.17 | 7.83 | -0.97 | 2.89 | 0.7 | 0.2 | 70.59 | -3.5647 | -47.38 | 0.06 | 0.8 | 4.22 |
| LQD | ISHARES IBOXX INVESTMENT GRA | 116.16 | 65.48 | -2.47 | 49.6 | -6.56 | 1.13 | -0.05 | 1.53 | -3.57 | 227.37 | 1.46 | 0.73 | 69.54 | -6.8443 | -51.06 | 0.19 | 0.86 | 8.96 |

## Sell Criteria

Selling of holdings is accomplished in two ways: one is when actively trading up and a holding is sold because it is being replaced by a holding that has better ranking measures, and two, when a holding hits its stop loss level.

## Tweaking the Model

A model that is based on sound principles using a rational approach to measuring trends, a strong set of reasonable rules, and the discipline to follow it, (especially, when it seems it isn't working) is the secret to a successful model process. Tweaking a model is the equivalent of creating destruction. The best models are the ones that are least sensitive to changes in their parameters.

There are times, however, when one of the measures just seems to steadily be losing its trend identification ability. I'm not saying you should never change a parameter or a model component, just don't start tinkering with the parameters—change the component. In this case my goal is to find a replacement that only makes a positive contribution to the model's historical performance with extremely little or no negative contribution.

## Model in Action

The following charts (Figures 15.9, 15.10, 15.11, and 15.12) show the stages of the weight of the evidence model over different time periods. The binary overlaid on the Nasdaq Composite Index is a simplified process that shows an uptrend whenever the Weight of the Evidence measure is greater than 50 and a downtrend whenever it is less than 50. This method shows when the measure is essentially invested (uptrend) and when it is defensive (downtrend). The lower plot is the weight of the evidence composite.

Remember: All of the financial theories and all of the market fundamentals will never be any better than what the trend of the market allows.

**FIGURE 15.9** Weight of the Evidence (1996–2012)

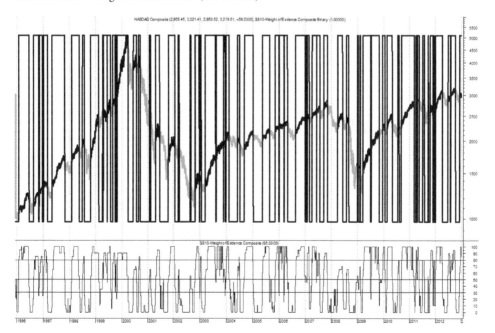

*Source:* Chart courtesy of MetaStock.

**FIGURE 15.10**   Weight of the Evidence (2007–2012)

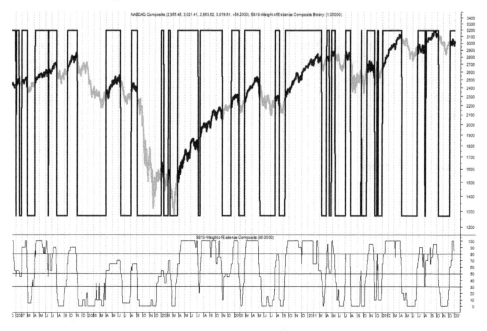

*Source:* Chart courtesy of MetaStock.

**FIGURE 15.11**   Weight of the Evidence (2011–2012)

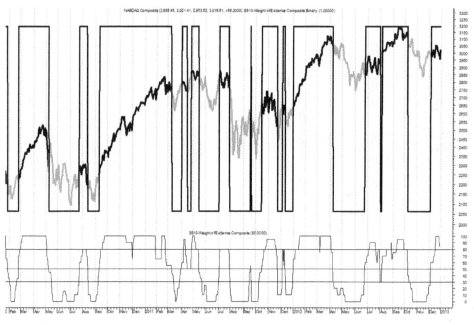

*Source:* Chart courtesy of MetaStock.

**FIGURE 15.12**   Weight of the Evidence (2012)

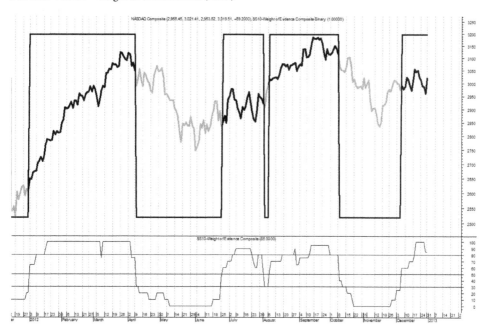

*Source:* Chart courtesy of MetaStock.

## Risk Statistics, Ratios, Stops, Whipsaws, and Miscellaneous

This is a wrap-up section that contains important information and concepts, but would have been out of place if put in one of the previous chapters. Risk statistics are generally good for two purposes: predicting the probability of future outcome and comparing two funds, managers, and so on. If you have read this far, you know I only think they are good for the latter—comparison purposes. When looking at historical returns and standard deviation, you will find that they are not constant, but dependent on the time frame being analyzed. Personally, using less than five years will produce statistics that are not significant for longer-term analysis. Risk statistics come in all sizes and shapes, but comparative risk-adjusted statistics are what we discuss here. These should always be calculated using exactly the same time frames for the two series you are analyzing. Plus it is good to do this over a number of different time frames, say 5, 7, 10, 15, and even 20 years. This section also covers whipsaws, fund expenses, stop losses, and turnover.

### Sharpe Ratio

The Sharpe Ratio was created by William Sharpe in the 1960s and introduced as an alternative to the reward-to-volatility ratio. Clearly, in this case, he is assuming volatility is standard deviation.

$$\text{Sharpe Ratio} = (\text{Mean} - \text{Risk Free Rate}) / \text{Standard Deviation}$$

Here is a simple example: let's say investment A has a return of 12 percent and a Standard Deviation of 10 percent, while investment B has a return of 18 percent and a Standard Deviation of 16 percent. Let's assume the Risk Free Rate is 3 percent. Then Investment A has a Sharpe Ratio of 0.90 ((12 − 3)/10). Investment B has a Sharpe Ratio of 0.9375 ((18 − 3)/16). Hence Investment B is a better investment based on this risk-adjusted statistic. The purpose of this example is to show that a higher standard deviation is acceptable if accompanied by a higher return.

## Sortino Ratio

Created by Frank Sortino and offered as an alternative to the Sharpe Ratio, it is simply the use of downside deviation in the denominator instead of standard deviation and instead of using the Risk Free return it uses a user-defined measure of minimal acceptable return. Downside deviation sounds reasonable, but you must be careful in its determination and assess it for the data in question. If you were to determine variability in a long period of data, the downside variation would be different than if you looked at a short term part of the data.

Sortino Ratio = (Mean − Minimal Acceptable Return) / Downside Deviation

The Minimal Acceptable Return can be set as a function relative to the Mean Return using a rolling return chart.

## Correlations, Alpha, Beta, and Coefficient of Determination

These were thoroughly covered in Chapters 13 and 14.

## Up and Down Capture

Personally, I think this statistic on performance is the most important of all of them. It measures the cumulative return of an investment compared to a benchmark's cumulative return in both up and down periods of the benchmark. If the value of the Up Capture is more than 100 percent, then it means that the investment captured more than 100 percent of the move when the benchmark advances. If the number is less than 100 percent, say 80 percent, then it means the investment only captured 80 percent of the up moves as the benchmark advanced. Down Capture works the same way only focusing on the downward moves of the benchmark.

For example, we have an Up Year with the Benchmark increasing 20 percent, the Up Capture of the investment is 60 percent, then the Investment made 20 percent × 60 percent = 12 percent. Assume a down year in which the benchmark declined by 40 percent, the Investment had a Down Capture of 80 percent, then the Investment returned 40 percent × 80 percent = 32 percent.

## Whipsaws

Trend following has one issue that will constantly plague the investor and usually at the most least-expected time, and that is whipsaws. I have to admit, I think it just takes experience to get used to whipsaws. I hate them, but I also know that trying to adjust a model based on sound principles so that the ones in the recent past are reduced or eliminated will lead to two things: one, the performance in the past will probably be reduced, and you have probably reduced the performance going forward and probably without actually changing the overall number of whipsaws. Trying to eliminate whipsaws will often create more and at the worst time—going forward.

### Up Market Whipsaw

A whipsaw can occur in both up and down markets. An up market whipsaw is when the market is trending higher, and then experiences a pullback in price such that it triggers a stop loss and a holding is sold. Shortly thereafter the market resumes its uptrend (see Figure 15.13). You follow your rules on the process of how to reinstate the equity exposure and you then purchase another asset to replace the one that was sold or you can repurchase the one that was sold as long as you are aware of wash sale rules.

**FIGURE 15.13** Up Market Whipsaw

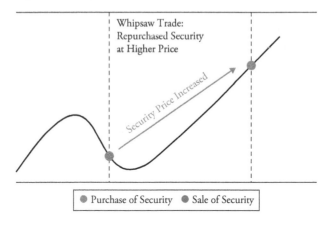

### Down Market Whipsaw

A down market whipsaw occurs in a downtrend after a bottom forms, your trend measures see an uptrend developing and calls for equity exposure so you buy based on your rules. Shortly thereafter the market reverses and the downtrend resumes and the security just purchased is at its stop loss and is sold. This is the most common type of whipsaw (see Figure 15.14) because when uptrends begin the Weight of the Evidence is usually low and your trade up rules are not yet into play. When legging into a new uptrend, your goals is liquid exposure—period.

**FIGURE 15.14**  Down Market Whipsaw

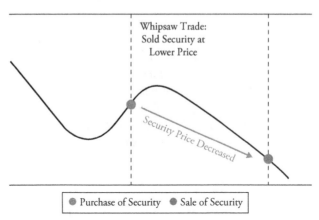

Whipsaw Trade:
Sold Security at
Lower Price

*Security Price Decreased*

● Purchase of Security   ● Sale of Security

## Stops and Stop Loss Protection

A stop loss is generally applied in an effort to reduce a portfolio's exposure to the risk of downside market moves. These are determined by a number of methods, a predetermined cumulative loss is reached or on a percentage of drawdown. Stops can be justified from behavior biases such as disposition effect and loss aversion. I think it can be stated that the use of stop loss protection will almost always reduce a portfolio's return, especially if the returns are not momentum driven. In other words, the use of stop losses in trend following is certainly better than in mean reversion strategies. Further, they provide an investor with discipline and the potential to reduce risk. Generally, though, the reality is that although many think they will improve performance, instead the real value of them is in overall risk reduction. On another note, trend following can be best served with using the reversal of trend as the stop loss technique. However, this would require some real stamina in the process as one can suffer significant losses before most trend-following methods will provide the risk reduction. Figure 15.15 shows how a moving stop loss system can work. This stop is based on a 5 percent decline in price from the highest close reached in the last 15 trading days (top oval). Therefore, that highest point reached in the past 15 days moves within the range of prices during those 15 days. In Figure 15.15 you can see the highest close was about midway back in the 15-day range, or 7 days ago to be exact. The plot at the bottom shows the percent decline from the moving 15-day highest close. Hence, once it drops below the second horizontal line at −5 percent (bottom oval) the stop is reached and the sell order is executed. Don't waste your time creating elaborate stop loss techniques if you aren't going to follow them. In my opinion, all stops are inviolable—period.

This stop loss technique works well because it protects the gains from momentum investing. However, there are situations in market action that would cause this stop loss to fail, and that is during a slow nonvolatile decline. Since the stop is based on the moving past (15 days in this example), it is conceivable that the price would decline and the stop would follow it down because the decline did not exceed the stop loss percentage. Although this is rare, it is certainly possible and must be addressed. One solution is to use a stop that is measuring the trend of the holding, such as the Trend

**FIGURE 15.15** Stop Loss Example

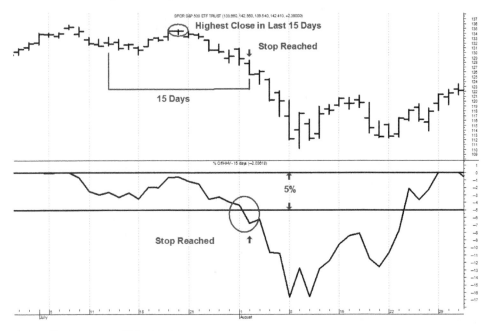

*Source:* Chart courtesy of MetaStock.

measure discussed in Chapter 14. This way, if the price was declining slowly and the percent from previous high value stop isn't working, the trend stop will catch it before the decline in price becomes an issue.

### Stop Loss Execution

This is easy! Execute it when it hits—period. Although it is easy to write this, very often managers fail to live up to this simple creed. I do not know how many times I have heard of a manager that holds a committee meeting when a stop is hit to decide whether to execute it. How truly sad! If you are going to spend time and effort in developing a stop loss process, then why would you question it when it occurs? To me, a stop loss is inviolable. Now there is an issue with stops and when they hit based on the time of day, but this can be dealt with in the rules of a good model. Here is an example of a stop loss process that considers the time of day. From rules, there is no trading during the first 30 minutes of the trading day. This has historically been referred to as *amateur hour* and probably not just appropriate for amateurs but professionals alike. There is often a lot of volatility just after the open as prices seek stability after watching the news and morning futures. I think it is just best to stand aside during this period. The rules also can cease all trading beyond one hour before the market closes. This period of time also has some volatility but often the time is justified for trade execution, depending on the size of the trade. In any case, the actual trading day is reduced from the market hours to help overcome the uncertainty during those periods and allow execution time.

When within the rules-based trading day (defined above), when a stop is hit, it is executed. However the execution process can also be defined with rules. For example, when a holding hits its predefined stop, an alert is sent to all involved in the trading process. This identification of a holding hitting its stop starts a 30-minute clock, which after 30 minutes, if the holding is still below its stop or goes below its stop for the remainder of the trading day, it is executed. The 30 minutes is designed to overcome the onslaught of breaking news, Internet, and constant media coverage throughout the day with the concern that occasionally the news is initially incorrect for whatever reason. Often a news story about a particular company can cause not only the company stock to decline, but the industry, the industry group, and even the sector that company is in to decline. If you were holding a technology sector ETF and Intel had a bad news blast, it could and probably would affect your technology holding. The 30-minute window from the stop being hit until it is executed allows any incorrect reporting to be corrected. Often you can see this in intra-day charts, a spike down, followed a few minutes later by a return to the previous price level. The bottom line is that you should have a process predefined on how to handle stops. It can be as simple or as complex as you feel comfortable with, but *you must follow it*.

## Mutual Fund Expenses

If you are trying to decide on which mutual fund to buy and are looking at objectives, such as growth, conservative, or small cap, you need to know this. Most of them hug a benchmark and performance is based on how they perform relative to that benchmark. If they beat the benchmark they call it alpha, and if they don't, they call it tracking error. Because most mutual fund managers are tied to a benchmark, expenses can become the only discernible difference among them.

You need to understand mutual fund expenses because so many times decisions on which fund to buy boils down to this factor. Expenses can cause you to forget the goal, which is to select the fund that will give you the total return you need. Below is Table 15.2, which shows three mutual funds, their total expenses, and total returns. Which mutual fund is delivering the most alpha?

Fund C clearly delivered the most alpha. If Fund C generated the same total return as the other two with a higher expense, then Fund C manager produces the most alpha of the three funds. However, if you are a momentum buyer like me, the above does not come into play. The concern about expense ratios comes into play when often that is the only delineation among managers who all follow the same objective.

**TABLE 15.2** Mutual Fund Expenses

|        | Total Fund Expenses | Total Return to Investor | Manager Performance (Alpha) |
|--------|---------------------|--------------------------|-----------------------------|
| Fund A | 0.25%               | 6.50%                    | ?                           |
| Fund B | 0.75%               | 6.50%                    | ?                           |
| Fund C | 1.25%               | 6.50%                    | ?                           |

## Turnover and Taxes

Turnover refers to the percentage of an investment vehicle's holdings that have been "turned over" or replaced with other holdings in a given year. Most unconstrained tactical models generally yield a high turnover.

> The turnover is based totally on market action.
>> Low volatility trends will not have high turnover.
>> Short whipsaw-like moves will have high turnover.
> Rarely are there any long-term gains or losses.
> Predominately there are short-term gains and losses.

A good model will not compromise its investment process with tax considerations. Plus there is no risk of getting a long-term gain that you did not participate in. This is a phenomenon most never realize can happen until it happens and then it is too late. Most mutual funds that follow an objective will hold issues for really long periods of time, upward of many years. If you purchase shares of an open-end mutual fund, and shortly thereafter the fund manager decides to sell one of their long-term holdings, you will realize the full long-term capital gains tax, and you never participated in the actual gains.
Remember: Taxes are the consequence of successful investing.

## Watching a Tactical Strategy over the Short Term

Most tactical unconstrained strategies are long term. Following them daily is insane. Following them even quarterly is misleading. Many tactical unconstrained strategies do not have a benchmark. This is critical to understand and convey. Almost the entire world of money managers is tied to benchmarking and rebalancing. Many tactical unconstrained strategies do neither. Often, because of one's investment model, it will be out of sync with the market, which is why comparing it to a benchmark like the S&P 500 on an improper basis (short term) is frustrating. You *must* realize that expecting it to track the daily, weekly, or even monthly direction of a benchmark is admitting that you do not understand this process.

## Benchmarking

Many funds/strategies are tied to a benchmark. In fact, I think most are tied to a benchmark. The goal of these managers is to try to beat the benchmark. Some do and some don't; yet when the number beating or failing to beat the benchmark is usually not worthy of comment, especially over time. I like to say that benchmarking is what you try to do when you have no idea what to do. The World of Finance is wrapped up in relative performance and comparison. Relative performance is a widely used investment tool, but often causes horrible investment decisions. If a client is told his or her account is up 15 percent, they are happy; until you tell them the market was up 20 percent. This often causes a client to search for a new fund or advisor who claims to beat the market. We all know that no one can legally make that promise but carefully worded marketing material can easily give the reader a subliminal message that makes them believe it can be done.

The cycle of performance chasing is the beginning of a vicious process of moving money from what is perceived to be a better performing fund or strategy. Sadly, these moves usually happen at the point in time when they should add to their current account instead of sell it. In the case of tactical unconstrained management, which is what the *Dancing with the Trend* strategy is, trying to select a benchmark to measure performance is losing sight of the strategy's goals and the client's investment horizon. The only benchmark that should matter is the strategy return required to meet your goals. Most will find that in their later years a strategy that meanders to the upside with minimal downside action will be their most comfortable ride. Benchmarking in the investing world is common, often used in sales and marketing, rarely of any true value to an investor who is not interested in a strategy that does not attempt to beat a benchmark. It is, however, human nature to try to measure and compares things; sadly that trait can cause poor results. In brief, benchmarking leads to chasing performance that generally leads to poorer performance.

## Full Cycle Analysis

If you would like an investment plan more oriented to your life span rather than your attention span, you probably would be better served with a tactical approach to the markets. The markets are not tied to the calendar, yet the world of finance is. Performance measures should be appropriate for the strategy, which means that tactical unconstrained should be measured over the full cycle of the market, whether it be top to top, or trough to trough. As an example, in Figure 15.16, a full cycle can be from A to C or from B to D.

## Actual Results from a Rules-Based Trend-Following Strategy—Dancing with the Trend

I am guilty of overkill with the multitude of charts and tables in the remainder of this chapter; however, I have a reason for it. First of all, the Dance with the Trend strategy does not have a benchmark. No benchmark exists for trend following that uses stops and treats cash as an asset class. Personally, I don't think there ever will be. Secondly, many people look at a wide variety of performance data and risk statistics and it seems logical to me to provide as many different "looks" as I can. Hopefully, I included one you are familiar with and can use. This section shows you the results

**FIGURE 15.16** Full Cycle Analysis

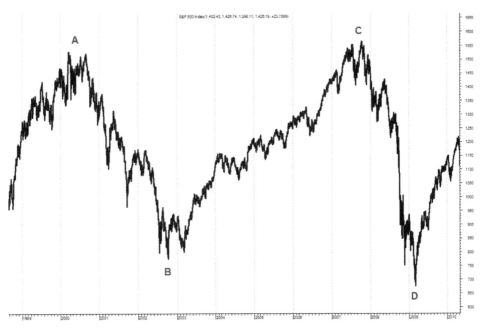

*Source:* Chart courtesy of MetaStock.

from the Dance with the Trend strategy, a rules-based strategy that uses a weight of the evidence approach to trend following, rules and guidelines, and strict discipline. The Dance with the Trend strategy began on December 31, 1996, with data through December 31, 2012. It has real results from a 17-year record of real money management; no back-tested results and no hypothetical results.

## Dance with the Trend Performance and Risk Comparison

The Dance with the Trend strategy is compared to S&P 500 Growth, S&P 500, S&P 500 Value, Russell 2000 Growth, Russell 2000, Russell 2000 Value, MSCI EAFE, and MSCI Emerging Markets. These categories cover large cap, small cap, and international.

Figure 15.17 shows the number of instances of drawdowns greater than 10 percent. The Dance with the Trend strategy had only two instances. All others had at least six.

Figure 15.18 shows the number of instances of drawdowns greater than 20 percent, which is also considered a bear market. The Dance with the Trend strategy had *no* drawdowns greater than 20 percent. Let me say that again. The Dance with the Trend strategy had *no* drawdowns greater than 20 percent.

**FIGURE 15.17**  Drawdowns Greater than 10 Percent

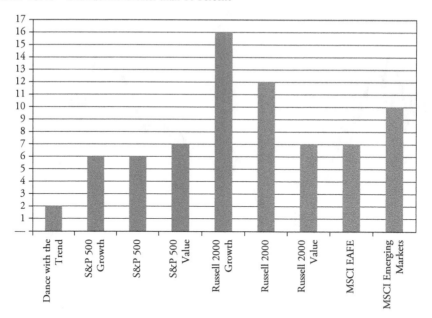

**FIGURE 15.18**  Drawdowns Greater than 20 Percent

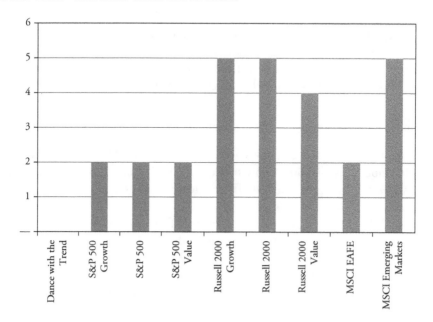

**FIGURE 15.19** Number of Months with Drawdowns Greater than 10 Percent

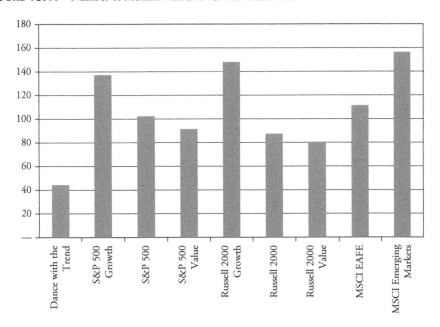

Figure 15.19 shows the total number of months spent in a drawdown of greater than 10 percent. The Dance with the Trend strategy had 42 months spent in a state of drawdown of greater than 10 percent, while others could be measured in decades.

Figure 15.20 shows the number of months in Bear Market territory. The Dance with the Trend strategy had zero months in a bear status. Zero!

Figure 15.21 shows the maximum drawdowns. The Dance with the Trend strategy had a maximum drawdown of −17 percent. Remember there were two giant bear markets during this period, each with drawdowns near −50 percent.

Figure 15.22 shows the average drawdowns. The average drawdown of the Dance with the Trend strategy was −5.1 percent.

Figure 15.23 shows the Ulcer Index, which is a measure of risk. The Dance with the Trend strategy had an Ulcer Index of only −7 percent.

## Dance with the Trend over a Full Market Cycle

Any strategy that is a trend follower that treats cash as an asset class and moves to cash during bad periods in the market does not have a benchmark. The only way to correctly measure performance for a strategy such as the Dance with the Trend strategy is over the full market cycle. The next three tables include the ubiquitous 60/40 strategy for comparison along with the also ubiquitous S&P 500 Index. When one does not

**FIGURE 15.20** Number of Months with Drawdowns Greater than 20 Percent

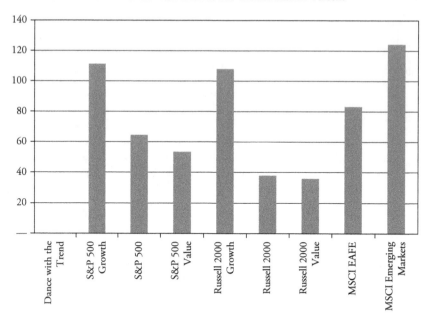

**FIGURE 15.21** Maximum Drawdown

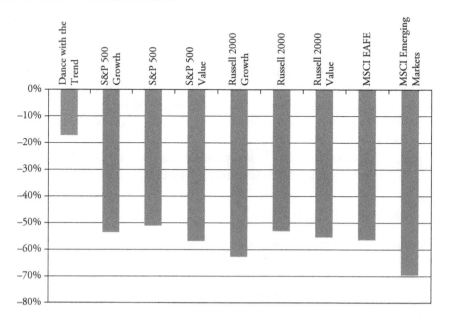

**FIGURE 15.22**  Average Drawdown

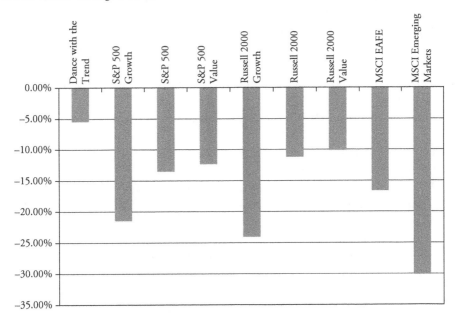

**FIGURE 15.23**  Ulcer Index

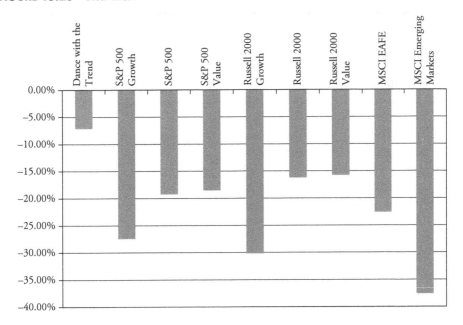

have a benchmark, at least something needs to be used. You can recall my comments on "The 60/40 Myth" in Chapter 3.

The following tables use many statistical and risk measures; their definitions are scattered throughout the book, but all are reproduced here for convenience.

Return—This is the annualized return, which is also the geometric mean of the returns.

Cumulative Return—This is the compound return of the series from the beginning date.

Standard Deviation—A measure of the average deviation of the returns from their mean (same as sigma).

Downside Risk—Also known as the *semi-standard deviation* as the sum is restricted to those returns that are less than the mean. Author note: Be careful here and be aware of the amount of data being analyzed. An inadequate amount of data would make this value unreliable.

Beta versus Market—This is the sensitivity of the series compared to that of a benchmark. A beta of one means the return series and the benchmark are similar.

Alpha versus Market—This is the mean of the excess returns of the series over beta times the benchmark. Author note: This is horribly overused in modern finance and very difficult to distinguish from returns derived from beta.

Sharpe Ratio—The annualized excess returns of the series divided by the annualized standard deviation.

Best Period Return—The maximum of the returns in the period of data analyzed.

Worst Period Return—The minimum of the returns in the period of the data analyzed.

Up Capture versus Market—This measures how well the series did in capturing the up periods of the benchmark.

Down Capture versus Market—This measures how well the series did in capturing the down periods of the benchmark.

Maximum Drawdown—The maximum compounded loss the series incurred during any period of measurement.

R-Squared versus Market—Shows how closely related to the benchmark the series is based on the variance of returns. This is also known as the *goodness of fit*.

Correlation versus Market—This measures how closely related the variance of the series is to the benchmark.

Table 15.3 shows the performance data for the first full bear/bull cycle in this century. When a risk statistic is compared to the market; that market is the S&P 500 Index.

Table 15.4 shows the Dance with the Trend strategy during the bull/bear cycle.

Table 15.5 shows the Dance with the Trend strategy since its conception.

**TABLE 15.3** Peak-to-Peak (April 2000–October 2007) Analysis

| | Return | Cumulative Return | Standard Deviation | Downside Risk | Beta vs. Market | Alpha vs. Market | Sharpe Ratio | Best Period Return | Worst Period Return | Up Capture vs. Market | Down Capture vs. Market | Maximum Drawdown |
|---|---|---|---|---|---|---|---|---|---|---|---|---|
| Dance with the Trend | 4.09% | 35.11% | 7.98% | 5.18% | 0.3673 | 3.23% | 0.51 | 10.78% | −6.12% | 51.29% | 29.62% | −11.82% |
| 60% S&P/40% BarCap Agg | 4.03% | 34.50% | 8.69% | 6.37% | 0.551 | 2.64% | 0.46 | 10.24% | −8.53% | 65.58% | 47.31% | −19.94% |
| S&P 500 Index | 1.92% | 15.36% | 15.61% | 11.84% | 1 | 0.00% | 0.12 | 15.39% | −17.28% | 100.00% | 100.00% | −43.76% |

**TABLE 15.4** Trough-to-Trough (October 2002–February 2009) Analysis

| | Return | Cumulative Return | Standard Deviation | Downside Risk | Beta vs. Market | Alpha vs. Market | Sharpe Ratio | Best Period Return | Worst Period Return | Up Capture vs. Market | Down Capture vs. Market | Maximum Drawdown |
|---|---|---|---|---|---|---|---|---|---|---|---|---|
| Dance with the Trend | 5.23% | 39.29% | 7.47% | 4.49% | 0.3186 | 4.56% | 0.7 | 10.78% | −4.30% | 52.72% | 18.15% | −6.39% |
| 60% S&P/40% BarCap Agg | 3.11% | 22.04% | 9.16% | 6.79% | 0.5847 | 1.84% | 0.34 | 10.24% | −11.33% | 66.66% | 54.28% | −27.36% |
| S&P 500 Index | 1.64% | 11.16% | 15.49% | 11.76% | 1 | 0.00% | 0.11 | 15.39% | −21.94% | 100.00% | 100.00% | −45.80% |

**TABLE 15.5** Since Inception Analysis: January 1996–December 2012 (Full History)

| | Return | Cumulative Return | Standard Deviation | Downside Risk | Beta vs. Market | Alpha vs. Market | Sharpe Ratio | Best Period Return | Worst Period Return | Up Capture vs. Market | Down Capture vs. Market | Maximum Drawdown |
|---|---|---|---|---|---|---|---|---|---|---|---|---|
| Dance with the Trend | 9.07% | 337.45% | 12.24% | 6.74% | 0.3983 | 6.24% | 0.74 | 28.93% | −6.12% | 57.41% | 22.66% | −15.22% |
| 60% S&P/40% BarCap Agg | 7.10% | 221.14% | 10.33% | 7.51% | 0.5723 | 2.65% | 0.69 | 12.91% | −11.33% | 64.34% | 51.00% | −27.36% |
| S&P 500 Index | 7.01% | 216.17% | 17.91% | 13.37% | 1 | 0.00% | 0.39 | 21.30% | −21.94% | 100.00% | 100.00% | −45.80% |

## Dance with the Trend with Other Asset Classes

The following tables show various risk statistics for the Dance with the Trend strategy compared to a wide variety of other asset classes. If a strategy such as the Dance with the Trend strategy does not have a benchmark, then this is a more valid method of comparing performance measures. Table 15.6 shows all of the risk statistics used in the previous tables with the addition of R-squared and Correlation.

## Dance with the Trend Return Analysis

Table 15.7 shows the various asset classes' performance over various time periods from 1 to 15 years.

## Dance with the Trend Upside Downside Analysis

Table 15.8 shows statistics for various periods relative to up and down markets as determined by the S&P 500 Index.

## Dance with the Trend Comparison with Style/Asset Classes

Table 15.9 shows the performance of the Dance with the Trend strategy against a host of various asset classes.

**TABLE 15.6** Risk/Return Table January 1996–December 2012: Summary Statistics

| | Return | Cumulative Return | Standard Deviation | Downside Risk | Beta vs. Market | Alpha vs. Market | Sharpe Ratio | Best Period Return | Worst Period Return | Up Capture vs. Market | Down Capture vs. Market | Maximum Drawdown | R-Squared vs. Market | Correlation vs. Market |
|---|---|---|---|---|---|---|---|---|---|---|---|---|---|---|
| Dance with the Trend | 9.07% | 337.45% | 12.24% | 6.74% | 0.3983 | 6.24% | 0.51 | 28.93% | −6.12% | 57.41% | 22.66% | −15.22% | 34.00% | 0.5831 |
| Nasdaq Composite Index | 7.10% | 221.12% | 28.45% | 20.33% | 1.3914 | −0.80% | 0.15 | 48.28% | −32.70% | 140.53% | 141.34% | −74.17% | 76.79% | 0.8763 |
| Dow Industrial Average | 7.98% | 268.99% | 16.87% | 12.60% | 0.8981 | 1.61% | 0.3 | 17.59% | −18.38% | 95.48% | 87.50% | −42.75% | 90.94% | 0.9537 |
| Russell 2000 Index | 7.46% | 239.60% | 22.36% | 16.43% | 1.1368 | 0.19% | 0.2 | 23.43% | −26.12% | 113.28% | 112.03% | −47.92% | 82.94% | 0.9107 |
| 30 Year Treasury | 7.20% | 225.87% | 15.92% | 9.42% | −0.4372 | 12.39% | 0.27 | 33.14% | −13.51% | −3.14% | −89.24% | −26.03% | 24.19% | −0.4918 |
| 10 Year Treasury | 6.06% | 171.79% | 8.54% | 5.42% | −0.2712 | 8.84% | 0.37 | 15.00% | −6.19% | 1.89% | −62.44% | −9.71% | 32.33% | −0.5686 |
| London Gold | 8.77% | 317.31% | 11.89% | 8.25% | −0.0865 | 10.28% | 0.49 | 14.56% | −12.62% | 23.49% | −41.14% | −34.98% | 1.70% | −0.1303 |
| US Cash Indices LIBOR | 3.42% | 77.06% | 1.14% | 0.82% | −0.0021 | 3.44% | 0.47 | 1.72% | 0.06% | 10.90% | −12.18% | 0.00% | 0.11% | −0.033 |
| CPI | 2.42% | 50.11% | 1.41% | 1.16% | 0.0122 | 2.32% | −0.33 | 2.64% | −3.41% | 8.34% | −7.26% | −3.41% | 2.40% | 0.1549 |
| S&P 500 Index | 7.01% | 216.17% | 17.91% | 13.37% | 1 | 0.00% | 0.23 | 21.30% | −21.94% | 100.00% | 100.00% | −45.80% | 100.00% | 1 |

385

**TABLE 15.7**   Return Analysis January 1996–December 2012 (Not Annualized If Less Than 1 Year)

|                       | 1 Year  | 2 Years | 3 Years | 4 Years | 5 Years | 10 Years | 15 Years |
|-----------------------|---------|---------|---------|---------|---------|----------|----------|
| Dance with the Trend  | 12.44%  | −0.73%  | 3.45%   | 3.86%   | 2.31%   | 4.73%    | 7.55%    |
| Nasdaq Composite Index| 17.75%  | 8.08%   | 11.34%  | 19.01%  | 3.79%   | 9.47%    | 5.19%    |
| Dow Industrial Average| 10.24%  | 9.31%   | 10.87%  | 13.71%  | 2.62%   | 7.32%    | 5.81%    |
| Russell 2000 Index    | 16.35%  | 5.59%   | 12.25%  | 15.81%  | 3.56%   | 9.75%    | 5.96%    |
| 30 Year Treasury      | 2.51%   | 17.85%  | 14.70%  | 2.80%   | 9.54%   | 7.46%    | 7.51%    |
| 10 Year Treasury      | 4.19%   | 10.48%  | 9.61%   | 4.42%   | 7.38%   | 5.58%    | 6.14%    |
| London Gold           | 5.49%   | 7.20%   | 14.09%  | 16.73%  | 14.14%  | 16.62%   | 12.12%   |
| US Cash Indices LIBOR | 0.46%   | 0.39%   | 0.38%   | 0.48%   | 1.07%   | 2.22%    | 3.10%    |
| CPI                   | 1.75%   | 2.37%   | 2.05%   | 2.24%   | 1.78%   | 2.43%    | 2.40%    |
| S&P 500 Index         | 16.00%  | 8.84%   | 10.87%  | 14.58%  | 1.66%   | 7.10%    | 4.47%    |

## Dance with the Trend Performance Comparison

Figure 15.24 shows the various asset classes from 1/1/1996 until 12/31/2012. The dotted line (Dance with the Trend) offers a fairly smooth ride. As one ages, this comfortable ride becomes more and more important. It is an investment ride that is easy to stick with over the years. Another wonderful advantage is it means that one could pull out almost all of their money at any time, independent upon market action. Think about that!

**FIGURE 15.24**   Asset Classes from 1/1/1996 until 12/31/2012

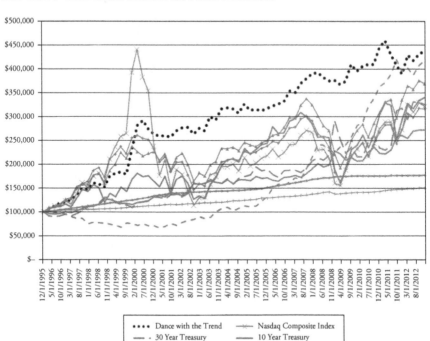

**TABLE 15.8** Upside/Downside Table January 1996–December 2012 (Single Computation)

| | # of Quarters | | Average Return (%) | | Average Return (%) vs. Market | | Quarter (%) | | 1-Year (%) | |
|---|---|---|---|---|---|---|---|---|---|---|
| | Up | Down | Up | Down | Up Market | Down Market | Best | Worst | Best | Worst |
| Dance with the Trend | 44 | 24 | 5.25 | −2.92 | 4.39 | −1.61 | 28.93 | −6.12 | 58.45 | −12.36 |
| Nasdaq Composite Index | 43 | 25 | 10.91 | −11.33 | 9.95 | −11.38 | 48.28 | −32.7 | 86.25 | −59.67 |
| Dow Industrial Average | 43 | 25 | 7.47 | −6.61 | 6.87 | −6.67 | 17.59 | −18.38 | 46.93 | −35.94 |
| Russell 2000 Index | 42 | 26 | 9.36 | −8.73 | 8.14 | −8.7 | 23.43 | −26.12 | 63.86 | −37.5 |
| 30 Year Treasury | 39 | 29 | 6.7 | −4.22 | −0.1 | 6.24 | 33.14 | −13.51 | 41.2 | −25.98 |
| 10 Year Treasury | 41 | 27 | 4.2 | −2.43 | 0.2 | 4.25 | 15 | −6.19 | 20.06 | −9.71 |
| London Gold | 40 | 28 | 6.41 | −3.59 | 1.95 | 2.96 | 14.56 | −12.62 | 43.01 | −21.41 |
| US Cash Indices LIBOR | 68 | 0 | 0.85 | 0 | 0.84 | 0.85 | 1.72 | 0.06 | 6.74 | 0.29 |
| CPI | 61 | 7 | 0.75 | −0.73 | 0.65 | 0.51 | 2.64 | −3.41 | 4.95 | −1.35 |
| S&P 500 Index | 45 | 23 | 7.16 | −7.77 | 7.16 | −7.77 | 21.3 | −21.94 | 49.77 | −38.09 |

**TABLE 15.9** Asset Performance Comparison from 12/31/1995 to 12/31/2012

| Style/Asset | Index | Growth of $100K | Return | Std. Dev. | Beta | Max. Drawdown |
|---|---|---|---|---|---|---|
| Small Cap Value | Russell 2000 Total Return Value | $453,220 | 9.30% | 20.71% | 0.94 | −50.35% |
| Trend Following | Dance with the Trend | $437,450 | 9.07% | 12.24% | 0.40 | −15.22% |
| Gold | London Gold Market Fixing Ltd | $417,310 | 8.77% | 11.89% | (0.09) | −34.98% |
| Long Bond | Barclays U.S. Treasury: 20+ Year | $364,910 | 7.91% | 13.82% | (0.36) | −21.40% |
| Small Cap | Russell 2000 Total Return Index | $336,530 | 7.40% | 22.35% | 1.14 | −47.93% |
| NASDAQ | Nasdaq Composite Index | $321,120 | 7.10% | 28.45% | 1.39 | −74.17% |
| Large Cap Growth | S&P 500 Growth | $318,910 | 7.06% | 18.71% | 1.01 | −53.40% |
| S&P 500 | S&P 500 Index | $316,170 | 7.01% | 17.91% | 1.00 | −45.80% |
| Large Cap Value | S&P 500 Value | $300,240 | 6.68% | 18.66% | 0.99 | −51.74% |
| Bond Index | Barclays US Agg Total Return Value | $270,980 | 6.04% | 3.48% | (0.07) | −2.44% |
| Small Cap Growth | Russell 2000 Total Return Growth | $227,640 | 4.96% | 26.40% | 1.33 | −58.21% |
| Emerging | MSCI Emerging Markets | $218,870 | 4.72% | 28.60% | 1.12 | −65.34% |
| International | MSCI Daily TR Gross EAFE USD | $210,380 | 4.47% | 20.37% | 1.00 | −51.78% |

## Mean Shifting

The Dance with the Trend model measures the trend of the market, then utilizes rules to scale into the trend, and maintains risk containment measures (stop loss) both absolute and relative, and when an uptrend is not identified, a cash position of up to 100 percent is utilized. There are two distribution concepts at play with this type of model. First the use of stop loss measures will reduce the downside variance and shift the return distribution mean to the right. Secondly, the baggage of trend following, known as *whipsaws* (see earlier in this chapter), will reduce the upside variance and shift the return distribution mean to the left. The benefit is that the mean shift to the right is much greater than the mean shift to the left, yielding a net shift to the right. (See Figure 15.25.)

Table 15.10 shows monthly return distributions for the Dance with the Trend strategy from 1996 to 2012, compared to the S&P 500. You can see that the average (mean) of returns for the Dance with the Trend strategy for this 17-year period was 0.65 percent versus 0.52 percent for the S&P 500, and with lower variability as denoted by St. Dev. (standard deviation/sigma). The more significant point is the minimum (Min) value for the strategy is only −5.84 percent versus the S&P 500 at −16.94 percent.

The top plot in Figure 15.25 is the monthly return distribution for the Dance with the Trend strategy from 1996 to 2012. The vertical axis shows the number of events that occurred at the various return levels. The shaded area is the 12-month moving average of those returns so that you can more closely relate to where the bulk of returns occurred. The second plot is the monthly return distribution of the S&P 500 over the exact same time period, also with the 12-month moving average shown. Notice the lack of negative returns (left side) on the top plot of the strategy compared to the S&P 500 in the lower plot. This ability to avoid downside returns provides a right shift (more positive) in the mean of all values. In the top plot there are two return values that have been truncated (two long lines that reach the top of the plot) in order to keep the values in the vertical axis the same as those in the

**TABLE 15.10**   Statistics from 1996–2012 Comparing Dance with the Trend to S&P 500

|          | Dance w/Trend | S&P 500 |
|----------|---------------|---------|
| Mean     | 0.65%         | 0.52%   |
| Std. Dev.| 3.46%         | 4.62%   |
| Min      | −5.84%        | −16.94% |
| Max      | 28.31%        | 10.77%  |

**FIGURE 15.25**  Distribution of Returns for Dance with the Trend versus S&P 500

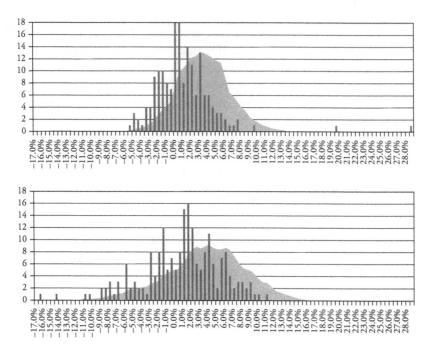

lower plot. There values are 33 and 29. I think it is clear that the Dance with the Trend strategy offers higher returns in addition to much fewer returns in the negative (left) realm.

That was a lot of performance comparisons. Hopefully, you were able to grasp the message that a rules-based trend-following strategy that uses stops and treats cash as an asset class is much better than many, if not most of the investment strategies being hyped by managers who only try to follow a benchmark.

# CHAPTER 16

# Putting Trend-Following to Work

What better way to see how all this information on rules-based trend analysis can actually be put to work and used in a successful practice: The following are interviews with Jud Doherty, president, Stadion Money Management, LLC, and Will McGough, VP Portfolio Management. Stadion is a money management company that, in 2004, *Defined Contribution* news named Advice Provider of the Year in the retirement plan industry. Stadion currently has more than $6 billion under management in separately managed accounts, six mutual funds, and retirement 401(k) plans.

When did you first get interested in the markets?

(Jud)   My first job out of college in 1991 was in 401(k) recordkeeping, which was an operational role. But it gave me exposure to the mutual fund world and insight into the behavior of the typical investor. To gain greater investment knowledge, I entered the CFA program, which led to the next phase of my career, which was institutional investment consulting.

(Will)   From a young age I decided to focus my studies on math over literature, after all there are only 10 basic numbers (counting 0) versus 26 letters, so the odds were in my favor! Mathematics was a natural segue to financial market interest as I grew older. I was also fortunate enough to have family members who tweaked my interest in the markets. My grandfather was a big IBD proponent and gave me a few shares of stock after I graduated from high school. Watching the volatility during the late 1990s/early 2000s I knew there had to be a better way to invest than to watch wild swings and P&L. Then, freshly out of school, I was supposed to study for the CFA program by getting to work early, but instead, spent all my time during the morning darkness studying the markets. Each day, the markets behave differently, which is essential in keeping the thirst for knowledge alive.

Can you describe the overall methodology of your approach to the markets?

(Jud)   I am a firm believer in active management to add safety, not return, and that a disciplined process is critical to success. Gut feelings, emotions, predictions, and forecasts may work once in a while, but are a long-term recipe for disaster.

(Will)    It's all about probabilities. We want to participate when the odds are in our favor of price continuing to go higher and want to protect against times when the odds are signaling detrimental price action. We do this from analyzing price trends, the strength of those trends via market breadth, which is equal weighted participation, and through relative strength, which is determined when speculative markets like small cap and emerging markets are leading the way. From there, we get an overall picture of market health, which we have broken down into various levels to drive asset allocation, security selection, and sell criteria metrics. The final key is knowing when to cut losses via sell criteria; there is no question that we have the discipline to follow this approach no matter how wrong it may feel at times.

How did you come up with the breadth indicators that you use today?

(Will)    Most of the measures we use are simple variations of classic indicators that are common to the technical analysis community.

How have these procedures done over the years?

(Jud)    Active management has underperformed since the lows of 2009, but this is to be expected. Anyone who has kept pace with the market the last few years should be questioned, because they likely have not made any moves that would (or will) protect their portfolio when the next inevitable bear market occurs.

(Will)    Trend following with momentum has the ability over the short term to disconnect from market performance. Whipsaws will eventually lead to underperforming bull markets, and large loss avoidance will make the strategy very appealing after bear markets. But it's the full market cycle that counts. After combining the strengths during bears and weaknesses during bulls the goal is to have market-like returns with unmarket-like volatility.

Have you made any changes to the procedures over the years?

(Jud)    Changes to philosophy and model have been nonexistent, but due to changing markets and opportunities, various indicators and components within our model have changed. For example, breadth will always be an indicator of market health in my opinion, but how breadth is calculated or measured may change over time based on index construction and market evolution.

(Will)    Changes are much akin to natural evolution. A Lexus today isn't the same Lexus as 20 years ago but it's still a Lexus. Stadion's investment philosophy is still the same and the tactical model still follows the same mandate. The beauty of our approach is that we are not reliant on a single indicator; it's the collective voice of our basket of indicators that guides us. Therefore, when research dictates a new method, calculation, or rule be added the plug-and-play nature of our approach means changes are along the fringe rather than at the heart of what we do.

What changes have you made and why?

(Will)    One example of a change is our relative strength measure. For many years, actually over a decade ago, we measured speculation by looking at exchanges, primarily, the NYSE versus Nasdaq. Over the years, listing requirements have changed and new vehicles like ETFs have come about causing the price indices that track these exchanges to be influenced by factors that were not a part of the original indicator thesis. Therefore, we moved to a pure common stock approach by measuring the same original intent by using the S&P 500 and Russell 2000.

What type of assets does Stadion manage; only mutual funds?

(Jud)    Stadion manages 401(k) accounts, collective investment trusts (CITs), separately managed accounts, and mutual funds. But the underlying philosophy of all of these vehicles is active management to protect during devastating bear markets.

Is your model used for all the assets or just some?

(Jud)    All assets we manage at Stadion are governed by strict rules, and in a team environment. Virtually all are managed actively/tactically, though we do have a small portion that is allocated strategically in our 401(k) accounts.

(Will)    As Stadion grows there could be different types of models and strategies but everything we do will be outlined by following a rules-based disciplined process.

Why do you think breadth does so well in a trend following model?

(Will)    Breadth is a derivative of price. The most common type of breadth is advancing versus declining issues, which looks at the number of stocks moving up or down in price across an index or exchange. When market cap or price-weighted indexes performance is driven by those higher weighted constituents in the face the equal weighted voice of the entire index you begin to see breadth divergences. This leading of price gives breadth merit in trend-following systems.

What do you think of the NYSE having about 50 percent of its issues as interest sensitive? Does that affect your model?

(Will)    Funny you mention that. Earlier when I talked about changes to our process the one item affecting our relative strength measure that I didn't bring up was interest-sensitive securities like preferred issues. Not only did this constituency affect our relative strength measure, but it was detrimental to our source of breadth. Since these securities would move contrary to more common equity stocks our breadth measures using NYSE data were affected.

Using a purer stock membership and speculative index in the Nasdaq has enhanced our trend following breadth measures.

You said that you look at only Nasdaq breadth data. Why? Is there any other breadth data that you use?

(Will)  Currently our approach is predicated off of Nasdaq market data. We believe the Nasdaq to represent the broadest, most speculative measure of risk in the U.S. market place. The Nasdaq has less stringent listing requirements so it has a natural downside bias over time as more securities go from the exchange than come to it, this allows periods of ample speculation to show more predominately than its bellwether brother NYSE.

What is the Ulcer Index?

(Will)  The Ulcer Index attempts to quantify risk around measuring drawdowns. Drawdowns are the true source of risk that investors face, not some normal distribution variance around a mean return.
Note from author: The Ulcer Index is also covered as a ranking measure in Chapter 14.

Do you care to comment on this? "Nobody can feed a family with reduced downside; however, it is far easier to recover from difficult periods."

(Jud)  Total return is what matters in the end. But if two strategies have identical returns and one of them has bigger drawdowns, most people simply can't tolerate that and will abandon the strategy. We believe lower drawdowns lead to better sleep at night and a higher likelihood of investors sticking with a given strategy. In other words, high drawdown equals strategy abandoning equals performance chasing equals lack of meeting investing goals.

(Will)  Most definitely, this is the value of compounding at its finest. To recover from a 20 percent loss takes a 33 percent return. To recover from a 5 percent loss takes a 5.3 percent return. It is much easier to recover from small losses than it is large losses. Most people focus on how much return they can get in upmarkets but the key to investing is really the loss avoidance.

I believe you said you would share some of the research that Stadion has done in regard to the indicators and models you mentioned earlier. How about it?

(Will)  Thanks Greg, let me show you two different ways we approach indicators and systems. The system part will actually reference this and your previous book on breadth and will fully disclose those indications. First, let me show you a specific trend following price indicator. This is a classic variation of common approaches. We call it "adaptive trend." Since it's proprietary I can't tell the exact formula but here is what it is: it is a midpoint moving average with a volatility-adjusted average true range band around it as a buy/sell trigger. As volatility and range expands the lower bound band tightens up for quicker exits and the exact happens for smooth trends, low volatility and more "standard" ATR allows more investible flexibility. Our Adaptive Trend indicator averages about four to five trades per year while only being invested approximately 60 percent of the time, which annualizing a return of about 14 percent from 1971 to 2012 (versus 8 percent for the Nasdaq). It has a peak drawdown of 30 percent, and an Ulcer Index (risk) of 7.5, which is about 20 percent of the risk buy-and-hold carries with the Nasdaq Ulcer index of 35. Our results include no return on cash and do not factor in for trading costs or slippage. Based on our actual trading data using ETFs for many years, our actual costs vary between 10 and 20 basis points per year. Figure 16.1 shows the equity line in the top plot, the adaptive trend index in the middle plot and the S&P 500 with adaptive trend in the lower plot. The binary of the signals is overlaid on the S&P 500 in the lower plot. You can clearly see it does an excellent job of picking market turns.

**FIGURE 16.1** Adaptive Trend

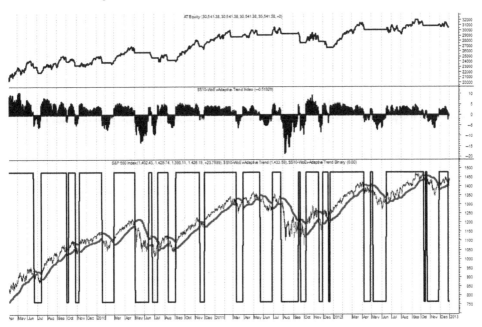

*Source:* Chart courtesy of MetaStock.

Figure 16.2 is a view of the equity line (top line) versus the Nasdaq Composite (lower line) over the longer term. As you can tell, chipping away at upmarkets but avoiding the bears is the key to success.

Next let me show you how to take trend following one step further. Building a basket of indicators to identify trends can be very helpful so let me explain. I'm going to make this one very simple. As you know, we are huge fans

**FIGURE 16.2**  Adaptive Trend versus Nasdaq Composite (1971–2012)

*Source:* Chart courtesy of MetaStock

of the work that the McClellans have done over the years. We also believe in the 5 percent and 10 percent exponential averages (39 and 19 day respectively). So let's take three longer-term indications to develop an environment for when trends should occur. Here is what we will use:

- Nasdaq McClellan Summation Index > 1000 (using the Miekka adjustment), formula in your book, *The Complete Guide To Market Breadth Indicators*.
- Ten percent Trend of Nasdaq New Highs > 10 percent Trend of Nasdaq New Lows, a 19-period exponential moving average of each breadth series (I think this is in your book also).
- Two-hundred-day exponential average of the Nasdaq Composite.

Table 16.1 is a summary of the stand-alone signal results, obviously better than buy and hold but none of them all that great.

Now if we start to combine them in a two-out-of-three and three-out-of-three format (see Table 16.2), we start to see remarkably less risky environments but with lower return. It's the classic risk/return trade off. But we do have a solution of keeping a lower risk environment while matching market return.

For this we now add an intermediate trend following signal (see Table 16.3), the 19/39 price oscillator on the Nasdaq Composite. Once we add this we can then build out a set of system rules. For the two of three with the price oscillator we will be 50 percent invested, for three of three without

**TABLE 16.1**   Component Performance versus Buy and Hold

|  | Compound Annual Return | Ulcer Index | Maximum Drawdown |
|---|---|---|---|
| Advance Decline | 7.50% | 9.5 | 33% |
| New High New Low | 10.50% | 21 | 60% |
| Price | 12% | 16 | 41% |
| Buy and Hold | 9.50% | 35 | 78% |

**TABLE 16.2**   Comparison of Two of Three and All Three to Buy and Hold

|  | Compound Annual Return | Ulcer Index | % Invested | Maximum Drawdown |
|---|---|---|---|---|
| Two of Three | 10.30% | 15 | 63% | 46% |
| Three of Three | 7.50% | 7 | 40% | 15% |
| Buy and Hold | 9.50% | 35 |  | 78% |

**TABLE 16.3**   System versus Buy and Hold Comparison

|  | Compound Annual Return | Ulcer Index | % Invested | Maximum Drawdown |
|---|---|---|---|---|
| Two of Three | 10.30% | 15 | 63% | 46% |
| Three of Three | 7.50% | 7 | 40% | 15% |
| Buy and Hold | 9.50% | 35 | 100% | 78% |
| System | 9.30% | 7.3 | 56% | 20% |

the oscillator 75 percent invested, and finally 100 percent invested when all components are on (3 of 3 for our basket and price trend oscillator positive). You can see from Table 16.3 that this system yielded a return close to Buy and Hold, but with considerably less risk as measured by the Ulcer Index, percent of time invested, and maximum drawdown. I think it is fairly clear this process reduces the risk and helps the return, which was the goal.

Any short bit of advice to investors that you would like to share?

(Jud)     Do not chase performance! It is almost a guarantee that the worst time to fire a manager is when you most want to!

(Will)     Investors need to understand what it is they want to accomplish by setting goals and staying within rules and boundaries of a process. By having a vision and process combined with the discipline to stick with it, whatever they seek to do will work as long as their methodology is sound and reasonable. For many, this takes many years, patience, and maturity to attain!

Thanks Jud and Will.

This concludes Part III.

# CHAPTER 17

# Conclusions

Technical analysis used to be greeted with as much enthusiasm as Jeffrey Skilling addressing the Better Business Bureau and was often referred to as a *black art*. It still is often called *charting*, which is not unlike referring to space flight as flying. Fortunately, those times have passed. The following quote from the Reverend Dr. Martin Luther King could easily be applied to a rules-based trend-following investment model, substituting model for man (he).

---

The ultimate measure of a man is not where he stands in moments of comfort and convenience, but where he stands at times of challenge and controversy.

*Dr. Martin Luther King*

---

Near the beginning of this book, I stated that this was not a storybook, but a compilation of ideas, concepts, and research from almost 40 years in the markets, primarily as a technical analyst. We started out by uncovering numerous facts that are routinely used in modern finance that simply do not meet the test of rigorous mathematics or logical scrutiny. Many things in finance are truly fiction or terribly flawed. Next we moved into a section that dealt with market facts, these were basically about how markets work and after covering the fiction and flaws, appeared relatively simple but were based on sound principles of logic and reason. A large section of the book introduced research on risk, and hopefully redefined what risk is. Research that used a simple process of filtered waves and time to determine if markets trended was presented across a wide range of data sets. The final part of the book, after hopefully convincing you that markets are unpredictable and that there are risk reduction techniques such as trend following that will make you a successful investor over the long term, introduced a rules-based trend-following model affectionately called "Dance with the Trend." Many examples of how to measure what the market was doing, with variable risk categories based on that weight of the evidence, were presented. Security ranking and selection methods were introduced along with a sample set of rules and guidelines to follow. In the end, hopefully, you realized that a rules-based model along with the discipline to follow it will help remove the human subjectivity and those horrible human emotions that we all have.

The story about Abraham Wald's work as a member of the Statistical Research Group during World War II can shed some light into money management (widely disseminated as Abraham Wald's Memo). Wald was tasked with damage assessments to aircraft that returned from service over Germany, and determined which areas of the aircraft structure should be better protected. He found that the fuselage and fuel systems of returned planes were more likely to be damaged than the engines. He made a totally unconventional assessment: Do not focus on the areas that sustained the most damage on these planes that returned, but focus on the essential sections that came back relatively undamaged, such as the engines. By virtue of the fact the planes returned, the heavily damaged areas did not contribute to the loss of the aircraft, but losing the engine would, and therefore would not return. Hence focus on more armor around the engines. For an airplane in battle, protect the essential parts and it will fly again. Investing is not unlike an airplane in battle: Protect the assets from destruction, such as large losses (drawdown), and the investor will live to invest again. Most of modern finance is focused on the nonessential parts.

---

Existing theories about the behavior of stock prices are remarkably inadequate. They are of so little value to the practitioner that I am not even fully familiar with them. The fact that I could get by without them speaks for itself.

*George Soros*, Alchemy of Finance, *1994*

---

As stated previously and often, my critique of much about modern finance is without offering any solutions. When someone complains to me about something, my usual response is that they need to offer a solution to validate their complaint. I am guilty of violating that principle in this book. Gaussian statistics are used extensively in finance because anyone who has taken mathematics, engineering, finance, or economics has learned them. Plus they are relatively simple to understand and while they have shortcomings do provide some understanding about distributions of market data, but never about the extremes. There are statistical techniques that deal with this shortcoming simply referred to as *power laws*. A number of papers present sufficient evidence to this concept. I have listed a few in the appendix, but an Internet search for "power laws in finance" will provide you with a host of works. You will quickly see that Benoit Mandelbrot (Chapter 3) started something.

For those who still believe that markets do not trend, here is a simple attempt to move you away from that belief. Trends exist because of the herding characteristics of humans. For example, limit orders and stop loss levels are usually set based on an incremental measure from a recent price. Robert Prechter provides an exceptional paper on this subject. (A104)

## Financial Advice

It is far from the purpose of this book to get into financial advice other than to blatantly state, "If you cannot control your emotions when making investment decisions, then seek help." Remember, experts cannot predict the market any better than anyone else, but they can offer a systematic approach to investing. They will assist in your switching/ abandoning of strategies for whatever reason and truly help with your behavior when it comes to the markets. Usually, they will also help your accountability so that you continue to make periodic contributions to your portfolio. Outside objectivity is also a benefit as the advisor can slow you down on your dash to follow the herd, and cause you to stick to your plan. The sad part is that most investors will wait too late in life to realize they need help. Wanting to act rational because you know you should, and doing so, are often far apart. Here are some simple questions to ask a potential advisor: how do you manage risk and how do you make investment decisions. Look for answers that involve a process.

Remember: It is not important to be right every time, but it is important to be right over time.

A return of your money; or a return on your money.

Performance tells you nothing about the risks assumed to attain that performance, risks that tend to show up later. It is better to manage risk than to just measure it.

According to William Bernstein successful investors need:

1. An interest in the process.
2. An understanding of the laws of probability and a working knowledge of statistics.
3. A firm grasp of financial history.
4. The emotional discipline to execute their planned strategy faithfully, come hell, high water, or the apparent end of capitalism as we know it.

## A Compilation of Rules and Guidelines for Investors

Over the years I have collected lists of rules, guidelines, steps, and so on written by various individuals for various reasons. Most of them were created by folks after they had spent decades in the business and were sharing some things they not only learned over that time, but also believed.

### Robert Farrell's 10 Rules for Investing

Robert Farrell was Merrill Lynch's technical analyst for many years. Here are his 10 rules for investing:

1. Markets tend to return to the mean over time. When stocks go too far in one direction, they come back. Euphoria and pessimism can cloud people's heads. It's easy to get caught up in the heat of the moment and lose perspective.
2. Excesses in one direction will lead to an opposite excess in the other direction. Think of the market baseline as attached to a rubber string. Any action too far in one direction not only brings you back to the baseline, but leads to an overshoot in the opposite direction.
3. There are no new eras—excesses are never permanent. Whatever the latest hot sector is, it eventually overheats, mean reverts, and then overshoots. Look at how far

the emerging markets and BRIC nations ran over the past six years, only to get cut in half. As the fever builds, a chorus of "this time it's different" will be heard, even if those exact words are never used. And of course, it—Human Nature—never is different.

4. Exponential rapidly rising or falling markets usually go further than you think, but they do not correct by going sideways. Regardless of how hot a sector is, don't expect a plateau to work off the excesses. Profits are locked in by selling, and that invariably will lead to a significant correction, which eventually comes.

5. The public buys the most at the top and the least at the bottom. That's why contrarian-minded investors can make good money if they follow the sentiment indicators and have good timing. Watch Investors Intelligence (measuring the mood of more than 100 investment newsletter writers) and the American Association of Individual Investors survey.

6. Fear and greed are stronger than long-term resolve. Investors can be their own worst enemy, particularly when emotions take hold. Gains "make us exuberant; they enhance well-being and promote optimism," says Santa Clara University finance professor Meir Statman. His studies of investor behavior show that "Losses bring sadness, disgust, fear, regret. Fear increases the sense of risk and some react by shunning stocks."

7. Markets are strongest when they are broad and weakest when they narrow to a handful of blue-chip names. Hence, why breadth and volume are so important. Think of it as strength in numbers. Broad momentum is hard to stop, Farrell observes. Watch for when momentum channels into a small number of stocks ("Nifty 50" stocks).

8. Bear markets have three stages—sharp down, reflexive rebound, and a drawn-out fundamental downtrend. I would suggest that as of August 2008, we are on our third reflexive rebound—the January rate cuts, the Bear Stearns low in March, and now the Fannie/Freddie rescue lows of July. Even with these sporadic rallies end, we have yet to see the long drawn out fundamental portion of the Bear Market.

9. When all the experts and forecasts agree—something else is going to happen. As Stovall, the S&P investment strategist, puts it: "If everybody's optimistic, who is left to buy? If everybody's pessimistic, who's left to sell?" Going against the herd as Farrell repeatedly suggests can be very profitable, especially for patient buyers who raise cash from frothy markets and reinvest it when sentiment is darkest.

10. Bull markets are more fun than bear markets, especially if you are long only or mandated to be fully invested. Those with more flexible charters might squeak out a smile or two here and there.

### James Montier (GMO)

Risk isn't a number and it isn't volatility, it's the permanent impairment of capital. Volatility creates the opportunity.

Leverage cannot turn a bad investment into a good one, but it can turn a good one bad.

Leverage limits staying power.

Often financial innovation is often just leverage in thinly veiled disguise.

## James Montier's Seven Immutable Laws of Investing

1. Always insist on a margin of safety.
2. This time is never different.
3. Be patient and wait for the fat pitch.
4. Be contrarian.
5. Risk is the permanent loss of capital, never a number.
6. Be leery of leverage.
7. Never invest in something you don't understand.

## My Rules

1. Turn off the TV and stop surfing the Internet for advice (stop the noise).
2. Develop a simple process, one that you can explain to anyone (mine is trend following).
3. Create a security selection process based on momentum.
4. Devise a simple set of prudent and reasonable rules and guidelines.
5. Follow your process with discipline; without it, you will fail.
6. If you do not have the discipline to do this, seek professional help from someone who does.
7. Do not be upset with yourself if you do not have the discipline at times; be proud of yourself for recognizing it.
8. Do not confuse luck with skill.
9. Listen and learn from the market—it is always right.
10. Read this list often.

It is never the indicator or the model; it is the user of those tools who is probably at fault.

> *"If I've learned a little*
> *My Grandad told me so*
> *It ain't so much the fiddle,*
> *It's the man who holds the bow."*

Cowritten by my favorite Texas musicians, John Arthur Martinez and Mike Blakely

## Secular Markets and the Efficiency Ratio

I want to show you that a number of the indicators/measures discussed in this book have other uses. For example, the Efficiency Ratio mentioned in Chapter 14 used to select the most efficient buy candidates can also be used to confirm market action, such as in Secular markets. Figure 17.1 shows the weekly Dow Industrials with the secular markets identified (only secular bears identified with no identification for the secular bulls) and the four-year Efficiency Ratio. In other words how efficient did the market move over a four-year period. You can see that secular bull markets are much more efficient (higher ER) than secular bear markets. This result is not surprising, but at least is now somewhat quantified.

**FIGURE 17.1**   Secular Markets and the Efficiency Ratio

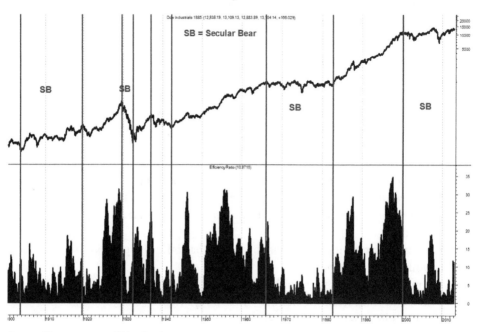

*Source:* Chart courtesy of MetaStock.

## The Rules-Based Trend-Following Model in October 1987

Okay, I always get asked this, how did the Dance with the Trend model perform on Black Monday, October 1987? First of all, this model was not in existence until the early 1990s, but I have data back to the late 1970s to show how it would have performed. As you can see the S&P 500 is the top plot in Figure 17.2 and the Weight of the Evidence is in the lower plot. The Weight of the Evidence began to decline the first week in September and was below 50 percent by September 10, 1987. While stops in the zone below 50 percent are extremely tight, it is highly probable that any money management at this time would be fully defensive in cash or cash equivalents. And this is over a month prior to the crash. Notice how just prior to the crash the Weight of the Evidence popped up slightly then dropped quickly prior to the crash.

**FIGURE 17.2**   Weight of the Evidence in 1987

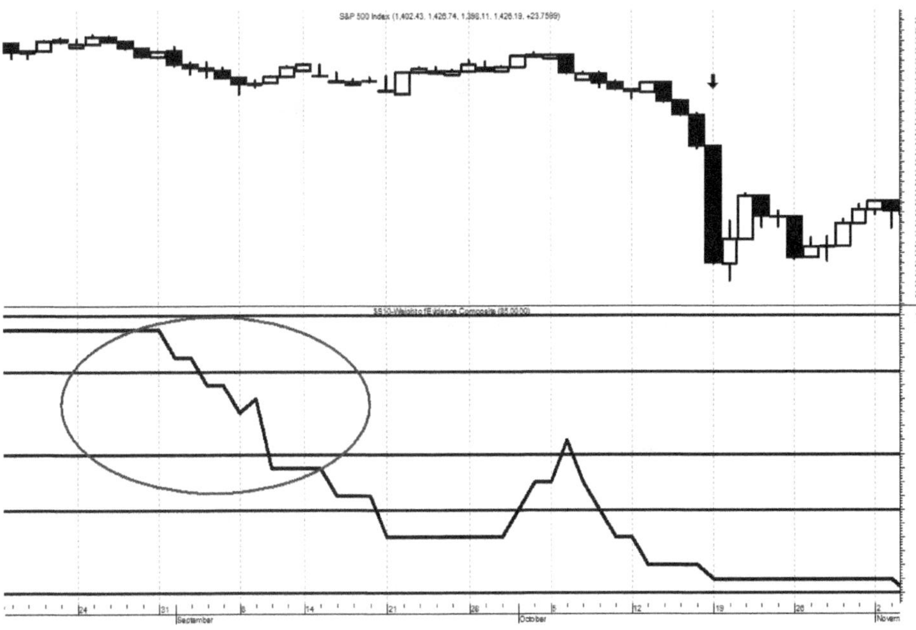

*Source:* Chart courtesy of MetaStock.

## The Flash Crash of May 6, 2010

Big market declines rarely occur while the market is making new highs. When one is a trend follower it means they *never* get out at the top and *never* get in at the bottom. A fact of life and one that is only apparent in the remarkably beautiful world of hindsight. Often I get a question along the lines of how do you handle panic selloffs, such as 1987, and the May 2010 Flash Crash. The year 1987 was explained previously. The Flash Crash on May 6, 2010, was a really scary day. The good news is that the market had peaked on April 23, 2010, and had been in a downtrend for two weeks prior to the Flash Crash, which I believe most have forgotten. In Figure 17.3 the April 23 peak is denoted by point A and the Flash Crash of May 6 by point B, nine trading days later. The Weight of the Evidence dropped from 100 into the second zone two days prior to May 6. Recall that when a zone changes, so do the stops on all holdings. This tightening of the stops took the holdings down to only one that remained on the morning of May 6. Recall also that all selling is done only when the individual holding hits its stop. The last holding was sold the morning of May 6 because it hit its stop. Luck? Of course there was some luck involved. If the crash had occurred a few days earlier, most of the holdings would have gotten clobbered. However, the trend peaked nine days before the Flash Crash and the system worked.

This event prompted some research into market action prior to crash days. The results were strong that rarely do markets crash while making new highs. February 27, 2007, was about the only time it happened.

**FIGURE 17.3**   Flash Crash and the Weight of the Evidence

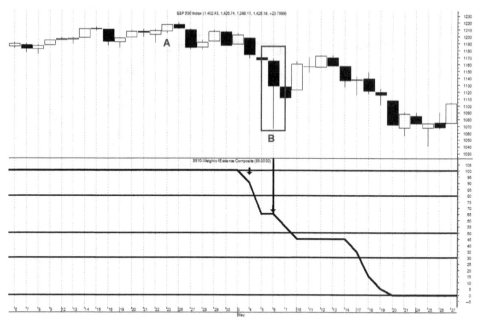

*Source:* Chart courtesy of MetaStock.

In today's complex markets, money management must remain focused on process, which helps control their investment philosophy and the nature of their client base. Controlling the process of investing is absolutely critical for long-term success in the markets. And my final quote from James Montier: "when athletes were asked what went through their minds just before the Beijing Olympics, the consistent response was a focus on process, and not outcome." (B43) Don't forget that.

## Final Observations

I want to avoid, even though it is tempting, repeating much of what I have elaborated on in this book, but some of the pontifications are so important in my opinion that I'm going to repeat a few. The goals of this book are numerous.

Understand how markets work and how they have worked in the past.
Understand the plethora of information that exists in modern finance that is just wrong.
Understand how the tools of modern finance work and their shortcomings.
Understand that you, as a human being, have terrible natural investment tendencies.
Understand what risk is.
Understand that most markets trend and those trends can be identified.

Understand that there are ways to use technical analysis to invest successfully over the long term.

And finally, understand that there are many techniques for investing, but until you grasp full control over your emotions and have exemplary discipline you will probably fail. Failure is how one can learn—hopefully.

Although this has been alluded to throughout this book, I'm going to put it as simply as I can. A rules-based trend follower never asks the questions: Which way is the market going to go? Are we near a top, a bottom, and so on? A trend follower doesn't need to know and shouldn't actually care other than inherent curiosity. We know that increasing capital by participation in up markets is favorable, there is still some joy associated with being totally defensive during down markets while most others are being clobbered. Although that may sound cruel to some, it alleviates some of the frustration of usually underperforming in volatile bull moves. It also falls nicely into a number of the behavioral traits outlined in Chapter 6.

I have injected many personal opinions in this book, most are opinions formed by learning about the markets over the past 40 years, and not all those periods were good, in fact, many were not good. I paid high tuition to learn some things. Once I learned to get my gut feelings out of the process, things got steadily better. I have challenged many things in modern finance and a few things in technical analysis. Again, just opinions as I cannot offer formal proof either way. There are two recommended reading lists in the appendix if you are just starting out, or if you are an old timer, maybe you will enjoy those recommendations also. And now:

## Dance with the Trend!

# Appendix A: Passive versus Active Management

Passive means that the investor or manager does not change the portfolio components except for occasional, usually based on the calendar, rebalancing to some preconceived ratio of stocks and bonds. Passive is prosaic and often is designed just to replicate the market. An active investor or manager is one who attempts to invest in top performing stocks or assets using some methodology to assist in that process. Often it is difficult to tell the difference between some active managers and their benchmark. They have become benchmark huggers, often because of career risk. This is not a complete list, but does address the most popular strategies and while there is some overlap in some strategies, that is not unexpected.

**Examples of Passive**

*Buy and hold.* The concept of long-only investments is usually based on fundamental research. For decades this was the much touted method to long-term success in the stock market, and, in fact, for most people, that is probably correct, especially if much of their holding period was during a secular bull market. Value investing is generally attributed to this type of investing. Sadly, buy and hold can be devastating during secular bear markets. Five of the strong arguments for buy and hold are:

1. The market goes up over the long run.
2. Equity returns will keep you ahead of inflation.
3. The market always recovers from bear markets.
4. Commissions, fees, and taxes are kept low.
5. No one can time the market's up and down moves.

This book is about why those arguments are false. Hopefully when you read them, you were aware that they are not strong arguments at all, but merely selling points for those who benefit from your decision to buy and hold.

*Strategic asset allocation.* A very popular process, which basically infers that the investor or manager sets up a portfolio of assets based on their individual risk to return measures. This concept has been the tenant of modern portfolio theory and, like buy and hold, works quite well in secular bull markets. The really sad part is that buy and hold probably will outperform strategic asset allocation in those secular bull markets. Strategic asset allocation almost always involves periodic rebalancing to the predetermined ratio. Personally, I find it hard to adapt to a strategy that sells its best performing assets and buys more of the worst. Peter Mauthe says strategic asset allocation does not have a tactic. Mauthe goes on to say that nothing gets better with neglect. My tire pressure is low, so I can be passive or active in attending to them. Health, relationships, customer relations, nothing I know of gets better with neglect. So why would my investments be any different?

Portfolio rebalancing seems flawed from its basic premise: selling the best performing assets and buying more of the worst performing assets. Or, selling the best and buying the worst hoping that mean reversion kicks in before you kick off.

*Dollar cost averaging.* The act of investing a fixed dollar amount on a periodic basis. This was addressed in more detail in Chapter 2.

## Examples of Active

*Momentum.* A concept that selects the top-performing assets based on their price performance. While this sounds good, the process does involve determining the period of time to use to measure that performance and usually involves some sort of ranking capability.

*Sector rotation.* Somewhat similar to a momentum strategy but restricted to market sectors and sometimes includes the industry groups. This technique is probably easier to put into practice because it involves fewer issues to monitor and measure. One of the problems with this strategy is that it cannot protect you from bear markets, only reduce the pain. If this strategy is long only and the goal is to remain fully invested, then it was described in Chapter 8.

*Alternatives.* These strategies usually come to fruition during the mid- to later years of secular bear markets, when investors realize that passive investing is no longer working. Futures, hedging, options, and a whole host of derivative products are used across the board in the alternatives category.

*Absolute return.* This falls under the Alternatives header and generally relates to strategies that are totally unconstrained in long, short, hedges, leveraged, and so on. They are not tied to any benchmark, hence, absolute return versus relative return.

*Tactical asset management.* This was listed last as this is essentially what this book is all about. Tactical asset management infers that the investor or manager is unconstrained not only in which assets, but when to invest in them.

Table A.1 gives brief comments on the various strategies. With the benefit of hindsight, the market can seem predictable; however, many of these strategies are more useful in describing the market's past than in anticipating its future.

**TABLE A.1** Pro and Con of Various Strategies

| Strategy | Pro | Con | Comments |
|---|---|---|---|
| Buy and Hold | Low cost as tries to avoid market timing and transaction expense. Assumes that asset prices always rise which is strongly supported by investment marketing. Much research showing that most indexes beat most active managers. Diversification is usually the justification. Generally tax efficient. | Asset prices do not always go up and at times have significant losses. The investor must ride the bad times in order to be invested in the good times. Those times could come at a really bad time in the investor's life. The investor must know who to allocate for diversification. The mere fact that there is no protection from bear markets resonates with most investors. | This is the simple solution for investors who want market returns but also understand they will also get market risks. |
| Strategic Asset Allocation | Can usually approach market like return from diversification into market performance. It certainly sounds good. | Similar to buy and hold in that no real protection from large downside moves in the market. The investor has to determine when and how often to rebalance the portfolio. | There is no proof that this can outperform their benchmarks consistently. Why pay for this gamble of small excess performance. |
| Dollar Cost Averaging | At least the investor is doing something by adding to fixed dollar amounts in down markets. Easy to set up with automatic contribution, plus it really sounds good. | Why buy more of something that is declining in value? Shouldn't you be buying what is rising? | Sometimes the only way to work with some 401(k) plans. Fails miserably in secular bear markets and horrible to endure near retirement. |
| Momentum | Always into the best performing assets. Usually a relative strength evaluation is used and then switching into the top group periodically. | Difficulty sets in when to switch out of a holding to one that is outperforming. Must have rules to overcome this or trading costs can get large. | This is a good way to avoid the large bear markets but it must be incorporated with rules to instill discipline in the process. |
| Sector Rotation | Usually always invested and often tied to a momentum selection strategy. When markets begin to become weak, can move into typically weak sectors such as utilities, healthcare, and staples. | Usually always invested and that means the holdings, even though they are in perceived defensive positions, can get hurt in bear markets. | If cash were one of the asset classes this would be an improvement. |

*(Continued)*

**TABLE A.1**  Continued

| Strategy | Pro | Con | Comments |
|---|---|---|---|
| Alternatives*/ Absolute Return | It has its day in the sun. Diversification by philosophy might apply to many. | Usually quite illiquid. Often can be viewed as black boxes. | Complex, plus an investor needs to know when to use and when not to use. Absolute return should be a goal, not an asset class or type of investment. |
| Tactical Asset Management | Often a rules driven process that tactically moves into assets based upon their relative performance. | Often is overly complex and can be done defensively or opportunistically. Can be expense and difficult to track with a benchmark. Rarely tax efficient. Whipsaws in trendless markets can hurt momentum strategies. | Performance for most of these should be measured over the full market cycle; that is, from market top to market top, or from trough to trough. |

*Alternative strategies can be further reduced to the following: Long/Short, Risk/Merger, Market Neutral, Convertible Arbitrage, Sector Focus, Event Driven, Real Estate, Managed Futures, Private Equity, and Venture Capital.

*Note:* Active management is quite broad. At one end it can be a manager who rebalances a portfolio once a year. This approach rarely uses stop loss protection and is always 100 percent invested, which means it does not ever hold cash or cash equivalents. At the other end of the spectrum is the tactical unconstrained manager, similar to my "Dancing with the Trend" strategy. This is an approach that utilizes stop loss protection, treats cash and cash equivalents as an asset class, and it determined to protect the downside.

# Appendix B: Trend Analysis Tables

The following tables on Trend Analysis are the same as those contained in Chapter 10 except here they are ordered by their Rank.

**TABLE B.1** Trendiness One Rank

| Trendiness | | Avg. | Up Trendiness | |
|---|---|---|---|---|
| Average | *Rank* | U/D | WtdAvg | Rank |

| | | Trendiness One | | | | | Trendiness Two | | | Trendless Analysis | | | |
|---|---|---|---|---|---|---|---|---|---|---|---|---|---|
| | | Trendiness | | Avg. | Up Trendiness | | While in Trend | | | | | | |
| | Index Name | Average | Rank | U/D | WtdAvg | Rank | Up/Tot | Dn/Tot | Up Rank | Up | Down | Trendless | Rank |
| C | U.S. Dollar Index | 95.16 | 1 | 1.08 | 102.65 | 101 | 51.85% | 48.15% | 105 | 49.34% | 45.82% | 4.84% | 109 |
| C | CRB Index | 92.69 | 2 | 1.42 | 131.59 | 87 | 58.45% | 41.55% | 98 | 54.17% | 38.51% | 7.31% | 108 |
| S | S&P Energy Sector | 92.31 | 3 | 2.52 | 232.75 | 15 | 71.59% | 28.41% | 33 | 66.08% | 26.23% | 7.69% | 107 |
| I | Australia All Ordinaries | 90.94 | 4 | 2.28 | 207.75 | 28 | 69.52% | 30.48% | 52 | 63.22% | 27.71% | 9.06% | 106 |
| I | Slovakia SAX | 90.31 | 5 | 1.28 | 115.54 | 95 | 56.08% | 43.92% | 100 | 50.65% | 39.67% | 9.69% | 105 |
| I | Chile IGPA General Index | 90.17 | 6 | 1.66 | 149.32 | 74 | 62.34% | 37.66% | 91 | 56.21% | 33.95% | 9.83% | 104 |
| I | MSCI EAFE | 89.91 | 7 | 1.99 | 178.96 | 52 | 66.56% | 33.44% | 75 | 59.85% | 30.06% | 10.09% | 103 |
| | NYSE Composite | 89.89 | 8 | 2.41 | 217.05 | 22 | 70.61% | 29.39% | 44 | 63.47% | 26.42% | 10.11% | 102 |
| | S&P 500 Index | 88.78 | 9 | 2.25 | 199.91 | 33 | 69.21% | 30.79% | 55 | 61.45% | 27.33% | 11.22% | 101 |
| | DJ Wilshire 5000 Composite | 88.07 | 10 | 2.62 | 230.54 | 16 | 72.34% | 27.66% | 29 | 63.70% | 24.36% | 11.93% | 100 |
| | Russell 2000 Value | 87.53 | 11 | 3.69 | 322.90 | 2 | 78.59% | 21.41% | 6 | 68.80% | 18.74% | 12.47% | 99 |
| S | Morgan Stanley Consumer Index | 87.52 | 12 | 2.96 | 259.01 | 9 | 74.68% | 25.32% | 16 | 65.36% | 22.16% | 12.48% | 98 |
| S | S&P Utilities Sector | 87.37 | 13 | 2.19 | 191.14 | 44 | 68.61% | 31.39% | 62 | 59.95% | 27.42% | 12.63% | 97 |
| I | S&P/TSX Composite (Canada) | 87.29 | 14 | 2.20 | 191.92 | 42 | 68.58% | 31.42% | 64 | 59.86% | 27.43% | 12.71% | 96 |
| S | S&P Healthcare Sector | 86.97 | 15 | 2.21 | 192.24 | 41 | 68.78% | 31.22% | 58 | 59.82% | 27.16% | 13.03% | 95 |
| | S&P 500 Total Return | 86.90 | 16 | 3.21 | 278.62 | 4 | 76.12% | 23.88% | 12 | 66.15% | 20.75% | 13.10% | 94 |
| | Value Line Index (Arithmetic) | 86.60 | 17 | 2.36 | 204.40 | 29 | 70.19% | 29.81% | 47 | 60.79% | 25.81% | 13.40% | 93 |
| | S&P 500 Tot Ret Inflation Adj | 86.25 | 18 | 3.05 | 262.89 | 8 | 75.15% | 24.85% | 13 | 64.82% | 21.43% | 13.75% | 92 |
| | Dow Industrials 1885 | 86.07 | 19 | 2.27 | 195.02 | 38 | 69.23% | 30.77% | 54 | 59.59% | 26.49% | 13.93% | 91 |

| | Index | | | | | | | | | | | | |
|---|---|---|---|---|---|---|---|---|---|---|---|---|---|
| | Major Market Index | 84.49 | 20 | 2.68 | 226.54 | 20 | 72.75% | 27.25% | 27 | 61.47% | 23.02% | 15.51% | 90 |
| | Value Line Index (Geometric) | 84.44 | 21 | 1.93 | 162.59 | 64 | 65.56% | 34.44% | 82 | 55.36% | 29.09% | 15.56% | 89 |
| I | Russell 3000 | 84.38 | 22 | 2.95 | 248.63 | 12 | 74.56% | 25.44% | 18 | 62.91% | 21.47% | 15.62% | 88 |
| | MSCI EM | 84.27 | 23 | 2.21 | 186.22 | 49 | 68.72% | 31.28% | 59 | 57.92% | 26.36% | 15.73% | 87 |
| S | Healthcare Index (S&P) | 84.22 | 24 | 1.94 | 163.54 | 62 | 66.04% | 33.96% | 79 | 55.62% | 28.60% | 15.78% | 86 |
| | S&P MIDCAP INDEX | 84.10 | 25 | 2.71 | 228.13 | 19 | 72.86% | 27.14% | 26 | 61.28% | 22.82% | 15.90% | 85 |
| I | Sri Lanka All Share | 83.98 | 26 | 1.29 | 108.17 | 98 | 56.21% | 43.79% | 99 | 47.21% | 36.77% | 16.02% | 84 |
| | S&P 100 Index | 83.97 | 27 | 2.27 | 190.61 | 46 | 69.33% | 30.67% | 53 | 58.22% | 25.76% | 16.03% | 83 |
| | Dow Jones Utilities | 83.77 | 28 | 2.43 | 203.64 | 30 | 70.76% | 29.24% | 41 | 59.28% | 24.49% | 16.23% | 82 |
| | Russell 1000 | 83.72 | 29 | 3.02 | 252.92 | 11 | 75.06% | 24.94% | 14 | 62.84% | 20.88% | 16.28% | 81 |
| | Russell 2000 | 83.02 | 30 | 2.07 | 171.63 | 56 | 67.34% | 32.66% | 70 | 55.91% | 27.11% | 16.98% | 80 |
| I | United Kingdom FTSE 100 | 82.77 | 31 | 2.53 | 209.34 | 24 | 71.56% | 28.44% | 34 | 59.23% | 23.54% | 17.23% | 79 |
| I | Malaysia KLSE Composite | 82.64 | 32 | 1.96 | 162.02 | 66 | 66.08% | 33.92% | 78 | 54.61% | 28.04% | 17.36% | 78 |
| S | S&P Industrials Sector | 82.49 | 33 | 2.05 | 169.05 | 58 | 66.98% | 33.02% | 71 | 55.25% | 27.24% | 17.51% | 77 |
| I | Switzerland Swiss Market | 82.10 | 34 | 2.79 | 229.22 | 18 | 73.27% | 26.73% | 23 | 60.16% | 21.94% | 17.90% | 76 |
| | Russell 2000 Growth | 82.05 | 35 | 2.31 | 189.76 | 47 | 69.62% | 30.38% | 51 | 57.13% | 24.92% | 17.95% | 75 |
| I | S&P/TSX 60 CAPPED (Canada) | 81.78 | 36 | 2.43 | 198.35 | 36 | 70.79% | 29.21% | 40 | 57.89% | 23.89% | 18.22% | 74 |
| S | AMEX Pharmaceutical Index | 81.68 | 37 | 1.74 | 142.38 | 80 | 63.58% | 36.42% | 87 | 51.93% | 29.74% | 18.32% | 73 |
| | NASDAQ Composite | 81.32 | 38 | 2.19 | 177.69 | 53 | 68.54% | 31.46% | 65 | 55.74% | 25.58% | 18.68% | 72 |
| S | S&P Telecomm Sector | 80.79 | 39 | 1.71 | 138.25 | 84 | 63.06% | 36.94% | 89 | 50.95% | 29.84% | 19.21% | 71 |
| | Russell 1000 Growth | 80.55 | 40 | 2.61 | 209.84 | 23 | 72.16% | 27.84% | 30 | 58.13% | 22.43% | 19.45% | 70 |
| | AMEX Composite | 80.49 | 41 | 3.38 | 271.90 | 6 | 76.98% | 23.02% | 8 | 61.97% | 18.53% | 19.51% | 69 |
| I | Chile IPSA | 80.43 | 42 | 1.63 | 131.41 | 88 | 61.97% | 38.03% | 95 | 49.84% | 30.58% | 19.57% | 68 |
| I | Peru Lima General | 80.33 | 43 | 1.78 | 142.75 | 79 | 63.81% | 36.19% | 86 | 51.26% | 29.07% | 19.67% | 67 |
| S | S&P Cons Staples Sector | 80.19 | 44 | 2.49 | 199.75 | 34 | 71.17% | 28.83% | 39 | 57.07% | 23.12% | 19.81% | 66 |
| | Dow Jones Composite | 78.81 | 45 | 2.49 | 196.51 | 37 | 71.23% | 28.77% | 38 | 56.13% | 22.68% | 21.19% | 65 |
| | S&P 400 Index | 78.80 | 46 | 3.01 | 237.45 | 13 | 74.59% | 25.41% | 17 | 58.78% | 20.02% | 21.20% | 64 |
| | Russell 1000 Value | 78.58 | 47 | 2.26 | 177.52 | 54 | 69.06% | 30.94% | 56 | 54.27% | 24.31% | 21.42% | 63 |
| | S&P 1500 INDEX | 78.57 | 48 | 2.58 | 202.70 | 31 | 71.79% | 28.21% | 32 | 56.41% | 22.16% | 21.43% | 62 |
| I | Netherlands AEX General | 78.28 | 49 | 2.45 | 191.77 | 43 | 70.74% | 29.26% | 42 | 55.37% | 22.90% | 21.72% | 61 |
| I | Belgium BEL-20 | 78.16 | 50 | 2.15 | 168.18 | 59 | 68.21% | 31.79% | 68 | 53.32% | 24.84% | 21.84% | 60 |
| I | Spain Madrid General | 78.14 | 51 | 1.79 | 140.12 | 82 | 64.01% | 35.99% | 85 | 50.02% | 28.12% | 21.86% | 59 |

*(Continued)*

415

**TABLE B.1** Continued

| | | Trendiness One | | | | | | Trendiness Two | | | Trendless Analysis | | | |
| | | Trendiness | | Avg. | Up Trendiness | | While in Trend | | | | | | | |
| | Index Name | Average | Rank | U/D | WtdAvg | Rank | Up/Tot | Dn/Tot | Up Rank | Up | Down | Trendless | Rank |
|---|---|---|---|---|---|---|---|---|---|---|---|---|---|
| I | Israel TA-100 | 77.53 | 52 | 2.57 | 199.63 | 35 | 71.90% | 28.10% | 31 | 55.75% | 21.78% | 22.47% | 58 |
| I | S&P/TSX 60 (Canada) | 77.47 | 53 | 2.50 | 193.45 | 40 | 71.32% | 28.68% | 37 | 55.25% | 22.21% | 22.53% | 57 |
| S | S&P Materials Sector | 77.15 | 54 | 2.01 | 154.98 | 72 | 66.66% | 33.34% | 74 | 51.43% | 25.72% | 22.85% | 56 |
| S | S&P Cons Discretionary Sector | 76.96 | 55 | 2.71 | 208.53 | 25 | 73.02% | 26.98% | 24 | 56.20% | 20.76% | 23.04% | 55 |
| | Dow Jones Stoxx | 76.85 | 56 | 2.53 | 194.67 | 39 | 71.39% | 28.61% | 35 | 54.86% | 21.99% | 23.15% | 54 |
| I | Austria ATX | 76.85 | 57 | 2.24 | 172.31 | 55 | 68.65% | 31.35% | 61 | 52.76% | 24.09% | 23.15% | 53 |
| I | Venezuela IBC | 76.70 | 58 | 1.70 | 130.78 | 89 | 63.02% | 36.98% | 90 | 48.34% | 28.37% | 23.30% | 52 |
| I | Japan Nikkei 225 | 75.65 | 59 | 1.95 | 147.74 | 75 | 65.66% | 34.34% | 80 | 49.67% | 25.98% | 24.35% | 51 |
| I | Global Dow | 74.55 | 60 | 1.95 | 145.64 | 77 | 65.57% | 34.43% | 81 | 48.88% | 25.67% | 25.45% | 50 |
| C | AMEX Oil Index | 74.51 | 61 | 1.96 | 146.23 | 76 | 66.24% | 33.76% | 77 | 49.36% | 25.15% | 25.49% | 49 |
| I | Philippines PSE Composite | 74.47 | 62 | 1.66 | 123.72 | 93 | 62.28% | 37.72% | 93 | 46.38% | 28.09% | 25.53% | 48 |
| S | S&P Financials Sector | 74.40 | 63 | 1.73 | 128.41 | 91 | 63.20% | 36.80% | 88 | 47.03% | 27.38% | 25.60% | 47 |
| I | Indonesia Jakarta Composite | 73.88 | 64 | 2.04 | 150.64 | 73 | 66.95% | 33.05% | 72 | 49.46% | 24.42% | 26.12% | 46 |
| I | Egypt CMA | 73.73 | 65 | 2.82 | 207.83 | 27 | 73.69% | 26.31% | 22 | 54.33% | 19.40% | 26.27% | 45 |
| I | Norway Oslo All Share Composite | 73.70 | 66 | 3.74 | 275.40 | 5 | 78.82% | 21.18% | 5 | 58.09% | 15.61% | 26.30% | 44 |
| I | Thailand SET | 73.51 | 67 | 1.88 | 138.19 | 85 | 64.99% | 35.01% | 83 | 47.77% | 25.73% | 26.49% | 43 |
| I | Johannesburg All Shares | 72.84 | 68 | 4.53 | 330.27 | 1 | 81.41% | 18.59% | 2 | 59.30% | 13.54% | 27.16% | 42 |
| S | S&P 500 Equal Weight | 72.75 | 69 | 2.19 | 158.98 | 69 | 68.66% | 31.34% | 60 | 49.95% | 22.80% | 27.25% | 41 |
| C | Silver Base Price Handy & Harman | 72.55 | 70 | 1.44 | 104.30 | 100 | 58.78% | 41.22% | 97 | 42.65% | 29.91% | 27.45% | 40 |
| I | Denmark Copenhagen 20 | 72.47 | 71 | 2.76 | 200.23 | 32 | 72.37% | 27.63% | 28 | 52.45% | 20.03% | 27.53% | 39 |
| I | S&P 600 Index | 71.77 | 72 | 2.55 | 183.16 | 50 | 71.37% | 28.63% | 36 | 51.23% | 20.55% | 28.23% | 38 |
| I | EURONEXT 100 | 70.41 | 73 | 3.67 | 258.45 | 10 | 77.86% | 22.14% | 7 | 54.82% | 15.59% | 29.59% | 37 |
| S | S&P Technology Sector | 70.34 | 74 | 2.05 | 144.50 | 78 | 66.92% | 33.08% | 73 | 47.07% | 23.27% | 29.66% | 36 |
| I | Viet Nam Index | 70.31 | 75 | 1.08 | 75.84 | 103 | 51.69% | 48.31% | 106 | 36.34% | 33.97% | 29.69% | 35 |
| I | Dow Jones Euro Stoxx | 70.26 | 76 | 2.37 | 166.81 | 60 | 69.78% | 30.22% | 50 | 49.03% | 21.23% | 29.74% | 34 |

| | | | | | | | | | | | | | |
|---|---|---|---|---|---|---|---|---|---|---|---|---|---|
| I | Swedish OMX 30 | 77 | 70.18 | 2.72 | 190.76 | 45 | 72.97% | 27.03% | 25 | 51.21% | 18.97% | 29.82% | 33 |
| I | Hong Kong Hang Seng | 78 | 69.98 | 2.22 | 155.21 | 70 | 68.60% | 31.40% | 63 | 48.01% | 21.97% | 30.02% | 32 |
| I | Czech Republic PX | 79 | 69.81 | 1.65 | 115.13 | 96 | 62.22% | 37.78% | 94 | 43.44% | 26.38% | 30.19% | 31 |
| I | France CAC 40 | 80 | 69.78 | 2.45 | 171.01 | 57 | 70.69% | 29.31% | 43 | 49.32% | 20.45% | 30.22% | 30 |
| | Dow Jones Transport | 81 | 69.39 | 2.24 | 155.18 | 71 | 68.29% | 31.71% | 67 | 47.39% | 22.00% | 30.61% | 29 |
| I | Taiwan Weighted | 82 | 69.20 | 1.82 | 125.61 | 92 | 64.06% | 35.94% | 84 | 44.33% | 24.87% | 30.80% | 28 |
| S | Morgan Stanley Cyclical Index | 83 | 69.12 | 2.32 | 160.59 | 67 | 68.48% | 31.52% | 66 | 47.33% | 21.78% | 30.88% | 27 |
| I | Mexico IPC | 84 | 68.41 | 3.35 | 229.30 | 17 | 76.30% | 23.70% | 11 | 52.19% | 16.21% | 31.59% | 26 |
| I | Germany DAX | 85 | 67.81 | 3.44 | 233.49 | 14 | 76.73% | 23.27% | 9 | 52.03% | 15.78% | 32.19% | 25 |
| I | Ibex 35 | 86 | 67.58 | 2.42 | 163.35 | 63 | 69.99% | 30.01% | 49 | 47.30% | 20.28% | 32.42% | 24 |
| I | Pakistan Karachi 100 | 87 | 67.51 | 2.06 | 139.15 | 83 | 66.54% | 33.46% | 76 | 44.92% | 22.59% | 32.49% | 23 |
| I | South Korea Seoul Composite | 88 | 67.39 | 1.59 | 107.17 | 99 | 61.19% | 38.81% | 96 | 41.24% | 26.15% | 32.61% | 22 |
| | DJ Wilshire US Small Cap | 89 | 66.74 | 3.12 | 208.53 | 26 | 74.27% | 25.73% | 19 | 49.57% | 17.18% | 33.26% | 21 |
| I | Singapore Straits Times | 90 | 65.83 | 1.67 | 109.63 | 97 | 62.30% | 37.70% | 92 | 41.01% | 24.82% | 34.17% | 20 |
| | NASDAQ 100 | 91 | 65.28 | 2.86 | 186.56 | 48 | 73.88% | 26.12% | 20 | 48.23% | 17.05% | 34.72% | 19 |
| I | Dow Jones Euro Stoxx 50 | 92 | 64.79 | 2.51 | 162.47 | 65 | 70.54% | 29.46% | 45 | 45.71% | 19.09% | 35.21% | 18 |
| S | DJ Wilshire REIT Total Return | 93 | 64.34 | 4.14 | 266.38 | 7 | 79.56% | 20.44% | 3 | 51.19% | 13.15% | 35.66% | 17 |
| | Italy FTSE MIB Index | 94 | 64.28 | 2.48 | 159.60 | 68 | 70.12% | 29.88% | 48 | 45.07% | 19.21% | 35.72% | 16 |
| S | Dow Jones Wilshire REIT | 95 | 64.13 | 3.46 | 221.59 | 21 | 76.41% | 23.59% | 10 | 49.00% | 15.13% | 35.87% | 15 |
| I | Finland HSE General Index | 96 | 63.57 | 2.09 | 133.08 | 86 | 67.49% | 32.51% | 69 | 42.90% | 20.67% | 36.43% | 14 |
| I | China Shanghai Composite | 97 | 62.87 | 1.17 | 73.82 | 104 | 54.10% | 45.90% | 103 | 34.01% | 28.86% | 37.13% | 13 |
| I | Greece General Share | 98 | 62.60 | 1.27 | 79.60 | 102 | 55.26% | 44.74% | 101 | 34.59% | 28.01% | 37.40% | 12 |
| I | S&P CNX NIFTY (India) | 99 | 62.26 | 2.88 | 179.06 | 51 | 73.86% | 26.14% | 21 | 45.99% | 16.27% | 37.74% | 11 |
| I | Norway Oslo OBX Top 25 | 100 | 60.77 | 4.88 | 296.50 | 3 | 82.86% | 17.14% | 1 | 50.36% | 10.41% | 39.23% | 10 |
| I | India BSE 30 | 101 | 57.04 | 2.29 | 130.77 | 90 | 68.93% | 31.07% | 57 | 39.32% | 17.72% | 42.96% | 9 |
| I | Argentina MerVal | 102 | 50.48 | 2.41 | 121.53 | 94 | 70.23% | 29.77% | 46 | 35.45% | 15.03% | 49.52% | 8 |
| C | Gold Base Price Handy & Harman | 103 | 49.21 | 1.20 | 59.26 | 105 | 54.64% | 45.36% | 102 | 26.89% | 22.32% | 50.79% | 7 |
| I | Hanoi SE Index | 104 | 49.16 | 0.44 | 21.73 | 109 | 31.12% | 68.88% | 109 | 15.30% | 33.86% | 50.84% | 6 |
| I | Brazil Bovespa | 105 | 48.29 | 3.44 | 165.90 | 61 | 74.77% | 25.23% | 15 | 36.11% | 12.18% | 51.71% | 5 |
| C | Gold Mining Stocks | 106 | 48.18 | 1.07 | 51.61 | 106 | 52.05% | 47.95% | 104 | 25.08% | 23.10% | 51.82% | 4 |
| C | Gold and Silver Mining | 107 | 38.35 | 0.90 | 34.66 | 107 | 48.11% | 51.89% | 108 | 18.45% | 19.90% | 61.65% | 3 |

*(Continued)*

**TABLE B.1**   Continued

| | Trendiness One | | | | | Trendiness Two | | | | | | |
| | Trendiness | | Avg. | Up Trendiness | | While in Trend | | | Trendless Analysis | | | |
| Index Name | Average | Rank | U/D | WtdAvg | Rank | Up/Tot | Dn/Tot | Up Rank | Up | Down | Trendless | Rank |
|---|---|---|---|---|---|---|---|---|---|---|---|---|
| C Gold Bugs (AMEX) | 32.56 | 108 | 1.04 | 33.76 | 108 | 51.30% | 48.70% | 107 | 16.70% | 15.85% | 67.44% | 2 |
| I Turkey ISE National-100 | 32.02 | 109 | 4.43 | 141.83 | 81 | 79.17% | 20.83% | 4 | 25.35% | 6.67% | 67.98% | 1 |
| **Statistics** | | | | | | | | | | | | |
| Mean | 74.81 | | 2.33 | 174.47 | | 68.04% | 31.96% | | 51.10% | 23.71% | 25.19% | |
| Average Deviation | 9.27 | | 0.56 | 44.70 | | 5.46% | 5.46% | | 7.42% | 4.39% | 9.27% | |
| Median | 76.96 | | 2.27 | 172.31 | | 69.21% | 30.79% | | 52.03% | 23.27% | 23.04% | |
| Minimum | 32.02 | | 0.44 | 21.73 | | 31.12% | 17.14% | | 15.30% | 6.67% | 4.84% | |
| Maximum | 95.16 | | 4.88 | 330.27 | | 82.86% | 68.88% | | 68.80% | 45.82% | 67.98% | |
| Sigma | 12.25 | | 0.77 | 58.11 | | 7.66% | 7.66% | | 10.28% | 5.92% | 12.25% | |
| Geometric Mean | 73.59 | | 2.20 | 161.93 | | 67.53% | 31.15% | | 49.70% | 22.93% | 22.50% | |
| Harmonic Mean | 72.03 | | 2.04 | 142.11 | | 66.92% | 30.41% | | 47.64% | 22.01% | 19.90% | |
| Kurtosis | 2.08 | | 1.30 | 0.52 | | 446.17% | 446.17% | | 245.72% | 191.06% | 207.66% | |
| Skewness | -1.24 | | 0.64 | -0.05 | | -148.50% | 148.50% | | -134.87% | 42.01% | 123.61% | |
| Trimmed Mean—20% | 76.18 | | 2.29 | 174.81 | | 68.78% | 31.22% | | 52.30% | 23.58% | 23.82% | |

418

# All Ranked by Trendiness One Up Trendiness Rank

**TABLE B.2** Up Trendiness Rank

| Trendiness | | Avg. | Up Trendiness | |
|---|---|---|---|---|
| Average | Rank | U/D | WtdAvg | Rank |

| | | Trendiness One | | | | | Trendiness Two | | | | Trendless Analysis | | | |
|---|---|---|---|---|---|---|---|---|---|---|---|---|---|---|
| | | Trendiness | | Avg. | Up Trendiness | | While in Trend | | | | | | | |
| | Index Name | Average | Rank | U/D | WtdAvg | Rank | Up/Tot | Dn/Tot | Up Rank | Up | Down | Trendless | Rank |
| I | Johannesburg All Shares | 72.84 | 68 | 4.53 | 330.27 | 1 | 81.41% | 18.59% | 2 | 59.30% | 13.54% | 27.16% | 42 |
| I | Russell 2000 Value | 87.53 | 11 | 3.69 | 322.90 | 2 | 78.59% | 21.41% | 6 | 68.80% | 18.74% | 12.47% | 99 |
| I | Norway Oslo OBX Top 25 | 60.77 | 100 | 4.88 | 296.50 | 3 | 82.86% | 17.14% | 1 | 50.36% | 10.41% | 39.23% | 10 |
| I | S&P 500 Total Return | 86.90 | 16 | 3.21 | 278.62 | 4 | 76.12% | 23.88% | 12 | 66.15% | 20.75% | 13.10% | 94 |
| I | Norway Oslo All Share Composite | 73.70 | 66 | 3.74 | 275.40 | 5 | 78.82% | 21.18% | 5 | 58.09% | 15.61% | 26.30% | 44 |
| I | AMEX Composite | 80.49 | 41 | 3.38 | 271.90 | 6 | 76.98% | 23.02% | 8 | 61.97% | 18.53% | 19.51% | 69 |
| S | DJ Wilshire REIT Total Return | 64.34 | 93 | 4.14 | 266.38 | 7 | 79.56% | 20.44% | 3 | 51.19% | 13.15% | 35.66% | 17 |
| S | S&P 500 Tot. Ret. Inflation Adj. | 86.25 | 18 | 3.05 | 262.89 | 8 | 75.15% | 24.85% | 13 | 64.82% | 21.43% | 13.75% | 92 |
| S | Morgan Stanley Consumer Index | 87.52 | 12 | 2.96 | 259.01 | 9 | 74.68% | 25.32% | 16 | 65.36% | 22.16% | 12.48% | 98 |
| I | EURONEXT 100 | 70.41 | 73 | 3.67 | 258.45 | 10 | 77.86% | 22.14% | 7 | 54.82% | 15.59% | 29.59% | 37 |
| I | Russell 1000 | 83.72 | 29 | 3.02 | 252.92 | 11 | 75.06% | 24.94% | 14 | 62.84% | 20.88% | 16.28% | 81 |
| I | Russell 3000 | 84.38 | 22 | 2.95 | 248.63 | 12 | 74.56% | 25.44% | 18 | 62.91% | 21.47% | 15.62% | 88 |
| I | S&P 400 Index | 78.80 | 46 | 3.01 | 237.45 | 13 | 74.59% | 25.41% | 17 | 58.78% | 20.02% | 21.20% | 64 |
| I | Germany DAX | 67.81 | 85 | 3.44 | 233.49 | 14 | 76.73% | 23.27% | 9 | 52.03% | 15.78% | 32.19% | 25 |
| S | S&P Energy Sector | 92.31 | 3 | 2.52 | 232.75 | 15 | 71.59% | 28.41% | 33 | 66.08% | 26.23% | 7.69% | 107 |
| I | DJ Wilshire 5000 Composite | 88.07 | 10 | 2.62 | 230.54 | 16 | 72.34% | 27.66% | 29 | 63.70% | 24.36% | 11.93% | 100 |
| I | Mexico IPC | 68.41 | 84 | 3.35 | 229.30 | 17 | 76.30% | 23.70% | 11 | 52.19% | 16.21% | 31.59% | 26 |
| I | Switzerland Swiss Market | 82.10 | 34 | 2.79 | 229.22 | 18 | 73.27% | 26.73% | 23 | 60.16% | 21.94% | 17.90% | 76 |

(*Continued*)

419

**TABLE B.2** Continued

| | Index Name | Trendiness One | | | | | Trendiness Two | | | Trendless Analysis | | | |
|---|---|---|---|---|---|---|---|---|---|---|---|---|---|
| | | Trendiness | | Avg. | Up Trendiness | | While in Trend | | | | | | |
| | | Average | Rank | U/D | WtdAvg | Rank | Up/Tot | Dn/Tot | Up Rank | Up | Down | Trendless | Rank |
| | S&P MIDCAP INDEX | 84.10 | 25 | 2.71 | 228.13 | 19 | 72.86% | 27.14% | 26 | 61.28% | 22.82% | 15.90% | 85 |
| | Major Market Index | 84.49 | 20 | 2.68 | 226.54 | 20 | 72.75% | 27.25% | 27 | 61.47% | 23.02% | 15.51% | 90 |
| S | Dow Jones Wilshire REIT | 64.13 | 95 | 3.46 | 221.59 | 21 | 76.41% | 23.59% | 10 | 49.00% | 15.13% | 35.87% | 15 |
| | NYSE Composite | 89.89 | 8 | 2.41 | 217.05 | 22 | 70.61% | 29.39% | 44 | 63.47% | 26.42% | 10.11% | 102 |
| | Russell 1000 Growth | 80.55 | 40 | 2.61 | 209.84 | 23 | 72.16% | 27.84% | 30 | 58.13% | 22.43% | 19.45% | 70 |
| I | United Kingdom FTSE 100 | 82.77 | 31 | 2.53 | 209.34 | 24 | 71.56% | 28.44% | 34 | 59.23% | 23.54% | 17.23% | 79 |
| S | S&P Cons Discretionary Sector | 76.96 | 55 | 2.71 | 208.53 | 25 | 73.02% | 26.98% | 24 | 56.20% | 20.76% | 23.04% | 55 |
| I | DJ Wilshire U.S. Small Cap | 66.74 | 89 | 3.12 | 208.53 | 26 | 74.27% | 25.73% | 19 | 49.57% | 17.18% | 33.26% | 21 |
| I | Egypt CMA | 73.73 | 65 | 2.82 | 207.83 | 27 | 73.69% | 26.31% | 22 | 54.33% | 19.40% | 26.27% | 45 |
| I | Australia All Ordinaries | 90.94 | 4 | 2.28 | 207.75 | 28 | 69.52% | 30.48% | 52 | 63.22% | 27.71% | 9.06% | 106 |
| | Value Line Index (Arithmetic) | 86.60 | 17 | 2.36 | 204.40 | 29 | 70.19% | 29.81% | 47 | 60.79% | 25.81% | 13.40% | 93 |
| | Dow Jones Utilities | 83.77 | 28 | 2.43 | 203.64 | 30 | 70.76% | 29.24% | 41 | 59.28% | 24.49% | 16.23% | 82 |
| | S&P 1500 INDEX | 78.57 | 48 | 2.58 | 202.70 | 31 | 71.79% | 28.21% | 32 | 56.41% | 22.16% | 21.43% | 62 |
| I | Denmark Copenhagen 20 | 72.47 | 71 | 2.76 | 200.23 | 32 | 72.37% | 27.63% | 28 | 52.45% | 20.03% | 27.53% | 39 |
| | S&P 500 Index | 88.78 | 9 | 2.25 | 199.91 | 33 | 69.21% | 30.79% | 55 | 61.45% | 27.33% | 11.22% | 101 |
| S | S&P Cons Staples Sector | 80.19 | 44 | 2.49 | 199.75 | 34 | 71.17% | 28.83% | 39 | 57.07% | 23.12% | 19.81% | 66 |
| I | Israel TA-100 | 77.53 | 52 | 2.57 | 199.63 | 35 | 71.90% | 28.10% | 31 | 55.75% | 21.78% | 22.47% | 58 |
| I | S&P/TSX 60 CAPPED (Canada) | 81.78 | 36 | 2.43 | 198.35 | 36 | 70.79% | 29.21% | 40 | 57.89% | 23.89% | 18.22% | 74 |
| | Dow Jones Composite | 78.81 | 45 | 2.49 | 196.51 | 37 | 71.23% | 28.77% | 38 | 56.13% | 22.68% | 21.19% | 65 |
| | Dow Industrials 1885 | 86.07 | 19 | 2.27 | 195.02 | 38 | 69.23% | 30.77% | 54 | 59.59% | 26.49% | 13.93% | 91 |
| | Dow Jones Stoxx | 76.85 | 56 | 2.53 | 194.67 | 39 | 71.39% | 28.61% | 35 | 54.86% | 21.99% | 23.15% | 54 |
| I | S&P/TSX 60 (Canada) | 77.47 | 53 | 2.50 | 193.45 | 40 | 71.32% | 28.68% | 37 | 55.25% | 22.21% | 22.53% | 57 |
| S | S&P Healthcare Sector | 86.97 | 15 | 2.21 | 192.24 | 41 | 68.78% | 31.22% | 58 | 59.82% | 27.16% | 13.03% | 95 |
| I | S&P/TSX Composite (Canada) | 87.29 | 14 | 2.20 | 191.92 | 42 | 68.58% | 31.42% | 64 | 59.86% | 27.43% | 12.71% | 96 |
| I | Netherlands AEX General | 78.28 | 49 | 2.45 | 191.77 | 43 | 70.74% | 29.26% | 42 | 55.37% | 22.90% | 21.72% | 61 |

| | | | | | | | | | | | | | |
|---|---|---|---|---|---|---|---|---|---|---|---|---|---|
| S | S&P Utilities Sector | 87.37 | 13 | 2.19 | 191.14 | 44 | 68.61% | 31.39% | 62 | 59.95% | 27.42% | 12.63% | 97 |
| I | Swedish OMX 30 | 70.18 | 77 | 2.72 | 190.76 | 45 | 72.97% | 27.03% | 25 | 51.21% | 18.97% | 29.82% | 33 |
| | S&P 100 Index | 83.97 | 27 | 2.27 | 190.61 | 46 | 69.33% | 30.67% | 53 | 58.22% | 25.76% | 16.03% | 83 |
| | Russell 2000 Growth | 82.05 | 35 | 2.31 | 189.76 | 47 | 69.62% | 30.38% | 51 | 57.13% | 24.92% | 17.95% | 75 |
| | NASDAQ 100 | 65.28 | 91 | 2.86 | 186.56 | 48 | 73.88% | 26.12% | 20 | 48.23% | 17.05% | 34.72% | 19 |
| I | MSCI EM | 84.27 | 23 | 2.21 | 186.22 | 49 | 68.72% | 31.28% | 59 | 57.92% | 26.36% | 15.73% | 87 |
| I | S&P 600 Index | 71.77 | 72 | 2.55 | 183.16 | 50 | 71.37% | 28.63% | 36 | 51.23% | 20.55% | 28.23% | 38 |
| I | S&P CNX NIFTY (India) | 62.26 | 99 | 2.88 | 179.06 | 51 | 73.86% | 26.14% | 21 | 45.99% | 16.27% | 37.74% | 11 |
| I | MSCI EAFE | 89.91 | 7 | 1.99 | 178.96 | 52 | 66.56% | 33.44% | 75 | 59.85% | 30.06% | 10.09% | 103 |
| | NASDAQ Composite | 81.32 | 38 | 2.19 | 177.69 | 53 | 68.54% | 31.46% | 65 | 55.74% | 25.58% | 18.68% | 72 |
| | Russell 1000 Value | 78.58 | 47 | 2.26 | 177.52 | 54 | 69.06% | 30.94% | 56 | 54.27% | 24.31% | 21.42% | 63 |
| I | Austria ATX | 76.85 | 57 | 2.24 | 172.31 | 55 | 68.65% | 31.35% | 61 | 52.76% | 24.09% | 23.15% | 53 |
| | Russell 2000 | 83.02 | 30 | 2.07 | 171.63 | 56 | 67.34% | 32.66% | 70 | 55.91% | 27.11% | 16.98% | 80 |
| I | France CAC 40 | 69.78 | 80 | 2.45 | 171.01 | 57 | 70.69% | 29.31% | 43 | 49.32% | 20.45% | 30.22% | 30 |
| S | S&P Industrials Sector | 82.49 | 33 | 2.05 | 169.05 | 58 | 66.98% | 33.02% | 71 | 55.25% | 27.24% | 17.51% | 77 |
| I | Belgium BEL-20 | 78.16 | 50 | 2.15 | 168.18 | 59 | 68.21% | 31.79% | 68 | 53.32% | 24.84% | 21.84% | 60 |
| I | Dow Jones Euro Stoxx | 70.26 | 76 | 2.37 | 166.81 | 60 | 69.78% | 30.22% | 50 | 49.03% | 21.23% | 29.74% | 34 |
| I | Brazil Bovespa | 48.29 | 105 | 3.44 | 165.90 | 61 | 74.77% | 25.23% | 15 | 36.11% | 12.18% | 51.71% | 5 |
| S | Healthcare Index (S&P) | 84.22 | 24 | 1.94 | 163.54 | 62 | 66.04% | 33.96% | 79 | 55.62% | 28.60% | 15.78% | 86 |
| I | Ibex 35 | 67.58 | 86 | 2.42 | 163.36 | 63 | 69.99% | 30.01% | 49 | 47.30% | 20.28% | 32.42% | 24 |
| | Value Line Index (Geometric) | 84.44 | 21 | 1.93 | 162.59 | 64 | 65.56% | 34.44% | 82 | 55.36% | 29.09% | 15.56% | 89 |
| I | Dow Jones Euro Stoxx 50 | 64.79 | 92 | 2.51 | 162.47 | 65 | 70.54% | 29.46% | 45 | 45.71% | 19.09% | 35.21% | 18 |
| I | Malaysia KLSE Composite | 82.64 | 32 | 1.96 | 162.02 | 66 | 66.08% | 33.92% | 78 | 54.61% | 28.04% | 17.36% | 78 |
| S | Morgan Stanley Cyclical Index | 69.12 | 83 | 2.32 | 160.59 | 67 | 68.48% | 31.52% | 66 | 47.33% | 21.78% | 30.88% | 27 |
| I | Italy FTSE MIB Index | 64.28 | 94 | 2.48 | 159.60 | 68 | 70.12% | 29.88% | 48 | 45.07% | 19.21% | 35.72% | 16 |
| | S&P 500 Equal Weight | 72.75 | 69 | 2.19 | 158.98 | 69 | 68.66% | 31.34% | 60 | 49.95% | 22.80% | 27.25% | 41 |
| I | Hong Kong Hang Seng | 69.98 | 78 | 2.22 | 155.21 | 70 | 68.60% | 31.40% | 63 | 48.01% | 21.97% | 30.02% | 32 |
| | Dow Jones Transport | 69.39 | 81 | 2.24 | 155.18 | 71 | 68.29% | 31.71% | 67 | 47.39% | 22.00% | 30.61% | 29 |
| S | S&P Materials Sector | 77.15 | 54 | 2.01 | 154.98 | 72 | 66.66% | 33.34% | 74 | 51.43% | 25.72% | 22.85% | 56 |
| I | Indonesia Jakarta Composite | 73.88 | 64 | 2.04 | 150.64 | 73 | 66.95% | 33.05% | 72 | 49.46% | 24.42% | 26.12% | 46 |
| I | Chile IGPA General Index | 90.17 | 6 | 1.66 | 149.32 | 74 | 62.34% | 37.66% | 91 | 56.21% | 33.95% | 9.83% | 104 |
| I | Japan Nikkei 225 | 75.65 | 59 | 1.95 | 147.74 | 75 | 65.66% | 34.34% | 80 | 49.67% | 25.98% | 24.35% | 51 |

*(Continued)*

**TABLE B.2** Continued

| | | Trendiness One | | | | | Trendiness Two | | | Trendless Analysis | | | |
| | | Trendiness | | Avg. | Up Trendiness | | While in Trend | | | | | | |
| Index Name | | Average | Rank | U/D | WtdAvg | Rank | Up/Tot | Dn/Tot | Up Rank | Up | Down | Trendless | Rank |
|---|---|---|---|---|---|---|---|---|---|---|---|---|---|
| C | AMEX Oil Index | 74.51 | 61 | 1.96 | 146.23 | 76 | 66.24% | 33.76% | 77 | 49.36% | 25.15% | 25.49% | 49 |
| I | Global Dow | 74.55 | 60 | 1.95 | 145.64 | 77 | 65.57% | 34.43% | 81 | 48.88% | 25.67% | 25.45% | 50 |
| S | S&P Technology Sector | 70.34 | 74 | 2.05 | 144.50 | 78 | 66.92% | 33.08% | 73 | 47.07% | 23.27% | 29.66% | 36 |
| I | Peru Lima General | 80.33 | 43 | 1.78 | 142.75 | 79 | 63.81% | 36.19% | 86 | 51.26% | 29.07% | 19.67% | 67 |
| S | AMEX Pharmaceutical Index | 81.68 | 37 | 1.74 | 142.38 | 80 | 63.58% | 36.42% | 87 | 51.93% | 29.74% | 18.32% | 73 |
| I | Turkey ISE National-100 | 32.02 | 109 | 4.43 | 141.83 | 81 | 79.17% | 20.83% | 4 | 25.35% | 6.67% | 67.98% | 1 |
| I | Spain Madrid General | 78.14 | 51 | 1.79 | 140.12 | 82 | 64.01% | 35.99% | 85 | 50.02% | 28.12% | 21.86% | 59 |
| I | Pakistan Karachi 100 | 67.51 | 87 | 2.06 | 139.15 | 83 | 66.54% | 33.46% | 76 | 44.92% | 22.59% | 32.49% | 23 |
| S | S&P Telecomm Sector | 80.79 | 39 | 1.71 | 138.25 | 84 | 63.06% | 36.94% | 89 | 50.95% | 29.84% | 19.21% | 71 |
| I | Thailand SET | 73.51 | 67 | 1.88 | 138.19 | 85 | 64.99% | 35.01% | 83 | 47.77% | 25.73% | 26.49% | 43 |
| I | Finland HSE General Index | 63.57 | 96 | 2.09 | 133.08 | 86 | 67.49% | 32.51% | 69 | 42.90% | 20.67% | 36.43% | 14 |
| C | CRB Index | 92.69 | 2 | 1.42 | 131.59 | 87 | 58.45% | 41.55% | 98 | 54.17% | 38.51% | 7.31% | 108 |
| I | Chile IPSA | 80.43 | 42 | 1.63 | 131.41 | 88 | 61.97% | 38.03% | 95 | 49.84% | 30.58% | 19.57% | 68 |
| I | Venezuela IBC | 76.70 | 58 | 1.70 | 130.78 | 89 | 63.02% | 36.98% | 90 | 48.34% | 28.37% | 23.30% | 52 |
| I | India BSE 30 | 57.04 | 101 | 2.29 | 130.77 | 90 | 68.93% | 31.07% | 57 | 39.32% | 17.72% | 42.96% | 9 |
| S | S&P Financials Sector | 74.40 | 63 | 1.73 | 128.41 | 91 | 63.20% | 36.80% | 88 | 47.03% | 27.38% | 25.60% | 47 |
| I | Taiwan Weighted | 69.20 | 82 | 1.82 | 125.61 | 92 | 64.06% | 35.94% | 84 | 44.33% | 24.87% | 30.80% | 28 |
| I | Philippines PSE Composite | 74.47 | 62 | 1.66 | 123.72 | 93 | 62.28% | 37.72% | 93 | 46.38% | 28.09% | 25.53% | 48 |
| I | Argentina MerVal | 50.48 | 102 | 2.41 | 121.53 | 94 | 70.23% | 29.77% | 46 | 35.45% | 15.03% | 49.52% | 8 |
| I | Slovakia SAX | 90.31 | 5 | 1.28 | 115.54 | 95 | 56.08% | 43.92% | 100 | 50.65% | 39.67% | 9.69% | 105 |
| I | Czech Republic PX | 69.81 | 79 | 1.65 | 115.13 | 96 | 62.22% | 37.78% | 94 | 43.44% | 26.38% | 30.19% | 31 |
| I | Singapore Straits Times | 65.83 | 90 | 1.67 | 109.63 | 97 | 62.30% | 37.70% | 92 | 41.01% | 24.82% | 34.17% | 20 |
| I | Sri Lanka All Share | 83.98 | 26 | 1.29 | 108.17 | 98 | 56.21% | 43.79% | 99 | 47.21% | 36.77% | 16.02% | 84 |
| I | South Korea Seoul Composite | 67.39 | 88 | 1.59 | 107.17 | 99 | 61.19% | 38.81% | 96 | 41.24% | 26.15% | 32.61% | 22 |

| | | | | | | | | | | | | |
|---|---|---|---|---|---|---|---|---|---|---|---|---|
| C | Silver Base Price Handy & Harman | 72.55 | 70 | 1.44 | 104.30 | 100 | 58.78% | 41.22% | 97 | 42.65% | 29.91% | 27.45% | 40 |
| C | U.S. Dollar Index | 95.16 | 1 | 1.08 | 102.65 | 101 | 51.85% | 48.15% | 105 | 49.34% | 45.82% | 4.84% | 109 |
| I | Greece General Share | 62.60 | 98 | 1.27 | 79.60 | 102 | 55.26% | 44.74% | 101 | 34.59% | 28.01% | 37.40% | 12 |
| I | Viet Nam Index | 70.31 | 75 | 1.08 | 75.84 | 103 | 51.69% | 48.31% | 106 | 36.34% | 33.97% | 29.69% | 35 |
| I | China Shanghai Composite | 62.87 | 97 | 1.17 | 73.82 | 104 | 54.10% | 45.90% | 103 | 34.01% | 28.86% | 37.13% | 13 |
| C | Gold Base Price Handy & Harman | 49.21 | 103 | 1.20 | 59.26 | 105 | 54.64% | 45.36% | 102 | 26.89% | 22.32% | 50.79% | 7 |
| C | Gold Mining Stocks | 48.18 | 106 | 1.07 | 51.61 | 106 | 52.05% | 47.95% | 104 | 25.08% | 23.10% | 51.82% | 4 |
| C | Gold and Silver Mining | 38.35 | 107 | 0.90 | 34.66 | 107 | 48.11% | 51.89% | 108 | 18.45% | 19.90% | 61.65% | 3 |
| C | Gold Bugs (AMEX) | 32.56 | 108 | 1.04 | 33.76 | 108 | 51.30% | 48.70% | 107 | 16.70% | 15.85% | 67.44% | 2 |
| I | Hanoi SE Index | 49.16 | 104 | 0.44 | 21.73 | 109 | 31.12% | 68.88% | 109 | 15.30% | 33.86% | 50.84% | 6 |

**Statistics**

| | | | | | | | | |
|---|---|---|---|---|---|---|---|---|
| Mean | 74.81 | 2.33 | 174.47 | 68.04% | 31.96% | 51.10% | 23.71% | 25.19% |
| Average Deviation | 9.27 | 0.56 | 44.70 | 5.46% | 5.46% | 7.42% | 4.39% | 9.27% |
| Median | 76.96 | 2.27 | 172.31 | 69.21% | 30.79% | 52.03% | 23.27% | 23.04% |
| Minimum | 32.02 | 0.44 | 21.73 | 31.12% | 17.14% | 15.30% | 6.67% | 4.84% |
| Maximum | 95.16 | 4.88 | 330.27 | 82.86% | 68.88% | 68.80% | 45.82% | 67.98% |
| Sigma | 12.25 | 0.77 | 58.11 | 7.66% | 7.66% | 10.28% | 5.92% | 12.25% |
| Geometric Mean | 73.59 | 2.20 | 161.93 | 67.53% | 31.15% | 49.70% | 22.93% | 22.50% |
| Harmonic Mean | 72.03 | 2.04 | 142.11 | 66.92% | 30.41% | 47.64% | 22.01% | 19.90% |
| Kurtosis | 2.08 | 1.30 | 0.52 | 446.17% | 446.17% | 245.72% | 191.06% | 207.66% |
| Skewness | −1.24 | 0.64 | −0.05 | −148.50% | 148.50% | −134.87% | 42.01% | 123.61% |
| Trimmed Mean—20% | 76.18 | 2.29 | 174.81 | 68.78% | 31.22% | 52.30% | 23.58% | 23.82% |

All Ranked by Trendiness Two Up Rank

**TABLE B.3**  Trendiness Two Up Rank

| | While in Trend | |
|---|---|---|
| Up/Tot | Dn/Tot | Up Rank |

| | Trendiness One | | | | | Trendiness Two | | | | | | |
|---|---|---|---|---|---|---|---|---|---|---|---|---|
| | Trendiness | | Avg. | Up Trendiness | | While in Trend | | | Trendless Analysis | | | |
| Index Name | Average | Rank | U/D | WtdAvg | Rank | Up/Tot | Dn/Tot | Up Rank | Up | Down | Trendless | Rank |
| I Norway Oslo OBX Top 25 | 60.77 | 100 | 4.88 | 296.50 | 3 | 82.86% | 17.14% | 1 | 50.36% | 10.41% | 39.23% | 10 |
| I Johannesburg All Shares | 72.84 | 68 | 4.53 | 330.27 | 1 | 81.41% | 18.59% | 2 | 59.30% | 13.54% | 27.16% | 42 |
| S DJ Wilshire REIT Total Return | 64.34 | 93 | 4.14 | 266.38 | 7 | 79.56% | 20.44% | 3 | 51.19% | 13.15% | 35.66% | 17 |
| I Turkey ISE National-100 | 32.02 | 109 | 4.43 | 141.83 | 81 | 79.17% | 20.83% | 4 | 25.35% | 6.67% | 67.98% | 1 |
| I Norway Oslo All Share Composite | 73.70 | 66 | 3.74 | 275.40 | 5 | 78.82% | 21.18% | 5 | 58.09% | 15.61% | 26.30% | 44 |
| I Russell 2000 Value | 87.53 | 11 | 3.69 | 322.90 | 2 | 78.59% | 21.41% | 6 | 68.80% | 18.74% | 12.47% | 99 |
| I EURONEXT 100 | 70.41 | 73 | 3.67 | 258.45 | 10 | 77.86% | 22.14% | 7 | 54.82% | 15.59% | 29.59% | 37 |
| AMEX Composite | 80.49 | 41 | 3.38 | 271.90 | 6 | 76.98% | 23.02% | 8 | 61.97% | 18.53% | 19.51% | 69 |
| I Germany DAX | 67.81 | 85 | 3.44 | 233.49 | 14 | 76.73% | 23.27% | 9 | 52.03% | 15.78% | 32.19% | 25 |
| S Dow Jones Wilshire REIT | 64.13 | 95 | 3.46 | 221.59 | 21 | 76.41% | 23.59% | 10 | 49.00% | 15.13% | 35.87% | 15 |
| I Mexico IPC | 68.41 | 84 | 3.35 | 229.30 | 17 | 76.30% | 23.70% | 11 | 52.19% | 16.21% | 31.59% | 26 |
| S&P 500 Total Return | 86.90 | 16 | 3.21 | 278.62 | 4 | 76.12% | 23.88% | 12 | 66.15% | 20.75% | 13.10% | 94 |
| S&P 500 Tot Ret Inflation Adj. | 86.25 | 18 | 3.05 | 262.89 | 8 | 75.15% | 24.85% | 13 | 64.82% | 21.43% | 13.75% | 92 |
| Russell 1000 | 83.72 | 29 | 3.02 | 252.92 | 11 | 75.06% | 24.94% | 14 | 62.84% | 20.88% | 16.28% | 81 |
| I Brazil Bovespa | 48.29 | 105 | 3.44 | 165.90 | 61 | 74.77% | 25.23% | 15 | 36.11% | 12.18% | 51.71% | 5 |
| S Morgan Stanley Consumer Index | 87.52 | 12 | 2.96 | 259.01 | 9 | 74.68% | 25.32% | 16 | 65.36% | 22.16% | 12.48% | 98 |
| S&P 400 Index | 78.80 | 46 | 3.01 | 237.45 | 13 | 74.59% | 25.41% | 17 | 58.78% | 20.02% | 21.20% | 64 |
| Russell 3000 | 84.38 | 22 | 2.95 | 248.63 | 12 | 74.56% | 25.44% | 18 | 62.91% | 21.47% | 15.62% | 88 |

| | Index | | | | | | | | | | |
|---|---|---|---|---|---|---|---|---|---|---|---|
| | DJ Wilshire U.S. Small Cap | 66.74 | 89 | 208.53 | 26 | 74.27% | 25.73% | 19 | 49.57% | 17.18% | 33.26% | 21 |
| | NASDAQ 100 | 65.28 | 91 | 186.56 | 48 | 73.88% | 26.12% | 20 | 48.23% | 17.05% | 34.72% | 19 |
| I | S&P CNX NIFTY (India) | 62.26 | 99 | 179.06 | 51 | 73.86% | 26.14% | 21 | 45.99% | 16.27% | 37.74% | 11 |
| I | Egypt CMA | 73.73 | 65 | 207.83 | 27 | 73.69% | 26.31% | 22 | 54.33% | 19.40% | 26.27% | 45 |
| I | Switzerland Swiss Market | 82.10 | 34 | 229.22 | 18 | 73.27% | 26.73% | 23 | 60.16% | 21.94% | 17.90% | 76 |
| S | S&P Cons Discretionary Sector | 76.96 | 55 | 208.53 | 25 | 73.02% | 26.98% | 24 | 56.20% | 20.76% | 23.04% | 55 |
| I | Swedish OMX 30 | 70.18 | 77 | 190.76 | 45 | 72.97% | 27.03% | 25 | 51.21% | 18.97% | 29.82% | 33 |
| | S&P MIDCAP INDEX | 84.10 | 25 | 228.13 | 19 | 72.86% | 27.14% | 26 | 61.28% | 22.82% | 15.90% | 85 |
| | Major Market Index | 84.49 | 20 | 226.54 | 20 | 72.75% | 27.25% | 27 | 61.47% | 23.02% | 15.51% | 90 |
| I | Denmark Copenhagen 20 | 72.47 | 71 | 200.23 | 32 | 72.37% | 27.63% | 28 | 52.45% | 20.03% | 27.53% | 39 |
| | DJ Wilshire 5000 Composite | 88.07 | 10 | 230.54 | 16 | 72.34% | 27.66% | 29 | 63.70% | 24.36% | 11.93% | 100 |
| | Russell 1000 Growth | 80.55 | 40 | 209.84 | 23 | 72.16% | 27.84% | 30 | 58.13% | 22.43% | 19.45% | 70 |
| I | Israel TA-100 | 77.53 | 52 | 199.63 | 35 | 71.90% | 28.10% | 31 | 55.75% | 21.78% | 22.47% | 58 |
| | S&P 1500 INDEX | 78.57 | 48 | 202.70 | 31 | 71.79% | 28.21% | 32 | 56.41% | 22.16% | 21.43% | 62 |
| S | S&P Energy Sector | 92.31 | 3 | 232.75 | 15 | 71.59% | 28.41% | 33 | 66.08% | 26.23% | 7.69% | 107 |
| I | United Kingdom FTSE 100 | 82.77 | 31 | 209.34 | 24 | 71.56% | 28.44% | 34 | 59.23% | 23.54% | 17.23% | 79 |
| | Dow Jones Stoxx | 76.85 | 56 | 194.67 | 39 | 71.39% | 28.61% | 35 | 54.86% | 21.99% | 23.15% | 54 |
| | S&P 600 Index | 71.77 | 72 | 183.16 | 50 | 71.37% | 28.63% | 36 | 51.23% | 20.55% | 28.23% | 38 |
| I | S&P/TSX 60 (Canada) | 77.47 | 53 | 193.45 | 40 | 71.32% | 28.68% | 37 | 55.25% | 22.21% | 22.53% | 57 |
| | Dow Jones Composite | 78.81 | 45 | 196.51 | 37 | 71.23% | 28.77% | 38 | 56.13% | 22.68% | 21.19% | 65 |
| S | S&P Cons Staples Sector | 80.19 | 44 | 199.75 | 34 | 71.17% | 28.83% | 39 | 57.07% | 23.12% | 19.81% | 66 |
| S | S&P/TSX 60 CAPPED (Canada) | 81.78 | 36 | 198.35 | 36 | 70.79% | 29.21% | 40 | 57.89% | 23.89% | 18.22% | 74 |
| | Dow Jones Utilities | 83.77 | 28 | 203.64 | 30 | 70.76% | 29.24% | 41 | 59.28% | 24.49% | 16.23% | 82 |
| I | Netherlands AEX General | 78.28 | 49 | 191.77 | 43 | 70.74% | 29.26% | 42 | 55.37% | 22.90% | 21.72% | 61 |
| I | France CAC 40 | 69.78 | 80 | 171.01 | 57 | 70.69% | 29.31% | 43 | 49.32% | 20.45% | 30.22% | 30 |
| | NYSE Composite | 89.89 | 8 | 217.05 | 22 | 70.61% | 29.39% | 44 | 63.47% | 26.42% | 10.11% | 102 |
| I | Dow Jones Euro Stoxx 50 | 64.79 | 92 | 162.47 | 65 | 70.54% | 29.46% | 45 | 45.71% | 19.09% | 35.21% | 18 |
| I | Argentina MerVal | 50.48 | 102 | 121.53 | 94 | 70.23% | 29.77% | 46 | 35.45% | 15.03% | 49.52% | 8 |
| | Value Line Index (Arithmetic) | 86.60 | 17 | 204.40 | 29 | 70.19% | 29.81% | 47 | 60.79% | 25.81% | 13.40% | 93 |
| I | Italy FTSE MIB Index | 64.28 | 94 | 159.60 | 68 | 70.12% | 29.88% | 48 | 45.07% | 19.21% | 35.72% | 16 |
| I | Ibex 35 | 67.58 | 86 | 163.36 | 63 | 69.99% | 30.01% | 49 | 47.30% | 20.28% | 32.42% | 24 |
| I | Dow Jones Euro Stoxx | 70.26 | 76 | 166.81 | 60 | 69.78% | 30.22% | 50 | 49.03% | 21.23% | 29.74% | 34 |

(Continued)

**TABLE B.3** Continued

| | Index Name | Trendiness One — Trendiness — Average | Trendiness One — Trendiness — Rank | Trendiness One — Avg. U/D | Trendiness One — Up Trendiness — WtdAvg | Trendiness One — Up Trendiness — Rank | Trendiness Two — While in Trend — Up/Tot | Trendiness Two — While in Trend — Dn/Tot | Trendiness Two — Up Rank | Trendless Analysis — Up | Trendless Analysis — Down | Trendless Analysis — Trendless | Trendless Analysis — Rank |
|---|---|---|---|---|---|---|---|---|---|---|---|---|---|
| I | Russell 2000 Growth | 82.05 | 35 | 2.31 | 189.76 | 47 | 69.62% | 30.38% | 51 | 57.13% | 24.92% | 17.95% | 75 |
| | Australia All Ordinaries | 90.94 | 4 | 2.28 | 207.75 | 28 | 69.52% | 30.48% | 52 | 63.22% | 27.71% | 9.06% | 106 |
| I | S&P 100 Index | 83.97 | 27 | 2.27 | 190.61 | 46 | 69.33% | 30.67% | 53 | 58.22% | 25.76% | 16.03% | 83 |
| | Dow Industrials 1885 | 86.07 | 19 | 2.27 | 195.02 | 38 | 69.23% | 30.77% | 54 | 59.59% | 26.49% | 13.93% | 91 |
| | S&P 500 Index | 88.78 | 9 | 2.25 | 199.91 | 33 | 69.21% | 30.79% | 55 | 61.45% | 27.33% | 11.22% | 101 |
| | Russell 1000 Value | 78.58 | 47 | 2.26 | 177.52 | 54 | 69.06% | 30.94% | 56 | 54.27% | 24.31% | 21.42% | 63 |
| I | India BSE 30 | 57.04 | 101 | 2.29 | 130.77 | 90 | 68.93% | 31.07% | 57 | 39.32% | 17.72% | 42.96% | 9 |
| S | S&P Healthcare Sector | 86.97 | 15 | 2.21 | 192.24 | 41 | 68.78% | 31.22% | 58 | 59.82% | 27.16% | 13.03% | 95 |
| I | MSCI EM | 84.27 | 23 | 2.21 | 186.22 | 49 | 68.72% | 31.28% | 59 | 57.92% | 26.36% | 15.73% | 87 |
| I | S&P 500 Equal Weight | 72.75 | 69 | 2.19 | 158.98 | 69 | 68.66% | 31.34% | 60 | 49.95% | 22.80% | 27.25% | 41 |
| I | Austria ATX | 76.85 | 57 | 2.24 | 172.31 | 55 | 68.65% | 31.35% | 61 | 52.76% | 24.09% | 23.15% | 53 |
| S | S&P Utilities Sector | 87.37 | 13 | 2.19 | 191.14 | 44 | 68.61% | 31.39% | 62 | 59.95% | 27.42% | 12.63% | 97 |
| I | Hong Kong Hang Seng | 69.98 | 78 | 2.22 | 155.21 | 70 | 68.60% | 31.40% | 63 | 48.01% | 21.97% | 30.02% | 32 |
| I | S&P/TSX Composite (Canada) | 87.29 | 14 | 2.20 | 191.92 | 42 | 68.58% | 31.42% | 64 | 59.86% | 27.43% | 12.71% | 96 |
| | NASDAQ Composite | 81.32 | 38 | 2.19 | 177.69 | 53 | 68.54% | 31.46% | 65 | 55.74% | 25.58% | 18.68% | 72 |
| S | Morgan Stanley Cyclical Index | 69.12 | 83 | 2.32 | 160.59 | 67 | 68.48% | 31.52% | 66 | 47.33% | 21.78% | 30.88% | 27 |
| | Dow Jones Transport | 69.39 | 81 | 2.24 | 155.18 | 71 | 68.29% | 31.71% | 67 | 47.39% | 22.00% | 30.61% | 29 |
| I | Belgium BEL-20 | 78.16 | 50 | 2.15 | 168.18 | 59 | 68.21% | 31.79% | 68 | 53.32% | 24.84% | 21.84% | 60 |
| I | Finland HSE General Index | 63.57 | 96 | 2.09 | 133.08 | 86 | 67.49% | 32.51% | 69 | 42.90% | 20.67% | 36.43% | 14 |
| | Russell 2000 | 83.02 | 30 | 2.07 | 171.63 | 56 | 67.34% | 32.66% | 70 | 55.91% | 27.11% | 16.98% | 80 |
| S | S&P Industrials Sector | 82.49 | 33 | 2.05 | 169.05 | 58 | 66.98% | 33.02% | 71 | 55.25% | 27.24% | 17.51% | 77 |
| I | Indonesia Jakarta Composite | 73.88 | 64 | 2.04 | 150.64 | 73 | 66.95% | 33.05% | 72 | 49.46% | 24.42% | 26.12% | 46 |
| S | S&P Technology Sector | 70.34 | 74 | 2.05 | 144.50 | 78 | 66.92% | 33.08% | 73 | 47.07% | 23.27% | 29.66% | 36 |
| S | S&P Materials Sector | 77.15 | 54 | 2.01 | 154.98 | 72 | 66.66% | 33.34% | 74 | 51.43% | 25.72% | 22.85% | 56 |
| I | MSCI EAFE | 89.91 | 7 | 1.99 | 178.96 | 52 | 66.56% | 33.44% | 75 | 59.85% | 30.06% | 10.09% | 103 |
| I | Pakistan Karachi 100 | 67.51 | 87 | 2.06 | 139.15 | 83 | 66.54% | 33.46% | 76 | 44.92% | 22.59% | 32.49% | 23 |

426

| | | | | | | | | | | | | | |
|---|---|---|---|---|---|---|---|---|---|---|---|---|---|
| C | AMEX Oil Index | 74.51 | 61 | 1.96 | 146.23 | 76 | 66.24% | 33.76% | 77 | 49.36% | 25.15% | 25.49% | 49 |
| I | Malaysia KLSE Composite | 82.64 | 32 | 1.96 | 162.02 | 66 | 66.08% | 33.92% | 78 | 54.61% | 28.04% | 17.36% | 78 |
| S | Healthcare Index (S&P) | 84.22 | 24 | 1.94 | 163.54 | 62 | 66.04% | 33.96% | 79 | 55.62% | 28.60% | 15.78% | 86 |
| I | Japan Nikkei 225 | 75.65 | 59 | 1.95 | 147.74 | 75 | 65.66% | 34.34% | 80 | 49.67% | 25.98% | 24.35% | 51 |
| I | Global Dow | 74.55 | 60 | 1.95 | 145.64 | 77 | 65.57% | 34.43% | 81 | 48.88% | 25.67% | 25.45% | 50 |
| I | Value Line Index (Geometric) | 84.44 | 21 | 1.93 | 162.59 | 64 | 65.56% | 34.44% | 82 | 55.36% | 29.09% | 15.56% | 89 |
| I | Thailand SET | 73.51 | 67 | 1.88 | 138.19 | 85 | 64.99% | 35.01% | 83 | 47.77% | 25.73% | 26.49% | 43 |
| I | Taiwan Weighted | 69.20 | 82 | 1.82 | 125.61 | 92 | 64.06% | 35.94% | 84 | 44.33% | 24.87% | 30.80% | 28 |
| I | Spain Madrid General | 78.14 | 51 | 1.79 | 140.12 | 82 | 64.01% | 35.99% | 85 | 50.02% | 28.12% | 21.86% | 59 |
| I | Peru Lima General | 80.33 | 43 | 1.78 | 142.75 | 79 | 63.81% | 36.19% | 86 | 51.26% | 29.07% | 19.67% | 67 |
| S | AMEX Pharmaceutical Index | 81.68 | 37 | 1.74 | 142.38 | 80 | 63.58% | 36.42% | 87 | 51.93% | 29.74% | 18.32% | 73 |
| S | S&P Financials Sector | 74.40 | 63 | 1.73 | 128.41 | 91 | 63.20% | 36.80% | 88 | 47.03% | 27.38% | 25.60% | 47 |
| S | S&P Telecomm Sector | 80.79 | 39 | 1.71 | 138.25 | 84 | 63.06% | 36.94% | 89 | 50.95% | 29.84% | 19.21% | 71 |
| I | Venezuela IBC | 76.70 | 58 | 1.70 | 130.78 | 89 | 63.02% | 36.98% | 90 | 48.34% | 28.37% | 23.30% | 52 |
| I | Chile IGPA General Index | 90.17 | 6 | 1.66 | 149.32 | 74 | 62.34% | 37.66% | 91 | 56.21% | 33.95% | 9.83% | 104 |
| I | Singapore Straits Times | 65.83 | 90 | 1.67 | 109.63 | 97 | 62.30% | 37.70% | 92 | 41.01% | 24.82% | 34.17% | 20 |
| I | Philippines PSE Composite | 74.47 | 62 | 1.66 | 123.72 | 93 | 62.28% | 37.72% | 93 | 46.38% | 28.09% | 25.53% | 48 |
| I | Czech Republic PX | 69.81 | 79 | 1.65 | 115.13 | 96 | 62.22% | 37.78% | 94 | 43.44% | 26.38% | 30.19% | 31 |
| I | Chile IPSA | 80.43 | 42 | 1.63 | 131.41 | 88 | 61.97% | 38.03% | 95 | 49.84% | 30.58% | 19.57% | 68 |
| I | South Korea Seoul Composite | 67.39 | 88 | 1.59 | 107.17 | 99 | 61.19% | 38.81% | 96 | 41.24% | 26.15% | 32.61% | 22 |
| C | Silver Base Price Handy & Harman | 72.55 | 70 | 1.44 | 104.30 | 100 | 58.78% | 41.22% | 97 | 42.65% | 29.91% | 27.45% | 40 |
| C | CRB Index | 92.69 | 2 | 1.42 | 131.59 | 87 | 58.45% | 41.55% | 98 | 54.17% | 38.51% | 7.31% | 108 |
| I | Sri Lanka All Share | 83.98 | 26 | 1.29 | 108.17 | 98 | 56.21% | 43.79% | 99 | 47.21% | 36.77% | 16.02% | 84 |
| I | Slovakia SAX | 90.31 | 5 | 1.28 | 115.54 | 95 | 56.08% | 43.92% | 100 | 50.65% | 39.67% | 9.69% | 105 |
| I | Greece General Share | 62.60 | 98 | 1.27 | 79.60 | 102 | 55.26% | 44.74% | 101 | 34.59% | 28.01% | 37.40% | 12 |
| C | Gold Base Price Handy & Harman | 49.21 | 103 | 1.20 | 59.26 | 105 | 54.64% | 45.36% | 102 | 26.89% | 22.32% | 50.79% | 7 |
| I | China Shanghai Composite | 62.87 | 97 | 1.17 | 73.82 | 104 | 54.10% | 45.90% | 103 | 34.01% | 28.86% | 37.13% | 13 |
| C | Gold Mining Stocks | 48.18 | 106 | 1.07 | 51.61 | 106 | 52.05% | 47.95% | 104 | 25.08% | 23.10% | 51.82% | 4 |
| C | U.S. Dollar Index | 95.16 | 1 | 1.08 | 102.65 | 101 | 51.85% | 48.15% | 105 | 49.34% | 45.82% | 4.84% | 109 |
| I | Viet Nam Index | 70.31 | 75 | 1.08 | 75.84 | 103 | 51.69% | 48.31% | 106 | 36.34% | 33.97% | 29.69% | 35 |

*(Continued)*

**TABLE B.3** Continued

| Index Name | Trendiness One | | | | | Trendiness Two | | | | | | |
| | Trendiness | | Avg. | Up Trendiness | | While in Trend | | | Trendless Analysis | | | |
| | Average | Rank | U/D | WtdAvg | Rank | Up/Tot | Dn/Tot | Up Rank | Up | Down | Trendless | Rank |
|---|---|---|---|---|---|---|---|---|---|---|---|---|
| C Gold Bugs (AMEX) | 32.56 | 108 | 1.04 | 33.76 | 108 | 51.30% | 48.70% | 107 | 16.70% | 15.85% | 67.44% | 2 |
| C Gold and Silver Mining | 38.35 | 107 | 0.90 | 34.66 | 107 | 48.11% | 51.89% | 108 | 18.45% | 19.90% | 61.65% | 3 |
| I Hanoi SE Index | 49.16 | 104 | 0.44 | 21.73 | 109 | 31.12% | 68.88% | 109 | 15.30% | 33.86% | 50.84% | 6 |
| **Statistics** | | | | | | | | | | | | |
| Mean | 74.81 | | 2.33 | 174.47 | | 68.04% | 31.96% | | 51.10% | 23.71% | 25.19% | |
| Average Deviation | 9.27 | | 0.56 | 44.70 | | 5.46% | 5.46% | | 7.42% | 4.39% | 9.27% | |
| Median | 76.96 | | 2.27 | 172.31 | | 69.21% | 30.79% | | 52.03% | 23.27% | 23.04% | |
| Minimum | 32.02 | | 0.44 | 21.73 | | 31.12% | 17.14% | | 15.30% | 6.67% | 4.84% | |
| Maximum | 95.16 | | 4.88 | 330.27 | | 82.86% | 68.88% | | 68.80% | 45.82% | 67.98% | |
| Sigma | 12.25 | | 0.77 | 58.11 | | 7.66% | 7.66% | | 10.28% | 5.92% | 12.25% | |
| Geometric Mean | 73.59 | | 2.20 | 161.93 | | 67.53% | 31.15% | | 49.70% | 22.93% | 22.50% | |
| Harmonic Mean | 72.03 | | 2.04 | 142.11 | | 66.92% | 30.41% | | 47.64% | 22.01% | 19.90% | |
| Kurtosis | 2.08 | | 1.30 | 0.52 | | 446.17% | 446.17% | | 245.72% | 191.06% | 207.66% | |
| Skewness | -1.24 | | 0.64 | -0.05 | | -148.50% | 148.50% | | -134.87% | 42.01% | 123.61% | |
| Trimmed Mean—20% | 76.18 | | 2.29 | 174.81 | | 68.78% | 31.22% | | 52.30% | 23.58% | 23.82% | |

There is no table for the Trendless Rank because it is inversely related to the Trendless One Rank.

## GICS Tables

**TABLE B.4**  Trendiness One Rank

| Trendiness | | Avg. | Up Trendiness | |
|---|---|---|---|---|
| Average | Rank | U/D | WtdAvg | Rank |

| | Trendiness One | | | | | Trendiness Two | | | | | | |
|---|---|---|---|---|---|---|---|---|---|---|---|---|
| | Trendiness | | Avg. | Up Trendiness | | While in Trend | | | Trendless Analysis | | | |
| GICs—Data up to and including 30 day Trends | Average | Rank | U/D | WtdAvg | Rank | Up/Tot | Dn/Tot | Up Rank | Up | Down | Trendless | Rank |
| 30 Consumer Staples | 92.37 | 1 | 2.75 | 254.00 | 7 | 71.59% | 28.41% | 10 | 66.13% | 26.25% | 7.63% | 94 |
| 3020 Food Beverage & Tobacco | 91.26 | 2 | 2.11 | 192.55 | 14 | 67.74% | 32.26% | 39 | 61.82% | 29.44% | 8.74% | 93 |
| 302020 Food Products | 91.05 | 3 | 2.47 | 225.13 | 9 | 67.82% | 32.18% | 38 | 61.75% | 29.30% | 8.95% | 92 |
| 3030 Household & Personal Products | 90.08 | 4 | 3.07 | 276.63 | 4 | 72.55% | 27.45% | 7 | 65.35% | 24.73% | 9.92% | 91 |
| 303010 Household Products | 89.36 | 5 | 2.91 | 259.99 | 5 | 70.23% | 29.77% | 17 | 62.76% | 26.60% | 10.64% | 90 |
| 35 Health Care | 88.65 | 6 | 2.05 | 181.62 | 19 | 68.78% | 31.22% | 24 | 60.97% | 27.68% | 11.35% | 89 |
| 302010 Beverages | 88.44 | 7 | 2.56 | 226.16 | 8 | 70.75% | 29.25% | 14 | 62.58% | 25.87% | 11.56% | 88 |
| 3520 Pharmaceuticals Biotechnology & Life Sci. | 87.44 | 8 | 1.50 | 131.53 | 65 | 60.29% | 39.71% | 79 | 52.72% | 34.72% | 12.56% | 87 |
| 352020 Pharmaceuticals | 87.14 | 9 | 1.65 | 143.93 | 59 | 62.72% | 37.28% | 68 | 54.65% | 32.49% | 12.86% | 86 |
| 301010 Food & Staples Retailing | 87.08 | 10 | 2.07 | 179.85 | 24 | 68.29% | 31.71% | 32 | 59.47% | 27.61% | 12.92% | 85 |
| 3010 Food & Staples Retailing | 87.08 | 11 | 2.07 | 179.86 | 23 | 68.30% | 31.70% | 31 | 59.47% | 27.61% | 12.92% | 84 |
| 3510 Health Care Equipment & Services | 86.01 | 12 | 1.95 | 167.89 | 29 | 66.79% | 33.21% | 45 | 57.45% | 28.56% | 13.99% | 83 |
| 551010 Electric Utilities | 85.91 | 13 | 1.72 | 147.86 | 52 | 65.61% | 34.39% | 59 | 56.37% | 29.54% | 14.09% | 82 |
| 55 Utilities | 85.80 | 14 | 1.93 | 165.27 | 30 | 68.61% | 31.39% | 27 | 58.87% | 26.93% | 14.20% | 81 |
| 2020 Commercial & Professional Services | 85.39 | 15 | 1.90 | 162.61 | 34 | 63.43% | 36.57% | 65 | 54.16% | 31.22% | 14.61% | 80 |

(*Continued*)

**TABLE B.4** Continued

| GICs—Data up to and including 30 day Trends | Trendiness One | | | | | | Trendiness Two | | | | Trendless Analysis | | | |
|---|---|---|---|---|---|---|---|---|---|---|---|---|---|---|
| | Trendiness | | Avg. | Up Trendiness | | | While in Trend | | | | | | | |
| | Average | Rank | U/D | WtdAvg | Rank | | Up/Tot | Dn/Tot | Up Rank | Up | Down | Trendless | Rank |
| 201010 Aerospace & Defense | 85.36 | 16 | 3.02 | 257.55 | 6 | | 74.37% | 25.63% | 4 | 63.48% | 21.88% | 14.64% | 79 |
| 25 Consumer Discretionary | 85.29 | 17 | 2.52 | 215.00 | 10 | | 71.17% | 28.83% | 12 | 60.70% | 24.59% | 14.71% | 78 |
| 202010 Commercial Services & Supplies | 85.15 | 18 | 1.93 | 164.33 | 32 | | 63.73% | 36.27% | 63 | 54.26% | 30.88% | 14.85% | 77 |
| 351010 Health Care Equipment & Supplies | 84.68 | 19 | 2.21 | 187.24 | 15 | | 68.91% | 31.09% | 23 | 58.35% | 26.33% | 15.32% | 76 |
| 2520 Consumer Durables & Apparel | 84.32 | 20 | 2.02 | 170.30 | 27 | | 66.22% | 33.78% | 51 | 55.84% | 28.48% | 15.68% | 75 |
| 20 Industrials | 84.22 | 21 | 2.33 | 196.04 | 13 | | 66.98% | 33.02% | 43 | 56.41% | 27.81% | 15.78% | 74 |
| 50 Telecommunication Services | 83.96 | 22 | 1.61 | 135.19 | 63 | | 63.06% | 36.94% | 67 | 52.95% | 31.01% | 16.04% | 73 |
| 2010 Capital Goods | 83.87 | 23 | 2.17 | 181.94 | 18 | | 65.99% | 34.01% | 54 | 55.35% | 28.52% | 16.13% | 72 |
| 2530 Consumer Services | 83.80 | 24 | 2.16 | 181.15 | 21 | | 67.54% | 32.46% | 40 | 56.60% | 27.20% | 16.20% | 71 |
| 501010 Diversified Telecommunication Services | 83.39 | 25 | 1.43 | 119.21 | 73 | | 61.54% | 38.46% | 75 | 51.32% | 32.07% | 16.61% | 70 |
| 253010 Hotels Restaurants & Leisure | 83.23 | 26 | 2.25 | 187.03 | 16 | | 68.47% | 31.53% | 29 | 56.99% | 26.24% | 16.77% | 69 |
| 2030 Transportation | 81.83 | 27 | 1.99 | 163.16 | 33 | | 65.96% | 34.04% | 55 | 53.98% | 27.85% | 18.17% | 68 |
| 351020 Health Care Providers & Services | 81.64 | 28 | 1.96 | 160.38 | 35 | | 68.12% | 31.88% | 34 | 55.61% | 26.03% | 18.36% | 67 |
| 151030 Containers & Packaging | 81.33 | 29 | 1.45 | 117.98 | 74 | | 58.80% | 41.20% | 84 | 47.82% | 33.51% | 18.67% | 66 |
| 4030 Insurance | 80.90 | 30 | 1.51 | 121.92 | 69 | | 61.31% | 38.69% | 76 | 49.60% | 31.30% | 19.10% | 64 |
| 403010 Insurance | 80.90 | 30 | 1.51 | 121.92 | 69 | | 61.31% | 38.69% | 76 | 49.60% | 31.30% | 19.10% | 64 |
| 15 Materials | 80.59 | 32 | 1.93 | 155.21 | 44 | | 66.66% | 33.34% | 47 | 53.72% | 26.87% | 19.41% | 63 |
| 151010 Chemicals | 80.09 | 33 | 2.28 | 182.47 | 17 | | 68.73% | 31.27% | 26 | 55.04% | 25.04% | 19.91% | 62 |
| 551020 Gas Utilities | 80.07 | 34 | 2.63 | 210.49 | 11 | | 69.30% | 30.70% | 20 | 55.49% | 24.58% | 19.93% | 61 |
| 302030 Tobacco | 79.85 | 35 | 2.26 | 180.11 | 22 | | 69.05% | 30.95% | 22 | 55.14% | 24.71% | 20.15% | 60 |

| | | | | | | | | | | | | |
|---|---|---|---|---|---|---|---|---|---|---|---|---|
| 2540 Media | 79.47 | 36 | 1.50 | 119.58 | 72 | 62.53% | 37.47% | 71 | 49.70% | 29.78% | 20.53% | 59 |
| 254010 Media | 79.47 | 37 | 1.51 | 119.60 | 71 | 62.54% | 37.46% | 70 | 49.70% | 29.77% | 20.53% | 58 |
| 252010 Household Durables | 79.40 | 38 | 1.87 | 148.85 | 51 | 65.79% | 34.21% | 58 | 52.23% | 27.17% | 20.60% | 57 |
| 101020 Oil Gas & Consumable Fuels | 79.38 | 39 | 1.84 | 146.14 | 56 | 66.64% | 33.36% | 48 | 52.89% | 26.48% | 20.62% | 56 |
| 201060 Machinery | 79.30 | 40 | 1.85 | 146.89 | 54 | 65.79% | 34.21% | 57 | 52.17% | 27.13% | 20.70% | 55 |
| 10 Energy | 78.03 | 41 | 1.99 | 155.47 | 42 | 68.37% | 31.63% | 30 | 53.36% | 24.68% | 21.97% | 54 |
| 303020 Personal Products | 77.78 | 42 | 2.56 | 199.00 | 12 | 71.63% | 28.37% | 9 | 55.72% | 22.06% | 22.22% | 53 |
| 2550 Retailing | 77.30 | 43 | 2.06 | 159.09 | 38 | 68.21% | 31.79% | 33 | 52.73% | 24.58% | 22.70% | 52 |
| 40 Financials | 77.26 | 44 | 2.00 | 154.38 | 47 | 63.20% | 36.80% | 66 | 48.83% | 28.43% | 22.74% | 51 |
| 252020 Leisure Equipment & Products | 77.14 | 45 | 1.66 | 127.86 | 67 | 62.53% | 37.47% | 72 | 48.23% | 28.91% | 22.86% | 50 |
| 201040 Electrical Equipment | 77.13 | 46 | 2.21 | 170.37 | 26 | 68.76% | 31.24% | 25 | 53.04% | 24.10% | 22.87% | 49 |
| 201050 Industrial Conglomerates | 76.91 | 47 | 2.02 | 155.64 | 40 | 66.19% | 33.81% | 52 | 50.91% | 26.00% | 23.09% | 48 |
| 252030 Textiles Apparel & Luxury Goods | 75.88 | 48 | 2.29 | 173.47 | 25 | 67.04% | 32.96% | 42 | 50.87% | 25.01% | 24.12% | 47 |
| 255010 Distributors | 75.33 | 49 | 2.00 | 150.35 | 49 | 58.62% | 41.38% | 85 | 44.16% | 31.17% | 24.67% | 46 |
| 551030 Multi-Utilities | 74.90 | 50 | 2.00 | 149.47 | 50 | 67.99% | 32.01% | 35 | 50.93% | 23.97% | 25.10% | 45 |
| 4010 Banks | 74.83 | 51 | 1.96 | 146.48 | 55 | 66.15% | 33.85% | 53 | 49.50% | 25.34% | 25.17% | 44 |
| 45 Information Technology | 74.68 | 52 | 1.95 | 145.32 | 58 | 66.92% | 33.08% | 44 | 49.98% | 24.71% | 25.32% | 43 |
| 401010 Commercial Banks | 74.65 | 53 | 1.67 | 124.87 | 68 | 62.60% | 37.40% | 69 | 46.73% | 27.92% | 25.35% | 42 |
| 203040 Road & Rail | 74.63 | 54 | 2.03 | 151.60 | 48 | 64.95% | 35.05% | 62 | 48.48% | 26.16% | 25.37% | 41 |
| 251010 Auto Components | 74.49 | 55 | 1.50 | 111.99 | 79 | 61.75% | 38.25% | 74 | 45.99% | 28.49% | 25.51% | 40 |
| 255040 Specialty Retail | 74.35 | 56 | 1.91 | 141.76 | 62 | 67.83% | 32.17% | 37 | 50.43% | 23.92% | 25.65% | 39 |
| 255030 Multiline Retail | 73.98 | 57 | 1.99 | 147.31 | 53 | 66.55% | 33.45% | 49 | 49.24% | 24.75% | 26.02% | 38 |
| 4510 Software & Services | 73.65 | 58 | 2.11 | 155.04 | 45 | 66.72% | 33.28% | 46 | 49.14% | 24.51% | 26.35% | 37 |
| 452020 Computers & Peripherals | 73.42 | 59 | 1.80 | 132.41 | 64 | 65.96% | 34.04% | 56 | 48.43% | 25.00% | 26.58% | 36 |
| 203010 Air Freight & Logistics | 73.07 | 60 | 1.31 | 95.46 | 85 | 58.16% | 41.84% | 87 | 42.50% | 30.57% | 26.93% | 35 |
| 2510 Automobiles & Components | 72.61 | 61 | 1.25 | 90.89 | 86 | 56.57% | 43.43% | 91 | 41.08% | 31.53% | 27.39% | 34 |
| 4020 Diversified Financials | 72.31 | 62 | 2.20 | 159.21 | 37 | 67.83% | 32.17% | 36 | 49.05% | 23.27% | 27.69% | 33 |
| 151050 Paper & Forest Products | 72.31 | 63 | 1.56 | 112.62 | 78 | 62.00% | 38.00% | 73 | 44.83% | 27.48% | 27.69% | 32 |
| 451020 IT Services | 72.15 | 64 | 2.51 | 181.40 | 20 | 70.36% | 29.64% | 15 | 50.77% | 21.39% | 27.85% | 31 |

(Continued)

**TABLE B.4** Continued

| GICs—Data up to and including 30 day Trends | Trendiness One | | | | | Trendiness Two | | | Trendless Analysis | | | |
|---|---|---|---|---|---|---|---|---|---|---|---|---|
| | Trendiness | | Avg. | Up Trendiness | | While in Trend | | | | | | |
| | Average | Rank | U/D | WtdAvg | Rank | Up/Tot | Dn/Tot | Up Rank | Up | Down | Trendless | Rank |
| 4520 Technology Hardware & Equipment | 72.01 | 65 | 2.34 | 168.20 | 28 | 70.79% | 29.21% | 13 | 50.98% | 21.04% | 27.99% | 30 |
| 201070 Trading Companies & Distributors | 72.01 | 66 | 1.99 | 143.65 | 60 | 65.61% | 34.39% | 60 | 47.25% | 24.77% | 27.99% | 29 |
| 4040 Real Estate | 71.02 | 67 | 4.44 | 315.56 | 2 | 79.66% | 20.34% | 2 | 56.57% | 14.45% | 28.98% | 28 |
| 404020 Real Estate Investment Trusts (REITs) | 70.96 | 68 | 4.11 | 291.71 | 3 | 77.97% | 22.03% | 3 | 55.33% | 15.63% | 29.04% | 27 |
| 151040 Metals & Mining | 70.80 | 69 | 1.49 | 105.56 | 80 | 61.06% | 38.94% | 78 | 43.23% | 27.57% | 29.20% | 26 |
| 451030 Software | 70.63 | 70 | 2.19 | 154.76 | 46 | 67.16% | 32.84% | 41 | 47.44% | 23.20% | 29.37% | 25 |
| 352030 Life Sciences Tools & Services | 69.80 | 71 | 4.52 | 315.72 | 1 | 81.86% | 18.14% | 1 | 57.14% | 12.66% | 30.20% | 24 |
| 401020 Thrifts & Mortgage Finance | 69.70 | 72 | 0.94 | 65.37 | 94 | 48.83% | 51.17% | 94 | 34.03% | 35.67% | 30.30% | 23 |
| 202020 Professional Services | 68.50 | 73 | 2.41 | 164.94 | 31 | 71.58% | 28.42% | 11 | 49.04% | 19.47% | 31.50% | 22 |
| 352010 Biotechnology | 67.26 | 74 | 1.73 | 116.08 | 76 | 63.71% | 36.29% | 64 | 42.85% | 24.41% | 32.74% | 21 |
| 201020 Building Products | 66.98 | 75 | 1.48 | 99.19 | 84 | 59.10% | 40.90% | 83 | 39.59% | 27.39% | 33.02% | 20 |
| 251020 Automobiles | 66.96 | 76 | 1.31 | 87.93 | 87 | 58.44% | 41.56% | 86 | 39.13% | 27.83% | 33.04% | 19 |
| 452010 Communications Equipment | 66.25 | 77 | 2.35 | 155.62 | 41 | 69.29% | 30.71% | 21 | 45.91% | 20.35% | 33.75% | 18 |
| 201040 Electronic Equipment Instruments & Components | 65.26 | 78 | 1.60 | 104.62 | 81 | 60.02% | 39.98% | 80 | 39.17% | 26.09% | 34.74% | 17 |
| 402030 Capital Markets | 64.42 | 79 | 2.48 | 159.53 | 36 | 73.91% | 26.09% | 5 | 47.62% | 16.81% | 35.58% | 16 |
| 201030 Construction & Engineering | 63.99 | 80 | 1.35 | 86.32 | 88 | 57.81% | 42.19% | 88 | 37.00% | 26.99% | 36.01% | 15 |
| 253020 Diversified Consumer Services | 63.50 | 81 | 1.35 | 85.72 | 89 | 56.94% | 43.06% | 90 | 36.16% | 27.34% | 36.50% | 14 |
| 402010 Diversified Financial Services | 63.06 | 82 | 1.58 | 99.86 | 83 | 59.82% | 40.18% | 81 | 37.72% | 25.33% | 36.94% | 13 |
| 402020 Consumer Finance | 62.47 | 83 | 2.34 | 145.90 | 57 | 72.17% | 27.83% | 8 | 45.09% | 17.39% | 37.53% | 12 |
| 4530 Semiconductors & Semiconductor Equipment | 62.35 | 84 | 1.29 | 80.13 | 91 | 55.88% | 44.12% | 92 | 34.84% | 27.51% | 37.65% | 11 |

| | | | | | | | | | | | |
|---|---|---|---|---|---|---|---|---|---|---|---|
| 203020 Airlines | 62.08 | 85 | 1.11 | 68.98 | 93 | 50.58% | 49.42% | 93 | 31.40% | 30.68% | 37.92% | 10 |
| 551050 Independent Power Producers & Energy Traders | 61.70 | 86 | 2.52 | 155.44 | 43 | 69.69% | 30.31% | 19 | 43.00% | 18.71% | 38.30% | 9 |
| 453010 Semiconductors & Semiconductor Equipment | 58.82 | 87 | 1.99 | 117.13 | 75 | 64.99% | 35.01% | 61 | 38.23% | 20.59% | 41.18% | 8 |
| 101010 Energy Equipment & Services | 58.81 | 88 | 1.94 | 114.02 | 77 | 68.49% | 31.51% | 28 | 40.28% | 18.53% | 41.19% | 7 |
| 501020 Wireless Telecommunication Services | 57.95 | 89 | 1.47 | 85.22 | 90 | 59.37% | 40.63% | 82 | 34.40% | 23.54% | 42.05% | 6 |
| 151020 Construction Materials | 54.73 | 90 | 1.35 | 73.74 | 92 | 56.97% | 43.03% | 89 | 31.18% | 23.55% | 45.27% | 5 |
| 452040 Office Electronics | 52.62 | 91 | 1.96 | 103.17 | 82 | 66.32% | 33.68% | 50 | 34.90% | 17.72% | 47.38% | 4 |
| 351030 Health Care Technology | 49.70 | 92 | 2.59 | 128.56 | 66 | 70.26% | 29.74% | 16 | 34.92% | 14.78% | 50.30% | 3 |
| 255020 Internet & Catalog Retail | 47.42 | 93 | 3.29 | 155.96 | 39 | 72.96% | 27.04% | 6 | 34.59% | 12.82% | 52.58% | 2 |
| 451010 Internet Software & Services | 46.82 | 94 | 3.07 | 143.62 | 61 | 69.81% | 30.19% | 18 | 32.69% | 14.14% | 53.18% | 1 |
| Mean | 75.23 | | 2.06 | 154.98 | | 65.87% | 34.13% | | 49.64% | 25.60% | 24.77% | |
| Average Deviation | 7.64 | | 0.41 | 36.42 | | 4.15% | 4.15% | | 6.36% | 3.32% | 7.64% | |
| Geometric Mean | 76.39 | | 1.97 | 150.30 | | 65.64% | 33.69% | | 50.14% | 25.73% | 21.57% | |
| Harmonic Mean | 75.91 | | 1.90 | 143.09 | | 65.40% | 33.21% | | 49.52% | 25.27% | 19.92% | |
| Kurtosis | -0.72 | | 5.60 | 1.67 | | 141.08% | 141.08% | | -12.26% | 110.32% | -72.25% | |
| Maximum | 92.37 | | 4.52 | 315.72 | | 81.86% | 51.17% | | 66.13% | 35.67% | 52.58% | |
| Mean | 73.07 | | 2.05 | 148.49 | | 65.84% | 35.09% | | 47.94% | 26.17% | 24.15% | |
| Median | 75.33 | | 1.99 | 150.30 | | 66.22% | 33.45% | | 49.70% | 26.03% | 24.12% | |
| Minimum | 7.64 | | 0.41 | 36.42 | | 4.15% | 4.15% | | 6.36% | 3.32% | 7.64% | |
| Sigma | 12.06 | | 0.64 | 50.32 | | 8.34% | 6.25% | | 9.17% | 5.24% | 10.05% | |
| Skewness | -0.63 | | 1.71 | 1.01 | | -21.78% | 21.78% | | -40.56% | -76.87% | 63.02% | |
| Trimmed Mean—20% | 76.21 | | 1.98 | 150.37 | | 65.93% | 34.07% | | 50.15% | 26.10% | 23.79% | |

**TABLE B.5** Up Trendiness Rank

| Trendiness | | Avg. | Up Trendiness | |
|---|---|---|---|---|
| Average | Rank | U/D | WtdAvg | Rank |

| GICs—Data up to and including 30 day Trends | Trendiness One | | | | | Trendiness Two | | | | | | |
|---|---|---|---|---|---|---|---|---|---|---|---|---|
| | Trendiness | | Avg. | Up Trendiness | | While in Trend | | | Trendless Analysis | | | |
| | Average | Rank | U/D | WtdAvg | Rank | Up/Tot | Dn/Tot | Up Rank | Up | Down | Trendless | Rank |
| 352030 Life Sciences Tools & Services | 69.80 | 71 | 4.52 | 315.72 | 1 | 81.86% | 18.14% | 1 | 57.14% | 12.66% | 30.20% | 24 |
| 4040 Real Estate | 71.02 | 67 | 4.44 | 315.56 | 2 | 79.66% | 20.34% | 2 | 56.57% | 14.45% | 28.98% | 28 |
| 404020 Real Estate Investment Trusts (REITs) | 70.96 | 68 | 4.11 | 291.71 | 3 | 77.97% | 22.03% | 3 | 55.33% | 15.63% | 29.04% | 27 |
| 3030 Household & Personal Products | 90.08 | 4 | 3.07 | 276.63 | 4 | 72.55% | 27.45% | 7 | 65.35% | 24.73% | 9.92% | 91 |
| 303010 Household Products | 89.36 | 5 | 2.91 | 259.99 | 5 | 70.23% | 29.77% | 17 | 62.76% | 26.60% | 10.64% | 90 |
| 201010 Aerospace & Defense | 85.36 | 16 | 3.02 | 257.55 | 6 | 74.37% | 25.63% | 4 | 63.48% | 21.88% | 14.64% | 79 |
| 30 Consumer Staples | 92.37 | 1 | 2.75 | 254.00 | 7 | 71.59% | 28.41% | 10 | 66.13% | 26.25% | 7.63% | 94 |
| 302010 Beverages | 88.44 | 7 | 2.56 | 226.16 | 8 | 70.75% | 29.25% | 14 | 62.58% | 25.87% | 11.56% | 88 |
| 302020 Food Products | 91.05 | 3 | 2.47 | 225.13 | 9 | 67.82% | 32.18% | 38 | 61.75% | 29.30% | 8.95% | 92 |
| 25 Consumer Discretionary | 85.29 | 17 | 2.52 | 215.00 | 10 | 71.17% | 28.83% | 12 | 60.70% | 24.59% | 14.71% | 78 |
| 551020 Gas Utilities | 80.07 | 34 | 2.63 | 210.49 | 11 | 69.30% | 30.70% | 20 | 55.49% | 24.58% | 19.93% | 61 |
| 303020 Personal Products | 77.78 | 42 | 2.56 | 199.00 | 12 | 71.63% | 28.37% | 9 | 55.72% | 22.06% | 22.22% | 53 |
| 20 Industrials | 84.22 | 21 | 2.33 | 196.04 | 13 | 66.98% | 33.02% | 43 | 56.41% | 27.81% | 15.78% | 74 |
| 3020 Food Beverage & Tobacco | 91.26 | 2 | 2.11 | 192.55 | 14 | 67.74% | 32.26% | 39 | 61.82% | 29.44% | 8.74% | 93 |
| 351010 Health Care Equipment & Supplies | 84.68 | 19 | 2.21 | 187.24 | 15 | 68.91% | 31.09% | 23 | 58.35% | 26.33% | 15.32% | 76 |

434

| | | | | | | | | | | | |
|---|---|---|---|---|---|---|---|---|---|---|---|
| 253010 Hotels Restaurants & Leisure | 83.23 | 26 | 2.25 | 187.03 | 16 | 68.47% | 31.53% | 29 | 56.99% | 26.24% | 16.77% | 69 |
| 151010 Chemicals | 80.09 | 33 | 2.28 | 182.47 | 17 | 68.73% | 31.27% | 26 | 55.04% | 25.04% | 19.91% | 62 |
| 2010 Capital Goods | 83.87 | 23 | 2.17 | 181.94 | 18 | 65.99% | 34.01% | 54 | 55.35% | 28.52% | 16.13% | 72 |
| 35 Health Care | 88.65 | 6 | 2.05 | 181.62 | 19 | 68.78% | 31.22% | 24 | 60.97% | 27.68% | 11.35% | 89 |
| 451020 IT Services | 72.15 | 64 | 2.51 | 181.40 | 20 | 70.36% | 29.64% | 15 | 50.77% | 21.39% | 27.85% | 31 |
| 2530 Consumer Services | 83.80 | 24 | 2.16 | 181.15 | 21 | 67.54% | 32.46% | 40 | 56.60% | 27.20% | 16.20% | 71 |
| 302030 Tobacco | 79.85 | 35 | 2.26 | 180.11 | 22 | 69.05% | 30.95% | 22 | 55.14% | 24.71% | 20.15% | 60 |
| 3010 Food & Staples Retailing | 87.08 | 11 | 2.07 | 179.86 | 23 | 68.30% | 31.70% | 31 | 59.47% | 27.61% | 12.92% | 84 |
| 301010 Food & Staples Retailing | 87.08 | 10 | 2.07 | 179.85 | 24 | 68.29% | 31.71% | 32 | 59.47% | 27.61% | 12.92% | 85 |
| 252030 Textiles Apparel & Luxury Goods | 75.88 | 48 | 2.29 | 173.47 | 25 | 67.04% | 32.96% | 42 | 50.87% | 25.01% | 24.12% | 47 |
| 201040 Electrical Equipment | 77.13 | 46 | 2.21 | 170.37 | 26 | 68.76% | 31.24% | 25 | 53.04% | 24.10% | 22.87% | 49 |
| 2520 Consumer Durables & Apparel | 84.32 | 20 | 2.02 | 170.30 | 27 | 66.22% | 33.78% | 51 | 55.84% | 28.48% | 15.68% | 75 |
| 4520 Technology Hardware & Equipment | 72.01 | 65 | 2.34 | 168.20 | 28 | 70.79% | 29.21% | 13 | 50.98% | 21.04% | 27.99% | 30 |
| 3510 Health Care Equipment & Services | 86.01 | 12 | 1.95 | 167.89 | 29 | 66.79% | 33.21% | 45 | 57.45% | 28.56% | 13.99% | 83 |
| 55 Utilities | 85.80 | 14 | 1.93 | 165.27 | 30 | 68.61% | 31.39% | 27 | 58.87% | 26.93% | 14.20% | 81 |
| 202020 Professional Services | 68.50 | 73 | 2.41 | 164.94 | 31 | 71.58% | 28.42% | 11 | 49.04% | 19.47% | 31.50% | 22 |
| 202010 Commercial Services & Supplies | 85.15 | 18 | 1.93 | 164.33 | 32 | 63.73% | 36.27% | 63 | 54.26% | 30.88% | 14.85% | 77 |
| 2030 Transportation | 81.83 | 27 | 1.99 | 163.16 | 33 | 65.96% | 34.04% | 55 | 53.98% | 27.85% | 18.17% | 68 |
| 2020 Commercial & Professional Services | 85.39 | 15 | 1.90 | 162.61 | 34 | 63.43% | 36.57% | 65 | 54.16% | 31.22% | 14.61% | 80 |
| 351020 Health Care Providers & Services | 81.64 | 28 | 1.96 | 160.38 | 35 | 68.12% | 31.88% | 34 | 55.61% | 26.03% | 18.36% | 67 |
| 402030 Capital Markets | 64.42 | 79 | 2.48 | 159.53 | 36 | 73.91% | 26.09% | 5 | 47.62% | 16.81% | 35.58% | 16 |
| 4020 Diversified Financials | 72.31 | 62 | 2.20 | 159.21 | 37 | 67.83% | 32.17% | 36 | 49.05% | 23.27% | 27.69% | 33 |
| 2550 Retailing | 77.30 | 43 | 2.06 | 159.09 | 38 | 68.21% | 31.79% | 33 | 52.73% | 24.58% | 22.70% | 52 |
| 255020 Internet & Catalog Retail | 47.42 | 93 | 3.29 | 155.96 | 39 | 72.96% | 27.04% | 6 | 34.59% | 12.82% | 52.58% | 2 |
| 201050 Industrial Conglomerates | 76.91 | 47 | 2.02 | 155.64 | 40 | 66.19% | 33.81% | 52 | 50.91% | 26.00% | 23.09% | 48 |

*(Continued)*

**TABLE B.5** Continued

| GICs—Data up to and including 30 day Trends | Trendiness One | | | | | Trendiness Two | | | Trendless Analysis | | | |
|---|---|---|---|---|---|---|---|---|---|---|---|---|
| | Trendiness | | Avg. | Up Trendiness | | While in Trend | | | | | | |
| | Average | Rank | U/D | WtdAvg | Rank | Up/Tot | Dn/Tot | Up Rank | Up | Down | Trendless | Rank |
| 452010 Communications Equipment | 66.25 | 77 | 2.35 | 155.62 | 41 | 69.29% | 30.71% | 21 | 45.91% | 20.35% | 33.75% | 18 |
| 10 Energy | 78.03 | 41 | 1.99 | 155.47 | 42 | 68.37% | 31.63% | 30 | 53.36% | 24.68% | 21.97% | 54 |
| 551050 Independent Power Producers & Energy Traders | 61.70 | 86 | 2.52 | 155.44 | 43 | 69.69% | 30.31% | 19 | 43.00% | 18.71% | 38.30% | 9 |
| 15 Materials | 80.59 | 32 | 1.93 | 155.21 | 44 | 66.66% | 33.34% | 47 | 53.72% | 26.87% | 19.41% | 63 |
| 4510 Software & Services | 73.65 | 58 | 2.11 | 155.04 | 45 | 66.72% | 33.28% | 46 | 49.14% | 24.51% | 26.35% | 37 |
| 451030 Software | 70.63 | 70 | 2.19 | 154.76 | 46 | 67.16% | 32.84% | 41 | 47.44% | 23.20% | 29.37% | 25 |
| 40 Financials | 77.26 | 44 | 2.00 | 154.38 | 47 | 63.20% | 36.80% | 66 | 48.83% | 28.43% | 22.74% | 51 |
| 203040 Road & Rail | 74.63 | 54 | 2.03 | 151.60 | 48 | 64.95% | 35.05% | 62 | 48.48% | 26.16% | 25.37% | 41 |
| 255010 Distributors | 75.33 | 49 | 2.00 | 150.35 | 49 | 58.62% | 41.38% | 85 | 44.16% | 31.17% | 24.67% | 46 |
| 551030 Multi-Utilities | 74.90 | 50 | 2.00 | 149.47 | 50 | 67.99% | 32.01% | 35 | 50.93% | 23.97% | 25.10% | 45 |
| 252010 Household Durables | 79.40 | 38 | 1.87 | 148.85 | 51 | 65.79% | 34.21% | 58 | 52.23% | 27.17% | 20.60% | 57 |
| 551010 Electric Utilities | 85.91 | 13 | 1.72 | 147.86 | 52 | 65.61% | 34.39% | 59 | 56.37% | 29.54% | 14.09% | 82 |
| 255030 Multiline Retail | 73.98 | 57 | 1.99 | 147.31 | 53 | 66.55% | 33.45% | 49 | 49.24% | 24.75% | 26.02% | 38 |
| 201060 Machinery | 79.30 | 40 | 1.85 | 146.89 | 54 | 65.79% | 34.21% | 57 | 52.17% | 27.13% | 20.70% | 55 |
| 4010 Banks | 74.83 | 51 | 1.96 | 146.48 | 55 | 66.15% | 33.85% | 53 | 49.50% | 25.34% | 25.17% | 44 |
| 101020 Oil Gas & Consumable Fuels | 79.38 | 39 | 1.84 | 146.14 | 56 | 66.64% | 33.36% | 48 | 52.89% | 26.48% | 20.62% | 56 |
| 402020 Consumer Finance | 62.47 | 83 | 2.34 | 145.90 | 57 | 72.17% | 27.83% | 8 | 45.09% | 17.39% | 37.53% | 12 |
| 45 Information Technology | 74.68 | 52 | 1.95 | 145.32 | 58 | 66.92% | 33.08% | 44 | 49.98% | 24.71% | 25.32% | 43 |
| 352020 Pharmaceuticals | 87.14 | 9 | 1.65 | 143.93 | 59 | 62.72% | 37.28% | 68 | 54.65% | 32.49% | 12.86% | 86 |
| 201070 Trading Companies & Distributors | 72.01 | 66 | 1.99 | 143.65 | 60 | 65.61% | 34.39% | 60 | 47.25% | 24.77% | 27.99% | 29 |
| 451010 Internet Software & Services | 46.82 | 94 | 3.07 | 143.62 | 61 | 69.81% | 30.19% | 18 | 32.69% | 14.14% | 53.18% | 1 |
| 255040 Specialty Retail | 74.35 | 56 | 1.91 | 141.76 | 62 | 67.83% | 32.17% | 37 | 50.43% | 23.92% | 25.65% | 39 |

| | | | | | | | | | | | |
|---|---|---|---|---|---|---|---|---|---|---|---|
| 50 Telecommunication Services | 83.96 | 22 | 1.61 | 135.19 | 63 | 63.06% | 36.94% | 67 | 52.95% | 31.01% | 16.04% | 73 |
| 452020 Computers & Peripherals | 73.42 | 59 | 1.80 | 132.41 | 64 | 65.96% | 34.04% | 56 | 48.43% | 25.00% | 26.58% | 36 |
| 3520 Pharmaceuticals Biotechnology & Life Sci. | 87.44 | 8 | 1.50 | 131.53 | 65 | 60.29% | 39.71% | 79 | 52.72% | 34.72% | 12.56% | 87 |
| 351030 Health Care Technology | 49.70 | 92 | 2.59 | 128.56 | 66 | 70.26% | 29.74% | 16 | 34.92% | 14.78% | 50.30% | 3 |
| 252020 Leisure Equipment & Products | 77.14 | 45 | 1.66 | 127.86 | 67 | 62.53% | 37.47% | 72 | 48.23% | 28.91% | 22.86% | 50 |
| 401010 Commercial Banks | 74.65 | 53 | 1.67 | 124.87 | 68 | 62.60% | 37.40% | 69 | 46.73% | 27.92% | 25.35% | 42 |
| 4030 Insurance | 80.90 | 30 | 1.51 | 121.92 | 69 | 61.31% | 38.69% | 76 | 49.60% | 31.30% | 19.10% | 64 |
| 403010 Insurance | 80.90 | 30 | 1.51 | 121.92 | 69 | 61.31% | 38.69% | 76 | 49.60% | 31.30% | 19.10% | 64 |
| 254010 Media | 79.47 | 37 | 1.51 | 119.60 | 71 | 62.54% | 37.46% | 70 | 49.77% | 29.77% | 20.53% | 58 |
| 2540 Media | 79.47 | 36 | 1.50 | 119.58 | 72 | 62.53% | 37.47% | 71 | 49.70% | 29.78% | 20.53% | 59 |
| 501010 Diversified Telecommunication Services | 83.39 | 25 | 1.43 | 119.21 | 73 | 61.54% | 38.46% | 75 | 51.32% | 32.07% | 16.61% | 70 |
| 151030 Containers & Packaging | 81.33 | 29 | 1.45 | 117.98 | 74 | 58.80% | 41.20% | 84 | 47.82% | 33.51% | 18.67% | 66 |
| 453010 Semiconductors & Semiconductor Equipment | 58.82 | 87 | 1.99 | 117.13 | 75 | 64.99% | 35.01% | 61 | 38.23% | 20.59% | 41.18% | 8 |
| 352010 Biotechnology | 67.26 | 74 | 1.73 | 116.08 | 76 | 63.71% | 36.29% | 64 | 42.85% | 24.41% | 32.74% | 21 |
| 101010 Energy Equipment & Services | 58.81 | 88 | 1.94 | 114.02 | 77 | 68.49% | 31.51% | 28 | 40.28% | 18.53% | 41.19% | 7 |
| 151050 Paper & Forest Products | 72.31 | 63 | 1.56 | 112.62 | 78 | 62.00% | 38.00% | 73 | 44.83% | 27.48% | 27.69% | 32 |
| 251010 Auto Components | 74.49 | 55 | 1.50 | 111.99 | 79 | 61.75% | 38.25% | 74 | 45.99% | 28.49% | 25.51% | 40 |
| 151040 Metals & Mining | 70.80 | 69 | 1.49 | 105.56 | 80 | 61.06% | 38.94% | 78 | 43.23% | 27.57% | 29.20% | 26 |
| 201040 Electronic Equipment Instruments & Components | 65.26 | 78 | 1.60 | 104.62 | 81 | 60.02% | 39.98% | 80 | 39.17% | 26.09% | 34.74% | 17 |
| 452040 Office Electronics | 52.62 | 91 | 1.96 | 103.17 | 82 | 66.32% | 33.68% | 50 | 34.90% | 17.72% | 47.38% | 4 |
| 402010 Diversified Financial Services | 63.06 | 82 | 1.58 | 99.86 | 83 | 59.82% | 40.18% | 81 | 37.72% | 25.33% | 36.94% | 13 |
| 201020 Building Products | 66.98 | 75 | 1.48 | 99.19 | 84 | 59.10% | 40.90% | 83 | 39.59% | 27.39% | 33.02% | 20 |
| 203010 Air Freight & Logistics | 73.07 | 60 | 1.31 | 95.46 | 85 | 58.16% | 41.84% | 87 | 42.50% | 30.57% | 26.93% | 35 |
| 2510 Automobiles & Components | 72.61 | 61 | 1.25 | 90.89 | 86 | 56.57% | 43.43% | 91 | 41.08% | 31.53% | 27.39% | 34 |
| 251020 Automobiles | 66.96 | 76 | 1.31 | 87.93 | 87 | 58.44% | 41.56% | 86 | 39.13% | 27.83% | 33.04% | 19 |
| 201030 Construction & Engineering | 63.99 | 80 | 1.35 | 86.32 | 88 | 57.81% | 42.19% | 88 | 37.00% | 26.99% | 36.01% | 15 |

*(Continued)*

**TABLE B.5** Continued

| GICs—Data up to and including 30 day Trends | Trendiness One | | | | | Trendiness Two | | | Trendless Analysis | | | |
|---|---|---|---|---|---|---|---|---|---|---|---|---|
| | Trendiness | | Avg. | Up Trendiness | | While in Trend | | | | | | |
| | Average | Rank | U/D | WtdAvg | Rank | Up/Tot | Dn/Tot | Up Rank | Up | Down | Trendless | Rank |
| 253020 Diversified Consumer Services | 63.50 | 81 | 1.35 | 85.72 | 89 | 56.94% | 43.06% | 90 | 36.16% | 27.34% | 36.50% | 14 |
| 501020 Wireless Telecommunication Services | 57.95 | 89 | 1.47 | 85.22 | 90 | 59.37% | 40.63% | 82 | 34.40% | 23.54% | 42.05% | 6 |
| 4530 Semiconductors & Semiconductor Equipment | 62.35 | 84 | 1.29 | 80.13 | 91 | 55.88% | 44.12% | 92 | 34.84% | 27.51% | 37.65% | 11 |
| 151020 Construction Materials | 54.73 | 90 | 1.35 | 73.74 | 92 | 56.97% | 43.03% | 89 | 31.18% | 23.55% | 45.27% | 5 |
| 203020 Airlines | 62.08 | 85 | 1.11 | 68.98 | 93 | 50.58% | 49.42% | 93 | 31.40% | 30.68% | 37.92% | 10 |
| 401020 Thrifts & Mortgage Finance | 69.70 | 72 | 0.94 | 65.37 | 94 | 48.83% | 51.17% | 94 | 34.03% | 35.67% | 30.30% | 23 |
| Mean | 75.23 | | 2.06 | 154.98 | | 65.87% | 34.13% | | 49.64% | 25.60% | 24.77% | |
| Average Deviation | 8.10 | | 0.43 | 35.77 | | 4.15% | 4.15% | | 6.59% | 3.55% | 8.10% | |
| Median | 76.39 | | 1.99 | 152.99 | | 66.65% | 33.35% | | 50.60% | 26.25% | 23.61% | |
| Minimum | 46.82 | | 0.94 | 65.37 | | 48.83% | 18.14% | | 31.18% | 12.66% | 7.63% | |
| Maximum | 92.37 | | 4.52 | 315.72 | | 81.86% | 51.17% | | 66.13% | 35.67% | 53.18% | |
| Sigma | 10.24 | | 0.62 | 50.36 | | 5.51% | 5.51% | | 8.36% | 4.76% | 10.24% | |
| Geometric Mean | 74.48 | | 1.98 | 147.41 | | 65.64% | 33.68% | | 48.89% | 25.08% | 22.71% | |
| Harmonic Mean | 73.65 | | 1.91 | 140.06 | | 65.40% | 33.20% | | 48.08% | 24.48% | 20.69% | |
| Kurtosis | 0.19 | | 4.49 | 1.70 | | 116.95% | 116.95% | | −43.07% | 68.53% | 19.41% | |
| Skewness | −0.71 | | 1.64 | 1.02 | | −23.65% | 23.65% | | −40.84% | −77.98% | 70.65% | |
| Trimmed Mean—20% | 76.02 | | 1.99 | 150.28 | | 65.98% | 34.02% | | 49.97% | 26.00% | 23.98% | |

**TABLE B.6** Trendiness Two Up Rank

| | While in Trend | | |
|---|---|---|---|
| **Up/Tot** | **Dn/Tot** | | **Up Rank** |

| | Trendiness One | | | | | Trendiness Two | | | Trendless Analysis | | | |
|---|---|---|---|---|---|---|---|---|---|---|---|---|---|
| | Trendiness | | Avg. | Up Trendiness | | | While in Trend | | | | | | |
| GICs—Data up to and including 30 day Trends | Average | Rank | U/D | WtdAvg | Rank | Up/Tot | Dn/Tot | Up Rank | Up | Down | Trendless | Rank |
| 352030 Life Sciences Tools & Services | 69.80 | 71 | 4.52 | 315.72 | 1 | 81.86% | 18.14% | 1 | 57.14% | 12.66% | 30.20% | 24 |
| 4040 Real Estate | 71.02 | 67 | 4.44 | 315.56 | 2 | 79.66% | 20.34% | 2 | 56.57% | 14.45% | 28.98% | 28 |
| 404020 Real Estate Investment Trusts (REITs) | 70.96 | 68 | 4.11 | 291.71 | 3 | 77.97% | 22.03% | 3 | 55.33% | 15.63% | 29.04% | 27 |
| 201010 Aerospace & Defense | 85.36 | 16 | 3.02 | 257.55 | 6 | 74.37% | 25.63% | 4 | 63.48% | 21.88% | 14.64% | 79 |
| 42030 Capital Markets | 64.42 | 79 | 2.48 | 159.53 | 36 | 73.91% | 26.09% | 5 | 47.62% | 16.81% | 35.58% | 16 |
| 255020 Internet & Catalog Retail | 47.42 | 93 | 3.29 | 155.96 | 39 | 72.96% | 27.04% | 6 | 34.59% | 12.82% | 52.58% | 2 |
| 3030 Household & Personal Products | 90.08 | 4 | 3.07 | 276.63 | 4 | 72.55% | 27.45% | 7 | 65.35% | 24.73% | 9.92% | 91 |
| 402020 Consumer Finance | 62.47 | 83 | 2.34 | 145.90 | 57 | 72.17% | 27.83% | 8 | 45.09% | 17.39% | 37.53% | 12 |
| 303020 Personal Products | 77.78 | 42 | 2.56 | 199.00 | 12 | 71.63% | 28.37% | 9 | 55.72% | 22.06% | 22.22% | 53 |
| 30 Consumer Staples | 92.37 | 1 | 2.75 | 254.00 | 7 | 71.59% | 28.41% | 10 | 66.13% | 26.25% | 7.63% | 94 |
| 202020 Professional Services | 68.50 | 73 | 2.41 | 164.94 | 31 | 71.58% | 28.42% | 11 | 49.04% | 19.47% | 31.50% | 22 |
| 25 Consumer Discretionary | 85.29 | 17 | 2.52 | 215.00 | 10 | 71.17% | 28.83% | 12 | 60.70% | 24.59% | 14.71% | 78 |
| 4520 Technology Hardware & Equipment | 72.01 | 65 | 2.34 | 168.20 | 28 | 70.79% | 29.21% | 13 | 50.98% | 21.04% | 27.99% | 30 |
| 302010 Beverages | 88.44 | 7 | 2.56 | 226.16 | 8 | 70.75% | 29.25% | 14 | 62.58% | 25.87% | 11.56% | 88 |

(*Continued*)

**TABLE B.6** Continued

| GICs—Data up to and including 30 day Trends | Trendiness One | | | | | Trendiness Two | | | Trendless Analysis | | | |
|---|---|---|---|---|---|---|---|---|---|---|---|---|
| | Trendiness | | Avg. | Up Trendiness | | While in Trend | | | | | | |
| | Average | Rank | U/D | WtdAvg | Rank | Up/Tot | Dn/Tot | Up Rank | Up | Down | Trendless | Rank |
| 451020 IT Services | 72.15 | 64 | 2.51 | 181.40 | 20 | 70.36% | 29.64% | 15 | 50.77% | 21.39% | 27.85% | 31 |
| 351030 Health Care Technology | 49.70 | 92 | 2.59 | 128.56 | 66 | 70.26% | 29.74% | 16 | 34.92% | 14.78% | 50.30% | 3 |
| 303010 Household Products | 89.36 | 5 | 2.91 | 259.99 | 5 | 70.23% | 29.77% | 17 | 62.76% | 26.60% | 10.64% | 90 |
| 451010 Internet Software & Services | 46.82 | 94 | 3.07 | 143.62 | 61 | 69.81% | 30.19% | 18 | 32.69% | 14.14% | 53.18% | 1 |
| 551050 Independent Power Producers & Energy Traders | 61.70 | 86 | 2.52 | 155.44 | 43 | 69.69% | 30.31% | 19 | 43.00% | 18.71% | 38.30% | 9 |
| 551020 Gas Utilities | 80.07 | 34 | 2.63 | 210.49 | 11 | 69.30% | 30.70% | 20 | 55.49% | 24.58% | 19.93% | 61 |
| 452010 Communications Equipment | 66.25 | 77 | 2.35 | 155.62 | 41 | 69.29% | 30.71% | 21 | 45.91% | 20.35% | 33.75% | 18 |
| 302030 Tobacco | 79.85 | 35 | 2.26 | 180.11 | 22 | 69.05% | 30.95% | 22 | 55.14% | 24.71% | 20.15% | 60 |
| 351010 Health Care Equipment & Supplies | 84.68 | 19 | 2.21 | 187.24 | 15 | 68.91% | 31.09% | 23 | 58.35% | 26.33% | 15.32% | 76 |
| 35 Health Care | 88.65 | 6 | 2.05 | 181.62 | 19 | 68.78% | 31.22% | 24 | 60.97% | 27.68% | 11.35% | 89 |
| 201040 Electrical Equipment | 77.13 | 46 | 2.21 | 170.37 | 26 | 68.76% | 31.24% | 25 | 53.04% | 24.10% | 22.87% | 49 |
| 151010 Chemicals | 80.09 | 33 | 2.28 | 182.47 | 17 | 68.73% | 31.27% | 26 | 55.04% | 25.04% | 19.91% | 62 |
| 55 Utilities | 85.80 | 14 | 1.93 | 165.27 | 30 | 68.61% | 31.39% | 27 | 58.87% | 26.93% | 14.20% | 81 |
| 101010 Energy Equipment & Services | 58.81 | 88 | 1.94 | 114.02 | 77 | 68.49% | 31.51% | 28 | 40.28% | 18.53% | 41.19% | 7 |
| 253010 Hotels Restaurants & Leisure | 83.23 | 26 | 2.25 | 187.03 | 16 | 68.47% | 31.53% | 29 | 56.99% | 26.24% | 16.77% | 69 |
| 10 Energy | 78.03 | 41 | 1.99 | 155.47 | 42 | 68.37% | 31.63% | 30 | 53.36% | 24.68% | 21.97% | 54 |
| 3010 Food & Staples Retailing | 87.08 | 11 | 2.07 | 179.86 | 23 | 68.30% | 31.70% | 31 | 59.47% | 27.61% | 12.92% | 84 |
| 301010 Food & Staples Retailing | 87.08 | 10 | 2.07 | 179.85 | 24 | 68.29% | 31.71% | 32 | 59.47% | 27.61% | 12.92% | 85 |
| 2550 Retailing | 77.30 | 43 | 2.06 | 159.09 | 38 | 68.21% | 31.79% | 33 | 52.73% | 24.58% | 22.70% | 52 |
| 351020 Health Care Providers & Services | 81.64 | 28 | 1.96 | 160.38 | 35 | 68.12% | 31.88% | 34 | 55.61% | 26.03% | 18.36% | 67 |
| 551030 Multi-Utilities | 74.90 | 50 | 2.00 | 149.47 | 50 | 67.99% | 32.01% | 35 | 50.93% | 23.97% | 25.10% | 45 |

440

| Industry | | | | | | | | | | | |
|---|---|---|---|---|---|---|---|---|---|---|---|
| 4020 Diversified Financials | 72.31 | 62 | 2.20 | 159.21 | 37 | 67.83% | 32.17% | 36 | 49.05% | 23.27% | 27.69% | 33 |
| 255040 Specialty Retail | 74.35 | 56 | 1.91 | 141.76 | 62 | 67.83% | 32.17% | 37 | 50.43% | 23.92% | 25.65% | 39 |
| 302020 Food Products | 91.05 | 3 | 2.47 | 225.13 | 9 | 67.82% | 32.18% | 38 | 61.75% | 29.30% | 8.95% | 92 |
| 3020 Food Beverage & Tobacco | 91.26 | 2 | 2.11 | 192.55 | 14 | 67.74% | 32.26% | 39 | 61.82% | 29.44% | 8.74% | 93 |
| 2530 Consumer Services | 83.80 | 24 | 2.16 | 181.15 | 21 | 67.54% | 32.46% | 40 | 56.60% | 27.20% | 16.20% | 71 |
| 451030 Software | 70.63 | 70 | 2.19 | 154.76 | 46 | 67.16% | 32.84% | 41 | 47.44% | 23.20% | 29.37% | 25 |
| 252030 Textiles Apparel & Luxury Goods | 75.88 | 48 | 2.29 | 173.47 | 25 | 67.04% | 32.96% | 42 | 50.87% | 25.01% | 24.12% | 47 |
| 20 Industrials | 84.22 | 21 | 2.33 | 196.04 | 13 | 66.98% | 33.02% | 43 | 56.41% | 27.81% | 15.78% | 74 |
| 45 Information Technology | 74.68 | 52 | 1.95 | 145.32 | 58 | 66.92% | 33.08% | 44 | 49.98% | 24.71% | 25.32% | 43 |
| 3510 Health Care Equipment & Services | 86.01 | 12 | 1.95 | 167.89 | 29 | 66.79% | 33.21% | 45 | 57.45% | 28.56% | 13.99% | 83 |
| 4510 Software & Services | 73.65 | 58 | 2.11 | 155.04 | 45 | 66.72% | 33.28% | 46 | 49.14% | 24.51% | 26.35% | 37 |
| 15 Materials | 80.59 | 32 | 1.93 | 155.21 | 44 | 66.66% | 33.34% | 47 | 53.72% | 26.87% | 19.41% | 63 |
| 101020 Oil Gas & Consumable Fuels | 79.38 | 39 | 1.84 | 146.14 | 56 | 66.64% | 33.36% | 48 | 52.89% | 26.48% | 20.62% | 56 |
| 255030 Multiline Retail | 73.98 | 57 | 1.99 | 147.31 | 53 | 66.55% | 33.45% | 49 | 49.24% | 24.75% | 26.02% | 38 |
| 452040 Office Electronics | 52.62 | 91 | 1.96 | 103.17 | 82 | 66.32% | 33.68% | 50 | 34.90% | 17.72% | 47.38% | 4 |
| 2520 Consumer Durables & Apparel | 84.32 | 20 | 2.02 | 170.30 | 27 | 66.22% | 33.78% | 51 | 55.84% | 28.48% | 15.68% | 75 |
| 201050 Industrial Conglomerates | 76.91 | 47 | 2.02 | 155.64 | 40 | 66.19% | 33.81% | 52 | 50.91% | 26.00% | 23.09% | 48 |
| 4010 Banks | 74.83 | 51 | 1.96 | 146.48 | 55 | 66.15% | 33.85% | 53 | 49.50% | 25.34% | 25.17% | 44 |
| 2010 Capital Goods | 83.87 | 23 | 2.17 | 181.94 | 18 | 65.99% | 34.01% | 54 | 55.35% | 28.52% | 16.13% | 72 |
| 2030 Transportation | 81.83 | 27 | 1.99 | 163.16 | 33 | 65.96% | 34.04% | 55 | 53.98% | 27.85% | 18.17% | 68 |
| 452020 Computers & Peripherals | 73.42 | 59 | 1.80 | 132.41 | 64 | 65.96% | 34.04% | 56 | 48.43% | 25.00% | 26.58% | 36 |
| 201060 Machinery | 79.30 | 40 | 1.85 | 146.89 | 54 | 65.79% | 34.21% | 57 | 52.17% | 27.13% | 20.70% | 55 |
| 252010 Household Durables | 79.40 | 38 | 1.87 | 148.85 | 51 | 65.79% | 34.21% | 58 | 52.23% | 27.17% | 20.60% | 57 |
| 551010 Electric Utilities | 85.91 | 13 | 1.72 | 147.86 | 52 | 65.61% | 34.39% | 59 | 56.37% | 29.54% | 14.09% | 82 |
| 201070 Trading Companies & Distributors | 72.01 | 66 | 1.99 | 143.65 | 60 | 65.61% | 34.39% | 60 | 47.25% | 24.77% | 27.99% | 29 |
| 453010 Semiconductors & Semiconductor Equipment | 58.82 | 87 | 1.99 | 117.13 | 75 | 64.99% | 35.01% | 61 | 38.23% | 20.59% | 41.18% | 8 |
| 203040 Road & Rail | 74.63 | 54 | 2.03 | 151.60 | 48 | 64.95% | 35.05% | 62 | 48.48% | 26.16% | 25.37% | 41 |

*(Continued)*

**TABLE B.6** Continued

| GICs—Data up to and including 30 day Trends | Trendiness One | | | | | Trendiness Two | | | | | | |
|---|---|---|---|---|---|---|---|---|---|---|---|---|
| | Trendiness | | Avg. | Up Trendiness | | While in Trend | | | Trendless Analysis | | | |
| | Average | Rank | U/D | WtdAvg | Rank | Up/Tot | Dn/Tot | Up Rank | Up | Down | Trendless | Rank |
| 202010 Commercial Services & Supplies | 85.15 | 18 | 1.93 | 164.33 | 32 | 63.73% | 36.27% | 63 | 54.26% | 30.88% | 14.85% | 77 |
| 352010 Biotechnology | 67.26 | 74 | 1.73 | 116.08 | 76 | 63.71% | 36.29% | 64 | 42.85% | 24.41% | 32.74% | 21 |
| 2020 Commercial & Professional Services | 85.39 | 15 | 1.90 | 162.61 | 34 | 63.43% | 36.57% | 65 | 54.16% | 31.22% | 14.61% | 80 |
| 40 Financials | 77.26 | 44 | 2.00 | 154.38 | 47 | 63.20% | 36.80% | 66 | 48.83% | 28.43% | 22.74% | 51 |
| 50 Telecommunication Services | 83.96 | 22 | 1.61 | 135.19 | 63 | 63.06% | 36.94% | 67 | 52.95% | 31.01% | 16.04% | 73 |
| 352020 Pharmaceuticals | 87.14 | 9 | 1.65 | 143.93 | 59 | 62.72% | 37.28% | 68 | 54.65% | 32.49% | 12.86% | 86 |
| 401010 Commercial Banks | 74.65 | 53 | 1.67 | 124.87 | 68 | 62.60% | 37.40% | 69 | 46.73% | 27.92% | 25.35% | 42 |
| 254010 Media | 79.47 | 37 | 1.51 | 119.60 | 71 | 62.54% | 37.46% | 70 | 49.70% | 29.77% | 20.53% | 58 |
| 2540 Media | 79.47 | 36 | 1.50 | 119.58 | 72 | 62.53% | 37.47% | 71 | 49.70% | 29.78% | 20.53% | 59 |
| 252020 Leisure Equipment & Products | 77.14 | 45 | 1.66 | 127.86 | 67 | 62.53% | 37.47% | 72 | 48.23% | 28.91% | 22.86% | 50 |
| 151050 Paper & Forest Products | 72.31 | 63 | 1.56 | 112.62 | 78 | 62.00% | 38.00% | 73 | 44.83% | 27.48% | 27.69% | 32 |
| 251010 Auto Components | 74.49 | 55 | 1.50 | 111.99 | 79 | 61.75% | 38.25% | 74 | 45.99% | 28.49% | 25.51% | 40 |
| 501010 Diversified Telecommunication Services | 83.39 | 25 | 1.43 | 119.21 | 73 | 61.54% | 38.46% | 75 | 51.32% | 32.07% | 16.61% | 70 |
| 4030 Insurance | 80.90 | 30 | 1.51 | 121.92 | 69 | 61.31% | 38.69% | 76 | 49.60% | 31.30% | 19.10% | 64 |
| 403010 Insurance | 80.90 | 30 | 1.51 | 121.92 | 69 | 61.31% | 38.69% | 76 | 49.60% | 31.30% | 19.10% | 64 |
| 151040 Metals & Mining | 70.80 | 69 | 1.49 | 105.56 | 80 | 61.06% | 38.94% | 78 | 43.23% | 27.57% | 29.20% | 26 |
| 3520 Pharmaceuticals Biotechnology & Life Sci. | 87.44 | 8 | 1.50 | 131.53 | 65 | 60.29% | 39.71% | 79 | 52.72% | 34.72% | 12.56% | 87 |
| 201040 Electronic Equipment Instruments & Components | 65.26 | 78 | 1.60 | 104.62 | 81 | 60.02% | 39.98% | 80 | 39.17% | 26.09% | 34.74% | 17 |
| 402010 Diversified Financial Services | 63.06 | 82 | 1.58 | 99.86 | 83 | 59.82% | 40.18% | 81 | 37.72% | 25.33% | 36.94% | 13 |

| Industry | | | | | | | | | | | |
|---|---|---|---|---|---|---|---|---|---|---|---|
| 501020 Wireless Telecommunication Services | 57.95 | 89 | 1.47 | 85.22 | 90 | 59.37% | 40.63% | 82 | 34.40% | 23.54% | 42.05% | 6 |
| 201020 Building Products | 66.98 | 75 | 1.48 | 99.19 | 84 | 59.10% | 40.90% | 83 | 39.59% | 27.39% | 33.02% | 20 |
| 151030 Containers & Packaging | 81.33 | 29 | 1.45 | 117.98 | 74 | 58.80% | 41.20% | 84 | 47.82% | 33.51% | 18.67% | 66 |
| 255010 Distributors | 75.33 | 49 | 2.00 | 150.35 | 49 | 58.62% | 41.38% | 85 | 44.16% | 31.17% | 24.67% | 46 |
| 251020 Automobiles | 66.96 | 76 | 1.31 | 87.93 | 87 | 58.44% | 41.56% | 86 | 39.13% | 27.83% | 33.04% | 19 |
| 203010 Air Freight & Logistics | 73.07 | 60 | 1.31 | 95.46 | 85 | 58.16% | 41.84% | 87 | 42.50% | 30.57% | 26.93% | 35 |
| 201030 Construction & Engineering | 63.99 | 80 | 1.35 | 86.32 | 88 | 57.81% | 42.19% | 88 | 37.00% | 26.99% | 36.01% | 15 |
| 151020 Construction Materials | 54.73 | 90 | 1.35 | 73.74 | 92 | 56.97% | 43.03% | 89 | 31.18% | 23.55% | 45.27% | 5 |
| 253020 Diversified Consumer Services | 63.50 | 81 | 1.35 | 85.72 | 89 | 56.94% | 43.06% | 90 | 36.16% | 27.34% | 36.50% | 14 |
| 2510 Automobiles & Components | 72.61 | 61 | 1.25 | 90.89 | 86 | 56.57% | 43.43% | 91 | 41.08% | 31.53% | 27.39% | 34 |
| 4530 Semiconductors & Semiconductor Equipment | 62.35 | 84 | 1.29 | 80.13 | 91 | 55.88% | 44.12% | 92 | 34.84% | 27.51% | 37.65% | 11 |
| 203020 Airlines | 62.08 | 85 | 1.11 | 68.98 | 93 | 50.58% | 49.42% | 93 | 31.40% | 30.68% | 37.92% | 10 |
| 401020 Thrifts & Mortgage Finance | 69.70 | 72 | 0.94 | 65.37 | 94 | 48.83% | 51.17% | 94 | 34.03% | 35.67% | 30.30% | 23 |
| Mean | 75.23 | | 2.06 | 154.98 | | 65.87% | 34.13% | | 49.64% | 25.60% | 24.77% | |
| Average Deviation | 8.10 | | 0.43 | 35.77 | | 4.15% | 4.15% | | 6.59% | 3.55% | 8.10% | |
| Median | 76.39 | | 1.99 | 152.99 | | 66.65% | 33.35% | | 50.60% | 26.25% | 23.61% | |
| Minimum | 46.82 | | 0.94 | 65.37 | | 48.83% | 18.14% | | 31.18% | 12.66% | 7.63% | |
| Maximum | 92.37 | | 4.52 | 315.72 | | 81.86% | 51.17% | | 66.13% | 35.67% | 53.18% | |
| Sigma | 10.24 | | 0.62 | 50.36 | | 5.51% | 5.51% | | 8.36% | 4.76% | 10.24% | |
| Geometric Mean | 74.48 | | 1.98 | 147.41 | | 65.64% | 33.68% | | 48.89% | 25.08% | 22.71% | |
| Harmonic Mean | 73.65 | | 1.91 | 140.06 | | 65.40% | 33.20% | | 48.08% | 24.48% | 20.69% | |
| Kurtosis | 0.19 | | 4.49 | 1.70 | | 116.95% | 116.95% | | −43.07% | 68.53% | 19.41% | |
| Skewness | −0.71 | | 1.64 | 1.02 | | −23.65% | 23.65% | | −40.84% | −77.98% | 70.65% | |
| Trimmed Mean—20% | 76.02 | | 1.99 | 150.28 | | 65.98% | 34.02% | | 49.97% | 26.00% | 23.98% | |

There is no table ranked on Trendless because it is inversely related to Trendiness One Trendiness Rank.

# Appendix C: Market Breadth

In 2006 McGraw-Hill published my book, *The Complete Guide to Market Breadth Indicators*. Breadth was an area I had spent a great deal of time on over the past 30-plus years. Breadth was almost totally ignored by the technical analysis community as most of the popular books on technical analysis usually only devoted a chapter to the subject of breadth. The book was in actuality a giant research project for me, one that took well over a year to complete even though I had been collecting breadth data and information since the 1980s. I tried to include every known breadth indicator or relationship in existence. I think I almost did that. The information following is from that book, and what I feel is the absolute most important part of the book. Enjoy!

## Why Breadth?

- It takes advantage of inefficient markets. If investors are irrational and prone to excessive optimism with the latest hot stocks and excessive pessimism with those issues that have suffered recently, then market capitalization weighting reflects those inefficiencies from its very definition of shares times price. Breadth, which is equal weighted, does not have that problem.
- Avoid heavy concentration into a few stocks. Market capitalization weighting often causes a large portion of a portfolio to be concentrated in only a few issues—concentration risk. Breadth totally avoids this.
- Get more exposure to small capitalization stocks. Merely by the concept of capitalization weighting, small stocks will have a smaller effect on the portfolio. True, they are generally considered riskier, but they have also had historically stronger performance. Breadth deals with large and small capitalization stocks equally.

Breadth analysis is like quantum mechanics, it does not predict a single definite result, instead it predicts a number of different possible outcomes, and tells us how likely each one will be. Breadth directly represents the market, no matter what the indices are doing. It is the footprint of the market and the best measure of the market's liquidity.

Most breadth indicators are at best, coincident indicators, and usually somewhat lagging. Any of the indicators that are smoothed with moving averages are certainly

445

lagging. Lagging means that the indicator is only telling you what is happening after it has happened. Lagging is not a problem, once you realize that picking exact tops and bottoms in the market is better left to gamblers. The confirmation of lagging indicators, however, is very important. Some breadth indicators, especially some of the ratios, can offer leading indications based upon the identification and use of previous levels or thresholds that are consistent with similar market action. An oscillator that reached a threshold level, either positive or negative, with consistency relative to market tops and bottoms is such an indicator. Many breadth indicators work in this manner.

## A Familiar Breadth Indicator

Most investors are familiar with the long-running Friday night show, *Wall Street Week*, on Public Broadcasting hosted by Louis Rukeyser, who, every week would comment on his elves (his term for technical analysts) and the Wall Street Week Index. What you may not have known is that this index was a composite of 10 indicators, three of which were breadth-based. Robert Nurock, long-time panelist and Chief Elf, created it. Robert Nurock was the editor of the *Astute Investor*, a technical newsletter for many years.

The Arms Index was one of the indicators in the Wall Street Week Index. A 10-day moving average was used with bullish signals given when it was about 1.2 and bearish when it was below 0.8. The advances minus the declines were used over a 10-day period and bullish signals were from the point where the index exceeds 1,000 to a peak and down to a point 1,000 below the peak. Bearish signals were just the opposite. The third breadth indicator used was the new highs compared to the new lows. For bullish signals an expansion of the 10-day average of new highs from less than 10 up to 10-day average of new lows. Similarly, bearish signals were an expansion of 10-day average of new lows from less than 10 until it exceeds the 10-day average of new highs.

## Breadth Components

Breadth components are readily available from newspapers, online sources, and so on and consist of daily and weekly statistics. They are: Advances, Declines, Unchanged, Total Issues, Up Volume, Down Volume, Total Volume (V), New Highs, and New Lows.

From one day to the next, any issue can advance in price, decline in price, or remain unchanged. Also any issue can make a new high or a new low. Here are more specific definitions:

> Advancing Issues or Advances (A)—Stocks that have increased in price from one day to the next, even if only by one cent, are considered as advancing issues or advances.

Declining Issues or Declines (D)—Stocks that have decreased in price from one day to the next are considered declining issues or declines.

Unchanged Issues or Unchanged (U)—Stocks that do not change in price from one day to the next are considered unchanged issues or unchanged.

Note: Prior to July 1997, stock prices were measured in eighths of a point, or about 12.5 cents as the minimum trading unit. In July 1997 the NYSE went from using eighths to sixteenths. This made the minimum trading unit about 6.25 cents. On January 2, 2002, they went to a decimalization pricing that made the minimum trading price equal to one cent (a penny).

Total Issues (TI)—This is the total of all issues available for trading on a particular exchange. If you added the advances, declines, and unchanged issues together it would equal the total issues.

Advancing Volume or Up Volume (UV)—This is the volume traded on a day for each of the stocks that are advancing issues. It is the total volume of all the advances.

Declining Volume or Down Volume (DV)—This is the total volume for all the declines for a particular day.

Total Volume (V)—This is the total volume of all trading for a particular day. Total volume is the sum of Up Volume, Down Volume, and Unchanged Volume. To find Unchanged Volume subtract the sum of Up Volume and Down Volume from the Total Volume. Total volume is not generally considered a breadth component, but is many times used in a ratio with the up or down volume to alleviate the increase in trading activity over long periods of time.

New High (H)—Whenever a stock's price reaches a new high price for the last 52 weeks it is termed a *new high*.

New Low (L)—Whenever a stock's price reaches a new low price for the last 52 weeks it is termed a *new low*.

Note: The NYSE new highs and new lows are now computed on a fixed 52-week moving time window starting on January 1, 1978. Before that, the new highs and new lows were computed on a variable time window of anywhere from two and a half months to 14 and a half months. This rendered the new high new low data prior to 1978 almost useless, and certainly confusing to use.

## Breadth versus Price

Breadth does not consider the amount or magnitude of price change. It also does not consider the number of shares traded (volume). And it does not consider the shares outstanding for individual stocks. Most stock market indices, such as the New York Stock Exchange Composite Index, the Nasdaq Composite Index, S&P 500 Index, the

Nasdaq 100, and so on, weigh each stock based on its price and number of outstanding shares. This makes their contribution to the index based on their value and are sometimes called market-value weighted indices or capitalization weighted indices. Because of this (at this writing), Microsoft, Qualcomm, Intel, Cisco, eBay, Nextel, Dell, Amgen, Comcast, and Oracle account for more than 40 percent of the Nasdaq 100 Index and its ETF, QQQQ. Ten percent of the components account for 40 percent of the price movement of the index. This can lead to an incorrect analysis of the markets, especially if some of these large cap stocks experience price moving events. Many times the reference to the large caps issues is that of the generals, while the small caps are referred to as the soldiers. As you will find out, the generals are not always the leaders.

Breadth treats each stock the same. An advance of $10 in Microsoft is equally represented in breadth analysis as the advance of two cents of the smallest, least capitalized stock. Breadth is truly the best way to accurately measure the liquidity of the market.

## The Difference between Daily and Weekly Breadth Data

You just cannot add up daily breadth data for the week to get the weekly data. Here is a scenario that will explain why (Table C.1).

Here's the narrative: An advance or decline for the week should be based on its price change from the previous Friday close to the close of the current week. It has absolutely nothing to do with the daily data. Take a single stock; its previous Friday close price was $12. On Monday it was up $1 to $13. It went up a dollar each day for the first four days of the week and closed on Thursday at $16. However on Friday it dropped $5 to $11. For the week it was down $1, which would be one decline for the week. However, on a daily basis, it accounted for four advances and one decline, or a net three advances.

John McGinley, past editor of *Technical Trends*, and sidekick of the late Arthur Merrill, sent this note: "I strongly believe that in creating weekly figures for the advance declines, one does not use the published weekly data for they disguise and hide what really went on during the week. For instance, imagine a week with 1,500 net advances one day and the other four days even. The weekly data would hide the devastation which occurred that dramatic day."

**TABLE C.1**   Daily Breadth versus Weekly Breadth

| Stock: XYZ Corp. | Day | Price | Daily A-D | Weekly A-D |
|---|---|---|---|---|
| | Friday | 12.00 | | |
| | Monday | 13.00 | +1 | |
| | Tuesday | 14.00 | +1 | |
| | Wednesday | 15.00 | +1 | |
| | Thursday | 16.00 | +1 | |
| | Friday | 11.00 | −1 | −1 |
| Total | | | +3 | −1 |

## Advantages and Disadvantages of Using Breadth

Consider a period of distribution (market topping process) such as 1987, 1999, 2007, 2011, and so on. As an uptrend slowly ends and investors seek safety, they do so by moving their riskier holdings such as small cap stocks, into what is perceived to be safer large cap and blue chip stocks. This is certainly a normal process and one that can't be challenged. However, the mere act of moving from small to large cap stocks causes the capitalization weighted (Nasdaq Composite, New York Stock Exchange Index, S&P 500) and price weighted (Dow Industrials) to move higher simply because of the demand for large cap issues. Breadth, on the other hand, begins to deteriorate from this action. It is said that breadth arrives at the party on time, but always leaves early. Another analogy is that the troops are no longer following the generals. There is a nice chart showing this concept in Figure 13.9.

Breadth data seems to not be consistent among the data providers. If you think about it, if a stock is up it is an advance for the day, so why is there a disparity? Some data services will not include all stocks on the exchange. They will eliminate preferred issues, warrants, rights, and so on. This is fine as long as they tell you that is what they are doing. In the past few years, the number of interest-sensitive issues on the New York Stock Exchange has increased so that they account for more than half of all the issues. These issues are preferred stocks, closed-end bond funds, electric utility stocks, to mention a few.

Many analysts such as Sherman and Tom McClellan, Carl Swenlin, and Larry McMillan use common stocks only breadth indicators. Richard Russell refers to it as an operating company–only index. Using stocks that have listed options available is another good way to avoid the interest sensitive issues, since most stocks that have listed options are common stocks.

Each breadth indicator seems to have its benefits and its shortcomings. The fact that breadth measures the markets in a manner not possible with price is the key element in these conclusions. Breadth measures the movement of the market, its acceleration and deceleration. It is not controlled by General Electric, Microsoft, Intel, Cisco, General Motors, and so on; any more than it is controlled by the smallest capitalized stock on the exchange.

Table C.2 shows the breadth components needed for calculation of the indicator, whether the indicator is better for picking market bottoms, market tops, trend analysis, and whether it is better for short- or long-term analysis. Keep in mind that short term is generally some period of time less than five to six months. Identification of a market bottom can be an event that can last only a few days or launch a giant secular bull market. In Table C.2, the terms short- and long-term refer to the frequency of signals as much as anything. A number of the long-term indicators are good for trend following; in Table C.2 if neither Bottoms nor Tops were checked, it was because the indicator is better at trend analysis.

Some indicators are better at Tops, Bottoms, and both; and at different times, but are only identified by Bottoms and/or Tops below. Great effort was made to determine if one appeared to be better at one or the other. If no difference could be ascertained, they were reported as being good for both Bottoms and Tops. Please keep in mind the nature of market bottoms versus market tops. Bottoms are generally sharp and quick and usually much easier to identify, whereas market tops are usually long periods of distribution where most market indices rotate through their peaks at different times. You will notice that considerably more indicators are noted as being good at Bottoms than at Tops. Add to that the subjective interpretation of the various indicators and the table that follows should be viewed as a beginning guide only.

## Table Columns

| | |
|---|---|
| A | Advances |
| D | Declines |
| U | Unchanged |
| TI | Total Issues |
| UV | Up Volume |
| DV | Down Volume |
| H | New Highs |
| L | New Lows |
| V | Total Volume |
| MKT | Market Index |

Note: If neither Bottoms nor Tops are checked (X), it means the indicator is better at trend analysis.

**TABLE C.2**  Breadth Indicators

Primary Indicators

| *AD Difference* | Breadth Components Used: | | | | | | | | | | Good for use at: Market | | Better for: Term | |
|---|---|---|---|---|---|---|---|---|---|---|---|---|---|---|
| | A | D | U | TI | UV | DV | H | L | V | MKT | Bottoms | Tops | Short | Long |
| Advances—Declines | X | X | | | | | | | | | X | | X | |
| AD Overbought/Oversold | X | X | | | | | | | | | X | | X | |
| Plurality Index | X | X | | | | | | | | | X | X | X | |
| AD—Fugler | X | X | | | | | | | | | X | X | X | |
| AD Line | X | X | | | | | | | | | | X | | X |
| AD Line—1% | X | X | | | | | | | | | | | X | |
| AD Line—Eakle | X | X | | | | | | | | | X | | | X |
| AD Line—Normailzed | X | X | | | | | | | | | X | X | X | |
| AD Line—Bolton | X | X | X | | | | | | | | | | | X |
| AD Line—Adj. Total Issues | X | X | | X | | | | | | | | | | X |
| Big Movers Only | X | X | | X | | | | | | | | | | X |
| AD Line Oscillator | X | X | | | | | | | | | X | X | X | |
| Absolute Breadth Index | X | X | | | | | | | | | X | X | X | |
| Absolute Breadth—Adj. | X | X | | X | | | | | | | X | X | | X |
| AD Power | X | X | | | | | | | X | | X | | | X |
| Coppock Breadth Indicator | X | X | | X | | | | | | | | X | | |
| Haurlan Index—Short Term | X | X | | | | | | | | | X | X | X | |
| Harulan Index—Med Term | X | X | | | | | | | | | X | X | X | |
| Haurlan Index—Long Term | X | X | | | | | | | | | | | | X |
| McClellan Oscillator | X | X | | | | | | | | | X | X | X | |
| McClellan Summation Index | X | X | | | | | | | | | X | X | | X |
| Merriman Breadth Model | X | X | | | | | | | | X | X | X | X | |
| Swenlin Breadth Mo. Osc. | X | X | | | | | | | | | X | X | X | |
| Swenlin Trdg Osc—Breadth | X | X | | | | | | | | | X | X | X | |
| Zahorchak Method | X | X | | | | | | | | X | | | | X |

| *AD Ratio* | A | D | U | TI | UV | DV | H | L | V | MKT | Bottoms | Tops | Short | Long |
|---|---|---|---|---|---|---|---|---|---|---|---|---|---|---|
| AD Ratio | X | X | | | | | | | | | X | X | X | |
| Breadth Thrust | X | X | | | | | | | | | X | | | X |
| Breadth Thrust Continuation | X | X | | | | | | | | | | | | X |
| Duarte's Market Thrust | X | X | | | | | | | | | X | | X | |
| Eliades Sign of the Bear | X | X | | | | | | | | | | X | | X |
| Hughes Breadth Mo. Osc. | X | X | X | | | | | | | | X | X | X | |
| Panic Thrust | X | X | | | | | | | | | X | | X | |
| STIX | X | X | | | | | | | | | X | X | X | |

*(Continued)*

**TABLE C.2**  Continued

Primary Indicators

| AD Miscellaneous | A | D | U | TI | UV | DV | H | L | V | MKT | Good for use at: Market — Bottoms | Tops | Better for: Term — Short | Long |
|---|---|---|---|---|---|---|---|---|---|---|---|---|---|---|
| Advances/Issues Traded | X |  |  | X |  |  |  |  |  |  | X |  | X |  |
| AD Divergence Oscillator | X | X | X |  |  |  |  |  | X |  |  |  |  | X |
| AD Diffusion Index | X |  |  | X |  |  |  |  |  |  | X |  | X |  |
| Breadth Climax | X | X | X |  |  |  |  |  |  |  | X | X |  | X |
| Declining Issues TRIX |  | X |  |  |  |  |  |  |  |  | X | X | X |  |
| Disparity Index | X | X |  |  |  |  |  |  | X |  |  |  |  | X |
| Dynamic Synthesis | X | X | X |  |  |  |  |  | X |  | X | X |  | X |
| Unchanged Issues |  |  | X |  |  |  |  |  |  |  | X |  |  | X |
| Velocity Index | X | X | X |  |  |  |  |  |  |  | X | X | X |  |

| HL | A | D | U | TI | UV | DV | H | L | V | MKT | Bottoms | Tops | Short | Long |
|---|---|---|---|---|---|---|---|---|---|---|---|---|---|---|
| New Highs—New Lows |  |  |  |  |  |  | X | X |  |  | X | X | X |  |
| New High New Low Line |  |  |  |  |  |  | X | X |  |  | X |  |  | X |
| New Highs & Lows Osc. |  |  |  |  |  |  | X | X |  |  | X | X | X |  |
| New Highs New Lows Derv. |  |  |  |  |  |  | X | X |  |  | X | X | X |  |
| New Highs/New Lows |  |  |  |  |  |  | X | X |  |  | X | X | X |  |
| New Highs & New Lows X |  |  |  |  |  |  | X | X |  |  |  |  |  | X |
| New Highs % Total Issues |  |  |  | X |  |  | X |  |  |  |  | X |  | X |
| New Lows % Total Issues |  |  |  | X |  |  |  | X |  |  | X |  |  | X |
| High Low Logic Index |  |  |  | X |  |  | X | X |  |  | X | X | X |  |
| High Low Validation |  |  |  |  |  |  | X | X | X |  | X | X | X |  |

| Volume | A | D | U | TI | UV | DV | H | L | V | MKT | Bottoms | Tops | Short | Long |
|---|---|---|---|---|---|---|---|---|---|---|---|---|---|---|
| Up Volume |  |  |  |  | X |  |  |  |  |  | X |  | X |  |
| Down Volume |  |  |  |  |  | X |  |  |  |  | X |  | X |  |
| Changed Volume |  |  |  |  | X | X |  |  |  |  | X | X | X |  |
| Up & Down Volume |  |  |  |  | X | X |  |  |  |  | X | X | X |  |
| McClellan Oscillator — Vol. |  |  |  |  | X | X |  |  |  |  | X | X | X |  |
| McClellan Summation—Vol. |  |  |  |  | X | X |  |  |  |  |  |  |  | X |
| Merriman Volume Model |  |  |  |  | X | X |  |  |  |  | X | X | X |  |
| Swenlin Volume Mo. Osc. |  |  |  |  | X | X |  |  | X |  | X | X | X |  |
| Swenlin Trading Osc.—Vol. |  |  |  |  | X | X |  |  | X |  | X | X | X |  |
| Up Vol. Down Vol. Line |  |  |  |  | X | X |  |  |  |  |  |  |  | X |
| Cumulative Volume Ratio |  |  |  |  | X | X |  |  |  |  | X | X | X |  |
| Up Down On Balance Vol. |  |  |  |  | X | X |  |  | X |  |  |  |  | X |
| Volume Percentage Ratio |  |  |  |  | X | X |  | X |  |  | X |  | X |  |
| Upside—Downside Volume |  |  |  |  | X | X |  |  |  |  | X | X | X |  |
| Upside/Downside Volume |  |  |  |  | X | X |  |  |  |  | X | X | X |  |
| Zweig Up Volume Indicator |  |  |  |  | X | X |  |  |  |  | X |  |  | X |

| Composite | A | D | U | TI | UV | DV | H | L | V | MKT | Bottoms | Tops | Short | Long |
|---|---|---|---|---|---|---|---|---|---|---|---|---|---|---|
| Arms' Index | X | X | | | X | X | | | | | X | X | X | |
| Arms' Open Index | X | X | | | X | X | | | | | X | X | X | |
| Bretz Trin-5 | X | X | | | X | X | | | | | X | X | X | |
| Cash Flow Index | X | X | | X | X | X | X | X | X | | | | | X |
| Comp. Tape Index—Short | X | X | | | X | X | X | X | | | X | X | X | |
| Comp. Tape Index—Med. | X | X | | | X | X | X | X | | | X | X | X | |
| Comp. Tape Index—Long | X | X | | | X | X | X | X | | | | | | X |
| Dysart Pos. Neg. Vol. | X | X | | | | | | | X | | | | | X |
| Eliades New TRIN | X | X | | | X | X | | | | | X | X | X | |
| Haller Theory | | | | | | | | | | | X | X | | X |
| Hindenberg Omen | X | X | | X | | | X | X | | X | | X | | X |
| Market Thrust | X | X | | | X | X | | | | | X | | X | |
| McClellan Osc.—Volume | X | X | | | X | X | | | | | X | X | X | |
| McClellan Sum.—Volume | X | X | | | X | X | | | | | | | | X |
| Moving Balance Indicator | X | X | | | X | X | | | | | X | | X | |
| Technical Index | X | X | | X | X | X | X | X | X | | | | | X |
| Titanic Syndrome—1988 | X | X | | X | X | | X | X | | | | X | | X |
| Titanic Syndrome—1991 | X | X | | X | X | | X | X | | | X | X | | X |
| Titanic Syndrome—1995 | X | X | | X | X | | X | X | | | X | X | | X |
| Trend Exhaustion Index | X | | | | | | X | | | | | X | | X |

| Secondary Indicators | A | D | U | TI | UV | DV | H | L | V | MKT | Bottoms | Tops | Short | Long |
|---|---|---|---|---|---|---|---|---|---|---|---|---|---|---|
| AD Differential—Mamis | X | X | | | | | | | | | X | X | X | |
| Hughes Breadth Mo. % Osc | X | X | X | | | | | | | | X | X | X | |
| Advances TRIX | X | | | | | | | | | | X | X | X | |
| New Highs New Lows % TI | | | | X | | | X | X | | | X | X | X | |
| New Highs Lows—Morris | | | | | | | X | X | | | | | | X |
| New High New Low Cohen | | | | | | | X | X | | | X | X | X | |
| Wkly New H New L Hayes | | | | | | | X | X | | | | X | | X |
| New Highs Hayes | | | | | | | X | X | | | | X | X | X |
| New Highs New Lows Burk | | | | | | | X | X | | | X | X | X | |
| Low High Logic | | | | X | | | X | X | | | | X | X | |
| Up Volume Detrended | | | | | X | | | | | | X | X | X | |
| Down Volume Detrended | | | | | | X | | | | | X | X | X | |
| Up Down Volume Oscillator | | | | | X | X | | | X | | X | X | X | |
| Zweig Double 9 Up Volume | | | | | X | X | | | | | X | | | X |
| Zweig Double 9 Down Vol. | | | | | X | X | | | | | X | | | X |
| Arms Index 21–55 Oscillator | X | X | | | X | X | | | | | X | X | X | |
| WTrin10 | X | X | | | X | X | | | | | X | X | X | |
| Market Thrust Oscillator | X | X | | | x | X | | | | | X | X | X | |
| Market Thrust Summation | X | X | | | X | X | | | | | X | X | | X |
| Technical Index ROC | X | X | | X | X | X | X | X | X | | X | X | X | |
| Trend Explosion Index | | X | | | | | | X | | | X | | | X |

## Favorite Breadth Indicators

Here is a list of breadth indicators that I believe are good ones to follow. Some are for daily analysis and some are used merely to be kept aware of their indications. There are some really good breadth indicators that have made some very good market calls over the years—they are marked as awareness only below. I try to avoid noisy indicators that require too much interpretation and very short term in nature.

| Breadth Indicator | When Used |
| --- | --- |
| Advance Decline Line | Long term and usually early |
| Advance Decline Line Normalized | Good breadth overbought oversold |
| Breadth Thrust | Awareness only |
| Eliades Sign of the Bear | Awareness only |
| New Highs New Lows Line | Long-term trend |
| New Highs New Lows | Intermediate trends |
| McClellan Oscillator | Short to intermediate |
| McClellan Summation with Miekka Adj. | Longer term and market staying power |
| Moving Balance Indicator | Very good for bottoms (oversold) |
| Swenlin Breadth Momentum | Short-term picture |
| Trend Exhaustion Index | Good for topping alert |
| Up Volume (smoothed) | Good for the beginning of market tops |
| WTrin10 | Short-term overbought oversold |
| Zahorchak Method | Good for trend following |
| Zweig Up Volume Indicators | Awareness only |

## New High New Low Validation Measure

During my research on breadth I became acutely aware that most analysts treated new highs and new lows in the same manner as they did with advances, declines, up volume, and down volume. A terrible mistake as I will attempt to explain. This will help validate and show how to interpret new high and new low data. If you consider the facts relating to new highs and new lows, you will see the necessity for this. A new high means that the closing price reached a high that it had not seen in the past year (52 weeks). Similarly, a new low is at a low not seen for at least a year. This indicator tries to identify when the new high or new low is determined to be good or bad using the following line of thinking.

Consider that prices have been in a narrow range for more than a year. Something then triggers an event that causes the market to move out of that trading range to the upside. This will immediately cause almost every stock that moves with the market to also become a new high. New highs are generally the force that keeps good up moves going. The new lows in this scenario will dry up, as expected. Now consider that the market has had a steady advance for quite some time. The number of new highs will generally continue to remain high as most stocks will rise with the market. Of course,

**FIGURE C.1**   New High New Low Validation

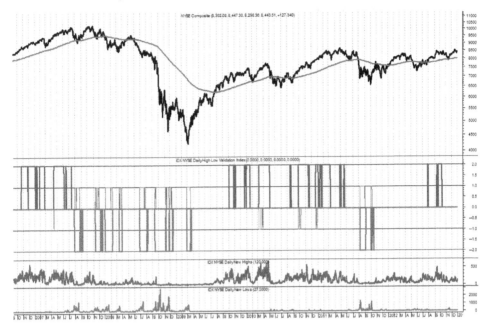

*Source:* Chart courtesy of MetaStock.

there will be drops as the market makes it corrections on its path to higher prices. When the number of new highs starts to dry up, you will probably notice that the number of unchanged issues starts to increase slightly because a lot of stocks will just cease to participate in the continuing rise. New lows will not happen for some time because the market is just starting to form a top. The number of new lows will increase as the market forms its broad top, while the number of new highs gets smaller and smaller. It will be the time frame of this topping action that determines when the new lows will start to kick in. Remember, you cannot have a new low until an issue is at a new low price over the last year.

When the market declines and you start to see fewer new lows, it means the market is losing its downside momentum. Why is this so? It is because some issues have already bottomed and are not continuing to make new lows. This is tied to the rotational effect, sometimes caused by various market sectors hitting bottoms at different times. Figure C.1 is an attempt to show this visually. Up spikes (solid line) equal to +2 represent good new highs. Up spikes (dashed line) equal to +1 represent bad new highs. Similarly, down spikes (solid line) at −2 equates to good new lows and −1 (dotted line) equates to bad new lows. You might read that again since it is not obvious. I wanted to keep the new highs as the up spikes and the new lows as the down spikes. Short up spikes are bad new highs and short down spikes are bad new lows. Bad, in this case, means they did not conform to the theory talked about above.

In Figure C.1 the top plot is the NYSE Composite index with a 252 day exponential average overlaid. The bottom plot is the new lows, the next to the bottom is the new highs, and the second from the top plot is the New High New Low Validation Measure. It is the plot that has the tooth-like moves both up and down. The top of the up moves is at a value of 2 and represents valid new highs. The bottom of the down moves is at –2 and represents valid new lows. The smaller up and down moves are at +1 and –1 and represent new highs and new lows, respectively, which are good, but not as good as the ones at +2 and –2. Although this is a great deal of information to put into a single chart in a black-and-white book, you can look at the validated periods and compare them to the top plot of the NYSE Composite and see that they do a really good job of pointing out new highs and new lows that are meaningful.

This method of trying to determine when the new highs and new lows are truly good ones, involves the rate of change of the market, a smoothed value of each component relative to the total issues traded, and their relationships with each other. For example, if the market is in a rally (rate of change high) and the new highs are increasing, any new lows that appear are not good ones. Similarly, if the market is in a downtrend, with high negative rate of change, then any new highs that appear are not good ones. The use of the term *good ones* refers to whether they are valid to use in any new high new low analysis.

# Appendix D: Recommended Reading

There are many great books available in the field of technical analysis and finance. However, I'm going to keep the list short and focused. The bibliography contains many other wonderful books on technical analysis, finance, and behavioral analysis, but if I had to pick a library of only four books, this is it.

## Getting Started List

Kirkpatrick, Charles D., and Dahlquist, Julie R., 2011, Technical Analysis, Pearson Education, Upper Saddle River, NJ.

Easterling, Ed., 2011, Probable Outcomes, Cypress House, Fort Bragg, CA.

Bernstein, Peter L., 1998, Against the Gods, John Wiley & Sons, New York.

Montier, James, 2010, The Little Book of Behavioural Investing, John Wiley & Sons, West Sussex, England.

## Additional Recommended Reading

I'm not sure why I started this list because there are so many great books on investing out there now that it is difficult to decide which to read. I guess I just answered my own dilemma as I have read many, if not most of them and these are the ones I personally would recommend because they complement this book.

Pring, Martin J., 1985, Technical Analysis Explained, McGraw-Hill, New York.

Bernstein, Peter L., 1992, Capital Ideas, John Wiley & Sons, Hoboken, NJ.

Makridakis, Spyros and Hogarth, Robin, 2010, Dance with Chance, Oneworld Publications, Oxford, England.

Mandelbrot, Benoit, 2004, The (Mis)Behavior of Markets, Basic Books, New York.

Shefrin, Hersh, 2002, Beyond Fear and Greed, Oxford University Press, New York.

Solow, Kenneth R., 2009, Buy and Hold Is Dead Again, Morgan James Publishing, Garden City, NY.

Tetlock, Phlip E, 2005, Expert Political Judgement: How Good Is It? How Can We Know? Princeton University Press, Princeton, NJ.

Fox, Justin, 2009, Myth of the Rational Market, HarperCollins, New York.

Coleman, Thomas S., 2012, Quantitative Risk Management, John Wiley & Sons, Hoboken, NJ.

Weatherall, James O., 2013, The Physics of Wall Street, Houghton Mifflin Harcourt Publishing, New York.

# Bibliography

## Academic Papers/Research Papers/Articles

(A1) 1741 Asset Management, "Are Stock Recommendations Useful?" Research Note Series 4/2012, retrieved from http://ssrn.com/abstract=2182731

(A2) Ambrosio, Frank J., "An Evaluation of Risk Metrics," Vanguard Investment Counseling and Research, retrieved from www.advisors.vanguard.com

(A3) Ang, Andrew, "Mean-Variance Investing," Asset Management, August 10, 2012, retrieved from http://ssrn.com/id2131932

(A4) Arnott, Rob, Hsu, Jason, Kalesnik, Vitali, and Tindall, Phil, "The Surprising Alpha from Malkiel's Monkey and Upside-down Strategies," October 10, 2012, retrieved from http://ssrn.com/abstract=2165563

(A5) Asness, Clifford, "An Old Friend: The Stock Market's Shiller P/E," November 2012, AQR Capital Management.

(A6) Barber, Brad M., Odean, Terrance, and Zhu, Ning, "Systematic Noise," April 2003.

(A7) Barber, Brad M., and Odean, Terrance, "All that Glitters: The Effect of Attention and News on Buying Behavior of Individuals and Institutional Investors," November 2006, retrieved from http://ssrn.com/id460660

(A8) Barber, Brad M., and Odean, Terrance, "The Behavior of Individual Investors," September 2011, retrieved from http://ssrn.com/abstract=1872211

(A9) Barberis, Nicholas, and Thaler, Richard, "A Survey of Behavioral Finance," September 2002, forthcoming in the Handbook of the Economics of Finance.

(A10) Bernstein, Peter L., "How Far Away is the Past; How Near is the Future?" Peter L. Bernstein, Inc., New York City presentation given to the Next Generation Asset Management conference in Washington, DC, on June 12–13, 2008.

(A11) Bodie, Zvi, "On the Risk of Stocks in the Long Run," Financial Analysts Journal, May–June 1995, 18–22.

(A12) Bogle, John C., "Black Monday and Black Swans," CFA Institute, 2008, retrieved from www.cfapubs.org

(A13) Bouchaud, Jean-Philippe, "Power Laws in Economy and Finance: Some Ideas from Physics," Science and Finance, August 7, 2000, 109–111.

(A14) Brinson, Gary P., Hood, L. Randolph, and Beebower, Gilbert L., "Determinants of Portfolio Performance," Financial Analysts Journal, January–February 1995, 133.

(A15) Carlos, Ann M., Fletcher, Erin, and Neal, Larry, "Share Portfolios and Risk Management in the Early Years of Financial Capitalism: London 1690–1730," Australian National University Discussion Paper No. 2012–2016, September 2012.

(A16) Chambers, David, and Dimson, Elroy, "Keynes the Stock Market Investor," March 5, 2012, retrieved from http://ssrn.com/abstract=2023011

(A17) Chen, Linda H., Jiang, George J., and Zhu, Kevin X., "Do Style and Sector Indexes Carry Momentum?" August 28, 2011, retrieved from http://ssrn.com/id2139210

(A18) Chrystal, K. Alec, and Mizen, Paul D., "Goodhart's Law: Its Origins, Meaning and Implications for Monetary Policy," November 12, 2001.

(A19) Clare, Andrew, Seaton, James, and Thomas, Stephen, "Breaking into the Blackbox: Trend Following, Stop Losses, and the Frequency of Trading: the Case of the S&P500," March 2012, retrieved from http://ssrn.com/abstact=2126476

(A20) Clare, Andrew, Seaton, James, Smith, Peter N., and Thomas, Stephen, "The Trend is Our Friend: Risk Parity, Momentum and Trend Following in Global Asset Allocation," August 15, 2012, retrieved from http://ssrn.com/abstract=2126478

(A21) Cremers, Martijn, and Petajisto, Antti, "How Active is Your Fund Manager?" Yale School of Management, retrieved from http://ssrn.com/abstract=891719

(A22) Cremers, Martijn, Petajisto, Antti, and Zitzewitz, Eric, "When Benchmark Indices Have Alpha: Problems with Performance Evaluation," June 5, 2008.

(A23) Crook, Michael, and Nick, Brian, "Equities for the Long Run: A New Look at the Future Equity Premium," 2012, retrieved from http://ssrn.com/abstract+2172796

(A24) Cullen, Grant, and Gasbarro, Dominic, "Systematic Risk and the Performance of Mutual Funds Pursuing Momentum and Contrarian Trades," retrieved from http://ssrn.com/abstract=1460353

(A25) Dagnino, George, "Sector Investing and Business Cycles," The Peter Dag Portfolio Strategy and Management, November 15, 2003.

(A26) Davis, Joseph, Aliaga-Diaz, Roger, and Thomas, Charles, "Forecasting Stock Returns: What Signals Matter, and What Do They Say Now?" Vanguard Research, October 2012.

(A27) Dichev, Ilia, Graham, John, and Rajgopal, Shiva, "Earnings Quality: Evidence from the Field," September 9, 2012, retrieved from http://ssrn.com/abstract=2103384

(A28) Edesess, Michael, "No More Stupid Forecasts!" July 5, 2011, retrieved from www.advisorsperspective.com//commentaries/index.php

(A29) Edesess, Michael, "What Fama and French's Latest Research Doesn't Tell Us," June 14, 2011, retrieved from www.advisorperspectives.com//commentaries/index.php

(A30) Epley, Nicholas, and Gilovich, Thomas, "The Anchoring-and-Adjustment Heuristic," Association for Psychological Sciences, 2006.

(A31) Eriksson, Kimmo, "The Nonsense of Math Effect," Judgment and Decision Making, Vol. 7, No. 6, November 2012, 746–749.

(A32) Estrada, Javier, "Black Swans, Market Timing, and the Dow," November, 2007, retrieved from http://ssrn.co/abstract=1086300

(A33) Falkenstein, Eric, "Risk and Return in General: Theory and Evidence," December 2009, retrieved from http://ssrn.com/abstract=1420356

(A34) Fama, Eugene F., "Market Efficiency, Long-term Returns, and Behavioral Finance," Journal of Financial Economics, October 3, 1997.

(A35) Fama, Eugene F., "The Behavior of Stock Market Prices," Journal of Business, Vol. 38, Issue 1 (Jan. 1965), 34–105.

(A36) Farmer, J. Doyne, and Geanakoplos, John, "Power Laws in Economics and Elsewhere," Santa Fe Institute, Santa Fe, NM, May 14, 2008.

(A37) Fidelity Market Analysis, Research & Education, "A Tactical Handbook of Sector Rotations," August 23, 2010.

(A38) Finger, Christopher C., "Language of Risk," RiskMetrics Group, Research Monthly, 2007.

(A39) Fong, Kingsley, Gallagher, David, and Lee, Adrian, "Who Win and Who Lose Among Individual Investors?" December 9, 2008, retrieved from http://ssrn.com/abstract=1343519

(A40) Gabaix, Xavier, "Power Laws in Economics and Finance," NBER Working Paper Series, No. 14299, September 2008.

(A41) Gajilan, Arlyn, "Worst Predictions," Newsweek.com, http://2010.newsweek.com/top-10/worst-predictions/jim-cramer.html

(A42) Goetzmann, William N., "An Introduction to Investment Theory," Yale School of Management, retrieved from http://viking.som.yale.edu/will/finman540/classnotes/class1.html

(A43) Goetzmann, William N., Ibbotson, Roger G., and Peng, Liang, "A New Historical Database for the NYSE 1815–1925: Performance and Predictability," Yale School of Management, July 14, 2000, retrieved from http://ssrn.com/abstract=236982

(A44) Ghysels, Eric, Horan, Casidhe, Moench, Emanuel, "Forecasting through the Rear-View Mirror: Data Revisions and Bond Return Predictability," Federal Reserve Bank of New York, Staff Report 581, November 2012, retrieved from http://ssrn.com/abstract=2175150

(A45) Han, Yufeng, and Zhou, Guofu, "Trend Factor: A New Determinant of Cross-Section Stock Returns," November, 2012, retrieved from http://ssrn.com/abstract=2182667

(A46) Haugen, Robert, and Baker, Nardin, "Commonality in the Determinants of Expected Stock Returns," Journal of Financial Economics, Summer 1996.

(A47) Hubner, Georges, "How Do Performance Measures Perform?" Journal of Portfolio Management, Summer 2007.

(A48) Hurst, Brian, Ooi, Yao, and Pedersen, Lasse, "A Century of Evidence on Trend-Following Investing, AQR Capital Management, Fall 2012.

(A49) Ioannidis, John P.A., "Why Most Published Research Findings Are False," PLoS Medicine, Vol. 2, Issue 8, August 2005, 0696–0701.

(A50) Jackson, Matthew O, "A Brief Introduction to the Basics of Game Theory," Stanford University, retrieved from http://ssrn.com/abstract=1968579

(A51) Jordan, Steven J., "Is Momentum a Self-Fulfilling Prophecy?" May 3, 2012, retrieved from http://ssrn.com/abstract=2188153

(A52) Kaminski, Kathryn M., and Lo, Andrew W., "When Do Stop-Loss Rules Stop Losses?" Swedish Institute for Financial Research, No. 63, May 2008.

(A53) Keller, Wouter, and van Putten, Hugo, "Generalized Momentum and Flexible Asset Allocation," draft v0.98, December 24, 2012 retrieved from http://ssrn.com/abstract=2193735

(A54) Kramer, Marc M., and Lensink, Robert, "The Impact of Financial Advisors on the Stock Portfolios of Retail Investors," August 29, 2012, retrieved from http://ssrn.com/abstract=2139491

(A55) Kraussl, Roman, and Sandelowsky, Ralph, "The Predictive Performance of Morningstar's Mutual Fund Ratings," August 17, 2007, retrieved from http://ssrn.com/abstract=963489

(A56) Lei, Adam Y.C., and Li, Huihua, "The Value of Stop Loss Strategies," January 29, 2009, retrieved from http://ssrn.com/abstract=1214737

(A57) Lewis, John, "Tactical Asset Allocation Using Relative Strength," Dorsey Wright Money Management, March 2012.

(A58) Lo, Andrew W., "Long-Term Memory in Stock Market Prices," Econometria, Vol. 59, No. 5, September, 1991, 1279–1313.

(A59) Maheu, John, McCurdy, Thomas, and Song, Yong, "Components of Bull and Bear Markets: Bull Corrections and Bear Rallies," American Statistical Association Journal of Business and Economic Statistics, Vol. 30, No. 3, July 2012, retrieved from http://ssrn.com/abstract=2171892

(A60) Malkiel, Burton G., "The Clustering of Exteme Movements: Stock Prices and Weather," CEPS Working Paper No. 186, February 2009.

(A61) Mangel, Marc, and Samaniego, Francisco J., "Abraham Wald's Work on Aircraft Survivability," Journal of the American Statistical Association, Vol. 79, Issue 386, June 1984, 259–267.

(A62) Manski, Charles, "Policy Analysis with Incredible Certitude," National Bureau of Economic Research, July 2010.

(A63) Markowitz, Harry M., "Foundations of Portfolio Theory," Baruch College, Nobel Lecture, December 7, 1990.

(A64) Mazzilli, Paul, "Tracking Tracking Error," Journal of Indexes, June 18, 2007.

(A65) McKay, Betsy, "Government's Standard Lumps Hunks, Athletes with Truly Obese," Wall Street Journal, July 23, 2002.

(A66) McLean, David, and Pontiff, Jeffrey, "Does Academic Research Destroy Stock Return Predictability?" University of Alberta and MIT Sloan School of Management, January 22, 2012, retrieved from http://ssrn.com/abstract=2156623

(A67) Montier, James, "Seven Sins of Fund Management," Dresdner Kleinwort Wasserstein, November 2005.

(A68) Montier, James, "The Seven Immutable Laws of Investing," GMO, March 2011.

(A69) Montier, James, "The Flaws of Finance," GMO, May 2012.

(A70) Nenkov, Gergana, MacInnis, Deborah J., and Morrin, Maureen, "How Do Emotions Influence Saving Behavior?" Center for Retirement Research at Boston College, Number 9–8, April 2009.

(A71) Park, JaeHong, Kumar, Alok, and Raghunathan, Rajagopal, "Confirmation Bias, Overconfidence, and Investment Performance: Evidence from Stock Message Boards," JEL Codes: G11, G12, July 12, 2010.

(A72) Peavy, John W., and Safran, Jason R., "How Efficiently Does the Stock Market Process News of Price Anomalies?" Journal of Investing 19.4, 2010, 122–127.

(A73) Phillips, Christopher, "The Active-Passive Debate: Bear Market Performance," Vanguard Investment Counseling and Research, retrieved from www.vanguard.com

(A74) Phillips, Christopher, "Market Indexes: Determining the Appropriate Benchmark," Vanguard Investment Counseling and Research, retrieved from www.advisors.vanguard.com

(A75) Phillips, Christopher, and Kinniry, Francis, "The Active-Passive Debate: Market Cyclicality and Leadership Volatility," Vanguard Investment Counseling and Research, retrieved from www.vanguard.com

(A76) Pompian, Michael M., "Introduction to Behavior Investor Types," Morningstar Advisor, January 29, 2009.

(A77) Pompian, Michael M., "Diagnosing Behavior Types," Morningstar Advisor, February 19, 2009.

(A78) Ricciardi, Victor, and Simon, Helen K., "What is Behavioral Finance?" Business, Education and Technology Journal, Fall 2000.

(A79) Risen, Jane L., and Gilovich, Thomas, "Another Look at Why People are Reluctant to Exchange Lottery Tickets," Journal of Personality and Social Psychology, Vol. 93, No. 1, 2007, 12–22.

(A80) Ritter, Jim, "Create a Hybrid Indicator," Stocks and Commodities, V.12:12, December 1992, 534.

(A81) Roll, Richard, "R-Squared," Journal of Finance, Vol. 43, Issue 3, Papers and Proceedings of the 47th Annual Meeting of the American Finance Association, Chicago, IL, December 28–30, 1987 (July 1988), 541–566.

(A82) Salganik, Matthew, Dodds, Peter, and Watts, Duncan, "Experimental Study of Inequality and Unpredictability in an Artificial Cultural Market," Vol. 311, Science, February 10, 2005.

(A83) Seiden, Sam, "Portfolio Diversification: Truth Versus Myth," SFO, April 2007.

(A84) Sewell, Martin, "History of the Efficient Market Hypothesis," UCL Dept. of Computer Science, January 20, 2011.

(A85) Shahidi, Alex, "Why a 60/40 Portfolio Isn't Diversified," April 24, 2012, retrieved from www.advisorperspectives.com

(A86) Shefrin, Hersh, "Behavioral Finance: Biases, Mean-Variance Returns, and Risk Premiums," CFA Institute, June 2007.

(A87) Shiller, Robert J., "Investor Behavior in the October 1987 Stock Market Crash: Survey Evidence," NBER Working Paper No. 2446, November 1987.

(A88) Shiller, Robert J., "From Efficient Market Theory to Behavioral Finance," Cowles Foundation Discussion Paper No. 1385, retrieved from http://cowles.econ.yale.edu/

(A89) Shiller, Robert J., "Human Behavior and the Efficiency of the Financial System," prepared for the Handbook of Macroeconomics, 1997.

(A90) Smith, David, and Faugere, Christophe, "Head and Shoulders above the Rest? The Performance of Institutional Portfolio Managers Who Use Technical Analysis," Dept. of Finance and Center for Institutional Investment Management, University of Albany, January 2013, retrieved from http://ssrn.com/abstract=2202060

(A91) Sortino, Frank A., and Forsey, Hal J., "On the Use and Misuse of Downside Risk," Journal of Portfolio Management, Winter 1996.

(A92) Sperber, Dan, "The Guru Effect," Springer Science+Business Media B.V., 2010.

(A93) Stangl, Jeffrey, Jacobsen, Ben, and Visaltanachoti, Nuttawat, "Sector Rotation over Business Cycles," Massey University, Department of Commerce, Auckland, New Zealand, retrieved from http://ssrn.com/abstract=999100

(A94) Stix, Gary, "A Calculus of Risk," retrieved from www.ge.infm.it/~ecph/bibliography/stix98.html

(A95) Tversky, Amos, and Kahneman, Daniel, "Rational Choice and the Framing of Decisions," Journal of Business, Vol. 59, No. 4, Pt. 2, 1986.

(A96) Tversky, Amos, and Kahneman, Daniel, "The Framing of Decisions and the Psychology of Choice," Science, Vol. 211, January 30, 1981.

(A97) Tversky, Amos, and Kahneman, Daniel, "Prospect Theory: An Analysis of Decision under Risk," Econometria, Vol. 47, No. 2, March 1979, 263–292.

(A98) Unknown Author(s), "The Value of Stop Loss Strategies," JEL Classification: C15, G11.

(A99) Unknown Author(s), "Is Portfolio Theory Harming Your Portfolio?" Executive Summary, retrieved from http://ssrn.com/abstract=1840734

(A100) Wilcox, Cole, and Crittenden, Eric, "Does Trend Following Work on Stocks?" Blackstar Funds, LLC, November 2005.

(A101) Zhu, Yingzi, and Zhou, Guofu, "Technical Analysis and Theory of Finance," Tsanghau University and Washington University in St. Louis, September 17, 2007.

(A102) Zweig, Jason, "If You Think Worst Is Over, Take Benjamin Graham's Advice," Wall Street Journal, May 26, 2009.

(A103) Kinnel, Russell, "Mind the Gap: Why Investors Lag Funds," Morningstar Direct, February, 4, 2013.

(A104) Prechter, Robert R., and Parker, Wayne, D., "The Financial/Economic Dichotomy in Social Behavioral Dynamics: The Socionomic Perspective," Journal of Behavioral Finance, Vol. 8, No. 2, retrieved from http://ssrn.com/abstract=1495051

(A105) Dobelli, Rolf, "News Is Bad for You—and Giving Up Reading It Will Make You Happier," Guardian, April 12, 2013.

(A106) Williams, Larry, "Larry Williams Trading Lesson 16," LnL Publishing, LLC, retrieved from www.ireallytrade.com/lessons/sixteen16.html

(A107) Williams, Dean, "Trying Too Hard," SVP, Batterymarch Financial, Keynote speech, Financial Analysts Federation Seminar, Rockford College, August 9, 1981.

(A108) Sewll, Martin, "Behavioural Finance," February 2007 (revised April 2010).

(A109) Sødahl, Lars O., "Systematic Elements in the Price Formation in Speculative Markets—A Test of 'The Mill Process,'" The Fifth Biennial Conference, Alternate Perspectives in Finance, Dundee, Scotland, July 2000.

## Books

(B1) Achelis, Steven B., 1995, Technical Analysis from A to Z, McGraw-Hill, New York.

(B2) Alexander, Michael A., 2005, Investing in a Secular Bear Market, iUniverse, Lincoln, NE.

(B3) Alexander, Michael A., 2000, Stock Cycles, Writers Club Press, Lincoln, NE.

(B4) Arbesman, Samuel, 2012, The Half-Life of Facts: Why Everything We Know Has an Expiration Date, Penguin Group, New York.

(B5) Ariely, Dan, 2008, Predictably Irrational, HarperCollins, New York.

(B6) Aronson, David, 2007, Evidence Based Technical Analysis, John Wiley & Sons, Hoboken, NJ.

(B7) Bernstein, Peter L., 1998, Against the Gods, John Wiley & Sons, New York.

(B8) Bernstein, Peter L., 1992, Capital Ideas, John Wiley & Sons, New York.

(B9) Bernstein, Peter L., 2007, Capital Ideas Evolving, John Wiley & Sons, Hoboken, NJ.

(B10) Brafman, Ori, and Brafman, Rom, 2008, Sway, Broadway Books, Random House, Inc., New York.

(B11) Bramly, Serge, Leonardo., 1994, The Artist and the Man, Penguin Books, New York.

(B12) Coleman, Thomas S., 2012, Quantitative Risk Management, John Wiley & Sons, Hoboken, NJ.

(B13) Coleman, Thomas S., 2011, A Practical Guide to Risk Management, CFA Institute.

(B14) Covel, Michael W., 2009, Trend Following, Pearson Education, Upper Saddle River, NJ.

(B15) Davis, Ned, 1991, Being Right or Making Money, Ned Davis Research.

(B16) Easterling, Ed., 2005, Unexpected Returns, Cypress House, Fort Bragg, NC.

(B17) Easterling, Ed., 2011, Probable Outcomes, Cypress House, Fort Bragg, NC.

(B18) Edesess, Michael, 2007, The Big Investment Lie, Berrett-Koehler Publishers, San Francisco, CA.

(B19) Fox, Justin, 2009, Myth of the Rational Market, HarperCollins, New York.

(B20) Fung, Kaiser, 2010, Numbers Rule Your World, McGraw-Hill, New York.

(B21) Gallati, Reto R., 2012, Investment Discipline, Balboa Press, Bloomington, IN.

(B22) Gilovich, Thomas, 1991, How We Know What Isn't So, Free Press, New York.

(B23) Gwartney, James, Stroup, Richard L., and Lee, Dwight R., 2005, Common Sense Economics, St. Martin's Press, New York.

(B24) Haugen, Robert A., 1999, The Inefficient Stock Market, Pearson Education, Upper Saddle River, NJ.

(B25) Katsenelsen, Vitaily N., 2007, Active Value Investing, John Wiley & Sons, Hoboken, NJ.

(B26) Katsenelsen, Vitaliy N., 2011, The Little Book of Sideways Markets, John Wiley & Sons, Hoboken, NJ.

(B27) Kirkpatrick, Charles D., and Dahlquist, Julie R., 2011, Technical Analysis, Pearson Education, Upper Saddle River, NJ.

(B28) Levitt, Steven D., and Dubner, Stephen J., Super Freakonomics, HarperCollins, New York.

(B29) Lo, Andrew, and Hasanhodzic, J., 2010, The Evolution of Technical Analysis, John Wiley & Sons, Hoboken, NJ.

(B30) Makridakis, Spyros G., 1990, Forecasting, Planning and Strategy for the 21st Century, Free Press, New York.

(B31) Makridakis, Spyros, and Hogarth, Robin, 2010. Dance with Chance, Oneworld Publications, Oxford, England.

(B32) Mandelbrot, Benoit, 2004, The (Mis)Behavior of Markets, Basic Books, New York.

(B33) Mauboussin, Michael J., 2012, The Success Equation, Harvard Business Review Press, Boston.

(B34) Mauldin, John, 2004, Bull's Eye Investing, John Wiley & Sons, Hoboken, NJ.

(B35) Mauldin, John, 2006, Just One Thing, John Wiley & Sons, Hoboken, NJ.

(B36) Mauldin, John, and Tepper, Jonathan, 2011, Endgame, John Wiley & Sons, Hoboken, NJ.

(B37) Martin, Peter G., and McCann, Byron B. 1989, The Investor's Guide to Fidelity Funds, John Wiley & Sons, New York.

(B38) Masonson, Leslie N., Buy Don't Hold, 2010, Pearson Education, Upper Saddle River, NJ.

(B39) Merrill, Arthur A., 1984, Behavior of Prices on Wall Street, Analysis Press, Chappaqua, New York.

(B40) Merrill, Arthur A., 1977, Filtered Waves Basic Theory, Analysis Press, Chappaqua, New York.

(B41) MetaStock Version 11 User Manual, Thomson Reuters.

(B42) Montier, James, 2007, Behavioral Investing, John Wiley & Sons, Hoboken, NJ.

(B43) Montier, James, 2010, The Little Book of Behavioural Investing, John Wiley & Sons, West Sussex, England.

(B44) Paulos, John Allen, 2003, A Mathematician Plays the Stock Market, Basic Books, New York.

(B45) Plummer, Tony, 2003, Forecasting Financial Markets, Kogan-Page, London, England.

(B46) Pring, Martin J., 1985, Technical Analysis Explained, McGraw-Hill, New York.

(B47) Pring, Martin J., 1993, Martin Pring on Market Momentum, International Institute for Economic Research and Probus Publishing.

(B48) Reinhart, Carmen M., and Rogoff, Kenneth S., 2009, This Time Is Different, Princeton University Press, Princeton, NJ.

(B49) Runyon-Haber, 1971, Fundamentals of Behavioral Statistics, Addison-Wesley, Boston.

(B50) Savage, Sam L., 2009, The Flaw of Averages, John Wiley & Sons, Hoboken, NJ.

(B51) Shefrin, Hersh, 2002, Beyond Fear and Greed, Oxford University Press, New York.

(B52) Sherden, William A., 1998, The Fortune Sellers, John Wiley & Sons, New York.

(B53) Shiller, Robert J., 2001, Market Volatility, MIT Press, Cambridge, MA.

(B54) Silver, Nate, 2012, The Signal and the Noise, Penguin Press, New York.

(B55) Singal, Vijay, 2004, Beyond the Random Walk, Oxford University Press, New York.

(B56) Solow, Kenneth R., 2009, Buy and Hold Is Dead Again, Morgan James Publishing, Garden City, NY.

(B57) Tetlock, Philip E., 2005, Expert Political Judgement: How Good Is It? How Can We Know? Princeton University Press, Princeton, NJ.

(B58) Vince, Ralph, 2007, Handbook of Portfolio Mathematics, John Wiley & Sons, Hoboken, NJ.

(B59) Weatherall, James Owen, 2013, The Physics of Wall Street, Houghton Mifflin Harcourt Publishing Company, New York.

(B60) Weinstein, Stan, 1988, Secrets for Profiting in Bull and Bear Markets, Dow Jones-Irwin, Homewood, IL.

(B61) Zahorchak, Michael G., 1977, The Art of Low Risk Investing, Van Nostrand Reinhold Company, New York.

(B62) Zweig, Jason, 2007, Your Money and Your Brain, Simon and Schuster, New York.

(B63) Zweig, Martin E., 1986, Winning on Wall Street, Warner Books, New York.

(B64) Anderson, Gary, 2012, The Janus Factor, John Wiley & Sons, Hoboken, NJ.

(B65) Derman, Emanuel, 2004, My Life As a Quant, John Wiley and Sons, Hoboken, NJ.

## Websites

(W1) Carl Swenlin—www.decisionpoint.com

(W2) www.stockcharts.com

(W3) Ed Easterling—www.crestmontresearch.com

(W4) Doug Short—http://advisorperspectives.com/dshort/

(W5) Tim Richards—www.psyfitec.com/ and http://www.psyfitec.com/p/list-of-behavioral -biases.html

(W6) Martin Sewell—www.behaviouralfinance.net/

(W7) www.cxoadvisory.com

(W8) Jason Goepfert—www.sentimentrader.com

(W9) www.multpl.com

(W10) www.jasonzweig.com

(W11) www.wolframalpha.com

# About the Author

Gregory L. Morris is senior vice president, chief technical analyst, and chairman of the Investment Committee for Stadion Money Management, LLC. He also serves as the chairman of the Station Trust Board. In this capacity Greg educates institutional and individual clients on the merits of technical analysis and why Stadion utilizes a technical rules-based model. Greg oversees the management of over $5.5 billion (2012) in assets in six mutual funds, separate accounts, and retirement plans. From December 2003 to May 2005, Greg served as a trustee and advisor to the MurphyMorris ETF Fund. He also served as treasurer and chief executive officer of MurphyMorris Money Management Co., the advisor to the fund.

Greg has written three books with McGraw-Hill: *The Complete Guide to Market Breadth Indicators*, a book introducing market breadth analysis for investors; a third edition (original edition in 1992) to his best-selling and vastly expanded *Candlestick Charting Explained*, released in March 2006; and *Candlestick Charting Explained Workbook*, which was published in December 2011. In 2011, Greg produced Japanese Candlestick Pattern Recognition software for Thomson Reuter's MetaStock. This is an add-on package that not only offers automatic identification of real patterns, but provides a sophisticated trend analysis measure and automatic support and resistance identification.

Greg is a member of the National Association of Active Investment Managers (NAAIM) where he currently chairs the Wagner Paper Contest, the American Association of Professional Technical Analysts (AAPTA), and the Market Technician's Association (MTA). During college he was a member of the American Institute of Aeronautics and Astronautics.

From 1996 to 2002, Greg was CEO of MurphyMorris, Inc., the leading provider of web-based market analysis tools, education, and commentary. MurphyMorris, Inc., was acquired by StockCharts.com, Inc., in October 2002. In 1999, Greg and three associates started MurphyMorris Money Management Co. to manage assets for individuals. This focus was later changed as the firm became the advisor to the MurphyMorris ETF Fund in January 2004, and later merged into the Stadion (PMFM) family of funds.

From 1994 to 1996, he was president of G. Morris Corporation, a Dallas, Texas headquartered business that provided products and services for investors and traders. His lead product was a series of more than 450 indicators and trading systems that supported most windows-based technical analysis software packages. From 1993 to

1994, Greg was part of MarketArts, Inc., which launched the first windows-based technical analysis software program, Windows on Wall Street.

In 1992 he published a book on Japanese candlestick analysis called *CandlePower*, now available in soft cover as *Candlestick Charting Explained* (McGraw-Hill). Widely recognized as an expert on candlesticks and the developer of candlestick filtering, he has lectured around the world on the subject. From 1982 until 1993, he worked in association with N-Squared Computing, producing more than 15 technical analysis and charting software titles, many of which are actively used today. In May 1989, he was awarded outstanding alumni for 1989 from Pratt County College.

Greg earned his pilot's license in 1967 and flew many versions of Cessna (Cessna 150 maximum takeoff weight = 1,500 pounds) and Mooney single-engine aircraft. During his seven years as a Navy pilot he flew the T2-C Buckeye, A-4J Skyhawk, and his favorite military jet, the F-4J Phantom. While in the Navy, he logged more than 240 carrier landings (103 at night) and exceeded twice the speed of sound. From 1978 to his retirement in 2004, Greg was a captain for Delta Air Lines flying the Boeing 727, Lockheed L-1011, McDonald Douglas MD-88, MD-90, Boeing 757, Boeing 767, and his favorite airliner, the McDonald Douglas MD-11 (maximum takeoff weight = 625,000 pounds). With his private pilot time, the Navy fighter pilot career (1971–1978), and airline career he accumulated 21,000 hours of flying time, and as he likes to say, never put a scratch on an airplane.

He graduated from the University of Texas at Austin in 1971, has a BS degree in Aerospace Engineering, has authored numerous investment-related articles, speaks at numerous seminars and investment groups, and has appeared many times on Financial News Network (FNN), Fox Business, CNBC, and Bloomberg TV. Greg was featured in *Investor's Business Daily* in December 2007, *Business Week* in July 2008, *Barron's* in January 2009, *Stocks and Commodities* in September 2009, and *Bloomberg Markets* in May 2011. Greg has been invited to Italy, Brazil, Vietnam, Canada, Hong Kong, Singapore, and China to lecture on the merits of technical market analysis. From 1971 to 1977, he was a Navy F-4 fighter pilot aboard USS *Independence* who was selected for, and graduated from, the Navy Fighter Weapons School known as Top Gun. Greg and his wife, Laura, live in the mountains of North Georgia in the summer and Central Texas in the winter.

# About the Online Resources

The author will update a number of the tables and figures in the book periodically at www.wiley.com/go/morrisinvesting (password: trend). He will also maintain a blog at either of these two locations: http://dance-with-the-trend.blogspot.com/ or http://dancewiththetrend.wordpress.com/ At the stage of wrapping up this book, he has not decided which blog service to use. Below is a list of Figures and Tables that will be updated.

## Figures

7.16 Secular Bull Markets since 1900
7.17 Secular Bull Market Composite
7.18 Secular Bear Markets since 1900
7.19 Secular Bear Market Composite
8.3 Secular Bear Market PE since 1900
8.4 Secular Bear Market PE Composite
8.5 Secular Bull Market PE since 1900
8.6 Secular Bull Market PE Composite
8.18 Twenty-Year Annualized Return of S&P 500 Price
8.19 Twenty-Year Annualized Total Return for S&P 500
8.20 Twenty-Year Annualized Total Return for S&P 500 Inflation Adjusted
8.22 Distribution of Inflation-Adjusted 20-Year Returns by Quartile
8.23 Distribution of Inflation-Adjusted 20-Year Returns by Decile
8.24 Distribution of Inflation-Adjusted 20-Year Returns by Standard Deviation
8.25 Distribution of Inflation-Adjusted 20-Year Returns by Percentage Ranges
11.8 S&P 500 Distribution of Drawdowns Greater than 15 Percent
11.9 S&P 500 Distribution of All Drawdowns
11.13 Dow Industrials Distribution of Drawdowns Greater than 15 Percent
11.14 Dow Industrials Distribution of All Drawdowns

## Tables

10.9 All Three Trend Analyses on All Indices
11.2 S&P 500 Drawdown Decline Data
11.3 S&P 500 Drawdown Recovery Data

# Index